Corpus Linguistics and Sociolinguistics

Language and Computers

STUDIES IN DIGITAL LINGUISTICS

Edited by

Christian Mair (*University of Freiburg, Germany*)
Charles Meyer (*University of Massachusetts at Boston*)

Editorial Board

VOLUME 82

The titles published in this series are listed at *brill.com/lc*

Corpus Linguistics and Sociolinguistics

A Study of Variation and Change in the Modal Systems of World Englishes

By

Beke Hansen

BRILL

RODOPI

LEIDEN | BOSTON

Cover illustration: Chris Curtis/Shutterstock.com

Library of Congress Cataloging-in-Publication Data

Names: Hansen, Beke, author.
Title: Corpus linguistics and sociolinguistics : a study of variation and
  change in the modal systems of world Englishes / by Beke Hansen.
Description: Leiden ; Boston : Brill, [2018] | Series: Language and computers
  : studies in digital linguistics, ISSN 0921-5034 ; volume 82 | Includes
  bibliographical references and index.
Identifiers: LCCN 2018035523 (print) | LCCN 2018045316 (ebook) | ISBN
  9789004381520 (Ebook) | ISBN 9789004381513 (hardback : alk. paper)
Subjects: LCSH: English language--Modality. | English language--Discourse
  analysis. | Corpora (Linguistics) | Sociolinguistics.
Classification: LCC PE1315.M6 (ebook) | LCC PE1315.M6 H36 2018 (print) | DDC
  425/.6--dc23
LC record available at https://lccn.loc.gov/2018035523

Typeface for the Latin, Greek, and Cyrillic scripts: "Brill". See and download: brill.com/brill-typeface.

ISSN 0921-5034
ISBN 978-90-04-38151-3 (hardback)
ISBN 978-90-04-38152-0 (e-book)

To my family for always believing in me

Contents

Acknowledgements

This book would have not been possible without the support of several people. First of all, I would like to thank my supervisor, Professor Lieselotte Anderwald, for giving me the opportunity to carry out my research project at her chair. I am grateful for her constant support, guidance, and patience throughout this project. Her advice, suggestions, and critical remarks have helped me to develop professionally and personally. I am also indebted to Professor Matthias Meyer, my second supervisor, for his support in this project, especially for his technical support with PERL. Special thanks are also due to Professor Christian Mair, who readily agreed to review my thesis as a third supervisor and who provided me with the opportunity to submit my book proposal to Brill.

I would also like to thank Philip Bolt, Kingsley Bolton, Joseph Hung, John Du Bois, Wallace Chafe, Charles Meyer, Sandra A. Thompson, Robert Englebretson, Nil Martey, Hongyin Tao, Paroo Nihilani, Ni Yibin, Anne Pakir, Vincent Ooi, S.V. Shastri, Gerhard Leitner and their teams for their huge effort in compiling the amazing databases on which my study is based. Of course, special thanks are also due to the people who have lent me their words for analysis as speakers in the ICE component corpora.

I also say thank you to my colleagues from the University of Kiel for their support and inspiring discussions, in particular Dr. Johanna Gerwin, Ingrid Paulsen, Benjamin Peter, Dr. David Reuter, Dr. Elisabeth Winkler, Vicki Allen, Robert Daugs, and Berit Johannsen. I would like to express special thanks to Professor Alena Witzlack-Makarevich for her support with R and to Dr. Karsten Schmidtke-Bode for encouraging me to analyse typological issues of modality. Furthermore, I would like to express my gratitude to Cord Christian Casper and Rob Raabe for distributing my questionnaires during their stays in Agra and Hyderabad. I am also very grateful to the participants of my questionnaire for sharing their knowledge with me. I would also like to express my gratitude to the audiences of ICAME 2015, ISLE 2016, and ICAME 2017 for helpful comments and suggestions. Furthermore, I am indebted to Rob Raabe, Dr. Johanna Gerwin, Benjamin Peter, Meike Ohm, Ina Rebers, Eva Schmidt, and Kristin Dreesen, who spent hours of carefully proofreading and meticulously commenting on my manuscript. I would also like to thank Maarten Frieswijk from Brill for his valuable help in the publication process.

Above that, I would like to express my gratitude to my family, in particular my grandma Christa Jürgensen and my late grandpa Ernst Jürgensen, my parents Anja and Hartmut Hansen, my sister Neele Büll, her husband Arne, and their son Bosse, and my brother Lewe-Drees Hansen, his wife Jule, and their son Bo, and Nati for their unconditional love and support. As part of my own little family, I would like to thank my partner Ulf Viehöfer, who was always by my side and supported me with great patience throughout. I am grateful for having him in my life. Last but not least, this list would not be complete without thanking Levke Beyer, Luisa Kampmeyer, Lena Keil, Katharina Peine, Marja Lamm, Konstanze Uhlen, Johanna Hinrichsen, Ricarda Messer, Marion Semmler, and Julia Sander for their close friendship.

Kiel, December 2017

Illustrations

Figures

Tables

Abbreviations

$	speaker code (in corpus examples)
1N	first person, non-generic reference
1SG	first person singular (in glosses)
2N	second person, non-generic reference
2PL	second person plural (in glosses)
3N	third person, non-generic reference
3SG	third person singular (in glosses)
AA	Austro-Asiatic (language family)
ACC.DEF	definite accusative (in glosses)
ADV	adverbial marker (in glosses)
AIC	Aikake's Information Criterion
AmE	American English
ARCHER	A Representative Corpus of Historical English Registers
AusE	Australian English
BahE	Bahamian English
B-BROWN	parallel corpus to BROWN with data from 1931
BLOB	parallel corpus to LOB with data from 1931
BlSAfE	Black South African English
BNC	British National Corpus
BrE	British English
BROWN	Brown University Standard Corpus of Present-Day American English
CamE	Cameroon English
CanE	Canadian English
CASE	Corpus of Academic Spoken English
CCE	Cameroon Corpus of English
CCIE	Contemporary Corpus of Indian English
CCJ	Corpus of Cyber-Jamaican
CCN	Corpus of Cyber-Nigierian
CEEC	Corpus of Early English Correspondence
CL	noun classifier (in glosses)
COCA	Corpus of Contemporary American English
COHA	Corpus of Historical American English
COLT	The Bergen Corpus of London Teenage Language
CONTE	Corpus of Early Ontario English
CookE	Cook Island English
CPSA	Corpus of Professional Spoken American English
C-US	Santa Barbara Corpus and FROWN

DAT	dative (in glosses)
DC-HKE	Diachronic Corpus of Hong Kong English
DCPSE	Diachronic Corpus of Present-Day Spoken English (with data from LLC and the spoken part of ICE-GB)
DEB	debitive (in glosses)
DECTE	Diachronic Corpus of Tyneside English
DEL	delimitative aspect (in glosses)
DICE	mini-corpus, consisting of a later part of DCPSE (with data from ICE)
DiCIE	Diachronic Corpus of Indian English
Dr	Dravidian (language family)
DSEU	mini-corpus, consisting of an early part of DCPSE (with data from LLC)
EAfE	East African English
EFL	English as a foreign language
ELF	English as a lingua franca
EModE	Early Modern English
EMPH	emphatic (in glosses)
ENL	English as a native language
ESD	English as a second dialect
ESL	English as a second language
FijiE	Fiji English
FLOB	Freiburg-LOB Corpus
FROWN	Freiburg BROWN Corpus of American English
FUT	future (in glosses)
G	subject with generic reference
GhanE	Ghanaian English
GloWbE	Corpus of Global Web-based English
HK	Hong Kong component of GloWbE
HKE	Hong Kong English
HON	honorifics (in glosses)
IA	Indo-Aryan (language family)
IC	Inner Circle
ICAME	International Computer Archive of Modern and Medieval English
ICE	International Corpus of English
ICE-AUS	International Corpus of English, Australian component
ICE-CAN	International Corpus of English, Canadian component
ICECUP	International Corpus of English Corpus Utility Program
ICE-EA	International Corpus of English, East African component
ICE-GB	International Corpus of English, Great Britain component
ICE-GH	International Corpus of English, Ghanaian component
ICE-HK	International Corpus of English, Hong Kong component

ICE-IND	International Corpus of English, Indian component
ICE-IND*	International Corpus of English, Indian component (revised version)
ICE-IRE	International Corpus of English, Irish component
ICE-JA	International Corpus of English, Jamaican component
ICE-NIG	International Corpus of English, Nigerian component
ICE-NZ	International Corpus of English, New Zealand component
ICE-PHI	International Corpus of English, Philippine component
ICE-SIN	International Corpus of English, Singaporean component
ICE-SL	International Corpus of English, Sri Lankan component
ICE-T&T	International Corpus of English, Trinidad and Tobago component
ICE-UG	International Corpus of English, Ugandan component (written only)
ICE-USA	International Corpus of English, US component (written only)
ICE-USA*	Santa Barbara Corpus of Spoken American English, International Corpus of English, US component (written only)
ICLE	International Corpus of Learner English
IDG	indigenous (strand)
IN	Indian component of GloWbE
IND	indicative (in glosses)
IndE	Indian English
INF	infinitive (in glosses)
IrE	Irish English
JamC	Jamaican Creole
JamE	Jamaican English
KenE	Kenyan English
L1	first language of a speaker
L1 (position)	first position to the left of a keyword
L2	second language of a speaker
L2 (position)	second position to the left of a keyword
LLC	London Lund Corpus of Spoken English
LModE	Late Modern English
LOB	Lancaster-Oslo-Bergen Corpus
LOC	locative (in glosses)
MalE	Malaysian English
M-co	Mossé-coefficient
MDA	multidimensional analysis
ME	Middle English
ModE	Modern English
NEC	necessity (in glosses)
NG	Nigerian component of GloWbE
NICE	'negation', 'inversion', 'code', 'emphasis'

NigE	Nigerian English
NIVE	non-native institutionalised varieties of English
NSM	Natural Semantic Metalanguage
NZE	New Zealand English
OE	Old English
OED	Oxford English Dictionary
OC	Outer Circle
OPT	optative (in glosses)
PAST	past tense (in glosses)
PCE	postcolonial English
PDE	Present-Day English
PFV	perfective aspect (in glosses)
Phil-BROWN	BROWN Corpus of Philippine English
PhilE	Philippine English
PL	plural (in glosses)
POS	parts-of-speech (tagged)
POS	possibility (in glosses)
POSS	possessive (in glosses)
PRES.INDEF	indefinite present (in glosses)
PROL	prolative (in glosses)
PRT	particle (in glosses)
PTCP	participle (in glosses)
R1 (position)	first position to the right of a keyword
R2 (position)	second position to the right of a keyword
SAfE	South African English
SamE	Samoan English
SBC	Santa Barbara Corpus of Spoken American English
SEA	Southeast Asian
SG	Singaporean component of GloWbE
SG	singular (in glosses)
SgE	Singapore English
SGEM	Speak Good English Movement
SLA	second-language acquisition
SPE	South Pacific Englishes
SPICE-Ireland	Systems of pragmatic annotation in ICE-Ireland
SrLE	Sri Lankan English
StE	Standard English
STL	settler (strand)
TanzE	Tanzanian English
TB	Tibeto-Burman (language family)

TrinE	Trinidadian English
UCREL	University Centre for Computer Corpus Research on Language
USAS	UCREL Semantic Analysis System
WALS	World Atlas of Language Structures
WE	World Englishes
WhSAfE	White South African English

CHAPTER 1

Introduction

The modal system of English is a well-researched area of English linguistics –
at least for first-language (L1) varieties. The situation is different for
second-language (L2) varieties of English, for which the modal system is still
under-researched (cf. Loureiro-Porto 2016, 144), although the situation has
slightly improved in recent years. This monograph addresses this research gap
by analysing variation and change in the modal systems of the L1 varieties British English (BrE) and American English (AmE) and the L2 varieties Hong Kong
English (HKE), Indian English (IndE), and Singapore English (SgE). This chapter defines basic terms and gives an overview of the structure of the book to lay
the foundation for the chapters that follow.

1.1 Modality, Mood, and Modal System

There is no definition of modality that is generally agreed upon. Huddleston
and Pullum, like many others, explain the term 'modality' with reference to
mood (cf. Huddleston & Pullum 2002, 172; cf. also Palmer 1979, 4). They state
that "[t]he distinction between mood and modality is like that between
tense and time [...]: mood is the category of grammar, modality a category of
meaning" (Huddleston & Pullum 2002, 171). As a semantic category, modality
embraces "notions such as ability, possibility, hypotheticality, obligation, and
the imperative meaning" (Depraetere & Reed 2006, 269). All these notions can
be subsumed under the notions 'possibility' and 'necessity', which is why some
linguists define modality as "a speaker's judgment that a proposition is possibly or necessarily true or that the actualization of a situation is necessary or
possible" (Depraetere & Reed 2006, 269; cf. also Huddleston & Pullum 2002,
173). Examples (1)–(4) serve to illustrate the four main aspects of the definition
(cf. Huddleston & Pullum 2002, 173, my emphases).

(1)   He *may* have written it himself.

(2)   He *must* have written it himself.

(3)   You *may* help her.

(4)   You *must* help him.

© KONINKLIJKE BRILL NV, LEIDEN, 2018 | DOI:10.1163/9789004381520_002

Example (1) shows the speaker's judgement that the proposition is possibly true, i.e. 'it is possibly true that he has written it himself'. Example (2) shows the speaker's judgment that the proposition is necessarily true, i.e. 'it is necessarily true that he has written it himself'. Example (3) shows the speaker's judgment that the actualisation is possible. This means it becomes possible that you help her because I give you the permission to do so (cf. Huddleston & Pullum 2002, 173). Example (4) shows the speaker's judgment that the actualisation is necessary, i.e. 'it is necessary that you help her'. The examples show that modality in English is expressed by a modal system including modal auxiliaries and semi-modals and that it is only rarely expressed by mood.[1]

1.2   Types of Modality

Considering the definition of modality introduced above, we can see that, apart from the binary distinction into possibility and necessity, the definition includes another two-fold distinction, i.e. into the truth of the proposition and actualisation of action. Coates uses the terms 'epistemic modality' and 'non-epistemic', i.e. 'root modality', to refer to these two types of modality (cf. Coates 1983, 18–22). Epistemic modality "is concerned with the speaker's assumptions or assessment of possibility and […] it indicates the speaker's confidence […] in the truth of the proposition expressed" (Coates 1983, 18). Epistemic *must*, for example, prototypically "conveys the speaker's confidence in the truth of what he [or she] is saying, based on a logical process of deduction from facts known to him [or her]" (Coates 1983, 41). Epistemic *must* can often be paraphrased with 'I'm sure/I confidently assume that' (cf. Coates 1983, 18), e.g. (5) to (7).

(5)   Speaker B ($B) I think it's a rare opportunity for a woman artist
       Speaker A ($A) I'm sure it *must be* (ICE-IND*:S1B-045)

(6)   In Jaipur then we have also we have a Birla Mandir and of course we've a Hawa Mahal in Jaipur it's pretty famous you *must have seen* photographs and all (ICE-IND*:S1A-008)

(7)   Yeah I think her sister uh Shammi *must be knowing* her sister well […] (ICE-IND*:S1A-058)

---

1   Note, however, that the mandative subjunctive has been shown to be well established in AmE (cf. Leech et al. 2009, 53) but less so in IndE where periphrasis with *should* is preferred (cf. Sedlatschek 2009, 281–289).

Examples (5) to (7) are typical examples of epistemic *must* from the subjective core, expressing a logical inference on the part of the speaker ('I confidently infer that x') (cf. Coates 1983, 41). In (5), the use of epistemic *must* expresses the speaker's strong confidence in the truth of the proposition and occurs in 'modal harmony'[2] with the phrase *I'm sure*. In (6), the speaker explicitly mentions the fact on which the inference is based; however, the strength of confidence is not explicitly stated in a phrase. The speaker instead confidently assumes that the addressee has seen the Hawa Mahal in Jaipur on photos because the palace is very famous. In (7), the speaker does not explicitly state why he assumes that Shammi knows her sister well. Epistemic *must* is less strong in (7) than in examples (5) and (6) because the speaker tones down the strength of confidence in the inference with the hedge *I think*. Apart from these subjective uses of epistemic *must*, there are also cases of objective uses that can be paraphrased with 'in the light of what is known, it is necessarily the case that x' (cf. Coates 1983, 41–42). An example of this rather rare usage is (8).

(8)   If this total is hundred then if this fifty that *must be* fifty If this is seventy-five that *must be* twenty-five (ICE-IND*:S2A-032)

In terms of syntactic features, we can find a co-occurrence of epistemic *must* with i) the perfect (cf. (6)), ii) the progressive aspect, iii) existential subjects, iv) stative verbs (cf. (5), (7), (8)), and v) inanimate subjects (cf. (5) and (8)) (cf. Coates 1983, 44). The epistemic reading of *must* occurs very often with perfect forms but root readings are also possible here in the sense of Standard English (StE) 'had to get', as (9) illustrates.

(9)   Poor Ashwini she didn't get admission in Delhi no because of the less percentage that she got she has got She got *must have got* atleast [sic!] eighty Then she would have got that admission here in Delhi (ICE-IND*:S1A-070)

Epistemic readings of *must* also have a strong tendency to co-occur with verbs in the progressive aspect. However, it should be taken into account that some English-as-a-second-language (ESL) varieties exhibit an extended use of the progressive, for example with stative verbs (cf. (7)) (cf. Rautionaho 2014, 199 for the extended use of stative progressives in IndE) and that not all examples of *must* followed by a verb in the progressive aspect are necessarily epistemic (cf. also Section 11.1 for methodological implications of this). This is why for a

---

2   The term 'modally harmonic combinations' was first introduced by Lyons (1977, 807) and
    initially only covered combinations of modal verb and modal adverb.

coding of the functions of *must* manual inspection of every concordance line is necessary. An example where the context is necessary to disambiguate the reading of *must* can be found in (10). In isolation, it is more likely that the sentence would be construed as epistemic (also because of the co-occurrence with the progressive), although in context it clearly represents a root use of *must* (paraphrased with 'it is necessary for').

(10) $A But the ladies who are sitting in the men's seat and they won't get up $B They won't get up $A So the men *must be standing* [...] (ICE-IND*:S1A-021)

The semi-modal verbs *have to, have got to,* and *need to* can also have an epistemic reading, although this is rare, cf. (11) to (13).

(11)   But after Tiananmen it's now become clear that this *has to* be a relationship based on mutual distrust [...] (ICE-HK:S1B-027)

(12)   Oh dear but oh I'm sure it's *got to* be pretty hard (ICE-HK:S1A-095)

(13)   As the culture of Hong Kong same as China-towns countries and urban areas in mainland China has been partially inherited from China, and partially influenced by other cultures, people *need to* face a very embarrassing situation that they want to maintain the traditional culture of Chinese but also want to march with foreign steps. (ICE-HK:W2A-008)

The second type of modality in Coates's classification is root modality. She argues that root modals form a coherent group that can be systematically distinguished from epistemic modals by syntactic criteria (e.g. root modals tend to co-occur with animate subjects, dynamic verbs, and the passive (cf. Coates 1983, 21)). While epistemic modality shows a cline of subjectivity, as illustrated with examples (5) to (8), root modality is marked by two interrelated clines from subjective to objective and strong to weak readings. Examples (14) and 15 illustrate the gradience found in the category of root modality.

(14)   "I don't want to go" "But you *must*" (ICE-SIN:W2F-019)

(15)   "Change is necessary but it *must* be evolutionary, not revolutionary", he said. (ICE-SIN:W2C-017)

Example (14) shows a strong subjective case of the core modal *must* with a high degree of speaker involvement, while example (15) is weak and more objective with less intense involvement on the part of the speaker. Despite the range of meanings expressed, Coates argues that all root modals are related and can be positioned on a cline, which is why she rejects tripartite distinctions that divide root modality up further, such as that made by Palmer (1979). Palmer subdivides Coates's root category into deontic and dynamic (cf. Palmer 1979, 36; cf. also Huddleston & Pullum 2002, 177–179 for a division into epistemic, deontic, and dynamic modality). Deontic modality refers to cases in which "conditioning factors are external to the person", whereas in dynamic modality the conditioning factors are internal to the person (cf. Palmer 2001, 70). Deontic modality therefore relates to instances where an obligation or permission from an external source is expressed, while dynamic modality relates to instances where an ability or willingness of the subject is expressed. This distinction works well for the modal *can*, where (16) refers to permission and can therefore be assigned deontic use, while (17) refers to ability and can therefore be assigned dynamic function.

(16)   You *can* go now. (deontic)

(17)   Sarah *can* speak French. (dynamic)

The distinction between deontic and dynamic readings with the modal *must* is sometimes difficult to draw, as Palmer himself also admits (cf. Palmer 1979, 58). Overall, dynamic *must* is rare, as it accounts for only about 6% in Collins's data from ICE-AUS, ICE-GB, and C-US.[3] Examples of dynamic *must* include instances where the necessity is conditioned by circumstances, e.g. (18), or instances where it describes an inner need of the subject, e.g. (19) (from Collins 2009a, 40–41). Instances such as in (19) are extremely rare, though.

(18)   Axon sprouting occurs from the proximal nerve end and *must* penetrate the fibrous tissue present at the nerve interface. (ICE-GB:W2A-026)

(19)   Dugongs are true mammals and *must* surface to breathe, and so they will inevitably be war casualties. (ICE-GB:W2B-029)

Other examples of the difficulty in distinguishing between deontic and dynamic *must* include instances where an action is not only necessitated by circumstances but also by a deontic source (i.e. the speaker), e.g. (15) (cf. also Depraetere & Verhulst 2008, 14–15; Collins 2009a, 41). The difficulty in distinguishing Palmer's deontic *must* and dynamic *must* suggests that they belong to the same category, i.e. that they "lie on a cline extending from strong 'Obligation' (the core) to cases at the periphery where the sense of 'Obligation' is extremely

---

3   This corpus consists of spoken data from the *Santa Barbara Corpus of Spoken American English* (SBC) and written data from FROWN.

weak [...]" (Coates 1983, 21). According to Coates, Palmer's distinction would therefore lead him to "choose arbitrary cut-off points, and to obscure the essential unity of the Root modals" (Coates 1983, 21). I agree with Coates's assumption that root modality forms a coherent group and I have therefore decided to use her bipartite distinction into epistemic and root modality (= deontic modality) for the purpose of this study. I will use the term 'deontic modality' in its broad meaning as a synonym for 'root modality' (cf. also Tagliamonte & Smith 2006, 345) and not in Palmer's sense as a subcategory of it. Building on the distinction between epistemic and root modality, my type of analysis does not account for relationships between deontic and dynamic readings or dynamic and epistemic readings, which is a benefit of applying the three-way distinction of modal meanings that Collins mentions (cf. Collins 2009a, 23). Apart from the two classifications detailed above, there are more approaches to modal meanings that are neatly summarised in Depraetere and Reed (2006, 227–279) and Van Linden (2012, 21–27).

1.3   Modal Verbs

The modal verbs *can, could, will/'ll, would/'d, may, might, shall, should,* and *must* are commonly used to express modality in English, together with the group of semi-modal verbs. Modal verbs form an identifiable subclass of the broader category of auxiliary verbs by showing properties that are characteristic of the class of auxiliary verbs and additional properties that are only typical of modal auxiliaries. Aside from the group of modal verbs, the group of auxiliaries also includes the primary verbs *be, do,* and *have.* All auxiliaries show the so-called NICE ('negation', 'inversion', 'code', 'ellipsis') properties (cf. Table 1), which distinguish them from lexical verbs (cf. Huddleston & Pullum 2002, 92–93; Palmer 1979, 8–10).

TABLE 1   Auxiliary verbs vs. lexical verbs (from Huddleston & Pullum 2002, 93, my emphases)

Auxiliary verb	Lexical verb	
He has seen it.	*He saw it.*	
*He **has not** seen it.*	**He saw not it.*	N
***Has he** seen it?*	**Saw he it?*	I
*He has seen it **and I have too.***	**He saw it and I saw too.*	C
*They don't think he's seen it **but he** HAS seen it.*	**They don't think he saw it but he SAW it.*	E

Auxiliaries take post-verbal negation with *not* or enclitic *n't* and, in contrast to main verbs, do not require *do*-support when negated and invert with the subject in interrogative sentences. They can occur in stranded position where a main verb has been omitted, i.e. "before a 'deletion site', a position vacated by elements deleted by ellipsis or moved to another place in the sentence." (Huddleston 1980, 69, 'code'). Furthermore, they carry emphatic stress to mark polarity contrasts ('ellipsis'). In addition to the four NICE properties, modal auxiliaries show distinctive features that mark them as a group and set them apart from the so-called primary verbs *be*, *do*, and *have* (cf. Quirk et al. 1985, 127–128; Huddleston & Pullum 2002, 106–107). Modal auxiliaries only have finite forms and cannot be combined with each other.[4] They do not show agreement with the subject and they trigger the bare infinitive. Modal auxiliaries occur in the apodosis of a remote conditional (*If you came tomorrow, you could help with the flowers.* vs. **If you came tomorrow, you were able to help with the flowers.*)[5] and show abnormal time reference in the past tense (e.g. *Could you tell me the time, please?*).

Must shows the NICE properties of auxiliaries and, in addition to these, all properties that are typical of modal auxiliaries except for those that presuppose a preterite form,[6] i.e. occurrence in the apodosis of a remote conditional[7] and abnormal time reference. *Must* will therefore be treated as a modal auxiliary in this study.

1.4   Semi-modal Verbs

Modality is not only expressed by the group of modal auxiliaries but also by periphrastic verbs, which take an intermediate status between auxiliaries and main verbs, as can be seen in Figure 1.

The scale shown in Figure 1 implies that there is no clear-cut opposition between auxiliary verbs and main verbs but a cline with several intermediate

---

4 Note, however, that some non-standard varieties have double modal constructions (cf. for example Beal 2004, 128).

5 In some cases, modal auxiliaries can also occur in the protasis of an *if*-clause (cf. Huddleston & Pullum 2002, 191 for *will* in if-clauses).

6 PDE *must* derives from the preterite form *moste*, which started to be used with present time reference in the ME period. The present tense use finally replaced the past tense use in LModE (cf. Denison 1998, 176). The modal can still be found with past time reference in reported speech, e.g. *He said he must come on Tuesday* (Palmer 2001, 76).

7 Nevertheless, rare cases exist, e.g. *If he stayed in the army, he must surely have become a colonel* (cf. Huddleston & Pullum 2002, 109).

(one verb phrase)	(a) **central modals**	*can, could, may, might, shall, should, will/'ll, would/'d, must*
	(b) **marginal modals**	*dare, need, ought to, used to*
	(c) **modal idioms**	*had better, would rather/sooner, be to, have got to,* etc.
	(d) **semi-auxiliaries**	*have to, be about to, be able to, be bound to, be going to, be obliged to, be supposed to, be willing to,* etc.
	(e) **catenatives**	*appear to, happen to, seem to, get + -ed* participle, *keep + -ing* participle, etc.
(two verb phrases)	(f) **main verb + non-finite clause**	*hope + to*-infinitive, *begin + -ing* participle, etc.

FIGURE 1   The auxiliary verb-main verb scale (adapted from Quirk et al. 1985, 137).

categories. This scale points to the process of grammaticalisation, i.e. "the change whereby lexical items and constructions come in certain contexts to serve grammatical functions and, once grammaticalized, continue to develop new grammatical functions" (Traugott & Hopper 2003, xv). As will be shown in Sections 6.1.1 to 6.1.4, the modal and semi-modal verbs of this study have all undergone grammaticalisation in their development. Quirk et al. place central modal verbs at the end point of the auxiliary-main verb scale, because they fulfil the NICE properties as well as typical properties of the group of modal auxiliaries, as discussed before. The group that resembles the central modals most are the marginal modal verbs *dare, need, ought to,* and *used to.* These can be used in modal function but also as main verbs, which is the reason why they are not placed in the category of central modals (cf. Quirk et al. 1985, 138). The next category is the group of modal idioms, including *had better, would rather/sooner, be to,* and *have got to.* This group of verbs includes auxiliaries plus infinitives, which are sometimes marked by *to* (cf. Quirk et al. 1985, 141). Modal idioms are similar to central modal verbs because they do not have non-finite forms (e.g. **I will have got to leave soon*). At the same time, modal idioms also differ from auxiliaries because they do not function as operators (**We haven't got to pay already, have we?*) (cf. Quirk et al. 1985, 141). The next category, the category of semi-auxiliaries, includes verbs such as *have to, be about to, be able to, be bound to, be going to, be obliged to, be supposed to,* and *be willing to.* These verbs fulfil modal and aspectual functions, which makes them similar to auxiliaries. Each consists of a primary verb (*be* or *have*) and is followed by the marked infinitive (cf. Quirk et al. 1985, 143). As these verbs have non-finite forms, they resemble main verbs more strongly in their syntactic behaviour (cf. Quirk et al. 1985, 144). Due to this fact they can provide suppletive forms in the defective paradigm of modal auxiliaries (cf. Quirk et al. 1985, 144). The last category, catenative verbs, includes verbs that have aspectual or modal meaning, similar to auxiliaries, but whose syntactic behaviour is more similar to main verbs (cf. Quirk et al. 1985, 146).

In the present study, I will use the cover term 'semi-modals' for those verbs that belong to Quirk et al.'s categories 'modal idioms' and 'semi-auxiliaries'. This means that I will refer to *have to, have got to,* and *need to* as 'semi-modals', although the modal idiom *have got to* differs syntactically from the more flexible semi-auxiliaries *have to* and *need to.* I will also depart from Quirk et al.'s classification of *need* as a marginal modal because I postulate two forms, i.e. the core modal verb *need* and the semi-modal verb *need to,* based on the historical development of these two forms (cf. Section 6.1.4 for the grammaticalisation of *need to*). The focus will be on the semi-modal *need to,* but I will also deal with the core modal verb *need* with regard to its intertwined history with the semi-modal *need to.*

Thus, I will adopt a binary classification of the verbs into central modals and semi-modals. The first group includes the modal verb *must,* which fulfils all NICE criteria and most criteria for modal auxiliaries. The second group includes the semi-modal verbs *have to, have got to,* and *need to.* It should be noted that the term 'semi-modals' is not consistently used in the literature. Biber et al. use the term 'semi-modals' as it is used in this study (cf. Biber et al. 1999, 484), while Collins uses the term 'quasi-modals' as a cover term for the group of verbs that is labelled 'semi-modals' in this study and refers to Quirk et al.'s modal idioms as 'semi-modals' (cf. Collins 2009a, 15–17). An alternative label for the group of verbs labelled 'semi-modals' in this study and 'quasi-modals' by Collins is

'periphrastic forms' (cf. Westney 1995, 11). The grouping of the semi-modal verbs
into one category is justified because they all occur with the marked infinitive
and are semantically related to the core modal verbs. This semantic affiliation
calls for an integrative investigation of the central modals with their semantically and functionally related semi-modals. Three major semantic categories
of modality can be distinguished: (1) permission/possibility/ability (*can, could,
may, might, be able to, be allowed to, be permitted to*), (2) obligation/necessity
(*must, should, (had) better, have (got) to, need to, ought to, be supposed to*), and
(3) volition/prediction (*will/'ll, would/'d, shall, be going to*) (cf. Biber et al. 1999,
485). I focus on the second category, i.e. the modal and semi-modals of obligation and necessity and restrict my analysis to strong obligation and necessity.

1.5   The (Socio-)Linguistic Variable Studied

This means I treat strong deontic modality as a linguistic variable, which can be
defined as two or more ways of "saying the same thing" (Labov 1972, 271). Linguistic variables can be found on all levels of linguistic analysis, for example the
realisation of the (ing)-variable in phonology, the different ways of forming the
comparative in morphology, different expressions for the same concept (e.g.
coke vs. *soda* vs. *pop*) on the lexical level, or the genitive alternation on the syntactic level. If the variants of a variable correlate with social factors (e.g. age, gender), we speak of a sociolinguistic variable. The sociolinguistic variable that will
be the focus in this study is strong deontic modality, which can be expressed by
the core modal verb *must* or the semi-modal verbs *have to, have got to*, and *need
to*, i.e. the variants of the variable deontic modality (cf. Figure 2). Unlike Biber
et al., I will deal with the semi-modal verbs *have to* and *have got to* separately
in this study due to their historical development (cf. Sections 6.1.2 and 6.1.3).

All four variants can be used to express strong obligation or necessity, as can
be seen in example sentences (20) to (23).

(20) Yes certainly atleast [sic!] you *must* uh attend the club once (ICE-
      IND*:S1A-001)

(21) [...] you *have to* speak in Oriya in order to be like them (ICE-IND*:S1A-010)

FIGURE 2   Strong deontic modality as a linguistic variable.

(22) Oh you *have got to* wait for your marks first (ICE-IND*:S1A-055)

(23) [...] if you want to communicate with people from other cities you *need to* know around uh ten fifteen languages (ICE-IND*:S1A-025)

Apart from the expression of deontic modality, the four variants can also express epistemic modality. While epistemic senses of *must* have existed since the end of the 14th century, epistemic senses of *have to*, *have got to*, and *need to* only emerged towards the end of the 20th century (cf. Sections 6.1.1–6.1.4). *Must* is therefore much more entrenched in its epistemic sense than any of the semi-modal verbs, which only rarely express epistemic readings, e.g. (11) to (13) (cf. also Mair 2006, 105; Depraetere & Verhulst 2008, 17; Close & Aarts 2010, 165). It is still debated whether *need to* has developed an epistemic sense or whether the root sense of *need to* may only imply epistemic modality in some cases. Very often, those examples that are given of an epistemic reading are ambiguous between the root and the epistemic reading, e.g. (13) (cf. also examples in Nokkonen 2006, 54–55).

Variation between *must, have to, have got to*, and *need to* is therefore less strong in epistemic modality, where *must* is the predominant variant used. Thus, strong variation between these variants can only be found in deontic modality. In order to establish functional equivalence, all variants were coded according to their function and only treated as variants of the same variable when they expressed the same meaning.

1.6   Subjectivity vs. Objectivity

The notions of subjectivity and objectivity have been used to explain the alternation between modal and semi-modal verbs (cf. Gramley & Pätzold 2004, 126); in particular with regard to the alternation between the core modal *must* and the semi-modals *have to* and *have got to* (cf. Quirk et al. 1985, 226; Huddleston & Pullum 2002, 206). The general assumption is that the core modal *must* expresses an obligation imposed by the speaker, while *have to* expresses an obligation that is external to the speaker, i.e. an "'external' necessity, originating in e.g. a rule or a regulation" (Depraetere & Verhulst 2008, 2). Westney gives examples (24) and (25) to illustrate the subjective reading of *must* and the objective reading of *have to* (cf. Westney 1995, 45, my emphases).

(24) My girl *must* be home by ten.

(25) My girl *has to* be home by ten.

In (24), the speaker is construed as the source of obligation. It is his or her will or interest that the girl is home by ten. In (25) instead, the deontic source is external to the speaker. The two major reference grammars of English, Quirk et al. (1985) and Huddleston and Pullum (2002), both mention the subjectivity-objectivity dimension as a distinguishing feature for the use of *have to/have got to* vs. *must*, e.g. the semi modal *have (got) to* "is often felt to be more impersonal than *must*, in that it tends to lack the implication that the speaker is in authority" (Quirk et al. 1985, 226) and "[*h*]*ave* and *have got* are most commonly used for deontic necessity [...]. Here they characteristically differ from *must* in being objective rather than subjective" (Huddleston & Pullum 2002, 206). The 'subjective' nature of modal verbs has also been adduced as an explanation for the use of the modal *must* in epistemic function because epistemic modality is considered to be inherently subjective. But the existence of objective epistemic uses (e.g. (8)) and semi-modal verbs with epistemic function (e.g. (11)-(13)) seriously challenge this line of argumentation (cf. also Westney 1995, 55–56).

As for deontic modality, the subjectivity-objectivity distinction seems to be more established. However, not all linguists agree that the semi-modal verbs *have to* and *have got to* tend to be used with an objective reading, as proposed by the two major reference grammars.[8] Coates, for instance, argues that *have got to* tends to be used subjectively and thus differs from *have to*, which only has an objective reading (cf. Coates 1983, 53;57). She suggests that this is one of the major differences between the semi-modal verbs, apart from the distinction that *have to* can be used with a habitual reading while this is not possible for *have got to* (and neither for *must*) (cf. Coates 1983, 57). Coates's postulation of a subjective reading for *have got to* goes against the clear association of semi-modal verbs with objectivity. She also finds examples of *must* with an objective reading that suggest that the modal verbs are not necessarily subjective (cf. also (15)). This means that the alternation between modal *must* and the semi-modal verb *have to* cannot be explained only along these lines.

Depraetere and Verhulst empirically analyse the claim of the association of *must* with subjectivity and *have to* with objectivity in their study on sources of modality (cf. Depraetere & Verhulst 2008). They classify examples of *must* and *have to* in ICE-GB according to their sources of obligation, which they divide into discourse-internal and discourse-external sources. Discourse-internal sources

---

8   The association between semi-modal verbs and objectivity also falls short in explaining the choice of *need to* over *must*, because the meaning of *need to* shows speaker involvement – although it has also developed objective uses lately (cf. Taeymans 2004; Nokkonen 2006).

are the speaker in affirmative sentences and the hearer in interrogative sentences (~subjective uses), while discourse-external sources include regulations, conditions, and circumstances (~objective uses) (cf. Depraetere & Verhulst 2008, 4). Their corpus findings show that both *have to* and *must* have discourse-internal and discourse-external sources and that the choice between them on the basis of different sources of obligation could not be corroborated (cf. Depraetere & Verhulst 2008, 23). They could only ascertain that *have to* is favoured with the discourse-external source 'circumstances' in their data from ICE-GB (cf. Depraetere & Verhulst 2008, 23–24). This is why they suggest that other factors, such as mode and strength of obligation, may have a stronger influence on the use of either verb, as *must* is more often used in written mode and "conveys necessity with more insistence than *have to*" (Depraetere & Verhulst 2008, 24; cf. also Sweetser 1990, 54 for the "irresistible force" associated with *must*).

These findings suggest that the alternation between root *must* and *have to* cannot only be explained with reference to differences in the source of obligation, but that other factors need to be taken into account as well. In addition, drawing a subjective-objective distinction in this study was deemed problematic because of the unfamiliarity with culture-specific rules, regulations, and moral principles in Hong Kong, India, and Singapore, which may lead to a 'culture-blind' imposition of categories from a 'Western' perspective and ultimately to circularity in coding. Another complicating factor in coding subjective and objective uses is that speakers are sometimes only the channel reporting an obligation necessitated by circumstances (cf. also the cases of *must* and *have to* with discourse-internal and discourse-external sources in Depraetere & Verhulst 2008, 14 or examples in Collins 2009a, 41). All of these arguments speak against adopting the subjective-objective distinction in this corpus-based study. Note, however, that Diaconu analyses the sources associated with *must*, *have to*, *have got to*, and *need to* on the basis of data from ICE-GB, ICE-JA, ICE-IND, and ICE-IRE by applying Depraetere and Verhulst's classification (cf. Diaconu 2012b, 131–175). Her study reveals that the modal and semi-modal verbs in ICE-JA, ICE-IND, and ICE-IRE show a similar distribution of functions to those in ICE-GB (cf. Diaconu 2012b, 174). Similarly to Depraetere and Verhulst, she also argues that register and formality differences "can usefully account for the competition and layering within strong obligation/necessity" (Diaconu 2012b, 175). These findings suggest that the exclusion of the factor 'source of obligation' as a predictor conditioning the choice of *must* over *have to* may be justified and that other factors probably play a more important role (cf. Section 4.3.1 for the language-internal and language-external factors that are analysed in this study).

1.7   Brief Overview of the Chapters

In order to systematically address questions of variation and change in the modal systems of L2 varieties of English, this study is divided into 11 chapters. This chapter introduced basic terminology for the study.

Chapter 2 provides an overview of previous studies on modal and semi-modal verbs in L1 and L2 varieties of English. The focus of this overview is on studies that analyse the domain of obligation and necessity, including corpus-based studies and sociolinguistic studies in the field. Finally, the overview concludes with the postulation of research desiderata and a proposal for a postcolonial research agenda in L2 varieties of English.

Chapter 3 develops the theoretical framework for the study and provides important sociohistorical background information about the development and status of English in Hong Kong, India, and Singapore. First, fundamental aspects of the two most influential models in the field of World Englishes (WE) are outlined, Kachru's (1985) Model of the Three Concentric Circles and Schneider's (2007) Dynamic Model, for the purpose of situating the varieties under analysis within these models. Second, Mufwene's (2001) Feature Pool Model and Biewer's (2015) adaptation of the model to the ESL context are described. Mufwene's (2001) model describes the restructuring process in the emergence of a new variety in terms of a competition-and-selection process between features that enter the pool from superstrate and substrate languages. Biewer (2015) identifies important selection features in the emergence of ESL varieties. The combination of the models and the description of the socio-historical background form the basis for understanding why the domain of obligation and necessity is shaped the way it is in the new varieties.

In Chapter 4, I detail the methodology of this study, which can best be described as 'sociolinguistic, and corpus-based', as I apply sociolinguistic methods to my corpus data and complement my corpus findings with qualitative findings from a sociolinguistic questionnaire in order to shed light on variation and change in the domain of obligation and necessity. As a prerequisite for the application of sociolinguistic methods to corpus data, I critically analyse the social structure of the data. Afterwards, I explain the process of data extraction and coding. I analyse variation in the domain by coding the variants according to language-internal and language-external factors, which have largely been neglected in the study of WE thus far. I finish the chapter by introducing multivariate analysis as the statistical model used for analysing the joint effect of language-internal and language-external factors on choice.

Chapter 5 introduces the overall findings concerning the regional variation in the use of *must, have to, have got to,* and *need to* in BrE, AmE, HKE, IndE, and SgE.

Chapter 6 discusses reasons behind the regional distribution identified in Chapter 5. The synchronic structure of the domain of obligation and necessity is analysed as a product of a competition-and-selection process of features. I have a closer look at the three sources that contribute features to the pool, which are the historical superstrate variety of BrE, the substrate languages, and the hypercentral variety AmE.

Having thoroughly analysed the input to the feature pool, I discuss four principles that may have guided the selection of features in Chapter 7. These are transfer principles, cultural motivations, SLA strategies, and cognitive principles.

Having taken a closer look at (regional) variation, I analyse changes in the modal system in Chapter 8, induced by the fact that diachronic studies on L1 varieties of English have shown that the modal domain is undergoing change. As there are currently no diachronic corpora available for the L2 varieties under study, I analyse the distribution of the variants with respect to age in order to provide apparent-time evidence for potential ongoing changes. The apparent-time studies are the first attempt to provide empirical evidence for recent change in the domain, which has so far simply been assumed on the basis of the development found in English-as-native-language (ENL) varieties.

Chapter 9 focuses on the alternation between the two main competitors in the field of strong deontic modality, *must* and *have to,* by analysing the joint effect of language-internal factors ('type of subject', 'verb semantics') and language-external factors (e.g. 'variety', 'text type', 'age', 'gender') on the choice between *must* and *have to.*

Chapter 10 summarises and discusses the main findings of this study and presents avenues for future research in a thematic conclusion of the study.

Chapter 11 discusses the methodological implications of the study for the wider corpus-linguistic community with reference to its contribution to the debate about big data and possibilities for the interface of corpus linguistics and sociolinguistics.

CHAPTER 2

Previous Research

This section gives an overview of previous corpus-based studies on the modal and semi-modal verbs of obligation and necessity. The overview starts with a summary of research on L1 varieties of English, where the modal system is generally well studied (Section 2.1) and continues with research on the modal system in L2 varieties of English (Section 2.2). After the literature overview, research desiderata will be formulated and a research agenda will be devised in Sections 2.3 and 2.4.

2.1 Studies on L1 Varieties of English

The modal system of L1 varieties of English is a well-researched area of linguistics, as is visible in the large number of synchronic descriptions, such as Ehrman (1966), Hermerén (1978), Palmer (1979), Coates (1983), and Westney (1995). Ehrman (1966) and Hermerén (1978) are synchronic studies on the semantics of the English central modal auxiliaries based on the *Brown University Standard Corpus of Present-Day American English* (BROWN corpus, Francis & Kučera 1979). Coates (1983) analyses the modal verb system of BrE instead, based on the *Lancaster-Oslo-Bergen Corpus* (LOB, Johansson, Leech & Goodluck 1978) and the *Survey of English Usage Corpus*, comprising over 1.5 million words. She investigates a representative sample of approximately 200 tokens of each modal verb in these corpora (cf. Coates 1983, 2). Her theory is often referred to as the framework for corpus-based studies on English modal verbs because of its detailed account of the semantics of the modal auxiliaries and its application to corpus data. In contrast to these corpus-based studies, Palmer (1979) and Westney (1995) are corpus-informed studies on the modal verbs in BrE. Palmer illustrates his findings with data from the *Survey of English Usage Corpus* "for heuristic and exemplificatory purposes only" (Palmer 1979, 21).

Apart from these synchronic studies on the modal system of standard and non-standard BrE and AmE, there are also investigations of modal and semi-modal verbs in other standard varieties of English. Collins is the first to broaden the scope of analysis by investigating the modals and semi-modals of obligation and necessity (*must, should, ought, need,* and *have (got) to*) in Australian English (AusE) based on the relatively small *Australian Corpus*, which comprises 225,000 words (cf. Collins 1991). He finds that *must* overall is more rarely used in AusE than in BrE (cf. Collins 1991, 153). Regarding the meaning of *must*, he finds a predominance of its epistemic reading over its deontic reading in AusE in contrast to an almost equal distribution in BrE (cf. Collins 1991, 154). *Have to* primarily expresses root readings in AusE, although epistemic readings can also be found, whereas *have got to* only shows root readings in his small corpus (cf. Collins 1991, 157).

Collins later presents a more comprehensive and more detailed study on the modals and semi-modals of obligation and necessity in AmE, BrE, AusE, and New Zealand English (NZE) in his article from 2005 (cf. Collins 2005). His study is based on the respective *International Corpus of English* (ICE) corpora (ICE-AUS, ICE-NZ, ICE-GB, Greenbaum 1996b); the data for AmE are retrieved from a makeshift corpus (C-US) in absence of a completed ICE-USA corpus. By including NZE in his semantic analysis of the modals of obligation and necessity, he shifts the focus to another (Antipodean) L1 variety. His findings show that C-US has the lowest frequency of *must*, pointing to the strong decrease of the core modal verb in AmE (cf. Collins 2005, 253–254). The frequency of *must* is higher in all other varieties, with the highest number found in ICE-NZ, followed by ICE-GB and ICE-AUS (cf. Collins 2005, 253). By contrast, the frequency of *have to* is highest in C-US, followed by ICE-AUS, ICE-GB, and ICE-NZ with the lowest frequency of the semi-modal verb (cf. Collins 2005, 253). The semi-modal verb *have got to* is instead more frequently used in ICE-AUS and ICE-GB than in ICE-NZ and C-US (cf. Collins 2005, 253). The semi-modal verb *need to* has the highest frequency in C-US and the lowest frequency in ICE-GB, with ICE-AUS and ICE-NZ ranging in between (cf. Collins 2005, 253). Collins also analyses the semantics of *must* and finds that root *must* is more often used in written language than in spoken language (cf. Collins 2005, 254). The highest frequency of root *must* can be found in NZE, followed by BrE and AusE, and the lowest frequency in AmE (cf. Collins 2005, 254). The frequency of epistemic *must* in written language is almost the same in AusE, BrE, and NZE, while it is comparatively low in AmE, where *must* is generally much more rarely used (cf. Collins 2005, 254). Root *have to* is more often found in spoken language than in written language, while epistemic *have to* is rare in both modes, except for some occurrences in NZE and AmE (cf. Collins 2005, 256). With regard to root *have got to*, Collins finds that it is more often used in spoken language than in written language in all corpora, with a particularly high frequency in AusE and BrE (cf. Collins 2005, 261). It is even more often used than the core modal *must* in the dialogue sections of ICE-AUS, ICE-GB, and ICE-NZ (cf. Collins 2005, 261). Its epistemic use is rare in all varieties under analysis (cf. Collins 2005, 261).

Collins further expands the scope of his studies by analysing the modal and semi-modal verbs of prediction and volition as well as the modal and

semi-modal verbs of possibility, permission, and ability, with data derived from
ICE-AUS, ICE-GB, and the *Santa Barbara Corpus of Spoken American English*
(SBC, Du Bois et al. 2000) (cf. Collins 2007a, 2007b). Important findings from
his earlier studies are synthesised in a monograph offering a comprehensive
study on regional variation and genre variation in the use of modal and semi-
modal verbs (cf. Collins 2009a). Apart from these studies, which analyse a wide
variety of modal and semi-modal verbs, there are also several studies that focus on specific members of the group, such as Taeymans's study on *dare* and
need in BrE, Nokkonen's studies on the semi-modal *need to* in BrE, and Lorenz's
study on the contracted semi-modal verbs *gonna*, *gotta*, and *wanna* (cf. Taeymans 2004; Nokkonen 2006, 2010, 2012, 2015; Lorenz 2013).

In addition to these synchronic studies, there is also an extensive body of
diachronic corpus-based research on the modal system of BrE and AmE (e.g.
Biber, Conrad & Reppen 1998; Krug 2000; Leech 2003; Smith 2003; Biber 2004;
Jankowski 2004; Leech et al. 2009; Leech & Smith 2009; Millar 2009; Close &
Aarts 2010; Leech 2011; Seggewiß 2012; Bowie, Wallis & Aarts 2013; Johansson
2013; Leech 2013; Mair 2015a).

Biber, Conrad, and Reppen analyse developments in the use of modal and
semi-modal verbs of obligation and necessity from the 17th to the 20th century in news, fiction, and drama based on ARCHER (*A Representative Corpus of
Historical English Registers*), LLC (*London Lund Corpus of Spoken English*), and
the BNC (*British National Corpus*) (cf. Biber, Conrad & Reppen 1998, 205–210).
These include the modal verbs *must* and *should* and the semi-modal verbs
have to, *have got to*, *need to*, *ought to*, and *be supposed to* (cf. Biber, Conrad &
Reppen 1998, 205). They find that in all registers "modals have generally been
more common than semi-modals over the last four centuries, but that relationship has been changing, with semi-modals becoming increasingly common"
(Biber, Conrad & Reppen 1998, 206–208). The semi-modal verbs are marked by
a gradual increase from the 17th to 20th century, with a particularly strong increase in the 20th century, the century where the modal verbs have decreased,
especially in drama (cf. Biber, Conrad & Reppen 1998, 208).

Another study that focuses on the interaction of register differences and
historical change is Biber (2004), who studies the developments in the use of
modal and semi-modal verbs in the different registers of ARCHER (drama, personal letters, newspaper prose, and academic prose) between 1650 and 1990.
He shows that the modal verbs *may*, *must*, *should*, *will*, and *shall* declined in
the last 50–100 years in all registers, while the semi-modal verbs increased,
especially in drama and letters (cf. Biber 2004, 199). With regard to the core
modal *must*, he finds that it actually increased in medical prose before its decline in frequency in the last 50 years (cf. Biber 2004, 210). The frequency of

the core modal remained relatively stable in personal letters but increased in newspaper prose (cf. Biber 2004, 210). Regarding the semi-modal *have to*, Biber finds a strong increase in use, especially in drama and personal letters (cf. Biber 2004, 203). Apart from changes in the frequency of the modal and semi-modal verbs, he also analyses the meanings of *must* and *have to* in personal letters and newspaper prose (cf. Biber 2004, 206–210). He finds that *must* was predominantly used in its deontic meaning in the 17th and 18th century in personal letters, while it carried epistemic and deontic meanings in the 20th century (cf. Biber 2004, 206–207). The increase in epistemic uses led to relative stability in the frequency of the modal verb in personal letters (cf. Biber 2004, 208). In newspapers, *must* was already used in deontic and epistemic readings in the 17th and 18th century, although its frequency was rare then (cf. Biber 2004, 208). With an increase in frequency in 20th century newspaper language, it was predominantly used in obligation readings (cf. Biber 2004, 209). The semi modal *have to* is primarily used in its deontic reading in personal letters from its rise in the late 18th century to the 20th century (cf. Biber 2004, 207–208).

Krug (2000) presents an in-depth study of the grammaticalisation and rise of the semi-modal verbs, with a focus on *be going to*, *have to*, *have got to*, *want to*, *need (to)*, *ought (to)*, and *dare (to)*, on the basis of the historical *Helsinki Corpus*, ARCHER, the BROWN family of corpora, and the BNC (cf. Krug 2000). The BROWN family of corpora is also the database used in studies by Leech (2003), Smith (2003), and Leech et al. (2009). These studies all indicate that the central modal verbs decreased while the semi-modal verbs increased in the period between 1961 and 1991. The studies also show that the trends are more pronounced in AmE than in BrE, which is why they are explained in the light of the process of 'Americanisation'. Furthermore, these studies prove that the decline of the core modal verbs is stronger in spoken language than in written language, which leads to the assumption that the process of 'colloquialisation', whereby written language starts to approximate spoken norms, is involved. Regarding the core modal and semi-modal verbs of strong obligation, these studies reveal that *must* decreased in the thirty-year period between 1961 and 1991. The decrease of *must* affects both readings, although its decline is sharper in its deontic sense than in its epistemic sense. This decline is explained by 'democratisation' (cf. Fairclough 1993), a process whereby overt markers of authority are avoided.[1] With regard to the semi-modal verbs *have to*, *have got to*, and *need to*,

---

1   Another study that links changes in the use of modal and semi-modal verbs to changes in society is Myhill's study on the development of the modal system in nine AmE plays from the period between 1824 and 1947 (cf. Myhill 1995). Myhill shows that the frequency of *must*, *should*, *may*, and *shall* declined after the Civil War, while the frequency of *got to*, *have to*,

the studies show that the frequency of *have to* remained relatively stable, which suggests that its rise has reached a saturation point. Furthermore, no significant increase of *have got to* could be observed in written language. By contrast, the frequency of *need to* increased dramatically towards the end of the 20th century. Apart from more general diachronic shifts in the frequencies of the modal and semi-modal verbs, Smith also analyses the impact of genre on linguistic change and shows that *must* decreased in all registers, while *have to* increased most strongly in the press section and is particularly frequent there as well as in fiction (cf. Smith 2003, 251). For the semi-modal *have got to*, Smith observes that its use is mostly restricted to press and fiction (cf. Smith 2003, 252). For *need to*, he finds that its rise can be detected in all registers; "[i]t appears to have no clear genre preferences" (Smith 2003, 252).

The claim about the rise of the semi-modal verbs and the decline of the core modal verbs has been further tested against data from the extended BROWN family. Leech and Smith, for example, analyse the frequency of modal and semi-modal verbs in BLOB, comprising BrE language data from 1931 (cf. Leech & Smith 2009). They show that the frequency of the core modal verbs remained relatively stable between 1931 and 1961 and that their decrease only set in after 1961 (cf. Leech & Smith 2009, 187). With regard to the semi-modal verbs, they demonstrate that the rise observed between 1961 and 1991 is a continuation of a trend which already existed in the previous thirty years between 1931 and 1961 in BrE (cf. Leech & Smith 2009, 189). Concerning the modal and semi-modal verbs of strong obligation, Leech and Smith show that the core modal *must* had already been decreasing between 1931 and 1961 in BrE before a sharp decrease set in between 1961 and 1991; this means "the decline of *must* shows an accelerating trend in the more recent period" (Leech & Smith 2009, 191). They point out that the frequency of *have to* increased sharply between 1931 and 1961 before the strong decrease of *must* (cf. Leech & Smith 2009, 190). The frequency development of *need to* shows an increase between 1931 and 1961, which becomes very steep in the period between 1961 and 1991 (cf. Leech & Smith 2009, 191).

---

ought, better, and *can* increased in this period (cf. Myhill 1995, 162). He argues that these frequency changes reflect changes in society, "the 'old' modals had usages associated with hierarchical social relationships, with people controlling the actions of other people, and with absolute judgments based upon social decorum, principle, and rules about societal expectations of certain types of people. The 'new' modals, on the other hand, are more personal, being used to, for example, give advice to an equal, make an emotional request, offer help, or criticize one's interlocutor" (Myhill 1995, 157). In another study, he analyses the functions of *must, have to,* and *have got to* and shows that *must* is associated with obligations deriving from social norms, while *have to* is associated with objective meanings, and *got to* with 'individual' meaning (cf. Myhill 1996).

Millar analyses the frequency of the modal and semi-modal verbs in the TIME magazine corpus, comprising data from 1923 to the present (cf. Millar 2009). His study is the only study that argues against a general decline of the core modal verbs, as he observes that "while certain modal verbs have fallen in frequency, the overall pattern is one of growth" (Millar 2009, 191). The growth in the group of core modal verbs is especially visible in the rise of *can*, *could*, and *may* (cf. Millar 2009, 199). But Millar's findings concerning the development of the core modal *must* do not contradict earlier findings, as his data also point to a strong decrease of the modal verb throughout the 20th century (cf. Millar 2009, 199). Furthermore, he also finds that its deontic sense is decreasing sharply, but, contrary to earlier findings, he observes a rise in frequency in its epistemic use (cf. Millar 2009, 203). With regard to the semi-modal verbs, he supports earlier findings about the rise of this group of verbs (cf. Millar 2009, 204). All semi-modal verbs of strong obligation (*have to*, *have got to*, and *need to*) are on the rise in the period between the 1920s and the 2000s (cf. Millar 2009, 204). His findings indicate that the rise in the use of the semi-modal *have to* is strongest between the 1930s and the 1940s (cf. Millar 2009, 204). *Need to* is the semi-modal verb that increased most strongly in the 20th century, while *have got to* is generally rare in the TIME corpus but marked by an increase in the 20th century (cf. Millar 2009, 204).

In a reply to Millar's study, Leech shows that the group of core modal verbs is on the decline in the 20th century, with an accelerated decline since the 1960s, by using data from the extended BROWN family from 1901 to 2006 for BrE and data from the *Corpus of Historical American English* (COHA) for AmE (cf. Leech 2011). His findings suggest that *must* has been on the decrease since 1931 and decreased most sharply after 1961 in BrE (cf. Leech 2011, 551). Based on COHA, he observes that *must* also decreased in AmE between 1910 and 2006, with a sharp decrease after the 1970s (cf. Leech 2011, 554). His data from the *Corpus of Contemporary American Englsih* (COCA) show that the trend continued in the period between 1990 and 2010 (cf. Leech 2011, 554). As Leech focuses on the development of the core modal auxiliaries in COCA, Johansson complements his study well by analysing the development of the semi-modal verbs of obligation and necessity in COCA (cf. Johansson 2013). He shows that the rise of *have to* seems to have come to a halt in the period between 1990–1994 and 2005–2008, while *need to* is still on the rise in COCA and is even more frequently used than *must* in contemporary AmE (cf. Johansson 2013, 375). The semi-modal *have got to* is only rarely used instead and decreased between 1990–1994 and 2005–2008 (cf. Johansson 2013, 375). Apart from analysing the diachronic development of the modal and semi-modal verbs, Johansson also analyses variation according to genre ('Spoken', 'Fiction', 'Magazine', 'News', 'Academic') (cf. Johansson 2013, 375–376). He observes that *have to* is the expression that is most often used across all registers except for academic prose, where *must* and also *need to* are more often used than *have to* (cf. Johansson 2013, 375–376). As *have to* and *have got to* are most often used in spoken language and least often in academic prose, Johannsson concludes that they are less formal than *must* and *need to*, which "are more compatible with the formality of writing in Academic prose" (Johansson 2013, 376).

In a study from 2013, Leech corroborates earlier findings according to which spoken language is more advanced in the two trends of the decline of the core modal verbs and the rise of the semi-modal verbs with data from the *Diachronic Corpus of Spoken Present-Day English* (DCPSE), which comprises spoken language data from the 1960s and 1990s (cf. Leech 2013). Furthermore, he gives supporting evidence for the rise of the semi-modal verbs by constructing an apparent-time scenario on the basis of the BNC demographically-sampled sub-corpus (cf. Leech 2013, 113). Mair (2015a) extends the diachronic analysis of the modal and semi-modal verbs in AmE to B-BROWN from 1931 and finds that "[t]he generalisation that modals are on the decline *as a category* [...] cannot be upheld for B-Brown, Brown and Frown" (Mair 2015a, 132). He finds an increase in the frequency of the group of core modal verbs between the 1930s and 1961 of 12%, which is followed by a decrease of 12% between 1961 and 1991 (cf. Mair 2015a, 131). With regard to the modal and semi-modal verbs of obligation and necessity, Mair observes that *must* shows an insignificant decrease between the 1930s and 1961 before it decreases drastically between 1961 and 1991 (cf. Mair 2015a, 131), confirming earlier tendencies that showed an accelerated decrease of the core modal verb towards the end of the 20th century. For the competing semi-modal *have to*, he shows a significant increase between B-BROWN and FROWN, with a strong rise in frequency between the 1930s and 1961 (cf. Mair 2015a, 137). While he does not find a significant increase of the semi-modal *have got to*, he observes a strong increase for the semi-modal verb *need to* in the period between the 1930s and 1991 (cf. Mair 2015a, 137). Further evidence about the decline of the core modal verbs and the rise of the semi-modal verbs in the 20th century comes from Jankowski's study on *must, have to, have got to*, and *got to* in British and American dramas (cf. Jankowski 2004). She uses variationist methodology to analyse the competition between the variants in the domain of deontic modality and finds that the proportion of *must* decreased in the period between 1902 and 2001, while the proportion of *have to* increased (cf. Jankowski 2004, 95). Regarding the semi-modal verb (*have*) *got to*, she finds that it only increased towards the end of the 20th century in BrE but not in AmE (cf. Jankowski 2004, 95). More recently, the trends of the decline of the core modal verbs and the rise of the semi-modal verbs have also been confirmed in spoken diachronic data from BrE (cf. Close & Aarts 2010; Seggewiß 2012; Bowie, Wallis & Aarts 2013).

While most of the diachronic studies analyse standard BrE and AmE, there are also some studies on changes in the use of the modal and semi-modal verbs of obligation in dialects of English. Tagliamonte, for example, studies the use of *must*, *have to*, and *(have) got to* in York English (cf. Tagliamonte 2004). She provides further indirect evidence about ongoing language change in deontic modality on the basis of apparent-time evidence. Her findings show that the proportion of *must* decreased from the oldest to the youngest age group, while the proportion of *have to* rose from the oldest to the youngest age group (cf. Tagliamonte 2004, 42). These findings point to a decrease of *must* and an increase of *have to* in real time in York English and thus confirm trends previously identified in diachronic studies. For the semi-modal verb *(have) got to*, she finds an increase in its share from the oldest to the youngest age group, suggesting an increase in real time (cf. Tagliamonte 2004, 42). Tagliamonte and Smith extend the scope of analysis to other dialects of English by analysing the domain of deontic modality in dialect data from England, Scotland, and Northern Ireland (cf. Tagliamonte & Smith 2006). Their study shows that "[m]ust is obsolescent and there is an unanticipated resurgence of *have to* alongside pan-dialectal grammatical re-organization" (cf. Tagliamonte & Smith 2006, 341). This reorganisation involves an encroachment of *have to* on the territory of *must* and a specialisation of *have got to* to contexts with subjects of indefinite reference (cf. Tagliamonte & Smith 2006, 341).

Apart from the analysis of British dialect data, Tagliamonte also investigates the domain of obligation and necessity in Toronto English together with D'Arcy (cf. Tagliamonte & D'Arcy 2007). Their findings similarly show a decrease of *must* and an increase of *have to* in apparent time (cf. Tagliamonte & D'Arcy 2007, 71). However, they do not find an increase of the other two semi-modal verbs *(have) got to* and *need to* (cf. Tagliamonte & D'Arcy 2007, 71). In another study together with Denis, Tagliamonte supplements the apparent-time study in Toronto English with three apparent-time studies with data from speakers of towns outside Toronto, namely Burnt River, Lakefield, and Belleville (cf. Tagliamonte & Denis 2014). They show an increase of *have to* in apparent time for Belleville and Burnt River, similar to that found for Toronto English (cf. Tagliamonte & Denis 2014, 107).

Fehringer and Corrigan present another variationist study on dialect data with their diachronic study of the modal and semi-modal verbs of obligation and necessity in Tyneside English, with data drawn from the *Diachronic Corpus of Tyneside English* (DECTE, 1960–2010) (cf. Fehringer & Corrigan 2015). Their findings reveal that *must* decreased in the period between 1960 and 2010 in its root sense but increased in its epistemic sense during that period, which they take as evidence for a trend towards monosemy for the modal verb (cf. Fehringer &

Corrigan 2015, 361). Their findings support earlier interpretations of synchronic findings by Trousdale (2003), who argued that simplification and redistribution processes are at work in the restructuring of the modal system of this dialect of English on the basis of recorded data from 20 informants. He shows, for example, that *must* is predominantly used in its epistemic sense in this variety of English ('simplification') and that the root sense of strong obligation is now predominantly expressed by the semi-modal verbs *have to, have got to*, and *gotta* ('redistribution') (cf. Trousdale 2003, 277–278; cf. also Beal, Burbano-Elizondo & Llamas 2012, 67). In line with this view, we can see a redistribution of root modality from modal *must* to the semi-modal verbs *have to, have got to*, and *need to*, with a rise in frequency of these expressions between 1960 and 2010 (cf. Fehringer & Corrigan 2015, 369). The data from DECTE show that *have to* and *have got to* are most often used as expressions of root modality in the time span between 1960 and 2010 and that *have got to* was more frequently used than *have to* in the earlier periods but not in the later period (cf. Fehringer & Corrigan 2015, 369). The decrease of *have got to* after its rise, or its 'twist of fate' as Tagliamonte and Smith (2006) call it, has also been observed in other studies, for example by Close and Aarts (2010).

Apart from these dialect studies, there are also diachronic studies on regional standard(ising) varieties of English other than BrE and AmE. Dollinger analyses developments in the use of modal and semi-modal verbs in early Canadian English (CanE) on the basis of the *Corpus of Early Ontario English* (CONTE), including language data from the late 18th century and the 19th century (cf. Dollinger 2008). During this period, he finds shifting distributions in the functions of *must* in CanE and BrE, with a decrease of the share of root *must* and an increase of the share of epistemic *must* (cf. Dollinger 2008, 220–222). Overall, CanE shows a lower proportion of epistemic *must* than BrE in all periods, which Dollinger interprets as a sign of its 'conservativeness' (cf. Dollinger 2008, 225). Apart from these findings concerning the core modal, he also shows that the semi-modal verb *have to* was on the increase in CanE during that period, even more strongly so than in BrE (cf. Dollinger 2008, 224).

Another study that analyses the modal system of an L1 variety of English is Rossouw and van Rooy's study on the use of modal and semi-modal verbs in 19th and 20th century South African English (SAfE) based on a corpus of letters, newspapers, and fiction (cf. Rossouw & van Rooy 2012). Their findings indicate that the frequency of modal verbs remained relatively stable throughout the 19th century and the first half of the 20th century, before a decrease set in in the second half of the 20th century (cf. Rossouw & van Rooy 2012, 16). Contrary to findings from other L1 varieties of English, their study on SAfE does not show the expected increase in the use of semi-modal verbs (cf. Rossouw & van Rooy 2012, 17). Their findings do not only differ from findings of other studies with regard to these overall trends but also with regard to individual developments of specific modal expressions. For the core modal verb *must*, they find, for example, that it does not decrease as strongly as in other varieties of English, presumably "because the social taboo against its perceived face-threatening strength appears not to be felt so strongly in South Africa" (Rossouw & van Rooy 2012, 23). In another study on WhSAfE, Wasserman and van Rooy show that *must* extended its meaning to denote median obligation in the period between the 1820s and the 1990s, probably due to contact with Afrikaans (cf. Wasserman & van Rooy 2014, 47–48).

Collins continues to extend research on the modal system to other L1 varieties of English with his diachronic study on AusE (cf. Collins 2014). He studies the use of the core modal verbs *must, should, ought to, will*, and *shall* and their semantically related semi-modal verbs *have to, have got to*, and *be going to* in AusE fiction from the period between 1800 and 1999 and compares his findings to data from the BrE and AmE fiction sections of ARCHER. He comes to the conclusion that AusE generally follows the pattern identified for BrE and AmE but is marked by a lower frequency of modal verbs and a "reluctance to embrace the quasi-modals as enthusiastically as users of American English" (Collins 2014, 7). As far as the modal and semi-modal verbs of obligation and necessity are concerned, he observes that *must* is generally less often used in AusE than in BrE and AmE and decreased between 1800–1849 and 1950–1999 (cf. Collins 2014, 15). This means "that AusE is isolated from the two older varieties in the relative smallness of its frequency for *must*" (Collins 2014, 15). Regarding the development of the senses of *must*, he finds that the share of epistemic *must* decreased while that of deontic *must* increased, which is unexpected given earlier findings about the development of the senses of *must* (cf. Collins 2014, 16). The general decrease of *must* contrasts strongly with the rise of the semi-modal *have to* in AusE, whose rate of increase is stronger than in BrE but weaker than in AmE in the 20th century (cf. Collins 2014, 12). For *have got to*, Collins records an increase in AusE and also in BrE and AmE, with the strongest increase in AmE (cf. Collins 2014, 14). While BrE and AmE show a similar pattern until the end of the 19th century, marked by a steep increase in the use of *have to* between 1850–1899 and 1900–1949, they take different routes of development thereafter, with a decrease in the frequency of the semi-modal verb in AmE between 1900–1949 and 1950–1999 and a continued (though more moderate) increase in BrE during this period (cf. Collins 2014, 14). AusE instead is marked by a gradual increase in the use of the semi-modal between 1800–49 and 1950–1999, although it tailed off towards the end of the 20th century (cf. Collins 2014, 14).

The overview of previous research on the modal systems in L1 varieties of English shows that modal and semi-modal verbs are undergoing language change, with a general decrease in the frequency of the core modal verbs and a simultaneous increase in the frequency of semi-modal verbs. The core modal verb *must* and the semi-modal verb *have to* generally follow this trend, with a decrease of *must* and an increase of *have to* in most L1 varieties of English. The frequency development of the semi-modal verb *have got to* instead does not follow the increase of the semi-modal verbs in all varieties of English. It seems to be involved in a declining trend in Northern American varieties of English but not in British varieties of English. By contrast, the semi-modal verb *need to* shows a strong increase in most varieties of English. Apart from the identification of these major frequency changes in the use of modal expressions of obligation and necessity, the findings also underline the importance of relating the changes in the frequency of forms to the functions fulfilled by them. Most studies show a sharp decline of the core modal *must* in its root sense rather than in its epistemic sense, while the semi-modal verbs are mostly restricted to deontic readings. Aside from variation through time, the findings of the studies also attest to the importance of analysing regional and stylistic variation by pointing to frequency differences in the use of modal and semi-modal verbs of obligation and necessity between varieties of English and in different genres.

2.2   Studies on L2 Varieties of English

Several structural descriptions suggest that L2 varieties of English also exhibit variation in the modal system (cf. Mesthrie 2008b, 626–627 for a summary). The descriptions indicate that the modal verb *would* shows an extended use in several ESL varieties to express politeness, tentativeness, and irrealis aspect in contexts where StE uses *will* (cf. Alsagoff & Lick 1998, 141 for SgE; Bautista 2004 for Philippine English (PhilE), Alo & Mesthrie 2008, 326 for Nigerian English (NigE); Bhatt 2008, 559 for IndE; Low 2010, 238–239 for SgE and Malaysian English (MalE)). While *would* can substitute for *will*, *will* can also substitute for *would* in some varieties, such as in NigE or BlSAfE (cf. Alo & Mesthrie 2008, 326; Mesthrie 2008a, 490). The use of *will* and *would* was analysed in corpus-based studies by Deuber for Trinidadian English (TrinE) and by Deuber et al. for TrinE, Fiji English (FijiE), IndE, SgE, Jamaican English (JamE), and Bahamian English (BahE) (cf. Deuber 2010; Deuber et al. 2012; Deuber 2014, 202–237). Deuber et al.'s quantitative and qualitative findings reveal variable use of the two modals, "with tokens of *would* appearing where only *will* occurs in British English and vice versa" (Deuber et al. 2012, 87).

Apart from variation in the use of modals of volition and prediction, variation has also been observed for modals of permission, possibility, and ability, such as in the use of the double modal *can be able* in some African Englishes (cf. Alo & Mesthrie 2008, 326 for NigE; Mesthrie 2008a, 490 for Black South

African English (BlSAfE). Furthermore, we can also see variation in the use of *can* and *could* (similar to the variation between *will* and *would* in the domain of prediction and volition) (cf. Bhatt 2008, 559 for IndE; Bowerman 2008, 477 for BlSAfE). The use of *can* and *could* in L2 varieties has also been analysed on the basis of corpus data by Deuber for TrinE and Hackert et al. for FijiE, IndE, SgE, TrinE, JamE, and BahE (the same set of varieties as in Deuber et al.'s 2012 study on *will* and *would*) (cf. Deuber 2010; Hackert et al. 2013). One of the main findings of Hackert et al.'s study is that Asian Englishes prefer non-past modals over past tense modals (in their case study *can* over *could*), whereas TrinE and BahE display the reverse behaviour (cf. Hackert et al. 2013).

Finally, variation has also been noted in the use of the modals of obligation and necessity. Alo and Mesthrie note for example that the double modal *must have to* can be found in NigE (cf. Alo & Mesthrie 2008, 326). Bowerman ascertains that the illocutionary force of *must* "has much less social impact in WhSAfE [White South African English] than in the other varieties of English, and often substitutes for polite *should/shall*" (Bowerman 2008, 477; cf. also Rossouw & van Rooy 2012, 23; Wasserman & van Rooy 2014, 47–48), which seems to apply more generally to varieties of English in Africa, South Asia, and Southeast Asia, as Mesthrie concludes in his synopsis on morphological and syntactic variation when he states that "in some varieties *must* does not generally carry the semantics of obligation or 'bossiness' understood in StE [sc. Standard English]" (Mesthrie 2008b, 627) (cf. also Section 7.2 for cultural motivations for this finding). Anecdotal evidence therefore suggests that variation across ESL varieties can also be found in the use of the modals of obligation and necessity, but it has rarely been analysed quantitatively and qualitatively on the basis of corpus data, with only some notable exceptions.

The first article that reports corpus findings about the modal systems of L2 varieties of English is Nelson's (2003) article on the use of *must, should, ought to, need to*, and *(have) got to* in spoken BrE, NZE, East African English (EAfE), IndE, JamE, and HKE. His study is based on the spoken parts of ICE-GB, ICE-NZ, and ICE-EA and a sample of 10 dialogues and 10 monologues from ICE-IND, ICE-JA, and ICE-HK, whose spoken sections were not yet available in their entirety at the point of his study. His findings show that *have to* is the most frequently used verb in the field in all corpora except in ICE-EA, where *should* is used with a higher frequency (cf. Nelson 2003, 27–29). He observes a particularly high frequency of *have to* in ICE-HK (cf. Nelson 2003, 28–29).[2] With regard

---

2 Note that Nelson subsumes *have to, have got to*, and *gotta* under one category as lexical variants but provides the frequency of each in the tables. As I treat *have to* and *have got to* separately in my corpus-based study, I report the frequency for them separately despite Nelson's categorisation (cf. Nelson 2003, 27).

to the semi-modal verb *need to*, he finds that JamE is characterised by a higher frequency of this semi-modal verb than all other varieties, while IndE shows a considerably lower frequency of this semi-modal verb (cf. Nelson 2003, 29). The frequency of *must* instead does not vary strongly between the varieties but shows considerable variation in the distribution of epistemic and root uses (cf. Nelson 2003, 30). Nelson finds that *must* predominates in its root function in all varieties, even though the shares of root and epistemic uses approach each other in BrE and NZE, while the deontic share is much larger in the other four varieties and particularly large in EAfE (Nelson 2003, 30). The respective shares of epistemic *must* are 43% for BrE and NZE, 30% for IndE, 18% for HKE, and only 9% for EAfE (cf. Nelson 2003, 30). In the case of JamE, Nelson's sample has no epistemic uses of *must* (cf. Nelson 2003, 31). This means that IndE is marked by a comparatively higher proportion of epistemic *must* than the other three ESL varieties. While Nelson finds strong differences in the distribution of the senses of *must*, he does not identify differences in the distribution of the senses of *should* and *have (got) to* in the varieties; both verbs predominantly express root modality (cf. Nelson 2003, 30–31).

Another early study on modal verbs in ESL varieties is Nkemleke's study of *must* and *should* in Cameroon English (CamE) (cf. Nkemleke 2005). His study is based on the *Cameroon Corpus of English* (CCE), comprising 1 million words, compiled in the period between 1992 and 1994 (cf. Nkemleke 2005, 48). The corpus contains written texts from 11 text categories ('official press', 'students' 'essays', 'miscellaneous', 'novels and short stories', 'private press', 'government memoranda', 'private letters', 'tourism', 'religion', 'official letters', and 'advertisement') (cf. Nkemleke 2005, 48). His study pursues two major aims: (1) identifying regional differences between CamE and BrE and (2) analysing register variation in the use of *must* and *should* in CamE.

He observes a lower frequency of epistemic *must* in CamE than in BrE, with a share of 21% in CCE compared to 31% in LOB. He further divides up the category of root modality into 'instruction', 'exhortation', 'intention', and 'necessity'. The first subcategory 'instruction' comprises 'performative' uses of *must*, in which the speaker obliges the hearer to do something, i.e. they can be paraphrased with 'I order you to x' (cf. Nkemleke 2005, 51). This type of *must* is only rarely used in BrE and is restricted to highly specific contexts, such as in law courts (cf. Nkemleke 2005, 52). However, his findings show that "[t]he use of performative *must* in Cameroon English is generalised" (Nkemleke 2005, 52). It is used in the text categories 'students' 'essays', 'private letters', and 'religion' (cf. Nkemleke 2005, 52). With regard to *should*, he finds – among other things – that it has a higher share of root uses in CamE than in BrE, with a share of 71% in CCE compared to a share of 51% in LOB (cf. Nkemleke 2005, 56).

This may suggest that the trend towards monosemy of *should* is more advanced in CamE than in BrE or it may simply reflect the time difference of approximately 30 years between CCE and LOB.

To add another study, Biewer analyses regional variation in the frequency of use and distribution of functions of the modal verbs but also of semi-modal verbs of obligation and necessity (cf. Biewer 2009). She takes into consideration the complete field of obligation and necessity, including modal and semi-modal verbs of strong and weak obligation (*must, have (got) to,* and *need to, should, ought to, supposed to,* and *need*) (cf. Biewer 2009, 48). She studies the use of these verbs in the South Pacific Englishes (SPE) Fiji English (FijE), Samoan English (SamE), and Cook Island English (CookE) and in the ENL varieties AmE, BrE, and NZE. Her case study is based on a newspaper corpus, comprising about 2.17 million words, with articles that were written in the period between 2004 and 2007 (cf. Biewer 2009, 47). Biewer supplements these data with press data from the ICE corpora of FIjiE, BrE, and NZE (cf. Biewer 2009, 47).

She finds that all varieties use *should* most often, followed by *have (got) to,*[3] *must,* and *need to* (cf. Biewer 2009, 48). However, the SPE show more variation in the frequency of individual modal and semi-modal verbs (cf. Biewer 2009, 48). In particular, FijiE is marked by high frequencies of *should* and *have to* (cf. Biewer 2009, 48). She also recognises that *ought to* and modal *need* "are effectively non-existent in South Pacific Englishes" (Biewer 2009, 49). After analysing the frequencies of the modal and semi-modal verbs, she zooms in on the semantic profiles of *should* and *must* (cf. Biewer 2009, 49–50). She finds that *should* predominantly expresses deontic modality in all varieties rather than epistemic or putative meaning (cf. Biewer 2009, 49; cf. also Nelson 2003, 31 and Nkemleke 2005, 56 for similar findings). Additionally, she proves that BrE and NZE pattern alike in that their share of deontic readings is lower than that found in the other varieties (cf. Biewer 2009, 49). The SPE FijiE and SamE are marked by a higher proportion of deontic readings and therefore pattern closely with AmE, while the proportion of deontic *should* in CookE is in between that of NZE and AmE (cf. Biewer 2009, 49). With regard to the modal *must,* she observes that the ENL varieties BrE and AmE use *must* with a lower frequency than the ESL varieties (cf. Biewer 2009, 50). She therefore considers the ENL varieties to be "more advanced in the decline of *must* than the other varieties" (Biewer 2009, 50). Regarding the distribution of the senses of *must,* she exposes a higher share of epistemic *must* in BrE, NZE, and CookE than in the other varieties (cf. Biewer 2009, 50). This means that the SPE as a group show a stronger deontic bias of *must* than the L1 varieties of English (cf. Biewer

---

3   Note that Biewer does not distinguish between *have to* and *have got to* in her analysis.

2009, 51). Based on her own and Nelson's (2003) findings, she argues that the deontic bias of *must* seems to represent a more general trend in ESL varieties (cf. Biewer 2009, 51). Those varieties that use deontic *must* more often in her study (i.e. FijiE and SamE) also show a higher co-occurrence of deontic *must* with verbs in the passive (cf. Biewer 2009, 50).

She analyses these findings with reference to three sources of variation: (1) exonormative influence, (2) second-language acquisition (SLA) strategies, and (3) substrate influence. Biewer argues that the same ranking in terms of frequency of the modal and semi-modal verbs indicates exonormative influence (cf. Biewer 2009, 51). She claims that the SLA process of simplification can account for the high frequency of *should* and the extremely low frequency of *ought to* and *need* in the SPE (cf. Biewer 2009, 51). She explains the widespread use of *must* with the passive in FijiE and SamE with substrate influence, as the use of the passive is a common strategy of softening a request in the local Oceanic substrate languages (cf. Biewer 2009, 51).

Biewer revisited the topic of SLA and ESL varieties in her 2011 article, where she analysed the same set of modal and semi-modal verbs as in her earlier study from 2009 but extended her scope of analysis beyond the SPE to three more New Englishes, namely the Asian varieties SgE, PhilE, and the African variety Ghanaian English (GhanE), again in comparison with the L1 varieties BrE, AmE, and NZE (cf. Biewer 2011). An extended version of the newspaper corpus that was used in her previous work serves as the database for her study. It comprises texts with three million words from the period between 2004 and 2009 (cf. Biewer 2011, 20–21).

In her study from 2009, she found that *should* was used with the highest frequency in all varieties and her study from 2011 points out that *should* is also most often used in SgE, PhilE, and GhanE (cf. Biewer 2011, 22). As far as the meanings of *should* are concerned, Biewer finds a higher frequency of putative *should* in GhanE and SgE, similar to the use of *should* in BrE and NZE (cf. Biewer 2011, 22). All the other varieties show a stronger tendency towards monosemy of *should*, with a high share of deontic *should* (cf. Biewer 2011, 24–25).

With regard to the frequencies of *have (got) to*, she finds a general preference for *have (got) to* over *must*, except in GhanE and SgE, where *must* is preferred over *have (got) to* (cf. Biewer 2011, 22). Biewer explains the high frequency of *must* in GhanE with differences in politeness strategies (cf. Biewer 2011, 25–26). In general, she finds that the core modal *must* is more often used in the ESL varieties than in BrE and AmE (cf. Biewer 2011, 25). Furthermore, Biewer shows that all varieties use deontic *must* more often than epistemic *must* (cf. Biewer 2011, 26). However, the share of deontic *must* is lower in BrE, NZE, and CookE, as compared to all other varieties (cf. Biewer 2011, 26). Regarding the less frequent expressions of obligation and necessity, she observes that those modal and semi-modal verbs that already have a marginal status in ENL varieties are further marginalised in ESL varieties (cf. Biewer 2011, 23). In her discussion of the findings, she pays special attention to shared characteristics of ESL varieties as potential products of SLA processes and lists the following characteristics.

> ESL varieties [...] show similarities that can be traced back to SLA constraints: greater variability among ESL than ENL, preference of one modal over others but not necessarily the same in all L2 varieties, restriction of the system in types and meaning, overusage and underusage.
>
> BIEWER 2011, 27

In particular, she explains the rare use of *ought to* in the ESL varieties by the SLA process of avoidance of redundancy as *ought to* is similar in meaning to *should*, and the more frequent use of deontic *must* with the Transfer to Somewhere Principle, as well as the Markedness Theory (cf. Section 7.3 for more details about her findings).

While Nelson's (2003), Nkemleke's (2005), and Biewer's (2009, 2011) studies focused on the frequencies and functions of modal and semi-modal verbs of obligation and necessity, Collins's (2009b) study deals with a broader range of modal and semi modal verbs but without further analysis of their functions. Collins studies the modal verbs *must, should, need, will,* and *shall* and the semi-modal verbs *have to, have got to, need to, be going to,* and *want to* in the four L1 varieties BrE, AmE, AusE, and NZE, and the five L2 varieties PhilE, SgE, HKE, IndE, and Kenyan English (KenE) (cf. Collins 2009b). He subsumes PhilE, SgE, and HKE under the category 'Southeast Asian Englishes' (SEA) in the frequency comparisons. He investigates the synchronic frequency distribution in the L2 varieties against the background of the changes identified in the L1 varieties based "[o]n the relatively safe assumption that the rise of the quasi-modals [...] is also occurring in the other Englishes of the world" (Collins 2009b, 285). In general, he observes that "[t]he IC [Inner Circle] varieties have a stronger predilection for the quasi-modals overall than do the OC [Outer Circle] varieties" (Collins 2009b, 285). AmE is the most 'advanced' variety, with the highest frequency of semi-modal verbs (cf. Collins 2009b, 285). The L1 variety most similar to AmE with regard to the frequency of semi-modal verbs is AusE, while the other two L1 varieties, BrE and NZE, are more 'conservative', i.e. they show a lower frequency of semi-modal verbs (cf. Collins 2009b, 285). Within the group of L2 varieties, he observes that the SEA varieties PhilE, SgE, and HKE are more 'advanced' in the rise of the semi-modal verbs than KenE and IndE (cf. Collins

2009b, 285). In terms of the decline of the modal verbs, he again finds that AmE is the most 'advanced' variety, with the lowest frequency of modal verbs (cf. Collins 2009b, 285–286). Once more, AusE patterns closely with AmE, while NZE is more similar to BrE (cf. Collins 2009b, 285–286). Within the group of L2 varieties, he finds that KenE has the most 'advanced' status, followed by IndE and the SEA varieties (cf. Collins 2009b, 285–286).

In a second step, Collins compares the frequencies of the semi-modal and core modal verbs in spoken language and written language (cf. Collins 2009b, 286–287). Based on the assumption that spoken language responds faster to changes than written language, he interprets synchronic speech to writing ratios diachronically to assess how far the varieties have advanced in the rise of the semi-modal verbs and the decline of the core modal verbs (cf. Collins 2009b, 286). As AmE has the highest number of semi-modal verbs in spoken language compared to written language, he concludes that AmE is again the most advanced variety in the rise of the semi-modal verbs (cf. Collins 2009b, 286). On the assumption that a high number of modal verbs in writing compared to speech signals 'conservatism', he shows that within the L1 varieties of English, NZE is most 'conservative', while AmE and AusE are more 'advanced' in the trend of the decline of the core modal verbs (cf. Collins 2009b, 287). With regard to the L2 varieties, he finds that "it is, surprisingly, IndE that emerges as the most advanced, followed by the SEA varieties and KenE" (Collins 2009b, 287).

Apart from these general findings, he also takes a closer look at the modal and semi-modal verbs of obligation and necessity. He shows that *have to* is the most frequently used semi-modal verb in the group of L2 varieties, while it only ranks second, after *going to*, in the L1 varieties of English (cf. Collins 2009b, 287). Within the groups, he identifies AmE as the most advanced L1 variety and the SEA varieties as the most advanced L2 varieties in terms of their synchronic frequencies of *have to* (cf. Collins 2009b, 287). With regard to *must*, his findings emphasise that the core modal is least often used in AmE, with 402 tokens per million words, and most often used in SgE, with 1,061 tokens per million words (cf. Collins 2009b, 286). As for the semi-modal verb *have got to*, he finds that it "is more readily embraced in the IC [Inner Circle] varieties [...] than in the OC [Outer Circle]" (Collins 2009b, 289). However, he also notes that L2 varieties are more likely to use the semi-modal verb in writing than the L1 varieties, which he explains with stronger adherence to prescriptive norms in L1 varieties (cf. Collins 2009b, 289). For the semi-modal verb *need to*, he finds a similar frequency across L1 and L2 varieties of English, with the highest frequencies of the semi-modal verb in AmE in the group of L1 varieties and the SEA varieties in the group of L2 varieties (cf. Collins 2009b, 289). Based on these findings, Collins concludes that AmE is driving the change of the rise of the quasi-modal verbs and the decline of the modal verbs "and that within the set of five OC [Outer Circle] Englishes, it is the SEA varieties that are most advanced in these trends" (Collins 2009b, 291).

In his follow-up study with Yao, Collins analyses the same set of modal and semi-modal verbs except for the modal *need* and the semi-modal *need to* in the same set of varieties (cf. Collins & Yao 2012). In addition to the varieties studied in his earlier work, Collins and Yao include the four L2 varieties of English JamE, NigE, MalE, and FijiE in their study (cf. Collins & Yao 2012). Even with more varieties included, they notice that AmE remains the most 'advanced' variety, with the highest frequency of semi-modal verbs of all varieties analysed (cf. Collins & Yao 2012, 44). Within the OC varieties, they observe that KenE and IndE are not only more 'conservative' than the SEA varieties but also more 'conservative' than the Caribbean varieties (cf. Collins & Yao 2012, 44). With regard to the frequency of core modal verbs, they note that JamE is the most 'advanced' variety of all L2 varieties, with the lowest frequency of core modal verbs in this variety. Conversely, SgE turns out to be the most 'conservative' variety of the L2 varieties (cf. Collins & Yao 2012, 44). More generally, they find that "[t]he OC [Outer Circle] varieties are considerably more conservative than the IC [Inner Circle]" (Collins & Yao 2012, 44).

They also compare speech vs. writing ratios in L1 and L2 varieties and find again that AmE is the most 'advanced' L1 variety, with the highest frequency of semi-modal verbs in speech and the lowest frequency of core modal verbs in writing (cf. Collins & Yao 2012, 44–45). For L2 varieties, they analyse speech vs. writing ratios for those varieties where spoken and written components of the corpora are available, i.e. the same L2 varieties as in Collins (2009b) plus JamE. They find the highest speech to writing ratio of semi-modal verbs in the L2 variety JamE (cf. Collins & Yao 2012, 44). With regard to the modal verbs, they find that all L2 varieties show a higher frequency of modal verbs in spoken language than the L1 varieties (except for the modal *shall*), which they regard as a sign of their 'vitality' in L2 varieties, "suggesting [...] that their rate of decline may be less marked – or at least delayed" (Collins & Yao 2012, 46). They consequently argue that the L1 varieties are more 'advanced' in the decline of the core modal verbs (cf. Collins & Yao 2012, 47). For the semi-modal verb of obligation *have to*, they observe that spoken JamE is characterised by a rather high frequency, whereas its frequency is low in the African varieties of English, NigE and KenE (cf. Collins & Yao 2012, 47). Generally, they conclude that those varieties that are at a later developmental stage in Schneider's (2007) model are those that are more 'advanced' in the trend of the rise of the semi-modal verbs, i.e. JamE is more advanced than KenE (cf. Collins & Yao 2012, 52). In the decline of the modal verbs, they find that AmE is most 'advanced' and that the L1 varieties have generally 'advanced' further than the L2 varieties in this process of linguistic change (cf. Collins & Yao 2012, 52).

Van der Auwera, Noël, and De Wit (2012) use the same methodology as Collins (2009b) and Collins and Yao (2012) in order to shed light on the developments of the core modal *need* and the semi-modal *need to* in the L1 varieties BrE and AmE and the L2 varieties HKE, PhilE, SgE, and IndE. In absence of diachronic corpora for the L2 varieties under analysis, they argue the ratio of use in the spoken and written section of the ICE corpora "provides a good basis for the formulation of hypotheses on diachronic change" (van der Auwera, Noël & De Wit 2012, 57). They assess the validity of Collins's (2005) methodology by testing the predictions made on the basis of the speech to writing distribution of *need* and *need to* in ICE-GB against the diachronic tendencies that have been observed on the basis of the LOB and the *Freiburg-LOB Corpus* (FLOB). They analyse the use of the core modal *need* and the semi-modal *need to* in negative and positive polarity contexts. They come to the conclusion that the core modal *need* is restricted to negative polarity contexts in BrE and AmE and that it decreased from 1961 to 1991 in BrE and AmE based on the data from the BROWN family of corpora (cf. van der Auwera, Noël & De Wit 2012, 60). *Need to*, on the other hand, increased during this period in negative polarity contexts but even more strongly so in positive polarity contexts (cf. van der Auwera, Noël & De Wit 2012, 60). As they find a lower frequency of *need* in negative polarity contexts in spoken language compared to written language and a higher frequency of *need to* in negative and positive polarity contexts in spoken language as opposed to written language, they conclude that the predictions on the basis of speech to writing comparisons mirror the tendencies identified in diachronic corpora (cf. van der Auwera, Noël & De Wit 2012, 65).

They then apply the same method to the ICE corpora ICE-HK, ICE-PHI, ICE-SIN, and ICE-IND and show that the modal *need* is not entirely restricted to negative polarity contexts, with some rare cases of positive polarity *need* in ICE-HK, ICE-IND, and ICE-SIN (cf. van der Auwera, Noël & De Wit 2012, 69). They note that the frequency of *need* is lower in the spoken section than in the written section in all ESL varieties, except for IndE (cf. van der Auwera, Noël & De Wit 2012, 69–70). This is why they hypothesise that "the frequency of *need* 'decreases' in Hong Kong, Philippine and Singapore English, but not in Indian English, where it 'increases'" (van der Auwera, Noël & De Wit 2012, 71). The frequency of the semi-modal verb *need to* instead has a higher frequency in spoken language than in written language but only in HKE and in IndE and not in PhilE and SgE (cf. van der Auwera, Noël & De Wit 2012, 70). This leads them to argue that "the frequency of *need to* 'rises' in Indian and Hong Kong English, but not in Philippine and Singapore English, where it 'drops' drastically" (van der Auwera, Noël & De Wit 2012, 71). With regard to the contexts in which *need to* 'is rising' in IndE and HKE, they observe that IndE shows a more substantial 'rise' in positive polarity contexts than in negative polarity contexts, similar to BrE, while the 'rise' in negative polarity contexts is stronger in HKE, dissimilar to BrE (cf. van der Auwera, Noël & De Wit 2012, 70).

In another paper by Collins, the focus is on the use of the semi-modal verbs. He analyses whether there is a correlation between the regional differences in the frequencies of the semi-modal verbs and "the different levels of tolerance that speakers of these Englishes display towards grammatical colloquialism" (Collins 2013, 155). His hypothesis is that those varieties where speakers are more tolerant of 'grammatical colloquialisms' display a higher frequency of semi-modal verbs. His hypothesis is closely linked to the postulation of 'colloquialisation', which is one of the explanations that have been put forward in earlier studies to explain the rise of the semi-modal verbs in ENL varieties (cf. Section 2.1) (cf. Leech 2003, 237). The process assumes that norms of written language are approaching norms of spoken language. As Collins's study is based on synchronic data, he does not speak of 'colloquialisation' but of 'colloquialism' to refer to the state evoked by the process of 'colloquialisation' (cf. Collins 2013, 155–156). Similarly, he also uses the terms 'Americanism' and 'grammaticism' rather than 'Americanisation' and 'grammaticalisation' (cf. Collins 2013, 156).

He takes the ratio of contraction of several verbs and the negator *not* as an indicator for a variety's 'colloquialism' and shows that L1 varieties of English use more contractions than L2 varieties of English (cf. Collins 2013, 159). Furthermore, he is able to show a correlation between a variety's rate of contraction and its frequency of semi-modal verbs. In fact, he finds the same ranking of the varieties in terms of their use of contractions as in their use of semi-modal verbs in his earlier study, with AmE showing most contractions and the highest number of semi-modal verbs, followed by AusE, NZE, and BrE (cf. Collins 2013, 159–160). In the group of ESL varieties, he demonstrates that the opposition between the more 'advanced' SEA varieties and the less 'advanced' varieties IndE and KenE (which he calls 'non-SEA') in the trend of the rise of the semi-modal verbs correlates with their rates of contraction (cf. Collins 2013, 160).

While Collins's study tries to shed light on the rise of the semi-modal verbs in terms of 'colloquialisation/colloquialism', Loureiro-Porto takes a closer look at 'grammaticalisation' by analysing the semi-modal verbs *have to*, *have got to*, *need (to)*, and *want to* in the private dialogue sections of ICE-GB, ICE-HK, and ICE-IND (cf. Loureiro-Porto 2016). First, she studies the frequency of the modal and semi-modal verbs. Second, she investigates their degree of grammaticalisation by analysing their semantic and morphosyntactic properties.

With regard to the frequencies of *must, have to, have got to, need (to)*, and *want to*, she observes a higher frequency of *must* in ICE-IND compared to ICE-HK and ICE-GB, a higher frequency of *have to* in ICE-HK and ICE-SIN, and a lower frequency of *have got to*, whereas *need (to)* occurs with a higher frequency in ICE-HK than in ICE-GB but with a lower frequency in ICE-IND than in ICE-HK and ICE-GB. For the emerging semi-modal verb *want to*, she finds that it is more often used in ICE-HK than in ICE-GB but less often used in ICE-IND (cf. Loureiro-Porto 2016, 147).

Loureiro-Porto then analyses the degree of grammaticalisation of these verbs by analysing their semantic and morphosyntactic properties. She observes that the core modal *must* is most frequently used to express epistemic meanings (cf. Loureiro-Porto 2016, 150–151). The frequency of epistemic *must* differs across varieties, with BrE using epistemic *must* with the highest frequency, followed by ICE-HK and ICE-IND, with the lowest frequency of epistemic *must* (cf. Loureiro-Porto 2016, 152). While in HKE and BrE the semi-modal verbs can also be employed in epistemic function, *must* is the only expression of logical necessity in IndE (cf. Loureiro-Porto 2016, 150). Loureiro-Porto identifies epistemic meanings of *have got to* and *got to* in BrE and HKE, although her example given for epistemic *got to* from ICE-HK does not seem to be an ambiguous example between epistemic and deontic readings but an example of idiomatic *get to know* (*Because we we we got to know him in our school*) (cf. Loureiro-Porto 2016, 154). She also gives one example of an epistemic meaning of *need*, which, however, also allows a deontic interpretation at closer inspection, as an anonymous reviewer of her article also remarks (cf. Loureiro-Porto 2016, 155). With regard to *need (to)*, she finds a clear association of modal *need* with negative polarity contexts and semi-modal *need to* with positive polarity contexts in BrE and IndE but notices two instances of modal *need* in positive polarity contexts in HKE (cf. Loureiro-Porto 2016, 155; cf. also earlier findings by van der Auwera, Noël & De Wit 2012, 69). With regard to the semantics of *want to*, she observes that the semi-modal verb is predominantly used in its volitional sense, however, it also expresses deontic meanings but only marginally so (with a share of 3.2% in BrE, 2.2% in HKE, 1.9% in IndE) (cf. Loureiro-Porto 2016, 156–157). Furthermore, *want to* can only be used in negative contexts to express a prohibition in BrE and HKE but not in IndE (cf. Loureiro-Porto 2016, 157). Loureiro-Porto also notes that *want to* can occur with inanimate subjects in HKE (cf. Loureiro-Porto 2016, 158). She interprets all these findings in terms of a higher degree of grammaticalisation of *want to* in BrE than in HKE, which in turn shows a higher degree of grammaticalisation of the semi-modal verb than IndE (cf. Loureiro-Porto 2016, 158).

Finally, Loureiro-Porto also takes a closer look at the morphosyntactic characteristics of the verbs. She argues that the higher rate of contractions of semi-modal verbs, which are overall very rare in the ICE data, suggests a higher degree of grammaticalisation, again in the order of BrE>HKE>IndE (cf. Loureiro-Porto 2016, 160). She also analyses selectional preferences for the subject and claims that *must* is the modal expression that has grammaticalised furthest in all varieties, as it co-occurs most often with third person subjects (cf. Loureiro-Porto 2016, 161). In addition, she also observes a co-occurrence of third person subjects and *need (to)* in IndE, suggesting a higher degree of grammaticalisation of this semi-modal verb here (cf. Loureiro-Porto 2016, 162). With regard to the selection of inanimate subjects as another indicator of auxiliarisation, she finds that *must* is most often used with inanimate subjects, which is in line with its high degree of grammaticalisation, while the semi-modal verb *want to* most often occurs with animate subjects, reflecting that it is less grammaticalised (cf. Loureiro-Porto 2016, 163). Finally, she also analyses the sentential complements of the verbs and finds that the semi-modal verb *need to* is used with a wider range of sentential complements in BrE and HKE, pointing again to a higher degree of grammaticalisation in these varieties than in IndE, where the semi-modal verb only occurs with a following marked infinitive with *to* and elided complements (cf. Loureiro-Porto 2016, 165–166). In IndE instead, the core modal *need* shows a higher degree of grammaticalisation, as it occurs more often with the bare infinitive here (cf. Loureiro-Porto 2016, 165). She argues that this "seem[s] to suggest that *need* persists as a core modal in IndE, while it is on the verge of disappearing in BrE and HKE" (Loureiro-Porto 2016, 167; cf. also earlier findings about *need* in IndE by van der Auwera, Noël & De Wit 2012, 69–70).

She concludes her findings with the general observation that the semi-modal verbs are more grammaticalised in BrE than in the two ESL varieties, and that they are more grammaticalised in HKE than in IndE in the group of ESL varieties (cf. Loureiro-Porto 2016, 167). The higher grammaticalisation of the semi-modal verbs leads to a stronger replacement of *must*, resulting in more variation in the system in HKE compared to IndE (cf. Loureiro-Porto 2016, 168). She explains the stronger divergence of IndE from BrE in light of Schneider's (2007) model by arguing that IndE diverged more strongly from BrE than HKE as a result of the earlier beginning of the 'Nativisation' phase in this variety compared to HKE, which was marked by an exonormative orientation until the 1960s (cf. Loureiro-Porto 2016, 168). She also adds that grammaticalisation may be closely intertwined with the process of colloquialisation, which is arguably more advanced in HKE than in IndE (cf. Loureiro-Porto 2016, 168). This claim is supported by Collins's study that takes contraction as an indicator of 'colloquialism' and shows that HKE is characterised by more contractions than IndE (cf. Collins 2013, 160). However, it is not entirely clear what Loureiro-Porto means by 'colloquialisation' because her data do not comprise written language, whose approximation to spoken norms is generally referred to by the term. If this definition of the term is applied, the patterning of ICE-HK and ICE-IND in Figure 13 in Chapter 4 shows indeed that there is a slight difference in the positions of the written components of ICE-HK and ICE-IND on the cline between spoken language and academic prose, with the written component of ICE-HK diverging less strongly from spoken norms than the written component of ICE-IND. However, given the database of her study, it may be that Loureiro-Porto rather refers to a 'more colloquial' character of spoken HKE compared to spoken IndE, a phenomenon that Mesthrie and Bhatt have described as 'hypercolloquial' language use with reference to SgE (cf. Mesthrie & Bhatt 2008, 114–115). This is also reflected in the orientations of the spoken components of ICE-HK and ICE-IND in Figure 13 in Chapter 4. Loureiro-Porto also mentions the third keyword for the explanation of the rise of the semi-modal verbs, 'democratisation', but leaves it to further research to analyse claims about linguistic democratisation in ESL varieties empirically (cf. Loureiro-Porto 2016, 169).

In another study, Mair analyses the modal and semi-modal verbs of obligation and necessity as one of the five variables with which he tries to position the usage profile of JamE in terms of its norm orientation towards BrE and AmE (cf. Mair 2009a, 2009b). The other variables he studies are *person(s)* as a synonym for *people*, presence or absence of subject-verb inversion in questions, the use of contractions, and quotative *be like*. As for the modals of obligation and necessity, he analyses the use of *must, have to, have got to*, and *need to* in the private dialogue sections of ICE-GB, ICE-NZ, ICE-IND, and ICE-JA, and SBC (cf. Mair 2009a, 50). Because of the changes identified in ENL varieties, he states that the modal verbs lend themselves particularly well "to assess the synchronic regional orientation of a New English with regard to British or American norms and also its degree of linguistic conservatism" (Mair 2009a, 50). Generally, he finds that NZE patterns more closely with BrE in the use of the modal and semi-modal verbs of obligation, while JamE patterns more closely with AmE (cf. Mair 2009a, 50–51). With regard to the semi-modal verb *have to*, he notices that it is more common in the New Englishes than in BrE (cf. Mair 2009a, 50). He tentatively mentions substrate influence on JamE from the equivalent expression in Jamaican Creole (JamC) (*hafi*) as a possible explanation for the high frequency of the semi-modal verb in JamE but states that this cannot explain the high frequencies found in the other New Englishes IndE and NZE (cf. Mair 2009a, 50). However, the existence of *hafi* in JamC may condition the low frequency of *have got to* in JamE (cf. Mair 2009a, 50). The usage pattern for JamE also shows a remarkably high frequency of innovative *need to* but a low frequency of *have got to* (cf. Mair 2009a, 50–51). By contrast, in IndE he finds a "markedly conservative profile, reflected in the high frequencies

for *must* and low frequencies for the innovative forms *need to* and *have got to*"
(Mair 2009a, 50).

In his second paper, he analyses the same modal and semi-modal verbs but
also takes a look at their frequencies in ICE-IRE (cf. Mair 2009b, 18). Irish English (IrE) shows a similar profile to the other New Englishes, with a somewhat
higher frequency of *must* and *have to* and a lower frequency of *have got to* than
BrE (cf. also Filppula 2014), which is rare in all varieties except in BrE and NZE
(cf. Mair 2009b, 18–19). The frequency of innovative *need to* is instead almost
the same in BrE and IrE (cf. Mair 2009b, 18). Again, what is most remarkable in
the frequency distribution of *need to* is the surprisingly high frequency found
in JamE (cf. Mair 2009b, 19). Mair explains that the comparatively later date
of compilation of ICE-JA in the early 2000s may be a possible explanation
for the differences observed between ICE-JA, ICE-IND, and ICE-NZ (cf. Mair
2009b, 19). Apart from these particular findings concerning the frequencies
of the modal and semi-modal verbs, Mair's studies are also interesting from
a methodological point of view because he analyses the corpora from a sociolinguistic perspective (cf. Section 11.2 for a discussion of the interface between
corpus linguistics and sociolinguistics). In this way, 'corpus linguistics meets
sociolinguistics' in his case studies, for example by analysing the speakers' age
and gender in the use of quotative *be like* (cf. Mair 2009a, 55–56, 2009b, 23).

Diaconu built on Mair's exploratory study of modal and semi-modals of obligation by presenting an in-depth study of *must, have to, (have) got to*, and *need
to* in BrE, AmE, IrE, JamE, and IndE on the basis of SBC and FROWN for AmE, and
the dialogue and written press text sections in ICE for the other varieties (cf. Diaconu 2012b). She finds that *have to* is the preferred variant in all varieties, but
that its frequency is particularly high in ICE-JA and ICE-IND, the ESD and ESL
varieties in her study (cf. Diaconu 2012b, 92). She claims that the high frequency
in both varieties suggests that *have to* "is taking over the meanings of its modal
counterpart in the two outer circle varieties more than in those from the inner
circle" (Diaconu 2012b, 92). Concerning the frequency of the semi-modal verb
have got to, she finds that it is only rarely used in JamE and IndE compared to a
more widespread use in the three L1 varieties (cf. Diaconu 2012b, 93). For *need
to*, however, she observes instead the highest frequency of use across all varieties in JamE, with the lowest frequency found in IndE (cf. Diaconu 2012b, 93–94).
Diaconu also analyses the distribution of *must, have to, have got to*, and *need to*
according to register (private dialogue vs. public dialogue) (cf. Diaconu 2012b,
97). She finds that the high frequency of *have to* in ICE-IND and ICE-JA as well
as the high frequency of *must* in ICE-IND compared to the other varieties can
be found in both text types (cf. Diaconu 2012b, 98). She therefore argues that
the patterns identified in the dialogue section reflect stable regional variation

(cf. Diaconu 2012b, 99–100). Diaconu also analyses the distribution of forms with regard to their semantics and finds that all markers of obligation and necessity show a predominance of root readings over epistemic readings (cf. Diaconu 2012b, 121–129). She shows the inherent preference of the L1 varieties of English for epistemic *must* over root *must* in the dialogue sections of the respective ICE corpora (cf. Diaconu 2012b, 123). But although *must* is more often used in root reading than in epistemic reading in ICE-IND, its epistemic use has a higher frequency than that found in all other varieties (cf. Diaconu 2012b, 123–124; contrary to the tendency identified by Loureiro-Porto 2016, 152).[4] With regard to the semi-modal verbs, Diaconu shows a clear preference for their root uses over epistemic uses in all varieties, as has also been identified in other studies on L1 and L2 varieties (cf. Diaconu 2012b, 124–125). Although the frequency of epistemic readings is generally very low, Diaconu finds some subtle differences in use. She observes that the Jamaican and Indian variety of English have a slightly higher frequency of epistemic *have to* than the ENL varieties, and that epistemic *have got to* is more often used in BrE and AmE, while epistemic *need to* is most frequently used in JamE (cf. Diaconu 2012b, 125–128).

Diaconu also analyses the modal and semi-modal verbs of obligation and necessity with regard to their sources of obligation by applying Depraetere and Verhulst's (2008) framework, which distinguishes between discourse-internal and discourse-external sources of obligation (cf. Diaconu 2012b, 131–164; cf. also Section 1.6). She finds that there is no correlation between the occurrence of *must*, *have to*, *have got to*, and *need to* and their sources of obligation (cf. Diaconu 2012b, 167). But she observes – among other things – a tendency to use *must* to express self-imposed obligation rather than speaker-imposed obligation in ICE-IND and ICE-JA and a tendency to use *have to* with discourse-internal sources of obligation in ICE-JA, pointing to an extension of *have to* to subjective readings (cf. Diaconu 2012b, 169–170).

Finally, Diaconu performs a multivariate analysis to shed light on the variation between the core modal *must* and the semi-modal *have to* (cf. Diaconu 2012b, 185–207). Her analysis shows that the use of *must* is correlated with third person subjects (cf. also Loureiro-Porto 2016, 161), verbs expressing activities or states (e.g. *run*, *know*) rather than verbs expressing accomplishment or achievement (e.g. *build*, *recognise*), formal text types as well as discourse-internal sources of obligation (cf. Diaconu 2012b, 198). Some of her findings are also presented in her two articles (cf. Diaconu 2012a, 2015). What is missing from Diaconu's study is the analysis of substrate influence on the encoding of

---

4 These differences may result from the fact that Loureiro-Porto (2016) analyses only the private dialogue section, while Diaconu (2012b) also analyses the public dialogue section of ICE.

epistemic and deontic modality as a possible source of present-day variability in ICE-JA and ICE-IND.

Substrate influence is, however, the main topic of Bao's analysis of the use of *must* in SgE (cf. Bao 2010; cf. also Bao 2015, 163–177). He analyses the functions of *must* in the private dialogue sections of ICE-GB, ICE-SIN, ICE-IND, and ICE-PHI and draws on Collins's (2005) findings on the distribution of *must* in SBC, and the dialogue sections of ICE-GB, ICE-AUS, and ICE-NZ as points of comparison. He finds a strong deontic bias of *must* in ICE-SIN, with a share of 84% of deontic *must*, compared to a share of deontic *must* of 35% in ICE-NZ, 37% in ICE-AUS, 38% in SBC, 44% in ICE-GB, 52% in ICE-PHI, and 60% in ICE-IND. He explains the divergent pattern of SgE with the process of convergence-to-substratum, "the phenomenon of English grammatical features converging in usage or function to the equivalent features in the linguistic substratum" (Bao 2010, 1729). He gives three reasons for this phenomenon: (1) Mandarin expresses deontic and epistemic modality with different expressions, (2) perfect contexts in which epistemic *must* predominantly occurs are rare in SgE, and (3) the equivalent expression of deontic *must* in Mandarin does not have the same grammaticalisation path from deontic to epistemic modality as English (cf. Bao 2010, 1731).

His findings suggest that SgE is the only ESL variety in his sample that displays such a strong deontic bias. Therefore, his data do not suggest that ICE-IND and ICE-PHI show the same deontic bias of *must* that was identified in earlier studies on other ESL varieties (e.g. EAfE, JamE, HKE, GhanE, CamE). This raises the question of why some ESL varieties show a deontic bias of *must* while others do not. If the structure of the substrate language plays a role, as Bao suggests, we would expect those varieties that do not show a strong deontic bias to have an equivalent of *must* in their substrate language(s) that encodes deontic and epistemic modality. However, this has not been analysed so far (cf. Section 6.2 for the analysis of the structures in the substrate languages of SgE, HKE, and IndE).

Another study on the modal system of an ESL variety is Imperial's study on *must* and *have to* in Philippine English (cf. Imperial 2014). His study analyses the competition between *must* and *have to* in ICE-PHI from a variationist perspective by studying the influence of language-internal and language-external factors on the choice between the two variants of deontic modality. As a result, his study shows – among other things – that *have to* is favoured in contexts with first and second person subjects, objective readings, and in spoken text types (cf. Imperial 2014, 11–12).

Herat's study on Sri Lankan English (SrLE), which is based on written corpus data from ICE-Sri Lanka (ICE-SL), COCA, and the BNC, is yet another study that deals with the use of *must* and *have to* (cf. Herat 2015). Her findings show that the semi-modal *have to* has a higher frequency than the modal *must* as an expression of deontic modality in SrLE (cf. Herat 2015, 112). As earlier studies on L1 varieties of English have also disclosed (cf. Section 2.1), she finds that the frequency of *must* and *have to* is also highly genre-dependent in SrLE, with *have to* showing the highest frequency in the less formal genre correspondence (cf. Herat 2015, 112). *Must* is unexpectedly used with the highest frequency in press reportage, which Herat interprets as a sign of the variety's 'conservativeness' (cf. Herat 2015, 113). In comparison with AmE and BrE, Herat notes that *have to* is used with a significantly higher frequency in SrLE than in BrE and AmE (cf. Herat 2015, 114), which ties in with earlier observations of a higher frequency of *have to* in other ESL varieties (cf. Collins 2009b, 285). Furthermore, she also observes that *have to* is preferred over *must* with first and second person subjects, while both variants of deontic modality occurred most often with third person subjects in ICE-SL (cf. also Imperial 2014, 11–12). She interprets her synchronic findings from a diachronic perspective and argues that *have to* is replacing *must* in SrLE (cf. Herat 2015, 120).

Apart from these synchronic descriptions of the modal system, which often aim at diachronic extrapolation, there are also some diachronic studies on modality in ESL varieties. Two of these studies were published in a special issue of the *Journal of English Linguistics* in 2014 on the topic of diachronic approaches to modality in WE (cf. Noël, van Rooy & van der Auwera 2014). The article by Collins, Borlongan, and Yao in this special issue deals with changes in the modal system of PhilE on the basis of Phil-BROWN (late 1950s to early 1960s) and the written part of ICE-PHI (early 1990s) (cf. Collins, Borlongan & Yao 2014). They use a preliminary version of Phil-BROWN that is supposed to match the composition of the BROWN corpus once it is finished (cf. Collins, Borlongan & Yao 2014, 71–72). On the basis of this corpus, they examine the frequency of the core modal verbs *may, might, must, shall,* and *should,* the marginal modal *ought to,* and the semi-modal verbs *be able to, be going to, be supposed to, have to, need to,* and *want to.* They decided to exclude the higher frequency modal verbs *can, could, will,* and *would* because they have a high frequency but do not show a strong decline in BrE and AmE, which is why they argue "that their inclusion would dissipate the results for the modals class as a whole" (Collins, Borlongan & Yao 2014, 73). Despite the exclusion of these modal verbs, they still retain the semantically related semi-modal verbs *be able to* and *be going to* in their analysis. They compare the data from PhilE to the diachronic findings for BrE and AmE from Leech et al.'s (2009) study.

Their study focuses on three aspects: (1) frequency changes in the use of modal and semi-modal verbs, (2) genre variation, and (3) changes in the distribution of the senses of the core modal verbs. With regard to frequency changes between the 1960s and 1990s, they show that the modal verbs decreased by 16% in PhilE, compared to a decrease of these verbs by 21% in BrE and 25% in AmE (cf. Collins, Borlongan & Yao 2014, 73). This means that PhilE "emerges as the most conservative of the three varieties" (Collins, Borlongan & Yao 2014, 73). With regard to the modal *must*, they observe a change in frequency of -24%, which is less dramatic than those found for BrE, with -29% and AmE, with -34% (cf. Collins, Borlongan & Yao 2014, 73). For the group of semi-modal verbs, Collins, Borlongan, and Yao note that it increased substantially from Phil-BROWN to ICE-PHI, with a change in frequency of +29%, which is even higher than those found for BrE, with +18% and AmE, with +20% (cf. Collins, Borlongan & Yao 2014, 75). They interpret the strong rise in PhilE in terms of the variety's orientation towards AmE (cf. Collins, Borlongan & Yao 2014, 75). Concerning the individual semi-modal verbs, they observe a change in the frequency of *have to* of +30%, which is significant, while the changes in the frequency of *have to* in BrE (+9%) and AmE (+3%) are not (cf. Collins, Borlongan & Yao 2014, 75). The frequency of *need to* shows a considerably stronger change in frequency in all varieties, with +125% in AmE, +267% in BrE, and +268% in PhilE (cf. Collins, Borlongan & Yao 2014, 75). They also trace the changes in the use of the modal and semi-modal verbs in different registers ('Press', 'Learned', and 'Fiction') and find that the core modal verbs decreased most strongly in the registers 'Learned' and 'Fiction' in PhilE, i.e. the registers that also suffered the strongest decline in AmE (cf. Collins, Borlongan & Yao 2014, 76). At the same time, the register 'Learned' also undergoes the highest rise in the use of semi-modal verbs (cf. Collins, Borlongan & Yao 2014, 77). Apart from register differences, they also analyse semantic differences in the use of the modal verbs. PhilE unexpectedly shows a stronger decrease of epistemic *must* than of deontic *must*, contrary to findings on BrE and AmE (cf. Collins, Borlongan & Yao 2014, 79). In interpreting their overall findings, they attribute the weaker decline of the core modal verbs to 'colonial lag' and the stronger increase in the frequency of the semi-modal verbs to exonormative orientation towards AmE usage patterns, which suggests to them that "PhilE writers have been striving to catch up with AmE over this period" (cf. Collins, Borlongan & Yao 2014, 85). However, with regard to individual modal and semi-modal verbs, they also observe signs of an endonormative orientation, for example in the comparatively high frequency of *shall* in PhilE (cf. Collins, Borlongan & Yao 2014, 85).

The second diachronic study of modality in WE is by van Rooy and Wasserman about WhSAfE and BlSAfE (cf. van Rooy & Wasserman 2014). They analyse the frequency of modal and semi-modal verbs to see whether the two ethnic varieties of SAfE become more similar in their use, based on the assumption that the settler (STL) and the indigenous (IDG) strands are becoming increasingly intertwined when a variety proceeds in Schneider's (2007) model (cf. Section 3.2). To this end, they analyse the frequencies of the core modal verbs *can, could, may, might, must, shall, should, will, would, need,* and *ought to* and the semi-modal verbs *be able to, be about to, be bound to, be to, be going to, had better, (have) got to, have to, need to, be supposed to,* and *want to* in written data (reportage, fiction, non-prose fiction) from the 1950s and the 2000s (cf. van Rooy & Wasserman 2014, 58). Rather than convergence, they discover increasing divergence between the two strands from the middle of the 20th century onwards. The frequencies of both modal and semi-modal verbs increased slightly in BlSAfE between the 1950s and the 2000s, while their frequencies decreased in WhSAfE in the same period (cf. van Rooy & Wasserman 2014, 61). They observe that the frequency of modal *must* does not show a significant decline in the period between the 1950s and the 2000s in BlSAfE and WhSAfE, contrary to the sharp decline of *must* in other varieties (cf. van Rooy & Wasserman 2014, 60). Furthermore, they observe that its deontic use predominates and that it is used to express strong obligations in BlSAfE, while it is also used for moderate obligation in WhSAfE, a use that is very rare in BlSAfE (cf. van Rooy & Wasserman 2014, 61–62). Concerning the semi-modal verbs of obligation and necessity, a significant change in frequency was only observed for *need to,* which increased dramatically, whereas *have to* and *have got to* did not show significant increases in BlSAfE and WhSAfE (cf. van Rooy & Wasserman 2014, 60). The findings suggest that the decline of the core modal verbs and the rise of the semi-modal verbs do not occur in all varieties of English, which challenges earlier assumptions by Collins (2009b) and Collins and Yao (2012) and emphasises the crucial importance of analysing this claim empirically.

Another diachronic study on the modal system in ESL varieties is by Noël and van der Auwera that was published in Collins's (2015) edited volume *Grammatical change in English world-wide* (cf. Noël & van der Auwera 2015). Noël and van der Auwera study developments in the dispersion rates of the modal verbs *can, could, may, might, must, shall, should, will,* and *would* and the semi-modal verbs *be going to, have to, (have) got to, need to, want to, be supposed to, used to,* and *be able to* between 1990 and 2010 (cf. Noël & van der Auwera 2015, 447). Their study is based on texts from five newspapers: the American newspapers *The New York Times* and *The Washington Post,* the British newspapers *The Times* and *The Guardian,* and the Hong Kong newspaper *South China Morning Post* (cf. Noël & van der Auwera 2015, 446). Their findings indicate that the dispersion of the modal and semi-modal verbs in HKE is more similar to the dispersion in BrE than to that in AmE, with a general decrease of the core modal verbs and a rise in the group of semi-modal verbs (cf. Noël & van der Auwera 2015, 460). With regard to the individual modal and semi-modal verbs of obligation and necessity, we can see, however, that *must* remained relatively stable in the period between 1990 and 2010, not showing a decrease of the modal verbs as was found for all other newspapers except for *The Washington Post* (cf. Noël & van der Auwera 2015, 461). The findings about the semi-modal verbs reveal that *have to* decreased from 1990 to 2010 in the *South China Morning Post*, while *got to* remained stable and *need to* increased (cf. Noël & van der Auwera 2015, 462). These findings show the importance of analysing genre differences in linguistic changes, a factor that has only recently received more attention in studies on modal and semi-modal auxiliaries (cf. Bowie, Wallis & Aarts 2013; Smith & Leech 2013, 83; Mair 2015a, 141).

2.3   Research Desiderata

The overview has shown that while most studies on the modal system in WE formulate hypotheses about ongoing language change, the majority is not based on diachronic data. Instead, these studies draw diachronic conclusions from synchronic frequencies and/or by comparing frequencies in spoken language and written language. This procedure is problematic for several reasons.

First, interpreting synchronic frequencies as signs for 'advancement' in the general trend of the decline of the core modal verbs and the rise of semi-modal verbs heavily relies on the supposition that the trend is indeed general and can be found in all varieties of English. This assumption has been called into question by recent diachronic findings which suggest that not all varieties of English seem to follow this trend (cf. van Rooy & Wasserman 2014). As a consequence, empirical studies about ongoing language change are necessary to prove the assumption.

Second, the method of interpreting synchronic frequency distributions in L1 and L2 varieties in terms of their advancement in the diachronic trend is dubious because it construes the present-day states of the historical input varieties as the ultimate goals of development. This means the varieties are placed on a developmental scale of advancement. In other words, the synchronic state of the ESL varieties is understood as a historical state of the ENL varieties. ESL varieties are construed as 'conservative' varieties that 'lag behind' the more 'advanced' ENL varieties. This type of construal implies hierarchisation and bears striking similarities with the construal of colonised people in 19th century colonial discourses (cf. Section 2.4 for more details).

Third, the method of comparing frequencies across speech and writing assumes that innovations necessarily spread from spoken language to written language and ignores the fact that linguistic innovations may originate in written language in changes from above. What is more, conventions and stylistic associations of spoken language and written language may differ in ESL varieties (cf. Xiao 2009 and the discussion in Section 4.3.1). In some varieties, spoken language is closer to written norms, which is why Mesthrie and Bhatt speak of 'register shift' (cf. Mesthrie & Bhatt 2008, 114; cf. also Figure 13 in Chapter 4). Taking this into account, it is no surprise that Collins, for example, finds a higher frequency of semi-modal verbs in L1 varieties of English than in L2 varieties of English (cf. Collins 2009b, 285).

Fourth, the comparison of frequencies in spoken and written language is not an established method of extrapolating diachronic change from synchronic variation. While it is certainly true that researchers had to rely on indirect methods of investigating diachronic change in New Englishes in the absence of diachronic corpora, they are definitely not restricted to comparisons across speech and writing, as van Rooy and Wasserman claim (2014, 54).

These issues clearly illustrate that it is, first of all, necessary to analyse empirically whether ESL varieties are indeed undergoing the same changes in the modal system as ENL varieties, as has been assumed in most of these studies. Furthermore, it needs to be tested whether the construal of ESL varieties as less 'advanced' varieties on their way towards the state of the ENL varieties can be supported by empirical evidence or remains a construal from the perspective of 'Western' researchers. The comparison of frequencies in spoken and written language does not seem to be the ideal method to find out about language change for the reasons outlined above. Therefore, alternative methods of analysing language change in New Englishes need to be sought. The first method that comes to mind is the apparent-time method, which draws conclusions about language change from synchronic frequency distributions across different age groups and is a far more established method than the comparison of frequencies in spoken and written language, as well as being one that has been successfully tested against real-time evidence. Despite its widespread use in sociolinguistics, apparent-time studies have not been conducted so far to analyse ongoing change in the modal systems in ESL varieties, although this is generally possible as metadata including the speakers' age are available for at least some corpora (cf. Section 8.1 for more details about the method and Section 8.3 for apparent-time findings about the modal system in HKE, IndE, and BrE).

The 'Western-biased' view of New Englishes does not only become apparent in the construal of these varieties as 'conservative' but also in the pre-occupation with cultural explanations for the rise of semi-modal verbs that emerged in ENL contexts and are not necessarily valid in ESL contexts, such as Americanisation, colloquialisation, and democratisation. This perspective necessarily leads to blindness for culture-specific explanations of variability in ESL varieties and, thus, ignores earlier findings that point to 'pragmatic indigenisation' in the use of modal and semi-modal verbs (cf. Section 7.2 for cultural motivations behind the use of modal and semi-modal verbs).

Another implication of this view on New Englishes is the focus on differences between the group of ENL and ESL varieties and between varieties within these two groups. The analytic entity is therefore the homogeneous 'variety', and internal variation within varieties is only rarely analysed. Studies on modal and semi-modal verbs have shown that their use differs strongly according to register, but most studies on the modal system in ESL varieties focus on basically two registers, dialogues and press texts. This leads to the fact that register differences in the use of modal and semi-modal verbs have rarely been studied in more detail in ESL varieties on the basis of ICE (but cf. Balasubramanian 2009, 197 on the basis of the *Corpus of Contemporary Indian English* (CCIE)). Moreover, while substrate influence has been analysed for specific phenomena in some varieties of English (e.g. the use of *must* in SgE), systematic analyses of correlations between the structures of ESL varieties and the structures of their substrate languages have been missing up to now (cf. Section 6.2 for an analysis of the modal systems in the substrate languages of HKE, IndE, and SgE). An analysis of the structures of substrate languages may help to answer the question why some ESL varieties behave differently than others, for example in the encoding of epistemic modality. Some earlier studies have shown that IndE seems to be characterised by a comparatively high frequency of epistemic *must*, which is why it is especially important to analyse the structures of the substrate languages of IndE and compare it to the structures of the substrate languages of SgE in order to investigate claims about substrate influence on the encoding of epistemic modality.

While substrate languages are clearly one important source of present-day variability, the historical state of the input variety may be equally important. Although this claim has been repeatedly made in the context of ESL varieties, it has rarely been empirically tested by reconstructing the historical input variety and comparing its structure to the synchronic structure of ESL varieties (cf. Section 6.1.7 for a discussion about a potential 'founder effect' in the modal system).

In those studies that take a closer look at variation between variants, the focus is on language-internal factors of variation (e.g. 'subject', 'verb type'). However, language-external factors such as 'mother tongue', 'age', and 'gender' of the speakers are equally important and need to be analysed more closely (cf. Chapter 9 for the influence of language-internal and language-external factors on the choice between *must* and *have to*).

The overview shows that most of the research gaps can be addressed by extending the analysis of language variation from language-internal factors to language-external factors. In this way, diachronic change can be analysed by integrating information about the age and gender of the speakers, register differences can be analysed by integrating information about the text types of ICE, and substrate influence can be analysed by integrating information about the mother tongue of the speakers. This means that corpus-based studies on the modal system in ESL varieties can profit from the methodological strengths of variationist sociolinguistic studies on the modal systems in ENL varieties. Therefore, a mixed methods approach is needed that combines corpus-linguistic techniques with sociolinguistic methods to tackle the most important open questions in the field. The transfer of sociolinguistic methods to corpus-based studies may ultimately also shift the focus from product-oriented to process-oriented descriptions of ESL varieties, for example by analysing the process of transfer behind the product of substrate influence or the processual nature behind the synchronic 'state' of the varieties in terms of age-related variation. This may enable us to catch a glimpse of how these varieties are constantly being made and remade by their speakers and it would help to prevent them from being perpetually construed and reified into static monolithic entities by researchers, even today.

2.4   Towards a Postcolonial Research Agenda

Having identified open research questions, it is also necessary to critically assess how research has 'traditionally' been conducted in the field of WE. As Section 2.2 has shown in great detail, in many studies on WE, BrE (or AmE) serves as the yardstick of comparison against which New Englishes are defined.

An illustrative example of the description of the structure of New Englishes against the background of the structure of BrE and AmE is Mesthrie and Bhatt's typological classification of New Englishes into two classes, 'preservers' and 'deleters' (cf. Mesthrie & Bhatt 2008, 90; cf. also Saraceni 2015, 82–83). Taking BrE and AmE as the standard of comparison creates a hierarchy of Englishes.

> In other words, it is difficult to sustain the argument that world Englishes are qualitatively equal if they are defined by how much they diverge from varieties that are considered 'standard' by virtue of having been codified in the Inner Circle.
>
> SARACENI 2015, 79

This means that studies taking BrE or AmE as the reference suffer from a negative definition of WE by tacitly subscribing to a '"deficit' view [...], making its looming presence felt through words like *omission, deletion, unusual,* which are used against words like *norms, required, rules, standard*" (Saraceni 2015, 87). This negative definition of New Englishes from the point of view of BrE (or AmE) is strongly reminiscent of the construction of the colonised people as the 'Other' in colonial discourses, the alterity that serves to construct the identity of the colonisers (cf. Ashcroft, Griffiths & Tiffin 2000, 9). The process of identity construction via differentiation from an alterity leads to a maximisation of difference. In the case of research on WE this means that our search for differences setting the New Englishes apart from BrE (or AmE) leads to a bias towards postulating differences rather than similarities between ENL and ESL varieties (cf. also Saraceni 2015, 79). Furthermore, the process of 'Othering' also leads to stereotyping the alterity, i.e. perceiving the alterity as a homogeneous entity without much internal differentiation, which facilitates the process of delineation. This process becomes visible in large-scale studies on intervarietal differences that regard New Englishes as entities without much internal differentiation. To develop a more 'postcolonial' research design, it is necessary to define New Englishes positively and not only in terms of divergence from L1 varieties. This can best be achieved by shifting the focus of analysis from BrE (or AmE) to the variety itself and explaining variation from within, which may eventually allow us to uncover the polylithic nature of ESL varieties.

Taking BrE (or AmE) as the standard of comparison has also led to essentialist descriptions of L1 and L2 Englishes in terms of binary oppositions, such as 'innovative' vs. 'conservative', 'advanced' vs. 'less advanced', 'leading' vs. 'lagging behind' (cf. also Section 7.2). Collins and Yao state for example that "the IC [Inner Circle] varieties are generally *more advanced* than the OC [Outer Circle]" (Collins & Yao 2012, 52, my emphasis). This statement evokes problematic associations in the study of postcolonial varieties of English because it bears striking similarity with colonial discourses of 'Eurocentric diffusionism', i.e.

> Europeans are seen as the 'makers of history'. Europe eternally advances, progresses, modernizes. The rest of the world advances more sluggishly, or stagnates: it is 'traditional society'. Therefore, the world has a permanent geographical center and a permanent periphery: an Inside and an Outside. Inside leads, Outside lags. Inside innovates, Outside imitates.
> BLAUT 1993, 1

If we substitute Europeans with BrE speakers and Europe with BrE in the quote above, we can easily see the legacy of contemporary descriptions of WE (cf. Barrett 2014, 209 for similar associations in descriptions of creoles as 'simple'). This also becomes visible in statements such as "objectively speaking, it is the metropolitan varieties that have innovated, whilst the New Englishes may have done nothing remarkable" (Mesthrie & Bhatt 2008, 115). Statements like these show that the contemporary description of New Englishes is closely interwoven with former colonial discourses about the speakers of these varieties.

The above-mentioned 'permanent geographical centre' and 'the permanent periphery' are visualised in Kachru's model of the Three Concentric Circles, i.e. the 'Inner Circle' as the 'permanent centre' and 'Outer Circle' as 'the permanent periphery' (cf. Kachru 1985; cf. Section 3.1 for a description of the model). Together with the Expanding Circle of English, comprising the English-as-a-foreign language (EFL) varieties, the model may be misinterpreted as visualising an old model of the world:

> there is a clear and definite center, but outside of it there is gradual change, gradual decline in degree of civilization or progressiveness or innovativeness, as one moves outward into the periphery.
>
> BLAUT 1993, 14

If these ideas are mapped onto the state of Englishes in Kachru's model, a cline of innovativeness develops from the most innovative ENL varieties via ESL varieties to EFL varieties, an idea that might not sound too unfamiliar to researchers in the field of WE. Blaut states that the idea of diffusionism in historical and geographical theorising is based on two maxims: "(1) Most human communities are uninventive. (2) A few human communities [...] are inventive and thus remain the permanent centers of cultural change or progress" (Blaut 1993, 14). If we rewrite the maxims by substituting communities with varieties and cultural change with linguistic change, the maxims ring a bell with the researcher in the WE paradigm: '(1) Most varieties of English are uninventive. (2) A few varieties of English are inventive and thus remain the permanent centres of linguistic change or progress'. This shows that although researchers explicitly acknowledge the emergence of internal norms in the form of local innovations in ESL varieties, they may tacitly subscribe to a diffusionist view on these varieties. While descriptions of New Englishes as 'conservative' only evoke these associations, the following description of the state of IndE makes them explicit:

> Last but not least, IndE as a second-language variety is defined as being in the *least favoured position* in this picture, namely *lagging behind* as the most *conservative* of all varieties under examination [...].
>
> DIACONU 2012B, 11, my emphases

The quote clearly shows that 'conservative' is the negatively marked member of the contrasting pair 'innovative' vs. 'conservative'. In this way, the dichotomies lead to a hierarchical differentiation because they imply superiority of the historical input varieties and thus reproduce colonial discourses about the speakers of these varieties, who are indexically linked to the varieties (cf. Blaut 1993, 17 for a list of contrastive pairs in definitions of the 'core' and the 'periphery'). The description of these varieties as 'conservative' echoes presentations of the colonized "as underdeveloped versions of Europeans and their civilization" (Hardt & Negri 2001, 126) in colonial discourses of the 19th century. This view is firmly grounded in the belief that the historical stages of the development of mankind are "present synchronically in the various primitive peoples and cultures spread across the globe" (Hardt & Negri 2001, 126; cf. also Blaut 1993, 16, who refers to this belief as the 'theory of our contemporary ancestors'). The metaphor 'synchrony of the non-synchronic' is sometimes also used to describe this belief system. If we search for the same belief system in linguistic research, we can again see striking parallels because former colonial varieties are sometimes conceived of as windows to a historical stage of BrE (cf. also Hackert 2014, 294). Sometimes the 'justification' for studying varieties of English is to enhance the knowledge about linguistic processes in BrE (or AmE). In postcolonial theory, this process is referred to as understanding one's identity through the alterity.

This view becomes most obvious in the use of the highly disputed notion of 'colonial lag'.[5] The first use of the term in linguistics goes back to Marckwardt in his study on AmE where he uses it to describe not only the state of the language but also the state of the nation itself (cf. Marckwardt 1958, 80). The notion has survived until today, probably also because it blends well with historical discourses about colonial people, as Görlach also observes when he states

> [t]he term 'colonial lag' was one of the most catching phrases applied to the modern language history of English, convincing since it appeared to describe what people had known all the time, viz. that colonials were not quite up-to-date and not conversant with modern metropolitan developments.
>
> GÖRLACH 1987, 55

This means that Eurocentric beliefs persist "long after the rationale for their acceptance has been forgotten [...] [and] that newer candidate beliefs gain acceptance without supporting evidence if they are properly Eurocentric" (Blaut 1993, 10).

---

5   Cf. Görlach (1987), who considers 'colonial lag' a myth that lacks linguistic evidence, and Hundt (2009) for a critical assessment of the usefulness of the notion in cases of differential language change.

The same discourses are also evoked by evolutionary models of language change, such as Schneider's (2007) Dynamic Model (cf. also Saraceni 2015, 55, cf. Section 3.2 for a description of the model). Hackert details the legacy of contemporary language ideologies in evolutionary models of English (cf. Hackert 2014). In the 19th century, evolutionary models of languages were employed to construct "hierarchies in which English and the English-speaking people inevitably came out on top" (Hackert 2014, 283). Evolution was equated with progress and language was considered to reflect a nation's social and economic advancement (cf. Hackert 2014, 293). The wider implication of this belief was "[t]he more highly developed a nation's way of life, the more highly developed its 'genius' and thus its language" (Hackert 2014, 286).

I argue that the 'Anglocentric' view of WE has probably gone unnoticed so far because most of the studies on WE come from the so-called 'Inner Circle',[6] where the descriptions are consonant with long-standing discourses about the speakers of these varieties. Repeated citational practices of New Englishes as less 'advanced' thus foster an indexical link between the two terms so that after a time one term is necessarily evoked by the other, even without explicit reference (cf. also Barrett 2014, 197). In this way, this type of construction of New Englishes becomes the norm that is not called into question, even in the absence of diachronic empirical evidence or by researchers that are not from the so-called 'Inner Circle'. Saraceni claims that

> [t]he normalizing effect of these dominant discourses can be so powerful that even researchers who operate *within* a non-Inner Circle sociolinguistic environment may feel compelled to follow representations that are defined by a gaze originating from well outside that very environment.
>
> SARACENI 2015, 98–99

It is important to note that by describing the 'conservativeness' of New Englishes without empirical evidence, researchers take an active part in establishing the norm that ultimately leads to the marginalisation of New Englishes and, by extension, to the marginalisation of their speakers (cf. also Barrett 2014, 198).[7]

---

6 There is an interesting parallel to research in postcolonial literatures, which has been criticised for its Eurocentricity and the way researchers from the 'West' capitalise on studies about 'Eastern' literature, thereby reproducing colonial power structures. But it has to be noted that there are also researchers from the respective countries both in postcolonial literatures and postcolonial Englishes.

7 The treatment of New Englishes in the framework of Universal Grammar by Mesthrie and Bhatt (2008, 96–107) also marginalises the speakers of these varieties because of "its normative assumptions about language based on a Eurocentric basis" (Barrett 2014, 205, who criticises basic assumptions of formal linguistics from a queer perspective).

Having analysed 19th-century colonial discourses, we can clearly see the historical burden of contemporary descriptions of postcolonial varieties as 'less advanced' varieties. The analysis also demonstrates in what way the WE paradigm can profit from an interdisciplinary perspective to critically question some of its underlying working assumptions. As there is hardly any empirical evidence for the claim that New Englishes are 'less advanced' in language change, the role of historical discourses cannot be underestimated and we have to ask ourselves:

> To what extent have we emancipated ourselves from the dominant 19th-century ideology in Europe that considered European languages and cultures as superior, more evolved, or more refined than their non-European counterparts?
>
> MUFWENE 2006, 4

Detecting similarities between 19th-century colonial discourses and contemporary descriptions of New Englishes can only be the first step in 'decolonising' research methods; the second step must be the development of a research design that implements some of the ideas of postcolonial theory. Based on the idea of 'giving voice' to those in the periphery in postcolonial theory, the New Englishes should become the analytical focus of study in this type of research. This means that the perspective on New Englishes has to change from an external perspective to an internal perspective, thereby moving the New Englishes from the periphery to the centre (cf. also Barrett 2014, 219). The analysis of variety-internal variation according to register, mother tongue, age, and gender of the speaker in this study could be an effective way of 'researching back' by producing empirical evidence rather than accepting unproven stereotypical descriptions that owe much to historical contingency.

2.5   Summary

The literature overview has revealed that the modal system of English is a well-researched area in L1 varieties, with many synchronic and diachronic studies (cf. Section 2.1). These studies show variation and change in the modal domain, by pointing to regional differences in use and ongoing language change. The real-time and apparent-time studies on the modal system in L1 varieties indicate a general decline of the core modal verbs and a rise in the frequency of the semi-modal verbs. The core modal *must* and the semi-modal verbs *have to* and *need to* follow this general trend, while the semi-modal verb *have got to* seems to be on the decrease in Northern American varieties of English, while its frequency remains relatively stable in BrE.

Against the background of these developments in L1 varieties of English, the modal domain has also attracted the interests of linguists working in the field of L2 varieties of English (cf. Section 2.2). However, they are faced with the challenge that no diachronic corpora are available as yet for most L2 varieties of English. Some linguists have interpreted synchronic frequency distributions of modal and semi-modal verbs in light of the diachronic processes in L1 varieties of English, while others have compared the ratio of modal and semi-modal verbs across speech and writing on the basic assumption that spoken language responds faster to changes. As this method is problematic for a number of reasons (cf. Section 2.3), a more established method of extrapolating change from synchronic variation is necessary in order to analyse language change in progress in L2 varieties of English. Ultimately, an application of sociolinguistic methods to L2 varieties can be the key to open questions, for example by using the apparent-time method to analyse ongoing language change in L2 varieties. Furthermore, the integration of other language-external factors, such as 'text type', 'gender', and 'mother tongue' of the speakers may help to answer more questions, for example concerning register variation in the modal domain, the nature of change, or potential substrate influence. Moreover, placing the ESL varieties at the centre of the study by defining them from within, i.e. in terms of their internal make-up rather than only in terms of their divergence from ENL varieties, may help to establish a more postcolonial research agenda in WE (cf. Section 2.4). This entails that constructions of ESL varieties as conservative varieties, which lag behind the state of ENL varieties, have to be avoided because they bear strong resemblance to long-standing colonial discourses about the speakers of these varieties and are not based on empirical evidence. Instead of perpetuating these discourses, empirical evidence about the development of ESL varieties has to be produced.

CHAPTER 3

The Theoretical Framework

This chapter provides the theoretical framework for the following study and introduces the socio-historical background of English in Hong Kong, India, and Singapore. First, I will describe the two predominant models in the field of WE, Kachru's (1985) Model of the Three Concentric Circles (Section 3.1) and Schneider's (2007) Dynamic Model (Section 3.2). I will situate the varieties under study in the models and describe the socio-historical background of English in Hong Kong, India, and Singapore by outlining important historical events that had an impact on the development of English in these countries (Sections 3.2.1–3.2.3). While these two models and the socio-historical background help us to enhance our understanding of the nature of the varieties, they do not provide us with a toolkit for analysing why the varieties are shaped the way they are. I will therefore draw on Mufwene's (2001) Feature Pool Model, which understands the development of creoles and other varieties of English in terms of a competition-and-selection process (Section 3.3). Biewer (2015) adapts this model to the ESL context in her study on SPE and identifies relevant selection principles that guide the choice between one variant and another (Section 3.4). Based on the socio-historical background of English in the varieties and a synthesis of the theoretical models, I will propose an integrated model for the description of modality in HKE, IndE, and SgE in the summary (Section 3.5).

3.1 Kachru's Three Concentric Circles Model

One of the most influential models of the historical spread of English around the world is Kachru's (1985) Model of the Three Concentric Circles of English (cf. Figure 3). This model conceives of the diffusion of English in three phases represented by three circles: the 'Inner Circle', 'the Outer Circle', and the 'Expanding Circle'. The three circles reflect differences in the spread of English, in the acquisition of English, and in the domains in which English is used (cf. Kachru 1985, 12).

The Inner Circle represents the historical basis for the spread of English and comprises regions in which English is the first language of the majority of the population. Countries belonging to the Inner Circle are for example the UK, the USA, Canada, and Australia (cf. Kachru 1985, 12). The Outer Circle accounts

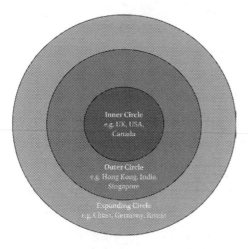

FIGURE 3
Kachru's Model of the Three Concentric
Circles (adapted from Crystal 1997, 54).

for the spread of English via colonisation by the Inner Circle countries and is therefore composed of former colonies, such as Hong Kong, India, and Singapore. English is not spoken as the first language in these countries but as a second language, very often in a multilingual setting (cf. Kachru 1985, 12). English is often recognised as one of the official languages and fulfils a wide range of functions in different domains (cf. Kachru 1985, 12–13). The Expanding Circle focuses on the spread of English as an international language. In contrast to Outer Circle countries, English did not arrive in these countries via colonisation but because of its importance as an international language (cf. Kachru 1985, 13). English has no official status in these countries and is not used as an intranational lingua franca. By contrast, it is learned at school and is used for international communication. Examples of countries belonging to this circle are China, Germany, and Russia. Kachru acknowledges that the boundaries between the circles are often not clear-cut and that some countries are difficult to place in the model, e.g. South Africa (cf. Kachru 1985, 13–14).

The number of speakers increases from the Inner Circle to the Expanding Circle. This might point to a possible change in the influence of non-native speakers on English, as English is used by more non-native speakers than native speakers today. However, a closer look at the norm orientation in non-native varieties of English reveals that Expanding Circle varieties are 'norm-dependent' upon the 'norm-providing' Inner Circle varieties (cf. Kachru 1985, 17). Consequently, the Expanding Circle shows an exonormative orientation towards external standards of use set by the Inner Circle varieties. This becomes apparent in the reliance on native speaker models in EFL contexts. The situation is different in Outer Circle varieties, which can develop their own norms of use. This is why they are called 'norm-developing varieties' (cf. Kachru 1985, 17). Varieties of the Outer Circle have a contradictory norm orientation that is both oriented towards external and internal standards (i.e. exonormative and endonormative) (cf. Kachru 1985, 17). While Kachru sees this ambivalent orientation as a characteristic of the Outer Circle varieties in general, Schneider considers norm orientation as a process that includes the gradual detachment from external norms to the embracement of internal norms in the formation of a new variety (cf. Schneider 2007, 49; cf. also Section 3.2). This observation reflects one of the strongest differences between the two models. Schneider's (2007) model provides a more process-oriented analysis of postcolonial varieties of English, while Kachru's (1985) model is more static, although it is based on a historical process. The perceived stasis of Kachru's (1985) model has probably also led to the mapping of the ENL-ESL-EFL distinction onto the model (cf. Strang 1970, 17–18), so that it is often adduced as a classification of the different types of English spoken around the world. The Inner Circle is taken as a shorthand for ENL varieties, the Outer Circle as a shorthand for ESL varieties, and the Expanding Circle correspondingly as a shorthand for EFL varieties.

Although it is generally recognised that Kachru's (1985) model has played an important role for the acknowledgment of the independent status of Outer Circle varieties, it has also been criticised (cf. Bruthiaux 2003; Jenkins 2003; Rajadurai 2005). One of the major criticisms raised against the model is that varieties are categorised primarily by geographical and political criteria that do not necessarily reflect the complex sociolinguistic situations in these countries (cf. Bruthiaux 2003, 161; Jenkins 2003, 17). This fact glosses over sociolinguistic similarities between countries that were colonised and those that were not (cf. Bruthiaux 2003, 166). Furthermore, as the model is based on nations rather than speakers, countries that have ENL and ESL speakers are difficult to place in the model (South Africa and Singapore being cases in point). By classifying varieties of English into three categories, the model focuses on differences between the circles rather than on differences within the circles, which consequently downplays the amount of internal heterogeneity within the three groups. Evidence of this can be found in the neglect of dialectal variation in Inner Circle varieties, the neglect of variation in terms of different levels of proficiency in Outer Circle varieties, or the neglect of differences in the range of functions fulfilled in Expanding Circle countries (cf. Bruthiaux 2003, 174). Differences in Outer Circle varieties in terms of the share of how many speakers know or use English for intra-ethnic communication are not addressed in the model either (cf. Bruthiaux 2003, 164; Jenkins 2003, 13–14; cf. Sections 3.2.1–3.2.3 for differences between Hong Kong, India, and Singapore with regard to these aspects). Moreover, due to the indefinite boundaries, the circles allow for transitions or 'grey areas' (cf. Jenkins 2003, 17), for example when English starts to be acquired as a first language in Outer Circle countries or assumes a wider range of functions in Expanding Circle countries. A last point of criticism that has been levelled against the model is that it places the Inner Circle varieties at the centre of the development even though their influence might not be as powerful after all (cf. Jenkins 2003, 18). This also implies a superiority of the Inner Circle varieties which was clearly not intended by Kachru (cf. also the discussion in Section 2.4 on colonial implications of the model).

> The very term 'inner circle' conjures up a host of connotations [...]: "confined to an exclusive group", "privy to inner knowledge", "inside information", "privileged information", "exclusive to a center; especially a center of influence".
>
> RAJADURAI 2005, 114

If we apply Kachru's model to the varieties under study, we can place BrE and AmE in the Inner Circle and HKE, IndE, and SgE in the Outer Circle. However, this classification needs further qualification. While IndE can be regarded a typical Outer Circle variety, HKE and SgE are less prototypical, as the descriptions of their status and function in Sections 3.2.1 to 3.2.3 will show. HKE and SgE are both at least at the margin of the category of Outer Circle varieties (cf. Figure 4). HKE can be considered approaching the outer boundary of the category that borders on the Expanding Circle varieties because English is predominantly used as an international means of communication. By contrast, English is the lingua franca among the different ethnic groups in Singapore, where it fulfils a broad range of functions and is also used in less formal situations. Furthermore, English has become the native language of some Singaporeans. All these characteristics pull Singapore more strongly towards the Inner Circle varieties. For the scope of this study however, only language data of ESL speakers are taken into consideration because speakers of ICE-SIN have been selected on the criterion that English is their L2.

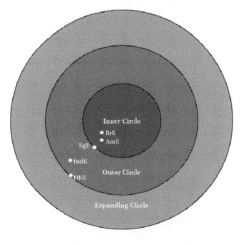

FIGURE 4
The status of HKE, IndE, and SgE in Kachru's (1985) Model of the Three Concentric Circles (adapted from Crystal 1997, 54).

The discussion shows that the classification of the varieties in terms of Ka-chru's model can only serve as a starting point because it does not do justice to the sociolinguistic reality in which English is used in these countries. This shortcoming can be overcome by applying Schneider's (2007) Dynamic Model to the varieties under study, which goes beyond a purely historical and geographical approach by incorporating sociolinguistic concepts in the evolution of postcolonial Englishes.

3.2   Schneider's (2007) Dynamic Model

Schneider's (2007) Dynamic Model is based on the idea that a common process underlies the formation of postcolonial Englishes (cf. Schneider 2007, 21).[1] His model postulates such a uniform process not only for the formation of varieties of former exploitation colonies but also for the formation of varieties of former settlement colonies (cf. Schneider 2007, 25). Consequently, Schneider's (2007) model includes ENL varieties such as AmE, AusE, and NZE alongside ESL varieties under the umbrella term 'postcolonial Englishes'. His model is based on the idea that the evolution of these varieties is driven by identity formations of the two groups that are involved in colonisation (cf. Schneider 2007, 29). These groups are the settler (STL) strand and the indigenous (IDG) strand, which represent the perspective of the colonisers and their descendants, as well as the colonised and their descendants, respectively (cf. Schneider 2007, 31). The two groups perceive themselves as clearly separate at the beginning of colonisation, but start to rewrite their identities when they realise that they will permanently share the territory (cf. Schneider 2007, 29–30). Their identities become more strongly intertwined and a new identity emerges. This identity reconstruction process has direct linguistic consequences, as the two groups use language as a symbolic means to express their identities. As soon as the identities of the two groups start to converge in a common identity, they begin to approximate each other's language. Schneider therefore claims "that to a considerable extent the emergence of PCEs [sc. postcolonial Englishes] is an identity-driven process of linguistic convergence" (Schneider 2007, 30). These changes in the identities of the two groups and their linguistic consequences evolve in five distinct stages, namely (1) Foundation, (2) Exonormative Stabilisation, (3) Nativisation, (4) Endonormative Stabilisation, and (5) Differentiation (cf. Schneider 2007, 30). Each stage is defined by characteristic settings of four parameters: (1) the socio-political background, (2) identity constructions, (3) sociolinguistic conditions of the contact setting, and (4) linguistic effects

---

1   For an earlier sketch of the model cf. Schneider (2003).

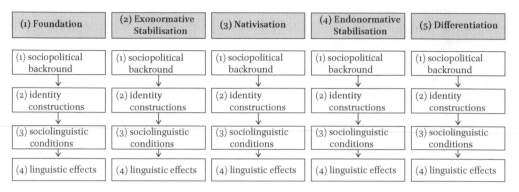

(1) Foundation	(2) Exonormative Stabilisation	(3) Nativisation	(4) Endonormative Stabilisation	(5) Differentiation
(1) sociopolitical backround	(1) sociopolitical backround	(1) sociopolitical backround	(1) sociopolitical backround	(1) sociopolitical backround
(2) identity constructions	(2) identity constructions	(2) identity constructions	(2) identity constructions	(2) identity constructions
(3) sociolinguistic conditions	(3) sociolinguistic conditions	(3) sociolinguistic conditions	(3) sociolinguistic conditions	(3) sociolinguistic conditions
(4) linguistic effects	(4) linguistic effects	(4) linguistic effects	(4) linguistic effects	(4) linguistic effects

FIGURE 5   Main aspects of Schneider's (2007) Dynamic Model.

(cf. Schneider 2007, 31). A causal relationship holds between the four parameters: the socio-political background shapes identity constructions, which determine the sociolinguistic conditions of the contact situation that bring about linguistic effects (cf. Schneider 2007, 30–31). The main aspects of the model are visualised in Figure 5. The stages of the model will be described by detailing the settings of the four parameters in each stage, beginning with the socio-political background and ending with the linguistic effects.

In the Foundation phase, English is introduced to a new territory by the STL strand, for example through the establishment of trading outposts or settlement emigration (cf. Schneider 2007, 33). In terms of identity constructions, it can be noted that the two strands regard themselves as entirely separate groups at this stage (cf. Schneider 2007, 33). Members of the STL strand identify themselves as representatives of Britain, while members of the IDG strand see "themselves as the only rightful residents [...] of the territory" (Schneider 2007, 34). The contact between the two groups is strongly restricted during this phase: "each group remains, operates, and continues to communicate predominantly within its own confines" (Schneider 2007, 34). Communication between the two strands only takes place for highly specific purposes, and bilingualism is limited to a few members of the IDG strand that interact with the STL strand (cf. Schneider 2007, 34–35). Regarding linguistic effects, this phase is characterised by the process of koinéisation in the STL strand because speakers of different British dialects come into contact (cf. Schneider 2007, 35). This process is especially prominent in settlement colonies, which have larger STL strands than exploitation or trade colonies (cf. Schneider 2007, 35). In trade colonies, we can instead observe the development of pidgin languages that serve as means of communication between the STL strand and the IDG strand for the purpose of trade (cf. Schneider 2007, 36). As contact between the two strands is restricted, the influence of the indigenous language(s) on English is weak and becomes only visible in toponymic borrowings at this stage (cf. Schneider 2007, 36).

In the second phase, which is referred to as 'Exonormative Stabilisation', the political situation stabilises through the establishment of colonies in the territories (cf. Schneider 2007, 36). This leads to the use of English in administrative, educational, and legal domains (cf. Schneider 2007, 36). Members of the STL strand still strongly identify themselves with their motherland, but compared to their compatriots who have not left their country of origin, they feel enriched by new cultural insights and hybrid identities emerge (cf. Schneider 2007, 37). The same feeling can be found in speakers of English in the IDG strand (cf. Schneider 2007, 37). In terms of the sociolinguistic setting of the contact situation, we can observe growing bilingualism in the IDG strand due to education and/or more regular contact with members of the STL strand (cf. Schneider 2007, 38). Members of the IDG strand learn English because the knowledge of English brings them social and economic advantages (cf. Schneider 2007, 38). At this stage, bilingualism is strongly restricted to the local elite, whose members often serve as middlemen between the colonial government and the colonised (cf. Schneider 2007, 38; cf. also Macaulay's *Minute on Education* in Section 3.2.2). This stage is also marked by the emergence of mixed marriages and descendants of these unions who may develop a hybrid identity (cf. Schneider 2007, 37). With regard to linguistic norms, the external standard of the STL strand serves as reference point but as emphasis is placed on the facilitation of interethnic communication at this stage, issues of correctness are rarely a subject of debate (cf. Schneider 2007, 38). Linguistically, changes in the use of English by the settlers can mostly be found at the lexical level in loan words for local animals and plants as well as for culture-specific customs and objects (cf. Schneider 2007, 39). The English variety spoken by speakers of the IDG strand starts to show structural features that have been transferred from the local language(s) (cf. Schneider 2007, 39–40). Grammatical innovations also occur at this stage but operate below the level of consciousness of members of the STL strand, who only judge the use of English by the speakers of the IDG strand in terms of its intelligibility (cf. Schneider 2007, 40).

The third phase is called 'Nativisation' and is according to Schneider "the most interesting and important, the most vibrant one" (Schneider 2007, 40). This is the stage where members of both strands start to rewrite their old identities and form new identities that conform with the new situation they find themselves in (cf. Schneider 2007, 40). Concerning the socio-political background, we can see that political independence becomes a central issue for the country, which is often also achieved at this stage (cf. Schneider 2007, 41). The STL strand slowly begins to strive towards cultural as well as linguistic independence as the close ties between them and their distant mother country loosen (cf. Schneider 2007, 41). It is at this stage that the STL and IDG strands interweave and a sense of a shared identity develops because "both parties consider themselves permanent residents of the same territory" (Schneider 2007, 41). The contact between the two strands increases and the STL and the IDG strands start to approximate each other. It is noteworthy that members of the IDG put more effort into this process, which becomes visible in the increasing number of ESL speakers in the IDG strand (cf. Schneider 2007, 42). Within the STL strand, a separation between innovative and conservative speakers appears (cf. Schneider 2007, 42). While innovative speakers use localisms as an expression of their new local identity, conservative speakers avoid linguistic innovations in favour of the external norm (cf. Schneider 2007, 42–43). The public controversy about falling standards (the so-called 'complaint tradition', cf. (183) in Chapter 11 for an example) initiated by conservative speakers is a typical sign of this process (cf. Schneider 2007, 43). Despite this trend, local forms gain increasing approval after some time. In terms of linguistic effects, we can see that the Nativisation phase brings about "the heaviest effects on the restructuring of the English language itself; it is at the heart of the birth of a new, formally distinct PCE [postcolonial English]" (Schneider 2007, 44). This restructuring takes place on different linguistic levels, including extensive borrowing at the lexical level and the emergence of a local accent at the phonological level (cf. Schneider 2007, 44). Restructuring processes at this stage even affect morphology and syntax as local grammatical constructions emerge (cf. Schneider 2007, 44). This means that the two strands start to converge linguistically and a new variety begins to emerge "which is a second language for some and a first language, incorporating erstwhile L2-transfer features, for others" (Schneider 2007, 45). The lexis-grammar interface seems to be especially open to restructuring in the early phases of indigenisation as shown in the emergence of innovative verb complementation patterns, hybrid compounds, local collocations, and idioms (cf. Schneider 2007, 46). Restructuring processes also extend to different conventions of language use with the emergence of local pragmatic norms (cf. Schneider 2007, 47).

The fourth stage, called 'Endonormative Stabilisation', is characterised by cultural and linguistic independence. It is commonly preceded by political independence or an 'event X', a "quasi-catastrophic political event" (Schneider 2007, 48–49), which results in a move towards a new cultural orientation. Fostered by the psychological separation from the motherland and the resulting new identity construction, members of the STL strand unite with members of the IDG strand: "this is the moment of the birth of a new nation" (Schneider 2007, 49). Internal differentiation in the community is de-emphasised for the sake of forging a more homogenous group identity (cf. Schneider 2007, 49). The distinct identity as one nation is reflected in the acknowledgement and use of the local variety of English that symbolises the new nation (cf. Schneider 2007, 49). The new variety is now accepted and the attitude of conservative speakers about declining standards has gradually disappeared (cf. Schneider 2007, 50). Typically, a shift from the label 'English in X' to the label 'X English' can be observed, which accounts for the distinctive status of the varieties (cf. Schneider 2007, 50). Another characteristic of this phase is the rise of literary creativity in the local variety of English (cf. Schneider 2007, 50). In terms of linguistic effects, it can be noticed that the distinct regional variety has stabilised in this phase (cf. Schneider 2007, 51). It is considered to be a largely homogenous entity and speakers tend to underplay heterogeneity (cf. Schneider 2007, 51). As a by-product of the emphasis on homogeneity, the variety often becomes codified in local dictionaries.

Stage 5 is the phase of 'Differentiation'. The new nation has stabilised as an independent country and "[a]s a consequence of external stability, there is now room for internal differentiation" (Schneider 2007, 53). Differences within the community are no longer de-emphasised for the benefit of a more encompassing national identity, as in the earlier phase 4, but explicitly acknowledged (cf. Schneider 2007, 53). With regard to identity constructions, members of the new nation see themselves as belonging to smaller locally defined communities (cf. Schneider 2007, 53). The identification with smaller subgroups leads to the establishment of dense networks between members of these subgroups. The networks enforce group-specific norms of use among their members that in turn symbolise group identity (cf. Schneider 2007, 53). Schneider therefore points out that the emergence of a new variety "is not the end point of linguistic evolution but rather a turning point from which something new springs: the stage of dialect birth" (Schneider 2007, 54).

The three postcolonial ESL varieties under study, HKE, IndE, and SgE have all entered or passed the third stage of Schneider's (2007) model. As the modal system is part of the grammar of English, the variety's advancement to stage 3 increases the probability that we may actually find instances of grammatical indigenisation that only occur when the intensity of contact between the two groups grows. Although all three varieties have reached phase 3 in their development, they differ in their advancement in Schneider's (2007) model, as will become evident in the description of the socio-historical background of English in Hong Kong, India, and Singapore in the following sections.

3.2.1   *English in Hong Kong*

Hong Kong became a British crown colony in 1842 after the First Opium War (1839–1842) under the Treaty of Nanking (cf. Evans 2016, 7). In the early years of colonisation, after English had become the official language in

1843, English took roots in government, law, education, and business affairs (cf. Setter, Wong & Chan 2010, 104). Knowledge of English spread through the establishment of missionary schools. However, access to these schools and thus access to English remained an asset for the elite for a long time (cf. Bolton 2000, 269). Between the establishment of Hong Kong as a British crown colony in 1842 and the annexation of the Kowloon peninsula in 1860, Hong Kong's population increased strongly (cf. Evans 2014, 580). The majority of people immigrating to Hong Kong were of Chinese origin who only planned to stay temporarily in the region (cf. Evans 2009, 284).

In 1898, the New Territories, Lantau Island and the adjacent northern lands, were leased to Britain for 99 years (cf. Setter, Wong & Chan 2010, 4). This annexation led to political stability in the territory and marks the onset of the phase of Endonormative Stabilisation (cf. Schneider 2007, 135).[2] In this period, the population of Hong Kong increased further, mainly through immigration from Guangzhou (formerly called 'Canton') (cf. Schneider 2007, 135). In the 19th and 20th century, the education system in Hong Kong was characterised by two separate strands, i.e. the Anglo-Chinese English-medium stream and the Chinese-medium stream (cf. Evans 2000, 186). After the Japanese occupation (1941–1945), the education system with the two streams re-emerged and Chinese-medium primary schools and English-medium secondary schools expanded (cf. Evans 2000, 186–187). As a consequence, more and more students were receiving Chinese-medium primary education but then moved on to English-medium schools for secondary education. English-medium education thus "transformed from a system intended for the Chinese elite in colonial society into one catering for the masses" (Evans 2000, 187) during this time.

The economy of Hong Kong changed rapidly in the 1960s. This period marks the onset of Nativisation of HKE. During this phase, Hong Kong developed "from a relatively poor refugee community to a wealthy commercial and entrepreneurial powerhouse" (Bolton 2000, 268). The tertiary sector of the economy was strengthened, resulting in an increased demand for proficiency in English (cf. Evans 2000, 199; Li 2008, 225; Setter, Wong & Chan 2010, 106). This growing demand and the hope that English-medium education would lead to socioeconomic advancement was reflected in the increase of enrolments in English-medium secondary schools during that period (cf. Evans 2000, 187). It needs to be borne in mind, however, that Cantonese or a mixed code between English and Cantonese was the norm even though these schools were nominally English-medium schools (cf. Evans 2000, 188; Bacon-Shone & Bolton 2008, 206;

---

2   See Evans (2009, 2014, 2015) for more details concerning the special status of HKE in Schneider's (2007) model.

Evans 2013, 304). The spread of English was further encouraged by the fact that the colonial government introduced free compulsory primary and secondary education after riots in 1966 and 1967 (cf. Bolton 2012, 225–226; Evans 2015, 403). This led to sustained expansion of English-medium education at the secondary level and increased bilingualism in the population (cf. Bacon-Shone & Bolton 2008, 27).

In 1974, Chinese[3] was declared the co-official language in *The Official Languages Ordinance*. Its position as official language was further strengthened in the Basic Law in 1984, which stated that English could be used in addition to Chinese (cf. Bolton 2012, 226–227). In the same year, the *Sino-British Joint Declaration* was signed that issued the handover of Hong Kong to the People's Republic of China as a Special Administrative Region (SAR) at the end of the lease in 1997 (cf. Setter, Wong & Chan 2010, 4). During the period between the 1970s and 1990s, several attempts were made to introduce Cantonese as the medium of instruction but parents and schools objected strongly to the proposals, so that the government did not implement the plans after all (cf. Bolton 2012, 231–232).

Since 1995, the government's official policy has been to educate a population that is biliterate in Cantonese and Putonghua (Mandarin) and trilingual in Cantonese, Putonghua, and English (cf. Bolton 2012, 228). In order to achieve this aim, the government decided shortly before the handover that Chinese should be the medium of instruction at junior secondary level (years 7–9) (cf. Evans 2013, 309). Only 114 schools in Hong Kong were allowed to continue teaching in English after proving that their students and staff were able to learn and teach effectively in English, while the remaining 307 schools had to implement the compulsory mother tongue policy (cf. Evans 2000, 185; Bolton 2012, 231; Evans 2013, 309). As the majority of schools were English-medium schools (at least nominally) before the handover, a large number of schools had to switch from English to Chinese as their medium of instruction. The policy spread discontent in the population. It was considered socially divisive because it would lead to the establishment of an elitist English-medium stream whose students "were perceived to enjoy an unfair advantage in life, while those forced to attend Chinese-medium schools were denied access to valuable linguistic capital" (Evans 2013, 309). The decision was, however, backed

---

3 Note that the term 'Chinese' is ambiguous and can refer to Putonghua (Mandarin) and Cantonese. In Hong Kong, the term 'Chinese' is usually interpreted as Cantonese and standard written Chinese with traditional Chinese characters (cf. also 'Chinese' as medium of instruction in Hong Kong, cf. Evans 2013, 306).

up by educational studies that showed that students learn better with mother tongue instruction than with instruction in an L2 (cf. Evans 2013, 309).

In June 1997, sovereignty over Hong Kong was transferred from Britain to China. Under the principle of 'one country, two systems', Hong Kong would enjoy a considerable amount of autonomy for 50 years after the handover, including the retention of its capitalist economic system (cf. Bolton 2003, 227; Bacon-Shone & Bolton 2008, 199). The reintegration of Hong Kong with China led to the introduction of Putonghua, the official language of the People's Republic of China, as a school subject and later as medium of instruction for Chinese subjects (cf. Evans 2013, 307). The teaching of Chinese subjects in Putonghua runs counter to the earlier aim of providing education in the mother tongue because Putonghua is an L2 for most Hong Kong students. The fine-tuning policy of the 'firm guidance' to schools on the medium of instruction at the end of the 2000s goes in the same direction because schools were now allowed to use English as the medium of instruction again "if 85% of the students in a particular class are in the top 40% of their age group academically" (Evans 2013, 315). This policy was implemented in 2010 and can be considered to be a reaction to economic and pragmatic needs, as Bolton explains.

> This loosening of government policy seems to have been motivated by a number of factors, including the desire of the business community to maintain Hong Kong's competitiveness as a centre for international commerce and finance, the pragmatic need to prepare students for a university education [...], as well as a groundswell of public opinion from many local parents.
>
> BOLTON 2012, 232

This also shows that English has not lost prestige after the handover as it still fulfils important functions in business, higher education, administration, and the legal system (especially in higher courts) (cf. Setter, Wong & Chan 2010, 112; Bolton 2012, 235). However, the role of Cantonese in most domains remains unchallenged and "*Putonghua* has yet to be heavy-handedly imposed" (Bolton 2012, 235).

The historical overview underlines that the early 1990s, the period in which ICE-HK was compiled, mark a politically vibrant period in between the Sino-British Joint Declaration in 1984 and the handover in 1997. During this period, English was the dominant language in secondary education (cf. Evans 2000, 186–187). It is also believed that Hong Kong people developed "a stronger 'Hong Konger' identity nested within a broader 'Chinese' identity" (Groves

2011, 35) in this period.[4] The development was stimulated by the change that people in Hong Kong were no longer only temporary residents as in earlier times but were, for the majority, born in Hong Kong and therefore called Hong Kong their home (cf. Bolton 2003, 117; Li 2008, 229).

Whether HKE already constituted a variety of its own in the early 1990s that was used to express this new identity is a highly-disputed issue and depends on the criteria that one chooses. At the linguistic level, Schneider claims that Nativisation processes set in at the beginning of the 1960s (cf. Schneider 2007, 135). However, in the 1980s, Luke and Richards still claim that "[t]here is no such thing [...] as Hong Kong English" (Luke & Richards 1982, 55), i.e. roughly twenty years after the onset of Schneider's Nativisation phase and a few years before ICE-HK was compiled. In a similar vein, Pang still asks whether HKE is a 'stillborn variety' in the early 2000s and distinguishes between 'localisation' and 'indigenisation' (cf. Pang 2003). In his terminology, 'localisation' refers to the emergence of distinct linguistic structures, while 'indigenisation' refers to "the acceptance by the local community of the existence of a local variety of a language" (Pang 2003, 12). He claims that English in Hong Kong has been localised but not indigenised because "[t]here are indeed well-documented features of Hong Kong English, but locals prefer to believe that they are not speaking a local variety [...]" (Pang 2003, 13). Approximately a decade after Pang's article, Groves still observes conflicting norm orientations, i.e. internal orientation in terms of actual language use and external orientation in terms of attitudes (cf. Groves 2011, 33). She therefore calls Hong Kong a case of 'linguistic schizophrenia' (Groves 2011, 33), a term proposed by Kachru for the ambivalent situation that speakers find themselves in when bilingualism spreads in the community (cf. Kachru 1983b). Groves takes the existence of conflicting norm orientations in Hong Kong as a first sign that HKE may be emerging as a

---

4   Weston argues instead that the relationship to Britain remains an important aspect of Hong Kong people's identity to dissociate themselves from mainland China (cf. Weston 2016, 680–681). The weakening of ties between the former colony and its colonial power is an assumed process in the emergence of a postcolonial variety but as Hong Kong did not gain independence but only experienced a change in sovereignty, it is therefore an atypical case of a postcolonial variety of English. The former colonial power is still seen as 'the lesser of two evils' and the relationship with it as a means of "safeguarding a local culture and identity that might otherwise be overwhelmed by the neighbouring country" (Weston 2016, 680; cf. also Setter, Wong & Chan 2010, 107). In a similar vein, Li suggests that the end of the British colonial rule leads to the abandonment of "the 'them vs. us' mindset directed toward the British and 'their' language" (Li 2008, 233; cf. also Lai 2008, 475). Furthermore, Joseph speculates that English may start to fulfil integrative functions in Hong Kong if Beijing tries to substitute Cantonese with Putonghua in Hong Kong in order to strengthen a pan-Chinese identity (cf. Joseph 2004, 159–161).

variety (cf. Groves 2011, 33), while Bolton and other researchers instead believe that HKE already existed as an autonomous variety at the beginning of the 2000s (cf. Bolton 2002; cf. also Bolton 2000, 2003; Gisborne 2009, 149). As can be seen from the dates of publication, the recognition of a distinct HKE variety is therefore a rather recent phenomenon (cf. (183) and (184) in Chapter 11 for speaker attitudes towards the status of HKE).

The variety of HKE represented in the ICE-HK corpus can therefore best be understood in terms of a 'nascent variety', which is why I will use the term 'Hong Kong English' rather than 'English in Hong Kong' in this study. In the early 1990s, the time of the compilation of ICE-HK, English functioned as the co-official language beside Cantonese. The data from the population census of 1991 indicate that 89% of the population spoke Cantonese as their usual language/dialect (cf. Figure 6). In light of these numbers, it is not surprising that Cantonese is the symbol of Hong Kong people's identity (cf. also Evans 2013, 307).[5]

Only 2% of the population spoke English as their usual language/dialect. The proportion of Putonghua was even lower, with 1% of the population using it as their usual language/dialect. The Chinese dialects make up 7% in total and their low frequency attests to their strong decline by 10% since 1911 (cf. Bacon-Shone & Bolton 2008, 31–32). In recent years, they have decreased even further to a proportion of 4% (cf. Bacon-Shone & Bolton 2008, 31). This means that Cantonese is the dominant language spoken in Hong Kong,

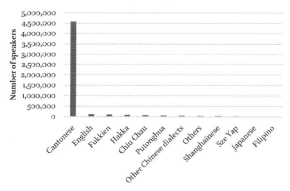

FIGURE 6   Number of speakers aged 5 and above by usual
             language/dialect (Hong Kong Census of
             Population 1991, Census and Statistics
             Department) (cf. Table 13 in the appendices).

---

5   Code-switching between English and Cantonese, called *mix* or *u-gay-wa* (lit. 'university talk'), among young (educated) people also seems to fulfil integrative functions in Hong Kong (cf. Schneider 2007, 138–139).

the language that is spoken at home and among intimates (cf. Li 2008, 197–198). Despite the dominant role of Cantonese, knowledge of English and Putonghua continues to spread (cf. Bacon-Shone & Bolton 2008, 43). While Cantonese fulfils integrative functions, the motivations to learn Putonghua and English are rather instrumental (cf. Pang 2003, 17; Setter, Wong & Chan 2010, 110–111).[6] Increasing contact to mainland China requires language skills in Putonghua (cf. Li 2008, 199), while international business relations require language skills in English. This is why Li describes the status of English in Hong Kong in terms of a 'value-added' language and argues that it fulfils typical functions of a high variety (H) in a diglossic setting, with Cantonese functioning as the low variety (L) (cf. Li 2008, 226). That English is not used for intranational communication makes the situation in Hong Kong different from the language situation in India or Singapore, where English also functions as an intranational means of communication between speakers of different languages. While in India, Hindi also fulfils the function of an interethnic lingua franca, especially in the north of the subcontinent, English is the only lingua franca between the Chinese, Malay, and Indian communities in Singapore (cf. Sections 3.2.2 and 3.2.3). Still, knowledge of English has spread in Hong Kong despite its more restricted functions from a mere 6% in 1931 to 45% in 2006 (cf. Bacon-Shone & Bolton 2008, 32). At the time of the compilation of ICE-HK, 32% of the population claimed knowledge of English, of these 2% used it as their usual language/dialect and 29% as another language/dialect (cf. Bacon-Shone & Bolton 2008, 32).

3.2.2   *English in India*

English in India has a long history. Despite its historical depth, it is still spoken by only a minority in India today, though given the nation's large population this minority constitutes a sizeable group of English speakers in the world (cf. Schneider 2007, 161). Its Foundation phase started in 1600, when Queen Elizabeth I granted a trade charter to the East India Company (cf. Mukherjee 2007, 164; Schneider 2007, 162). This led to the establishment of trading posts, which attracted English merchants throughout the 17th century (cf. Mukherjee 2010, 168). Missionaries also arrived in this period and spread knowledge of English further by the establishment of English-medium schools (cf. Mukherjee 2007, 164; Schneider 2007, 162–163). In this early stage, contact between the STL strand and the IDG strand was restricted to interactions between

---

6   Note, however, that Lai argues that English in Hong Kong has developed an identitary function after the handover "from [...] an international language into a marker of Hong Kong identity" (Lai 2008, 473).

English merchants, missionaries, and soldiers and a few indigenous people (cf. Mukherjee 2010, 168–169).

The situation changed when the East India Company defeated the last independent viceroy of Bengal in the Battle of Plassey in 1757 and the indigenous population realised that the British would stay in the country (cf. Mukherjee 2007, 164; Schneider 2007, 163). This victory marks the beginning of the expansion of British control to the whole subcontinent, the onset of the second stage of Endonormative Stabilisation. In the second half of the 18th century, the East India Company gradually transformed "from an economic organization to a political power" (Schneider 2007, 163). Roughly 100 years after the Battle of Plassey, the indirect rule over India through the East India Company changed to direct rule of the British Crown after the Great Rebellion (cf. Schneider 2007, 164; Sedlatschek 2009, 14–15). In the decades before and after the turn of the century, a considerable number of missionary schools were established and early discussions about the medium of instruction were held between the 'Orientalists', who favoured education in the indigenous languages and the 'Anglicists', who favoured education in English (cf. Schneider 2007, 164; cf. (185) in Chapter 11 for the perpetuation of arguments of this controversy until today). In 1835, Thomas Macaulay strongly advocated English-medium instruction in his *Minute on Education* with the aim of establishing

> a class who may be interpreters between us and the millions whom we govern – a class of persons, Indian in blood and colour, but English in taste, in opinions, in morals and in intellect.
>
> cited in KACHRU 1983a, 22

The British government decided to promote Macaulay's vision, which clearly served the needs of the British and not those of the indigenous population. A considerable number of English-medium schools were established that further spread knowledge of English in the class of Indians that were trained for public offices (cf. Mukherjee 2007, 165, 2010, 170). While indigenous languages partially remained the media of instruction in primary education, English became the uncontested medium of instruction in secondary and tertiary education (cf. Mukherjee 2010, 170). It did not only spread as the medium of instruction, but also as a language of administration, creative writing, and the media through the circulation of English newspapers at the end of the 19th century (cf. Sedlatschek 2009, 16). It is also during this period that English started to be used in more informal conversations between English-educated Indians (cf. Sedlatschek 2009, 16).

From the onset of the third stage of Nativisation at the beginning of the 20th century onwards, English was fulfilling more and more functions of a second language (cf. Schneider 2007, 166). The number of students enrolled in English-medium education grew in the early 20th century and it became soon visible that the introduction of English to form a class of subordinates turned the scales against the Empire with the incessant striving for self-government (cf. Sedlatschek 2009, 17). Mukherjee comments,

> [m]ost ironically from the British point of view, it was the English language as a pan-Indian communicative device in multilingual India that made it possible for Indian intellectuals from all over the subcontinent to agitate jointly against British rule.
>
> MUKHERJEE 2007, 166

English therefore also became the language of resistance against the British Raj (cf. Sedlatschek 2009, 17). Since independence in 1947, the English language has further strengthened its role despite attempts to discard the colonial language (cf. Sedlatschek 2009, 18). Hindi was declared the national language of India after independence, as it was the language with the highest number of speakers (and still is, cf. Figure 8) (cf. Sedlatschek 2009, 18). The new constitution allowed for a gradual shift from English to Hindi, as English had firmly established itself in administration, education, and the legal system (cf. Sedlatschek 2009, 18). English was assigned the status of an additional language for 15 years in the new constitution in 1950 before its planned abolition (cf. Sedlatschek 2009, 18). However, English was never officially abolished because speakers of Dravidian languages, who predominantly live in the non-Hindi speaking southern states of India (cf. Figure 9), firmly rejected the choice of Hindi as a national language and favoured English "as a more neutral linguistic choice" (Sedlatschek 2009, 18). The rejection of Hindi as a national language gradually evolved into violent protests in the language riots of the 1960s (cf. Mukherjee 2010, 172).[7] Even before the planned substitution of English with Hindi, the Indian Parliament therefore passed the *Official Languages Act* and its amendments in 1963 and 1967 that secured the status of English as a co-official language (often also labelled 'associate (additional) official language') (cf. Schneider 2007, 166; Sedlatschek 2009, 19).

---

7 Mukherjee argues that the language riots of the 1960s can be considered the event X in the evolution of IndE, i.e. the event that triggers Endonormative Stabilisation (cf. Mukherjee 2010, 171–172).

In terms of language teaching, India follows a policy of trilingualism with the so-called *Three Language Formula* that was finally accepted in 1968 (cf. Sedlatschek 2009, 20). It aims at teaching the regional mother tongue, English, and Hindi for non-Hindi speakers and another modern Indian language for Hindi speakers (cf. Sedlatschek 2009, 20). However, the policy has not been successfully implemented because Hindi speakers from the north were opposed to learning a Dravidian language, while speakers of Dravidian languages in the south refused to learn Hindi (cf. Schneider 2007, 166). The function of English as an administrative language is therefore not challenged by any other Indian language. English-medium education also remained popular despite the fact that English was no longer the obligatory medium of instruction (cf. Sedlatschek 2009, 20).

According to Schneider, IndE is still at the end of Nativisation but shows early characteristics of the Endonormative Stabilisation stage, which are however "disputable or weak" (Schneider 2007, 171). Among these 'early symptoms of phase 4' are an increasing acceptance of the local form of English and the emergence of literary creativity in English (cf. Schneider 2007, 171–172). However, other signs of the fourth stage of Schneider's (2007) model are still missing, such as homogenisation and codification, which is why Schneider places IndE in the third stage of his model (cf. Schneider 2007, 171–172). By contrast, Mukherjee argues that present-day IndE has reached the fourth stage of Schneider's (2007) model but still carries traces of phase 3 (cf. Mukherjee 2007, 168–170, 2010, 173).

In order to shed light on aspects of this controversy, I conducted a language attitude survey with 53 participants in 2015 (cf. Section 4.2) to see whether speakers of IndE show a positive attitude toward their local variety, a characteristic feature of phase 4 (cf. Section 3.2). My data reveal that IndE is recognised as a distinct variety by roughly three quarters of the respondents (cf. Item 1 in Figure 7). Roughly the same proportion considers IndE to be different from BrE (cf. Item 2 in Figure 7). With regard to identity functions fulfilled by IndE, 61% of the participants agree or strongly agree that IndE can give them a feeling of belonging and only 23% agree or strongly agree that English cannot give them a feeling of belonging (cf. Items 3 and 7 in Figure 7). In terms of norm orientations, the majority agrees or strongly agrees that they speak IndE (66%), while roughly half of the respondents agrees or strongly agrees that they speak BrE, while only 23% try to speak AmE (Items 4, 6, and 8). This means that BrE is chosen if an exonormative model is chosen, which may have to do with language ideologies because 47% consider BrE to be 'more correct' than AmE, while 57% consider AmE to be 'more colloquial' than BrE (cf. Items 5 and 9 in Figure 7).

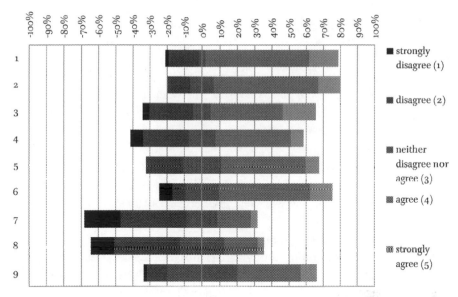

FIGURE 7   Language attitudes towards IndE (cf. Table 14 in the appendices).

1.   Indian English is a standard variety of English such as Australian English, Canadian English, or American English.
2.   Indian English is different from British English.
3.   Indian English originates from the Indian people, so it can give me a feeling of belonging.
4.   As an Indian, I try to speak British English.
5.   American English is more colloquial than British English.
6.   As an Indian, I try to speak Indian English.
7.   I do not feel that I belong to any English-speaking community, because English is not my mother tongue.
8.   As an Indian, I try to speak American English.
9.   British English is more correct than American English.

The questionnaire data indicate that IndE speakers do not only recognise that they speak a distinctive local variety of English but also accept it as their norm of speaking. The exonormative orientation towards BrE is still visible, as can be seen from the fact that half of the respondents try to speak BrE. However, most respondents orient themselves towards local norms, which is also visible in the number of participants who strongly agree that they speak IndE, a figure twice as high as the number of speakers who strongly agree that they speak BrE. This suggests a gradual dissolving of BrE norms. But if an exonormative variety is chosen as the norm, it is clearly BrE and not AmE. In terms of the integrative functions of IndE, we can see that English can give the majority of respondents a feeling of belonging, which might indicate a change ever since Schneider's postulation that IndE does not function as an identity marker (cf. Schneider 2007, 167). While the answers of the respondents support the entry of IndE into the phase of Endonormative Stabilisation, we need to be cautious not to generalise these findings to all speakers of IndE, because the sample is small (N=53) and not representative of the whole population with regard to the social characteristics of the speakers (cf. Section 4.2). Furthermore, the language attitude data can most likely not be projected back to the early 1990s when ICE-IND was compiled because the increasing acceptance by the majority of its speakers seems to be a rather recent phenomenon.

In the early 1990s, English was used by members of the middle and upper class of India's population as an intranational link language in more formal domains such as education, administration, business, and the media but also in less formal domains among family and friends (cf. Mukherjee 2007, 158; Sedlatschek 2009, 24). Despite the wide range of functions it fulfils, it is likely that it did not (yet) fulfil identity functions at that time (cf. Schneider 2007, 167). Schneider argues that this was hampered by the predominant role of Hindi in India (cf. Figure 8) and the fact that only a small minority spoke English (cf. Schneider 2007, 167). Only 0.02% of the population spoke English as a native language in 1991. Estimates of how many people spoke English as a second language in India at that time range from conservative estimates of 5% to 30% (cf. Tully 1997, 157; Kachru 2005, 14–15). But even if the conservative figure of 5% is accepted, this translates to 42 million speakers of IndE in 1991.[8] Consequently,

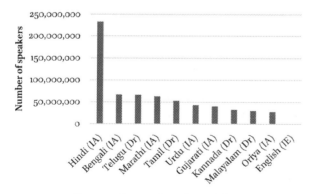

FIGURE 8   Ten most frequently spoken mother tongues in
            India (India Census of Population 1991, Govern-
            ment of India, Ministry of Home Affairs) (cf.
            Table 15 in the appendices).

---

8 This estimate seems reasonable, given that Sailaja estimates that 64 million people use
   English in India at the beginning of the 21st century (cf. Sailaja 2009, 3).

English was spoken by a great number of speakers, although they still constitute a minority in India itself. IndE is not a homogenous variety but displays regional and social variation (cf. Schneider 2007, 168, cf. Section 6.2 for regional variation, Chapters 8 and 9 for social variation). Regional varieties of English partially result from interference from the different L1s of the speakers (cf. also Kachru 1983a, 73–74), which is why labels such as 'Hindi English' or 'Telugu English' have found their way into descriptions of IndE (cf. Schneider 2007, 170; Lange 2017, 17–18; cf. also Figure 38 in Chapter 6). Figure 8 shows the number of speakers for the ten most frequently spoken mother tongues in India in 1991.

In the early 1990s as today, English existed in a multilingual environment in India, where languages from basically four different language families were spoken, i.e. from the Indo-Aryan language family, the Dravidian language family, the Tibeto-Burman language family, and the Austro-Asiatic language family. Figure 9 shows the regional distribution of the four language families in India.

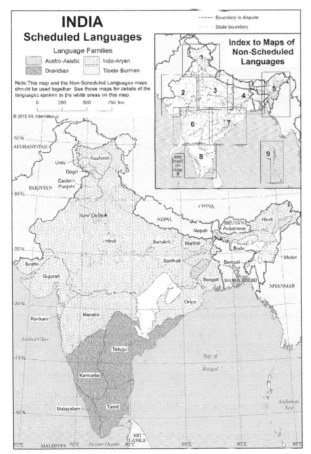

FIGURE 9
The regional distribution of
India's scheduled languages
(from the 19th edition of
Ethnologue).

As can be seen, the Indo-Aryan languages are predominantly spoken in the north while the Dravidian languages are prevalent in the south. Languages of these two language families make up 95% of the languages spoken in India (cf. Schilk 2011, 5). Of India's ten most frequently spoken mother tongues in 1991, Hindi, Bengali, Marathi, Urdu, Gujarati, and Oriya belong to the Indo-Aryan languages, while Telugu, Tamil, Kannada, and Malayalam are from the Dravidian language family (cf. Figure 8).

3.2.3   *English in Singapore*

The history of English in Singapore dates back to the early 19th century. This means English arrived in Singapore in the same time period as in Hong Kong. Its roots are therefore not as deep as those of IndE, which can be dated back to the 17th century. English arrived in Singapore when the British established a trading post on the island of Singapore in 1819 (cf. Schneider 2007, 153). At that time, Singapore was characterised by a small population (cf. Bao 2015, 15). The establishment of the trading post led to an influx of immigrants with a consequent rapid increase in population (cf. Schneider 2007, 153). Most of the early immigrants came from Malacca and Penang, which also formed part of the Straits Settlement to which Singapore belonged since 1826 (cf. Bao 2015, 15). Apart from the Chinese immigrants, there was also considerable immigration from southern India (cf. Schneider 2007, 154). Since 1836, the Chinese have formed the largest ethnic group, followed by the Malays, and the Indians (cf. Bao 2015, 16–17). The group of Europeans only constituted a minority of the immigrants from 1819 to 1836 (cf. Bao 2015, 16). This ethnic composition has lasted until today. During the early periods of colonisation, Singapore was clearly divided along ethnic lines, which was also visible in the spatial confinement of the communities (cf. Bao 2015, 21). Communication within the 'enclaves' took place in the dominant languages of the communities, whereas communication across enclaves was established through Bazaar Malay (cf. Bao 2015, 21). The local lingua franca Bazaar Malay is a Malay-based pidgin that was heavily influenced by the southern Chinese dialect Hokkien (cf. Gupta 1998, 109).[9] Apart from Bazaar Malay, Baba Malay, another variety of Malay, was spoken by the Straits-born Chinese, the descendants of Chinese immigrants who came to the Malay Archipelago (also called Peranakans)[10] (cf. Gupta 1998, 125).

In 1867, Singapore became a British colony. The date marks the onset of the stage of Exonormative Stabilisation of English in Singapore (cf. Schneider

---

9   Bao argues that a pidginised form of English was also used at that time as a lingua franca
       that preceded the emergence of SgE (cf. Bao 2015, 23).
10   Cf. Lim (2014) for the role of the Peranakans in the evolution of SgE.

2007, 154). During this phase, the population was transient in nature until the turn of the century and marked by a strong gender imbalance, with a demographic preponderance of male residents as a result of the massive influx of Chinese male migrant labourers (cf. Bao 2015, 17). Knowledge of English was largely restricted to the European settlers and a few Singaporean residents (cf. Gupta 1998, 108–109). This means that although bilingualism spread in the population, it was still limited to the local elite (cf. Schneider 2007, 154). English expanded further through the establishment of more English-medium schools in the second half of the 19th century (cf. Schneider 2007, 154). Europeans and Eurasians formed the largest group of students in English-medium schools (cf. Gupta 1998, 116). The only Chinese students were Straits-born Chinese (cf. Gupta 1998, 116). Teachers were mostly Eurasians or Indians, only about a quarter of teachers were British (cf. Gupta 1998, 124). In the early 20th century, Chinese students started to attend English medium schools whose mother tongues were predominantly Hokkien and Cantonese (cf. Gupta 1998, 116; Schneider 2007, 154). In the middle of the 20th century, Malay children also entered English-medium schools (cf. Gupta 1998, 116). During this time, English-medium schools spread but did not yet surpass Chinese-medium schools until the 1950s (cf. Gupta 1998, 116).

The Japanese occupation of Singapore in World War II suspended Britain's colonial rule for three years (cf. Schneider 2007, 155). After the Japanese interregnum, the British re-assumed power over Singapore but the Singaporean population sought independence, most strongly voiced by the People's Action Party (PAP) (cf. Schneider 2007, 155). This ultimately led to independence in 1965 after a period of self government in 1959 and a short union with Malaysia (cf. Schneider 2007, 155). These historical events initiated the Nativisation phase in Singapore in 1945. After independence in 1965, Singapore's economy transformed rapidly in the 1970s, which can be seen as the trigger for the onset of Endonormative Stabilisation of SgE (cf. Schneider 2007, 155). The country transformed into a modern economic centre and Singaporeans developed "a unique and novel identity which has combined European and Asian components" (Schneider 2007, 155–156). This is expressed by SgE, with its "world language character [that] expresses the country's global outreach [...], and its distinctively local shape [...] [that] ties up with the country's location and traditions" (Schneider 2007, 160). This means that unlike HKE and IndE, SgE fulfils identity functions, which is why Wong claims that English "in many ways functions like a *de facto* national language" (Wong 2014, 2) in Singapore. Apart from its intranational function, English also links Singaporeans to the world and is seen as the language of modernity (cf. Wong 2014, 2).

The government declared four languages official languages after independence. These are English, Mandarin, Malay, and Tamil (cf. Wong 2014, 1; Bao 2015, 19). Since 1966, the government's language policy has been one of 'ethnicity-based bilingualism', fostering knowledge in English and the ethnic 'mother tongues' (cf. Schneider 2007, 156; Bolton & Ng 2014, 310). Mandarin, Malay, and Tamil represent the 'mother tongues' of the three main ethnic groups, the Chinese, the Malays, and the Indians (cf. Gupta 1998, 117). Malay additionally has had the official status of national language since Singapore's short-lived reunion with Malaysia in 1963 (cf. Bolton & Ng 2014, 309; Wong 2014, 1). A speaker is assigned an ethnic mother tongue on the basis of the ethnicity of his or her father (cf. Gupta 1998, 117). In this way, Malay children are assigned Malay as their 'mother tongue', Chinese children are assigned Mandarin, and Indian children are assigned Tamil (cf. Gupta 1998, 117; Bolton & Ng 2014, 310). It needs to be mentioned, however, that the 'mother tongue' that is assigned to an ethnic group is not always the same as the first language of the speakers and may in some cases actually be a second language for the speakers. Disparity between the ethnically assigned 'mother tongue' and the *de facto* mother tongue of the speakers is more widespread in the Indian and Chinese communities than in the Malay community. Tamil was assigned to the Indian community because the early Indian immigrants came from the southern Indian state of Tamil Nadu, whose population predominantly speaks Tamil (cf. Bolton & Ng 2014, 312; cf. Figure 9). But today Indians in Singapore come from diverse regions of India and therefore may have a language other than Tamil as their mother tongue. Furthermore, Mandarin is not the heritage language of the Chinese because the immigrants used to speak Chinese dialects such as Hokkien, Cantonese, and Teochew (cf. Bolton & Ng 2014, 312; Wong 2014, 1). The Chinese dialects have decreased strongly in Singapore, which is partly a result of the introduction of Mandarin as the medium of instruction in Chinese schools that were established in the beginning of the 20th century and the successful *Speak Mandarin Campaign* that was launched in 1979 (cf. Bolton & Ng 2014, 310; Bao 2015, 19). The campaign encourages the use of Mandarin among the Chinese community and has effectively led to an intra-ethnic language shift from the Chinese dialects to Mandarin (cf. Bolton & Ng 2014, 310).

While the three 'mother tongues' were initially also supposed to function as media of instruction in schools, the last schools that offered non-English medium instruction had to be closed in 1980 because student enrolments had decreased drastically (cf. Bao 2015, 28). Thus, English became the universal medium of instruction (cf. Bolton & Ng 2014, 309). As English spread further in the population, complaints arose about falling standards, which is why the government launched the *Speak Good English Movement* (SGEM) in 2000 (cf. Bolton & Ng 2014, 310). This movement was also a reaction to the spread of Singlish in the population (cf. Bolton & Ng 2014, 310). Singlish (also 'Colloquial SgE') is a distinctive local variety of English that is marked by strong influence from Chinese, and which is predominantly used in informal contexts. Although the SGEM strongly rejects the use of Singlish, it carries covert prestige as an identity marker for Singaporeans (cf. (186) and (187) in Chapter 11 for instantiations of conflicting views on Singlish in web content).

The language policies that aimed at promoting English-bilingual speakers unintentionally led to the spread of English as a home language, which increased from around 2% in 1957 to 32% in 2010 (cf. Bolton & Ng 2014, 311). The Chinese and Indian communities have shown a stronger adoption of English as a home language than the Malay community (cf. Bolton & Ng 2014, 312). In the Indian community, English has even surpassed Tamil as the home language, while Mandarin is still the predominant home language in the Chinese community in 2010 (cf. Bolton & Ng 2014, 312). Despite the stronger retention of Malay in the Malay community, this group also shows an increased use of English. Consequently, all ethnic groups are undergoing language shift to English (cf. Schneider 2007, 157). As a result, "English has gone from the language of the elite to an interethnic lingua franca to the primary language of modern Singapore" (Bao 2015, 33). English therefore functions not only as an international language but also as an interethnic and increasingly intra-ethnic language (cf. also Wong 2014, 3).

In the 1990s, when ICE-SIN was compiled, the Chinese were the dominant ethnic group in Singapore, with 78% of the population being Chinese, 14% Malay, and 7% Indian (cf. Singapore Census of Population 1990, Singapore Department of Statistics). At that time, all Chinese dialects taken together still constituted the dominant group of languages spoken at home, at ca. 40% (cf. Figure 10); this figure dropped below 20% in 2010. Hokkien (19%) was still the most frequently spoken Chinese dialect in 1990, followed by Teochew (9%), and Cantonese (8%). Mandarin, the official ethnic mother tongue of the Chinese, was spoken by roughly a quarter of the population as the language of the home, already indicating the success of the *Speak Mandarin Campaign*. The next language most frequently spoken at home was English, spoken by roughly 20% of the population. Malay was spoken by 14%. Tamil and other Indian languages were spoken by only 3%.

Figure 10 shows that the Chinese dialects still played an important role in the Singaporean context in 1990. However, taken separately no language has a higher share of speakers than Mandarin. This indicates that Mandarin was already the dominant language of the Chinese community in 1990, a tendency that has been strengthened in more recent years (cf. Bao 2015, 21). When discussing language data from the 1990s, it is therefore advisable to take Mandarin as the most important language in contact with English (cf. Gupta 1998, 125–126).

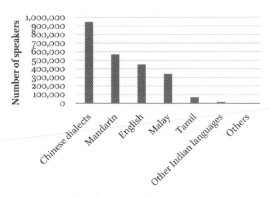

FIGURE 10   Resident population aged 5 years and
             above by language most frequently spoken
             at home (Singapore Census of Population
             1990, Singapore Department of Statistics)
             (cf. Table 16 in the appendices).

As I am predominantly interested in the language contact taking place in the
minds of the speakers, I will analyse Mandarin as one of the substrate language
of modern SgE, despite historically motivated criticism against this procedure
(cf. Lim & Ansaldo 2016, 126). As the brief sketch of the development of English
in Singapore has shown, Bazaar Malay and Baba Malay were the principal historical substrate languages in the formative period of SgE. However, although
the influence of Baba Malay on SgE is often mentioned, especially with regard
to a possible founder effect by the Peranakans (cf. Lim 2014), there is no evidence that grammatical restructuring in SgE is influenced by Baba Malay (cf.
Bao 2015, 30). Another reason why it makes sense to analyse the influence of
a Chinese substratum on SgE is that Bazaar Malay and Baba Malay were both
already strongly influenced by Chinese because Hokkien functioned as their
substratum (cf. Bao 2015, 35). At the same time, the effect of Hokkien was also
more direct as it functioned as secondary historical substrate, together with
the Chinese dialects Teochew and Cantonese (cf. Gupta 1998, 125). If the structure of the Chinese dialects Hokkien and Cantonese is compared to Mandarin
(cf. example (26) from Bao 2015, 20), we can see that their morphosyntax is
similar and that the mutal unintelligibility between the Chinese dialects predominantly results from phonological and lexical differences.

(26) Hokkien   gua   khi   hit-kieng   chai-kuan.
      Cantonese   ngo   hoey   kor-kan   ts'ai-gun.
      Mandarin   wǒ   qú   nà-jiān   cài-guǎn.
                     I   go   that-CL   restaurant.
      'I am going to that restaurant.'

The negligible differences between the dialects in terms of their morphosyntax, the linguistic level of interest for this study, therefore further warrant the decision to analyse Mandarin as an example of the Sinitic substrate of modern SgE. Apart from Mandarin, I will also analyse the influence of Malay and Tamil on the structure of SgE in Sections 6.2 and 7.1. Given the ethnic make-up of the Singaporean society in 1990, however, the influence of Malay and Tamil on SgE is likely to be weaker than that of Mandarin.

3.3   Mufwene's (2001) Feature Pool Model

The position of the varieties in Schneider's (2007) Dynamic Model shows that all varieties have reached phase 3, which means that we can expect grammatical restructuring processes to have taken place. In order to describe these restructuring processes in more detail, I will draw on Mufwene's (2001) Feature Pool Model.[11]

His model is part of a more comprehensive model that transfers knowledge from population genetics to the evolution of languages. Evolution in this model does not imply progress in any way but simply "long-term changes undergone by a language (variety) over a period of time" (Mufwene 2001, 12). This model suggests an analogy between a language and a species (cf. Mufwene 2001, 145). More precisely, language is seen as "a Lamarckian species, whose genetic makeup can change several times in its lifetime" (Mufwene 2001, 16). Language is also conceived of as a parasitic species that is dependent upon its hosts, "i.e. its speakers, on the society they form, and on the culture in which they live" (Mufwene 2001, 16). This highlights the importance of circumscribing the role and functions that English has in Hong Kong, India, and Singapore (cf. Sections 3.2.1–3.2.3). As part of the analogy between languages and species, Mufwene analyses language change in terms of competition and selection of features in a pool (cf. Figure 11). The linguistic features roughly correspond to genes in biology (cf. Mufwene 2001, 16). But unlike genes, these features are not only transferred in a vertical and unidirectional manner but also horizontally and bidirectionally (cf. Mufwene 2001, 16).

The arrows in the upper part show the input to the feature pool. The grey arrows represent input from superstrate languages and the white arrow

---

11   Note that Schneider also makes use of Mufwene's (2001) Feature Pool Model and provides a concise list of potential selection principles at work in the formation of postcolonial Englishes, including demography, frequency of forms, historical depth, markedness, salience, transparency and regularity, status of the speakers, identity-marking functions of linguistic forms, and similarities and differences between L1 and L2 forms and patterns (cf. Schneider 2007, 110–111).

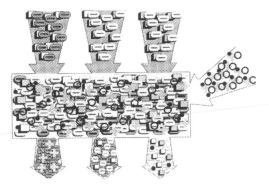

FIGURE 11   Mufwene's Feature Pool
                    Model (from Mufwene
                    2001, 6).

represents input from a substrate language. Mufwene argues that the restructuring processes that take place in the feature pool are ultimately the same
in the formation of koinés, creoles, and other contact varieties of English, although substrate languages only play a role in the formation of the latter two
(cf. Mufwene 2001, 4–6). In the case of creoles and contact varieties of English,
therefore, both the superstrate language and the substrate language feed features to the pool; more precisely the idiolects of speakers of these languages
contribute features to the pool. The idiosyncratic forms that individuals contribute compete with each other in the feature pool and those features that are
selected are recombined in the output in a way that differs from the structure
of the input languages, i.e. the structure of the creole or the structure of the
contact variety differs from both the structure of the superstrate and the structure of the substrate, as can be seen in the lower part of Figure 11 (cf. Mufwene
2001, 4–5). If features are repeatedly selected by several speakers, they may
become conventionalised and establish themselves as features of the newly
emerging variety (cf. van Rooy 2010, 8–9).

Mufwene compares the restructuring process that takes place to genetic re-
combination in biology but notes that transmission proceeds first and foremost
at the horizontal level rather than at the vertical level (cf. Mufwene 2001, 12).
Features may become modified during the selection process that is similar to
'blended inheritance' in biology, so that the emerging creole or variety may
also have features that were neither part of the lexifier nor of the substrate
languages. The modifications result from 'imperfect replication' that speakers make when they accommodate to each other in conversations or adapt to
new communicative needs (cf. Mufwene 2001, 11). During this process, both
'inheritance and recreation' take place, i.e. features of the input are used but
they are "undone and redone a few times" (Mufwene 2001, 24) and create a
new variety. This variety can differ from the input in qualitative but also in

quantitative terms, for example due to different frequencies of variants or different rankings of constraints of variants (cf. Mufwene 2001, 151). An increase in frequency of a variant can for instance result from an extension of its function by way of substratum influence (cf. Mufwene 2001, 160).

The competition-and-selection process does not take place in a vacuum but depends on the ecology of the contact situation, which includes internal and external factors (cf. Mufwene 2001, 21–22). Factors that determine the ecology of the language contact situation can be internal or external. The internal ecology involves, for example, the structural characteristics of the languages that serve as input and similarities between them (cf. Biewer 2015, 82; cf. also Lim 2009, 100). The socio-historical background is relevant to the external ecology of the contact situation, including, for example, the demographic make-up of the communities that are in contact and the power relations that hold between them (cf. Lim 2009, 100). Although the distinction between internal and external ecology is useful in theory, it is often blurred in reality because the two types of ecology interact strongly, for example "[e]xternal ecology causes changes but the nature of these is determined in part by structural characteristics (i.e., internal ecology) of the evolving system" (Mufwene 2001, 192). External and internal ecology come together in the minds of the speaker, whose language use is simultaneously shaped by aspects of both (cf. Mufwene 2001, 195). Despite the intricate interweaving of the two aspects of ecology, the theoretical distinction between the two is useful because it helps to unravel the relationship between language-internal and language-external factors of the contact situation. In the case of the variable under study, this means that it is important to analyse the language-internal competition between the group of modal and semi-modal verbs and their functions as well as language-external factors that affect this language-internal competition-and-selection process. I have described the socio-historical background of the English language in Hong Kong, India, and Singapore to provide an overview of important aspects of the external ecology of the contact situation (cf. Sections 3.2.1–3.2.3). In Sections 7.2 and 7.3, I will deal with the influence of culture and SLA principles, which also belong to the external ecology of the contact situation, on the restructuring process. The analyses of the roles of transfer and general cognitive principles instead belong to the internal ecology of the contact situation (cf. Sections 7.1 and 7.4). The interrelationship between internal and external ecology becomes immediately obvious because general cognitive principles and SLA as well as transfer and culture interact strongly in the restructuring process.

Apart from the integration of the context in which a new variety develops, another benefit of the Feature Pool Model is that it pays attention to the internal ecology of the historical varieties that served as input to the new variety, rather than only to the internal ecology of the present-day variety. This means that the historical state of the input at the time of early contact is reconstructed on the assumption that the 'founder principle' applies. This principle holds that varieties are strongly shaped by the structural features of the variety that served as the historical input in the formation of these varieties (cf. Mufwene 2001, 28–29). Although the founder principle is often mentioned in studies on WE, the state of the historical input variety is rarely reconstructed (cf. Section 6.1.7 for a discussion of the founder effect in the use of modal and semi-modal verbs of obligation and necessity).

The model is a valuable analytical tool because it analyses the evolution of new varieties in terms of a competition-and-selection process from a feature pool that is fed by the superstrate and the substrate languages. However, it is generally less accurate in the description of selection principles that determine the competition-and-selection process (cf. also Lange 2012, 67). Although Mufwene makes reference to cognitive factors as relevant selection principles throughout his monograph (cf. Mufwene 2001, 31–32, and *passim*), his treatment of their effects on the selection is less detailed. The only general observation he makes is:

> the more common or frequent, the more salient, the more regular, or the more transparent alternatives were favoured over the less common or frequent, less salient, less regular, or the opaque alternatives [...].
>
> MUFWENE 2001, 57

Apart from frequency, salience, regularity, and transparency, he also mentions markedness, which is related to frequency (cf. Mufwene 2001, 32). Additionally, he postulates that those features of the lexifier that are structurally similar to features in the substrate have a higher chance of being selected for the emerging variety (cf. Mufwene 2001, 31). His rather general selection principles, which are particularly relevant to creole formation, provide a valuable starting point but need to be specified and expanded for the ESL context (cf. also Biewer 2015, 83).[12] Given the criticism raised against the model in creole studies (cf. Plag 2011; McWhorter 2012) – the area for which it had originally been developed – it could well be that the Feature Pool Model turns out to be a more powerful analytical tool for the study of dialect formation than for the study of creole formation.

---

12   Cf. Winford (2017) for a discussion of the relationship between WE and creoles.

3.4 Biewer's (2015) Adapted Feature Pool Model

This is at least what Biewer's study suggests in which she applies the Feature Pool Model to the formation of ESL varieties by analysing the structure of the SPE FijE, SamE, and CookE. She takes a closer look at the following selection principles that may condition the choice of one feature over another in the competition-and-selection process: (1) transfer, (2) socio-cultural motivations, (3) SLA processes, and (4) cognitive processes (cf. Biewer 2015, 86–114).

In the formation of ESL varieties, local substrates are important contributors to the feature pool beside superstrate languages (cf. 6.1 and 6.2 for the description of the structure of the historical superstrate variety and the structures of the substrate languages). As English is spoken as a second language in Hong Kong, India, and Singapore, the L1s of the speakers play an important role. Speakers compare the structures of their L1s to the structures of their L2s and may transfer patterns from their L1s to features of their L2s if they perceive them to be similar (cf. Biewer 2015, 98) (cf. Section 7.1 for the role of transfer in the restructuring of the modal systems of HKE, IndE, and SgE).

Apart from transfer, socio-cultural motivations may also have an impact on the selection process. These may include the intensity of contact, language attitudes, social identity, accommodation, and cultural motivations (cf. Biewer 2015, 103–110). As the descriptions of the socio-historical background of English in Hong Kong, India, and Singapore have shown, the intensity of contact between the IDG strand and the STL strand was limited in the beginning but increased over the course of colonisation. However, ENL speakers always remained a minority in Hong Kong, India, and Singapore, which is why innovative features of L2 speakers have a relatively better chance of becoming established in these varieties than the innovative features of IDG speakers in settlement colonies where ENL speakers were in the majority. Another important social factor that has an impact on the selection process is language attitude. If there is no acceptance of the local variety in the population, salient structural features of this variety may be avoided (cf. Biewer 2015, 104–105). Due to the fact that people in Hong Kong had the strongest exonormative orientation in the early 1990s, we can expect a stronger orientation towards BrE norms because of a positive attitude towards BrE and a rather negative attitude towards their own local variety. Conversely, in SgE, we can expect a more positive attitude towards the local variety, which can foster the selection of local variants. These variants can then function as identity markers, such that the use of localisms may index association with the local group (cf. Biewer 2015, 105). However, this factor is probably less relevant to the restructuring of the modal domain, where local features are probably less salient. Another factor that guides the selection process is accommodation in the way that speakers attune to each other's language use in conversations, which may lead to linguistic convergence (cf. Biewer 2015, 105). Finally, cultural motivations can also play an important part in the evolution of a new variety because speakers make the variety fit their immediate communicative needs in the local culture (cf. Biewer 2015, 107). Interactions between individuals are therefore embedded in the cultural context that may differ from the cultural background in which English is used in Britain. Differences can, for example, relate to social roles and politeness strategies (cf. Biewer 2015, 107; cf. Section 7.2 for cultural motivations in the restructuring of the modal system).

Apart from transfer and socio-cultural motivations, SLA strategies can also play a role in the formation of new varieties as English is learnt as a second language in school (cf. Biewer 2015, 92–96). Learners adhere to contradictory production principles. On the one hand, they try to be as economical as possible when they speak, which becomes obvious in regularisations (cf. Terassa 2018, 159–182 for a study on regularisation in ESL varieties) and avoidance of redundant markers. On the other hand, they try to be explicit by maximising salience and transparency, for example when they use resumptive pronouns to increase salience or lexical markers to express tense (cf. Biewer 2015, 93–95; cf. Section 7.3 for a discussion of SLA principles in the restructuring of the modal systems in HKE, IndE, and SgE).

Finally, more general cognitive processes that are not restricted to learning situations play a role, too. These include "general aspects of human perception, language processing and speech production" (Biewer 2015, 86). These aspects lead to universal tendencies in the world's languages. They therefore also presumably matter in the selection of features from the pool. These cognitive principles include frequency, perceptual salience, markedness, and transparency. Those variants that are more frequent in the language system and are more frequently used by speakers have a selectional advantage over those that are infrequent and more rarely used by speakers (cf. Biewer 2015, 86). This is because variants with a high frequency are more deeply entrenched in speakers' minds (cf. Schneider 2007, 110). Variants that are perceptually more salient are also more likely to be chosen than those that are less salient (cf. Biewer 2015, 87). These include free morphemes and variants that occur in an exposed position in the sentence, i.e. at the beginning or end (cf. Biewer 2015, 87). This means that free morphemes are more likely to be selected than bound morphemes when both are employed in the same function. Furthermore, variants that are unmarked are more likely to be selected than variants that are marked (cf. Biewer 2015, 88). Markedness is usually specified with reference to the structure of the world's languages, unmarked variants are "those variants [...] that are common to many of the world's languages, less complex in structure, and in general more frequent than their marked opposites" (Biewer 2015, 88). This means that unmarked variants are the default option, i.e. "those which come naturally and those which are embedded in a systematic relationship with other, related forms" (Schneider 2007, 111). Markedness is therefore strongly related to frequency. In a language contact situation, where language contact takes place in the minds of the speakers, the structure of the world's languages may not determine the markedness of a variant but rather the structure of the input varieties that the speaker has access to (cf. Mufwene 2001, 58). This may mean that varieties can favour a cross-linguistic marked variant if it is the unmarked variant relative to the structure of the input language (cf. Section 7.1 for the discussion about the transfer of epistemic readings in IndE, a marked choice in the world's languages but not in the contact setting of Dravidian languages and Indo-European English). The tendency that unmarked variants are more frequently selected than marked variants often works against the principle of perceptual salience, as unmarked forms are often perceptually less conspicuous than marked ones (cf. Biewer 2015, 88). Another cognitive selection principle concerns complexity: "formally less complex variants are more likely to be selected than more complex ones" (Biewer 2015, 89). This also relates to the fact that unmarked forms are more frequent than marked forms and shows the intricate relationship between these cognitive processes. Cognitive complexity is also related to the principle of markedness because unmarked variants are often cognitively easier to process (cf. Biewer 2015, 89). This is why less complex variants are more often selected than more complex ones. Finally, transparency may also play a role in the selection process in the sense that transparent variants are more likely to be chosen than non-transparent ones (cf. Biewer 2015, 90). Transparent variants are those variants whose form is only associated with one meaning (cf. Biewer 2015, 90) (cf. Section 7.4 for the role of transparency in the restructuring of the modal system). In sum, these cognitive principles lead to a slightly modified version of Mufwene's statement mentioned earlier: "the more common or frequent, the more salient, [the 'more' unmarked,] the more regular, or the more transparent" variants are, the more likely it is that they will be selected (Mufwene 2001, 57).

The different selection principles proposed by Biewer represent hypotheses that are based on observations of tendencies and not categorical rules (cf. Biewer 2015, 84). Furthermore, the principles can interact with each other. They may at times run counter to each other or reinforce each other another time. There may also be a ranking of these principles in the way that one principle may override another if they conflict. Schneider claims that language-external factors probably have a stronger effect on the selection process than language-internal factors (cf. Schneider 2007, 110). This may lead to the assumption that cultural motivations can override language-internal cognitive processes (cf. Biewer 2015, 107). I will discuss the interaction between the principles with reference to restructuring processes in the modal domain in Section 7.5.

3.5   Summary

This chapter introduced the theoretical framework and the socio-historical background of English in Hong Kong, India, and Singapore. First of all, the varieties of English were placed in Kachru's (1985) Model of the Three Concentric Circles (cf. Section 3.1). The Outer Circle of the model comprises varieties that emerged in former colonial territories. Varieties of this circle are called 'norm-developing' varieties, which suggests that HKE, IndE, and SgE may develop their own norms of use that are semi-independent from the varieties of the Inner Circle. On the basis of the model, we can therefore assume that the varieties under study show restructuring processes in the modal system that are not reliant on the 'norm-providing' Inner Circle varieties, unlike the varieties of the Expanding Circle that are 'norm-dependent'. However, categorising the varieties merely in terms of Outer Circle varieties neglects differences between the varieties with regard to their status. While IndE can be considered a prototypical Outer Circle variety, HKE and SgE are less prototypical. The functions of English in Hong Kong resemble those of Expanding Circle varieties while those of Singapore resemble those of Inner Circle varieties.

In order to account for the differences between the varieties, I drew on Schneider's (2007) Dynamic Model, which allowed me to position the varieties in terms of their stages in their developments on the uniform trajectory from Foundation to Differentiation (cf. Section 3.2). All varieties under study have entered or passed the third stage of the model, called 'Nativisation'. This means that we can expect grammatical restructuring processes to have taken place, a process for which increased contact between the STL strand and the IDG strand is a prerequisite. As can be seen in Figure 12, however, the varieties differ in their advancement in the model.

Schneider argues that HKE reached phase 3 in the 1960s (cf. Schneider 2007, 135). Most studies about HKE from the beginning of the 21st century (cf. Pang 2003; Groves 2011) report a persisting strong exonormative orientation, which suggests that HKE had not progressed far in the Nativisation stage in the early 1990s, when ICE-HK was compiled. IndE has progressed further than HKE because the Nativisation phase had already set in at the beginning of the 20th

FIGURE 12   The position of HKE, IndE, and SgE in the 1990s in Schneider's (2007) Dynamic Model.

century, which means that it was deeply nativised in the early 1990s and early signs of phase 4 could be detected. SgE by contrast, reached the stage of Endonormative Stabilisation in the 1970s (cf. Schneider 2007, 155).[13]

The description of the socio-historical background of English in Hong Kong, India, and Singapore has shown that the varieties emerged in very different contexts (cf. Sections 3.2.1–3.2.3). While English has official status in all countries, its functions vary strongly. It is predominantly used for international communication in Hong Kong but functions as an intranational means of communication in India and Singapore. While language policies have restricted the role of English in Hong Kong, for example through the introduction of Chinese-medium education, language policies have boosted its role in Singapore. Additionally, whereas English fulfils instrumental functions in Hong Kong and India, it performs integrative functions in Singapore as an expression of a pan-ethnic identity. Hong Kong and Singapore can be considered to mark the end points on a scale, with IndE occupying the middle ground, despite being somewhat closer to SgE than to HKE in terms of the functions of English fulfilled on the subcontinent. In terms of the substrate languages, however, HKE and SgE align more closely as they both have a Sinitic substrate language, while IndE has many different, predominantly Indo-Aryan and Dravidian languages as its substrates. The selection of the varieties therefore provides an interesting test case for the explanatory power of the Dynamic Model and the analysis of substratum influence in restructuring processes in the modal domain.

While Kachru's (1985) and Schneider's (2007) models help us to describe the varieties and the contexts in which they have developed, they do not provide us with a framework for analysing why the varieties are structured the way they are. This is why Mufwene's (2001) Feature Pool Model was introduced in Section 3.3. It analyses the restructuring process involved in the evolution of new

---

13   More recent findings even suggest that SgE shows early traces of Differentiation along ethnic lines (cf. Lim 2000; Leimgruber 2009; Leimgruber & Sankaran 2014). Unfortunately, the ICE-SIN corpus does not provide metadata about the speakers, which makes it impossible to analyse whether grammatical variation in the modal system is correlated with ethnicity. Schröter uses the *Grammar of Spoken Singapore English Corpus* to throw light on ethnic variation in SgE in the use of null subjects (cf. Schröter 2018, 186–187).

varieties in terms of a competition-and-selection process between features that are fed into the pool by the superstrate variety BrE and the substrate languages. Biewer's (2015) formulation of selection principles further enhances the explanatory power of the model by identifying relevant selection principles in the formation of ESL varieties. Those selection principles that might prove to be relevant for the study were detailed in Section 3.4. I therefore propose to combine the strengths of the different models to arrive at an integrated model which may provide us with a more comprehensive view for the study of grammatical restructuring in the three ESL varieties HKE, IndE, and SgE.

Methodology

The grammatical variation of modal and semi-modal verbs of strong obligation and necessity in BrE, AmE, HKE, IndE, and SgE was defined as the object of investigation in Section 1.5. Thus, while the 'what' of this study has been clarified, the 'how' still needs some further explanation. Studies on the use of modal and semi-modal verbs of obligation in different varieties of English have shown that regional differences are quantitative rather than categorical in nature (cf. Sections 2.1 and 2.2), which is why I chose a corpus-linguistic approach to variation (cf. also Kortmann 2006, 603; Biewer 2011, 7). In Section 4.1, I will give an introduction to the ICE corpora as the database for my study. I will take a closer and also more critical look at their comparability in order to take possible biases in the data into account, which need to be addressed as the backdrop against which the data will be analysed and interpreted later. A considerable benefit of the carefully constructed ICE corpora for the purpose of this study is the availability of rich metadata about the speakers for some ICE corpora (cf. also Section 11.1.1). In Section 4.1.1, I will provide details about the ICE metadata and review sociolinguistic studies that have been conducted on the basis of them. In Section 4.1.2, I will analyse the social make-up of ICE-HK and ICE-IND* – the two ESL corpora I used for sociolinguistic investigations – by exploiting their metadata. Apart from the ICE corpora, I also used answers to a questionnaire as a data source for my study to enhance the corpus data with speakers' attitudes and perceptions on language use. I will briefly discuss the design of the questionnaire in Section 4.2. After discussing the databases in the first two subsections, I will continue with the description of the coding procedure adopted in this study. First, the envelope of variation of the dependent variable, i.e. contexts in which a choice between the variants is in theory possible, will be described in Section 4.3. In Section 4.3.1, I will then introduce the language-internal and language-external independent variables according to which the tokens of the dependent variable were annotated. After that, logistic regression as the statistical model used to account for the variation between the main competitors of strong obligation, *must* and *have to*, will be presented in Section 4.3.2. With logistic regression modelling, the effects of both language-internal and language-external variables on the dependent variable can be analysed simultaneously. Furthermore, this type of analysis is also used in (variationist) sociolinguistics and therefore also realises the sociolinguistic corpus-based approach of this study.

© KONINKLIJKE BRILL NV, LEIDEN, 2018 | DOI:10.1163/9789004381520_005

4.1   The ICE Corpora

In 1988, Sidney Greenbaum proposed an 'international computerised corpus of English' in *World Englishes* (cf. Greenbaum 1988) with the aim of complementing existing corpora on BrE and AmE by compiling corpora of other ENL varieties and of ESL varieties and corpora representing spoken as well as written language. To ensure comparability, these corpora were originally supposed to be collected in the same time period and supposed to adhere to a common design. Three decades after Greenbaum's (1988) proposal, the initial idea of an international corpus of English has been put into practice with 16 available ICE-corpora representing the English spoken in Australia, Canada, East Africa, Ghana, Great Britain, Hong Kong, India, Ireland, Jamaica, New Zealand, Nigeria, the Philippines, Singapore, Sri Lanka, Uganda, and the USA.[1] Apart from these, new corpora are still being compiled, e.g. ICE-Scotland, ICE-Gibraltar, and ICE-Puerto Rico. All corpora follow the same design, with a predominance of spoken texts comprising 60% of the respective corpora. The spoken texts are further divided into dialogues and monologues. Dialogues are divided into private and public dialogues and monologues into unscripted and scripted. The written part is divided into non-printed and printed texts. Non-printed texts include student writing and letters, while academic writing, popular writing, reportage, instructional writing, persuasive writing, and creative writing are included in the category of printed writing. Table 2 gives an overview of the common design of the ICE corpora (cf. also Greenbaum 1991, 6; Nelson 1996 for more details about the ICE corpus design).

The numbers in brackets indicate the number of texts that are included in each text category. Each component corpus has 500 texts of 2,000 words each, accounting for 1 million words in total (cf. Greenbaum 1996a, 5). Most of the texts are from the 1990s, although a few corpora contain more recent material (cf. Greenbaum 1996a, 6).[2] The ICE corpora represent 'educated English' from adult speakers (18 or above) "who have received formal education through the medium of English to the completion of secondary school" (Greenbaum 1996a, 6). However, some speakers who did not receive secondary education in English were also included because of their public status (e.g. politicians) (cf. Greenbaum 1996a, 6). The speakers and writers of the texts are 'natives' of

---

1   Only the written part is available for ICE-Nigeria (ICE-NIG), ICE-SL, ICE-Uganda (ICE-UG), and ICE-USA so far.

2   ICE-JA includes material from the 2000s, and ICE-GHA, ICE-NIG, and ICE-UG contain material from the 2010s.

TABLE 2   The common design of the ICE corpora (source: http://ice-corpora.net/ice/
design.htm, last access: 19/02/2018)

Mode	Type 1	Type 2	Type 3	File name
Spoken (300)	Dialogues (180)	Private (100)	Face-to-face conversations (90)	S1A-001 to S1A-090
			Phone calls (10)	S1A-091 to S1A-100
		Public (80)	Classroom lessons (20)	S1B-001 to S1B-020
			Broadcast discussions (20)	S1B-021 to S1B-040
			Broadcast interviews (10)	S1B-041 to S1B-050
			Parliamentary debates (10)	S1B-051 to S1B-060
			Legal cross-examinations (10)	S1B-061 to S1B-070
			Business transactions (10)	S1B-071 to S1B-080
	Mono-logues (120)	Unscripted (70)	Spontaneous commentaries (20)	S2A-001 to S2A-020
			Unscripted speeches (30)	S2A-021 to S2A-050
			Demonstrations (10)	S2A-051 to S2A-060
			Legal presentations (10)	S2A-061 to S2A-070
		Scripted (50)	Broadcast news (20)	S2B-001 to S2B-020
			Broadcast talks (20)	S2B-021 to S2B-040
			Non-broadcast talks (10)	S2B-041 to S2B-050
Written (200)	Non-printed (50)	Non-professional writing (20)	Student essays (10)	W1A-001 to W1A-010
			Exam scripts (10)	W1A-011 to W1A-020
		Correspon-dence (30)	Social letters (15)	W1B-001 to W1B-015
			Business letters (15)	W1B-016 to W1B-030
	Printed (150)	Academic writing (40)	Humanities (10)	W2A-001 to W2A-010
			Social sciences (10)	W2A-011 to W2A-020
			Natural sciences (10)	W2A-021 to W2A-030
			Technology (10)	W2A-031 to W2A-040

TABLE 2   The common design of the ICE corpora (*cont.*)

Mode	Type 1	Type 2	Type 3	File name
		Non-academic writing (40)	Humanities (10)	W2B-001 to W2B-010
			Social sciences (10)	W2B-011 to W2B-020
			Natural sciences (10)	W2B-021 to W2B-030
			Technology (10)	W2B-031 to W2B-040
		Reportage (20)	Press news reports (20)	W2C-001 to W2C-020
		Instruction-al writing (20)	Administrative writing (10)	W2D-001 to W2D-010
			Skills & hobbies (10)	W2D-011 to W2D-020
		Persuasive writing (10)	Press editorials (10)	W2E-001 to W2E-010
		Creative writing (20)	Novels & short stories (20)	W2F-001 to W2F-020

the variety represented by the respective corpus. Nelson explains the underlying definition of 'nativeness' as follows:

> 'Native' for our purposes means either that they were born in the country concerned, or if not, that they moved there at an early age and received their school education through the medium of English in that country.
> NELSON 1996, 28

The speakers and writers therefore have to meet three criteria, i.e. they have to be 18 years or older, need to have received secondary education in English, and have to be natives of the variety concerned.

Apart from these three necessary criteria for inclusion, the compilers "attempted to include as full a range as possible of the social variables which define the population" (Nelson 1996, 28). This means they tried to include speakers of various age groups, male as well as female speakers, and speakers from different regions. However, as the corpora were not primarily designed for sociolinguistic studies but rather for cross-varietal comparisons of standard

Englishes, their sociolinguistic structure is not representative of the structure of the population as a whole (cf. Nelson 1996, 28), and it is worth investigating the respective ICE corpora with regard to their social make-up (cf. Section 4.1.2).

One of the major aims of the ICE project was to create comparable corpora for ENL and ESL varieties. The same collection period and the common design of the corpora were supposed to ensure comparability between the corpora. But as some ICE teams joined the ICE project later, a time gap of 25 years separates the earlier ICE corpora from the later ICE corpora if we take the older texts from ICE-IND dating from 1991 and the most recent texts from ICE-Uganda (ICE-UG) dating from 2016 as reference points. Mair notices problems of comparability between the ICE corpora when analysing features undergoing rapid linguistic changes, such as the use of *be like* (cf. Mair 2009b, 23–24). Apart from these intercorpora differences, most corpora also show intracorpus differences with an internal diachronic dimension of up to 10 years, e.g. ICE-JA with texts from the early 1990s to the early 2000s.[3] Höhn (2012) makes use of this internal diachronic dimension in her analysis of the quotative system. As the new quotatives have rapidly found their way into Englishes around the world, the time gap in the compilation of the texts in ICE-JA is wide enough to analyse changes in the use of quotatives between the different collection periods (1990–1994, 1995–2001, and 2002–2005). She shows, for example, that the major rise in the frequency of *be like* occurs between the period 1995–2001 and 2002–2005 in ICE-JA. For future research based on ICE, it may be worth exploring whether the assumed disadvantage of differences in the compilation period between corpora can also be turned into an advantage, for example by tracing the state of features that are said to be involved in a process of 'language drift' in ICE corpora from different sampling periods, or also the global spread of features such as the new quotative *be like* ('the globalisation of vernacular variation', cf. Meyerhoff & Niedzielski 2003). In terms of comparability, it is necessary to be aware of the different sampling periods when features are analysed across all ICE corpora, especially when the feature is undergoing language change (cf. also Mair 2009b, 23–24). Postulating that IndE is a 'conservative variety' (cf. Collins 2009b, 285) based on a comparison of frequencies across all ICE corpora should therefore be viewed with caution, and explanations of differences should at least take the comparatively early compilation date of ICE-IND into account.

---

3   I would like to thank Professor Christian Mair for making the ICE-JA metadata available to me, which allowed me to identify the collection dates of the texts.

In terms of corpus structure, the ICE corpora generally adhere to the common design outlined in Table 2. However, in some cases compilers had to deviate from the common design, for example in the compilation of ICE-East Africa (ICE-EA). This corpus differs from other ICE corpora in size and structure. It is about one and a half times bigger than the other ICE corpora (cf. Beal 2012, 161), because it has two separate written parts for Kenya and Tanzania. But the two varieties are merged in one spoken part, which contains 250 texts from both varieties. This means that the spoken part of ICE-EA represents the English language spoken in two countries and that it is also smaller than the spoken parts of other ICE corpora, which are made up of 300 texts. The spoken part also differs with regard to the category face-to-face conversation. Schmied explains that it is difficult to obtain data for this category because "[t]he vast majority of the direct conversations in ICE-GB would simply not be conducted in English [sc. in East Africa]" (Schmied 1996, 185) but in the mother tongue (cf. also Lange 2017, 17). Furthermore, the compilers of ICE-EA changed the structure by including the category 'written as spoken', which includes 50 texts. The written part is made up of two components, i.e. one for Kenya and one for Tanzania, and has the usual size of 200 texts. The written part also differs from the common design, as some categories are not represented such as 'skills & hobbies'. Schmied explains that this category is particularly problematic in an African context, as "many of the concepts in this category are alien to many Third World cultures and the corresponding texts are imported from the First World" (Schmied 1996, 188). While some categories are simply not representative of the uses English is put to in these countries, other categories are available but are not always comparable in terms of their function. Schmied mentions African newspapers as a case in point, which may for example take over functions of the text category 'creative writing' that are associated with the medium 'book' in ENL varieties (cf. Schmied 1996, 189). In spoken language, the structure of dialogues may also differ strongly from ENL dialogues, which usually show an interactive back-and-forth between the participants rather than a succession of monologues, as is the case in some dialogues in ICE-EA (cf. Schmied 1996, 189). While ICE-EA probably diverges most strongly from the common design, we can also find smaller deviations in other ICE corpora. Whereas the compilers of ICE-EA modified the structure of the text categories and excluded categories that were not representative of the English spoken in East Africa, the compilers of ICE-HK apparently followed a different strategy by filling the complete category 'spontaneous commentaries' with commentaries on horse racing by BrE and AusE speakers. And although the information on the nationality of the speakers is available in the metadata, their speech is not marked as extra-corpus material in the respective text files, which makes these speakers part of the ICE-HK corpus.

Researchers who want to compare the language use of ESL varieties and AmE face the additional difficulty that for the ICE corpus of the USA only the written sub-corpus is available. This means that features of spoken language cannot be compared on the basis of ICE. One way of solving this problem is by using the SBC (cf. Collins 2007b; Collins & Yao 2012; Diaconu 2012b). This corpus has 249,000 words collected in the early 2000s (2000–2005) and most of the texts are private direct conversations in intimate settings, such as between family members and close friends. SBC is therefore comparable to the private dialogue section in ICE but does not match the spoken component in its entirety, as monologues are comparatively rare in SBC. As a consequence, the language used in SBC is more colloquial than the language used in the spoken part of ICE. Again, it is crucial to take this difference into account when analysing features that may show differences according to formality or that undergo language changes which may originate in the spoken language. Statements on the more 'advanced' state of the AmE variety in terms of its leading role in linguistic changes should therefore always be judged against its representation through SBC, which includes more informal and also more recent language data.

Another factor that may influence comparability is the different nature of spoken and written language in ENL varieties and some ESL varieties. Some ESL varieties show what has been termed 'register shift', i.e. "the influence of written norms upon speech" (Mesthrie & Bhatt 2008, 114).[4] Kachru states that "[s]poken SAE [South Asian English] does not sound *conversational*, as the spoken medium has been seldom taught as an academic discipline in the South Asian educational system" (Kachru 1983a, 42). Especially IndE has often been associated with a 'bookish' style, whereas SgE is considered to show the opposite trend towards 'hypercolloquial' language use in situations where more formal language use is required from a StE perspective (cf. Mesthrie & Bhatt 2008, 114–115). Early anecdotal evidence about differences in the nature of spoken language in ESL varieties has been empirically analysed with the help of multidimensional analysis (MDA) by Xiao (2009) and an n-gram analysis by Heller (2014). Both studies show the divergence of ICE-IND from other ICE corpora. Xiao uses Biber's (1988) multidimensional analysis to analyse differences between the ICE corpora with regard to register (cf. Xiao 2009, 442). He shows

---

4 It is interesting to note that this shift is a strong counter-force to the process of 'colloquialisation', which is deemed to be under way in ENL varieties (e.g. Mair 2006, 190).

that IndE has the lowest score for Factor 1 ('interactive casual discourse vs. informative elaborate discourse') in almost all text categories, "meaning that it is less interactive but more elaborate" (Xiao 2009, 443). Linguistic features that lead to a high score for Factor 1 are those associated with an involved interactive style, e.g. verbs of communication, boosters, discourse markers, or contracted forms (cf. Xiao 2009, 429). Linguistic features that lead to a low score for Factor 1 are those that are associated with a more elaborate, informational style, e.g. nominalisations, general/abstract terms, or passives (cf. Xiao 2009, 429). This supports the earlier anecdotal evidence about the 'bookish' style of IndE. Heller (2014) uses Biber et al.'s (1999) lexical bundle categories to analyse differences between corpora in terms of register. As some lexical bundles are more likely to occur in conversation, while others are more likely to occur in academic prose, Heller (2014) is able to position corpora on a continuum between conversation and academic prose. Figure 13 shows the position of the spoken and written components of ICE-GB, ICE-USA, ICE-HK, ICE-IND, and ICE-SIN on the continuum between conversation and academic prose.[5]

As can be seen in Figure 13, the spoken component of ICE-IND is remarkably different from all other spoken ICE corpora under analysis. Its deviation

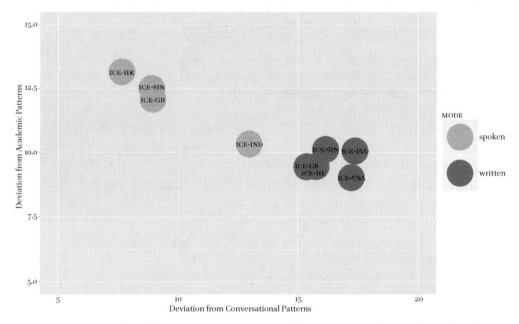

FIGURE 13   The spoken and written components of ICE-GB, ICE-USA, ICE-HK, ICE-IND, and ICE-SIN on the continuum between conversation and academic prose.

5   I would like to thank Benedikt Heller for providing me with his analysis of the corpora I analyse in this study.

from academic patterns is less strong than that of the other corpora, which ties in with Xiao's (2009) findings which show that the spoken component of ICE-IND is less interactive and more elaborate than other ICE corpora. These findings provide first empirical evidence for the written nature of spoken IndE and should be taken into account in comparative studies on ICE that include ICE-IND. With regard to the written nature of spoken language, Mesthrie and Bhatt provide an informed comment.

> It is not necessarily the case that New Englishes are being more formal when they use such terms [sc. *demise* for 'death' and *pain in one's bosom* for 'pain in one's chest']; they appear so only to outsiders expecting met-ropolitan norms [i.e. BrE, AmE].
>
> MESTHRIE & BHATT 2008, 114

Furthermore, these findings warn against extrapolating diachronic change from the comparison of spoken and written language (cf. Collins 2009b; Collins & Yao 2012; van der Auwera, Noël & De Wit 2012) in ICE-IND. The often cited 'conserva-tiveness' of IndE in comparative studies that extrapolate language change from comparisons of spoken and written language based on ICE should therefore be carefully judged against the backdrop of its 'conceptual writtenness' when mea-sured against StE spoken norms.

Another potential difference between the corpora may lie in their sociolinguis-tic composition. Comparability between the corpora is inevitably compromised by differences between the speakers with regard to social factors.

> It is unreasonable to expect compilers of the corpora to match speakers or writers exactly in the whole range of biographical features, such as sex, age, educational level, occupation or replicate the types of relationships between speakers in conversations in each corpus in exactly the same proportions.
>
> GREENBAUM 1996a, 5

As social factors such as age, gender, and mother tongue play a role in language variation and change, the social make-up of the ICE corpora under investigation will be analysed in more detail in Section 4.1.2 in order to account for possible differences between the corpora.

To summarise, we can see that the ICE "project has attempted to achieve con-formity, but complete identity between the corpora is not possible" (Greenbaum 1996a, 5). It is important to spot these differences when conducting research based on the ICE corpora in order to identify genuine differences between varieties that exist irrespective of differences in corpus structure. With regard to the corpora used in this study, we need to be aware that the strong 'innovative' tendency of AmE in language change is at least amplified by its representation by the more informal SBC. As changes in the modal domain are more conspicuous in spoken language, we can assume that these changes are more marked in SBC than in the other spoken ICE corpora that contain more formal spoken language (e.g. in the monologues). IndE probably appears more 'conservative' in linguistic changes on the basis of ICE-IND because of an earlier date of compilation, its written nature of spoken language, and its composition according to the age of the speakers (cf. Section 4.1.2). The differences between the corpora should be kept in mind and findings should be interpreted taking these differences into consideration but it also needs to be emphasised that despite these issues of comparability, the corpora are "sufficiently similar to justify global comparisons" (Greenbaum 1996a, 5).

4.1.1   The ICE Metadata and Sociolinguistics

As mentioned before, the ICE corpora contain 60% spoken language and a large number of texts in the private dialogue category. The language used in private dialogues is probably closest to what sociolinguists call the 'vernacular', the most informal unmonitored speech of a speaker, at least in ENL varieties. In the ESL contexts, the 'vernacular' is typically not a variety of English but the mother tongue of the speakers (cf. also Sridhar & Sridhar 1982, 95–96). Here, choosing to speak English already marks a formal choice because private dialogues are usually held in the L1 of the speaker (cf. also Mair 2009a, 46 for the situation in Jamaica). In Hong Kong, for example, private conversations are conducted in Cantonese, the common mother tongue for the majority of the population while English is used in more formal contexts (cf. Section 3.2.1). Due to the functions English performs in these societies and the acquisition of English through formal education, English may be marked by higher formality in ESL varieties than in ENL varieties. Furthermore, those speakers that are represented in ICE belong to the more highly educated strata of society and speak a standardised educated variety of English. As ICE represents the local acrolect or emerging standard, it could be assumed that variation may be rather limited because it does not take into account the basilectal and mesolectal range of speakers (cf. the discussion in Section 11.1). Nevertheless, studies on ICE have shown that variation in the emerging standard can be observed, which may partially be explained by social factors (cf. Section 11.2 for the relationship between sociolinguistics and corpus linguistics). To analyse the effect of these factors, information about these factors needs to be made available to the researcher (cf. Section 11.1.1 on data richness).

In his 1990 article in *World Englishes*, Greenbaum elaborates on the idea of an international corpus of English, which would also include biographical data of the speakers, making these additional metadata available for retrieval (cf. Greenbaum 1990, 80). But not all ICE teams seem to have been able to implement this plan, and those that have, differ in their way of doing so. The corpora therefore vary in terms of (1) availability and (2) accessibility of the metadata. Some ICE corpora such as ICE-SIN do not provide any information about the speakers at all, other ICE corpora such as ICE-JA and ICE-SL provide information about the speakers upon request, while yet others make the metadata directly available to the researcher in the lexical version of the corpora (e.g. ICE-HK, ICE-IND). If the metadata are available, they may still differ strongly from each other in the way they are stored and retrieved.

The metadata in ICE-GB are integrated in ICECUP, the software which was specifically developed for ICE-GB. This software allows the researcher to filter concordances according to the language-external variables 'text category', 'gender', 'age', and 'education'. This facilitates the integration of language-external variables in studies on variation because one can easily determine the percentage of use by different social groups of different variants. However, the integration of the metadata in ICECUP makes it impossible to directly align the concordances with all biographical details of a speaker (including age, gender, education), which would have been possible if the metadata had been available in a separate file or had been given before every utterance. As it is not possible to count the number of words per speaker, the number of words per social group can consequently not be determined (such as the number of words spoken by females as compared to males) in order to establish the balance of the corpus and in order to use the word count as the basis for normalising frequencies.

ICE-HK and ICE-IND are not analysable with ICECUP; the metadata are accessed differently here. While ICE-HK provides an Excel spreadsheet listing all information about the texts and the speakers/writers of the texts, ICE-IND has a separate header file for every file of the corpus. This makes the alignment of the data rather time-consuming – at least if it is not done automatically. Manual alignment of the data was considered to be necessary in light of the mismatches identified between the text data and the metadata in the case of ICE-IND. In order to make future studies of other variables and their correlation with social categories on the ICE-IND corpus possible, I exported the information from the header files to an Excel spreadsheet. This table served as the input for the insertion of the metadata to the text files. I gave each speaker in a file a unique speaker ID (e.g. S1A-001A for speaker $A in file S1A-001) because the speaker ID $A does not unambiguously identify one particular

TABLE 3   Example of a mismatch of information in the text data and metadata in ICE-IND

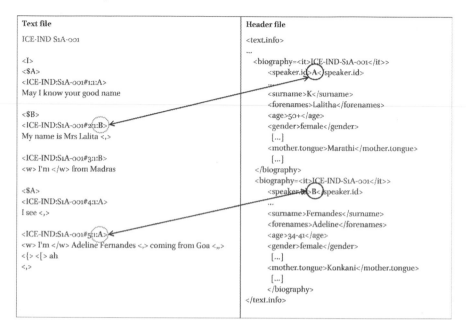

Text file	Header file
ICE-IND S1A-001	<text.info>
	...
<I>	<biography=<it>ICE-IND-S1A-001</it>>
<$A>	<speaker.id>A<>speaker.id>
<ICE-IND:S1A-001#1:1:A>	...
May I know your good name	<surname>K</surname>
	<forenames>Lalitha</forenames>
<$B>	<age>50+</age>
<ICE-IND:S1A-001#2:1:B>	<gender>female</gender>
My name is Mrs Lalita <,>	[...]
	<mother.tongue>Marathi</mother.tongue>
<ICE-IND:S1A-001#3:1:B>	[...]
<w> I'm </w> from Madras	</biography>
	<biography=<it>ICE-IND-S1A-001</it>>
<$A>	<speaker.id>B<>speaker.id>
<ICE-IND:S1A-001#4:1:A>	...
I see <,>	<surname>Fernandes</surname>
	<forenames>Adeline</forenames>
<ICE-IND:S1A-001#5:1:A>	<age>34-41</age>
<w> I'm </w> Adeline Fernandes <,> coming from Goa <,,>	<gender>female</gender>
<{> <[> ah	[...]
<,>	<mother.tongue>Konkani</mother.tongue>
	[...]
	</biography>
	</text.info>

speaker in a file but can refer to any speaker marked by $A, e.g. speaker $A in
S1A-001 or speaker $A in S1A-002. The unique speaker ID was used as the key to
integrate speaker information in the text files on an utterance basis by way of
which the PERL program inserted the information given in the table before the
utterances of the respective speaker in the text file. During the process of pre-
editing, I noticed several mismatches between the text data and the metadata
in ICE-IND. A quick look at the first file in the spoken section already reveals
a typical mismatch. Here, speaker $B introduces herself with "My name is Mrs
Lalita" and speaker $A with "I'm Adeline Fernandes". In the metadata, however,
speaker ID A is given to a "K. Lalitha [sic!]" and speaker ID B is given to "Ade-
line Fernandes" (cf. Table 3).

Some mismatches are, of course, more problematic than others. In this case,
the dialogue partners differ with regard to two of three social characteristics
(age and mother tongue). In other cases, speakers only differ with regard to
one social characteristic, such as in S1A-014, where the two speakers have a
different mother tongue (Bengali vs. Telugu) but are both females between 26
and 33 years of age. In other cases, the dialogue partners are reversed in the
metadata but have the same social characteristics, such as in S1A-038 with two

TABLE 4   Example of inconsistent use of speaker ID in text file in ICE-IND

Text file	Header file

ICE-IND S1B-063	<text.info>
	[...]
	    <biography=<it>ICE-IND-S1B-063</it>>
	        <speaker.id>A</speaker.id>
	        [...]
	        <surname>Singh</surname>
	        <forenames>B.P.</forenames>
	        <age>50+</age>
	        <gender>male</gender>
	        <nationality>Indian</nationality>
	        [...]
	        <occupation>Advocate</occupation>
	        [...]
	    </biography>
	    <biography=<it>ICE-IND-S1B-063</it>>
	        <speaker.id>B</speaker.id>
	        <communicative.role>witness
	        </communicative.role>
	        <surname>Valmiki</surname>
	        <forenames>Gora Ravan</forenames>
	        <age>21-25</age> [*age added → text information]
	        <gender>male</gender>
	        <nationality>Indian</nationality>
	        [...]
	    </biography>
	</text.info>

<I> <$A> <ICE-IND:S1B-063#1:1:A> Next <,,> <@> Gora </@> <,> <@> Ravan </@> <,> <@> Valmiki </@> [...] <,,> twenty-four years age <,,> [...] <$B> <ICE-IND:S1B-063#12:1:B> Now look here your name is <@> Gora </@> <,> <ICE-IND:S1B-063#13:1:B> Are you known by any other name <,,> ? [...] <$A> <ICE-IND:S1B-063#16:1:A> My real name is <@> Sunil </@> [...] <ICE-IND:S1B-063#17:1:A> However <,> I am also known <,,> by name <@> Gora </@> [...] <$B> <ICE-IND:S1B-063#21:1:B> On twenty-four eight eighty <,> twenty-eight four eighty-one where were you staying <,> ?	

males from the age group 26–33 with the mother tongue Kannada. In yet other cases, all the characteristics of the speakers differ, such as in S1A-060.

Another problem which became obvious during the alignment of text files and metadata was the inconsistent use of speaker codes in one and the same text. The dialogue between an advocate and a witness in text S1B-063 starts with an introduction of the witness named Gora Ravan Valmiki (cf. Table 4). Speaker $A introduces the witness with "Next Gora Ravan Valmiki [...] twenty-four years age". The advocate is assigned speaker code $B in the ensuing conversation when he says "Now look here your name is Gora", while the witness receives speaker code $A ("My real name is Sunil [...] However I am also known by name Gora"). Once again, when this information is compared to the metadata, it becomes apparent that speaker code $B is wrongly assigned to the witness (Gora Ravan Valmiki, 24), while speaker code $A is assigned to the advocate (B.P. Singh, 50+).

These kinds of mismatches are highly problematic if one wants to analyse correlations between linguistic features and social categories. To make the ICE-IND metadata available for sociolinguistic studies on IndE, I revised the metadata with the help of the information given in the text files in the form of introductions, greetings, and addresses. This procedure was deemed most appropriate once it transpired that receiving first-hand information on the compilation process of the text data and the corresponding metadata from the corpus compilers themselves was not possible. Information from an internal guideline for the creation of file header information seems to justify this procedure because the assignment of the speaker ID in the text file seems to precede the creation of the metadata (cf. Nelson 1991, 14). Information from the metadata in ICE-IND* indicate that the files were collected in this order. For example, the recording date of the text file S1A-016 is 1996 but information in the free comments section show that the corpus compilers had access to information about the speaker later than this year ("moved to [...] Pittsburgh (USA) (2000 to date)").

The rather time-consuming alignment of text data and metadata is probably the reason why the sociolinguistic potential of the ICE metadata has not been fully realised yet (cf. Diaconu 2012b, 57). There are only a few studies which make systematic use of the ICE metadata to study variation and change in ENL and ESL varieties (cf. Section 11.2.1 for the potential and limitations of these types of studies). Facchinetti (2003), Mair (2009a, 2009b), Fuchs and Gut (2012, 2015), Höhn (2012), Lange (2012), Schweinberger (2012), and Parviainen and Fuchs (2015) are notable exceptions in this area. Facchinetti (2003) uses speaker information on age, gender, and education in ICE-GB to analyse the use of the modal verb *may*. She finds no effect of gender, as males and females use *may* with roughly the same frequency (cf. Facchinetti 2003, 319). In terms of age, Facchinetti found a higher frequency with speakers of 46–65 but explains that this correlation is probably rather a result of the strong representation of speakers in this age group in text categories that favour the use of *may* such as public dialogue (cf. Facchinetti 2003, 319–320). The educational level of the speaker seems to have an effect on the use of *may* with a higher frequency of the modal verb in more highly educated speakers (cf. Facchinetti 2003, 320). Mair (2009a, 2009b) analyses – among other variables – the use of the new quotative *be like* in JamE with regard to the social factors age and gender.[6] He finds a positive correlation between the use of quotative *be like* and younger female speakers in ICE-JA (cf. Mair 2009a, 55). Fuchs and Gut (2012) examine the effect of social variables on the use of the ten most frequent intensifiers in the ICE corpora GB, IRE, CAN, NIG, IND, SIN, and PHI. One of their findings is that female speakers use more boosters than male speakers in most text types. Höhn (2012) analyses the quotative system (*say, be like, go*) in ICE-JA and ICE-IRE with regard to the language-internal factors 'grammatical person' and 'content of the quote', and the language-external factors 'register', 'collection period', and

---

6   Rosenfelder (2009) also analyses the language-external factors 'age' and 'gender' in a study on rhoticity in JamE but finds no significant effect of these social factors on /r/-realisation.

'gender of the speaker'. She finds that female speakers use *be like* more often than male speakers in the private dialogues of ICE-JA, while there is no gender difference in ICE-IRE in the use of quotative *be like* (cf. Höhn 2012, 282–283). Schweinberger (2012) also analyses *like* in IrE but does not restrict his analysis to quotative uses of *like* but includes all tokens of *like* as a discourse marker. He shows that the use of *like* depends heavily on the formality of the text type, with more informal text types favouring the use of *like* (cf. Schweinberger 2012, 190). He also analyses the effect of age on the use of *like* and finds a decrease of *like* with increasing age, suggesting an increase in real time (cf. Schweinberger 2012, 193). The gender difference in the use of *like* is not significant but if the interaction between age and gender is analysed, a gender-specific age pattern of use emerges, with males favouring the use of *like* in general, except for the age group 26–33, where female speakers use more instances of *like* than male speakers (cf. Schweinberger 2012, 193).

Lange (2012) is the first monograph-length study that uses information from the ICE metadata to account for possible extra-linguistic factors of variation. She uses speaker information about age, gender, education, and mother tongue to shed light on syntactic variation in spoken IndE. She finds correlations between topicalisation and gender. Female speakers use topicalisation (e.g. (27)) more often than male speakers.

(27) *My birthday party* <,,,> you arrange [...] Whereas *your birthday party* I'll arrange (ICE-IND:S1A-003)

Lange shows that IndE uses *only* and *itself* as presentational focus markers in addition to their uses as restrictive focus marker in the case of *only* and as reflexive pronoun and intensifier in the case of *itself* (cf. Lange 2012, 189–190). (28) and (29) illustrate the use of *itself* and *only* as presentational focus markers, here as a means of focusing the preceding adverbials of time (cf. also (175) in Chapter 11).

(28) Last year also uh I did one refresher course *in the month of June itself* and uh the duration of that was was actually twenty-four days (ICE-IND:S1A-075)

(29) Somehow like no it's very hot Like *in the afternoon only* it is burning The skin is burning like whereas in Goa we have the cool climate (ICE-IND:S1A-001)

Lange finds that the use of presentational *itself* and *only* correlates with age; younger speakers use presentational *only* and *itself* more often than older speakers, pointing to an increase of these uses in real time (cf. Lange 2012, 191). Furthermore, the use of presentational *only* is correlated with the educational level of the speakers in the way that *only* is underrepresented with speakers who hold a higher educational degree (Master's degree, PhD) and overrepresented with speakers who are graduates or who have received secondary education. Lange (2012) compares the proportions of the use of linguistic features by speakers with specific social characteristics (e.g. female/male) to their proportion in the corpus as a whole to assess the distribution of the feature. When a feature is 'underrepresented' in a certain group, it has a lower proportion of use than the proportion of the group with a certain social characteristic in the corpus suggests. In my own analyses, I decided to normalise the tokens of a specific feature on the basis of the number of words spoken by the specific social group in order to factor in differences in the length of utterances of the individuals. I also used a revised version of ICE-IND, which I call ICE-IND*, with corrections in the alignment of the text data and metadata. These mismatches were not identified in earlier studies, probably as a result of automatic alignment of the files.

Fuchs and Gut (2015) investigate the influence of the social factors age, gender, ethnic group of the speakers as well as the effect of text category on the use of the progressive in NigE. They show that age is a significant factor in the use of the progressive; younger speakers use the progressive more often than older speakers, while gender is not a significant factor in the use of the progressive. In terms of ethnicity, Fuchs and Gut find a higher frequency of the progressive with Yoruba speakers than Igbo speakers of NigE (cf. Fuchs & Gut 2015, 382). Text category also emerges as a significant factor, with more informal and more persuasive text categories favouring the use of the progressive. They take the distribution according to age as an indicator of ongoing language change in the direction of the rise of the progressive, as is also the case in ENL varieties (cf. Hundt 2004; Smitterberg 2005). Parviainen and Fuchs (2015) analyse *only* as a focus marker (and the focus marker *also*) with regard to age and gender in IndE, HKE, and PhilE. They find a more widespread use of presentational marker *only* in younger speakers and also show that female speakers use *only* as a focus marker more often than male speakers. They conclude that this distribution is indicative of linguistic change in progress and that the change is spreading from IndE as the 'super-central variety' to other Asian Englishes.

These studies show that the integration of social factors enhances analyses on variation and change in New Englishes by identifying significant correlations between social factors and the dependent variables under analysis (cf. Section 11.2.2 for research potential beyond this type of 'first-wave' research). For some variables in ESL varieties, similar patterns of social variation were identified to those found in ENL varieties, e.g. the higher frequency of the progressive by younger speakers (cf. the rise of the progressive in ENL varieties, Hundt 2004; Smitterberg 2005) or the higher frequency of quotative *be like* by young female speakers (cf. Tagliamonte & D'Arcy 2004 for ENL varieties). The integration of the metadata also introduces more idiosyncratic, variety-specific factors to the analysis. The factor 'mother tongue of the speaker' is very important in language contact situations and is particularly useful in the analysis of ESL varieties in multilingual settings, such as IndE, NigE, or Tanzanian English (TanzE). The ICE metadata are therefore a rich resource for the analysis of social variation in ESL varieties. But before one starts to analyse variation according to social factors in ESL varieties, the social make-up of the sample in the respective ICE corpora needs to be analysed with regard to its balance and representativeness (cf. also Tagliamonte 2006, 23–24).

4.1.2   The Social Structure of ICE-HK and ICE-IND*

As explained above, the ICE corpora were not primarily intended for sociolinguistic studies (cf. also Mair 2009a, 41). Their "focus was on regional variability in standard English, on the documentation of the New Englishes [...], and on stylistic variation" (Mair 2009a, 41). This is why it is sensible to analyse their social make-up before conducting sociolinguistic studies, as "the entire corpus will be undetectably biased for any relevant factors by the language of the social group which provided the majority of the texts" (Bauer 2002, 104). It is important to be aware of these biases, especially if one studies variables undergoing change. The social structure may have an impact on the overall 'behaviour' of the corpus in comparative studies with ICE, for example if corpora are biased towards younger female speakers that may be leading the way in some linguistic changes. Furthermore, it is important to analyse the representativeness of the social categories with regard to the society as a whole.

To find out more about the social structure of ICE-HK and ICE-IND*, the number of words per speaker was determined by means of a PERL script.[7] The script made use of the regular pattern with which speakers are marked in ICE (e.g. $A) and excluded extra-corpus material marked with <X> from the count, as well as textual mark-up and content mark-up (cf. (30)).

(30)   <$B> <ICE-IND:S1A-001#21:1:B> Even in Madras also we have <indig> na </ indig> <,> uh sea-shore <,> and after three <w> O'clock </w> <,> uh in the afternoon we have a very cool breeze and we enjoy that <,> sea breeze like anything (ICE-IND*:S1A-001)[8]

---

7   I would like to thank Professor Matthias Meyer for his support in the writing of the PERL script.
8   In the following linguistic examples, I excluded the mark-up where it was not relevant to the discussion to improve the legibility of the study.

The script summed up the number of words per speaker per file, which would not have been possible with standard concordance programs, which normally only allow the user to calculate the number of words per file. In a further step, the number of words per speaker was aligned with the information given in the respective metadata files. The alignment was less time-consuming with the ICE-HK corpus, which provides the metadata in one table, whereas the ICE-IND* metadata are stored separately for each file.

I decided to count the number of words that speakers with certain social characteristics contributed rather than to count the number of speakers with the respective social characteristic (in contrast to the method adopted in Lange 2012) in order to take differences in the length of utterances into account. This avoids overstating the representation of social categories of speakers who are less talkative. Consequently, the word count more accurately reflects the sociolinguistic make-up of the corpora in respect of actual contributions to the corpus and was used as a baseline for calculating normalised frequencies. I then analysed the ICE corpora with regard to their balance, i.e. whether the sample is diverse enough regarding the contributions of the speakers in terms of age, gender, and mother tongue, and their representativeness, i.e. whether the sample represents structures in the society as a whole (cf. also Section 11.1). As English is learnt at school and is predominantly spoken by educated people from the upper social classes, the sample shows a bias towards the social background of English speakers in these societies.

Information on the age of the speakers is available for 88% of the speakers in the spoken section of ICE-HK. The graph in Figure 14 depicts the word count in the spoken section of ICE-HK in relation to the number of words contributed by each age group.

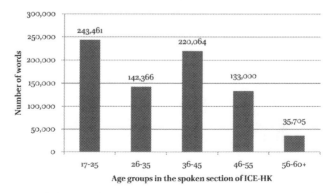

FIGURE 14   Corpus balance with regard to the social dimension age in the spoken section of
             ICE-HK.

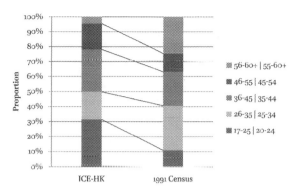

FIGURE 15   Representativeness of spoken ICE-HK with regard to the social dimension age as
             measured against data from the 1991 Census (cf. Table 17 in the appendices).

Concerning the balance of the corpus, we can see that all age groups are represented in the corpus, which is the prerequisite for the application of the
apparent-time method to ICE-HK. However, some age groups clearly contribute more words than others. The youngest age group contributes the highest
number of words with 243,461 words, while the oldest age group contributes
the lowest number of words with 35,705 words to the spoken part of ICE-HK, as
can be seen in Figure 14. With regard to the representativeness of ICE-HK, the
proportion of words spoken in ICE-HK by the respective age group was compared to the proportion of people of the whole population aged over 20 from
the 1991 population census (Hong Kong Census of Population 1991, Census
and Statistics Department). The age groups in ICE-HK do not match the age
groups in the census perfectly (cf. the key in Figure 15) but they correspond
well enough to allow for rough comparisons, as can be seen in Figure 15.

    The youngest age group (17–25) is overrepresented in ICE-HK with 31%, as
compared to the share of the 20–24 age group which, according to the 1991 Census, comprises 11% of the social demographic. By contrast, the oldest age group
is underrepresented in ICE-HK, with a share of only 5%, as compared to a share
of 25% in the society as a whole. Furthermore, the 25–34 age group has a higher
proportion in Hong Kong society with 30% than the proportion of 18% of the
contributions by this age group in ICE-HK may suggest. The representations of
age groups 36–45 and 46–55 roughly correspond to the proportions of these
age groups in Hong Kong society. The analysis of the representativeness of ICE-
HK with reference to the census from 1991 shows that ICE-HK is biased towards
the youngest age group, which needs to be taken into account in studies that
analyse variables undergoing change. This bias becomes even more obvious
when we compare the ICE-HK age structure to that of ICE-IND* with regard to
balance and representativeness.

Information about the gender of the speakers is available for 99.5% of the speakers in ICE-HK, and the two genders are almost equally distributed with reference to their contributions to the spoken section of ICE-HK.[9] Female speakers contribute slightly fewer words than male speakers with 46% of the total word count. This gender balance therefore also allows us to analyse gender-related variation in ICE-HK (cf. Figure 16).

Given that Hong Kong's society has a 50% male-female gender balance, the ICE-HK gender distribution in terms of number of words per gender matches the distribution of the genders 'on the ground' (cf. Figure 17) and is balanced as well as representative. However, this balance cannot be found in all text types of the corpus. The private dialogue section is, for example, marked by an overrepresentation of female speakers; here, females contribute 81% of the words.

With regard to the balance and representativeness of the social dimension 'mother tongue', it can be said that the clear majority of speakers in ICE-HK have Cantonese as their mother tongue, as is also the case in the population as a whole. However, we can find some speakers with an L1 other than Cantonese. These speakers are marked as extra-corpus material in all cases except for the speakers in the spontaneous commentaries (S2A-001-020). These speakers have English as their L1 and speak BrE or AusE as their mother tongues.

Information on age is provided for 432 speakers in ICE-IND*, i.e. for roughly half of the speakers in the corpus. The age structure in ICE-IND* is marked by

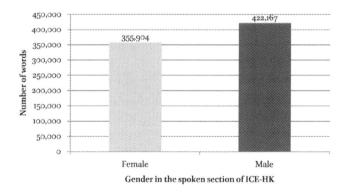

FIGURE 16   Corpus balance with regard to the social dimension gender in the spoken section of ICE-HK.

---

9   I prefer the term 'gender', i.e. the social construction of biological sex, although the metadata are probably based on the self-report about the speakers' biological sex rather than on their socially perceived and constructed masculinity or femininity (cf. Section 4.3.1; cf. also Labov 2001, 263).

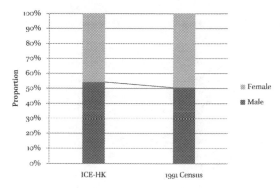

FIGURE 17   Representativeness of spoken ICE-HK with regard to the social dimension gender
as measured against data from the 1991 Census (only people aged 20 or above) (cf.
Table 18 in the appendices).

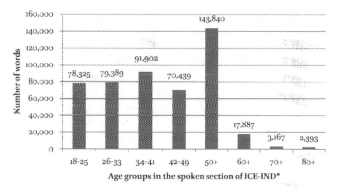

FIGURE 18   Corpus balance with regard to the social dimension age in the spoken section of
ICE-IND*.

a high number of words by speakers of the 50+ age group, who contribute 30%
of the total word count in ICE-IND* (cf. Figure 18).

In order to account for the representativeness of the ICE-IND* data with regard to the distribution of age groups in the corpus, I consulted the 1991 Census
of India, which provides the number of people for every age from 1 year to above
100 years. Based on these data, I recreated the ICE-IND* age categories to make
the data comparable. I therefore excluded all people under 18. These speakers
form a very large group in the age structure of India, constituting 43% of the
population, as India's age structure has the shape of the classical population
pyramid, with a decreasing number of people with increasing age. Figure 19
shows a comparison of the age structure found in ICE-IND* and that found in
India's population as a whole for people above 18.

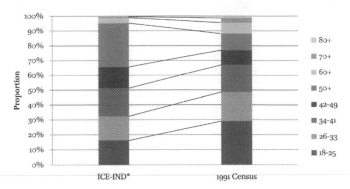

FIGURE 19   Representativeness of spoken ICE-IND* with regard to the social dimension age
as measured against data from the 1991 Census (cf. Table 19 in the appendices).

The youngest age group (18–25) is underrepresented in ICE-IND*, with a
share of 16%, as compared to 29% in India's population. The shares of the
middle-aged age groups (26–33, 34–41, and 42–49) in ICE-IND* correspond
roughly to their proportions in India's population, with 16%, 19%, and 14% in
ICE-IND* respectively as compared to 20%, 18%, and 10% in the census. The
50+ age group, however, is strongly overrepresented in the ICE-IND* data with
30%, as compared to only 11% in the census data. The oldest age groups (60+,
70+, 80+) roughly show the same shares in ICE-IND* as in India's population
as a whole and are only slightly underrepresented with 4%, 1%, and 0% in
ICE-IND* as compared to 7%, 3%, and 1% in the census data. The age structure has important ramifications for studies based on ICE-IND*, as the spoken
sub-corpus of ICE-IND* most strongly represents the speech of older speakers
(50+), so that the 'conservative' nature of IndE attested in some studies based
on ICE (e.g. Mair 2009a, 50) may be compounded by the overrepresentation of
this age group, which contributes a higher number of conservative forms than,
for example, the underrepresented youngest age group. The bias towards conservative rather than innovative forms in the distribution of forms undergoing
language change may therefore also be due to the age structure in ICE-IND*.
If the ICE-IND* corpus had been collected on the basis of representativeness
according to age group, the language use represented in ICE-IND* would probably be more 'innovative'. This line of argumentation is, of course, only valid if
we can find the same general patterns of variation across age groups in IndE as
those that have been found in L1 varieties of English.

   Gender is another important social dimension for this study as the behavior
of females and males may tell us something about the type of language change.
ICE-IND* provides information about the gender for 676 speakers. This means
that the social dimension of gender is specified for roughly 77% of the speakers
in the spoken section of ICE-IND*. Compared to the availability of information

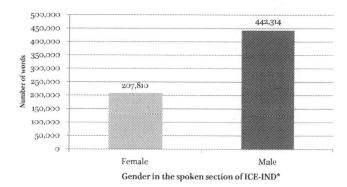

FIGURE 20   Corpus balance with regard to the social dimension gender in the spoken section of ICE-IND*.

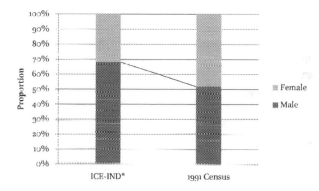

FIGURE 21   Representativeness of spoken ICE-IND* with regard to the social dimension gender as measured against data from the 1991 Census (only people aged 18 or above) (cf. Table 20 in the appendices).

about the age and mother tongue of the speakers, information on gender is more readily available. The speech of both genders is represented in ICE-IND*, although females contribute fewer words to the spoken part of ICE-IND* than male speakers, as can be seen in Figure 20.

Regarding the representativeness of gender for India's population as a whole, we can see that the gender balance in the population of India in 1991 is not achieved in the spoken component of ICE-IND*, measured by the number of words per gender in the complete spoken section of ICE-IND*. Here, we can see a clear overrepresentation of male speakers (cf. Figure 21), with females only having a share of 32%.

A more fine-grained analysis of the gender distribution according to text categories reveals that the share of females in the private dialogue section (S1A) matches the gender distribution found in the population as a whole, with 50% of words contributed by female speakers. Females are also fairly well represented in the text type of scripted monologues (S2B), with 43% of the total word count. However, they are underrepresented in the public dialogue sections (S1B), with only 21%, and even more greatly underrepresented in the unscripted monologues section (S2A), with a mere 11%. These differences clearly show the gender bias in connection with access to certain public domains and may reflect actual underlying gender differences in the domains associated with the text types (cf. Section 8.3 for gender-specific patterns of change which may be related to the restricted access of women to English). It also means that gender and text type may in some cases interact in complex ways for cultural reasons and that the understanding of biases in the data is a prerequisite for accounting for these complex interactions. What is more, the analysis of the ICE-IND* gender structure has shown that male speakers contribute significantly more words and therefore have a greater impact on the structure of the spoken section. If a feature is analysed that is involved in language change from below, the overrepresentation of male speakers can again lead to a more 'conservative' picture of IndE, as females tend to lead changes from below (cf. Labov 2001, 279–283; cf. also Section 4.3.1).

Another important social dimension of varieties of English which emerged in multilingual settings such as India is the mother tongue of the speakers. Out of 881 speakers listed in my database for ICE-IND*, information about the mother tongue is given for 374 speakers (42%). In total, 22 different languages can be found in the ICE-IND* metadata, as can be seen in Figure 22. I subsumed speakers of Marwari and Bhojpuri under Hindi to facilitate comparison with the census data that classify these regional languages as dialects of Hindi.

Figure 22 shows that the number of words contributed by the speakers of the 22 different languages varies greatly. Speakers of Marathi and Kannada contribute the largest number of words to the spoken part of ICE-IND*, followed by speakers of Hindi, Tamil, Malayalam, Telugu, Punjabi, and Konkani, who also contribute a substantial number of words. Speakers of a large number of languages (Tulu, Assamese, Khasi, Nepali, etc.) only contribute a limited number of words to the corpus. Knowing about this distribution makes it possible to analyse correlations between variants and those languages that contribute enough words to make statistical claims. The distribution of a small number of languages with very large numbers of speakers and many languages with very small numbers of speakers is also characteristic of India's multilingual language situation as a whole (cf. Section 3.2.2).[10]

---

10   India's multilingual situation is clearly understated by only referring to the first languages of the speakers, as most speakers are proficient in more than one language. In addition to those speakers that give Hindi as their mother tongue, the total number of speakers of Hindi is around 337 million, which attests to its status as a lingua franca. This means 40% of the Indian population knows Hindi.

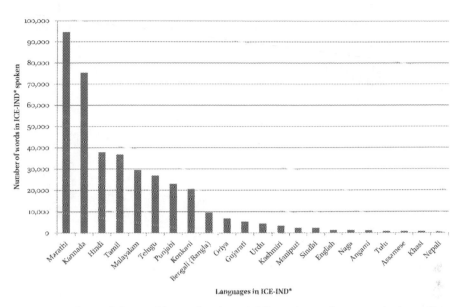

FIGURE 22   Corpus balance with regard to the social dimension mother tongue in the spoken
section of ICE-IND* (cf. in Table 21 the appendices).

The *Ethnologue* gives a total number of 461 different languages for India, of
which 447 are living and 14 are extinct.[11] These languages belong to four major
language families: (1) Indo-Aryan, (2) Dravidian, (3) Tibeto-Burman, and (4)
Austro-Asiatic. The two major language families in India are the Indo-Aryan
and Dravidian language families. These language families are distributed along
a north-south divide, with the Indo-Aryan language families in the north and
the Dravidian languages in the south of India. Languages of the Tibeto-Burman and Austro-Asiatic family are clearly in the minority and are only found in
specific areas. ICE-IND* features the four major language families, and the relatively small number of words spoken by speakers of languages of the Tibeto-
Burman and Austro-Asiatic families reflects their size in terms of speakers. If
we go down to the level of individual languages, we can see several similarities
but also major differences between the sample of ICE-IND* and the population as a whole. The 1991 Census of India lists the number of speakers for 216
different mother tongues that have more than 10 million speakers and their
percentage of the whole population.[12] Most of the languages represented in

11   http://www.ethnologue.com/country/IN (last access: 19/02/2018).
12   The data are available online at: http://www.censusindia.gov.in/DigitalLibrary/Table
       Series.aspx (last access: 01/02/2017) under 'Social & Cultural Tables'. It was not possible to
       retrieve information on the distribution of the mother tongue by age, which would have
       allowed me to exclude speakers below 18

ICE-IND* also rank among the 22 most common languages in the census. However, their ranking is not the same, as can be seen in Table 5.

TABLE 5   Comparison of the distribution of mother tongues in ICE-IND* and the 1991 Census data

L1	Language family	N words (corpus)	N speakers (census)	Percentage (corpus)	Percentage (census)
Marathi	IA (Indo-Aryan)	94,757	62,421,442	24.59	7.44
Kannada	Dr (Dravidian)	75,465	32,590,177	19.58	3.89
Hindi	IA	37,853	233,432,285	9.82	27.84
Tamil	Dr	36,787	52,886,931	9.55	6.31
Malayalam	Dr	29,487	30,325,637	7.65	3.62
Telugu	Dr	26,905	65,900,723	6.98	7.86
Punjabi	IA	23,023	23,085,063	5.97	2.75
Konkani	IA	20,616	1,723,264	5.35	0.21
Bengali (Bangla)	IA	9,683	66,552,894	2.51	7.94
Oriya	IA	6,785	27,586,476	1.76	3.29
Guj(a)rati	IA	5,246	40,335,889	1.36	4.81
Urdu	IA	4,437	43,358,978	1.36	5.17
Kashmiri	IA	3,347	33,845	0.87	0.004
Manipuri	TB (Tibeto-Burman)	2,365	1,270,038	0.61	0.15
Sindhi	IA	2,298	1,551,384	0.60	0.19
English	IE	1,348	178,598	0.35	0.02
Naga	TB	1,280	n/a	0.33	n/a
Angami	TB	1,069	58,567	0.28	0.01
Tulu	Dr	727	1,550,334	0.19	0.19
Assamese	IA	722	12,962,721	0.19	1.55
Khasi	AA (Austro-Asiatic)	672	700,047	0.17	0.08
Nepali	IA	475	2,075,746	0.12	0.25
Total		385,347	838,567,936[a]	100	100

[a]Number of speakers of all mother tongues included in census.

The most striking differences between ICE-IND* and the population as a whole
can be found in the representation of the three languages with the highest
word count in ICE-IND*: Marathi, Kannada, and Hindi. Marathi is the language
with the highest number of words in ICE-IND*, roughly contributing a quarter of the words to the spoken section. By contrast, speakers of Marathi make
up only about 7% of the population as a whole. The contribution of words to
ICE-IND* by speakers of Marathi therefore does not match the distribution
in the population, so that speakers of Marathi are strongly overrepresented
in the corpus. This overrepresentation of Marathi is due to the fact that the
ICE-IND project for the compilation of the spoken part was situated at Shivaji
University in Maharashtra, a state in the west of India, whose official language
is Marathi (cf. also Lange 2012, 82).

Speakers of Kannada are also strongly overrepresented in the corpus, contributing roughly one fifth of the total word count while only making up 4% of
the population as a whole. The overrepresentation of Kannada is probably also
"an accidental by-product of the sampling procedure" (Lange 2012, 82). Many
recordings of the private dialogue section come from Mysore, a city in the
southwestern state of Karnataka, whose official language is Kannada (cf. Lange
2012, 82). The other Dravidian languages Tamil, Malayalam, and Telugu are also
overrepresented in ICE-IND*, although to a smaller extent. The strongest difference between the corpus composition of ICE-IND* and the composition in
the society with regard to the L1s of the speakers is the underrepresentation of
Hindi in ICE-IND*. Speakers of Hindi contribute only roughly 10% to ICE-IND*
although they constitute 28% of the population in terms of number of speakers. The other major Indo-Aryan languages Bengali, Oriya, Guj(a)rati, and Urdu
are also underrepresented in ICE-IND*, while Punjabi, Konkani, Kashmiri, and
Sindhi are overrepresented in ICE-IND*, as can be seen in Table 5. Concerning
language families, the comparison shows that the Dravidian languages (Dr) are
overrepresented, while the Indo-Aryan languages (IA) are underrepresented
in ICE-IND* as compared to the 1991 Census. However, the share of Tibeto-
Burman (TB) and Austro-Asiatic languages (AA) in ICE-IND* matches their
status as minority languages in India. The comparison of corpus structure
and census data has important consequences for discussions of substrate influence for studies on ICE-IND. Rather than only taking Hindi as the 'default'
substrate language based on the large number of speakers in India's population (e.g. cf. Calle-Martín & Jesús 2017), Marathi and Kannada should also be
taken into consideration. Depending on the variable studied, the differences
between Hindi and Marathi may be less profound because of their common
ancestry. However, neglecting the Dravidian language Kannada in discussions
about substrate influence may not do justice to the dataset at hand. Ideally,

discussions on substrate influence should be refined by a more data-driven approach that takes correlations between linguistic features and L1s as possible symptoms of substrate influence. These correlations may then guide the way to influential substrate languages in varieties of English that have emerged in multilingual settings (cf. Section 6.2 for an attempt of such an approach and cf. Section 3.2.2 for the language situation in India).

As the speakers of ICE were not selected on the basis of social factors representative of the Indian society as a whole (cf. Nelson 1996, 28), we cannot expect the corpora to represent the social categories of those found in the population as a whole. Although sociolinguistic studies were not the primary goal of ICE, this section has shown that the structure of the sample in ICE-HK and ICE-IND* allows for the analysis of variation along social dimensions. Speakers with a broad range of social characteristics have been included. However, their representation in the corpus does not always match social reality as some speakers with particular social characteristics are overrepresented. Identifying these biases in the internal social make-up is therefore a prerequisite for understanding the 'behaviour' of the corpora in their entirety.

To summarise, we have seen that the social structure of ICE-HK is marked by an overrepresentation of younger speakers and an underrepresentation of older speakers. In terms of gender distribution, ICE-HK matches the almost equal distribution of male and female speakers in the population. The clear majority of speakers in ICE-HK have Cantonese as their mother tongue, which also matches the distribution in the population as a whole. The social structure of ICE-IND* is marked by an underrepresentation of younger speakers and an overrepresentation of speakers aged over 50. Furthermore, female speakers are underrepresented in ICE-IND*. With respect to the mother tongues of the speakers, we can identify an underrepresentation of Hindi, the language with the highest number of speakers in India, and an overrepresentation of Marathi and Kannada. More generally, we have seen that the Indo-Aryan languages are underrepresented while the Dravidian languages are overrepresented.

If these findings are linked to the question of comparability between the ICE corpora, we can see that the structure of ICE-IND* compared to ICE-HK at least fuels discussions on the 'conservative' nature of IndE, as IndE may indeed come across as more 'conservative' than other Englishes because (1) ICE-IND was compiled relatively early, (2) its spoken language resembles written language, (3) it overrepresents speakers of older age groups, and (4) it overrepresents male speakers. ICE-HK instead may appear more 'innovative' compared to ICE-IND* because (1) it overrepresents younger speakers and (2) has a higher proportion of female speakers. In variables that undergo changes from below, ICE-IND* may therefore have a higher frequency of older variants than ICE-HK if we can expect the same patterns of variation according to age and gender that have been found in L1 varieties of English.

4.2   Questionnaire

Apart from the corpus data, I also used data from two questionnaire studies conducted in March 2015 and August 2015 that I designed to gain insight into speakers' perspectives on variation in the use of expressions of obligation and necessity. I created two versions of the questionnaire (cf. Figure 61 and Figure 62 in the appendices), which I adapted in parts, for example in order to provide discourse completion tasks that represent situations in the everyday life of the students surveyed in March 2015 vs. those of the adults surveyed in August 2015. Most items were the same, so that I could increase my total number of participants in the second round of distribution. I excluded items from the second questionnaire where the standard deviation of the answers given was high and substituted them with questions that elicited free text answers.

In total, 53 speakers completed the two questionnaires. The majority (N = 35) were students enrolled in a Master's class of English Studies at the Dayal Bagh Educational Institute in Agra in Uttar Pradesh, a state in the northern region of India. Most of these speakers had Hindi as their mother tongue, which is why Hindi is strongly represented in the sample (N = 30). The survey was also distributed in Hyderabad, state capital of Telangana in the southeast region of India, where the Dravidian language Telugu is predominantly spoken, which is why the majority of the speakers interviewed in the second round had Telugu as their mother tongue (N = 8). The sample also includes four speakers that indicate English as their mother tongue, two Urdu speakers, and one speaker each of Marathi, Nepali, Tamil, Telugu/Tamil, Hindi/Punjabi, and English/Hindi, and two speakers who did not specify their mother tongue. The sample has a strong gender imbalance, with 50 female speakers, 1 male speaker, and 2 speakers who did not specify their gender. Furthermore, it is also biased towards younger speakers with a mean age of 24 years. With regard to occupations represented in the survey, the sample includes 33 students enrolled in an English master's programme and nine teachers, one doctor, one executive, one hostess, and eight participants who did not specify their occupation. It therefore must be critically assessed that the majority of participants, the students and teachers of the English master's programme, have probably developed an increased language awareness with regard to the English language. As a result, they may hold different views on the English language than speakers of IndE without such metalinguistic awareness (cf. also Krug & Sell 2013, 78–79 for the choice of participants in sociolinguistic questionnaires and interviews). The unbalanced sample in terms of mother tongue, gender, age, and occupation of the participants only represents a very small segment of the population and does not allow me to reach more general conclusions about IndE speakers. On the other hand, the large group of (young) academics fits the speaker profile targeted in ICE quite well. Despite the limitations due to the size and balance of the sample, the questionnaire data may therefore still constitute a first step towards the integration of speaker judgments into the research design in order to complement corpus findings.

First of all, I was interested in their language attitudes towards different varieties of English, especially towards IndE because a positive evaluation of IndE may be an important indicator of the stage of 'Endonormative Stabilisation' in Schneider's (2007) model (cf. Section 3.2). In this stage, "[t]he existence of a new language form is recognized, and this form has lost its former stigma and is positively evaluated" (Schneider 2007, 50). In order to find out about the perception of a new language form and language attitudes towards it, the participants rated several statements about different varieties of English on a five-point Likert scale, from 'strongly agree' to 'strongly disagree'. The choice allows participants to indicate that they are indifferent about the statement, which means they are not forced to take a stand as would be the case in a four-point or six-point scale (cf. Krug & Sell 2013, 78). I created some of the statements based on corpus findings for search terms such as "Indian English", "British English", "American English", or "English". Speaker A in text S2A-047, Jayaprakash Shinde (University Teacher, affiliated with the *Linguistics Society of India*), for example, addresses the status of IndE and defines it as a distinct variety of English in (31).

(31)   Now the conclusion arrived at were *Indian English* is not a substandard English it is not pidgin English it is not just British English with a few Indian spices added to it it has its own distinct identity (ICE-IND*:S2A-047)

In text S1A-015, more language attitudes towards varieties of English can be identified. For example, the speakers address the question of 'ownership' of a language and rights that go along with 'ownership'. In this case, the right to bring about changes in the language is considered a privilege of L1 speakers of English.

(32)   <$A> Yet even in those things [sc. in AmE and BrE] there may be some slight changes because their mother tongue is uh English and they are authorised to bring changes depending upon the daily usage
       <$B> Uhm English
       <$A> Whereas it is our cultivated language foreign language *we are not authorised to bring changes in grammar* and all those things (ICE-IND*:S1A-015)

These are only some examples that show different academic and non-academic discussions about IndE and I used them as a starting point to formulate statements that may reveal the language attitudes of the speakers with regard to the distinctiveness of English in India, the ownership of English, and the identity functions fulfilled by the Indian variety of English for Indian people. I adapted some of the statements from Zhang's language attitude study on HKE (cf. Zhang 2014, 108). I discussed the findings regarding IndE as a distinct variety and the attitudes towards IndE and other varieties of English in Section 3.2.2 in more detail. One of the major findings was that the answers of the participants showed a positive evaluation of IndE. While this was an interesting observation by itself, it could not be used as an explanation for variation in the use of modal and semi-modal verbs (cf. the speakers' language awareness of variation in the modal domain discussed below). Furthermore, it is impossible to transfer the attitude of Indian speakers towards their variety in 2015 to speakers represented in ICE-IND from the early 1990s, as changes in language attitude may have occurred since then.

The remaining parts of the survey were designed to gather information about the object of study, i.e. the use of *must, have to, have got to*, and *need to*. In the discourse completion task, I was primarily interested in what forms speakers of some Indo-Aryan languages (e.g. Hindi) used to express epistemic modality, because these speakers showed a lower proportion of epistemic *must* (as detailed in Section 6.2). Furthermore, I wanted to ascertain what other deontic expressions are used to express a strong recommendation that is of benefit to the hearer, and a request that is not beneficial to the hearer. Above that, I was interested in finding out about the associations speakers have of *must, have to, have got to, gotta*, and *need to*, for example whether speakers relate certain variants to BrE or AmE, to spoken language or written language, to formal language or informal language. I used the corpus findings from BrE, AmE, and IndE to determine whether speakers accurately identified the correlations of the variants. For example, the corpus findings showed that the distribution of *must* varies according to region, with BrE using more tokens of *must* than AmE. The association of *must* with BrE was therefore considered 'accurate'. In terms of correlations between the variants and mode and formality, I used the findings from IndE, so that a correlation between *must* and spoken language was counted as accurate, because the data from ICE-IND* show a higher frequency of root *must* in spoken language with a Mossé-coefficient (M-co) of 61 compared to an M co of 52 in written language (as opposed to BrE with an M-co of 25 in spoken mode vs. an M-co of 68 in written language). The accurate identification of correlations between the variants and their distribution according to variety, mode, and formality almost never exceeded the 50% mark in a task that had a 50% chance of accurate identification (ticking the box vs. not ticking it). This may

mean that the participants are not consciously aware of the distribution of variants, so that these variants are not open for active manipulation by the speakers
(for example, the use of *have got to* in order to express 'Britishness').

Apart from the distribution according to variety, mode, and formality, I was
also interested in the social perception of obligations, especially those expressed with the core modal *must.* I therefore asked the participants to rank
people according to their personality characteristics when they say *You must
help me out with this.* I used descriptors for personality traits that participants
had used in free text answers in my pilot study. Some of these descriptors are
also employed in other language attitude studies (cf. Preston 1999; Bernaisch
& Koch 2016). The participants ranked the personality characteristics of the
speakers according to the following bipolar pairs: 'friendly – unfriendly',
'sincere – insincere', 'helpful – unhelpful', 'educated – uneducated', 'proficient –
not proficient', 'authoritative – not authoritative', 'close – distant', 'confident –
insecure', 'experienced – inexperienced', 'young – old'. Friendliness, sincerity,
and helpfulness represent solidarity characteristics of a speaker, education,
proficiency, and experience represent aspects of the perceived competence of
a speaker, while authority, distance, confidence (and age) represent aspects
related to the status of a speaker. We would expect 'Anglo' English speakers to
rank a speaker who uses the sentence *You must help me out with this!* high on
the status dimensions but low on the solidarity dimensions because the use of
the modal verb is associated with authority and strong imposition by others.
The question is whether this correlation can also be found in speakers of IndE.

I used the qualitative findings from the questionnaire to supplement my
quantitative study from the corpus analyses, interspersing the qualitative
findings wherever they threw interesting light on the quantitative findings,
especially when the questionnaire data gave me an insight into culturally
shaped views about the use of the variants in social practices (cf. Section 7.2).
The questionnaire was therefore taken as a supplement to the corpus findings
about variation in the use of expressions of deontic modality.

4.3   Extracting the Dependent Variable

Having discussed the databases of my study, I would like to continue with the
description of data extraction from these databases by explaining the retrieval
of the dependent variable in this section and the coding of the independent
variables in the next section.

In Section 1.5, I explained that I will deal with deontic modality as a variable
realised by the variants deontic *must, have to, have got to,* and *need to.* These
variants can only be in variation in declarative affirmative sentences in the

present tense, which is why the analysis is restricted to these tokens and invariant tokens were excluded, such as tokens of *must, have to, have got to*, and *need to* in sentences with negation (e.g. (33) and (34)). The main competitors *must* and *have to* do not have the same scope of negation. While *must* takes internal negation, i.e. the modal has scope over the negator, *have to* takes external negation, i.e. the negator has scope over the modal. *Must* negates the main verb and therefore the negation applies to the proposition ('necessary that not'). *Have to* negates the auxiliary verb and therefore negation applies to the modality ('not necessary that') (cf. also Anderwald 2002, 38 for modal auxiliaries and scope of negation). *Must not* therefore expresses a prohibition while *not have to* expresses the absence of an obligation. Hence, example sentences (33) and (34) are not equivalent semantically and have therefore been excluded from the analysis.

(33) We *must not* forget their contribution to India. (ICE-IND*:W1A-001) ('necessary that not')

(34) Yes you *don't have to* pay ten thousand rupees loan (ICE-IND*:S1A-020) ('not necessary that')

Furthermore, tokens of *must, have to, have got to*, and *need to* in interrogative sentences were excluded from the analysis, such as (35) and (36). All expressions occurred only rarely in the interrogative but *must* was even more rarely used than the semi-modal verbs, so that variation was highly restricted in interrogative sentences (cf. also Huddleston & Pullum 2002, 205).

(35) What *must* we do if we do decide not to teach English or learn English any more? (ICE-IND*:S2B-041)

(36) Uh so how much *do we have* to pay (ICE-IND*:S1A-049)

Furthermore, I excluded past tense forms and non-finite forms of the semi-modal auxiliaries such as (37) and (38), because *must* does not have these forms.[13]

(37) But uh the family relationship required the man uhn the father to fix that she *had to* marry that fellow (ICE-IND*:S1A-069)

(38) I'll teach them in English of course, I'*ll have to* be very careful in the choice of words that I am going to use (ICE-IND*:S1A-078)

---

13 Note, however, that *must* may have past time reference in indirect speech, e.g. *I told him he must be home early* ('had to') from Quirk et al. (1985, 128), as already mentioned in Section 1.3.

In the case of *have to* and *have got to*, I also excluded non-modal tokens where possessive *have*/*have got* co-occurred with following infinitive marker introducing a purpose (e.g. (39) and (40), cf. Section 6.1.2 for the relationship between this construction and deontic *have to*). As I also included tokens of *have got to* where *have* was omitted, the results for *have got to* had to be filtered for lexical uses of *get*, e.g. (41) with following prepositional phrase or (42) with idiomatic *get to know*. The idiomatic expression *have to do with*/*have got to do with* was also excluded from my analysis, e.g. (43) and (44).

(39) I know we have to study but *what right do they have to stop* us from restrict us from all things all these things (ICE-IND*:S1A-052)

(40) [...] I am pleased to enclose a write-up of our Company and *the services we have to offer* for your attention (ICE-SIN:W1B-023)

(41) She *has got to the trip* for falling sick only (ICE-IND*:S1A-012)

(42) I *got to know* these people by joining the student bodies such as societies and clubs. (ICE-HK:W1B-009)

(43) So it *has to do with* culture also (ICE-IND*:S1A-036)

(44) That is a large part of the uh marketing uh functions because everything to do *got to do with* uh to go from petrol to diesel to uh L P G and so on (ICE-SIN:S2A-046).

I also excluded some rare cases where the modal *must* and semi-modal *have to* co-occurred such as in example sentences (45) to (47) (it is notable that (47) is from the text category of administrative writing). Although these double modals only occurred rarely, they may point to learner strategies that are employed to maximise salience (cf. also Williams's principles in Section 7.3 on SLA principles and the explanation by Biewer 2011, 19 for the occurrence of *can be able to* in some ESL varieties).

(45) And I think I *must have to* go to there (ICE-HK:S1A-080)

(46) We *must have to* invite uh so many cooks [...] (ICE-IND*:S1A-005)

(47) [...] the mission *must have to* be implementation-worthy at all levels (ICE-IND*:W2D-001)

Finally, I also excluded tokens of *must, have to, have got to*, and *need to* in unclear passages whose content I could not reconstruct, e.g. (48).

(48) So if you impose uh wage constraint you *have to be again uh* <unc> *one-word* </unc> again is extremely difficult to implement [...] (ICE-HK:S1B-022)

I decided to keep tokens of *must* in formulaic expressions, for example, tokens where *must* is followed by verbs of saying, because variation with its main competitor *have to* is also possible in these contexts as example sentences (49) and (50) show.

(49) It's really jolly good *I must say* (ICE-HK:S1A-047)

(50) Okay now *I have to say* what is retailing profit (ICE-HK:S2A-053)

Diaconu excludes these formulaic expressions because of their performative function (cf. Diaconu 2012b, 26). However, the corpus data show that variation does occur, despite the fact that these expressions are formulaic. Excluding these examples may result in the underestimation of the entrenchment of *have to* in the varieties because the replacement of *must* with *have to* in these constructions may point to a later stage of grammaticalisation, as has also been suggested by Tagliamonte and D'Arcy (2007, 73). Variation in the use of *must* and *have to* in these contexts is therefore relevant to the analysis of the competition between *must* and *have to*, and their distribution may give us an idea of the progress of grammaticalisation in the varieties. With this procedure, I extracted 8,881 tokens of *must, have to, have got to*, and *need to* from ICE-GB, SBC, ICE-USA, ICE-HK, ICE-IND*, and ICE-SIN and classified these tokens according to (up to) 12 independent variables.

4.3.1   *Coding the Independent Variables*

I coded the variants according to the language-internal factors: (1) function of the modal verb, (2) reference of the preceding subject, (3) grammatical person of the preceding subject, (4) the verb, and (5) semantics of the following verb. The language-external factors are coded according to the categories of: (6) variety, (7) mode (written/spoken), (8) text category, (9) age of the speaker, (10) gender of the speaker, (11) L1 of the speaker, and (12) speaker.

As regards function, I distinguished between epistemic and root modality as outlined in Section 1.2. This distinction was necessary to guarantee functional equivalence between the variants. Generally, competition between the variants is strong in root modality but less strong in epistemic modality, where *must* is the major variant used. However, the encoding of epistemic modality with the modal *must* seems to be subject to regional variation, with strong differences in the use of epistemic *must* across the varieties studied (cf. Section 5.1).

In order to operationalise the notion of strength of obligation, I coded those tokens of *must, have to, have got to*, and *need to* that express a root reading according to three language-internal variables: reference of the preceding subject, grammatical person of the subject, and semantics of the following verb (cf. also Jankowski 2004, 98). In terms of reference of the subject, I additionally distinguished generic vs. non-generic readings of the subject. (51) and (52) show the generic and non-generic reading in NPs, respectively, while (53) and (54) show examples of pronouns in generic and non-generic function (cf. Section 11.1 for issues involved in coding subject reference in varieties with variable article use).

(51) Because of each have a feeling going on that uh *girls* must be given some higher education till their marriage (ICE-IND*:S1A-088)

(52) *The youngsters under Azharuddin* must take this opportunity and establish their worth in the team. (ICE-IND*:W2E-009)

(53) Once people give you oranges *you* must give ang pows right (ICE-SIN:S2B-035)

(54) *You* must take us to Banglore someday introduce us to your husband as well as your sons (ICE-IND*:S1A-031)

Coates analyses the meaning of root *must* in the form of a cline from strong obligation to weak obligation (cf. Coates 1983, 32). In terms of this cline, obligations and necessities expressed towards subjects with a generic reading are weaker than those expressed towards subjects with a non-generic reading, where a particular referent can be identified. Within the group of subjects with a non-generic reading, the strength of obligation varies depending on the person of the subject. I therefore coded the subject according to first person, second person, and third person without a distinction in number. Obligations are strongest with second person subjects as in (55) and weakest with third person subjects as in (57); obligations with first person subjects as in (56) range in between the two poles of the cline (cf. also Leech et al. 2009, 114, who state that "the implication of personal imposition is likely to be uppermost" in first and second person subjects compared to third person subjects).

(55) *You must* do something! (ICE-SIN:W2F-001)
      → strong obligation

(56) Actually I plan to stop here one you know but I haven't reached two thou-
      sand words so *I must* carry on alright (ICE-SIN:S1B-015)
      → medium obligation

(57) Ya lah that that's it like she must *she must* do her research all lah
      (ICE-SIN:S1A-097)
      → weak obligation

The grammatical person of the subject and the reference are closely related, for
example in the case of first person subjects that tend to have a definite reading
(in 91% of the cases in the dataset used for Chapter 9; the generic cases occurred
with the first person plural pronoun *we*). As I was interested in operationalising
the force of the obligation, I decided to code the subjects according to their reference first and coded those that had a non-generic reading according to the grammatical person. I therefore used the following four categories: "G" (generic), "1N"
(first person, non-generic), "2N" (second person, non-generic), and "3N" (third
person, non-generic) (cf. also Jankowski 2004, 99–100 for the same procedure).

     Apart from the subject that precedes the modal or semi-modal verb, the type
of verb also plays an important role, as it makes a difference what the speaker
asks the hearer to do. Verbs of activity can be said to express a stronger sense of
obligation than stative verbs (cf. Jankowski 2004, 98), cf. the stronger obligation
expressed in (58) with the dynamic verb *play*, vs. the weaker obligation (necessity) expressed in (59) with the stative verb *have* from Coates (1983, 34, my emphases) at the extreme poles of the cline from strong obligation to weak obligation.

(58) "You *must play* this ten times over", Miss Jarrova would say, pointing with
      relentless fingers to a jumble of crotchets and quavers. (Lanc1-G332)

(59) Clay pots *must have* some protection from severe weather. (Lanc1-403)

In order to account for possible differences in the modals' and semi-modals'
selection of verbs, I used the semantically tagged version of the ICE corpora,
which is an annotated version of the corpora on the basis of the USAS tagset
(cf. Archer, Wilson & Rayson 2002; cf. Table 22 in the appendices). This tagset
has been created by researchers at the *University Centre for Computer Corpus
Research on Language* (UCREL). It works on the basis of POS-tagged corpora
by assigning semantic tags to words on the basis of a comprehensive tagset (cf.
Table 22 in the appendices). I had a closer look at each tag and recoded those
verbs whose semantics was not correctly identified by the tagger and tagged
the data from SBC (ICE-USAS*) because these were not tagged semantically.
The USAS tagset is not specifically designed for the tagging of the semantics of

verbs but is used to code the semantics of every word in a corpus. And while
Levin's (1993) *English verb classes and alternations* has become the standard
reference for grouping verbs according to common semantic but also syntactic
criteria, its classification turned out to be problematic for this analysis.
I was primarily interested in the semantics of the verbs, and verbs that carried
similar meanings were, for example, sometimes assigned to a class based on
their similar syntactic behaviour such as the verb class 'verbs with predicative
complement', which comprises verbs such as *know* and *remember*. Although, of
course, semantic and syntactic criteria of verbs are often closely intertwined
and can often not be analysed separately from each other, I was mainly interested in a semantic tagging of the verbs rather than a syntactic tagging.
I therefore chose to work with the USAS tagset, which tags words according to
their semantics, so that the verbs *know* and *remember* are semantically coded
as 'mental actions and processes' (top-level category X) rather than as 'verbs
with predicative complement', as was the case in Levin's (1993) categorisation.
The USAS tagset has 21 top-level labels, as can be seen in Table 6.

TABLE 6   Top-level labels in the UCREL Semantic Analysis System (from Archer, Wilson &
             Rayson 2002, 2)

A	B	C	E
General and abstract terms	The body and the individual	Arts and crafts	Emotion
F	**G**	**H**	**I**
Food and farming	Government and public	Architecture, housing, and the home	Money and commerce in industry
K	**L**	**M**	**N**
Entertainment sports, and games	Life and living things	Movement, location, travel, and transport	Numbers and measurement
O	**P**	**Q**	**S**
Substances, materials, objects, and equipment	Education	Language and communication	Social actions, states, and processes
T	**W**	**X**	**Y**
Time	World and environment	Psychological actions, states, and processes	Science and technology
Z			
Names and grammar			

These labels comprise words that belong to the same semantic field, "that are related by virtue of their being connected at some level of generality with the same mental concept" (Archer, Wilson & Rayson 2002, 1). The categories of the tagset were initially loosely based on McArthur's *Longman Lexicon of Contemporary English*, "as this appeared to offer the most appropriate thesaurus type classification of word senses for this kind of analysis" (Archer, Wilson & Rayson 2002, 2). The tagset has been changed over time and now comprises the 21 top-level categories shown in Table 6. The 'neat' structural organisation of concepts by use of most letters of the alphabet may lead to the assumption that the structure of the alphabet has been forced on the semantic structure of concepts and that the categorisation is therefore artificial. This may be a valid point of criticism regarding the structure of the tagset. However, at least for the purposes of my analysis, the semantic tagging of the verbs following the modal and semi-modal verbs seemed to be a good starting point for the analysis of possible differences in the selection of verbs with specific meanings. The top-level categories are further divided into more fine-grained categories (cf. Table 22 in the appendices, Archer, Wilson & Rayson 2002) that make it possible to analyse collocational patterns between the modal and semi-modal modal verbs and specific verbs such as *be*, which has a separate tag (A3). The coding of the subject and the coding of the following verb allowed me to account for properties in the syntactic slots preceding and following the modal and semi-modal verbs. The coding of the subject was the first step in the operationalisation of the notion of strength of obligation, and the coding of the semantics of the verb was the second step. It can be argued that activity verbs such as those in the categories M (e.g. *go, come*) and S (e.g. *allow, help*) in the USAS tagset (cf. Table 6) are stronger in their obligational force than stative verbs such as those in the categories A (e.g. *be, have*), Q (e.g. *say, confess*), and X (e.g. *know, remember*). The semantic categorisation also proved more valuable than a two-fold distinction according to the lexical aspect of the verb because it was possible to account for finer semantic distinctions within the categories of stative and dynamic verbs. The finer sub-categorisation of the tagset proved especially helpful in categories that contained a broad range of verbs such as category A, which includes – among other verbs – the auxiliaries *be, have*, and *do*. The coding of the language-internal factors 'subject' and 'verb semantics' helped me to operationalise the strength of obligation, so that examples of the type in (60) with non-generic second person subject and a following (implied) action verb such as *go* were likely to represent instances of strong obligation; examples of the type in (61) with generic third person subjects and the following stative verb *be* were likely to represent instances of weak obligation.

(60) "I don't want to *go*" "But *you must*" (ICE-SIN;W2F-010)

(61) "Change is necessary but *it must be* evolutionary, not revolutionary," he
      said. (ICE-SIN:W2C-017)

The tagset therefore provided a mid-level type of categorisation between the
broad categorisation according to lexical aspect and the fine coding for individual verbs. As mentioned above, it therefore not only allowed for a more
fine-grained analysis of the semantics of the verbs but also helped to group
the verbs into larger categories, because the coding according to individual
verbs showed that there were only a few verbs that occurred more often, while
the majority of verbs only occurred a few times in the corpus (cf. the classical 'A-curve pattern', Kretzschmar 2002, 102). The different types therefore only
had very few tokens in most of the cases, which made it difficult to analyse
emerging patterns without subsuming them in broader categories. The same
problem occurs for some categories in the analysis based on the USAS tagset
(cf. Table 22 in the appendices, cf. the discussion of the findings from the multivariate analysis in Chapter 9).

     In order to be able to account for regional variation, I first coded the tokens
of *must, have to, have got to*, and *need to* for the varieties BrE, AmE, HKE, IndE,
and SgE. Following that, I also coded the tokens according to mode, which is
another important factor for the alternation between modal and semi-modal
verbs and also for the use of epistemic *must* vs. root *must*. Semi-modal verbs
are more often used in spoken language than in written language, and 'colloquialisation' has therefore been proposed as an explanation for the rise of
semi-modal verbs in BrE and AmE (cf. Leech 2004b, 75). Epistemic *must* is also
more common in spoken language than in written language (cf. Coates 1983,
48). Within spoken and written mode, differences according to text type can be
observed, with the text type private dialogue (S1A) at the informal end and academic writing (W2A) at the formal end of the formality cline. The use of modal
and semi-modal verbs differs strongly according to text type. Biber finds the
highest frequency of semi-modal verbs in conversation, followed by fiction,
news, and academic prose (cf. Biber 2004, 191). Biber et al. show that the use
of epistemic *must* also varies according to register (cf. Biber et al. 1999, 494).
Epistemic *must* is more often used than root *must* in conversations, while this
pattern is reversed in academic prose (cf. Biber et al. 1999, 494). Coates finds
a similar pattern with a higher frequency of epistemic *must* than root *must*
in informal spoken language, while root *must* is consistently more frequently
used in formal spoken language, language written to be spoken, and written
language (cf. Coates 1983, 48). As stated above, the ICE text types differ in their
degree of formality. Fuchs and Gut propose a classification of the ICE text
types according to formality, which can be seen in Table 7. Their classification

is based on intuition and not on the analysis of linguistic features in the different categories, "since it has not yet been established which linguistic features correlate with formality in New Englishes" (Fuchs & Gut 2015, 378).

Huber uses five criteria to distinguish written text types of ICE-Ghana (ICE-GH) according to their formality:

> (1) the setting of text production and consumption, (2) the technical circumstances of text production such as time pressure during composition or publication status, (3) the educational level of the composer, (4) the educational level of the addressee and (5) the closeness to spoken language.
>
> HUBER 2014, 98

He groups social letters (W1B), press reports (W2C), and novels (W2F) under the category 'least formal', non-academic writing (W2B) and administrative writing (W2D) under the category 'more formal', and examination scripts (W1A) and academic writing (W2A) under the category 'most formal'. Huber classifies only the written text types of ICE-GH and uses a three-point scale, while Fuchs and Gut classify written and spoken text types of ICE-Nigeria (ICE-NIG) and use a five-point scale. This makes it somewhat difficult to compare the two classifications

TABLE 7 Classification of ICE categories according to formality (adapted from Fuchs & Gut 2015, 378)

Formality index	Text type
1	Face-to-face conversations (S1A), phone calls (S1A), social letters (W1B)
2	Broadcast interviews (S1B), non-academic writing (W2B), skills and hobbies (W2D)
3	Non-broadcast talks (S2B), broadcast talks (S2B), broadcast discussions (S1B), spontaneous commentaries (S2A), classroom lessons (S1B), parliamentary debates (S1B), unscripted speeches (S2A), press editorials (W2E), novels and short stories (W2F)
4	Broadcast news (S2B), business transactions (S1B), business letters (W1B), press news reports (W2C)
5	Academic writing (W2A), administrative writing (W2D), student essays (W1A), examination scripts (W1A)

but some basic differences in the relative ordering of the written text types can be identified nonetheless. Huber's categorisation differs from Fuchs and Gut's categorisation in that he assigns less formality to press reports (W2C), novels (W2F), and administrative writing (W2D) but more formality to non-academic writing (W2B). Both categorisations have in common that they classify social letters (W1B) as one of the most informal text types, while they rank academic writing (W2A) and examinations scripts (W1A) highest in degree of formality.

While Fuchs and Gut's classification is based on intuition and Huber's criteria for the classification are largely based on language-external factors, Xiao calculates the frequency of 141 linguistic features that "are functionally related and relevant to language variation research" (Xiao 2009, 424) to identify differences between the text types represented in ICE. He applies a refined version of the multidimensional analysis, which was first developed in Biber (1988) to the five ICE corpora ICE-GB, ICE-HK, ICE-IND, ICE-PHI, and ICE-SIN. Based on the co-occurrence of linguistic features, descriptive factor groups are identified along which the text types in ICE vary. One of these factors is 'interactive casual discourse vs. informative elaborate discourse' (cf. Xiao 2009, 429). Linguistic features that are typical of interactive discourse such as the discourse markers *ah* or *bravo* or boosters are loaded positively on this factor as well as more casual features such as contracted forms or *that*-deletion (cf. Xiao 2009, 429). Linguistic features that are typical of informative elaborate discourse are negatively loaded on this factor (cf. Xiao 2009, 429). Linguistic features associated with informative discourse are nominalisations or the attributive use of adjectives (cf. Xiao 2009, 429). The passive is an example of a linguistic feature that is more often used in elaborate style than in casual style (cf. Xiao 2009, 429). Factor 1 "provides an empirically valid formality scale with the positions of the individual genres established on the basis of a large set of linguistic features" (Bernaisch 2015, 95). Xiao shows that the 12 ICE registers differ according to Factor 1, i.e. whether they are interactive and casual or informative and elaborate. Private conversations are the most interactive and casual, whereas academic writing is the most informative and elaborate. This supports Fuchs and Gut's classification, who assign a formality index of 1 (least formal) to private conversations and a formality index of 5 (most formal) to academic writing. Xiao's analysis also ties in with Huber's classification of academic writing among the most formal text types in written ICE. Xiao's analysis shows that spoken text types are generally more interactive and less elaborate than written text types, except for creative writing and scripted monologues (cf. Xiao 2009, 436), as can be seen in Figure 23.

Basically, five groups can be found from most interactive casual discourse to most informative elaborate discourse: (1) private dialogue (S1A), (2) public dialogue (S1B), creative writing (W2F), and unscripted monologue (S2A),

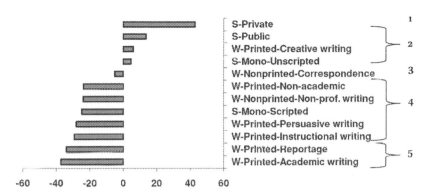

FIGURE 23   The 12 ICE registers according to Factor 1 based on several ICE corpora
(from Xiao 2009, 436, © 2009 The Author(s). Journal compilation
© 2009 Blackwell Publishing Ltd.)

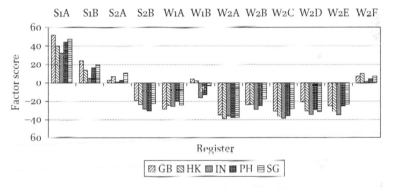

FIGURE 24   The 12 ICE registers according to Factor 1 in different ICE corpora
(from Xiao 2009, 442, © 2009 The Author(s). Journal compilation
© 2009 Blackwell Publishing Ltd.)

(3) correspondence (W1B), (4) non-academic writing (W2B), non-professional writing (W1A), scripted monologues (S2B), persuasive writing (W2E), and instructional writing (W2D), and (5) reportage (W2C) and academic writing (W2A). Again, we can see that private dialogues and printed academic writing form the end points of the cline. The analysis also shows that creative writing patterns closely with spoken text types, as was expected due to the representation of dialogues in this genre, which leads to a more widespread use of linguistic features associated with interactive discourse. Scripted monologues instead pattern with the written text types non-academic and non-professional writing, which is also in line with their composition, i.e. written to be spoken. The same five groups can be found if the analysis is conducted separately in the ICE corpora, as can be seen in Figure 24. What is remarkable

here is that ICE-IND is less interactive and more elaborate in almost all registers (cf. also the discussion about the comparability of ICE-IND with the other corpora in Section 4.1).

As can be seen in Figure 24, Xiao (2009) analyses the 'broad' text categories of ICE, while Fuchs and Gut (2015) also account for variation within these broad text categories, as for example in the text category correspondence (W1B), which includes social letters but also business letters. They give social letters a formality index of 1 while assigning a formality index of 4 to business letters.

Bernaisch also draws attention to differences within this text category and finds a markedly different pattern in ICE-IND compared to ICE-GB (cf. Bernaisch 2015, 99–100). He analyses the frequency of 21 lexical formality markers (e.g. *above mentioned, hence, regarding*) in ICE-GB, ICE-IND, and ICE-SL (cf. Bernaisch 2015, 93). He shows that ICE-GB has a considerably higher frequency of formality markers in business letters than in social letters. However, ICE-IND shows an almost equal distribution of formality markers in business letters and social letters, so that social letters contain more formality markers than would be expected from the distribution found in ICE-GB (cf. Bernaisch 2015, 100). The higher formality of social letters is also reflected in Figure 24, where ICE-IND shows the highest negative factor score in the category correspondence (W1B). The studies show that there is strong intravarietal variation but also intervarietal variation in terms of the formality of the text types.

As the frequency of epistemic *must* and of modal and semi-modal verbs are known to vary according to formality, the tokens of *must, have to, have got to,* and *need to* were coded according to text type. The coding procedure included three levels with increasingly fine-grained coding (cf. the three levels in Table 2). The most coarse-grained text categorisation divided the texts in ICE into four categories: (1) Dialogue (S1), (2) Monologue (S2), (3) Non-printed (W1), and (4) Printed (W2), whereby dialogues represent the most informal text type and printed texts the most formal text type. The second coding, a mid-level categorisation of the text types, divided the texts into 12 categories, with private conversations representing the most informal language and academic writing the most formal language. These 12 categories were then further divided into 32 text types, for example, dividing the mid-level category correspondence (W1B) into social letters and business letters. The text types of ICE were taken as the basis for coding rather than an a priori classification according to formality, to avoid overlooking intervarietal differences according to text type. As the comparison between Fuchs and Gut's (2015) and Huber's (2014) classification of the text types in ICE according to formality shows, there is no generally accepted classification. The classification of some text types differs quite strongly. Press

reports (W2C) are a case in point, ranking highly in formality in Fuchs and
Gut's (2015) but among the least formal text types in Huber's (2014) classification (cf. also the discussion of this text type in the alternation between *must*
and *have to* in Section 9.3). The difference in the classifications can probably
be traced back to differences in the method adopted. Xiao's (2009) method
is arguably the most sophisticated method to analyse text type differences in
ICE and will therefore be used as the basis for the interpretation of variation
in terms of text type. In line with his analysis, I would therefore regard press
news reports as a more formal text type. Xiao (2009) did not include SBC in his
MDA, which I used as a substitute for the missing spoken part of ICE-USA. Xiao
and McEnery (2005) use MDA to analyse differences between three genres:
conversation, speech, and academic prose based on SBC, the *Corpus of Pro-
fessional Spoken American English* (CPSA), and the *Freiburg BROWN Corpus of
American English* (FROWN) respectively. They use data from SBC for the genre
'conversation' and 'speech' (and additionally 12 texts from CPSA for the genre
'speech') and the category J from FROWN for the genre 'academic prose'. They
show that conversation has a high value for the factor 'Involved vs. informational' (i.e. interactive vs. informational above), followed by the genre 'speech'
and 'academic prose' as less involved and more informational. These findings
indicate that the conversations in SBC show similar linguistic features to the
dialogues in ICE (S1), while the speeches can be regarded as equivalents to the
texts in the monologue section in ICE (S2). In order to be able to account for
text type differences in SBC, I coded the text files in SBC on the basis of the
text categories found in ICE. I used the content of the files as a guide to decide
whether the dialogues are private or public and whether the monologues are
unscripted or scripted.

Due to the virtual absence of diachronic corpora, "the working environment
for diachronic corpus-linguistics is still relatively poor [in New Englishes]"
(Mair 2015a, 140). Currently, there are no diachronic corpora available for HKE,
IndE, and SgE, but they are in the making (cf. Section 11.1.1). The idea of a new
generation of ICE corpora ('ICE 2.0') to add a historical dimension to the ICE
project is currently also being discussed in the ICE community (for example,
in the 2015 workshop "The future of the International Corpus of English" at
ICAME 36 (*International Computer Archive of Modern and Medieval English*)).
The current lack of diachronic corpora makes real-time studies of language
change impossible, but the metadata that are available for some of the ICE
corpora provide the possibility to analyse variation across different age groups
in order to construct an apparent-time scenario, a method developed in sociolinguistics (cf. Chapter 8; cf. Section 11.2 for the interface between corpus
linguistics and sociolinguistics). To this end, I coded the age of the speaker for

every token of *must, have to, have got to,* and *need to* in the spoken section of
ICE-HK, ICE-IND*, ICE-GB,[14] and of SBC. As mentioned above, the metadata
for ICE-SIN are not available, which is why it was not possible to analyse sociolinguistic variation according to age, gender, and mother tongue in SgE. ICE-
HK, ICE-IND*, ICE-GB, and SBC provide information about the speakers but
are differently coded according to age. While ICE-HK differentiates between
ten age groups (17–20, 21–25, 26–30, 31–35, 36–40, 41–45, 56–50, 51–55, 56–60,
60+), ICE-IND* differentiates between eight age groups (18–25, 26–33, 34–41,
42–49, 50+, 60+, 70+, 80+), ICE-GB differentiates between four age groups
(18–25, 26–45, 46–65, 66+), and SBC does not have predefined age groups but
provides the exact age for each speaker. The age groups therefore differ across
the corpora. This makes it difficult to directly compare developments across
varieties but still makes it possible to account for internal developments in the
variety and to identify broad tendencies across varieties. In the case of ICE-
IND, the age groups sometimes also vary within the corpus, and some speakers
were not assigned to the respective age groups. I recoded those speakers and
aligned them with five large age groups (including the less well represented
age groups 60+, 70+, and 80+ in the age group 50+) in order to avoid smaller
overlapping categories.

    The distribution of variants according to age may show different patterns.
With stable variables, a curvilinear pattern is typical, characterised by a widespread use of non-standard forms in younger and older speakers and limited
use of non-standard forms in middle-age groups (cf. Downes 2005, 224). This
pattern has usually been explained by differences in the societal pressure to
conform to the standard between different age groups. As the middle-aged
group is involved in the workforce, pressures to conform to standard language
are arguably greatest here, which is why we can see the pattern of a 'middle-
aged trough'. With variables that undergo language change, we can identify
a different pattern. Here, the proportion of innovative variants decreases
with increasing age, while the proportion of conservative variants increases
with age.

    Analysing the distribution of *must, have to, have got to,* and *need to* ac-
cording to age can help us to identify ongoing language change. We can investigate for example whether the core modal *must* is also decreasing in ESL

---

14   The information about the age of the speakers is not directly retrievable from a separate
      metafile in ICE-GB but integrated in ICECUP, which only allows subsetting specific data-
      sets according to social parameters. I therefore aligned the concordances with speaker
      information on the basis of the subsets of the concordances according to the four age
      categories and the two gender categories.

varieties or whether the semi-modal verb *have to* is increasing. Furthermore, we can investigate changes in the use of *must* in terms of its two senses. So, while *must* decreased in frequency in ENL varieties in real time from 1960 to 1990 in both its deontic and epistemic senses (cf. Leech et al. 2009, 88), the proportion of epistemic *must* was on the rise from 1960 to 1990 from 25% to 34% in written BrE (cf. Leech et al. 2009, 285 based in Leech 2003, 233). Leech's findings are based on the coding of every third example of *must* in FLOB and LOB (cf. Leech 2003, 232). Smith's analysis of all tokens in LOB and FLOB supports the rise in the proportion of epistemic *must* from 26% to 32% (cf. Smith 2003, 257). My analysis of frequency changes in the senses of *must* shows that the proportion of epistemic *must* remained stable at 24% between 1900–1949 and 1950–1999 in the British component of AR-CHER, although the frequency of *must* decreased overall in this period. Findings based on spoken data indicate that epistemic *must* is generally more common in spoken language, as was mentioned above and that the rise of epistemic *must* is stronger here. Leech et al. find a rise in the proportion of epistemic *must* from 36% to 44% on the basis of DSEU (1960s) and DICE (1990s) (Leech et al. 2009, 285). Leech also finds a strong rise from 40% to 49% from SEU-mini-sp (1960) to ICE-GB-mini-sp (1990) (cf. Leech 2003, 233). These findings suggest that *must* is undergoing language change; its overall frequency is declining, while the proportion of its epistemic use is increasing. Conversely, the semi-modal verb *have to*, which is predominantly used in its deontic sense, is rising in frequency in BrE and AmE (cf. Krug 2000, 79; Leech 2003, 229; Smith 2003, 248–249; Leech et al. 2009, 97–99; Close & Aarts 2010, 175; cf. also Section 2.1). An apparent-time scenario can shed light on possible similar developments in ESL varieties.

As gender is another important social dimension in language variation and change, I coded the tokens of *must*, *have to*, *have got to*, and *need to* according to the gender of the speaker. As mentioned earlier, I prefer the term 'gender', although the information in the metadata is probably based on the self-report about the speakers' biological sex or on the assignment of gender on the basis of their sex by the corpus compilers rather than on their socially constructed and perceived masculinity or femininity (cf. also Labov 2001, 263). Equating biological sex with socially constructed gender is problematic for two reasons. First, it presupposes the construction of a female identity by females clearly demarcated from a male identity constructed by male speakers. Second, the assignment of a person to a gender category on the basis of the biological sex they are born with underestimates the agency of the speaker in the construction of their gender identity (cf. Eckert 1996 for the employment of pronunciation differences in the active construction of a female identity, cf. Section

11.2.2 for avenues for corpus-based sociolinguistic research of the third wave).[15] However, the focus of this study is not on the construction of gender in specific communities of practice with an ethnographic approach, but the analysis of language variation and change in the use of modal and semi-modal verbs of obligation and necessity in different regional varieties of English with corpus data. This is why broad gender patterns that have been identified in sociolinguistic studies of the first wave are of prime interest because they can give us evidence about whether the variable is stable or changing. Furthermore, as the two genders differ with regard to their use of innovative variants in different types of language change, the distribution of variants according to gender can give us information about the type of language change involved. Gender patterns may even point to differences in the establishment of a new linguistic form, as gender patterns are supposed to neutralise once a change has been widely accepted by the community (cf. Labov 2001, 309; cf. also discussion in Section 9.4). Labov identifies three patterns of language variation according to gender:

(1) For stable sociolinguistic variables, women show a lower rate of stigmatized variants and a higher rate of prestige variants than men.

LABOV 2001, 266

(2) In linguistic change from above, women adopt prestige forms at a higher rate than men.

LABOV 2001, 274

(3) In linguistic change from below, women use higher frequencies of innovative forms than men do.

LABOV 2001, 292

The difference in female behaviour between principles (1) and (2) as opposed to principle (3) led to the formulation of the 'gender paradox': "Women conform more closely than men to sociolinguistic norms that are overtly prescribed, but conform less than men when they are not" (Labov 2001, 293). If the distribution of the variants according to age suggests ongoing language change, the distribution of gender can therefore give us evidence about the type of change. As changes in the use of the modal and semi-modal verbs most likely run below the level of consciousness, we would expect female speakers

---

15   In studies which analyse variables that are actively used by speakers to express their gender identity, it would therefore make sense to use gender as the dependent variable in multivariate analyses.

to lead the rise of innovative *have to* in a change from below, at least in 'Western' societies. In varieties where the change is well established, we would expect a neutralisation of the gender pattern over time. However, it needs to be tested whether the gender patterns that have been formulated on the basis of varieties of English that emerged in 'Western' contexts can be transferred to varieties that have developed in different cultural contexts. It may well be that the behaviour of male and female speakers in linguistic change is mediated by their gender roles in society (cf. Section 8.3). If females only have restricted access to education, it follows that they also have restricted access to the emerging standard of English, which may be the prerequisite for acting as linguistic innovators in these societies.

Another social dimension that is relevant to the study of language variation and change in ESL varieties is, of course, the first language of the speakers. I therefore coded the tokens of *must, have to, have got to*, and *need to* in ICE-HK and ICE-IND* according to the mother tongue(s) of the speaker. The speakers in ICE-HK were almost exclusively L1 speakers of Cantonese, except for some English speakers that were not coded as extra-corpus material. This reflects the language situation in Hong Kong quite well. The language situation in India is marked by a high number of different languages (as detailed in Section 3.2.2), the majority of which come from the Indo-Aryan language family and the Dravidian language family. This linguistic diversity in India makes it difficult to pinpoint possible sources of substrate influence, which is why I coded the tokens according to the L1s of the speakers and also according to the language family in order to account for possible typological differences in the varieties spoken by speakers of languages that belong to different language families.

Furthermore, I also coded my data according to the speaker by assigning a personalised speaker ID (e.g. S1A-001A) to each speaker to be able to account for idiolectal variation. I additionally recorded each verb that followed the tokens of the modal and semi-modal verbs. The independent variables 'speaker' and 'verb' are random effects, "i.e. variables whose levels in the study do not cover all possible levels in the population" (Gries 2013, 333). As I had a high number of different speakers and different verbs in my dataset, it is, however, unlikely that individual outliers will affect the overall results, at least in the case of the major variants *must* and *have to*. As for minor variants such as *have got to* in ICE-HK, idiosyncratic language use may skew the findings (cf. the apparent-time study for HKE in Section 8.3). To summarise, I coded the dependent variable according to the following independent variables.

Language-internal:
- function (0 position) (epistemic vs. root)
- subject (L1 position)

- grammatical person (1st, 2nd, 3rd)
- subject reference (generic, non-generic)
- verb (R1 position)
  - verb (*go*, *say*, etc.)
  - verb semantics (different levels of fine-graining: semantics1, semantics2, semantics3)

Language-external

- variety (ICE-GB, ICE-USA*, ICE-HK, ICE-IND*, ICE-SIN)
- mode (spoken vs. written)
- text type (different levels of fine-graining: type1, type2, type3)
- age of the speaker (in different age categories)
- gender of the speaker (female vs. male)
- L1 of the speaker (Hindi, Marathi, Kannada, etc.)
- language family of L1 (Indo-Aryan, Dravidian, Tibeto-Burman, Austro-Asiatic)
- speaker

4.3.2 *Multivariate Analysis*

Variationist sociolinguistics adopted logistic regression early on as the statistical model behind programmes such as VARBRUL and GoldVarb (cf. Cedergren & Sankoff 1974). The use of logistic regression is not only common among sociolinguists nowadays but has also spread to other areas of study (cf. Speelman 2014, 488). Today an increasing number of researchers are using major statistical packages such as R or SPSS when they want to perform a logistic regression, because they offer more flexibility than VARBRUL and GoldVarb (cf. also Johnson 2009).

Logistic regression is a statistical model for estimating the relationship between a categorical dependent variable and (continuous or categorical) independent variables. In the most basic type of a categorical variable, the variable can take on two values, e.g. success vs. failure, female vs. male, pregnant vs. not pregnant. This type of variable is called a binary variable. A logistic regression that estimates the probability of occurrence of one of two values based on one or more independent variables is called binary logistic regression. The frequency distribution of *must, have to, have got to*, and *need to* in Figure 26 in Chapter 5 indicates that the major competition in the domain of deontic modality is between the variants *must* and *have to*. Although *have got to* and *need to* also fall under the broad category of deontic modality, they are much more marginal variants of the variable strong deontic modality than *must* and *have to* (cf. discussion in Section 5.2.2). Due to the specialised uses of *have got to* and *need to*, it can be argued that the dependent variable has only two possible outcomes, i.e. *must* vs. *have to*. We can therefore use binary logistic regression to identify relevant independent variables (also: predictors, here: subject, age, gender) and their effect on the dependent variable.[16] The decision for a binary logistic regression is furthermore warranted because the method "is well suited to deal with the type of unbalanced datasets that are typical of Corpus Linguistics" (Speelman 2014, 487). The method can therefore deal with the overrepresentation of female speakers in the private dialogue section in ICE-HK, or the underrepresentation of female speakers in the public dialogue section of ICE-IND* (cf. Section 4.1.2). For my dataset, logistic regression can be used to estimate the probability of *must* as opposed to *have to* given the independent variables: subject, verb semantics, variety, text type, age of the speaker, and gender of the speaker. *Must* and *have to* are possible in all contexts although with different degrees of probability. This is why the dataset only includes tokens that can theoretically occur in variation. Knock-out contexts where the choice is categorical such as future forms, where *have to* is the only choice, are excluded from the dataset (cf. the envelope of variation in Section 4.3). Logistic regression can measure the effect of one independent variable on the dependent variable while at the same time controlling for effects of other independent variables (cf. Levshina, Geeraerts & Speelman 2014, 206). The independent variables that have an effect on the choice between *must* and *have to* were identified by a backward stepwise selection procedure based on the Akaike's Information Criterion (AIC):

> [T]he AIC [...] is one measure that relates the quality of a model to the number of predictors it contains [...]. If two models explain data equally well, then the model with fewer predictors will have a smaller AIC.
>
> GRIES 2013, 261

The AIC therefore guarantees that the most parsimonious model, the model that can account for variation with the fewest predictors, will be selected ('Occam's razor'). Logistic regression modelling will be discussed more fully in Chapter 9, where regression models for the alternation between *must* and *have to* will be presented and discussed.

4.4   Summary

This methodological chapter outlined the 'sociolinguistic corpus-based approach' adopted in this study, which was considered most effective in order

---

16   'Effect' is understood as a correlation between an independent variable and a dependent variable and does not necessarily entail a causal relationship.

to address not only regional variation in the use of the modal and semi-modal verbs of obligation and necessity but also variety-internal variation, which has been largely neglected in studies of ESL varieties so far. The ICE corpora were chosen as the database for the study because their rich metadata are particularly suitable for this approach (cf. also Section 11.1.1). The structural and social make-up of the ICE corpora were analysed more closely in Section 4.1 to gain a more profound understanding of the data sources at hand and to identify biases in the data that may affect comparability between the ICE corpora. In addition to the corpus data, the study also makes use of questionnaire data to integrate a speaker perspective on language use, which is why the design of the questionnaire was briefly introduced in Section 4.2. In addition to that, the chapter also outlined methodological considerations in the processes of extracting the dependent variable, coding of the independent variables, and modelling the impact of the latter on the former in terms of binary logistic regression in Section 4.3.

CHAPTER 5

Obligation and Necessity in ENL and ESL

This section introduces the frequency distribution findings for *must, have to, have got to*, and *need to*, and the distribution of their senses from the corpus-based study of the ENL varieties BrE and AmE and the ESL varieties HKE, IndE, and SgE.[1] Figure 25 shows the 'big picture', the distribution of all forms of *must, have to, have got to*, and *need to* in declarative affirmative sentences in the corpora ICE-GB, ICE-USA*, ICE-HK, ICE-IND*, and ICE-SIN without specifying their functions.

The frequency distribution first of all indicates that the ESL varieties are marked by a much higher frequency of modal and semi-modal verbs of obligation and necessity overall.[2] All forms taken together, the frequency of these verbs is about 1.5 times higher in the ESL varieties than in the ENL varieties. If we take a look at the frequency of all expressions of obligation and necessity according to variety, we can see that ICE-USA* has the lowest frequency overall, with an M-co of 138, followed by ICE-GB, with an M-co of 154, whereas the frequencies are much higher in ICE-IND*, ICE-SIN, and ICE-HK, with an

---

1 Cf. Terassa (2018) and Schröter (2018) for two studies that are based on the same selection of Asian ESL varieties. Terassa (2018) analyses morphological simplification processes, in particular the omission of past tense and plural marking as well as regularisation processes in the past tense marking of irregular verbs and the use of mass nouns as count nouns. She uses the smaller ICE and the bigger GloWbE corpus as her databases (cf. Section 11.1) and effectively enhances her corpus-based data with experimental data from a perception experiment. She convincingly discusses her findings not only with regard to the well-known dimensions of substrate influence and institutionalisation but also with regard to the way these interact with frequency effects. Schröter (2018) is a variationist study on null subjects in spoken IndE, HKE, and SgE based on the direct conversation section of the respective ICE corpora. She uses multivariate analyses to shed light on linguistic and extra-linguistic factors ('coreferential coordination', 'clause type', 'position', 'person', 'reference', 'switch reference', 'persistence', 'verb phrase', 'gender', 'age', 'language family') that condition subject pronoun realisation in these varieties in comparison to BrE. She discusses her findings in light of language contact by adopting a typological perspective on null subjects and in light of Nativisation in terms of Schneider's (2007) Dynamic Model.

2 Note that Balasubramanian's findings about the frequencies of modal and semi-modal verbs in BrE/AmE and IndE point in the opposite direction, with *must, have to*, and *have got to* being used 1.5 times more frequently in BrE/AmE than in IndE (cf. Balasubramanian 2009, 197). The differences between her findings and my findings may be related to the fact that her findings are based on data from the CCIE, which are more recent and different from the data of ICE-IND. The differences may point to ongoing changes in the modal domain, which will be discussed in more detail in Chapter 8 on the basis of apparent-time findings.

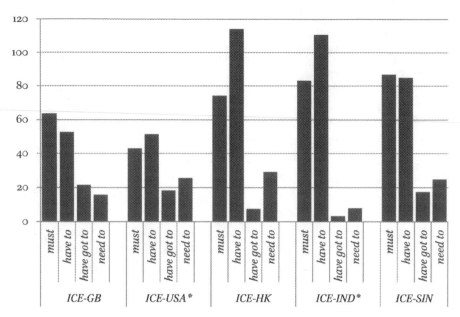

FIGURE 25   Modal and semi-modal verbs of obligation and necessity in ICE-GB, ICE-USA*,
ICE-HK, ICE-IND*, and ICE-SIN, normalised frequency per 100,000 words (cf.
Table 23 in the appendices).

M-co of 205, 214, and 225 respectively. Although the varieties pattern according
to their types (ENL vs. ESL), this does not mean that the groups are homogeneous. Each variety shows an individual profile with regard to the structure of
the field of strong deontic modality. Depending on the verb under analysis,
the frequencies show different relationships between the varieties. Within the
group of ESL varieties, the general tendency that can be observed is that ICE-
HK and ICE-IND* show a similar usage profile, while the profile of ICE-SIN
differs from the two ESL varieties in many respects. However, we can also find
cases where ICE-HK and ICE-SIN pattern more closely.

A closer look at the frequency of *have to* shows that it is used with an M-co
of 114 in ICE-HK, an M-co of 111 in ICE-IND*, and an M-co of 85 in ICE-SIN,
compared to an M-co of only 53 in ICE-GB and an M-co of 51 in ICE-USA*.
This means that *have to* is used more than twice as often in ICE-HK and ICE-
IND* than in ICE-USA* and is about 1.5 times more common in ICE-SIN than in
ICE-USA*. The frequency of *have to* in ICE-SIN places this variety between the
group of ENL and ESL varieties, with on M-co of 85 that is slightly above the
mean frequency of *have to*, at an M-co of 83.

The high frequency of the semi-modal *have to* in ICE-HK and ICE-IND* does
not preclude a high frequency of the core modal verb *must* in these varieties.

The core modal verb *must* is more often used in ICE-HK and ICE-IND*, with an M-co of 74 and 83 respectively compared to an M-co of 64 in ICE-GB and an M-co of 43 in ICE-USA*. The highest frequency of *must* can be found in ICE-SIN, with an M-co of 87. This means that *must* is more than twice as frequent in ICE-SIN as in ICE-USA* (the difference is significant at the p<0.0001 level, Log-likelihood test).

While ICE-SIN and ICE-USA* differ strongly with regard to the frequency of *must*, they behave alike in the frequency of *have got to*, with a frequency at an M-co of 18. However, SgE differs strongly from the other two ESL varieties in this regard because *have got to* is only rarely used in HKE and IndE, with an M-co of 8 in ICE-HK and an M-co of 3 in ICE-IND* respectively. The ENL variety BrE instead has the highest frequency of *have got to*, with an M-co of 22.

With regard to the semi-modal verb *need to*, we can identify a distinct pattern of use in ICE-IND*, which shows a very low frequency, with an M-co of 8 compared to the ENL varieties ICE-GB, with an M-co of 16 and ICE-USA*, with an M-co of 26, and the other ESL varieties, ICE-HK, with an M-co of 29, and ICE-SIN, with an M-co of 25. What is remarkable here is that ICE-HK and ICE-SIN even show a higher frequency of the semi-modal than ICE-GB, despite its rather recent emergence (cf. Section 6.1.4).

The frequency distribution of the forms reveals that the structure of the field of strong deontic obligation in the ESL varieties differs strongly from that of BrE, which is contrary to expectation, given that the New Englishes developed on the basis of a BrE historical input variety (cf. Section 6.1.5 for the reconstruction of the state of the historical input variety). Generally, ESL varieties are marked by a much higher frequency of all modal and semi-modal verbs of strong obligation than the ENL varieties. It could be argued that differences in verb complementation patterns may account for differences in the use of modal and semi-modal verbs between ENL and ESL varieties (cf. also Leech 2013, 110). In ENL varieties, finite constructions are being gradually replaced by infinitive constructions (cf. Leech 2013, 110), while some observations in ESL varieties point to the opposite direction, i.e. towards the 'fossilisation' of *that*-complements (cf. Selinker 1972, 216). This would imply that there are more contexts in ESL varieties in which modal and semi-modal verbs can be used, e.g. *There is a need that I must have all the time a combination* [...] (ICE-IND*:S2A-042). Examples like this, where *must* could be replaced by an infinitive construction, are however rare in ICE-IND*. Furthermore, a quantitative analysis did not confirm the hypothesis that New Englishes are marked by a more widespread use of finite verb complementation (cf. Schneider 2012, 80). This is why I will search for other reasons behind the higher frequency of *must* and *have to* in the ESL varieties. Despite the considerably higher frequency in

ESL varieties, they show similar rankings to ENL varieties, with *must* and *have to* among the more frequent verbs and *have got to* and *need to* among the less frequent verbs. With regard to the relationship between *must* and *have to*, ICE-USA*, ICE-HK, and ICE-IND* show a higher frequency of *have to* than *must*, while the reverse distribution can be found in ICE-GB and ICE-SIN, where *must* is used with a higher frequency than *have to*. In order to understand the frequency distribution of these forms better, it is necessary to analyse the functions fulfilled by these forms in order to account for underlying regional variation in the encoding of epistemic and root modalities (cf. Section 1.2).

5.1   Regional Variation in Epistemic Modality

Figure 26 shows the regional distribution of the modal and semi-modal verbs according to their functions. Forms with a root reading are marked dark grey, forms with an epistemic reading are marked grey, and unclear cases are marked light grey. What becomes immediately obvious is that the semi-modal verbs *have to*, *have got to*, and *need to* rarely function as markers of epistemic modality in any of the varieties. The core modal verb *must* is the verb that is most often used in epistemic function in all varieties of English (cf. also Mair

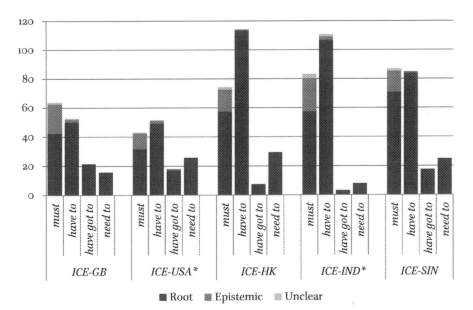

FIGURE 26   Modal and semi-modal verbs of obligation and necessity and their senses in
               ICE-GB, ICE-USA*, ICE-HK, ICE-IND*, and ICE-SIN, normalised frequency
               per 100,000 words (cf. Table 24 in the appendices).

2006, 105; Depraetere & Verhulst 2008, 17; Close & Aarts 2010, 176), although with strong differences in the frequency of use. But even for *must*, the deontic function dominates.

The highest frequency of epistemic *must* can be found in ICE-IND*, with an M-co of 23, closely followed by ICE-GB, with an M-co of 20. ICE-HK and ICE-SIN roughly have the same frequency, with an M-co of 15 and 14 respectively. The lowest frequency of epistemic *must* was found in ICE-USA*, with an M-co of 11. The low frequency of epistemic *must* in ICE-USA* is probably a result of differences in the structure of ICE-USA* compared to the other ICE corpora, as it only contains 249,000 words of spoken language and 400,000 words of written language, which leads to a share of 40% spoken language. The ICE corpora show exactly the reverse composition; with 60% spoken language (cf. Section 4.1 for the design of the ICE corpora). The difference in the distribution of epistemic *must* between ICE-USA* and the ICE corpora therefore points to register differences in the use of epistemic *must*, as also noted by Biber et al., who show a predominance of epistemic *must* in conversation, but a preponderance of root *must* in academic prose (cf. Biber et al. 1999, 494). The distribution of epistemic *must* in the spoken corpora can be seen in Figure 27.

Figure 27 shows that BrE uses epistemic *must* with an M-co of 22. In spoken AmE, the frequency of epistemic *must* is lower than that found in BrE, with

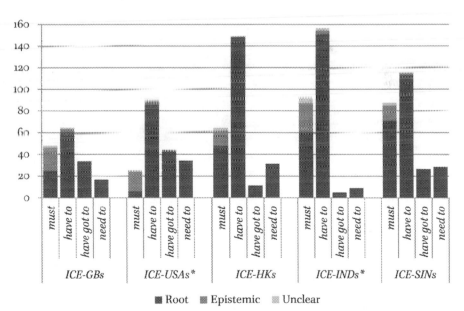

FIGURE 27 Modal and semi-modal verbs of obligation and necessity and their senses in the spoken section of ICE-GB, ICE-USA*, ICE-HK, ICE-IND*, and ICE-SIN, normalised frequency per 100,000 words (cf. Table 25 in the appendices).

an M-co of 18. This also has do with the fact that *must* is generally more rarely used in spoken AmE than in spoken BrE. However, this difference is probably even more pronounced because of comparability issues between ICE-GB and ICE-USA* (SBC). SBC is primarily composed of informal private dialogues, which disfavour the use of the modal verb *must*.

If we disregard the frequency of epistemic *must* in ICE-USA* for the moment and focus on the frequencies found in ICE-GB and the three L2 corpora, we can see that ICE-IND* has the highest frequency of epistemic *must*, with an M-co of 26. In ICE-HK and ICE-SIN, epistemic *must* is much more rarely used at an M-co of 14. This means that we can identify two groups of varieties with regard to the frequency of epistemic *must* in spoken language (disregarding ICE-USA* for now). The first group includes ICE-GB and ICE-IND*, which use epistemic *must* with a frequency of an M-co of 22 or higher. The second group includes ICE-HK and ICE-SIN, which use epistemic *must* with a frequency of an M-co of 14. This grouping is confirmed by Log-likelihood tests, which show that ICE-GB and ICE-IND* do not behave significantly differently to each other but are significantly different to ICE-HK and ICE-SIN. ICE-HK and ICE-SIN, in turn, pattern alike (cf. Calle-Martín & Jesús 2017, 98 for a similar pattern in zero marking of verbs with third person singular subjects). The grouping of the corpora is visualised in Figure 28.

If we now take a look at the distributions of *must* according to root and epistemic modalities, we can see that all varieties show a profile that is markedly different from the other varieties (cf. Figure 29). ICE-USA* behaves markedly differently to all the other corpora under analysis, with a comparatively large proportion of epistemic *must* (75%). The distribution found in ICE-USA*, with a share of epistemic uses at 75% is almost the mirror image of the distribution found in ICE-HK, where root *must* accounts for 77% of the uses of *must* (cf. Figure 29). The strong divergence of ICE-USA* is probably again a result of differences in the corpus structure between the spoken part of this corpus and the spoken components of ICE. As mentioned in Section 4.1, the spoken component of ICE-USA*, SBC, differs considerably from the spoken components

FIGURE 28   The patterning of the spoken corpora with regard to the frequency of epistemic
             must.

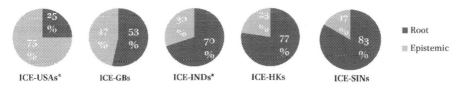

FIGURE 29   The proportion of epistemic *must* in ICE-USAS*, ICE-GBS, ICE-INDS*, ICE-HKS, and ICE-SINS, excluding unclear cases.

of ICE in that it is primarily composed of private conversations, a register that is known to favour the use of epistemic *must* (cf. Biber et al. 1999, 494). The distribution also indicates that *must* has decreased most strongly in its root sense in AmE (cf. Leech et al. 2009, 88–89). While the spoken component of ICE-USA* is marked by a predominance of epistemic *must*, ICE-GB, ICE-IND*, ICE-HK, and ICE-SIN all show a prevalence of deontic *must*, although the share of deontic *must* varies markedly between these varieties (cf. Figure 29). In this group, ICE-GB has the lowest share of deontic *must*, which means in turn that it has the highest share of epistemic *must*, at 47%. In ICE-SIN, at the other end of the scale, the share of epistemic *must* is lowest at 17%. ICE-IND* and ICE-HK lie between these two extremes, with a proportion of epistemic *must* of 30% and 23% respectively

The distributions of all varieties are markedly different to each other at the $p<0.05$ level when tested by pairwise chi-square tests. With regard to the grouping of varieties in terms of their frequencies of epistemic *must* in Figure 28, it can be seen that those varieties that have a higher frequency of epistemic *must*, BrE and IndE, are characterised by a larger share of epistemic *must*, while those varieties with a lower frequency of epistemic *must*, HKE and SgE, have a smaller share of epistemic *must*. ICE-HK and ICE-SIN show a strong deontic bias of *must*, whereas ICE-IND* has a larger share of epistemic *must* than ICE-SIN, even though this share is not as large as the shares found in ICE-GB or even ICE-USA*. If we adopt a threshold of $p<0.0001$, we can see that the differences between ICE-IND* and ICE-HK, and ICE-HK and ICE-SIN are not significant. This might point to the fact that a lower share of epistemic *must* is characteristic of L2 varieties (cf. Biewer 2011, 26).

Although epistemic *have to* is only infrequently used to express epistemic modality, its frequency distribution reveals a similar pattern to that found for the frequency of epistemic *must*, which may point to more general differences in the encoding of epistemic modality between the varieties. ICE-USA* shows the highest frequency of epistemic *have to*, with an M-co of 5. This finding squares well with Coates's observations that epistemic *have to* "is still felt to be an Americanism" (Coates 1983, 57). The second-highest frequencies of epistemic *have to* can be found in ICE-IND* and ICE-GB, with an M-co of 3 in both varieties. In ICE-HK and ICE-SIN instead, epistemic *have to* is used much more rarely than in the other varieties, with an M-co of 1 and 2 respectively. This shows again that ICE-IND* patterns more closely with ICE-GB in the encoding of epistemic modality, while ICE-HK and ICE-SIN show a similar usage profile, which differs more strongly from ICE-GB. With regard to epistemic *have got to*, we can observe that it is almost non-existent in all varieties except for spoken AmE, though the frequency is also not particularly high here, with an M-co of 2.

If Schneider's (2007) model is applied to these findings (cf. Section 3.2), we can see that ICE-HK does not pattern as expected. As HKE is in an earlier stage of Schneider's model than IndE and SgE, we would expect it to pattern more closely with BrE, the exonormative model for HKE. Instead it shows a similar frequency of epistemic *must* to SgE. SgE behaves as expected by Schneider's (2007) model by showing a low frequency of epistemic *must* and a strong deontic bias that could be an indicator of the development of an internal norm in this variety.[3] Schneider's (2007) model also seems to have explanatory value for the fact that there is no significant difference between the distributions of *must* in ICE-IND* and ICE-HK at the $p<0.0001$ level. Both varieties are in the third stage of the model, called 'Nativisation', although HKE is at the beginning of the stage, while IndE is approaching the end (cf. Sections 3.2.1 and 3.2.2). Although the stage of the varieties in Schneider's (2007) model may explain part of the findings, it does not explain why HKE and SgE pattern alike in terms of the frequency of epistemic *must*, two varieties at different stages in the model. This shows that there is no simple explanation for the differences in the encoding of epistemic modality between ICE-GB and ICE-IND*, and ICE-HK and ICE-SIN. This is why other factors have to be analysed that may help to explain the regional variation found in the distribution of the functions of *must*. Potential sources for this regional variation may be the historical state of the superstrate variety BrE or the structure of the substrate languages, whose analysis seems especially promising, given the similarities identified between HKE and SgE, two varieties with a Sinitic substrate. These potential sources of present-day variability will be discussed in more detail in Sections 6.1 and 6.2.

If we now compare the frequency of epistemic *must* and its proportion of all instances of *must* in spoken and written language (cf. Figure 27 and Figure 30), we can see that the frequency of epistemic *must* in ICE-GB is slightly lower in written language than in spoken language, with an M-co of 19 compared to an

---

3 Note, however, that the development of an internal norm does not necessarily mean divergence from ENL norms (cf. also the findings on the preposition *into* in ENL, ESL, and EFL varieties of English by Edwards & Laporte 2015).

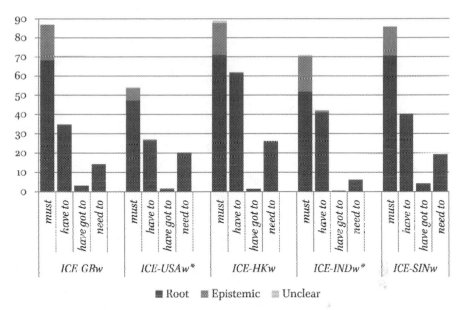

FIGURE 30   Modal and semi-modal verbs of obligation and necessity and their senses in the
written sections of ICE-GB, ICE-USA*, ICE-HK, ICE IND*, and ICE-SIN, normalised frequency per 100,000 words (cf. Table 26 in the appendices).

M-co of 22. As *must* is generally more often used in written language than in spoken language, the proportions of epistemic *must* differ strongly according to mode, with 21% in written language and 47% in spoken language. Similar tendencies can be found in AmE, but as the decline of *must* is more advanced in this variety, the frequency in spoken language is lower than that of ICE-GB. In the spoken component of ICE-USA*, epistemic *must* is more than twice as often used than in the written component of ICE-USA*, with an M-co of 18 compared to an M-co of 7. In terms of the proportions of epistemic *must*, the difference between spoken and written language is more pronounced in AmE, with a proportion of 75% in the spoken part of ICE-USA* compared to a mere 12% in the written part of ICE-USA*. The findings for AmE therefore also clearly indicate that epistemic *must* is a feature of spoken language in ENL varieties.

If we now turn to the frequencies of epistemic *must* in the ESL varieties, we can see that epistemic *must* is actually slightly less frequently used in spoken HKE, with an M-co of 14 compared to an M-co of 17 in written HKE. The difference in the proportion of epistemic *must* between written language and spoken language is less pronounced in HKE than in BrE and AmE, with 19% in written language compared to 23% in spoken language. In ICE-IND*, we can observe a similar distribution to ICE-GB, with an M-co of 26 in spoken language compared to an M-co of 19 in written language. In terms of the proportions, we can observe a slightly higher share of epistemic *must* in the spoken section, with a proportion of 30% compared to 26% in written language. In ICE-SIN, we find almost the same frequencies of epistemic *must* in the spoken and written section, with an M-co of 14 in the spoken part and an M-co of 15 in the written section of ICE-SIN. The proportions of epistemic *must* are also strikingly similar, with a share of 17% and 18% in spoken and written language respectively. These findings indicate that ICE-HK and ICE-SIN display a deontic bias of *must*, irrespective of mode, while this deontic bias cannot be attested for ICE-IND* in either spoken or written language.

5.2   Regional Variation in Root Modality

Striking regional variation can be found in the encoding of both epistemic and root modality. The frequency of root *must, have to, have got to,* and *need to* is roughly 1.5 times higher in ESL varieties than in ENL varieties, as we have seen in Figure 26.

5.2.1   *The Main Competitors:* Must *and* have to

If we take a look at the entire corpora (including spoken and written language), we can see that the semi-modal verb *have to* and the modal verb *must* are the main competitors in the field of strong deontic modality in all varieties and that *have to* is more often used than *must* in all varieties (cf. Figure 26). But the frequencies in the complete corpora also indicate that *have to* and *must* are roughly two times more frequently used in the ESL than in the ENL varieties. The frequency of root *have to* ranges from an M-co of 49 in ICE-USA* to an M-co of 113 in ICE-HK. ICE-GB shows a similar frequency to that found in ICE-USA*, with an M-co of 50, while the other two ESL varieties, IndE and SgE, use the semi-modal verb with a higher frequency, with an M-co of 107 and an M-co of 84 respectively. This means that the frequencies of *have to* in ICE-HK and ICE-IND* are more than twice as high than the frequencies found in ICE-USA* and ICE-GB. One could assume that the high frequency of *have to* results in a low frequency of use of the core modal verb *must*, in a process of displacement, but the frequency distribution of *must* does not indicate such a scenario.

The frequency of root *must* ranges from an M-co of 31 in ICE-USA*, the lowest frequency, to an M-co of 71 in ICE-SIN, the highest frequency. The frequency in ICE-GB is somewhat higher than that of ICE-USA*, with an M-co of 42, showing that *must* is still more commonly used in BrE today than in AmE, where it has decreased more drastically than in BrE (cf. also Biber et al. 1999,

488; Leech et al. 2009, 79). The frequency of root *must* in the other two ESL varieties, HKE and IndE, is about the same with an M-co of 57. This means that the ESL varieties are united in the greater use of both the semi-modal *have to* and the core modal *must*. Contrary to expectation, both *must* and *have to* are used more often, which suggests that a process of replacement is not taking place. As the use of modal and semi-modal verbs differs strongly according to mode, it makes sense to compare the frequency distribution of root *must* and *have to* in spoken and written language.

Figure 27 shows that *have to* is generally preferred over *must* in the spoken components of all corpora. The difference in the frequency of *have to* between the ENL and ESL varieties is even more pronounced in spoken language, with a difference of an M-co of 90 between the frequency in ICE-GB (with an M-co of 61) and the frequency in ICE-IND* (with an M-co of 151). ICE-USA* shows a higher frequency than ICE-GB with an M-co of 86, while the frequencies found in ICE-HK and ICE-SIN are much higher than those found in ICE-USA* and ICE-GB, with an M-co of 148 and an M-co of 113 respectively. The widespread use of *have to* does not lead to a lower frequency of *must* in spoken language, as can be seen in Figure 27. Both verbs are used with a higher frequency in ESL varieties than in ENL varieties. The contrast between the two types of varieties is especially strong if the frequencies of ICE-SIN and ICE-USA* are compared. In the spoken part of ICE-SIN, *must* is used with an M-co of 71, while it is only used with an M-co of 6 in SBC, showing the result of the drastic decline of the core modal in spoken AmE. The other ESL varieties, HKE and IndE, also show a higher frequency of appearance of root *must* (with an M-co of 48 and an M-co of 61 respectively), whereas in ICE-GB, the frequency of use of root *must* is only about half the frequency of that found in ICE-HK, with an M-co of 25.

In written language, the differences between the varieties are less pronounced (fitting quite well with what Mair has called 'convergence in writing, divergence in speech', Mair 2007, 84) (cf. Figure 27 and Figure 30). *Must* is more often used than *have to* in writing in all varieties under analysis. Its frequency ranges from an M-co of 47 in the written part of ICE-USA* to an M-co of 71 in the written part of ICE-HK. This means a difference of an M-co of 24, compared to a difference of an M-co of 42 in spoken language. The frequency found in ICE-GB and ICE-SIN is similar to the frequency found for ICE-HK, with an M-co of 68 and 71 respectively. ICE-IND* has a lower frequency with an M-co of 52, which is however still higher than that of ICE-USA*. The frequency of *have to* also fluctuates less strongly across the varieties in the written sections, from an M-co of 27 in ICE-USA* to an M-co of 62 in ICE-HK, i.e. a difference of an M-co of 35 compared to a difference of an M-co of 62 in spoken language. In the written part of ICE-GB, *have to* is used with an M-co of 35, while ICE-IND* and ICE-SIN use it slightly more frequently, with an M-co of 41 and an M-co of 40 respectively. This means that the ESL varieties show a higher frequency of *must* and *have to* than the ESL varieties in spoken and written language.

5.2.2   *More Marginal Members:* Need to *and* have got to

Must and *have to* were shown to be the main competitors in the field of strong deontic modality. However, apart from these two expressions of strong deontic modality, the semi-modal *need to* and *have got to* are also used in this function, though less frequently.

If we take a look at the data from all corpora (cf. Figure 26), including spoken and written language, we can see that innovative *need to* surprisingly has the highest frequency in ICE-HK, with an M-co of 29, followed by ICE-USA*, with an M-co of 26, and ICE-SIN, with an M-co of 25. The frequency in ICE-GB is lower, with an M-co of 16 and lowest in ICE-IND*, with an M-co of only 8. This means that *need to* is used 3.7 times more often in ICE-HK than in ICE-IND*.

In spoken language, ICE-USA* has the highest frequency, with an M-co of 34, followed by ICE-HK, with an M-co of 31, and ICE-SIN, with an M-co of 29. The frequency of the semi-modal verb is again lower in ICE-GB, with an M-co of 17 and lowest in ICE-IND*, with an M-co of 9. This shows that ICE-HK and ICE-SIN have a similar usage pattern while ICE-IND* behaves differently. The high frequency found in AmE is probably closely linked again to the corpus structure of SBC, which includes a large amount of private conversations that are highly interactive, favouring the use of the semi-modal verb (cf. Nokkonen 2012, 136). Given that the private conversations are less interactive in ICE-IND* (cf. the discussion in Section 4.1), it comes as no surprise that the semi-modal verb *need to* is used with such a low frequency in this variety. What is remarkable, however, is the widespread use of innovative *need to* in ICE-HK and ICE-SIN, which is unexpected given its rather recent emergence in BrE (cf. Section 6.1.4).

In written language, we can identify again a similar pattern, with ICE-HK, ICE-USA*, and ICE-SIN ranking high in the frequency of *need to*, with an M-co of 26, an M-co of 20, and an M-co of 19 respectively. The frequency of *need to* in ICE-GB is again lower, with an M-co of 14 and again lowest in ICE-IND*, with an M-co of 6. This means that in the group of ENL varieties, AmE has a higher frequency of *need to* than BrE. A somewhat higher frequency of *need to* in AmE has also been observed by Seggewiß for the time period 1950–1990 in ARCHER (cf. Seggewiß 2012, 80–81). But Leech et al. only found a higher frequency of *need to* in AmE in 1961, but a higher frequency in BrE in 1991 (cf. Leech et al. 2009, 286).

When the contexts are analysed where *need to* slowly enters the territory of *must*, we can see that it occurs with second person non-generic subjects and verbs expressing psychological actions, states, and processes (i.e. category X in the USAS tagset, cf. Table 6 in Chapter 4), especially in dialogues, such as in the example given in (62).

(62) I think you *need to focus* now on one aspect whether it's impacts whether it's just temperature whether it's rainfall (ICE-GB:S1B-007)

In these contexts, *need to* functions as a more polite expression of obligation than *must*, because the obligation is phrased in terms of the benefit to the hearer (cf. also Smith 2003, 260; Nokkonen 2006, 37). As *need to* has also developed objective uses, it also enters the territory of *have to*, especially in contexts with third person non-generic subjects and verbs of the semantic category X, e.g. (63).

(63) For example, in the case of ER and relational models, *it needs to know* how a relationship and its attributes are stored in the relations. (ICE-SIN:W2A-037)

Although an initial encroachment of *need to* can be observed in these particular contexts, its frequency does not suggest that it is a strong rival of either *must* or *have to* in any of the varieties (yet).

A similar observation can be made with regard to deontic *have got to*, whose frequency is the lowest of all expressions of obligation and necessity. Its frequency in all corpora amounts to an M-co of 66, which is lower than that found for *need to*, with an M-co of 103. The frequency of *must* is roughly four times higher than the frequency of *have got to*, with an M-co of 259 and the frequency of *have to* is even six times higher, with an M-co of 403. If the frequency of *have got to* is analysed in the individual varieties, we can see that *have got to* is used with the highest frequency in ICE-GB, with an M-co of 21, followed by ICE-SIN, with an M-co of 18, and ICE-USA*, with an M-co of 17 (cf. Figure 26). In ICE-HK and ICE-IND* instead *have got to* is used with a remarkably low frequency, with an M-co of 7 and an M-co of 3 respectively.

Have got to is associated with informality and it is therefore primarily a feature of spoken language, as becomes obvious when we compare Figure 27 and Figure 30. In spoken language, the frequency of *have got to* is highest in ICE-USA*, with an M-co of 42, followed by ICE-GB, with an M-co of 33. Again, issues of comparability between the spoken sections of ICE-USA* and ICE-GB have to be taken into account (cf. Section 4.1). As the spoken section of ICE-USA*, SBC, contains mostly private dialogues, its language is more informal than that of the complete spoken section of ICE-GB, which also contains public dialogues, as well as scripted and unscripted monologues. This may mean that the higher frequency of *have got to* found in ICE-USA* may be an artefact of differences in the corpus structure, rather than an indicator of regional variation between spoken AmE and spoken BrE. In order to enhance comparability, Seggewiß studied the frequency of *have got to* in spoken BrE and spoken AmE only on the basis of the private dialogue section of ICE-GB and SBC and found that *have got to* is actually more common in BrE, which is why she calls it a 'syntactic Briticism' (cf. Seggewiß 2012, 75). The same regional distribution, the preference of *have got to* in BrE, was also found by Biber et al. and Mair (cf. Biber et al. 1999, 487–488; Mair 2009b, 18–19).

Thus, Mair notes that *have got to* "is somewhat more common in BrE than in most other varieties, including British-derived New Englishes" (Mair 2015a, 138) (cf. also Filppula 2014 for the low frequency of *have got to* in IrE). If we take a look at the frequency of *have got to* in the spoken sections of the ESL corpora, we can see that Mair's claim is also supported by the data of this study. In HKE and IndE, *have got to* is used with a very low frequency, with an M-co of 11 and an M-co of 5 respectively. The frequency in ICE-SIN is higher than the frequencies in the other two ESL corpora, with an M-co of 27, but it is still lower than the frequency found in ICE-GB. The frequency of *have got to* in written language shows that it is almost non-existent here, clearly indicating its restriction to spoken language. This restriction is especially strong in ICE-HK, ICE-USA*, and ICE-IND*, which use *have got to* with an M-co of 2, 1, and 0.5 respectively. In ICE-SIN the frequency of *have got to* is instead higher, with an M-co of 4, even higher than the frequency observed in ICE-GB, with an M-co of 3 (cf. Section 4.1 for the 'hypercolloquial' character of SgE). The frequencies of *have got to* in spoken and written language therefore show that ICE-SIN is marked by a more widespread use of this semi-modal, similar to the ENL varieties but different from the other two ESL varieties.

However, as the frequency of *have got to* is low compared to the other expressions of obligation and necessity, it has to be mentioned that *have got to* is not a full-fledged rival of either *must* or *have to*. A closer look at the contexts in which *must*, *have to*, and *have got to* occur indicates that *have got to* only encroaches on the territory of *must* and *have to* in dialogues. Here, it tends to occur in contexts with first person non-generic subjects and with verbs that express movement, location, travel, and transport (category M in the USAS tagset, cf. Table 6 in Chapter 4), as in example (64).

(64) *I've got to go* or else or else I won't be able to catch the lecture
(ICE-SIN:S1A-069)

However, even in these contexts it is not as frequent as *must* or *have to*, which shows that it has not made substantial inroads in their territories yet. Considering the findings about *need to* and *have got to*, we can see that the competition in strong deontic modality is essentially restricted to *must* and *have to*.

5.3 Summary

The findings show that the frequency of modal and semi-modal verbs of obligation and necessity is generally higher in ESL varieties than in ENL varieties. The higher frequency is especially noticeable in the greater use of the two main markers of obligation and necessity, *must* and *have to*. The two more marginal members, *need to* and *have got to*, show different patterns of use in the varieties, generally pointing to a more widespread use of *need to* in the two varieties HKE and SgE but not in IndE and a more widespread use of *have got to* in SgE but not in the other two ESL varieties.

The distribution according to the senses has shown that *must* is the major variant used to express epistemic modality while the semi-modal verbs *have to*, *have got to*, and *need to* only rarely fulfil this function. But the varieties differ considerably with regard to their frequencies and proportions of epistemic *must*. The general pattern that has been observed in spoken language and written language is that IndE behaves similarly to BrE, while SgE and HKE are different from BrE by showing a low frequency of epistemic *must* and a strong deontic bias in the functional distribution of *must*. Explanations for this pattern will be sought in the structure of the historical input variety and the structure of the substrate languages (cf. Sections 6.1 and 6.2 respectively).

In the encoding of root modality, we have seen that the core modal verb *must* and the semi-modal verb *have to* are the main competitors in the domain of deontic modality in both ENL and ESL varieties, which calls for an analysis of the direct competition between these two variants (cf. the multivariate analysis in Chapter 9). Although *must* and *have to* are the main competitors in both types of varieties, the frequency of use differs radically between ENL and ESL varieties. The ESL varieties use both verbs with a considerably higher frequency than the ENL varieties, thus suggesting no replacement of *must* by *have to*. The frequency distribution therefore suggests that speakers of the ESL varieties express obligation and necessity more often than speakers of ENL varieties, but why? I will seek an answer to this question by taking a look at cultural differences in obligation practices in Section 7.2. In addition to that, the analysis of the frequencies in spoken and written language has shown that the use of *must* and *have to* varies strongly according to mode. This highlights the importance of analysing their use in both spoken and written language and also in different registers (cf. text type as one of the independent variables in the multivariate analysis in Chapter 9).

It has also been demonstrated that the semi-modal verbs *need to* and *have got to* are only marginal members in the field of strong deontic modality in all varieties. With regard to the frequency of the semi-modal verb *need to*, we can see that the varieties HKE and SgE pattern with the ENL varieties BrE and AmE, while IndE is marked by a distinct pattern with a considerably lower frequency of *need to* compared to the other varieties. As ICE-HK and ICE-SIN share a comparatively high frequency of *need to*, it seems plausible to analyse substrate influence as a possible reason behind this similarity (cf. Sections 6.2 and 7.1).

The distribution of the frequency of *have got to* showed that it is mostly restricted to spoken language. Here, it is used most often in the ENL varieties BrE and AmE and the ESL variety SgE, while it is only very rarely used in HKE and IndE. This distribution may be related to the more restricted functions of English in Hong Kong and India compared to the functions of English in Singapore (cf. Sections 3.2.1–3.2.3) as well as the rather recent grammaticalisation of *have got to* (cf. Section 6.1.3). Furthermore, the restricted use of *have got to* in HKE and IndE may point to simplification processes of the modal system, which are typical of SLA processes (cf. Section 7.3). In general, it has to be noted, however, that neither *have got to* nor *need to* are full-fledged competitors of *must* or *have to* (yet).

The findings of the corpus-based study have shown that each variety is characterised by an individual usage profile. The various aspects of the profiles are similar and different to aspects of the profiles of other varieties, which results in a complex web of relationships between the varieties. While the group of ESL varieties shares a higher frequency of the main markers of obligation and necessity, *must* and *have to*, they differ in their use of epistemic *must*. In the frequency of epistemic *must*, IndE unites with BrE, while HKE unites with SgE by having a much lower frequency than BrE. The two groups also differ with regard to the functional distribution of *must*, with the Sinitic-influenced varieties showing a strong deontic bias. In the use of *need to*, we can observe again a grouping of HKE and SgE but this time they also pattern alike with the ENL varieties. Then again, we can spot a similar behaviour of HKE and IndE, with the avoidance of *have got to*, thus differing from BrE, AmE, and SgE. These complex relationships between the varieties suggest that there is no simple explanation for the similarities and differences identified between the varieties and that more than one factor is likely to be involved in the restructuring of the field of strong obligation, as will be discussed in the next chapter.

The Feature Pool of Obligation and Necessity

The previous chapter introduced the state of the domain of obligation and necessity in HKE, IndE, and SgE and compared this state to the ENL varieties BrE and AmE, based on data from ICE-HK, ICE-IND*, ICE-SIN, ICE-GB, and ICE-USA* (cf. parts marked in bold in Figure 31). This chapter will analyse the underlying processes that contributed to the corpus findings with the help of the Feature Pool Model as proposed by Mufwene (2001) for the emergence of creole languages and applied to the ESL context by Biewer (2015). The corpus findings can be regarded as the product of competition-and-selection processes between features in the different ESL varieties (cf. Part A in Figure 31). It needs to be noted that our description of the varieties is mediated by the respective corpora (this is represented by the dotted arrows in Part A of Figure 31). As shown in Section 4.1.2, there are notable differences in the social composition of the corpora such as, for example, the predominance of younger speakers in ICE-HK as opposed to the predominance of older speakers in ICE-IND* or the written nature of the spoken part of ICE-IND. We therefore need to keep

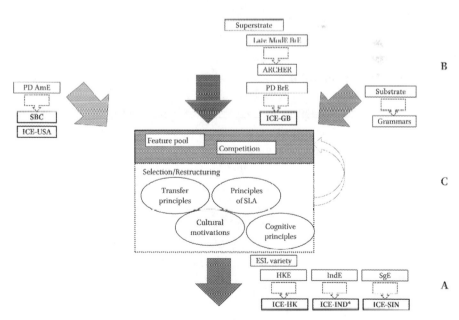

FIGURE 31   The Feature Pool Model (adapted from Biewer 2015, 114).

© KONINKLIJKE BRILL NV, LEIDEN, 2018 | DOI:10.1163/9789004381520_007

these differences in mind when we take the respective ICE-corpora as representatives for the respective ESL varieties.

The starting point of the competition-and-selection process mentioned above is the contribution of features from different sources, whose selection is conditioned by various principles. In the case of the varieties under analysis, three sources can be identified that contribute features to the pool (cf. Part B in Figure 31), i.e. (1) the historical input variety of BrE, (2) the respective substrate language(s), and (3) present-day AmE. IndE, SgE, and HKE developed in language contact situations with a historical variety of BrE as the superstrate and indigenous languages as the substrates. Apart from the BrE superstrate, AmE may also function as input to the new varieties as the "hyper-central variety" in the 'World System of Standard Englishes' (Mair 2013, 261) today. This section models this threefold contribution of variants to the feature pool by reconstructing the input of (1) the historical BrE input variety on the basis of ARCHER in Section 6.1, (2) the relevant substrate languages on the basis of reference grammars in Section 6.2, and (3) AmE in Section 6.3. This allows us to analyse the relative impact of the diachronic superstrate variety of BrE, the substrate languages of the varieties, and the hypercentral variety AmE, which are possible sources of present-day variability beside variability in the present-day input variety that was discussed in Chapter 5. After the respective input to the feature pool has been clarified, principles will be discussed, which guide the selection of features in Chapter 7 (cf. Part C in Figure 31).

6.1 BrE Historical Input

BrE forms the superstrate of the New Englishes under investigation (cf. Sections 3.2.1–3.2.3). Although most studies relate the structure of the New Englishes to the structure of present-day BrE as the input variety, it needs to be taken into account that present-day BrE differs from the input variety of the period of colonisation (cf. Mesthrie 2006, 277). The structure of the field of obligation and necessity has been reorganised over time and the diachronic development of the domain manifests itself in a 'layering' of forms synchronically (cf. Hopper 1991, 22). These layers represent historical stages in the grammaticalisation of the four verbs. All verbs have undergone a process whereby they changed from lexical words to function words. As function words, they first expressed root meanings and then developed epistemic meanings on the basis of these uses. Their shared development can be summarised in the following grammaticalisation path (cf. (65)).

(65) lexical word → function word (modal marker) → deontic modal marker → epistemic modal marker

Within the field of obligation and necessity, *must* is the oldest layer (66), followed by *have to* (67), *have got to* (68), and more recently by *need to* (69). Their particular grammaticalisation paths are outlined in (66) to (69) and detailed in Sections 6.1.1 to 6.1.4.

(66) *must*
     <'measure' → permission → *obligation/necessity* → wish → *inferred necessity* (cf. Table 8)

(67) *have to*
     <'own' → *obligation/necessity* → *inferred necessity* (cf. Table 9)

(68) *have got to*
     <'take hold of' ›'own' → *obligation/necessity* → *inferred necessity* (cf. Table 10)

(69) *need to*
     <'compel'/'be necessary' → absence of obligation (modal) → *obligation/ necessity* (semi-modal) → *inferred necessity* (semi-modal) (cf. Table 11)

The high frequency of the oldest layer, the core modal *must*, in ICE-IND* and ICE-SIN and the low frequency of the more recent layer, the semi-modal *have got to*, in ICE-IND* and ICE-HK suggest that searching for explanations in the historical state of the input variety BrE might be fruitful. This approach is supported by Mesthrie's call "for a less substratophile interpretation of New English variability" (Mesthrie 2006, 279) by analysing variability in the input variety as a possible contributing factor to variability in New Englishes.

This chapter therefore traces the historical development of the core modal *must* and the semi-modal verbs *have to*, *have got to*, and *need to* in the respective historical varieties of BrE. The focus will be on the dating of the emergence of the modal and semi-modal verbs in their root and epistemic senses, which represent synchronic layers in the system. The description of the historical development of these modal and semi-modal verbs in BrE will help to clarify the structure of the domain of obligation and necessity in the input variety at the time of the first contact between the STL and the IDG strands in Schneider's second phase, called 'Exonormative Stabilisation' (cf. Section 3.2). This phase is characterised by increased contact between the STL and the IDG strands, which results in the promotion of bilingualism (cf. Schneider 2007, 37–38). During this phase, "the external norm, usually written and spoken British English as used by educated speakers, is accepted as a linguistic standard of reference" (Schneider 2007, 38). As grammatical restructuring only takes place when contact between the groups increases, the state of the historical input variety will be outlined for the periods in which the varieties entered the second stage in Schneider's (2007) model, rather than the first stage of 'Foundation'.

India, Hong Kong, and Singapore reached this phase at different points in time. India entered the second phase in 1757 when the status of the East India Company changed "from an economic organization to a political power" (Schneider 2007, 163) after the Battle of Plassey. Singapore reached the second phase in 1867 when the Straits Settlement was declared a crown colony of Britain (cf. Schneider 2007, 154). The beginning of the second stage occurred about thirty years later in HKE and is marked by the Convention for the Extension of Hong Kong Territory in 1898 (cf. Schneider 2007, 135).

The state of the input variety at the time of colonisation is often assumed to have a strong impact on the structures of varieties of English in former colonial settings (cf. Mufwene 1996, 84, 2001; Mesthrie 2006, 277; van Rooy 2010). To test whether the varieties under study show signs of the founder effect, the structure of the domain of obligation and necessity will be described for the different points in time when IndE, SgE, and HKE entered the second phase. The description of the historical development of the domain of obligation and necessity in the period from 1750–1899 will be supported by data drawn from ARCHER (1600–1999).

6.1.1   *The Grammaticalisation of* must

Must is one of the nine core modal verbs of Present-Day English (PDE). As a member of the category of auxiliaries, it possesses the so-called NICE properties (cf. Palmer 1979, 8–10) and additional features of the modal verb category (cf. Section 1.3). PDE *must* can express two modal meanings, 'obligation/necessity' and 'inferred certainty'. These two meanings have survived until today and represent two stages in the development of *must* on its path from permission to obligation, to wish, to inferred certainty. Table 8 presents an overview of the grammaticalisation of *must* from Old English (OE) to Modern English (ModE) (examples from Traugott 1972, 198, my emphasis).

Historically, PDE *must* derives from the Germanic preterite-present verb *motan*, whose etymology is not entirely clear (cf. Standop 1957, 67). *Motan* is assumed to be a lengthened ō-grade of the Germanic base of *mete* (s.v. "mote, v.¹", OED online version 2002), which goes back to the Indo-European root

TABLE 8   The grammaticalisation of *must*

	motan <mete	'measure'
1	*He mot gan.* 'I permit him to go.'	permission
2	*He mot gan.* 'He must/is obliged to go.'	obligation/necessity
3	*Mote I long liuen.*	wish
4	*They must be married by now.*	inferred certainty

*med-, which means 'to mete', 'to measure' (cf. Standop 1957, 67). This reconstruction can explain the Gothic meaning of *gamotan* 'to find room'. However,
it is less transparent how this meaning is connected to the permission and obligation sense (cf. Standop 1957, 67). The permission sense is the oldest sense
of *motan* and can be found in early OE texts such as in (70).

(70) 7^1 þonne rideð ælc hys weges mid ðan feo,   7   hyt *motan*
      and then   rides each his way   with the money and it   may/are
                                                                 permitted
                                                                 to
      habban eall.
      have   all
      'and then each goes his own way with the money and can keep all of it'[2]

This sense existed until the end of the Middle English (ME) period when it was
gradually substituted by *magan* ('may'), which first appeared in the second
half of the 13th century (cf. Visser 1969, 1795). *Magan* finally replaces *motan* in
the sense of 'be allowed to' in the beginning of the 16th century, according to
Visser (1969, 1791). Denison claims that the loss of the permission reading of
must was already completed in the ME period (cf. Denison 1993, 303), which is
in line with Traugott, who dates the end of the permission reading to 1400 (cf.
Traugott 1972, 198).

    The second step in the development of *must* is its obligation reading, which
arose in later OE (c.1000);[3] a reading which *must* still carries today (cf. Traugott &
Dasher 2002, 132), e.g. (71).

---

1   The numeral 7 is used as an abbreviation for *and* in some editions of OE texts because of its
    similarity to the Tironian shorthand for *and* ⟨7⟩.
2   Alfred *Orosius* 21.4, translation by Traugott (1972, 71–72).
3   Traugott and Dasher's dating of the root reading in c.1000 and epistemic reading in c.1300 is
    probably based on the OED online version 2000 (cf. Traugott & Dasher 2002, 121).

(71) Hraþe seoþðan wæs æfter mundgripe mece geþinged, þæt hit sceaden-
     mæl scyran *moste*, cwealmbealu cyðan.
     'but he might reckon deadly fetters, twisted by hand, assured for him; that
     after seizure the sword would be prescribed, the patterned blade should
     settle it, make known a violent death'[4]

Several explanations have been put forward to explain the change from permission to obligation. One of these explanations is that the sense of obligation
may have developed from the use of *mote* in negative contexts, "where the two
senses ('may not', 'must not') coincide closely" (s.v. "mote, *v*.", OED online version 2000), i.e. the senses 'not permitted to' and 'obliged to not', e.g. (72).

(72) hie   sculon   simle   stician   on ðam hringum &   næfre *ne*
     they   should   always stick   to the rings   and never not
     moton him   beon   ofatogene.
     ought   from-them   be   taken-off
     'they should always be attached to the rings and should never be removed'[5]

Another explanation is given by Standop, who regards 'ordained by fate/God'
as the underlying sense of *motan* in its permission and obligation reading (cf.
Standop 1957, 75). To be allowed by fate or God to perform an action is considered to be equivalent to be obliged to perform the action (cf. Standop 1957,
75). Standop tries to link the permission and obligation meaning to the Indo-
European root **med-* ('to measure') when he states that the process of 'meting
out' needs to be understood within the social context in which rights ('permission') and duties ('obligation') are given to the people (cf. Standop 1957, 75).
Visser suggests an interaction between the two explanations by claiming that
the development of the obligation sense might have been strengthened by the
use of *mote* in negative contexts (cf. Visser 1969, 1797).[6] The discussion shows
that the oldest sense of *mote* is its permission sense out of which the obligation
reading developed in later OE.
    During the ME period up to the end of the 16th century, *motan* was also
used to express a wish (cf. Traugott 1972, 198).[7] This use was also replaced

---

4 *Beowulf* 1939–40, translation by Swanton (1978, 127).
5 Alfred *Curs Pastoralis* 171.17, translation by Traugott (1989, 51).
6 Traugott claims that Visser favours Standop's explanation and thus implicitly postulates the
   mechanism of conventionalisation of implicature (cf. Traugott 1989, 51, fn.14; cf. Visser 1969,
   1797).
7 Note that Standop and Visser claim that this usage is much older (cf. Standop 1957, 78; cf.
   Visser 1969, 1795). Visser gives quotations of this usage from the OE period (cf. Visser 1969,
   1769).

by *may*, which occurred in the second half of the 13th century for the first time and became more accepted in the beginning of the ModE period (cf. Visser 1969, 1795). Plank dates the loss of the wish sense to later ME/EModE (cf. Plank 1984, 344).

The last step in the semantic development of *must* is its epistemic use, which developed in the ME period; this is the second meaning of PDE *must* besides obligation (cf. Traugott 1972, 198; Traugott & Dasher 2002, 132). This type of *must* is used whenever the speaker makes a "confident inference" (Coates 1983, 5) and is therefore also called "inferential" (Leech et al. 2009, 87) or "illative" *must* (Visser 1969, 1810), e.g. (73).

(73) They *must* be married by now.

Traugott and Dasher state that early sporadic attestations of epistemic *must* can be found in ME, and that epistemic uses become more firmly established at the end of ME and the beginning of EModE (cf. Traugott & Dasher 2002, 132).[8] Traugott and Dasher propose the 13th century as the beginning of epistemic uses of *must* and use the earliest OED quotation (74), which allegedly contains epistemic *must* (s.v. "must, *v.*[1], 8a", OED online version 2003) from 1250 as support (cf. Traugott & Dasher 2002, 129).

(74) He *moste* kunne muchel of art, þat þu woldest ȝeue þer of part.[9]
'He would-have-to know much (of) art, that you would yield part of this [lit.: there of part].'

Traugott and Dasher translate (74) with "He must know much of art since you are willing to give part of it" (cf. Traugott & Dasher 2002, 129) and claim that the context for (74) is epistemic as the speaker concludes 'he must know a lot about art' on the basis of the protasis 'you are willing to give part of it' (cf. Traugott & Dasher 2002, 135). If the context of this quote from *Floris and Blauncheflur* is taken into consideration, however, *moste* turns out to carry root meaning rather than epistemic meaning. The context points to a generic *he* as a subject who must know a lot of tricks to make Blauncheflur give a part of her flower to him. The deontic reading is furthermore strengthened by a translation with

---

8   They claim that there were rare cases of epistemic use in OE texts (cf. Traugott & Dasher 2002, 121) and early sporadic uses in ME (cf. Traugott & Dasher 2002, 129).

9   *Floris and Blancheflur*, Cambridge MS, 521, translation by Warner (1993, 175), *moste* can be found in three (C, A, Cott.) of the four MSS. This line is taken from the Cambridge MS (MS Gg. 4. 27. 2), which is the oldest MS from c.1300 (cf. Hausknecht 1885 for a critical version of the poem).

shul in the later Trentham manuscript: *She shul konne ful muche of art.*[10] Warner also doubts that (74) is an example of epistemic *must* (cf. Warner 1993, 174). If this first attestation of *must* is disregarded, the next attestations of epistemic *must* are from the end of the 14th century, e.g. (75) from 1380 (cf. Warner 1993, 175) and (76) from 1385 (cf. Visser 1969, 1810).

(75) yif preisynge make gentilesse, thanne *mote* they nedes ben gentil that been preysed[11]
      'If praising creates nobility, then they who are praised must necessarily be noble'

(76) He that doth good and doth nat goodly ... *must* nedes be badde.[12]
      'He who does good and does not do it in a good way ... must necessarily be bad.'

These examples support Visser's claim that epistemic *must* "has been of frequent occurrence from the last part of the fourteenth century" (Visser 1969, 1810). Examples (75) and (76) also point to the importance of the collocation of epistemic *must* with the adverb *nedes*[13] in the development of epistemic *must* (cf. Traugott & Dasher 2002, 135). Visser gives several early examples of epistemic *must*, the large majority of which are colligated with *nedes* or later on with *needs*, with the last example of this collocation from 1673 (cf. Visser 1969, 1810–1811). This is also the last example of this collocation given in the OED (s.v. "must, *v.*[1], 8a", OED online version 2000), and this dating squares well

---

10   Trentham MS., fol. 98 a; vellum, c.1440, Note, however, that Warner gives Visser as a reference for his claim that *should* could also be used epistemically at the end of the ME period to refer to something highly probable with the first attestation in 1450 (type: *To-day should be an ideal one for the London skaters*) (cf. Warner 1993, 175; cf. Visser 1969, 1636). It is questionable whether epistemic *must* and epistemic *should* can be regarded as equivalent in terms of semantics, which strengthens the root reading in (74).

11   ?a1425 (c1380) Chaucer, Boece III, Prosa 6.41. It is interesting to take a look at the Latin original, in which the impersonal expression *necesse est* is translated by the common collocation *mote nedes*: *Quodsi claritudinem praedicatio facit, illi sint clari necesse est qui praedicantur* [...]. The influence of the Latin original on English translations is controversial. However, gauging from these examples, Latin *necesse* could have been a strengthening factor in the establishment of the collocation *mote nedes*. This, however, needs further research.

12   c1385 Usk, *Testament of Love* (Skeat) 109, 90.

13   Traugott states that epistemic *must* emerges "in the environment of a strongly epistemic adverb, such as *nedes* 'without doubt' [...]" (Traugott 1989, 42).

with Traugott's claim that *must* with strong epistemic meaning only starts to be used without the adverb in the 17th century (cf. Traugott 1989, 42), e.g. (77).

(77) the fruit *must* be delicious, the tree being so beautiful[14]

The OED gives one earlier attestation of epistemic *must* without a reinforcing adverb from 1590 (s.v. "must, $v.^1$, 8a", OED online version 2000), and Visser gives an example from 1598 (cf. Visser 1969, 1810). These examples help to specify the time of occurrence of epistemic *must* without reinforcing *nedes* to the end of the 16th and beginning of the 17th century.

The historical development of *must* shows that root *must* has been in common use since late OE and that epistemic *must* came into the English language at the end of the 14th century, usually accompanied by a reinforcing adverb. Epistemic *must* started to be used without a reinforcing adverb in the 17th century. All in all, this means that *must* had already long been established in its deontic sense in BrE when it functioned as the input variety in India, Hong Kong, and Singapore. *Must* was also well established in its epistemic sense with a reinforcing adverb when English was brought to India, Hong Kong, and Singapore in the 18th and 19th century. Epistemic *must* without a reinforcing adverb was a relatively recent innovation and can be expected to have been rare.

6.1.2   *The Grammaticalisation of* have to

Besides *must*, the semi-modal *have to* also carries obligation/necessity and inferred certainty readings today. The grammaticalisation process of the semi-modal *have to* involves several stages. Van der Gaaf (1931) is the first to describe the stages in the development of deontic *have to* in his seminal paper on *beon* and *habban* followed by an infinitive. Visser follows van der Gaaf's (1931) account of the development of the semi-modal and distinguishes between three types of *have* in the development towards the semi-modal *have to* (cf. Visser 1969, 1474).[15] Type A can be found in sentences with the structure *have* + object + infinitive such as *He had non heir to succeed*, in which *have* functions as a lexical verb denoting possession (cf. Visser 1969, 1474). Type B has the same syntactic structure as type A but *have* can express obligation in addition to possession, e.g. *I have a large feeld to erie* ('I have a large field to plough', cf. Visser 1969, 1474). This means that the person owns a large field and that it is his or her duty to plough it (cf. also van der Gaaf 1931, 182). In type C *have* denotes

---

14   Visser (1969, 1810), 1623 Middleton, *Spanish Gipsie* I, i, 16.
15   These stages are also discussed in Mitchell (1985, 401), Brinton (1991, 10–11), and Fischer (1994, 137–138).

obligation only and is followed directly by the infinitive such as in *You will have to sell your house* (cf. Visser 1969, 1474).

Heine offers the most recent adaptation of the traditional account of the development of deontic *have to* outlined by van der Gaaf (1931), Visser (1969), and Brinton (1991) (cf. Heine 1993, 42). He explains semantic changes in the development of *have* on the path from possession to obligation in five stages. Heine's stages of the development of the canonical example of *I have to write a letter* will be used for further reference (cf. Heine 1993, 42). In addition to his five stages, I will include epistemic uses of *have to* as the sixth stage in the development of *have to* because deontic uses gave rise to epistemic uses (cf. Table 9).

The first stage in Heine's account of the development is *have* in the possession schema as a full verb meaning 'own', 'possess' in a simple declarative sentence with direct object (cf. Heine 1993, 42).

The second stage shows that semi-modal *have to* developed in special contexts in which the possession schema was followed by a purpose adjunct (cf. Heine 1993, 41). *Have* is still a full verb at this stage governing the direct object to which the infinitive is added as an adverbial adjunct (cf. van der Gaaf 1931, 180; Visser 1969, 1476; Brinton 1991, 10; Heine 1993, 42; Fischer 1994, 137). The construction carries the purposive meaning 'to have something (somebody) for a certain purpose' (van der Gaaf 1931, 180).[16]

TABLE 9   The grammaticalisation of *have to* (adapted and extended on the basis of Heine 1993, 42)

<*have*	'own'
1 *I have a letter.*	possession
2 *I have a letter to mail.*	purpose: possession + purpose/goal adjunct
3 *I have a letter to write.*	the possessive meaning of *have* has been bleached out
4 *I have to write a letter.*	obligation/necessity, *have to* now functions as a unit lexeme
5 *I have to write.*	the object complement can now be deleted
6 *This has to be your husband.*	inferred certainty

---

16   The order of the constituents of this construction was variable in OE, nowadays it is invariable *have* + object + infinitive, e.g. *he has a good name to lose* (cf. van der Gaaf 1931, 186).

The possessive meaning became weakened (cf. van der Gaaf 1931, 182; Brinton 1991, 10; Łęcki 2010, 87) when the purpose adjunct referred to an action in the future, as in the example sentence of stage 3, "since the letter is not yet written and hence cannot be in the possession of the speaker" (Krug 2000, 56).[17] At this stage of the development, possession and obligation readings came to exist side-by-side (cf. van der Gaaf 1931, 182; Visser 1969, 1477; Fischer 1994, 138). The syntactic relations between the constituents is still that found in stage one, in which the direct object is still dependent on *have* (cf. Brinton 1991, 11).

In the transition from stage 3 to stage 4, the primary possessive meaning becomes obscured so that *have* started to express only obligation (cf. van der Gaaf 1931, 186; Brinton 1991, 11; Fischer 1994, 138; Łęcki 2010, 88). This change is accompanied by changes in the syntactic relations. The object is moved and syntactic reanalysis has taken place (cf. Krug 2000, 55).[18] The NP object is now an argument of the infinitive and *have* fills the position directly before the infinitive and becomes an auxiliary "to all intents and purposes" (van der Gaaf 1931, 184). *Have* and *to* function as a unit lexeme now, expressing obligation only. The closer bond between *have* and the infinitive becomes evident in assimilated spellings <hafta> and <hasta> and by the fact that adverbs can usually not be inserted between *have* and *to* (cf. Krug 2000, 57). The transition from stage 3 to stage 4, namely from discontinuous *have to* to continuous *have to*, is "the most important step in the grammaticalization of the construction" (Krug 2000, 56).

The transition from stage 4 to stage 5 has been either analysed as generalisation to intransitive verbs (cf. Brinton 1991, 12; Krug 2000, 58) or deletion of the object (cf. Fleischman 1982, 59; Heine 1993, 42). Generalisation seems to be more plausible as far as examples of *have to* with a following intransitive verb are concerned (cf. Krug 2000, 58).[19] Once *have to* was established as a modal marker denoting obligation, it also developed epistemic readings in a sixth stage and thus followed the common grammaticalisation path from root to epistemic readings, which was also taken by the modal verb *must* (cf. Bybee & Pagliuca 1985; Traugott 1989; Sweetser 1990).

---

17   Fischer et al. argue against the development towards a more bleached *have* and show that *have* already carried a bleached relational meaning in OE similar to existential *be* (cf. Fischer et al. 2000, 300).

18   'Syntactic reanalysis' is also referred to as 'boundary shift', 'restructuring' (cf. also Krug 2000, 55), or 'rebracketing' (cf. Brinton 1991, 13).

19   Visser also objects to the suggestion that the construction with intransitive verb or transitive verb without expressed object derives from the construction with direct object (cf. Visser 1969, 1485). According to him, this suggestion is "unprovable and improbable" (Visser 1969, 1485).

This section focuses on the transition from stage 3 to stage 4 when *have to* started to be used as a semi-modal denoting deontic obligation only and the development of epistemic meanings once the deontic meanings had become established. Although the development of *have to* following the stages outlined above is generally acknowledged (cf. van der Gaaf 1931; Visser 1969, 1474; Brinton 1991, 10–12; Heine 1993, 42; Fischer 1994, 137–138), the trigger for the transition from stage 3 to stage 4 is highly disputed. While van der Gaaf, Visser, Brinton, and Heine argue that semantic changes triggered the grammaticalisation of *have*, Fischer argues that syntactic changes initiate its grammaticalisation. The different approaches to the grammaticalisation of *have* resulted in different datings with regard to the emergence of its deontic meaning.

As explained above, van der Gaaf argues that semantic changes of the verb *have* induced the word order change in stage 4 (cf. van der Gaaf 1931, 184). When the possessive meaning of *have* was lost, *have* "also ceased to be a verb of complete predication, and it became to all intents and purposes an auxiliary of predication" (van der Gaaf 1931, 184), occurring in auxiliary position before the infinitive. In this scenario of change, "grammaticalization proceeds along a path of semantic change; the syntactic changes are subordinate to it, following hard on the heels of the semantic changes" (Fischer et al. 2000, 294). As van der Gaaf sees semantic changes prior to syntactic changes, he does not use the change in word order as a criterion for dating the emergence of obligative *have to* but instances in which he can find root meanings (cf. van der Gaaf 1931, 184). He argues that *have* already started to be used with obligation meaning in late OE (cf. van der Gaaf 1931, 182).[20] His examples from OE are, however, debatable, e.g. example (78) could be interpreted to represent stage two, in which both possession and obligation meanings exist side-by-side.

(78)   Uton we geþencean hwylc handlean we him forþ *to* berenne *habban*[21]
       'Let us remember what recompense we have to offer him'

Visser's categorisation of (78) under his type B supports this (cf. Visser 1969, 1477).[22] The OED also lists (78) under the meaning 'to possess as a duty or thing

---

20   Łęcki also argues for the existence of obligative *have* in OE by giving the following example: *To þæs tocyme ealle men to arisanne hi habbað mid heora lichaman & to agyldanne synd be agnum gescead* ('With his [sc. Jesus'] advent all men have to arise with their bodies and pay back for their deeds') (cf. Łęcki 2010, 108–109). However, this example seems to be a literal translation of the Latin *habēre* plus infinitive construction.

21   Van der Gaaf (1931, 182), Blickl. *Hom.*, p.91.

22   Łęcki also sees (78) as an example of the second stage of the development of *have* (cf. Łęcki 2010, 88).

to be done' (s.v. "have, *v.*7a", OED online version 2000), which would then make it an instance of possession and obligation reading rather than obligation reading only.[23] Mitchell also sees (78) as an example of the OED meaning 'to possess as a duty or thing to be done' (cf. Mitchell 1985, 401). Van der Gaaf's third example from OE (79) (cf. van der Gaaf 1931, 182), which is supposed to show the obligation reading is also questionable, especially if one takes into account that this example translates the Latin future active participle *bibiturus sum*, which rather points to a future meaning ('I am about to drink') than an obligation reading.[24]

(79) Mage gyt drincan þone calic ðe ic *to* drincenne *hæbbe*?[25]
       'Can you drink the goblet which I have to drink?'

The discussion shows that it is doubtful that the occurrence of obligative *have to* can already be dated to OE and supports Bock and Mitchell, who deny that the obligation reading can already be found in OE (cf. Bock 1931, 165; Mitchell 1985, 402).

Visser also argues for a semantically driven change of word order when he states that *have* loses its possessive sense and therefore becomes "merely a function word" (Visser 1969, 1478). He states that the development of the obligative construction (his type C) from the constructions type A ('possession') and type B ('possession and obligation') proceeded very slowly and that "it is not possible to ascertain when exactly the idiom appeared for the first time [...]" (Visser 1969, 1478). Visser uses the change in word order as the criterion to date the obligation reading of *have* because instances of *have* + infinitive + object exclusively express obligation (cf. Visser 1969, 1478; cf. also van der Gaaf 1931, 184; Brinton 1991, 11). Working on this assumption, Visser states that there are

---

23 The third edition of the OED online version 2015 lists (78) under the meaning 'expressing something that is to be done or needs to be done, as a duty, obligation, requirement, etc.' and classifies the *to*-infinitive as an object complement "specifying what needs to be done to the object" (s.v. "have, *v.*8a", OED online version 2015).

24 Cf. Łęcki, who also identifies a future reading of *hæbbe* in (79) (cf. Łęcki 2010, 107) and Plank for *have to* with future meaning (cf. Plank 1984, 320) as well as the remark in the OED "in early use the construction may occasionally approach a periphrastic or modal future in sense rather than more narrowly implying obligation" (s.v. "have, *v.*42a", OED online version 2015). Krug argues that obligation and future readings are contiguous as "obligation often points to the future because the predicate action is typically not actualized" (Krug 2000, 91). See also the future and obligation meaning of Mandarin *yào* in Section 6.2.

25 Van der Gaaf (1931, 182), Matthew XX, 22.

no instances of obligative *have* before 1200,[26] that it was still infrequent in ME[27] before it gained ground in ModE (cf. Visser 1969, 1478; cf. also van der Gaaf 1931, 184). Visser gives the first example of this usage from c.1225 (cf. Visser 1969, 1479):

(80) Ancre *naueð*   *to* witene buten hire   &   hire meidenes.[28]
      if   have-not to   know   but   herself and her   maidservants
      'Nuns have only to know themselves and their maidservants.'

The example is supposed to show the modal obligation reading only. Arguably, however, this example could also be an instance of *have to* with possessive and obligation meaning (Visser's category B).[29] This interpretation relies on the understanding of possession in a broader sense also listed in the OED, which gives the example *the king has subjects*, a context which is comparable to the context above (s.v. "have, *v.*2a", OED online version 2000).[30] Consequently, ME uses of obligative *have to* seem to be rare, and this might be the reason why the OED gives as its first attestation a quote from 1579 (s.v. "have, *v.*7c", OED online version 2000).

(81) He told him he *had* not *to* beleue that the couetousnes of Virginio ... had moued Ferdinand.[31]

---

26   Visser gives one example which could be an instance of *have to* with obligation reading before 1200, Blickl. *Hom.* III, 24: *Nænig man nafaþ to don modelico gestreon her on worlde* (cf. Visser 1969, 1478). This example seems to be debatable, especially if one takes other manuscripts into account which read: [...] *nænig man on worlde toðæs mycelne welan nafað, ne toðon modelico gestreon her on worlde* [...] ('No man on the world has so much weal, or such magnificent riches here in the world'). The manuscript rendered by Visser has the phrase *nafaþ to don* instead of *nafað, ne toðon*. The context suggests, however, that *nafað, ne toðon* is the more plausible wording if one takes a look at the preceding phrase which contains the form *toðæs* in a parallel construction and working on the assumption that the text contains rhetorical flourish.

27   Van der Gaaf gives only five instances before 1500 (cf. van der Gaaf 1931, 184).

28   Cf. Visser (1969, 1479), Ancr. R., Nero 31,9. The translation is supported by Jespersen, who sees *hire & hire meidenes* as the direct object of *haueð* and *buten* as the adverb (*ne ... buten =* 'but, only') and van der Gaaf, who assumes that *non* has been omitted (cf. Jespersen 1940, 204–205; van der Gaaf 1931, 184). Other manuscripts have the verb *to lokin* after *have* which would also support the interpretation that *have* carries obligative in addition to possessive meaning.

29   "In this type *to have* means 'to have something or somebody to look after or attend to'. It expresses duty, obligation in addition to possession" (Visser 1969, 1477).

30   Cf. also Fischer (1994, 151–152) for the different types of meanings expressed by *have*, for example that *have* can carry relational meaning which does not necessarily have to be one of literal possession.

31   G. Fenton tr. F. Guicciardini *Hist. Guicciardin* i, 8.

The assumption that ME uses of obligative *have* are rare and only become more firmly established in ModE is in line with Brinton's (1991) account of the development of obligative *have*. Brinton's (1991) thorough analysis traces the stages of the grammaticalisation process of *have* from full verb to operator with examples taken from the *Helsinki Corpus*. Brinton follows the traditional account of the development of the semi-modal verb *have to* by arguing that the PDE structures *I have a paper to write* and *I have to write a paper* both originate from the structure *have* + object + infinitive with *have* as a full verb with possessive meaning (cf. Brinton 1991, 2). Brinton (1991) describes three different stages in the development of *have* as an auxiliary.

Her analysis starts from the possessive structure of *have* prototypically followed by a concrete object to which the infinitive is attached as an optional adjunct (cf. Brinton 1991, 14; cf. Heine's second stage). *Have* functions as a full verb and can be substituted by synonymous verbs of possession such as *own* (cf. Brinton 1991, 15). Its meaning generalises in the OE period when *have* starts to occur with abstract objects (cf. Brinton 1991, 16).

In the second stage of the development, generalised *have* occurs in predicative structures in which the infinitive functions as an obligatory object complement, e.g. *nu ic longe spell hæbbe to secyenne* ('now I have a long story to tell').[32] The object is the future patient of the action expressed by the infinitive and the subject is both the subject of *have* and the infinitive. The meaning does not depend on the meaning of *have* alone but on the combination of generalised *have* with the infinitive (cf. Brinton 1991, 16). The meaning of the infinitive is one of non-past activity, i.e. an action which is not yet accomplished. In combination with *have*, this means that "one 'has' a non-past activity, which means that one still has it to do, either as a necessity [...], or as an obligation [...]" (Bybee & Pagliuca 1985, 73). Brinton argues "that the construction has a combined possessive and modal sense resulting from the generalised meaning of *habban* and the syntactic function of the predicative structure" (Brinton 1991, 19), which is in line with van der Gaaf's stage 2 possession and obligation reading and Visser's category B (cf. van der Gaaf 1931, 181–182; Visser 1969, 1474). During the ME period *have* gradually loses its possessive sense and occurs with intransitive infinitives, inanimate subjects, and abstract objects, which do not carry a strictly possessive interpretation (cf. Brinton 1991, 20–23). Brinton therefore argues that *have* starts to grammaticalise in ME by extending its range to more and more contexts but does not grammaticalise fully until EModE (cf. Brinton 1991, 23). All three types of *have*, i.e. in possessive, predicative, and periphrastic structure, can still occur in *have* + object + infinitive word order during the ME

---

32   eOE tr. Alfred, Orosius, *Hist.* (BL Add.) II, viii, 53.

period (cf. Brinton 1991, 23). The word order *have* + infinitive + object becomes more frequent in ME and is restricted to modal meaning (cf. Brinton 1991, 24).

In EModE, the two word orders undergo a differentiation of meaning so that both constructions can express obligation, however differently, with "one expressing the obligation to accomplish a result and the other expressing the obligation to perform an action" (Brinton 1991, 25). For example, *I have a paper to write* expressed an 'obligation to accomplish a result' whereas *I have to write a paper* expressed an 'obligation to perform an action'. This semantic differentiation led to syntactic reanalysis in which either the object NP + infinitive (*a paper to write*) or *have* + infinitive (*have to write*) is a constituent (cf. Brinton 1991, 25). Those constructions which express an 'obligation to accomplish a result' show the word order *have* + NP + infinitive, in which the NP and the infinitive form a constituent, while those constructions which express an 'obligation to perform an action' show the word order *have* + infinitive + NP, in which *have* and the infinitive form a constituent. *Have* occurs in the position of an auxiliary as a modifier of the infinitive in those constructions in which *have* and the infinitive build a constituent. *Have* is more fully grammaticalised in these constructions and restricted to obligation meaning, while it is less grammaticalised in constructions of the type *have* + object + infinitive, whose "meaning is less restricted, encompassing meanings of possession as well as obligation" (Brinton 1991, 25). All in all, Brinton (1991) also argues that semantic changes led to the grammaticalisation of *have* in the EModE period.

The reverse line of argumentation, namely that a syntactic change led to a semantic change is put forward by Fischer (1994), who argues that a change in word order from OV to VO in infinitival clauses triggered the grammaticalisation of *have*. Fischer (1994) also illustrates her findings with examples drawn from the *Helsinki Corpus*. She states:

> I do not see a slow, uninterrupted, gradual grammaticalisation process from possessive *have* to semi-modal *have to*, as envisaged by most linguists who have worked on this topic, such as van der Gaaf (1931), Visser (1969), Brinton (1991), but rather a more sudden spurt towards semi-modality (which can still be considered as a grammaticalisation process), occasioned by a change in basic word order, which put the hapless *have* next to the infinitive making escape, as it were, impossible.
>
> FISCHER 1994, 137

As Fischer (1994) argues for a syntactically driven change as the trigger for the grammaticalisation of *have*, she criticises van der Gaaf's (1931), Visser's (1969), and Brinton's (1991) account of the development, which sees semantic changes as the cause of its grammaticalisation. In order to support her argument, Fischer argues against occurrences of obligative *have* before late ME (cf. Fischer 1994, 151). She argues that van der Gaaf's (1931), Visser's (1969), and Brinton's (1991) understanding of the meaning of full verb *have* is unduly restrictive and criticises that they assign the meaning of obligation to all instances that do not show *have* in a strictly possessive sense (cf. Fischer 1994, 151). By contrast, Fischer proposes a broader reading of *have* "with a range of meanings centered around the notion of possession" (Fischer 1994, 151). Indeed, the basis of her argument "hinges on the exceptionally wide view she takes of 'possession', which rules out 'obligation' readings for all HAVE TO examples prior to Early Modern English" (Krug 2000, 264). Fischer draws attention to a continuum of meanings, with concrete possession on one extreme pole and a relational meaning on the other end of the continuum (cf. Fischer 1994, 151–152). Thus, many examples given as instances of the possession and obligation reading in van der Gaaf (1931), Visser (1969), and Brinton (1991) can be captured with this understanding of *have*.

On the basis of this broader reading of *have*, Fischer argues that these instances belong to the first stage, in which *have* only denotes possession, albeit in a very wide sense. Accounting for the occurrence of *have* with intransitive infinitives is another problem she faces with her account, as *have* with intransitive infinitives rules out a strictly possessive interpretation. She argues that the examples given by Brinton for *have* with intransitive infinitive turn out to be transitive on closer inspection with implied objects (cf. Fischer 1994, 143; Brinton 1991, 20–21). Fischer et al. also argue that all examples given for *have* with intransitive infinitive from ME are actually examples of the possessive structure (cf. Fischer et al. 2000, 299). Fischer's (1994) criticism of Brinton's (1991) account of the development needs to be seen against the backdrop of her own account, which sees syntactic changes in the word order as the trigger for the grammaticalisation of *have*. This account does not permit any root readings before the change in word order as this would imply the reverse development.

The main point of her criticism of earlier studies on *have to* is the difficulty in distinguishing the different types of *have* plus infinitive constructions in the absence of any formal indicators (cf. Fischer 1994, 138). Fischer et al. argue that the interpretation of the syntactic relations "depends ultimately on the interpretation of *have* as conveying either possession or obligation" (Fischer et al. 2000, 294), which leads to circularity in the argument. To escape this circularity, she proposes a different scenario, suggesting "that it is indeed a change in word order which set off the process of grammaticalisation" (Fischer 1994, 146). She argues that a change in word order was crucial to the grammaticalisation of *have* as it led to the juxtaposition of *have* and the infinitive, which then triggered the grammaticalisation of *have* (cf. Fischer 1994, 146).

In early ME a change in word order from SOV to SVO occurred, which changed the structure of constructions with *have* and infinitive to subject-NP *have* object-NP *to*-infinitive in both main and subclauses. The order is not problematic as long as the NP object clearly belongs to *have*, i.e. syntactically and thematically. However, when the object shows a stronger thematic link to the infinitive, it needed to shift to post-infinitival position to comply with the SVO word order.[33] If the object has a closer link to the infinitive, a syntactic reanalysis takes place in which the object NP is syntactically reanalysed as the object of the infinitive. This change occurred in late ME, when the shift from SOV to SVO word order reached infinitival clauses so that the word order became subject-NP *have to*-infinitive object-NP in these sentences (cf. Fischer 1994, 149). This juxtaposition of *have* and *to*-infinitive paved the way for the grammaticalisation of *have*, which now occurred in auxiliary position before the infinitive according to Fischer (1994, 149). Consequently, she dates the beginning of the grammaticalisation of *have to* in EModE after the change of word order in infinitival clauses had occurred in late ME (cf. Fischer 1994, 154).

What becomes obvious from the review of previous studies is that the relative order of the stages in the development of the semi-modal *have to* from possession over possession/obligation to obligation is undisputed (cf. van der Gaaf 1931; Visser 1969; Brinton 1991; Heine 1993; Fischer 1994). By contrast, the dating of the emergence of obligative *have* is strongly disputed. The existence of obligative *have* in OE as proposed by van der Gaaf (1931) and Łęcki (2010) needs to be rejected, as the closer examination of their examples has shown. Following Visser, Brinton, and Fischer, early instances of obligative *have to* seem to occur in ME, before it becomes more fully established in EModE (cf. Visser 1969, 1478; Brinton 1991, 27; Fischer 1994, 154). Despite the different explanations assumed for the grammaticalisation of *have* as either a process triggered by semantic changes or syntactic changes, all these accounts share the assumption that the critical period of grammaticalisation begins in EModE (cf. also Krug 2000, 54).

In his corpus-based grammaticalisation study, Krug agrees that the grammaticalisation process of *have to* begins in EModE but shows that a substantial increase in its frequency occurs much later, i.e. in the middle of the 19th century (cf. Krug 2000, 80). Mair argues that this "delayed-increase pattern" (2004, 129) seems to apply more generally by showing a time lag between the

---

33   The question arises whether this is ultimately also a semantic explanation in this syntactically driven change of grammaticalisation.

grammaticalisation of *going to, start* plus gerund and infinitive, and *help* plus infinitive and their rise in discourse frequency. Krug traces the frequency of *have to* in the BrE drama and fiction section of ARCHER from 1600 to 1990 in 50-year intervals (cf. Krug 2000, 79). His findings indicate that the frequency of *have to* is relatively low, until it rises sharply in the middle of the 19th century in the BrE drama section of ARCHER, "where the incidence rose almost sixfold [...] compared to the previous 50 years" (Krug 2000, 80). His findings for BrE fiction show a similar trend (cf. Krug 2000, 79). However, compared to the development in BrE drama, the increase is more gradual and less steep. He sees the cause for the grammaticalisation of *have to* in the semantic process of subjectification, which led to syntactic reanalysis with first attestations of adjacent *have* and *to* from c.1200 (cf. Krug 2000, 74). Krug states that contiguous *have to* was still rare in EModE and typically used in apokoinou structures often co-occurring with verbs of saying, such as *tell* (cf. Krug 2000, 74). For this reason, he explains the emergence of obligative *have to* in collocations with verbs of saying from a usage-based perspective (cf. Krug 2000, 100). These contexts do not permit a strictly possessive reading and the hearer therefore draws the pragmatic inference that "some internal or external force obliges the speaker to say something" (Krug 2000, 101). This inference "gradually lead[s] to the expansion of contexts in which *have to* is used, which in turn brings about the gradual conventionalization of the modal meaning" (Krug 2000, 101). The expansion of *have to* to other verbal complements becomes visible in the frequency rise of the construction in the middle of the 19th century (cf. Krug 2000, 101).

In a further stage of the development of *have to* as a semi-modal, an epistemic reading developed from its root reading. Although Brinton and Łęcki argue for the emergence of an epistemic sense of *have to* as early as ME (cf. Brinton 1991, 22–23; Łęcki 2010, 130–131), the epistemic sense seems to have emerged much later. Brinton and Łęcki maintain that epistemic readings already occurred in ME when *have* started to be used with inanimate subjects (cf. Brinton 1991, 22–23; Łęcki 2010, 130–131). However, on closer inspection their examples turn out to be deontic rather than epistemic. Fischer also rejects the examples given by Brinton as examples of epistemic *have to* (cf. Fischer 1994, 144; Brinton 1991, 22–23). Brinton gives (82) as a later example of epistemic *have to* from 1950 (cf. Brinton 1991, 5), which is taken from Visser's examples of deontic *have to* (cf. Visser 1969, 1486).

(82) Through the years she sensed that something like this *had to* happen some day.[34]

---

34   1950 Th. Pratt, *The Tormented Fawcett Public*, 36.

This example is debatable as it "is not unambiguously epistemic" as Denison remarks (cf. Denison 1998, 172). This discussion suggests that epistemic *have to* is a fairly recent phenomenon, as the first OED attestation in (83) from 1967 also indicates (s.v. "have", *v.*7d, OED online version 2000).[35]

(83) That *had to* be the most bizarre Grey Cup game ever.

This epistemic reading of the semi-modal is still only rarely used today (cf. Palmer 1979, 46; Coates 1983, 57–58; Krug 2000, 90). Krug only finds two instances of epistemic *have to* in the 20th century BrE drama section of ARCHER (cf. Krug 2000, 89). Coates claims that epistemic *have to* "is still felt to be an Americanism" (Coates 1983, 57). On the other hand, Quirk et al. state that it is also common in BrE (cf. Quirk et al. 1985, 145). However, in both varieties *must* is the usual choice when expressing logical necessity (cf. Coates 1983, 58), while *have to* is predominantly used in its deontic sense today (cf. Krug 2000, 89; cf. also my findings in Section 5.1).

The description of the historical development of *have to* reveals that early instances of obligative *have to* started to occur in ME, that the process of grammaticalisation emerges in the EModE period, and that a major rise in frequency only occurred in the second half of the 19th century. This means that *have to* was still used with a low frequency when India entered the second phase in 1757. Singapore entered the second phase in 1867, i.e. around the time when the major frequency increase of *have to* set in. When Hong Kong entered the second phase in 1898, the substantial rise in frequency had already taken place. The description of the development of *have to* also shows that epistemic *have to* probably only entered the language in the second half of the 20th century and was therefore not yet part of the inventory of the respective input varieties.

6.1.3   *The Grammaticalisation of* have got to
A more recent layer in the modal domain of obligation and necessity is the semi-modal *have got to*. Etymologically PDE *get* goes back to the Old Aryan root **ghed*, **ghod* 'to seize', 'take hold of' (s.v. "get, *v.*", OED online version 2012). In PDE, *have got* can denote stative possession and, when followed by an infinitive, root and epistemic meanings. *Have got* in its stative possession sense gave

---

35   The OED online version 2015 gives an earlier attestation from the *New York Times* from 1961: *My belief in The Times' infallibility ... was finally toppled by your endorsement of Mayor Wagner in the Democratic primary. You just have to be joking.* It is interesting to see cross-linguistic similarities with Spanish, where *tener que* (lit. 'have that') has also developed epistemic uses (cf. van der Auwera, Ammann & Kindt 2005, 259).

TABLE 10   The grammaticalisation of *have got to* in comparison to the grammaticalisation
of *have to*

	have got to		*have to*
	get < **ghed, ghod*	'take hold of'	*have* < 'own'
1	*I have got a letter.*	possession	*I have a letter.*
2			*I have a letter to mail.*
3	no reanalysis	(analogy to *have to*)	*I have a letter to write.*
4			*I have to write a letter.*
5	*I have got to write.*	obligation/necessity	*I have to write.*
6	*I've got to write.*	contraction	
7	*I got to write.*	omission of *have*	
	I gotta write.	coalescence	
8	*This has got to be your husband.*	inferred certainty	*This has to be your husband.*

rise to the obligation reading in analogy to *have to*. More recently, *have got to* has also developed an epistemic reading on the basis of the deontic reading. The grammaticalisation path of *have got to* in comparison to that of *have to* can be seen in Table 10.

The stative possessive reading of *have got* enters the language at the beginning of the 17th century (cf. Gronemeyer 1999, 25).[36] There are two different accounts of how *have got* entered the language in the sense of 'stative possession' (cf. Visser 1973, 2202, fn.2; Fodor & Smith 1978, 46; Schulz 2012, 129–130).

---

36   Visser and Plank also argue for a dating of possessive *have got* after the 16th century (cf. Visser 1973, 2202; Plank 1984, 338). However, Jespersen, Crowell, and Webster give examples of possessive *have got* from the 16th century (cf. Jespersen 1954, 47–48, Crowell 1959, 280; Webster's 1989 s.v. "have got" (Perrault et al. 1989). Łęcki finds even earlier examples of the stative possessive meaning in late ME "whose context may suggest a possessive interpretation" (Łęcki 2010, 139). Nevertheless, his examples do not exclude a dynamic reading of *get*. The first attestation of possessive *have got* in the OED dates from 1600 but has also been questioned by Rice (1932, 288). Gauging from the examples given in the relevant literature, the end of the 16th and beginning of the 17th century seems to be a plausible period for the occurrence of possessive *have got*.

One account sees *have got* in the meaning of 'have'/'possess' derived from the present perfect tense of *get* (cf. Plank 1984, 338; Visser 1973, 2202; Gronemeyer 1999, 26; Schulz 2012, 139). The dynamic reading 'have acquired' is the older meaning of the construction from which the stative meaning 'have'/'possess' is derived (cf. Visser 1973, 2202). The older meaning 'have acquired' shows the original meaning of *get*, which expresses the 'onset of a possession', i.e. ingressive + 'have' (cf. Gronemeyer 1999, 19).[37] *Get* is thus an "aspectual variant of *have* meaning 'come to have/possess'" (Gronemeyer 1999, 19). The present perfect tense gives rise to the meaning of 'stative possession' referring to "the consequent state of an earlier event" (Gronemeyer 1999, 4), enabled by the pragmatic inference that "once you get something, you are in possession of it" (Łęcki 2010, 139).[38] The perfect tense adds the contextual meaning that an action of the past is of current relevance to the present, which is incompatible with the 'ingressive' aspect inherent in *get*. This is why the ingressive aspect is cancelled and *get* becomes equivalent to present *have* in these constructions (cf. Gronemeyer 1999, 26).

The second account assumes that *got* has been inserted in possessive *have* contexts as a form of strengthened *have* (cf. Jespersen 1954, 47–48; Crowell 1959, 284).[39] Jespersen links *got* insertion in possessive *have* contexts to the rising frequency of *have* as an auxiliary, which led to the gradual loss of the possessive meaning, so that speakers felt the need to differentiate between the auxiliary use of *have* and its lexical use in the sense of 'possess' (cf. Jespersen 1954, 47–48). To show the meaning difference of the two types of *have*, they inserted *got* after *have* to strengthen the possessive meaning and formally distinguish it from the auxiliary use of *have* (cf. Jespersen 1954, 47–48). The question arises why *get* in its original dynamic meaning was chosen as a reinforcer for stative possessive *have*. Jespersen can partially answer this question, as he sees the semantic change of dynamic *get* to stative possessive *get* in the present perfect as the prerequisite for its insertion after possessive *have* (cf. Jespersen 1954, 47–48).

---

37   On the basis of 500 instances of *get* in the *Helsinki Corpus*, Gronemeyer suggests that the polysemous lexical item *get* has one underlying sense from which all other senses are derived (cf. Gronemeyer 1999, 11), which is composed of an aspectual ingressive component and the stative verb *have*, i.e. *get* = ingressive + 'have' ('come to possess') in constructions in which *get* is followed by an NP (ultimately going back to the meaning 'seize', Gronemeyer 1999, 35).

38   See Schulz (2012) for a more detailed account of the development of the stative possessive sense of *have got* as a conventionalisation of implicature.

39   Crowell refers to Bartlett (1848) as the source of this account (cf. Crowell 1959, 280). Although Crowell (1959) explicitly speaks of a 'substitution' process of *have* by *have got* several times in his article, he seems to have insertion in mind (Crowell 1959, 284).

Crowell also argues in favour of *got*-insertion in contexts in which *have* is reduced (cf. Crowell 1959, 280).[40] According to him, *got* is inserted in these contexts as a 'pattern preserver' to signal the verb in the subject + verb pattern (cf. Crowell 1959, 282–283). The discussion shows that the development of stative possessive *have got* cannot be explained without reference to the meaning of *get* in the present perfect.

The stative possessive meaning of *have got* gave rise to its deontic meaning. Gronemeyer claims that the development of the obligation reading of *have got to* is based on an analogical mapping with *have to* and was favoured by the established stative possession meaning of *have got* (cf. Gronemeyer 1999, 34). Gronemeyer explains this process as a case of 'intraference' (cf. Gronemeyer 1999, 34), in which "[d]ifferent elements of the same language can interfere with each other if they share enough linguistic substance, in particular meaning" (Croft 2000, 148). This means that *have got* and *have* were both used in the stative possessive reading and therefore showed semantic equivalence so that the deontic reading of *have* followed by an infinitive was also imposed on *have got* followed by an infinitive. In addition to its stative possessive sense, *have got* then also started to be used in the deontic sense 'be obliged to'. Krug also follows this line of argumentation.

> [I]t is not unlikely that by semantic analogy to (i.e. on the model of) the older HAVE TO construction HAVE GOT extended its range of complements from nominal complements (as in *I've got a house*) to infinitival ones (as in *I've got to go*).
>
> KRUG 2000, 64

He assumes two conflicting forces in the development of obligative *have got* which led to the insertion of *got*, i.e. "processing constraints and chunking" (Krug 2000, 64). Krug argues that the high frequency of co-occurrence of personal pronouns and *have* makes them possible candidates for coalescence so that *have* is contracted and attached to the pronoun ('chunking') (cf. Krug

---

40   Schulz does not agree with Crowell's (1959) and Krug's (2000) account of the development of *have got* as *got* insertion in reduced possessive *have* contexts, as she cannot find historical evidence for contracted possessive *have* before 1600 and only few contractions after 1600 (cf. Schulz 2012, 135). Schulz (2012) seems to misunderstand Krug's explanation (cf. Krug 2000, 64–65). Krug does not deal with contracted possessive *have* contexts but with contracted deontic *have* contexts. Thus, he does not deal with the development of the stative possessive reading of *have got*, which is the topic of Schulz's (2012) article. Her criticism regarding the insertion of *got* should therefore only be directed towards Crowell (1959), who assumes *got* insertion in contracted possessive *have* contexts.

2000, 64). However, this coalescence is hindered by processing constraints as contracted *have* forms cannot do justice to the greater semantic weight of obligation leading to processing problems and hindering understanding (cf. Krug 2000, 64–65). The 'processing constraints' work against 'chunking' and *got* is inserted after contracted *have* contexts. As *have got* already carried the meaning of stative possession synonymously to *have*, it was now used in other contexts in which *have* was also used, such as deontic *have to*, especially in order to strengthen *have* when it was contracted. Krug claims that "*got* comes to be inserted as a reinforcer in those cases where HAVE is reduced" (Krug 2000, 65). The question then arises what Krug means by 'reinforcement' (cf. Krug 2000, 64). As he focuses on the development of deontic readings, a semantic reinforcement by the insertion of *got* would mean strengthening the possessive meaning of contracted *have* (cf. Krug 2000, 64–65). This, however, does not happen in deontic *have* contexts, which express 'obligation' and not 'possession'. The term 'reinforcer' (Krug 2000, 65) is therefore used to refer to reinforcement by the addition of phonetic material[41] and not to refer to semantic strengthening.[42] The development of deontic *have got to* in analogy to deontic *have to* implies that *have got to* did not undergo the same development as *have to* (outlined in Section 6.1.2), although syntactic reanalysis is equally plausible for *have got to* (cf. Krug 2000, 63).[43] This account of the development of *have got to* is supported by the fact that discontinuous deontic *have got to* seems to be very rare or even absent until the 19th century (cf. Krug 2000, 65).[44] It therefore appears "that contiguous HAVE GOT TO with a deontic sense entered the language directly. That is to say, no previous bi-clausal structures need to be posited" (Krug 2000, 73). That *have got to* has taken the same steps in its development as *have to* seems furthermore unlikely because even the earliest attestations of deontic *have got to* occur with intransitive infinitives. This suggests that *have got to* "enters the language as late as stage (v) of the stages identified for HAVE TO" (Krug 2000, 66).

---

41   This interpretation of strengthening is in line with Łęcki, who analyses *got* as "mere phonetic substance inserted between HAVE and TO" (Łęcki 2010, 141).

42   Schulz's summary of Krug's account of the development of deontic *have got* seems to misunderstand the term 'reinforcer' in terms of semantic strengthening (cf. Schulz 2012, 132–133). This misunderstanding possibly stems from Crowell's statement that *got* was inserted because of semantic equivalence to *have* in possessive *have got* contexts (cf. Crowell 1959, 284).

43   Cf. Krug (1998) for the opposite line of argumentation, in which object movement and syntactic reanalysis are used to explain the development of deontic *have got to*.

44   Visser gives the following example of discontinuous *have got to* from 1884 with obligation reading in addition to possession reading: *I consider that I have got a bone to pick with Providence about that nose* (Rider Haggard, Dawn iv, 1884) (cf. Visser 1969, 1477).

Obligative *have got to* appears to enter written language at the end of the 19th century. The OED gives the first examples of deontic *have got to* from 1865 and 1875, i.e. examples (84) and (85) (s.v. "get, v.24", OED online version 2012). Gronemeyer also gives these occurrences as evidence for the development of the root sense of *have got to* in the late 19th century (cf. Gronemeyer 1999, 33).

(84) The first thing I've *got to* do is grow to my right size again.[45]

(85) This *has got to* be learned.[46]

This dating is also in line with Visser's first attestation of deontic *have got to* from 1860 (cf. Visser 1969, 1479).[47]

(86) he always remembers when I've *got to* take my doctor's stuff[48]

Krug suggests an earlier date for the first occurrence of obligative *have got*,[49] which can already be found in Dickens's *Oliver Twist* from the late 1840s in representations of non-standard speech (cf. (87), cf. Krug 2000, 62). Krug argues that this occurrence "suggests that HAVE GOT TO must have existed in spoken English for some time by then" (Krug 2000, 62).

(87) 'Never did, sir!' ejaculated the beadle. 'No, nor nobody never did; but she's dead, we've *got to* bury her;...'[50]

Anderwald even finds evidence for the existence of *have got to* before Dickens's examples from 1837 in negative comments on the semi-modal *have got to* in American grammars from 1827 and 1832 (cf. Anderwald 2016, 230). Based on this, she concludes that deontic *have got to* must have already been established at the beginning of the 19th century (cf. Anderwald 2016, 230). Example

---

45   1865 Carroll, *Alice in Wonderland*.
46   1875 Twain in *Atlantic Monthly*.
47   Jespersen also dates the first occurrences of deontic *have got to* to the middle of the 19th century (Jespersen 1954, 51). Beaconsfield L 223 *I have got to see the Bishop tomorrow morning* (1870 Disraeli, *Lothair*).
48   Eliot, *Mill on the Floss* I, IX.
49   Visser also states that *have/had got to* + infinitive "did not come into general use until the third decade of the 19th century" (Visser 1973, 2411), which would approximate Krug's dating of deontic *have got to* (cf. Krug 2000, 62) but does not give an example to support this claim.
50   1837/38 Dickens, *Oliver Twist* v, 80.

(88) supports this claim, as it was published in 1830 but composed prior to the author's death in 1818.

(88) Remember that you *have got to* love God, or else you perish for ever.[51]

If compared to the development of *have to* (cf. Table 10), *have got to* enters the language at stage 5 of the development of *have to* and then grammaticalises further than *have to* (cf. Krug 2000, 72). In stage 6 of its development, *have got to* undergoes contraction of *have*, e.g. *you've got to look* (cf. Krug 2000, 72). In stage 7, *have* is deleted altogether (e.g. *you got to be careful*) and finally or parallel to the sixth and seventh stages, a coalescence of *got* and the infinitive marker *to* can be identified and is represented in the orthographic form <gotta>, e.g. *you gotta run* (cf. Krug 2000, 72; cf. Lorenz 2013 for a study on semi-modal contractions). This form resembles the grammatical behaviour of the core modal verbs more closely (cf. Krug 2000, 72).[52] Denison states that the omission of *have* starts in the 20th century and gives (89) as the first example of invariant *got to* from 1909 (cf. Denison 1998, 173).

(89) 'I don't know', said Dickie, 'but we *got to* do it som'how.'[53]

Łęcki agrees with Denison's dating of *have* omission starting in the first half of the 20th century (cf. Łęcki 2010, 142). However, the OED gives an even earlier attestation from 1884 (s.v. "get, *v.*24b", OED online version 2012):

(90) We *got to* dig in like all git-out.[54]

---

51   1830 *Memoirs of Henry Obookiah*. Note that Łęcki gives an even earlier example from 1827: *I have got to work after Fuseli for a little Shakespeare* (Blake, *The Letters of William Blake*) (cf. Łęcki 2010, 141). Note, for AmE, Hull's grammar from 1829 already comments on *I have got to go* as an incorrect expression (cf. Webster's 1989, s.v. "have got" no.2).

52   Mair (2014) shows that *have got to* has further grammaticalised in contemporary AmE, where *got to* has been reanalysed as a monomorphemic main verb and starts to appear with *do*-support, e.g. *I don't care what people say. I don't got to explain myself to nobody, man* (COCA, Press, example taken from Mair 2014, 57).

53   1909 Nesbit, *Harding's Luck*, v.105.

54   Twain, *Adventures Huckleberry Finn*, xxxviii, 325. Example sentence (90) is part of a representation of non-standard spoken AmE. The context contains other non-standard features, such as the use of *ain't got* and multiple negation in the preceding sentence: 'We *ain't got no time to bother over that*,' he says. Cf. also Mair on the three variants of *have got* in negative contexts in North AmE, the 'standard variant' *have not got*, the 'traditional vernacular variant' *ain't got*, and the 'modern-vernacular variant' *don't got/doesn't got* (cf. Mair 2014, 63–64).

The first attestation of contracted *gotta* in the OED can be found in 1924 (cf. (91), s.v. "gotta, *v.*", OED online version 2012).

(91) He ... went forward as if to take her arm. 'You *gotta* come along,' I heard.[55]

Today obligative *have got to* is frequently used but considered informal (cf. Krug 2000, 63). Krug shows that its frequency is one and a half times higher than the frequency of *must* in present-day spoken BrE and calls the rise of *have got to* "a success story" (Krug 2000, 63).

As *must* and *have to*, *have got to* has also acquired an epistemic sense (cf. Gronemeyer 1999, 5). The root sense is, however, the predominant sense (cf. Gronemeyer 1999, 5). The epistemic sense of *have got to* seems to have entered the English language in the second half of the 20th century, as example (92) from 1961 demonstrates.[56] Denison claims that epistemic *have got to* spread from AmE to BrE (cf. Denison 1998, 172).

(92) This *has got to* be some kind of local phenomenon.[57]

The historical development of *have got to* shows that it only emerged in its deontic sense in the first half of the 19th century, after India entered the second phase of Schneider's (2007) model, and that it was still rare when the Exonormative Stabilisation phase started in Singapore and Hong Kong (cf. Sections 3.2.1–3.2.3). Thus deontic *have got to* was not in the input variety of BrE when interaction between STL and IDG strand increased in the second phase of the development of IndE. Deontic *have got to* was still infrequent in the input variety of BrE when Singapore and Hong Kong entered the second phase. The major rise in the frequency of *have got to* occurred around 1900 (cf. Krug 2000, 81). Neither reduced deontic *got to* nor contracted deontic *gotta* were part of the input variety BrE to all three varieties. Epistemic *have got to* developed long after IndE, SgE, and HKE reached the second phase and was therefore not part of the input variety either.

---

55   1924 Buchan, *Three Hostages*, xviii, 263. This sentence also appears in direct speech and the spelling probably represents the use of contracted *got to* in spoken language.

56   Łęcki claims that the epistemic meaning of *have got to* occurs roughly a century earlier in Charles Dickens's *Great Expectations* from 1861: '*I could have told you that, Orlick.*' *'Ah!' said he, drily. 'But then you've got to be a scholar.'* (cf. Łęcki 2010, 141). This example is difficult to classify and a lexical reading cannot entirely be ruled out (in the sense of 'you have become a scholar').

57   Cf. Gronemeyer 1999, 6; Harmon 1961, *The Planet with No Nightmare*.

6.1.4   *The Grammaticalisation of* need to

Need to is the last modal marker that enters the field of obligation and necessity. The different stages of its grammaticalisation path from a lexical verb to an epistemic semi-modal verb can be seen in Table 11.

While Visser traces the origin of present-day *need* to the impersonal OE verb *(ge)neodan* (cf. Visser 1969, 1424), more recent studies on *need* trace its origin to an OE personal verb *neodian/neadian* that means 'compel', 'force' (cf. van der Auwera & Taeymans 2006, 41; Loureiro-Porto 2009, 141).[58] The OED lists this verb under *need, v.*[1] 'compel', 'force', separate from *need, v.*[2] 'to be necessary' (s.v. "need, *v.*[1]" and s.v. "need, *v.*[2]", OED online version 2003). However, Molencki, van der Auwera and Taeymans, and Loureiro-Porto subscribe to the view that *need, v.*[1] and *need, v.*[2] are manifestations of one and the same verb in OE that was used with both meanings 'compel', 'force' and 'to be necessary' (cf. Molencki 2002, 378; van der Auwera & Taeymans 2006, 41; Loureiro-Porto 2009, 143). Loureiro-Porto gives several reasons for treating both uses together: (1) they both derive from the OE noun *nid*, (2) the OE verbs *neodian* and *neadian* are synonyms in OE, (3) the semantics of both verbs are related,[59] and (4) both verbs have the same form in ME (*neden*), where *need, v.*[1] is ultimately replaced by *need, v.*[2] (cf. Loureiro-Porto 2009, 143). The semantic relatedness of the two uses leads to the argument that the impersonal use 'to be necessary for' (*neodian*) developed from the personal use 'compel', 'force' (*neadian*) (cf. van

TABLE 11   The grammaticalisation of *need to*

<neodian/neadian	'compel', 'be necessary'
1 *Hys selfe may do that, he nede commaunde non other* rise of the group of semi-modal verbs	absence of obligation (modal)
2 *Boris needs to sleep ten hours every night for him to function properly.*	obligation/necessity (semi-modal)
3 *That needs to be time-consuming.*	inferred certainty (semi-modal)

---

58   The OED suggests *(ge)neodian* as the base form (s.v. "need, *v.*2", OED online version 2003; cf. also the discussion in van der Auwera and Taeymans 2006, 39–40).

59   Nokkonen provides an example of a bridging context between the two meanings of *need, v.*1 ('compel') and *need, v.*2 ('be necessary'), where *need, v.*1 occurs in the passive (cf. Nokkonen 2015, 25).

der Auwera & Taeymans 2006, 41) (cf. (93) from van der Auwera and Taeymans 2006, 40, my emphasis).

(93) Eft   se   pap *nedde* þone abbud Adrianus þæt he
     afterwards   the   pope compel the   abbot Adrianus that he
     Biscophade   onfenge
     office of bishop take up
     'Afterwards the pope forced the abbot Adrianus to take up the office of bishop'.

The use of *neodian* with the meaning 'to be necessary' (*need, v.²*) developed in late OE according to van der Auwera and Taeymans, and Nokkonen (cf. van der Auwera & Taeymans 2006, 40; Nokkonen 2015, 24). Loureiro-Porto shows that the use of *need, v.²* already becomes more frequent than that of *need, v.¹* from the middle of the ME period onwards (period M3 1350–1420), while *need, v.¹* has its last attestation in the same period after declining sharply from late OE onwards (cf. Loureiro-Porto 2009, 144). The last attestation in the OED dates from the end of the 15th century.

According to the OED, the history of the verb *need, v.²* is marked by two major developments. First, the verb undergoes a change from impersonal to personal use. Second, the lexical verb *need* develops modal characteristics. In OE, *need* is used as a lexical verb in impersonal constructions (cf. Warner 1993, 203), i.e. with the person or thing affected in the dative ('something is necessary for someone/something'), e.g. (94) (from Nokkonen 2015, 25, my emphasis).

(94) [...] it *nedis to* hym to do many gud werkis.[60]
     'he needs to do many good works'

This use was still found in ME "in the types *Me nedeth* + infinitive, *it nedeth* (*to*) *me* + infinitive and *it nedeth* + infinitive" (Visser 1969, 1424). These constructions favoured the infinitive marker *to* (or *for to*) (cf. Visser 1969, 1424). According to Visser, personal uses of *need* developed in the first centuries of ME, most likely as a result of the loss of dative endings on nouns (*me nedeth →
I need*), which also affected other verbs such as *like* (cf. Visser 1969, 1425). The development of personal uses of *need, v.²* resulted in ambiguous statements between the 'force, compel' reading of *need, v.¹* and the 'necessary' reading of *need, v.²*; *I needed him* could mean 'I forced him' or 'I had need of him' (cf. van

---

60   1340 Hampole, *Prose Treatises* (EETS), IX, 32, 10.

der Auwera & Taeymans 2006, 45). This ambiguity may have been a factor that conditioned the demise of *need, v.*[1] (cf. Nokkonen 2015, 27). First instances of the personal use of *need* with marked infinitive occurred towards the end of the 14th century according to Visser (1969, 1425–1426), e.g. (95) with marked infinitive with *for to*.

(95) More þan he *nediþ* for *to* have.[61]
      'More than he needs to have'.

An example of the personal use of *need* followed by the *to*-infinitive is given in (96) from the beginning of the 15th century (from Nokkonen 2015, 27, my emphasis).

(96) A welle also, at whiche many folk her water fecche, *Nedethe to* have the larger mouthe.[62]

First attestations of the use of personal *need* with bare infinitive can also be found towards the end of the 14th century, as in (97) from 1390.

(97) þou maiȝt not longe endure, And *nedes* dye.[63]
      'You must not long endure and need to die'.

The use of personal *need* with bare infinitive increased in the 15th century (cf. Nokkonen 2006, 35). The development of this use is closely intertwined with the gradual loss of the preterite-present verb *þurfan*, which was the OE equivalent of present-day personal *need* (cf. Visser 1969, 1423; van der Auwera & Taeymans 2006, 46).[64] It was used in non-assertive contexts to express the absence of obligation and necessity and was followed by the bare infinitive, e.g. (98).

---

61   1380 Wyclif, *Select English Works*. III, 348.
62   1412 Hoccleve, *De Reg. Princ.* 16.
63   1390 In a Pistel (in Brown, *Relig. Lyr.* XIVth C.) 75.
64   Molencki (2002) gives a detailed account of the relationship between *dearr* and *þearf* in OE, which were still clearly distinct auxiliaries then. They represented exceptional members of the group of preterite-present verbs (also called 'pre-modals') in that they were mostly restricted to non-assertive contexts and could sometimes occur with third person marking. In this way, OE *þearf* was not dissimilar to PDE *need*. Molencki (2002, 379) also shows that similar processes of replacement occurred in other Germanic languages.

(98) gif   he   gewitnesse   hæbbe,   ne   *þearf*   he   ðæt   geldan[65]
     if   he   knowledge   has   NEG   need   he   that   pay
     'if he knows that he is not bound to pay by law'[65]

It was ousted by *need* by the end of the 15th century (although it survived longer in some dialects) because of a state of homonymy with the OE preterite-present *durran* ('dare') (cf. Molencki 2002, 378). While the form was taken over by *dare*, the meaning of OE *þurfan* was taken over by *need*,[66] whose frequency in non-assertive contexts started to rise.[67] *Need* thereby replaced OE *þurfan* and filled the gap in the meaning of negative *must* (cf. Nokkonen 2015, 27). As a result, most of the early instances of personal *need* with bare infinitive are found in non-assertive contexts.[68] *Need* then developed an irregular form without third person marking (cf. Nokkonen 2006, 35), probably a generalised form of the subjunctive (cf. Barber 1997, 178). Molencki ascribes the development of modal characteristics of *need* to its new role as a substitute for *þurven*, which had modal characteristics (cf. Molencki 2002, 379). In this way, *need* started to be used with modal characteristics in the 16th century. This dating is in line with Barber, who gives (99) from the OED as the first attestation of modal *need* from 1538 (cf. Barber 1997, 178).

(99) Hys selfe may do that, he *nede* commaunde non other.[69]

Warner (1993) and Nokkonen (2006) also support the view that early uses of *need* with modal characteristics can be found in the 16th century. Barber states that the modal use of *need* has been common since then (cf. Barber 1997, 179) and Krug finds that Shakespeare already strongly prefers the modal use of *need* over its lexical use (cf. Krug 2000, 202).

---

65   c.890–901 Alfred *Laws* Introduction c. 28.
66   The replacement in the verbal domain was preceded and probably catalysed by a comparable replacement in the nominal domain, i.e. by the replacement of *þearf* by *neod* (cf. van der Auwera & Taeymans 2006, 48–49).
67   It is interesting to note that *dare* – like *need* – can also function as a main verb and as an auxiliary verb in PDE (cf. van der Auwera & Taeymans 2006, 46–47).
68   Non-assertive contexts include interrogative sentences, negative sentences, sentences with negative adverbs (*hardly*, *scarcely*, etc.), conditional clauses, and clauses with universal quantifiers (e.g. *all*) (cf. Taeymans 2004, 98). Van der Auwera, Noël, and De Wit refer to these contexts as 'negative polarity contexts' (cf. van der Auwera, Noël & De Wit 2012, 55).
69   1538 Bale, *Thre Lawes*, 1629. The newer version of the OED from 2003 dates this quote 10 years later (?1548).

Today the situation from Shakespeare's times has been completely inverted with a strong preference for *need* with main verb characteristics over *need* with modal characteristics (cf. Quirk et al. 1985, 138; Krug 2000, 202–203). Taeymans's study on a sample of the BNC shows that the ratio of modal *need* to main verb use *need* is about 1:8.3 (84:701) in written English and 1:21.3 (40:852) in spoken English (cf. Taeymans 2004, 103). She describes the development of *need* as 'oscillating' between main verb and modal verb status (cf. Taeymans 2004, 97). The development from modal verb to lexical verb status may at first sight go against the assumed unidirectionality of grammaticalisation processes (cf. Taeymans 2004, 104). However, as lexical *need* coexisted with modal *need* at all times (cf. Taeymans 2004, 98), this chain of development can therefore more adequately be described as 'retraction' (cf. Haspelmath 2004, 33–35; Loureiro-Porto 2009, 216) rather than as the development of a more lexical variant on the basis of a more grammatical variant, which would indeed go against the unidirectionality hypothesis of grammaticalisation. What we see then is a "'short-lived innovation'" (Taeymans 2004, 104) of the modal *need* and a subsequent retraction of this form in favour of the lexical verb *need*, so that "we are now confronted with a situation where modal usage has almost disappeared in favour of the semi-modal construction" (Taeymans 2004, 104). Where the modal *need* occurs, it is restricted to non-assertive contexts, while the semi-modal verb *need to* is unrestricted in its use (cf. Quirk et al. 1985, 138).

Diachronic studies on the development of the modal *need* and the semi-modal *need to* show that *need* is declining in its modal use and rising in its use as a main verb. Krug provides apparent-time evidence for the rise of *need* with main verb characteristics based on the BNC (cf. Krug 2000, 202–203; cf. also Nokkonen 2010, 58). The rise of *need to* in the second half of the 20th century was also identified in studies based on the BROWN quartet of corpora, which show a substantial increase in frequency between the 1960s and the 1990s for both BrE and AmE, and a simultaneous decrease in the frequency of the modal verb *need* (cf. Leech 2003, 229; Smith 2003, 248–249; Leech et al. 2009, 93–94). Müller also identifies a rise of the semi-modal *need to* between 1950–1960 and 1994–2004, and a simultaneous decrease of the modal *need* in this period based on the OED (cf. Müller 2008, 77). The period of 1950–1960 marks a turning point in the development of the modal *need* and semi-modal *need to*, as the main verb use surpasses the frequency of the modal use for the first time (cf. Müller 2008, 77).

Syntactically, the rise of *need to* takes place in affirmative contexts (cf. Smith 2003, 260), i.e. in contexts where the semi-modal could be a possible rival to *must, have to*, and *have got to*, e.g. (100) from van der Auwera and Plungian (1998, 80, my emphasis).

(100) Boris *needs to* sleep ten hours every night for him to function properly.

In line with Smith's (2003) findings, Nokkonen calls the use of *need to* in positive polarity contexts "a novelty" (Nokkonen 2006, 35). Taking this new context of use into account, Smith argues that *need to* can function as a deontic marker similar to *must* and *have to*:

> it can acquire the force of an imposed obligation, but – something which does not apply to the other markers – the writer or speaker can claim that the required action is merely being recommended for the doer's own sake.
>
> SMITH 2003, 260

In this way, the speaker "can downplay his/her own authority" (Nokkonen 2006, 37), which leads to a more indirect and therefore more polite way of expressing an obligation than subjective *must*. In this way, the obligation use of *need to* becomes established via pragmatic inference (cf. (101) from Leech 2004a, 102, my emphasis).

(101) You *need to* get a hair-cut.

The development from participant-internal to participant-external uses is supported by data from Müller, who attributes the rise of *need to* from 1950 onwards to the rise in its most recent use as a marker of obligation/necessity (cf. Müller 2008, 86). Tagliamonte and D'Arcy date the first occurrence of *need to* with an obligation/necessity meaning to the middle of the 19th century based on the OED (cf. Tagliamonte & D'Arcy 2007, 51, my emphasis).

(102) They *need to* be taught ... how vain are those objects.[70]

However, the updated version of the OED shows several earlier instances of *need to* with an obligation/necessity reading in assertive contexts (s.v. "need, *v.*[2], 10a", OED online version 2003), such as (103) from 1398. Nokkonen dates the first uses of *need to* with a general necessity reading towards EModE, slightly later than (103) (cf. Nokkonen 2015, 30, my emphasis).

---

70   1842 R.I. Wilberforce, *Rutilius and Lucius*, 116.

(103)   A good phisician *nediþ to* loke wel a-boute and be ful ware.[71]

The difference in the dating of early attestations of *need to* between Tagliamonte and D'Arcy and the OED probably stems from differences in the frequency
of *need to* in affirmative contexts in the different periods. *Need to* was polarity
neutral before the EModE period and then increased its use in non-assertive
contexts, so that by the end of Late Modern English (LModE) *need to* was predominantly used in non-assertive contexts (cf. Nokkonen 2015, 28). From the
end of LModE onwards, the use of *need to* in affirmative contexts increased
gradually and in PDE *need to* is polarity neutral again (cf. Nokkonen 2015, 28).
And although the use of *need to* in affirmative contexts had already started to
increase from the end of LModE onwards, a substantial increase only occurred
after 1950 (cf. Leech 2003, 229; Smith 2003, 248–249; Müller 2008, 81; Leech et
al. 2009, 97).[72]

   This point in time also marks the end point of the "formative period" of
several semi-modal verbs (cf. Krug 2000, 169), which leads Leech et al. to argue
that *need to* developed from the transitive main verb *need* "as part of the more
recent wave of grammaticalization which has given us new semi-modals such
as WANT *to*" (Leech et al. 2009, 94). This line of argumentation maintains that
need to has developed independently from modal verb *need* and "is not the
variant of modal *need(n't)*" (cf. Leech et al. 2009, 94), which is why the two
should be treated separately. The development of lexical *need* as a member of
the group of emerging modals may have been supported by noun constructions such as *a need to do something* (cf. Leech et al. 2009, 94). This approach
may also explain why *need to* can occur in assertive contexts, whereas modal
need is restricted to non-assertive contexts (cf. Leech et al. 2009, 94). Müller
also treats *need to* as an emergent modal and supports her argument by showing that *need to* does not take over functions of modal *need* (cf. Müller 2008,
86). As *need to* occurs in non-assertive contexts with an obligation/necessity
reading and therefore shares syntactic and semantic characteristics with modal and semi-modal verbs of obligation and necessity, it should be considered a
PDE rival to *must, have to*, and *have got to* rather than the lexical counterpart to
modal *need* in affirmative contexts. This is why I will only include *need to* in my
analyses and exclude modal *need* in further discussions, although I included
it in the historical description in order to address the intertwined history between modal *need* and semi-modal *need to*.

---

71   1398 J. Trevisa tr. Bartholomaeus Anglicus, *De Proprietatibus Rerum* (BL Add.), f. 102.
72   Millar's study based on the TIME corpus suggests an earlier rise (starting after the 1930s)
       of *need to* in AmE newspaper language (cf. Millar 2009, 204).

Like the other modal and semi-modal verbs in the field, *need to* has also developed epistemic readings as Nokkonen's studies based on the BROWN quartet for written BrE and LLC, COLT (*The Bergen Corpus of London Teenage Language*), and the BNC for spoken BrE reveal (cf. Nokkonen 2006, 2010, 2012). One of her examples from the demographically sampled part of the BNC is given in (104) (from Nokkonen 2012, 134, my emphasis).

(104) Sue: It's, it's the, the
      Kevin: it's the follow up it's the phone calling.
      Sue: Yeah.
      Kevin: and the follow up of cases.
      Sue: Yeah.
      Kevin: that *needs to* be time consuming[73]

However, epistemic meanings are still rare, an additional characteristic which aligns *need to* with the other semi-modal verbs of obligation and necessity (cf. Sections 6.1.2 and 6.1.3 on *have to* and *have got to*). There seems to be a clear specialisation of meanings in that the semi-modal verbs almost categorically denote root meaning, while epistemic meanings seem to be restricted to the core modal verb *must*.

To summarise, the form *need to* was already part of the input variety when IndE, SgE, and HKE entered the second phase of Schneider's (2007) model, however it was not yet used as a rival to *must, have to,* and *have got to* as its use in affirmative contexts only increased after the middle of the 20th century. Epistemic readings of *need to* cannot have been part of the historical input varieties either.

6.1.5   *Summary: The BrE Input Variety*

The overview of the historical development of the modal and semi-modal verbs of obligation shows that the domain has been reorganised over time. The oldest layer *must* already had deontic meaning in late OE. *Must* develops its epistemic reading at the end of the 14th century in collocation with a rein-forcing adverb and starts to be used in its epistemic sense without reinforcing adverb in the 17th century. The grammaticalisation of *have to* begins in the EModE period but a major rise in the frequency of *have to* occurs only in the second half of the 19th century. Deontic *have got to* enters the English language in the first half of the 19th century but does not increase in frequency until 1900. The most recent layer of the deontic markers is *need to*. Although first

---

73   H5E 707.

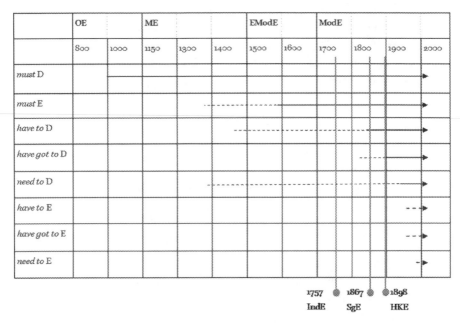

	OE		ME			EModE		ModE			
	800	1000	1150	1300	1400	1500	1600	1700	1800	1900	2000
must D											
must E											
have to D											
have got to D											
need to D											
have to E											
have got to E											
need to E											

1757 ● 1867 ● ●1898
IndE   SgE   HKE

FIGURE 32   The historical state of the modal domain of obligation and necessity in the input
variety BrE.

attestations could be found at the end of the 14th century, it does not rise in
frequency in affirmative contexts until the second half of the 20th century. All
of the semi-modal verbs under analysis have also developed epistemic uses
towards the end of the 20th century. However, these uses are rare for all semi-
modal verbs under investigation and have only recently been identified for
need to. Figure 32 gives an overview of the historical state of the input variety
BrE at the beginning of the second phase in IndE, SgE, and HKE.

When IndE entered the second phase in 1757, *must* had already been part of
the BrE variety for a long time in its deontic sense, and its epistemic sense was
also firmly established. *Have to* was still infrequent at this point in time and
only used in its deontic sense. *Have got to* was not yet part of BrE, neither in its
deontic nor in its epistemic sense. Early instances of *need to* with a necessity/
obligation reading were already present, but *need to* had not grammaticalised
yet.

When SgE entered the second phase in 1867, *must* was, of course, still part
of the input in its deontic and epistemic sense. Deontic *have to* rose strongly in
its frequency in the middle of the 19th century and was probably not as infrequent as in the IndE input anymore. First instances of deontic *have got to* entered the written language in the first half of the 19th century in BrE. The major

rise in its frequency occurred around 1900 at least in written language. *Have got to* may therefore have been part of the BrE input variety but was probably still infrequently used when SgE entered the second phase. The same is true for deontic *need to*, which only rose in frequency after 1950. Epistemic readings of the semi-modal verbs were not present in 1867 at all.

When HKE entered the second phase in 1898, *must* had been established for a long time in its deontic and epistemic senses and the major rise in the frequency of *have to* had already occurred in the middle of the 19th century. Deontic *have got* was still rarely used, since the major rise in its frequency occurred only shortly after HKE entered phase 2. *Need to* was not yet frequently used in its deontic sense in 1898 and epistemic uses of *have to*, *have got to*, and *need to* were not yet part of the input variety BrE at this point.

6.1.6 *Frequency Patterns after Grammaticalisation*

As the overview in Figure 32 shows, *must* was already used in its root as well as its epistemic reading when IndE, SgE, and HKE entered the second phase of 'Exornormative Stabilisation'. However, while dating the emergence of variants and their senses can give us a general idea about the variants and senses which were potentially part of the input variety, it cannot tell us anything about the frequency distribution of the senses, once they have become established. Quantitative diachronic data for the distribution of the senses of *must* in the 18th and 19th century are relatively scarce, as most studies on the relationship between the two senses of *must* are restricted to the 20th century (cf. Leech 2003; Smith 2003; Leech et al. 2009). While these studies show that *must* decreases most strongly in its root meaning (Leech 2003, 233; Smith 2003, 248–249; Leech et al. 2009, 87–88), it is unclear whether the trend of the decrease of root *must* already started in the 18th and 19th century when IndE, SgE, and HKE entered the second phase.

The only data available for frequency changes in the use of the two senses of *must* in the 18th and 19th century come from Biber (2004) and Dollinger (2008). Biber gives several examples to illustrate the expansion of the meaning of *must* in the letter section of ARCHER from predominantly root meaning in 17th- and 18th-century letters to both root and epistemic meanings in the 20th century (cf. Biber 2004, 206–207). In 17th- and 18th-century newspapers, *must* was already used in root and epistemic senses but became restricted to root uses by the 20th century (cf. Biber 2004, 208–209). Dollinger analyses the development of the senses of *must* in BrE between 1750–1799 and 1800–1849 in the letter, newspaper, and journal section of ARCHER as part of his study on the development of the modal auxiliaries in CanE (cf. Dollinger 2008, 205–226). His study shows that root uses are on the decline from 1750–1799 to 1800–1849, while epistemic senses are on the rise (cf. Dollinger 2008, 220–222). This overview shows that quantitative studies on the development of the senses of *must* are missing for the period under question, i.e. 1757–1898. In order to close the gap, a quantitative analysis on the frequency development of the senses of *must* was carried out based on the basis of the periods 1750–1799 and 1850–1899 of the BrE component of ARCHER 3.2.

Apart from the research gap identified for this particular time period, quantitative studies on the development of the senses are generally scarce and usually only cover a short period of time depending on the researcher's focus (cf. Gotti et al. 2002, 173–174; Leech 2003, 233; Smith 2003, 257; Biber 2004, 206–210; Dollinger 2008, 220–222; Leech et al. 2009, 285; Close & Aarts 2010, 176–177), which is why coherent long-term studies based on one database are missing. In order to close this research gap, I coded all instances of *must* (N=2,170) according to their meanings in the BrE section of ARCHER 3.2 between 1600 and 1999 (cf. Figure 33).[74] While the existing studies on the development of the senses of *must* all point to a relative increase in the epistemic use of *must* for the

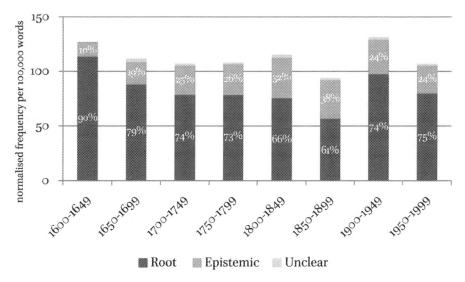

FIGURE 33   Development of *must* in its root and epistemic meaning between 1600 and 1999 in ARCHER, normalised frequency per 100,000 words (cf. Table 27 in the appendices).

---

74   I excluded all instances of negated *must* from my analysis because they were almost categorically deontic except for a few examples of epistemic *mustn't* at the beginning of the 19th century such as *Guernsey must not be a very comfortable residence for a stranger* (1809_anon_j5b).

respective periods, my study based on the BrE section of ARCHER 3.2 shows that epistemic senses of *must* do not rise steadily, neither in terms of their share nor in terms of their relative frequency. On the whole, the 20th century seems to be the 'odd one out' in the general tendency with a re-emergence of root readings as compared to the earlier centuries represented in ARCHER 3.2, as can be seen in Figure 33. Changes in the distributions of deontic and epistemic *must* between 1850–1899 and 1900–1949 are significant at the p<0.001 level (2×2 χ^2 test).

For the purposes of the study, the developments between the time periods of 1750–1799 and 1850–1899 are of particular relevance because they can provide the database for the analysis of BrE at the time of input for IndE in 1757, for SgE in 1867, and HKE in 1898, respectively. ARCHER is the only corpus available for the period under investigation and comprises only written language. However, it lends itself well to this analysis as it represents the kind of English typical of the more formal contexts of use in the colonies. Figure 34 shows the development of *must* between 1750–1799 and 1850–1899. The findings indicate that *must* is declining overall from a text frequency of 108 tokens per 100,000 words to a text frequency of 93 tokens per 100,000 words (M-co). The text frequency of *must* in its root sense decreases from 79 tokens to 57 tokens (M-co). The share of root uses also decreases from 73% to 61%. Epistemic uses are, instead, on the rise with an increased text frequency from 28 tokens to 35 tokens (M-co) and a relative increase from 26% to 38%. The changes in the distributions of deontic *must* and epistemic *must* are significant at the p<0.01 level (2×2 χ^2 test).

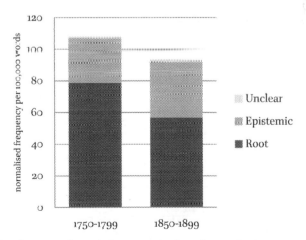

FIGURE 34   Development of *must* in its root and epistemic meaning between 1750–1799 and 1850–1899 in ARCHER, normalised frequency per 100,000 words (cf. Table 28 in the appendices).

6.1.7   *Founder Effect?*

The preceding sections clarified the state of the input variety at the time when IndE, SgE, and HKE entered the second phase in Schneider's (2007) model. If the founder principle has explanatory value for the synchronic variability of the varieties under investigation, we would expect to find correlations between the state of the historical BrE input variety and the synchronic state of the new varieties. As the domain of obligation and necessity has been reorganised in between the points in time when IndE, SgE, and HKE entered the second phase of Schneider's (2007) model, we would expect IndE, SgE, and HKE to show differences according to the state of the input variety. In order to assess the role of the BrE input variety on synchronic variability, the findings of the preceding section will now be compared to the findings for IndE, SgE, and HKE based on the synchronic ICE corpora from Chapter 5.

In the case of *must*, we would expect ICE-IND* to have a higher frequency of *must* than ICE-HK, as *must* is on the decline in BrE between 1757 and 1898, the points in time when IndE and HKE entered the second phase, respectively. This hypothesis is borne out by the ICE data. However, the high frequency of *must* in ICE-SIN does not fit the picture. There is also no correlation between the distribution of the senses of *must* in IndE, SgE, and HKE and their respective BrE input variety.[75] The shift towards more epistemic uses between 1750–1799 and 1850–1899 does not seem to have affected IndE, SgE, and HKE. IndE has the highest text frequency of epistemic uses with 23 tokens per 100,000 words, while ICE-SIN and ICE-HK show a markedly lower text frequency of epistemic *must* with 14 and 15 tokens per 100,000 words, respectively, although they entered the second phase much later. If we assume that the founder principle holds, we would expect a lower frequency of epistemic *must* in ICE-IND* compared to ICE-SIN and ICE-HK.

The findings for root *have to* have shown that ICE-SIN has the lowest frequency of *have to* with 84 tokens per 100,000 words, followed by ICE-IND* with 107 tokens, and ICE-HK with 113 tokens. Figure 35 shows the state of the historical input variety with regard to the frequency of deontic *have to* with data drawn from the British component of ARCHER 3.2, including all forms of *have to*.

---

75   As some may consider the onset of stage 2 of Schneider's (2007) model a rather arbitrary date in time for the reconstruction of the historical input variety (despite the justification given above), it is important to note that the overall picture does not change when the states of the historical input varieties of the Foundation phase or the Exonormative Stabilisation phase of Schneider's (2007) model are taken as reference points for each variety. Even then, there is no correlation between the state of the historical input varieties and the present-day state of the varieties in terms of their distributions of the senses of *must*.

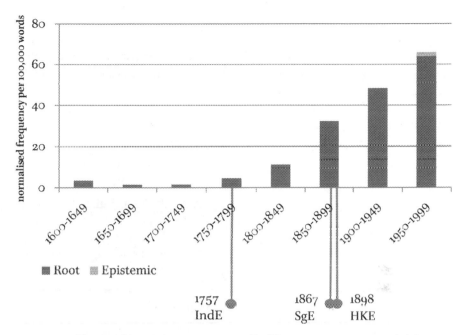

FIGURE 35   The rise of *have to* in ARCHER, normalised frequency per 100,000 words (cf. Table 29 in the appendices).

As can be seen in Figure 35, IndE entered the second phase before the major increase in the frequency of *have to* in 1850, while SgE and HKE entered the second phase after the major increase. The very high frequency of *have to* in ICE-HK may therefore indeed be linked to the state of the input variety. However, IndE entered the second phase almost a century earlier than HKE and shows a comparable frequency of use, which cannot be explained along the same lines. The almost equal distribution of *must* and *have to* in ICE-SIN also calls for an alternative explanation (cf. Figure 25 in Chapter 5). The nature of the input variety can, however, explain the low frequency of epistemic *have to* in all three varieties because epistemic *have to* was not part of the input variety at the time when IndE, HKE, and SgE entered the second phase.

The low frequency of root *have got to* in ICE-IND* can be linked to the state of the historical input variety (cf. Figure 26 in Chapter 5). When IndE entered the second phase of Schneider's (2007) model, root *have got to* was not yet part of the input. The frequency of root *have got to* in SgE is considerably higher, even higher than the frequency of *have got to* in ICE-HK (cf. Figure 26 in Chapter 5). SgE entered the second phase in 1867 after the first attestations of root *have got to* in the BrE input variety but before the major rise in its frequency around 1900. HKE entered the second phase in 1898 but shows a lower frequency of *have got to* than SgE. These findings cannot be explained by the nature of the input variety. However, the low frequency of epistemic *have got to* in all three varieties can be explained by the nature of the BrE input variety, as epistemic *have got to* was not part of the input variety.

The low frequency of *need to* in ICE-IND* may also be linked to the state of the BrE input variety, as *need to* was only rarely used in its root meaning in 1757 (cf. Figure 26 in Chapter 5). However, this state did not change when SgE and HKE entered the second phase, in 1867 and 1898, respectively. The unexpectedly high frequency of root *need to* in SgE and HKE (cf. Figure 26 in Chapter 5) therefore also needs further explanation. However, the low frequency of epistemic *need to* in all varieties does not come as a surprise given that epistemic *need to* was not part of the BrE input variety in any of the varieties under analysis. These findings suggest that the nature of the input variety can only partially explain the synchronic state of the domain of obligation and necessity in ICE-HK, ICE-IND*, and ICE-SIN.

It has to be kept in mind that the quantitative analysis is limited to data drawn from ARCHER, which is considered to be an adequate representation of the input variety because of the context of acquisition. As standard BrE was transmitted in the educational context, formal written standard BrE from the respective period was considered the most adequate representation of the input. Schneider's claim about the preservation of standard patterns in exploitation colonies and the absence of non-standard variants such as multiple negation justifies such a modelling of the input variety (cf. Schneider 2007, 101). But, although the classroom was "the main site at which world Englishes were forged" (Mesthrie 2006, 286), it still needs to be borne in mind that formal standard BrE was not the only input of the new varieties (cf. Mesthrie 2006, 277). The historical input was quite diverse and also contained non-standard language.[76] This is why the target language is best understood as "a varied and 'moving' target" (Mesthrie 2006, 277).

Despite these limitations, the representation of the historical input variety on the basis of ARCHER was instructive. The historical reconstruction of the domain of obligation and necessity gives us an empirical basis for postulating variants in the feature pool. It can go a long way towards explaining the

---

76   The input of non-standard speech was probably rather limited in the case of IndE. Mesthrie refers to Piggin, who states that most missionaries belonged to the upper socio-economic classes in the case of India (cf. Mesthrie 2006, 283–284). As social class variation and regional variation are correlated (cf. Trudgill 2000, 30), we can assume that the input variety was therefore close to the standard dialect.

minority variants. But not all variants can be accounted for by the structural make-up of the BrE input variety. As HKE, IndE, and SgE developed in language contact situations, the structural make-up of the relevant substrate languages needs to be taken into account next.

6.2 Substrate Languages

Substrate languages are important contributors to the feature pool in language contact situations. They contribute features with specific structural and semantic characteristics. Those features that are deemed to be equivalent in form and meaning are possible candidates for substratum influence on the L2, which is why the structure as well as the semantics of the L1 features expressing deontic obligation and epistemic necessity will be analysed in this section. A contact-linguistic perspective on modal markers is furthermore warranted by the fact that contact-induced restructurings of modal systems is quite common in the world's languages. Typological studies have shown that modal expressions are readily borrowed or calqued (cf. van der Auwera, Ammann & Kindt 2005, 260–261).

As Chapter 5 has shown, there are remarkable differences between the varieties with regard to the modal and semi-modal verbs of obligation and necessity. On the whole, all ESL varieties show a higher frequency of modal and semi-modal verbs of obligation and necessity as compared to the ENL varieties BrE and AmE. This finding will be further explored in Section 7.2, where the role of cultural factors in language variation and change will be discussed in more detail. The analysis of the senses of the modal and semi-modal verbs of obligation and necessity shows notable differences between the varieties with regard to the frequency of epistemic *must* (cf. Section 5.1). While BrE and IndE pattern alike in the frequency of epistemic *must*, HKE and SgE are marked by a significantly lower frequency than the latter two and show a strong deontic bias, with *must* only rarely expressing logical necessity here. As HKE and SgE both have a Sinitic language as their substrate language, analysing substrate influence as a possible explanation for the deontic bias of *must* seems promising. While the two Sino-Tibetan languages Cantonese, the substrate language of HKE, and Mandarin, one of the substrate languages of SgE are not mutually intelligible and are therefore sometimes deemed to be different languages rather than dialects of Chinese, their grammatical structure is similar (cf. Matthews & Yip 1994, 4; cf. also Section 3.2.3).

Apart from differences in the encoding of epistemic necessity, there are also differences in the encoding of deontic necessity. Here we can also observe a similar pattern in the use of *need to* in HKE and SgE as opposed to IndE. This also calls for an analysis of substrate influence. *Need to* has only recently become a rival of *must* and *have to* in affirmative contexts, as Section 6.1.4 has shown. Its recency lets one suspect that it is only rarely used in the ESL varieties, as is indeed the case in IndE. However, this hypothesis is not borne out by the data for ICE-HK and ICE-SIN, where *need to* is used with a comparatively high frequency (with an M-co of 29 and 25, respectively), even higher than the frequency of this semi-modal in BrE (with an M-co of 16, cf. Figure 26 in Chapter 5).

The differences between the varieties are less striking in the case of deontic *must* and *have to*, the two main competitors in the field of obligation and necessity in all varieties. Although *must* and *have to* are used with a markedly higher frequency in the three ESL varieties as compared to BrE and AmE, they share a similar distribution with the ENL varieties in that *have to* is preferred over *must* in all varieties being analysed (cf. Chapter 5). These similarities – especially between HKE and IndE – rather point to other mechanisms at work than substrate influence. Although it is possible that a similar outcome may be produced by similar structures in the substrate languages, it is more likely that universal cognitive processes and learner mechanisms underlie these similarities. If this line of argumentation is adopted, SgE with a comparatively higher proportion of *must* than HKE and IndE shows a divergent pattern.

In order not to rule out substrate influence a priori, I will describe the equivalents to English *must* and *have to* in Cantonese and Mandarin that may explain the unexpectedly divergent use in HKE and SgE. I will try to unravel the myriad interactions between relevant structures in the substrate languages and their equivalent structures in the ESL variety. In order to do this, I will perform a close analysis of the expressions of obligation and necessity in Cantonese for HKE, Mandarin, Malay, and Tamil for SgE, and the Indo-Aryan languages Hindi, Marathi, Konkani, and Malayalam, and the Dravidian languages Kannada, Tamil, and Telugu for IndE on the basis of relevant reference grammars. I restricted the analysis of the various mother tongues of the speakers of ICE-IND* to those where 20 or more tokens of epistemic and deontic *must* could be found. The description of the structure of the substrate languages will form the basis for the analysis of substratum influence by way of transfer in Section 7.1. With this procedure, I try to respond to Mesthrie's call for a more sophisticated treatment of substrate influence as an explanation for variation in L2 varieties of English (cf. Mesthrie 2008b, 634).

However, it needs to be noted that the approach adopted can only partially meet the complexities found in reality. The choice for Mandarin, Malay, and Tamil as the substrate languages of SgE are cases in point. Although these languages play an important role for present-day SgE, other languages that were involved in the actual formation of SgE are considered to have had a stronger impact such as Bazaar Malay, Hokkien, Teochew, and Cantonese (cf. Lim & Ansaldo 2015, 107–108; cf. also Section 3.2.3). However, as I was primarily interested in the cognitive process of transfer, I focused on the language contact taking place in the minds of the speakers. This means, my analysis of substrate influence on SgE is necessarily restricted to the synchronic language situation, which neglects the substrate languages involved in the earlier formation of SgE. This is of course problematic given the assumption that those speakers that shifted early to English were the ones who brought features from their substrate languages to the emerging L2 (cf. the 'Shifter Principle', Siegel 2008, 151). However, where functional descriptions of these substrate languages are available, they are usually from this or the 20th century, so that it is difficult to obtain information about the historical varieties of the relevant substrate languages that would allow me to analyse their influence on the emerging variety of English. Using Mandarin as the most important substrate languages for SgE is furthermore warranted by the fact that the Chinese dialects do not differ strongly in their morphosyntax (cf. Bao 2015, 20; cf. also Section 3.2.3).

The first hypothesis underlying the analysis of the substrate languages is that Cantonese (HKE) and Mandarin (SgE) do not have a feature that exhibits both deontic and epistemic readings in one form; while (at least some of) the substrate languages of IndE have a homomorphic feature that is associated with deontic and epistemic functions. The second hypothesis is that Cantonese and Mandarin have a formal and/or functional equivalent to *need to*, which has led to the unexpectedly high frequency of this semi-modal verb in HKE and SgE despite its recency as a deontic marker in BrE. The third hypothesis is that Mandarin has a structure which is equivalent to English *must*, which may have boosted its frequency in SgE.

The *World Atlas of Language Structures* (WALS, Haspelmath et al. 2005; Dryer & Haspelmath 2013) gives an overview of how the various languages of the world encode deontic (or 'situational' in their terminology)[77] and epistemic meanings (cf. van der Auwera & Ammann 2005, 312–313, van der Auwera & Ammann 2013). WALS categorises the languages of the world into: (1) languages that have one form[78] encoding both deontic and epistemic readings in the expression of possibility and necessity ('high overlap'), (2) languages

---

77   The term 'situational' is used to describe that the necessity is part of the situation in root modality, which is not the case in epistemic modality (cf. also van der Auwera, Ammann & Kindt 2005, 250). It therefore refers to the fact that root modality takes narrow scope while epistemic modality takes wide scope.

78   Note that the use of the vague term 'form' rather than the more precise 'modal verb' is used to cover all forms of modal expressions in languages, be they suffixes (as in the case of Dravidian Tamil, cf. (123) and (124)) or adverbs in the case of epistemic modality in Cantonese (cf. (116)). Some typologists suggest that the expression of modality by verbs

that encode both meanings in one form but either for necessity or for possibility ('some overlap'), and (3) languages that have no form which encodes both
meanings ('no overlap'). English, for example, shows 'modal polyfunctionality' (van der Auwera, Ammann & Kindt 2005, 249) in possibility and necessity
by using the same form to encode both deontic and epistemic readings, and
therefore falls into category (1), as examples (105) and (106), and (107) and (108)
from van der Auwera and Ammann (2013, my emphases) show.

Possibility

(105) You *may* go home now. (deontic)

(106) Bob *may* be mistaken about the cause of the accident. (epistemic)

Necessity

(107) You *must* go home now. (deontic)

(108) Terry *must* be from Northumberland. (epistemic)

Languages that fall into category (2) have an identical form that encodes
both readings but only for possibility or for necessity. Van der Auwera and
Ammann (2013) provide Hungarian as an example of this category, which
shows only identical forms for possibility but not for necessity, e.g. (109) and
(110).

Possibility

(109) *Haza*   **lehet**   *men-*   *n-*   *em?*   (deontic)
       to.home   may   go-   INF-   1SG
       'Am I allowed to go home?'

(110) **Lehet,**   *hogy*   *jöv-*   *ök.*   (epistemic)
       May   that   come-   IND.PRES.INDEF.1SG
       'I may be coming'.

---

is also a specific characteristic of European languages (cf. van der Auwera, Ammann &
Kindt 2005, 262).

Languages that fall into category (3) do not have markers that encode both deontic and epistemic readings, neither for possibility nor for necessity. Van der Auwera and Ammann (2013) give Evenki as an example of this category, which shows different forms for both readings for possibility, (111) and (112), and necessity (113) and (114).

Possibility

(111) *Ulguchen-* ***d'enge*** *bejetken amakan emc- d'e   n.*   (deontic)
      tell-   PTCP   boy   soon   come- FUT- 3SG
      'The boy who will be able to tell will come soon'.

(112) *Ga-*   ***na-***   *m.*   (epistemic)
      take-   POS-   1SG
      'Maybe I take/took recently'.

Necessity

(113) *Minggi- girki-   v   ilan-   duli- chas- tuli   suru-*
      my   friend- 1SG.POSS three- PROL hour- PROL go.away-
      mechin- *in.*   (deontic)
      NEC-   3SG.
      'My friend must go/leave in three hours'.

(114) *Su   tar   asatkan-   me   sa:-   **na-**   s.*   (epistemic)
      you   that   girl-   ACC.DEF   know   NEC-   2PL
      'You probably know that girl'.

The languages of type (1) with an overlap for both possibility and necessity such as English are in the minority if all languages of the world are taken into account and clearly cluster in Europe, as Figure 36 adapted from WALS shows. Typological studies show that only few languages in Europe do not exhibit multifunctionality in both possibility and necessity (Armenian, Catalan, Georgian, Hungarian, Welsh), which is why polyfunctionality in possibility and necessity "qualifies as an SAE [Standard Average European] feature" (van Olmen & van der Auwera 2016, 367; cf. also van der Auwera, Ammann & Kindt 2005, 247). Outside Europe, however, van der Auwera, Ammann, and Kindt only found the feature in one fifth of the world's languages based on an extended analysis of 241 languages (cf. van der Auwera, Ammann & Kindt 2005, 255; cf. Figure 36).

In WALS, there are only 36 languages attested with an overlap for both possibility and necessity (1) (black circles), 66 with an overlap for either possibility or necessity (2) (grey circles), and 105 with no overlap (3) (white circles). If we take a look at the distribution in Asia, we can see a mixed picture, which mirrors the general distribution of the languages of the world, with the highest number of languages showing no overlap, followed by languages with some overlap, and those with an overlap for possibility and necessity clearly in the minority. As far as the substrate languages of HKE, SgE, and IndE are concerned, we can find a partial overlap for either possibility or necessity in Cantonese, a complete overlap for possibility and necessity for Mandarin, and all three categories for the various substrate languages of India, with a complete overlap attested for the Dravidian languages Kannada and Telugu, partial overlap for Malayalam, Tamil, and Indo-Aryan Hindi, and no overlap for Marathi and Punjabi.

The information given in WALS can only function as a starting point because the category of necessity also includes weak necessity markers, i.e. equivalents of *should*, and overlap in the category of necessity may constitute an overlap for weak necessity but not for strong necessity, the case we are interested in. And in cases where some overlap is attested (category (2)), the information given in WALS does not tell us whether this overlap is in the domain of possibility or

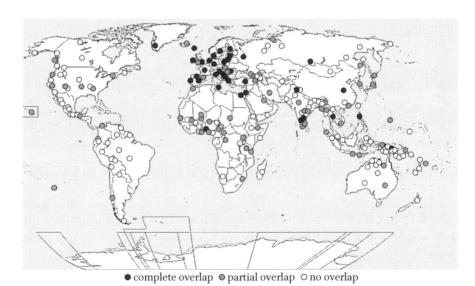

● complete overlap ◉ partial overlap ○ no overlap

FIGURE 36   Feature 76A Overlap between situational and epistemic modal marking adapted
            from WALS online (URL: http://wals.info/feature/76A#2/16.6/146.1 (last access:
            11/04/2018), cf. also van der Auwera & Ammann 2005, 312–313).

necessity. As our focus is on expressions of strong necessity, we need to scruti-
nise further whether the overlap is attested for possibility or necessity, and if it
is attested for necessity, whether it is attested for strong necessity. A typological
analysis of 241 different languages of the world suggests that only roughly one
tenth show an overlap of forms in necessity (cf. van der Auwera, Ammann &
Kindt 2005, 255). The necessary language data for closer inspection are provided by reference grammars of the respective languages.

Cantonese (IIKE) is assigned to category (2) in WALS, i.e. it is supposed to
show an overlap for either possibility or necessity. In Cantonese, necessity is
expressed by *yiu*, which can be used as a main verb to mean 'want' or 'need' (cf.
the discussion on the identification of *yiu* with English *need* below) or as an
auxiliary, which is similar to English *have to* in its meaning. The equivalent of
English *must* is expressed by *yiu* and the modal adverb *yātdihng* ('definitely'),
e.g. (115) (cf. Matthews & Yip 1994, 233, my emphases).

(115)   *Léihdeh   léuhng   go   **yātdihng   yiu**   gin-   háh   mihn.* (deontic)
      you-PL   two   CL   definitely   must   meet   DEL   face
      'You two really must get together'.

The epistemic sense of *must* is not expressed by the same construction but by
yātdihng haih, the modal adverb meaning 'definitely' and a form of 'be', e.g.
(116) (cf. Matthews & Yip 1994, 233, my emphasis).

(116)   *Kéuih   **yātdihng**   haih   mgéidāk-   jó   lak.* (epistemic)
      s/he   definitely   is   forget   PFV   PRT
      'He must have forgotten'.

The markers for strong necessity and epistemic necessity therefore do not
overlap in Cantonese, and epistemic notions of logical necessity are not expressed verbally at all but by an adverb and the verb in the indicative.[79] This

---

79   The attested partial overlap in WALS probably refers to the overlap of weak necessity
    markers (similar in meaning to English *should*). Here, we can find the same form *yīnggōi*
    realising both meanings, e.g. the deontic reading in *Léih yīnggōi sīusām dī* ('You should be
    more careful'.) and the epistemic meaning in *Ngódeih yīnggōi chā-mdō sei dím dou* ('We
    should be there [at] about four'.) (cf. Matthews & Yip 1994, 235). *Yīnggōi* is furthermore
    interesting from a cross-linguistic perspective, as *gōi* can be traced back to the lexical verb
    with the meaning of 'own' and therefore follows the same path as English *have to*, albeit
    apparently with a weaker meaning. Whether this similarity is linked to the high frequency
    of *have to* in ICE-HK is open to speculation. If an identification of *yīnggōi* with *have to*

is an interesting observation as the speaker is not marking his or her opinion from fact in the verb in these contexts at all.

According to WALS, Mandarin (SgE) shows an overlap for both possibility and necessity. However, this overlap does not seem to be present in expressions of strong necessity, as examples (117) and (118) from Bao (2010, 1732, my emphases) show.

(117) *women*   ***bixu***   *jianchi*   *zhenli*   (deontic)
        we   must   abide.by   truth
        'We must abide by the truth'.

(118) *zhe*   *er*   ***yiding***   *you*   *ren*   *lai*   *guo.*   (epistemic)
        this   place   certainly   have   person   come   PRT
        'This place, someone must have been here'.

As in Cantonese, we see that deontic notions of necessity are expressed by different linguistic forms than epistemic notions of necessity. And again, we see that epistemic readings are expressed by the indicative and an adverb of manner meaning 'definitely'. Apart from Mandarin, speakers of SgE may also have Austronesian Malay or Dravidian Tamil as their first languages (cf. also Section 3.2.3). Bao analyses the structure of Malay expressions of deontic and epistemic necessity and argues that Malay uses two different expressions to encode these two modalities, i.e. *mesti* for deontic modality as in (119) and *tentu* for epistemic modality as in (120) (cf. Bao 2015, 172, my emphases).

(119) *saya*   ***mesti***   *pergi*   *sekarang.*   (deontic)
        I   must   go   now
        'I must go now'.

(120) ***tentu***   *dia*   *datang.*   (epistemic)
        certain   she   come
        'She must be coming'.

While *tentu* is the usual way of expressing epistemic modalities, *mesti* can sometimes also be employed for the same function, which would mean that

---

really does take place, we would also expect a transfer of the epistemic function to *have to*, which is not borne out by the data.

Malay has an identical form for expressing these two meanings.[80] However, Bao informs us that *mesti* is only rarely used as an epistemic marker and is therefore first and foremost a deontic marker (cf. Bao 2015, 172). Ho Abdullah gives (121) and (122) to illustrate the overlap of forms (cf. Ho Abdullah 1993, 25, my emphases).

(121)   awak   ***mesti***   *lulus*   *ujian*   *memandu*   *itu.*   (deontic)
        you   must   pass   test   driving   that
        'There is an obligation for you to pass that driving test'.

(122)   awak   ***mesti***   *lulus*   *ujian*   *memandu*   *itu.*   (epistemic)
        you   must   pass   test   driving   that
        'I confidently infer that you will pass that driving test'.

As stated above, this overlap only occurs rarely in Malay (cf. also Ho Abdullah 1993, 25). However, overlap seems to be the usual case in Tamil, as examples (123) and (124) (from Asher 1985, 167;171, my emphases) show (cf. also Schiffman 1999, 88).

(123)   avan   *aŋke*   *pooka-*   ***ŋum***   (deontic)
        he   there   go-   DEB
        'He must go there'.

(124)   *ganeecan*   *ippa*   *mannaarkuṭiyile -*   *irukka-*   ***ŋum***   (epistemic)
        Ganesan   now   Mannargudi-LOC   be-   DEB
        'Ganesan must be in Mannargudi now'.

Speakers of Tamil, the ethnic language assigned to the Indian community in Singapore, are in the minority in Singapore as compared to speakers of Mandarin and Malay. Most of the residents are Chinese, and Mandarin therefore probably has the strongest influence on today's SgE (cf. also discussion in Section 3.2.3).

Tamil is, however, more prominent as one of the mother tongues of speakers from ICE-IND*. The Dravidian language Tamil is more strongly represented in ICE-IND*, it is the fourth in the ranking after Marathi, Kannada, and Hindi in

---

80   Ho Abdullah mentions *pasti* as another marker of epistemic necessity (cf. Ho Abdullah 1993, 26).

terms of number of words (cf. Section 4.1.2). As described in Section 3.2.2, India is a multilingual country, where languages from different language families are spoken. Most languages in India belong to the two major language families of the Dravidian languages and the Indo-Aryan languages. Languages that belong to the Dravidian language family are for example Kannada, Tamil, and Telugu, while Hindi, Konkani, and Marathi are languages of the Indo-Aryan language family. By exploiting the information on the speakers' mother tongues from the metadata, I was able to identify 22 different substrate languages in the spoken section of ICE-IND* in Section 4.1.2. The question arises whether there are differences between the substrate languages in the encoding of epistemic and deontic necessity and whether these differences can be related to differences between the two major language families. A meta-comment on IndE from the corpus by speaker A in text S1A-028 (Pramodini N., assistant professor of linguistics) shows that regional variation according to the language family may play a role in the formation of different IndE dialects (cf. (125)).

(125)   And there will be *different types of Indian English* Indian English one two three and so on. There must be different types of Indian Englishes because we have different varieties of languages spoken here in India varieties means different families of languages spoken here in India.

As Figure 37 shows, there are only subtle differences between speakers of the two major language families in the expression of root and epistemic meanings in the spoken section of ICE-IND*. The difference between speakers of the two different language families with regard the distributions of deontic and epistemic *must* is not significant at the p<0.05 level (2×2 χ^2 test).

It could be that these subtle differences are the end product of a levelling process of former, more substantial differences between the Indo-Aryan and Dravidian varieties of English. This levelling process may have occurred through continuous use of English as a lingua franca between the speakers of Indo-Aryan and Dravidian languages, especially in the South, where English rather than Hindi is used as a lingua franca. So, speakers of Indo-Aryan varieties of English may have developed *must* with epistemic necessity reading over time through continuing contact with speakers of Dravidian varieties. Van der Auwera and Ammann (2013) mention a similar case in West Greenlandic, where an overlap of deontic and epistemic possibility probably emerged through contact with Danish. Schilk also mentions the joint influence of a wide range of L1s on the emerging IndE variety, with the possibility that features that have their origins in one specific L1 stabilise in the emerging variety and are

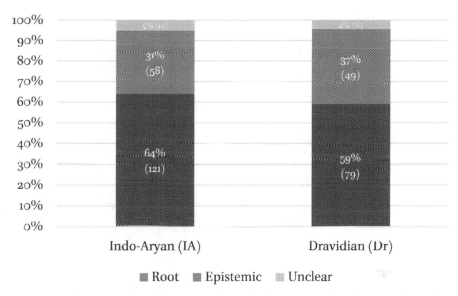

FIGURE 37   Root and epistemic meanings of *must* in the spoken section of ICE-IND* according to language family.

used by speakers that do not necessarily speak this language (cf. Schilk 2011, 12). This also ties in with Lange's description of South Asia as a *sprachbund* due to convergence of Indo-Aryan and Dravidian languages (cf. Lange 2012, 55–57).

If we perform a more fine-grained analysis at the level of the languages of the speakers by analysing the distribution of epistemic and deontic *must* in the English varieties of speakers with L1s with 20 tokens or above (cf. Lange 2017, 17–18 for the deconstruction of the notion 'Indian English' into 'Marathi English' and 'Tamil English' by speakers), we can see the distribution in Figure 38.

Splitting the data up according to the mother tongues of the speakers leads to smaller categories and smaller observed values, so that statistical testing becomes problematic in some cases (cf. absolute frequencies in Figure 38). The differences between the languages are not significant at the p<0.05 level (2×2 χ^2 test), although a pattern can be identified. Speakers with a Dravidian language background (Kannada, Tamil, and Telugu) all show a higher proportion of epistemic *must* than speakers with an Indo-Aryan language background (Hindi and Konkani). However, speakers of Marathi as speakers with an Indo-Aryan language background do not show the same tendency as speakers of the other Indo-Aryan languages.

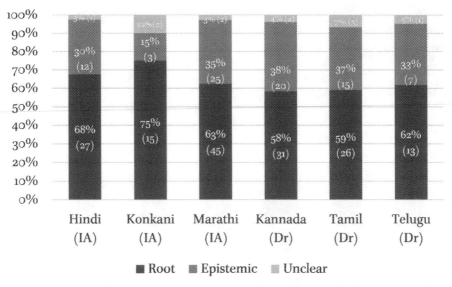

FIGURE 38   Root and epistemic meanings of *must* in the spoken section of ICE-IND* according to L1.

The Dravidian language Kannada was categorised as having identical forms
for the expression of deontic and epistemic possibility and necessity in WALS
(cf. Figure 36), and a closer look at reference grammars reveals that Kannada uses *beeku* to encode deontic and epistemic necessity, as examples (126)
and (127) show (from Schiffman 1983, 73, my emphases; cf. also Sridhar 1990,
239–241).

(126)   *niiv*   *naaLe*   *ill-*   *ir-*   ***beeku.***   (deontic)
        you   tomorrow   here   be   must/should[81]
        'You must/should be there tomorrow'.

(127)   *niiv*   *avarn*   *nooD-*   *ir-*   ***beeku.***   (epistemic)
        you   him   seen   have   must
        'You must have seen him'.

As already mentioned above, Tamil is also one of the substrate languages of
Singapore and also shows an identical form for the expression of epistemic

_____

81   Note that *beeku* can denote weak and strong obligation and therefore has *must*
       and *should* as its English equivalents.

and deontic modality. Telugu patterns like the other Dravidian languages analysed and also has one form to encode both meanings, e.g. (128) and (129) (from Krishnamurti & Gwynn 1985, 226, my emphases; cf. also Subrahmanyam 1974, 154).

(128)   cepp-   **aali**   (deontic)
         tell-   must
         'One must tell'.

(129)   ceppi-   uND-   **aali**   (epistemic)
         tell.PAST   be   must
         'One must have told'.

To summarise, all of the Dravidian substrate languages whose speakers contributed 20 or more tokens of *must* in the spoken section of ICE-IND* (Kannada, Tamil, Telugu) show an overlap of forms expressing epistemic and deontic necessity.[82] Having analysed the three Dravidian languages more closely, we can now turn to the three Indo-Aryan languages Hindi, Konkani, and Marathi.

Kachru does not mention an overlap of forms for deontic and epistemic necessity in Hindi (Kachru 1980, 45). For the deontic necessity meaning, *honā*[83] and *parnā*[84] are used as in (130) and (131) (from Kachru 1980, 50, my emphases).

(130)   mujhko   agle-   sāl   banāras   zarūr   jānā   **hai**. (deontic)
         I.DAT   next   year   Banaras   certainly go   is
         'I must go to Banaras next year'.

(131)   pitāji kī   āgyā hai, shādī   mẽ jānā hī   **paṛega**. (deontic)
         father HON of order is   wedding in go   EMPH have will
         'It is father's order, I will have to attend the wedding'.

---

82   The Dravidian language Malayalam, which was not included because it showed fewer than 20 instances of *must* also shows an overlap of forms for the encoding of epistemic and deontic necessity (cf. Andronov 1996, 180–181).

83   Note that the structure in Hindi with dative plus *be* is structurally similar to *have* in the sense that this structure also signifies possession (cf. also German dialects *mir ist* = 'I have').

84   *Paṛnā* literally means 'fall'. The obligation construction with *paṛnā* is also impersonal. In (131), the dative first personal pronoun *mujhko* ('me') is probably implied.

She explains that *honā* is used to express an internal compulsion, while *paṛnā* is used to express an external compulsion (cf. Kachru 1980, 50). The internal obligative *honā* is therefore probably more similar to the semi-modal *need to* in its semantics than to either English *must* or *have to*. *Paṛnā* instead is similar to *must* and *have to* in its deontic meaning, but it is not used to express epistemic necessity. Instead, Hindi uses expressions with *be* in the future form to express epistemic necessity and thus does not show modal marking at all, e.g. (132) (from Kachru 1980, 45, my emphases).

(132) *darvāzā*   *khulā*   *hai,*   *sonā*   *ghar*   *mẽ*   **hogī.**   (epistemic)
       door   open   is   Sona   house   in   be will
       'The door is open, Sona must be at home'.

Marathi has several impersonal constructions, which are used according to the modal strength intended (cf. Pandharipande 1997, 435–436). A similar construction to (130), an impersonal construction with *be* expressing an inner need, is considered to be the weakest in meaning, "since it is interpreted as closest to the intention of the agent and least burdensome" (Pandharipande 1997, 435). The strongest construction instead can also imply that someone has to fulfil an obligation, although he or she may not want to, e.g. (133) (from Pandharipande 1997, 436).

(133) **mala**   *bhāratālā*   *dzāwa,*   **lāgel.**   (deontic)
       I.DAT   India.DAT   go.OPT.3SG   must.FUT.3SG
       'I will have to go to India (i.e. even if I do not want to)'.

Again, the same construction is not used to express an epistemic meaning. Instead, several linguistic means are employed to express degrees of certainty: (a) adverbs such as *nakkī* 'definitely/certainly', *agdi* 'surely', and *dzarūr* 'decidedly', (b) the emphatic particle *-ts*, and (c) auxiliaries with aspectual markers (cf. Pandharipande 1997, 439). In terms of degree of certainty, the adverbs expressing certainty and the emphatic particle *-ts* rank higher than expressions employing auxiliaries and aspect marking. To conclude, the Indo-Aryan languages Hindi and Marathi show no overlap of forms in the expression of epistemic and deontic modality. I was not able to find any information about the encoding of epistemic and deontic necessity in Konkani, the third Indo-Aryan language whose speakers produced more than 20 tokens of *must* in the spoken section of ICE-IND*. Given that Konkani derived from Marathi, it is likely that it shows a similar structure as Marathi with no overlap of forms.

Figure 39 summarises the typological differences in the encoding of epistemic and deontic necessity. We can identify two types: type 1 includes those languages that show an overlap of forms for deontic and epistemic necessity, and type 2 includes those languages that show no overlap of forms. English and the Dravidian languages belong to type 1. For the sake of simplicity, Kannada, which has the highest word number of the Dravidian languages in ICE-IND*, represents all Dravidian languages here. The Sino-Tibetan languages Cantonese and Mandarin represent type 2, as well as the Austronesian language Malay and the Indo-Aryan languages, here represented by Marathi, the Indo-Aryan language with the highest number of words in ICE-IND*.

If the findings of this section are compared to the findings in Chapter 5, we can find a clear correlation between the type of encoding of deontic and epistemic necessity in the substrate languages and the use of epistemic *must* in the English varieties. ICE-HK and ICE-SIN showed a lower frequency of epistemic *must* and a strong deontic bias in the functional distribution, whereas ICE-IND* patterned similarly to ICE-GB, showing a higher frequency and also a

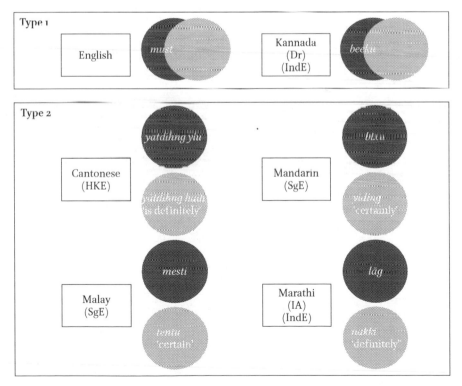

FIGURE 39   Encoding of root (dark grey) and epistemic senses (light grey) in English and the substrate languages of IndE, HKE, and SgE.

higher share of epistemic *must*. This finding can be linked to the separate encoding of deontic and epistemic meanings in two forms in Cantonese (HKE), Mandarin and Malay (SgE), as opposed to the encoding of deontic and epistemic meanings in one form in the Dravidian languages of India. We can therefore surmise that those varieties with a substrate language encoding deontic and epistemic necessity in one form tend to use epistemic *must* more often.

The type of encoding does not only correlate with these intervarietal differences but also with intravarietal differences in the case of ICE-IND*. IndE is an interesting case in point here, as it has substrate languages of both types. The Dravidian languages show an overlap of forms, while the Indo-Aryan languages analysed here show no overlap. As shown in Figure 37, there is indeed a subtle difference in the use of epistemic *must* between speakers of Dravidian languages and speakers of Indo-Aryan languages, with the speakers of Dravidian languages having a slightly higher proportion than speakers of Indo-Aryan languages. If we go down to the level of languages (cf. Figure 38), we can clearly see that speakers of those languages that encode deontic and epistemic readings in one form (Kannada, Tamil, Telugu) show a higher proportion of epistemic *must* than speakers of those languages that do not encode the two modalities in one form (Hindi, Konkani) with the only exception of Marathi. This exception may be a result of a process of secondary selection. Speakers of Dravidian languages may have contributed instances of *must* with epistemic meaning to the feature pool first, from which speakers of Indo-Aryan substrates may then have selected forms of epistemic *must* in a second step (cf. Lange 2012, 230, who found a similar case of fusion in the adoption of the Hindi indigenous tags *no/na* by speakers of Dravidian languages). It could also be that the structures of Marathi and Kannada have converged in some areas due to long-standing language contact between the two languages (cf. Gumperz & Wilson 1971). While we can see a clear correlation between the use of epistemic *must* and the speakers' L1s, it is still unclear how the positive or negative functional transfer took place. This will be discussed in Section 7.1, where transfer as one of the selection principles will be discussed in more detail.

Having analysed the expressions of logical necessity in the substrate languages more closely, we now turn to the different expressions of deontic necessity. Within the group of expressions of deontic necessity, *need to* sticks out as it patterns alike in ICE-HK and ICE-SIN as opposed to ICE-IND* (cf. Figure 26 in Chapter 5). Its high frequency in ICE-HK and ICE-SIN, even higher in ICE-HK than in both ENL varieties (cf. Figure 26 in Chapter 5), is unexpected, given that it has only recently emerged as a rival to *must* and *have to* (cf. Section 6.1.4).

As already mentioned above, Cantonese uses *yiu* as an equivalent to English *have to*, which is reinforced by the adverb *yātdihng* to express the meaning of *must*, e.g. (134) and (135) (from Matthews & Yip 1994, 233, my emphases).

(134) *Ngóhdeih   gām-máahn   **yiu**   chēut   heui   sihk.*
        we   tonight   need   out   go   eat
        'We have to eat out tonight'.

(135) *Nī   fūng   seun   yātdihng   **yiu**   léih   chīm   méng   sīn   yáuh-haauh.*
        this CL   letter definitely   need   you   sign   name   first   have-validity
        'This letter must have your signature in order to be valid'.

As can be seen in the gloss of (134) and (135), *yiu* literally means 'need' (or 'want'). It occurs as a main verb with a following noun and as an auxiliary with a following verb, where it can mean either 'have to' as in (134) or 'need to', as in (136) (from Matthews & Yip 1994, 234, my emphases).

(136) *Léih   **yiu**   hohk   dāk   faai   dī   sīn   dāk   ga!*
        you   need   learn   ADV   fast   a-bit   only   okay   PRT
        'You need to learn a bit faster, you know'.

We can find a similar use of Mandarin *xūyào*, which may express 'need' as a main verb and is also used as an auxiliary preceding a verb meaning 'need to', e.g. (137) and (138) (from Li & Thompson 1989, 178).

(137) *women   **xūyào**   fēijī.*
        we   need   airplane
        'We need airplanes'.

(138) *women   **xūyào**   jiàshǐ   fēijī.*
        we   need   pilot   airplane
        'We need to pilot airplanes'.

We can see that both Cantonese and Mandarin show forms expressing 'need' that can be used as main verbs followed by an NP or as auxiliaries when followed by a VP. When followed by a VP, Cantonese *yiu* and Mandarin *xūyào* are similar in meaning to English *need to* (rather than modal *need*) by referring to necessity. Cantonese *yiu* and Mandarin *xūyào* therefore bear syntactic and semantic similarities to English *need* followed by an NP in main verb function and *need to* followed by a VP in auxiliary function. This variable use of verbs in the functions of main verb and auxiliary verb, depending on the syntactic nature of the following constituent, does not seem to exist in the Dravidian languages of ICE-IND*, which usually employ invariant auxiliaries or bound morphemes (suffixes) to encode deontic modality (cf. examples (123), (126), and (128)). These invariant auxiliaries are not used as main verbs and are therefore more akin to core modal verbs in English in their form. Furthermore, they do not show a semantic equivalent for English *need to* in auxiliary function. It may well be that the syntactic and semantic similarity with Cantonese *yiu* and Mandarin *xūyào* has led to the high frequency of *need to* in HKE and SgE. Furthermore, it may also have contributed to the high frequency of the semi-modal verb *have to* in the case of HKE, as *have* and *have to* behave according to the same pattern described above in being employed in main verb function denoting possession and in auxiliary function denoting necessity. However, the same line of argumentation would then also apply to *have got to*, which also shows a main verb and auxiliary function but is not used with a high frequency in HKE. As *have got to* is associated with more colloquial contexts, it is not comparable to *have to*, which is why its rare use is more likely conditioned by the functions English fulfils in Hong Kong. English is the language used in formal contexts, whereas Cantonese is used in everyday conversation as the common language of the residents of Hong Kong (cf. Section 3.2.1). Informal conversations between friends and family, which are usually marked by a strong use of colloquial expressions, are simply not conducted in English but in Cantonese, the common language of Hong Kong people.

Due to the similar behaviour of SgE and HKE in terms of the rare use of epistemic *must* and the comparatively widespread use of semi-modal *need to* (cf. Figure 26 in Chapter 5), relevant structures in the substrate languages Mandarin and Cantonese were analysed more closely based on the assumption that these languages show typological similarities due to their common ancestry. In the case of the distribution of deontic *must* and *have to*, an unexpected pattern becomes visible, as HKE and SgE differ significantly from each other, while HKE and IndE show a similar distribution. SgE shows an idiosyncratic pattern here, as it has the highest text frequency of *must* with 71 tokens per 100,000 words (M-co), as compared to 57 tokens per 100,000 words in HKE and IndE (cf. Figure 26 in Chapter 5). This difference calls for a closer inspection of the encoding of strong obligation in Mandarin and Cantonese. As already mentioned earlier, the equivalent of *must* is *bìxū* in Mandarin Chinese according to Bao (cf. Bao 2010, 1731).

Li and Thompson list several auxiliaries under the meaning of 'must', *bìxū* is among them and additional forms such as *děi*, *bìyào*, or *bìděi* are given (cf. Li & Thompson 1989, 183); Lin only mentions *děi* as an auxiliary denoting 'have to' (cf. Lin 2001, 102). However, although Li and Thompson mention different forms for the meaning of 'must', 'ought to', they do not specify which variant is used in which cases, so that it remains unclear whether *bìxū* and *děi* fulfil the same functions and if so, whether there are any restrictions on their use. Wiedenhof also lists several auxiliaries for the expression of 'must', 'have to': *yào*, *děi*, *bìděi*, *bìxū*, *bìxūyáo*, and *xūyào* (cf. Wiedenhof 2015, 166–170). *Yào* can mean (1) 'want to', (2) 'be going to', 'will', 'shall', and (3) 'must', 'have to' (cf. Wiedenhof 2015, 166, my emphasis).

(139) Tāmen *yào* fāzhǎn jīngijì.
       'They want to develop the economy'.
       'They are going to develop the economy'.
       'They have to develop the economy'.

Děi and *bìděi* are less frequently employed in written language and are only used as auxiliaries (cf. Wiedenhof 2015, 170).[85] Their preference for less formal contexts makes them similar to English *have to* (cf. also Lin's 2001 translation of *děi* with 'have to').[86] *Bìxū* and *děi* differ in terms of modal strength expressed; *bìxū* expresses strong obligation, while *děi* expresses median obligation (cf. Halliday & McDonald 2004, 339).[87] *Bìxū* is used in formal language, such as in legal texts, similarly to modal *must* (cf. Ross & Sheng Ma 2006, 71). *Xūyào* and the more colloquial *bìxūyáo* are equivalent to 'need to' in meaning and syntactic behaviour, as they can also be used as transitive verbs expressing 'need' (cf. Wiedenhof 2015, 170). *Xūyào* can mean 'need to' in auxiliary function but also 'must', 'have to'. Written conventions distinguish between the two meanings of the auxiliary but "[i]n spoken Mandarin, both usages appear to serve as interpretations of a single meaning" (Wiedenhof 2015, 170). It therefore seems as if the conversational implicature of an imposed obligation of English *need to* is part of the conventional meaning of Mandarin *xūyào*. Mandarin *bìxū* and *děi* are probably equivalents to English *must* and *have to* respectively. They differ in terms of their formality and modal strength.

---

85   Ross and Sheng Ma explain that *bìxū* and *bìděi* are more formal than *děi* (cf. Ross & Sheng Ma 2006, 71).

86   This preference also makes *děi* and *bìděi* similar to English *have got to*. *Děi* is furthermore similar to deontic *have got to* in that it derives from a main verb meaning 'obtain' (*dé*) (cf. Wiedenhof 2015, 170).

87   This meaning differs from the meaning given in Wiedenhof, who states that *bìxū* is synonymous with *xūyào* ('need to') (cf. Wiedenhof 2015, 170). However, *xūyào* may also mean 'must', 'have to' in Mandarin.

The equivalents in Cantonese also seem to differ in modal strength. The meaning of 'have to' is expressed by *yiu* in Cantonese, which may be reinforced by a modal adverb such as *yātdihng* to denote 'must' ('definitely have to') (cf. Matthews & Yip 1994, 233). Consequently, both languages distinguish between two deontic markers in terms of strength, assigning weaker modal strength to the equivalent of *have to* as compared to the equivalent of *must*. The use of the respective markers in Mandarin is furthermore conditioned by mode (spoken/written), so that the equivalent of *have to* is less often used in written language. This distribution is also typical of the semi-modal *have to* in English, which is used with a higher frequency in spoken language, although it has also found its way into written language (cf. Section 9.3). Based on the shared preference of *děi* and *have to* for less formal language in Mandarin and English, it is no surprise that *have to* also shows a preference for the spoken mode in SgE, as can be seen in Figure 40. However, the same is true for all other varieties under analysis, though the preference is not equally strong across the varieties. What is more striking is the significantly higher frequency and proportion of *must* in the spoken part of ICE-SIN as compared to the spoken part of ICE-GB, as shown in Figure 41.

If *must* can be considered to be the equivalent of *bìxū*, it is possible that it is also associated with a stronger sense of obligation/necessity as compared to *have to* in SgE, which makes the finding even more astonishing because it

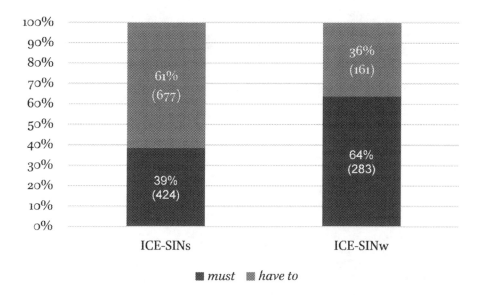

FIGURE 40   The distribution of *must* vs. *have to* according to mode (spoken vs. written) in
ICE-SIN (differences are significant at the $p<0.0001$ level, 2×2 χ^2 test).

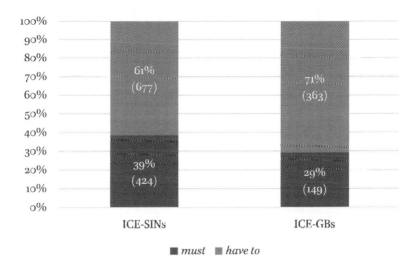

FIGURE 41   The distribution of *must* vs. *have to* in the spoken part of ICE-GB and ICE-SIN
(differences are significant at the p<0.001 level, 2×2 χ^2 test).

means that speakers of SgE express strong obligations more often than BrE
speakers. The structure of the substrate language does not provide a plausible
explanation why *must*, the equivalent of *bìxū*, is used with such a high frequency in spoken SgE, which is why other factors will be investigated in order
to account for this finding (cf. Section 7.2 for possible cultural reasons). While
the structure of the substrate language may not account for the comparatively
higher frequency of *must* in ICE-SIN, it may partially explain the distribution
of *must* and *have to* in ICE-HK. ICE-HK shows a considerably higher proportion
of *have to* as compared to ICE-SIN. A partial explanation for the high proportion of *have to* in ICE-HK may lie in the encoding of 'must' and 'have to' in
Cantonese, where the default form is arguably *yiu*, which is strengthened by
an adverb to denote a stronger sense of obligation, usually paraphrased with
'must' in the respective reference grammars. In this sense, *have to* may be the
default choice in HKE for expressing obligation and necessity. However, other
factors also seem to play a role such as SLA principles, which will be explored in
Section 7.3.

   To summarise, we have seen clear correlations between the type of encoding of epistemic and deontic obligation and necessity in the substrate languages and the frequency of epistemic *must* in the ESL varieties; those varieties that
have a substrate language that encodes epistemic and deontic readings in one
form show a higher frequency of epistemic *must*. The structure of the substrate
language may also partially account for the comparatively high frequencies of

need to in ICE-HK and ICE-SIN because both Cantonese and Mandarin have a verb that expresses 'need' as a transitive main verb and 'need to' when used in auxiliary function. Those varieties with an equivalent form to English *need* and *need to* therefore show a higher frequency of the semi-modal verb. In the case of the divergent pattern of SgE *must*, no clear correlation could be identified between the widespread use of *must* in SgE and the use of *bìxū* in Mandarin. This is why other factors will be taken into account for the variety-specific use of *must* in SgE (cf. Section 7.2).

The close analysis of the structure of the domain of obligation and necessity in the substrate language on the basis of reference grammars was necessary in order to postulate features that the substrate languages contribute to the feature pool. The level of detail in the description of the domain of obligation and necessity varies from grammar to grammar. While some grammars contain little information on the domain of obligation overall (some only provide a list of auxiliaries and their meaning), other grammars contain rich information about fine distinctions between the different deontic markers, often along the lines of the subjective-objective distinction. However, it is difficult to exploit this information to account for possible transfer of these pragmatic characteristics to the modal and semi-modal verbs of obligation and necessity in ESL varieties. I decided not to code the instances of *must* and *have to* according to subjective and objective uses because this type of pragmatic coding requires comprehensive knowledge about the cultural context, in particular about social, moral, and religious norms in these societies. Without this knowledge, pragmatic coding may lead to 'Western' interpretations of 'non-Western' situations and may unconsciously reproduce prior findings from ENL varieties (cf. also Section 1.6). As I decided not to code the instances of *must* and *have to* according to subjective and objective uses in the ESL varieties, I also decided not to describe the different variants with regard to this distinction in the relevant substrate languages, although this information was available in several grammars (e.g. Jain 1995, 222). While the amount of information provided was over-specified for the pragmatic meanings of the different variants for the purposes of this study, the opposite was sometimes also the case. The reference grammars are synchronic descriptions of the languages and only rarely give information about language change, which may also play a role in the domain of obligation and necessity in these languages. Furthermore, the grammars do not provide information about the frequency of use, which seems to be crucial in some cases (cf. the rare but possible use of Malay *mesti* as an epistemic marker). Despite these limitations, the grammars are invaluable resources for the study of second-language varieties of English, because they provide relevant information for postulating variants in the substrate languages that also feed into the feature pool. The corpus study on BrE, AmE, HKE, IndE, and SgE pointed to similarities between HKE and SgE, which could be correlated with the structures of the domain of obligation and necessity in their substrate languages. These correlations between the deontic bias of *must* and the encoding of epistemic necessity in the substrate languages and the high frequency of *need to* and equivalent structures in the substrate language are indicative of substrate transfer. How this transfer takes place will be explored in Section 7.1.

6.3 AmE Influence

Mair conceives of standard AmE as "the hub of the 'World System of Englishes'" (Mair 2013, 260), which influences the development of all other varieties of English. This influence is referred to as 'Americanisation' (cf. Leech & Smith 2009, 185) and is often used as an explanatory factor for language change, as in the case of the decline of the modal verbs. Here, AmE is most advanced in the decline of the modal verbs, with BrE following its lead (explicitly called 'follow-my-leader' pattern, cf. Leech et al. 2009, 253). In order to take possible AmE influence on the ESL varieties into account, I will briefly sketch regional differences between BrE and AmE in the use of *must, have to, have got to*, and *need to*.

As can be seen in the comparison of Figure 27 and Figure 30 in Chapter 5, regional differences between the ENL varieties BrE and AmE are stronger in spoken language than in written language ('convergence in writing, divergence in speech', Mair 2007, 84). The spoken data of AmE, ICE-USAS* (SBC), are marked by a lower frequency of *must* and a higher frequency of *have to* as compared to ICE-GB. The regional difference is related to the stronger decline of *must* in AmE as compared to BrE (cf. Leech et al. 2009, 74), but is probably overstated due to differences between ICE-GB and SBC in terms of corpus structure and compilation time because SBC contains more informal (i.e. more private direct conversations) and more recent data than ICE-GB from 2000–2005 (cf. also Section 4.1). Despite these caveats, the general tendency is clear: AmE has a lower frequency of *must* and a higher frequency of *have to*. If *must* is used, it predominantly fulfils the function of an epistemic marker in spoken AmE; AmE is the only variety under analysis that has a higher proportion of epistemic *must* than deontic *must*.

Apart from the main competitors in the domain of obligation and necessity, more marginal members also show differences in use across varieties as in the case of *have got to*. "In speech, it is somewhat more common in BrE than in most other varieties, including the British-derived New Englishes" (Mair 2015a,

138). However, although used with a lower frequency in AmE, it has grammaticalised further here, as becomes visible in its frequent use as reduced *gotta*, as opposed to BrE, where it is more often used in full or contracted form with *have*, based on data from the conversation part of ICE-GB and SBC (cf. Seggewiß 2012, 127).[88] Seggewiß relates the avoidance of *have got to* in AmE to the social stigma associated with it (cf. Seggewiß 2012, 128; cf. also the context of use of early attestations of *have got to* in Section 6.1.3). The comparatively higher frequency of *have got to* in BrE matches diachronic findings for the development of *have got to* in the two regional varieties BrE and AmE. The two varieties show a diametrically opposed diachronic trend, with an increase in BrE in the 20th century and a decrease in AmE, as Jankowski's real-time study on her *British and American Play Corpus* shows (cf. Jankowski 2004, 95; cf. Section 2.1). She distinguishes *have got to* from reduced *got to* and shows that *got to* declines towards the end of the century in AmE, while it is still on the rise in BrE (cf. Jankowski 2004, 95). Studies based on the (extended) BROWN family show similar trends, with an increase of *have got to* in BrE and a decrease in AmE, although the differences are not significant here (cf. Leech et al. 2009, 286; Mair 2015a, 139). Apparent-time studies by Tagliamonte and Tagliamonte and D'Arcy support the general tendency for BrE and North American varieties of English, with an increase of *have got to* in York English and a decrease in Toronto English (cf. Tagliamonte 2004, 42; Tagliamonte & D'Arcy 2007, 71).

A synchronic regional comparison of *need to* based on the conversation part of ICE-GB and SBC shows that *need to* is used with a higher frequency in spoken AmE as compared with spoken BrE (cf. Seggewiß 2012, 129). This pattern can also be observed if the data from SBC are compared to the complete spoken section of ICE-GB (cf. Figure 27 in Chapter 5). Here again, we have to take into account that the differences may be stronger due to the fact that SBC mostly contains dialogues that are more interactive than monologues and therefore favour the use of *need to* (cf. Nokkonen 2015, 176). Diachronic studies based on the BROWN family show a steep increase in the use of semi-modal *need to* in written BrE and AmE (cf. Mair 2015a, 136–137).

---

88   Note that Figure 27 in Chapter 5, which shows a higher frequency of *have got to* in AmE as compared with BrE, cannot be directly compared to Seggewiß's (2012) findings, as it is based on the complete spoken section of ICE-GB and SBC and not only on the conversation section in ICE-GB. In terms of text type comparability, it makes sense to compare SBC with the conversational part of ICE-GB only. However, I decided to include the complete spoken section of ICE-GB, as my focus is not on the regional difference between AmE and BrE but between these varieties and the ESL varieties, and this allows me to account for text type differences between BrE and the British-derived varieties in my study.

To summarise, regional characteristics of spoken AmE in the domain of obligation and necessity as compared to spoken BrE are a comparatively lower frequency of the core modal *must*, with 25 tokens of *must* per 100,000 words in ICE-USAS* (SBC) compared to 48 tokens of *must* per 100,000 words in ICE-GBs. Furthermore, AmE is also marked by a higher proportion of epistemic *must*, with 75% in ICE-USAS* compared to 47% in ICE-GBs. With regard to the semi-modal verbs, AmE shows a higher frequency of *have to* and *need to* as compared to BrE. *Have got to* is less frequently used in AmE than in BrE but is more often used in its contracted form *gotta*. In order to find correlations with AmE rather than BrE, we take the structure of the domain of obligation and necessity in the spoken part of the corpora as a reference point (cf. Figure 27 in Chapter 5), given that regional variation is stronger in spoken English than in written English ('convergence in writing, divergence in speech', cf. Mair 2007, 84). We can see similarities and differences in the use of verbal expressions of obligation and necessity between AmE and the ESL varieties under analysis. The ESL varieties share the higher frequency of *have to* with AmE. SgE and HKE also resemble AmE in the more widespread use of *need to*. IndE does not align with AmE in this case but shows a similar behaviour in the lower frequency of *have got to* than in BrE. HKE also shows a low frequency of *have got to* and both IndE and HKE show a decrease of *have got to* in apparent time (cf. Section 8.3), which also aligns them with AmE, where a decrease of this variant was also observed towards the end of the 20th century. Instead, SgE patterns with the ENL variety BrE with regard to the use of *have got to*, whose frequency in ICE-SIN is comparable to that in ICE-GB, with an M-co of 27 compared to an M-co of 33. While the contracted form *gotta* cannot be found in ICE-IND* at all and occurs only three times in ICE-HK, we can find 13 instances of contracted *gotta* in ICE-SIN, i.e. about 7% of all forms of *have got to* in this corpus, a much smaller proportion than the 69% found for AmE (cf. Seggewiß 2012, 126). The ESL varieties differ most strongly from AmE in their greater use of *must* and the comparatively higher proportion of its deontic sense.

As we can see, some correlations exist between the structure of the domain in AmE and those of HKE, IndE, and SgE, although I would argue that these correlations do not imply direct causation. The uniform behaviour of all ESL varieties in the higher frequency of *have to*, irrespective of their orientation towards ENL varieties rather points to more general mechanisms at work, including learner mechanisms and cognitive processes, than to the influence of AmE. At least a conscious process of 'Americanisation' can be ruled out, as the regional frequency differences between BrE and AmE are very likely below the level of consciousness for the speakers of ESL varieties and are not available for active manipulation by the speakers. My questionnaire data show that 14% of the respondents associate *have to* with AmE, 31% associate it with BrE, while the majority does not associate it with either of these varieties. The higher frequencies of *need to* are probably also not related to AmE influence. As the previous section has shown, the higher frequency of *need to* in HKE and SgE can be correlated with the existence of similar verbs in their respective substrate languages. This is why substrate influence may have a higher explanatory force than AmE influence.

In Section 5.2.2, it was shown that the semi-modal *have got to* is less frequently used in spoken AmE than in spoken BrE. It has been argued that the high frequency of the semi-modal verb in the spoken corpora (cf. Figure 27 in Chapter 5) does not indicate regional difference. It rather seems to be an artefact of the corpus structure of SBC, which is largely composed of informal conversations. Spoken AmE is therefore marked by a comparatively lower frequency of this semi-modal verb, a characteristic it shares with spoken HKE and IndE. This surface similarity is probably also not directly related to AmE influence but rather to a 'prestige barrier' (cf. Leech & Smith 2009, 189) that seems to be less relevant in BrE than in British-derived varieties of English, as the semi-modal seems to be rare in several British-derived varieties (e.g. AmE, IrE, HKE, and IndE) (cf. Figure 26 in Chapter 5). Its overall infrequency suggests that British-derived varieties of English are more susceptible to prescriptive pressures than BrE, as has been claimed before for written AmE (cf. Leech et al. 2009, 104; Leech & Smith 2009, 189). That *have got to* attracted negative prescriptive comments in usage guides is therefore also relevant to the discussion of this semi-modal in the New Englishes.[89] Prescriptive rules are usually part of second-language learning in the classroom and students are taught the standard variety, usually on the basis of the written word (cf. also Schneider 2007, 101 for the exceptional use of non-standard features in scholastic ESL varieties). *Have got to* probably originated in non-standard speech (cf. Krug 2000, 62) and although it is not considered non-standard anymore, it is still considered informal and therefore probably avoided in the New Englishes. As English is the second language for most of the speakers in the New Englishes, it is hypothesised that they adhere to prescriptive norms more closely, especially speakers of varieties in earlier developmental stages of Schneider's (2007) model, where the norm-orientation is towards the norms of the input variety. This may explain why HKE and IndE show a low frequency of *have got to*, whereas SgE shows a higher frequency as a variety that has entered Schneider's

---

89   Cf. Rice (1932) for some examples of prescriptive comments about *have got*.

(2007) fourth stage of Endonormative Stabilisation (cf. Section 3.2.3). However, if the distribution of *have got to* according to age is taken into account, the empirical data do not speak in favour of prescriptivism as an explanatory factor in HKE, as we can see a gradual monotonic decrease in HKE rather than a steep decrease in the middle-aged groups (cf. Section 8.3). The higher frequency of *have got to* in SgE is therefore more likely linked to the functions English fulfils in Singapore (cf. Section 3.2.3), and the similarities between AmE and the ESL varieties in the use of *have got to* are probably not the result of a process of 'Americanisation'.

This section outlined regional characteristics of the domain of obligation and necessity in AmE as compared to BrE and searched for correlations between the structures of AmE and HKE, IndE, and SgE. Although several surface similarities were identified, it was argued that these similarities probably do not imply causation, so that the influence of AmE seems to be rather limited with regard to the structure of the field of obligation and necessity, while the structure of the historical input variety and the structure of the substrate languages seem to have contributed more substantially to the feature pool and therefore seem to be more important sources for present-day variability.

6.4   Summary

This chapter analysed the threefold input to the feature pool in the domain of obligation and necessity in HKE, IndE, and SgE by (1) reconstructing the structure of the historical BrE input variety in Section 6.1, (2) analysing the structures of the substrate languages in Section 6.2, and (3) analysing the synchronic structure of present-day AmE as the hypercentral variety of English in Section 6.3.

The state of the superstrate variety was reconstructed for the time periods when the ESL varieties entered the second stage of their developments, called 'Exonormative Stabilisation'. The analysis showed that *must* was already used in deontic and epistemic functions at that time and that the epistemic function was on the rise between 1750–1799 and 1850–1899. As IndE entered the second phase in 1757 and SgE and HKE entered the second phase in 1867 and 1898, a founder effect for the more widespread use of epistemic *must* in IndE was ruled out. The reconstruction of the historical input variety was also inconclusive with regard to the frequency of *have to* in the varieties. While the high frequency of *have to* in ICE-HK may be an indicator of a possible founder effect because HKE entered the second phase after the major increase in the frequency of this semi-modal verb, the frequency distribution in ICE-IND* and

ICE-SIN do not blend in well with this explanation. The analysis of the state of the historical input variety was, however, instructive for the explanation of the low frequency of the minority variants *have got to* and *need to* in IndE, because these variants were not yet part of the historical variety of BrE that served as the input variety to IndE. Furthermore, the rather recent emergence of epistemic meanings of the semi-modal verbs may also be the reason behind their low frequency in the ESL varieties.

As the analysis of the historical state of the superstrate variety left several findings unexplained, the structures of the substrate languages were analysed in order to account for the influence on the structures of the feature pools by these important contributors. The analysis showed that the encoding of deontic and epistemic modality in one form correlated with the frequency of epistemic *must* in the ESL varieties. It also showed that varieties whose L1s have a structure that is semantically and syntactically similar to the semi-modal verb *need to* show a higher frequency of this semi-modal verb.

As a third contributor of variants, the structure of the domain of obligation and necessity in AmE was analysed as it fulfils the role of a hypercentral variety and is considered to influence other varieties around the world. Several surface similarities between AmE and the ESL varieties, such as the high frequency of *have to* and the low frequency of the semi-modal *have got to*, were identified but it was argued that these correlations do not imply causation, i.e. they are probably not the result of a direct influence of AmE on the ESL varieties.

CHAPTER 7

Selection Principles in the Feature Pool

Having clarified the structure of the domain of obligation and necessity in the historical input variety of BrE, the relevant substrate languages, and the 'hypercentral' variety AmE as the main contributors to the feature pool in the last chapter, we can now turn to relevant selection principles that are at work in the selection of one feature over another (cf. Part C in Figure 31 in the preceding chapter). The findings of the corpus study in Chapter 5 pointed to similarities between specific ESL varieties, in the group of ESL varieties, and between ESL varieties and ENL varieties. SgE and HKE behaved similarly with regard to the frequency and deontic bias of *must* and the high frequency of *need to*, which were deemed to be indicative of substrate influence via transfer. How this functional transfer takes place will be analysed in Section 7.1 on substrate transfer.

Apart from these similarities between HKE and SgE as opposed to IndE, there are also similarities between these ESL varieties as opposed to the ENL varieties. All ESL varieties differ significantly from the ENL varieties in that they show a considerably higher frequency of markers of strong deontic obligation and necessity, including a higher frequency of the core modal verb *must*. These differences in frequency are probably not related to shared features in the substrate languages but rather point to cross-cultural differences in obligation practices, which is why this finding will be further analysed in Section 7.2 on cultural motivations as selection principles for certain features.

The ESL varieties also show a similar behaviour in the preference for *have to* over *must* and in the smaller proportion of epistemic uses of *must*. HKE and IndE, which are at an earlier stage in Schneider's (2007) model, show a low frequency in the use of *have got to*, which may point to simplification processes typical of learner varieties. On the whole, the similarities between the ESL varieties may be indicative of SLA mechanisms, which will be discussed in Section 7.3.

Despite these differences based on the status of the variety as first-language or second-language variety, we can also find similarities between the two types of varieties (the so-called 'common core', cf. Quirk et al. 1985, 16). If the distribution in the complete corpora is considered (cf. Figure 26 in Chapter 5), it can be seen that both ENL and ESL varieties prefer the use of deontic *have to* over deontic *must* and use deontic *must* more often than epistemic *must*, which

© KONINKLIJKE BRILL NV, LEIDEN, 2018 | DOI:10.1163/9789004381520_008

may be indicative of universal cognitive mechanisms at work, irrespective of the type of variety.[1] These principles will be discussed in Section 7.4.

7.1   Transfer Principles

In Section 6.2, I had a closer look at the structures of the substrate languages in order to account for similarities in the use of modal and semi-modal verbs in ICE-HK and ICE-SIN as opposed to ICE-IND*. ICE-HK and ICE-SIN are both marked by a low frequency of epistemic *must* but a high frequency of *need to* compared to ICE-IND* (cf. Chapter 5). The differences in the frequencies of epistemic *must* and *need to* correlate with differences in the structures of the substrate languages (cf. Section 6.2), which points to substratum influence. As the term 'substratum influence' is used to describe the end product of a process, it leaves open the process occurring in the minds of the speakers that leads to the product (cf. also Siegel 2008, 105). Siegel suggests that one process behind substratum interference is 'transfer', "a type of cross-linguistic influence that takes place in the minds of individuals" (Siegel 2008, 105). He distinguishes between two types of transfer: (1) syntactic or 'word order' transfer and (2) functional transfer (cf. Siegel 2008, 107–108). The second type of transfer, functional transfer, which he defines as "the use of L2 forms with L1 grammatical properties" (Siegel 2008, 108), seems to be of special relevance to the explanation for the different frequencies of epistemic *must* and the semi-modal *need to*.

The apparent-time findings indicate that epistemic *must* is rising initially (i.e. from the oldest to the middle-aged groups of speakers) in both HKE and IndE (cf. Section 8.3). The monotonic increase suggests a gradual linguistic change that is typical of grammaticalisation. It seems that HKE and IndE both follow the grammaticalisation path from deontic to epistemic modality at the beginning. Although *must* seems to follow the grammaticalisation path from deontic to epistemic modality in both varieties, it seems to be less grammaticalised in HKE, judging from its low frequency in this variety. In addition, both

---

1   Note that there are strong register differences in terms of the frequency distribution of *must* and *have to* and epistemic *must* (cf. Biber et al. 1999, 489;494). The influence of text type on the alternation between *must* and *have to* will be considered as one of the factors in the multivariate analysis (cf. Chapter 9). The distribution of *must* according to functions shows a predominance of epistemic *must* in conversations and a predominance of deontic *must* in academic prose (cf. Biber et al. 1999, 494). In the present analysis, a predominance of epistemic *must* in spoken language was only identified for AmE based on data from SBC (cf. Figure 27 in Chapter 5).

varieties show a decrease in the frequency of epistemic *must* in the younger age groups. A closer look at the grammaticalisation processes of the equivalent expressions for *must* in the substrate languages seems promising in order to account for the different degrees of grammaticalisation of *must* in HKE and IndE.

The polysemy of words with deontic and epistemic meanings as the result of grammaticalisation from deontic to epistemic readings can be found in many languages of the world (cf. Figure 36 in Chapter 6; cf. Bybee & Pagliuca 1985, 66; Traugott 1989, 36; Sweetser 1990, 50; Traugott & König 1991, 209; Bybee, Perkins & Pagliuca 1994, 195). This grammaticalisation path is not only attested for the English language (cf. Section 6.1.1 above for more details of the rise of epistemic *must*) and related languages but also for languages from unrelated language families such as Dravidian or Finno-Ugric languages (cf. Sweetser 1990, 90; cf. Figure 36 in Chapter 6). This suggests that a universal cognitive process triggers the grammaticalisation from deontic to epistemic meaning (cf. also van der Auwera, Ammann & Kindt 2005, 255).

In the case of *must* two kinds of mechanisms are usually discussed in the relevant literature: (1) conventionalisation of implicature (cf. Traugott 1989; Hopper & Traugott 1993; Traugott & Dasher 2002) and (2) metaphor (cf. Sweetser 1990). Traugott explains the development of epistemic meanings with the process of conventionalisation of an implicature (cf. Traugott 1989, 51). She argues that the implicature of deontic *must* entails that the speaker will actually do what he or she is obliged to do and this therefore leads to the emergence of its epistemic reading. Sweetser (1990) instead claims that the underlying mechanism of semantic change from deontic to epistemic meanings is best understood as metaphorical mapping. Her understanding of this process goes back to Lakoff and Johnson, who define metaphor as a mechanism of "understanding and experiencing one kind of thing in terms of another" (Lakoff & Johnson 1980, 5). In the case of *must*, speakers map the structure of their sociophysical world onto their 'mental world', i.e. they "view logical necessity [...] as being the mental analogue of sociophysical force" (Sweetser 1990, 30). This means, speakers understand the mental force expressed by epistemic *must* in terms of the sociophysical force expressed by deontic *must*. This analogy becomes also visible in collocations such as *a strong argument*. The occurrence of deontic and epistemic *must* in largely mutually exclusive environments (e.g. epistemic *must* with progressive aspect or perfect) is a strong argument in favour of metaphor as the underlying process of semantic change. Furthermore, the metaphorical mapping of the two domains seems to be less culture-specific than the conventionalisation of implicature typically is and may therefore better explain the widely attested cross-linguistic evidence for forms with an ambiguous reading between root and epistemic modality.

As mentioned above, many languages follow the grammaticalisation path from deontic to epistemic modality, but not all languages do so. I argue that those varieties of English spoken by speakers of an L1 that exhibit this grammaticalisation path show a more widespread use of epistemic *must* than those varieties of English with an L1 whose equivalent for *must* does not follow this path. As we are dealing with the transfer of meanings rather than the transfer of forms, the process can best be understood in terms of 'pattern replication' rather than 'matter replication' (cf. Matras & Sakel 2007, 4). Matras and Sakel define 'matter replication' as "the actual adoption of a structure from another language for circulation in the recipient system" and 'pattern replication' as "a shift in meaning or in the distribution of existing structures" (Matras & Sakel 2007, 4). In 'matter replication', forms from a source language are transferred to a recipient language (e.g. 'borrowings' such as Hokkien *kiasu* 'selfish attitude' in SgE in (140)). In 'pattern replication', meanings from a model language are transferred to words of the replica language. This phenomenon is also called 'structural convergence', 'pattern transfer', or 'calque' (cf. Heath 1984, 367). In the area of grammar, we can find pattern replication in terms of transfer of grammatical meanings from the model language (M) to the replica language (R) (cf. Heine & Kuteva 2005, 2). Grammatical replication as pattern replication therefore differs from matter replication because the form of the L1 is not transferred but the function of a form in the model language is grafted onto a form that is considered to be equivalent in the replica language. Defined this way, 'grammatical replication' takes place when two languages are in contact and one language is restructured in terms of another language. In the case of second-language varieties of English, however, we are not only dealing with two languages that are in contact but with the restructuring of a newly emerging variety on the basis of contact with another variety of English, i.e. the superstrate variety, and substrate languages (cf. the Feature Pool Model in Figure 31 in Chapter 6).

The question that needs to be addressed is how the structure of the substrate language can actually have an influence on the frequency of epistemic *must*. In order to find an answer to this question, I will take the substrate languages Kannada (IndE) and Mandarin (SgE) as exemplary cases because these languages represent the two types of substrate languages that can be distinguished in terms of their encoding of deontic and epistemic modalities (cf. Figure 39 in Chapter 6). Kannada (IndE) has one form that encodes both readings, while Mandarin (SgE) has two different forms for deontic and epistemic modality. Other languages that are typologically similar to Kannada are the other two Dravidian languages Tamil and Telugu, while the Indo-Aryan languages Marathi, Konkani, Hindi (IndE), the Austronesian language Malay (SgE), and the Sino-Tibetan language Cantonese (HKE) are typologically similar to Mandarin.

The analysis of Kannada and Mandarin can therefore be applied to the other languages that were classified as type 1 or type 2 respectively (cf. Figure 39 in Chapter 6).

The equivalent of *must* in the Dravidian language Kannada, *beeku*, is ambiguous between deontic and epistemic reading, which is the result of a grammaticalisation process from deontic to epistemic modality. As discourse situations in which *must* is employed in its deontic function are more frequent than discourse situations in which *must* is used in its epistemic function, L2 speakers of English are likely to acquire modal verbs with deontic readings earlier than modal verbs with epistemic readings (cf. also Section 7.4 for frequency as an important cognitive selection principle). Thus, speakers of Kannada first map $beeku_D$ with $must_D$ based on the similarity between the forms in their more concrete obligational meaning (and probably also based on the formal similarity of their invariant form, although *beeku* differs from *must* in that it is used post-verbally, cf. Andersen's 1983, 178 'Transfer to Somewhere Principle', which holds that transfer will take place if there is a similar structure in the L1). The equivalence is therefore first established "on semantic/functional rather than on syntactic or other structural parameters" (Heine & Kuteva 2005, 229). This becomes obvious in cases where the substrate language expresses deontic modality with different linguistic means than with free morphemes, such as with the suffix -*ɳum* in Tamil that represents the equivalent of *must* (cf. (123)). Apart from situations where speakers want to express necessity in which they map $beeku_D$ and $must_D$, speakers may also want to express logical inference. In this case, they retrieve the relevant expression in their L1, i.e. $beeku_E$, and based on the prior mapping of $beeku_D$ and $must_D$, they transfer the epistemic meaning of $beeku_E$ onto *must* (cf. Figure 42). This order of development is in line with the sequence identified by Matras.

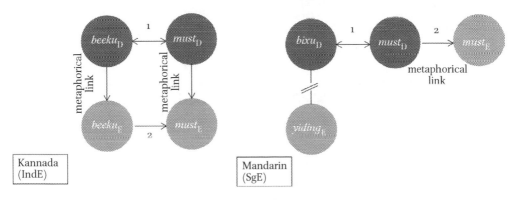

FIGURE 42 Mapping of form and function by Kannada L1 speakers compared to Mandarin L1 speakers.

> Speakers will inevitably direct their attention to the more concrete meaning when searching for a match in the replica [...]. The match will then lead to the emergence of a more abstract meaning.
>
> MATRAS 2009, 238–239

In addition to this, research on learner varieties of English has shown that "learners strive, at least initially, to maintain mapping-transparency, associating a single semantic feature with a single form" (Williams 1987, 181–182) and only add further meanings to the form. This extension of *must* to epistemic contexts may be regarded as a spontaneous replication of *beeku$_E$* initially but the use of *must$_E$* may quickly become conventionalised once the speaker realises that *must* is also polysemous in English, based on additional input from ENL varieties (cf. Heine & Kuteva 2010, 88).

In Mandarin, however, we can expect the speaker to identify *bìxū* with deontic *must* based on their similar meanings (and similar syntactic behaviours in terms of their invariant, preverbal use) (cf. Figure 42). But *bìxū* has only a deontic reading and has no formal equivalent that can also carry an epistemic reading (cf. also Bao 2010, 1732). Instead, the adverb *yiding* ('certainly') fulfils the epistemic function of *must* in Mandarin (cf. also Bao 2010, 1732). In this case, no metaphorical link which may lead to the mapping of the epistemic reading onto *must* exists. In other words, "[t]he environment in which English evolves into Singapore English lacks the metaphorical glue that binds the epistemic *must* with the deontic *must*" (Bao 2010, 1736). This is why speakers may express epistemic readings with linguistic means other than the modal *must*, for example with adverbs that are equivalent to Mandarin *yiding*, such as *certainly* (cf. also Section 7.3 for the lexical expression of modality in SLA).

Bao also accounts for the deontic bias of *must* in SgE in terms of substratum influence. He calls the type of substratum influence 'convergence-to-substratum', which "refer[s] narrowly to the phenomenon of English grammatical features converging in usage or function to the equivalent features in the linguistic substratum" (Bao 2010, 1729).[2] This process roughly corresponds to Siegel's (2008) 'functional transfer' but differs in perspective by focusing on the emerging ESL variety rather than the substrate languages. Bao gives three reasons for the 'convergence-to-substratum' process involved in the use of *must* in SgE: (1) epistemic and deontic modality are not expressed by the same modal auxiliary in Chinese and Malay, (2) the perfect form is used more rarely in SgE

---

2 Bao explains 'convergence-to-substratum' with bilingualism as a form of priming in which the speaker is predisposed to another language on the basis of his or her knowledge of other languages (cf. Bao 2016).

than in BrE, a context where epistemic *must* is often used in BrE, and (3) the grammaticalisation path from deontic to epistemic modality is absent in the Chinese equivalent of *must*. The first and third reasons are related, because the polysemy of a form denoting deontic and epistemic modality is the synchronic product of a diachronic grammaticalisation process. Apart from these two reasons that were also identified as relevant in the analysis above, Bao observes that the tendency towards deontic use is furthermore strengthened by the decline of the perfect in SgE, which leads to a decrease in epistemic *must* where BrE has epistemic *must have V-en* contexts (cf. Bao 2010, 1735).

Despite all these reasons for the deontic bias of *must*, the existence of epistemic *must* in SgE and the initial rise of epistemic *must* in HKE in apparent time suggest that speakers of these varieties may also develop epistemic uses of the modal *must* over time on the basis of input from the superstrate variety. The initial rise in frequency of epistemic *must* proceeds much more slowly in HKE than in IndE, where the shared grammaticalisation path triggers a faster development of epistemic *must* (cf. Section 8.3 for the apparent-time findings). The presence of the grammaticalisation path in the L1 of the speaker may thus act as a catalyst for the emergence of epistemic readings of *must*. This means that speakers who are familiar with this polysemy adopt epistemic *must* more readily in their second-language variety because substrate and superstrate languages contribute the polysemous form to the feature pool and it therefore has a greater chance of being selected in the restructuring process of the emerging ESL variety. Speakers of languages that do not have the grammaticalisation path can instead only draw on the structure of the superstrate to restructure their variety of English. This line of argumentation is supported by findings from SLA studies, which show that learners with an L1 containing comparable structures to the L2 acquire these structures faster than learners whose L1s do not have equivalent structures (cf. Siegel 2008, 108). The gradual rise of the proportion of epistemic *must* in apparent time from the oldest age groups to the middle-aged groups in ICE-HK and ICE-IND* suggests a process of ongoing grammaticalisation rather than the transfer of the result of a grammaticalisation process, i.e. the 'wholesale transfer' of *must* in both readings.

IndE speakers with a Dravidian language, such as Kannada, as their L1 replicate the structure of their L1 in their L2 (i.e. their ESL variety). This is referred to as 'L1>L2 replication' (Heine & Kuteva 2005, 237–238). Here, the second language of the speakers is the replica language that is restructured according to the first language that serves as the model language. Note that the L2 in this scenario is not the superstrate language BrE but the emerging variety (cf. also Siegel 2008, 122 for the emerging pidgin as the L2 in transfer). The superstrate variety BrE, however, is also important because it has the same structure as the

L1 and therefore reinforces the replication (in a process that could be called 'superstrate reinforcement' in analogy to 'substrate reinforcement'). In varieties with substrate languages that do not share the grammaticalisation path from deontic to epistemic with English, 'L1>L2 replication' can be ruled out as an explanation for the emergence of epistemic *must*. Here, epistemic *must* emerges due to the influence of the superstrate variety BrE, but only at the beginning before it decreases in frequency (cf. the analysis of the decrease of *must* according to function in Section 8.3).

If grammaticalisation takes place in the varieties whose L1s do not have a grammaticalisation path from deontic to epistemic modality, we would expect that the time of colonisation also plays an important role. The longer the varieties are in contact with the superstrate variety, the more grammaticalised should *must* be. As the period of colonisation was shorter in Hong Kong and Singapore than in India, it is hypothesised that epistemic *must* had less time to develop in these varieties of English. The Foundation phase of English in India already started in 1600 and it entered the phase of Exonormative Stabilisation in 1757 (cf. Section 3.2.2; cf. Schneider 2007, 162–166). If the second phase is taken as the starting point, the phase in which contact between the STL and the IDG strand increases, and independence in 1947 as the end point, we can identify a time depth for the English variety spoken in India of 190 years (and even longer, because English still plays an important role in post-independence India). If we compare this to the length of colonisation in Hong Kong and Singapore, we can see that English came to these territories much later, i.e. at the beginning of the 19th century, in 1819 in Singapore and 1841 in Hong Kong. These varieties therefore also entered the second phase of their development around a century later than IndE, in 1867 in Singapore and 1898 in Hong Kong (cf. Schneider 2007, 154;135). Singapore gained independence in 1965, while Hong Kong was returned to China in 1997 (cf. Schneider 2007, 136;155). The varieties of English therefore had about 100 years to develop and are still developing, because English is still spoken in these countries and has even expanded its functions considerably in Singapore. This may mean that *must* had more time to grammaticalise in IndE and its frequency may therefore reflect a later stage of the development than that found in HKE or SgE. This suggests that IndE and HKE reflect different stages in the process of linguistic change, something that also becomes visible when we compare the peaks of the frequency of epistemic *must* in both varieties. While the age group 36–45 in HKE shows a peak in frequency with an M-co of 17, this figure is higher for the 26–33 age group in IndE with an M-co peak of 37 (cf. Section 8.3). This could signify that the higher frequency of epistemic *must* in this age group in IndE could also have to do with the time depth of the English variety in India. IndE simply had more time to develop epistemic uses than the variety of English spoken in Hong Kong. Furthermore, the structures of some speakers' Lis act as catalysts for the development of epistemic readings of *must* in this variety.

To support the argument that substrate influence may play an important role for the distribution of deontic and epistemic modality, further cross-linguistic evidence is needed that shows a correlation between the structures of other ESL varieties and their substrate languages. PhilE could prove to be an interesting case in point. So far, researchers have produced conflicting evidence with regard to a potential deontic bias of the modal *must* in this variety of English. While Bao finds no such bias, with a proportion of 48% of epistemic uses (cf. Bao 2010, 1731), Collins, Borlongan, and Yao's findings indicate a deontic bias, with 72% deontic *must* in the 1960s and 81% in the 1990s in PhilE (cf. Collins, Borlongan & Yao 2014, 80). These dissimilar findings can be (partly) explained by differences in the databases. While Bao analyses the spoken private conversations of ICE-PHI, Collins, Borlongan, and Yao take written data from Phil-BROWN and ICE-PHI as their database. As epistemic uses of *must* are generally more common in spoken than in written language, Bao's findings of a larger proportion of epistemic *must* therefore correspond to expectation. As my argument is based on the semantic analysis of all instances of *must* in the complete spoken section of ICE, Bao's data are not directly comparable to my data, which is why only the investigation of the complete spoken section of ICE-PHI including private and public dialogues and monologues might throw further light on the presence or absence of a deontic bias in spoken PhilE. After such an analysis, it would be interesting to see whether the languages of the Philippines are typologically similar or different in the encoding of strong deontic and epistemic modality. Given that almost all languages of the Philippines belong to one major language family, the Malayo-Polynesian language family, it could well be the case that they behave similarly.

Further corroboration for the line of argumentation that substrate influence plays a role in the formation of the deontic bias of *must* comes from Nelson's data that indicate that HKE shows not such a strong deontic bias in the use of *should* compared to other ESL varieties (cf. Nelson 2003, 31), which may be related to the fact that Cantonese *yīnggōi* ('should') can also be used in epistemic function (cf. footnote 79 in Section 6.2). It would also be interesting to include varieties of English that emerged in Africa in the analysis to test whether their structures support the explanation given above. WALS, for example, shows an overlap for necessity and possibility in Yoruba, one of the most important of the 520 languages spoken in Nigeria according to the *Ethnologue*, and ICE-NIG also provides information about the mother tongues of some speakers that allows the influence of the structures of speakers' L1s on the variety of English spoken in Nigeria to be analysed. This may be especially interesting, because the various languages of Nigeria belong to different language families (compare the case of IndE and the use of epistemic *must* by speakers of languages from the Dravidian language family vs. speakers of languages from the Indo-Aryan language family in Section 6.2).

We observed that similarities between the structures of the substrate language and superstrate variety proved to be important for the use of epistemic *must*. Similarities between the substrate languages and the superstrate BrE also seem to be the underlying reason for the comparatively high frequencies of the semi-modal verb *need to* in HKE and SgE compared to IndE (cf. Section 6.2). The high frequency of this semi-modal is contrary to expectation, given its rather recent emergence as a competitor of *must*, *have to*, and *have got to* in affirmative contexts (cf. Section 6.1.4). In Cantonese and Mandarin, forms that express 'need' can be used as main verbs followed by an NP and as auxiliaries followed by a VP (cf. (137) and (138) for examples of Cantonese *xūyào* in both meanings). In this way, they are semantically and syntactically similar to English *need* in main verb function, and the semi-modal *need* with following infinitive marker *to*. The Dravidian languages of India do not show this twofold use of a verb that can express 'need' as a main verb but can also be used to modify a main verb to express a necessity to do something. These languages (usually) employ invariant auxiliaries or bound morphemes to express a necessity to do something that are restricted to auxiliary uses. This means that there is no form that is semantically and syntactically similar to main verb *need* and auxiliary *need to* in these languages to facilitate the emergence of *need to* in IndE. Another reason for the low frequency of *need to* in IndE may be that ICE-IND* is less interactive in almost all registers than all other corpora, and interactivity of a register was shown to correlate with a higher frequency of this semi-modal verb (cf. Figure 24 in Chapter 4; cf. Nokkonen 2012, 136).

The discussion has shown that syntactic and semantic similarities between the respective substrate language and the superstrate variety BrE are a necessary prerequisite for the process of transfer to occur (cf. also Schneider 2007, 111). As the Dravidian languages are similar to English in their use of a polysemous form for the expression of deontic and epistemic modality (cf. also van der Auwera, Ammann & Kindt 2005, 258), speakers of (Dr) IndE adopt epistemic uses of epistemic *must* more readily, leading to a higher overall frequency of epistemic *must* in these varieties compared to varieties spoken by speakers whose L1 does not employ one form for both functions. While Dravidian languages are more similar with regard to the encoding of deontic and epistemic modality, which leads to a similar use of *must* in the emerging ESL variety, Sinitic languages are similar to English in their use of an expression of 'need' in main verb and auxiliary verb function. This is why speakers of theses languages use the semi-modal *need to* more often in their varieties of English, such as HKE and SgE, than those speakers that do not have a semantic and syntactic equivalent of 'need' and 'need to' in their L1s.

7.2   Cultural Motivations

Almost every introductory textbook about WE and most forewords to studies on linguistic features in WE mention culture as an important factor for the linguistic indigenisation of English in these varieties, as the following examples show (my emphases).

> A nativised, accultured or indigenised variety of English is thus one that has been *influenced by the local cultures* in which it has developed.
>
> KIRKPATRICK 2007, 7

> 'Indigenisation' refers to the acculturation of the TL [target language] to localised phenomena, be they *cultural*, topographic or even linguistic (in terms of local grammatical, lexical and discourse *norms*).
>
> MESTHRIE & BHATT 2008, 11

> [sc. The term indigenised Englishes] refers to those varieties which have developed in ESL contexts and have become *adapted to their cultural environment* [...].
>
> SEARGEANT 2012, 172

For the purpose of this section, culture can be broadly defined "as the shared, socially learned knowledge and patterns of behaviour characteristic of some group of people" (Bailey & Peoples 2013, 37). We can see the linguistic expression of cultural knowledge most obviously at the lexical level in borrowings, such as Hokkien *kiasu* referring to 'the fear of losing out' (cf. (140)) or Malay *baju kurong* referring to 'a Malay dress for women' in SgE. Beside borrowings, we can also find English-English compounds in SgE that refer to local cultural concepts or practices, such as *hawker stall*, or the more recent *hawker centre* for 'open-air food stalls and complexes' (cf. (141)), or *red packet* (cf. (142)) for 'an envelope of money that people give as a gift on special occasions such as weddings, graduation, or birth'.

(140) Our understanding of *kiasu* is someone who wants to win at all cost (ICE-SIN:S1B-029)

(141) Although some would wax nostalgic over the loss of open-air dining op-portunities in *hawker stalls* around Hokkien Street, Chinatown or the Cuppage Road Car Park, they soon welcomed the cleaner, more orderly and hygienic milieux of *hawker centres* [...]. (ICE-SIN:W2B-003)

(142) During her old age, she still came to my mother's home every Chinese New Year to pay an annual visit. On these occasions, I always gave her a *red packet* of two hundred dollars, knowing that she needed the money for her large brood. (ICE-SIN:W2B-020)

Schneider states that "the question of whether any grammatical properties can possibly be accounted for as manifestations of a particular culture is a challeng-ing but unresolved issue" (Schneider 2007, 88). To my knowledge, only a few lin-guists have accounted for grammatical variation in terms of cultural differences. Olavarría de Ersson and Shaw (2003), for example, give a cultural explanation for differences in verb complementation. They analyse the verb complementation of *provide, furnish, supply, entrust*, and *present* and find that BrE speakers prefer the use of *provide so. with sth.* (*He provided them with money*), while IndE speak-ers prefer the use of *provide sth. to so.* (*He provided money to them*). They also analyse the use of *pelt, shower, pepper*, and *bombard* and find that BrE speakers again prefer the use of the construction *pelt so. with sth.*, while IndE speakers prefer *pelt sth. at so.* as a construction. In other words, BrE speakers more often select the construction that foregrounds the subject; IndE speakers more fre-quently choose the construction that foregrounds the object. They link this to possible differences in the construction of the self, which is seen as "the center of the world" in Anglo cultures, while it is seen "as a part or a small object in a larger whole" (Olavarría de Ersson & Shaw 2003, 159) in South Asian cultures.

Other than this tentative cultural explanation, the question of the interre-lationship between grammar and culture has received little to no attention in corpus-based research on grammatical variation in WE. This has probably to do with the nature of grammatical studies in WE. These studies are very often large-scale comparative studies (cf. Sections 2.2 and 11.1) that compare the use of a feature across a wide variety of ENL and ESL varieties, very often in ten or more varieties of English that have emerged in very different cultural con-texts. This type of research has clearly been shaped by the availability of the comparable ICE corpora (cf. Section 4.1). Currently, 16 corpora are available in total. And the ICE corpus project has not been finished yet; even more corpora are being compiled at the moment. Additionally, newer mega-corpora such as

GloWbE push research even further into the direction of large-scale comparative studies (cf. Section 11.1 for a discussion about ICE and GloWbE).

In these studies, the present-day state of the former input variety serves as
the point of departure for an analysis of variation in ESL varieties. Variation is
therefore construed in terms of difference from the so-called parent variety.
And in return the present-day state of the former input variety is construed as
the ultimate 'goal' of development, especially in studies that focus on variables
undergoing language change. Very often, ESL varieties are understood as 'lagging behind' the more advanced ENL varieties, as can be seen in the following
quotes (cf. also Section 2.4).

> Last but not least, IndE as a second-language variety is defined as being
> in the *least favoured position* in this picture, namely *lagging behind* as the
> *most conservative* of all varieties under examination [...].
>
> DIACONU 2012b, 11, my emphases

> The OC [Outer Circle] varieties are considerably *more conservative* than
> the IC [Inner Circle].
>
> COLLINS & YAO 2012, 44, my emphases

> [T]he IC [Inner Circle] varieties are generally *more advanced* than the
> OC [Outer Circle].
>
> COLLINS & YAO 2012, 52, my emphases

> What this may suggest is that PhilE [Philippine English] writers have
> been striving to *catch up* with AmE over this period.
>
> COLLINS, BORLONGAN & YAO 2014, 85, my emphases

These descriptions clearly show the Anglocentric perspective on New Englishes
and evoke problematic associations in the field of postcolonial Englishes (cf.
also Section 2.4). This Anglocentric perspective may lead to blindness for indigenisation processes that differ from those ongoing in ENL varieties, because
variation in these ESL varieties is understood in terms of variation in ENL varieties. This perspective is especially problematic when cultural explanations for
language variation and change that originate in ENL varieties are transferred
to ESL contexts. This is the case in attempts to transfer the notion of 'democratisation' (cf. Fairclough 1993) to ESL varieties in studies on modal verbs. In
Anglo cultures, obligations expressed with the modal verb *must* constitute a
threat to the hearer's negative face wants, because the speaker is construed
as the deontic source of obligation and imposes his or her will on the hearer.
This creates a hierarchy of power between the speaker and the addressee, so

that the speaker assumes a higher position in the hierarchy than the addressee. This explains why *must* is associated with a forceful tone in 'Western' societies and consequently avoided (cf. Smith 2003, 259). Its decline has usually been explained with cultural changes towards more 'democratic ways of speaking', also labelled 'democratisation' in 'Western' societies (cf. Fairclough 1993). This has arguably also led to a rise in the use of the semi-modal verb *have to*. In obligations expressed with *have to*, the speaker is not identified as the deontic source, the obligation deriving instead from external sources. The concept of non-imposition therefore lies at the heart of the process, which seems to be a particularly 'Western' concept. This problem becomes quite apparent once one tries to systematically integrate this cultural explanation to findings on modal verbs in WE, which is usually not done in studies that only mention 'democratisation' as a keyword (cf. Rajalahti, Parviainen & Klemola 2012; Loureiro-Porto 2013; Diaconu 2015, 146).

Apart from democratisation as a cultural explanation for linguistic variation and change, it may well be that there are subtler cultural differences that are less noticeable at first sight, that may also have an impact on linguistic structure. The question therefore arises whether the frequency differences shown in Figure 26 in Chapter 5 are indicators of cross-cultural differences in the sense that a higher frequency points to a higher cultural salience of the action that is expressed in the society (cf. Wierzbicka 1997, 11–12; cf. also Wong 2014, 36). This gives rise to the questions: Are there cultural differences in marking facts from opinion that may account for the high frequency of epistemic *must* in ENL varieties compared to the low frequency of epistemic *must* in ESL varieties? Are there cultural differences in obligational practices that may account for the high frequency of the modal and semi-modal verbs of obligation in ESL varieties and in particular the high frequency of root *must* in SgE? Wong states that

> [o]ne of the more striking features of Anglo English seems to be its strong emphasis on the distinction between facts and opinions [...]. It follows that Anglo English speakers refrain from expressing uncertainties as certainties and treat facts with utmost care.
>
> WONG 2014, 216

One of the linguistic means to mark opinions from facts is the use of epistemic phrases (e.g. *I think, I guess, I suppose*) (cf. Wierzbicka 2006, 295). Wierzbicka argues that the rise in the frequency of epistemic phrases occurred due to the emphasis on the distinction between facts and opinion during the British Enlightenment period, for example in the works by John Locke (cf. Wierzbicka 2006, 295). Epistemic phrases such as *I think* are employed to mark what one thinks from what one knows, e.g. *I think Bill is in Sydney now* vs. *Bill is in Sydney now*, where the sentence with the hedge *I think* expresses an opinion, while the simple declarative sentence expresses a fact (cf. Wierzbicka 2006, 204). It can be argued that a similar relationship holds between modally marked sentences and sentences that are not marked modally, e.g. *Bill must be in Sydney now* vs. *Bill is in Sydney now*. The sentence without epistemic *must* implies that the speaker is reporting a fact, while the sentence with epistemic *must* implies that the speaker does not report a fact but a (strong) opinion. Wong formulates the following Natural Semantic Metalanguage (NSM) script (cf. (143)) (cf. Wierzbicka 1991 for the NSM approach) to explain the Anglo script for marking opinions from facts (cf. Wong 2010, 2939).

(143) Anglo script
    I can't say about something, "it is like this" if I don't know that it is like this,
    I can say "it is like this" if I know that it is like this

Wong suggests that this script is typical of 'Anglo' Englishes but not typical of Singlish or of more formal varieties of SgE (cf. Wong 2014, 219), as the 'corresponding' Singaporean script in (144) shows.

(144) Singaporean script
    I can't say about something, "it is like this" if I know that it is not like this
    if I know that it can be like this,
        I can say, "it is like this"

The main difference between the two scripts "seems to be that Anglo English speakers do not assume anything without evidence while Singapore English speakers tend to make assumptions until evidence suggests otherwise" (Wong 2010, 2939). As a consequence, the distinction between opinion and fact is often not marked by linguistic means (cf. Wong 2014, 216), which is why it may be the case that contexts where we would expect epistemic *must* from an Anglo English perspective are not modally marked at all in SgE. The Singaporean way of (not) marking fact from opinion seems to be the norm if all cultures of the world are taken into account and can also be found in India, while the 'Anglo' way of marking fact from opinion is rather the exception (cf. Wong 2014, 228–229). In my questionnaire with speakers of IndE, I used the following discourse completion task in order to elicit epistemic *must* but also other forms that may be used in these contexts. I asked the participants to imagine the following situation: "You are at home with your flatmate and the doorbell rings. It's 3 o'clock in the afternoon and one of your friends wanted to come around at 3 o'clock. What would you say to your flatmate as the doorbell rings?". 21% used a modal (*must, may, would*) and another 21% used the indicative without a modal such as *She's here* or *Oh! My friend has come*. A minority option at 7% was the use of an epistemic hedge such as *I think*,

I guess. In 15%, a paraphrase was used such as in *I opens* [sic!] *the door with a smile, receives him/her and politely say that we are going out for an urgent work.*

The rest construed the situation differently, which became obvious in their choice of the imperative in 29% of the cases, such as *Open the door (please)* or *Go get the door,* or in their use of questions in 7% of the cases, such as *Can you please go and open the door or else I will go open the door.* Anglo English speakers are not likely to construe the situation in this way, because they would find it inappropriate to tell the flatmate to open the door for their own guests. Although this is only anecdotal evidence based on a questionnaire conducted with 53 participants, it is quite striking that over a third of my participants construed the situation reciprocally and deems it appropriate to tell the flatmate what to do in this situation. From an Anglo perspective, the imperative addressed to their flatmate would clearly constitute a face-threatening act in Brown and Levinson's (1987) terms. Kirkpatrick also addresses different pragmatic norms involved in the use of the imperative in Slavic cultures compared to 'Anglo' cultures and shows how differences in pragmatic use can lead to cross-cultural misunderstandings when he says that a "Russian apparently ordering an Australian to 'Open the window' might not be heard with complete equanimity" (Kirkpatrick 2015, 464).

Brown and Levinson's (1987) politeness theory has been strongly criticised for its Anglo bias, for example by Wierzbicka (1985), who has repeatedly warned against mistaking 'Anglo' English for the human norm (cf. Wierzbicka 2006, 11–13). Central to their theory is the concept of face, the 'public self-image' of an individual. Face is composed of two aspects, positive and negative face. Positive face is defined as "the want of every member that his [or her] wants be desirable to at least some others" (Brown & Levinson 1987, 62), i.e. the desire of every individual to be approved and appraised by others. Negative face is defined as the desire of every individual that "his [or her] actions be unimpeded by others" (Brown & Levinson 1987, 62). In other words, the individual wants to be free from the imposition of others. Cross-cultural research has shown that the concept of negative face is not a valid one for several 'Eastern' societies, as it "presupposes that the basic unit of society is the individual" (Matsumoto 1988, 405).

The difference in the emphasis on negative face wants may be relevant to the discussion of the use of *must* in Anglo varieties of English as opposed to SgE. Apart from the replacement of the modal verb by the semi-modal verb *have to* that has been mentioned earlier, orders or requests may also be redressed with the use of indirect speech acts to avoid a face-threatening act, e.g. (145) as opposed to (146).

(145) Could you possibly do something about it?

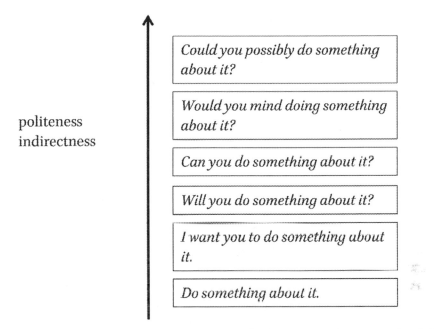

Could you possibly do something about it?

Would you mind doing something about it?

Can you do something about it?

Will you do something about it?

I want you to do something about it.

Do something about it.

politeness
indirectness

FIGURE 43   Correlation between indirectness and politeness in 'Anglo' varieties of English
            (cf. Leech 1983, 108).

(146) Do something about it.

The indirect request in (145) is considered more polite in Anglo cultures than the direct speech act in the form of an imperative in (146). In general, we can see a positive correlation between indirectness and politeness (cf. Leech 1983, 108).

However, this correlation does not seem to exist in Singlish, the basilectal variety of SgE, as Wong informs us (cf. Wong 2014, 173).[3] Here, the imperative is routine and unremarkable and not considered impolite (cf. Lee-Wong 2000, 75; Wong 2014, 153). Wong states that: "Anglo notions of not being 'pushy' or 'bossy' do not seem germane [to Singlish speakers] and Singlish speakers do not see the need to sound hypothetical and tentative when they want someone to do something" (Wong 2014, 172). Sentences such as *You carry my bag in* do not seem to be associated with impoliteness and the use of imperatives is not restricted to family and friends but it is also used among strangers, as the customer-client interaction in (147) shows. The background for (147) is that the customer wants the shop assistant to remove all the tags on a pair of jeans she has just bought (cf. Wong 2014, 174).

(147) This one you remove everything because I want to wear straightaway.

---

3 See also Meierkord (2016) and Kachru (2017) for similar observations in request strategies employed by speakers of Ugandan English and of IndE.

Lee-Wong shows that the majority of speakers prefer to express impositions 'in a direct bald-on record strategy', for example in the use of the imperative or simple declarative sentences such as *I'm taking your bike* (cf. Lee-Wong 2000, 206). These strategies are not considered rude but are socially acceptable. In the ICE-SIN corpus, we can find a widespread use of imperatives in interactions in the private dialogue section. The following imperatives are used in a situation where two people prepare their lunch meal: *You fry the luncheon meat first lah because I need time to cut up the beans*; *You hang around there do some work wash the dishes*; *assist me in cooking*; *well open the can open the can*; *give me a bowl*, or *please wash the bowl* (ICE-SIN:S1A-064).

The modal *can* is sometimes added as a tag question after the imperative in sentences such as *Do this, can?* (cf. Wong 2014, 155) or forms part of an interrogative (*Can you do this?*). While the interrogative with *can* is very often used in Singlish, the interrogative with *could* is less often used (cf. Wong 2014, 153). Wong argues that the interrogative with *can* in SgE does not have the same pragmatics as the interrogative with *can* in Anglo varieties of English (cf. *Can you do something about it?* in Figure 43; cf. Wong 2014, 154). The interrogative with *can* in Singlish asks the addressee about his or her abilities to do something and the underlying assumption is that the addressee will do what the speaker asks him to if he or she can do it (cf. Wong 2014, 154). The modal is therefore also often used in order to say that one is able to do something (*Can.* or *Can lah.*). The will of the speaker is not in focus but his or her abilities. The differences in the use of the modal *can* in these types of utterances shows in what way modal verbs may be subject to local pragmatic norms of use, which speakers may subconsciously transfer (cf. also Kirkpatrick 2012, 20). This transfer is very likely in ESL situations where usually speakers from the same cultural background interact and where an external pragmatic norm would probably be considered 'artificial'. The *can*-interrogative is comparable to the BrE use in interrogatives such as *Can you pass me the salt?*. However, it only seems to be used with small impositions in BrE.

The differences in the use of the modal *can* lead us to the question of whether the modal verb *must* is also subject to different pragmatic norms in SgE compared to BrE or AmE. Research on other varieties of English has shown that *must* "does not generally carry the semantics of obligation or 'bossiness' understood in StE [sc. Standard English]" (Mesthrie 2008b, 627). For example, *must* "has much less social impact in WhSAfE [White South African English] than in other varieties of English, and often substitutes for polite *should/shall*" (Bowerman 2008, 477). This finding and my findings about SgE suggest that *must* may carry a different pragmatic meaning in different varieties of English. In 'Anglo' societies, an order or request expressed by *must* clearly threatens the negative face of the hearer. But as negative face wants are less prominent in 'Eastern' societies, obligations with *must* may not constitute a face-threatening act in these types of societies.

I' as hearer is not overly concerned with this notion of 'imposition' by S [sc. the speaker] because H [sc. the hearer] is related to S as a member of a larger whole, the society.

LEE-WONG 2000, 311

This explanation points to differences in the construal of the self in relation to others as the source of differences in pragmatic norms that lead to a greater use of *must*, because it is less restricted in terms of its pragmatics. With this in view, it is highly interesting to note that Leech suggests 'Individualisation' as a synonym for the process of 'democratisation' (cf. Leech 2003, 237).

Markus and Kitayama's (1991) comprehensive metastudy about the cultural construction of self found that people from different cultures have markedly different self-constructions and that these can influence experience. Anglo cultures are marked by an independent construal of the self (cf. upper part of Figure 44) (other terms used for these cultures are 'individualist', 'egocentric', 'separate', 'autonomous', 'idiocentric', and 'self-contained', cf. Markus &

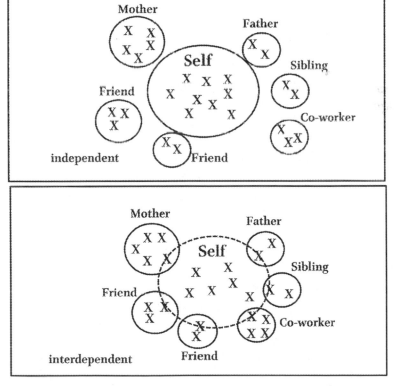

FIGURE 44   Independent vs. interdependent construal of self (adapted from Markus
             & Kitayama 1991, 226).

Kitayama 1991, 226). Individuals in cultures with an independent construal of self place a high value on autonomy. They try to maintain independence from others by attending to the self. They see themselves as a self-contained unit with relatively invariable internal attributes that are independent from others (marked by the Xs in Figure 44) (e.g. *I am creative.*). Many Asian cultures instead show an interdependent construal of self, they perceive the self as intimately connected with the group (cf. lower part of Figure 44) (other terms used for these cultures are 'sociocentric', 'holistic', 'collective', 'allocentric', 'ensembled', 'constitutive', 'contextualised', 'connected', and 'relational', cf. Markus & Kitayama 1991, 227). Here, the internal attributes of the self are variable and situation-bound (marked by the Xs that are at the intersection between the self and others) (e.g. *I am polite in front of my professor*, cf. Markus & Kitayama 1991, 226). Individuals in these cultures do not see themselves as bounded units (marked by the dashed lines of the circles in Figure 44), because "it [sc. the self] changes structure with the nature of the particular social context" (Markus & Kitayama 1991, 227). The self is defined by the interpersonal relationships it has, which is why in these cultures the emphasis is on attending to the needs of others, fulfilling one's role, and balanced interrelationships (cf. also Gao & Ting-Toomey 1998, 6). Individualism instead may even carry negative associations of selfishness (cf. Gao & Ting-Toomey 1998, 8). The different associations with individualism are epitomised in proverbs, while the Americans say "the squeaky wheel gets the grease", the Japanese say "the nail that stands out gets pounded down" (Markus & Kitayama 1991, 224).

Markus and Kitayama give an example of a typical interaction in interdependent cultures (cf. Markus & Kitayama 1991, 229). They describe a situation in which somebody prepares a sandwich for a friend and asks his or her friend: "Hey, Tom, what do you want in your sandwich? I have turkey, salami, and cheese" and Tom responds: "Oh, I like turkey". This script is quite familiar to members of a culture with an independent construal of self. The speaker gives the hearer a choice, because the speaker assumes that the hearer has a right to choose according to his or her own preferences. The same question asked in countries with an interdependent construal of self would create confusion and speakers might answer "I don't know", which does not commit them to anything. In these cultures, it is the responsibility of the speaker to fulfil the perceived needs of the addressee. So in this case the host is supposed to anticipate the speaker's choice and might say: "Hey Tomio, I made you a turkey sandwich because I remember that last week you said you like turkey more than beef" and Tomio may thank the host and confirm the choice. This type of reciprocal interaction is, of course, not practiced with every individual in interdependent cultures, it "will be most characteristic of relationships with 'in-group' members" (Markus & Kitayama 1991, 229).

The example shows in what way one and the same situation may be perceived completely differently by speakers with different cultural backgrounds. From an Anglo perspective, the first example is the unmarked situation, because the hearer is free from the imposition of the speaker and is given a choice. The second example, instead, is the marked situation and may come across as imposing to members of Anglo cultures, because the speaker decides for the hearer without giving him or her a choice. In cultures with an interdependent construal of self, however, the situation is not considered imposing but shows an act of caring for the needs of the other.

> An independent behaviour exhibited by a person [...] is likely to be based on the premise of underlying interdependence and thus may have a somewhat different significance than it has for a person from an independent culture.
>
> MARKUS & KITAYAMA 1991, 227

If we transfer this situation to obligational practices, we can see differences in the conceptualisation of obligation based on differences in the construal of self. Obligations expressed with *must* are perceived as situations in which the speaker tells the hearer what to do because, given the speaker's will in independent cultures, the hearer supposes that the speaker wants him or her to do the action. This implies that the hearer is not free from the imposition of the speaker and it therefore constitutes a face-threatening act to the hearer's negative face. He or she is not autonomous in this situation and the speaker enters the hearer's territory. In cultures with an interdependent construal of self instead, the hearer supposes that the speaker tells him or her what to do because the speaker knows that it is good for him or her (cf. the situation with the sandwich).

This means that obligations are differently perceived by speakers from cultures with different construals of the self (cf. also Nwoye 1992, 316–317 for impositions in the Igbo society). Oyserman, Coon, and Kemmelmeier state that "[t]he core element of collectivism is the assumption that groups bind and mutually obligate individuals" (Oyserman, Coon & Kemmelmeier 2002, 5). This means that mutual obligations constitute the unmarked case in these societies, whereas they constitute the marked case in Anglo cultures, where individuals strive for independence. This is why the acts of caring for others by Chinese people may be "(mis)interpreted as acts of encroachment and overstepping" by speakers of cultures with an independent construal of self (Gao & Ting-Toomey 1998, 28). In a similar vein, Wong states:

> From an Anglo perspective, [...] it might seem that the Singaporean re-
> quester is being unacceptably 'imposing' or even forceful, and that the
> addressee is obliging and does not exercise personal autonomy.
>
> WONG 2004, 239–240

The interaction in (148) from ICE-SIN may illustrate this cultural difference.
Here, the speaker wants the hearer to go and explicitly says that it is beneficial
to the hearer, although the hearer does not want to go.

(148) I can feel her heart beating. Her arms grow tight around me and she is
      crying. "I don't want to go" "But you *must*" " Must I?" "We've been through
      this before, Ariel", I remind her gently. For your own good, darling. Or for
      mine. (ICE-SIN:W2F-019)

This may reflect that individuals are more likely to act in response to social
norms and other people's will than in response to their own wishes, so that
expectations of others take precedence over their own will (cf. also Wong 2004,
239).

> Actions are viewed as arising from relations or interactions with others;
> they are a product of obligations, responsibilities, or commitments to
> others and are thus best understood with respect of these interpersonal
> relations.
>
> MARKUS & KITAYAMA 1991, 232

In interdependent societies, "[s]elf assertion is not viewed as being authentic,
but instead as being immature" (Markus & Kitayama 1991, 229). This contrasts
strongly with Anglo cultures, where independence from others is considered
a sign of maturity (e.g. visible in leaving the parents' house at a certain age).
In these cultures, the underlying assumption is that actions are guided by the
hearer's own volition, as becomes obvious in the following NSM script from
Wong (2004, 234).

(149) Anglo script for the motivation to do something
      [people think like this]
      when I do something, it is good if I do it because I want to do it not be-
      cause someone else wants me to do it

India's culture is also considered to be marked by an interdependent construal
of the self. I was therefore especially interested in the associations of the modal
verb *must* in IndE. This is why I asked the 53 participants in my questionnaire
to rank the personality characteristics of a person who says *You must help me*

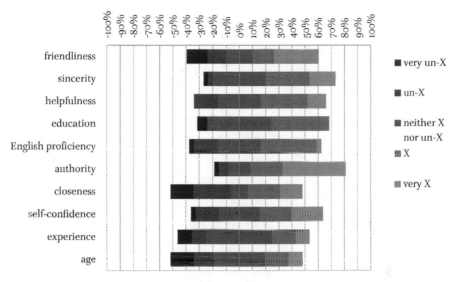

FIGURE 45   Personality characteristics associated with *must* in the sentence *You must help me out with this!* (cf. Table 30 in the appendices).

out with this! with regard to friendliness, sincerity, helpfulness, education, English proficiency, authority, closeness, self-confidence, experience, and age. The personality characteristics were chosen on the basis of free text answers given to more open questions in a pilot study with speakers from HKE, IndE, and SgE. The findings from my questionnaire show that the utterance is clearly associated with a speaker in authority, because 72% consider the speaker to be 'authoritative' or 'very authoritative' (cf. Figure 45). However, this does not mean that the speaker is perceived as 'unfriendly' as a consequence; 50% perceive the speaker as 'friendly' or even 'very friendly' compared to 29% who perceive the speaker as 'unfriendly' or 'very unfriendly'. Furthermore, the use of *must* in the utterance above is associated with a sincere person, because 53% imagine a 'sincere' or 'very sincere' speaker behind the utterance, while only 6% think the person is 'insincere' or 'very insincere'. Of course, the validity of these findings are compromised by the task design, because it runs the risk of overlooking situational differences in the use of *must*, for example differences with regard to the social distance between speaker and hearer. The situation the participants have in mind may then clearly have an influence on their ranking of the personality characteristics.

Of course, the descriptors are culturally-laden, too, which becomes most obvious in the ranking of *must* as 'authoritative' but at the same time as 'very friendly' by several speakers, two descriptors that almost preclude each other for Anglo speakers. This difference may have to do with cultural differences in terms of the importance of role relationships in the construal of the self:

"The conceptions of the Chinese self are [...] situated in, explained by, and governed by complex hierarchy and role relationships" (Gao & Ting-Toomey 1998, 17). Lee-Wong finds that Chinese subjects evaluate requests from a person with a higher status either as neutral or positive (cf. Lee-Wong 2000, 301). This probably has to do with the Confucian understanding that "knowing one's own position and behaving accordingly are taken to be fundamentals of a regulated society" (Sun 2006, 128). Biewer makes a similar observation for the Fijian and Samoan societies, where "people may not object to the strong force of a request coming from a person of high social status" (Biewer 2015, 108). Nkemleke shows that *must* is also more often used as a performative in religious texts, private letters, and student essays in CamE compared to its more restricted use in BrE predominantly in court procedures (cf. Nkemleke 2005, 52). Biewer explains the more widespread use of *must* with "a difference in the perception and expression of strong obligation in the two societies" (Biewer 2011, 19). This may equally apply to SgE, where requests may not be perceived as a threat to the autonomy of the speaker but rather as an appeal to the hearer's positive face in the way that mutual obligations strengthen the interconnectedness of the self. This also ties in with Wong, who states:

> They [sc. Singlish speakers] feel a cultural need to tell their addressees what to think and what to do. It is in this way that they feel connected with each other or perhaps even needed. Otherwise, the interaction might appear too formal and distant for the unmarked situation.
> WONG 2014, 259

After this discussion, we may see part of the findings shown in Figure 26 in Chapter 5 in a different light and we may go beyond Anglocentric explanations such as 'colonial lag' for the high frequency of *must*. Differences in the social practice of requests may lead to differences in the frequency of words that are associated with the social practice, depending on whether these situations are pragmatically marked or not. Obligations are less marked in Singapore, a culture with an interdependent construal of self, which may at least partially explain why the frequency of modal markers of obligation and necessity is higher here. This means that variation in the use of modals in L2 varieties "may result from different cultural perceptions of modality and different cultural rules in dealing with each other" (Biewer 2011, 20). What this analysis has also shown is that Anglo Englishes are, of course, also accultured and it may well be that these varieties constitute the marked case in cultures of the world, which means that researchers in WE have compared the ESL varieties against the typologically marked case. The discussion shows that it is important for speakers of English to understand "that different varieties of English encode different cultural norms and that such an understanding is crucial for successful inter-cultural communication" (Kirkpatrick 2015, 468).

The notions 'Anglo', 'Western' 'Eastern', 'non-Western' that were used in this section are clearly reductionist and assume homogeneity where in reality we find considerable heterogeneity. Of course, cultures are more complex and cannot be neatly distinguished along the two lines I discussed above. But the central aim of this chapter was to show that 'Western' cultural explanations cannot be considered to represent universal explanations which can then be easily transferred to varieties of English which have after all emerged in radically different cultural settings. This may at least help to avoid transferring cultural explanations for language change without scrutinising their applicability, for example in the case of the transfer of the culturally-laden concept of linguistic 'democratisation', even though this may be an appropriate explanation of societal changes towards more democratic ways of interaction in 'Western' societies.

This section has shown that there may be cultural differences in the marking of facts from opinion, which may (additionally) account for the low frequency of epistemic *must* in HKE and SgE. The section has also shown that *must* may not carry the same pragmatic force in HKE, IndE, and SgE as in 'Anglo' varieties due to the interdependent construal of the self in the ESL varieties I analysed. This section only analysed cultural differences associated with the use of modal and semi-modal verbs and the question remains in what way cultural explanations may play a role in studies on other language features. Clearly, more research is needed to find out how exactly the acculturation of English mentioned in several quotes at the beginning of this section surfaces in Englishes around the world.

7.3   Principles of SLA

ESL varieties are rarely discussed in terms of learner varieties, although these varieties are also non-native varieties of English. The lack of analyses of ESL varieties with respect to SLA was identified as a 'paradigm gap' early on by Sridhar and Sridhar (1982). The very basic similarity between ESL and EFL varieties lies in their origin as learner varieties. Both varieties may show features that develop in the learning process. But while ESL learner phenomena may stabilise over time "and turn into acceptable features of a newly developing variety in the socio-cultural setting in which the variety is used" (cf. Biewer 2011, 12; cf. also Buschfeld 2013, 59), learner features in EFL varieties are considered to be errors produced by speakers who have not (yet) achieved native speaker competence (cf. also Sridhar & Sridhar 1982, 94). This means that "fossilization is put on a level with feature nativization" (Buschfeld 2013, 59) in any joint description of EFL and ESL varieties, which explains why researchers of WE have refrained from applying concepts from SLA research to ESL varieties. Despite strong differences between EFL and ESL varieties (e.g. in terms of use, functions, relative stability, norm orientation, and acculturation, cf. also Section 3.1), EFL and ESL both develop via formal instruction at school as learner varieties. ESL varieties may therefore show typical characteristics of learner varieties, especially in the early stages of their development (cf. Mesthrie & Bhatt 2008, 156; cf. Buschfeld & Kautzsch 2017 for an integrated approach to EFL and ESL varieties). This is why SLA processes may account for some of the variation found in ESL varieties.

Williams (1987) attempts to bridge the gap identified by Sridhar and Sridhar (1982) by adopting an integrated approach to ESL varieties and learner varieties. Her analysis is grounded in the following observation:

> Certain forms [...], which are found in NIVEs [sc. non-native institutionalised varieties of English], strongly resemble forms found in learner languages, and at one time may, in fact, have been the result of individual language acquisition.
> WILLIAMS 1987, 163

She argues that learners simultaneously apply conflicting production principles, i.e. they try to find a compromise between economy of production and explicitness (or 'hyperclarity' in Williams's terminology, cf. Williams 1987, 169). She divides the principle of economy of production into two sub-principles, i.e. regularisation and selective production of redundant markers. She discusses invariant question tags, the loss of the mass/count noun distinction, the extension of the progressive aspect to stative verbs, SVO order in questions, and the omission of third person singular marking as cases of regularisation, i.e. the reduction of irregularities (cf. Williams 1987, 170–173). The lack of plural marking, past tense marking, and pronoun omission are discussed as instances of avoidance of redundancy in contexts where marking is dispensable because the relevant information can be reconstructed from the context (cf. Terassa 2018 for a corpus-based account of plural omission after quantifiers and numerals and past tense omission in the context of time adverbials). She goes on to discuss other features in terms of the principle of hyperclarity, which she divides into two sub-principles: (1) the principle of maximum transparency and (2) the principle of maximum salience (cf. Williams 1987, 178). Transparency relates to the one-to-one mapping of form and meaning, which is for example

maximised by the lexicalisation of completion by the adverb *already*. The use
of resumptive pronouns in relative clauses (e.g. *The guests who I have invited
them have arrived*), or pronouns following noun phrases (*My cousin he didn't go
to college*) are instead discussed as applications of the principle of maximum
salience, as the pronouns maximise the salience of the referents (cf. Williams
1987, 190–191).

More recently, Nesselhauf (2009) has also adopted a combined approach to
the analysis of ESL varieties and learner varieties based on the observation of
similarities between institutionalised varieties of English and learner varieties
of English (cf. Nesselhauf 2009, 3).[4] Nesselhauf analyses co-selection phenomena in the ENL variety BrE based on ICE-GB and the BNC, in the ESL varieties
KenE, IndE, SgE, and JamE on the basis of ICE, and in the learner varieties of
English spoken in Bulgaria, Czechoslovakia, the Netherlands, Finland, France,
Germany, Italy, Poland, Russia, Spain, and Sweden on the basis of the *International Corpus of Learner English* (ICLE). She studies the use of competing collocations (e.g. *play a role* vs. *play a part*), the semantic prosody of *have intention*
(with a preference for negative contexts in ENL varieties but positive contexts
in EFL varieties), complementation of nouns, and collocations of verbs and
prepositions (e.g. *discuss about*) (cf. Nesselhauf 2009, 4). Nesselhauf generally finds that the pattern of use in ESL varieties represents a state between
that of ENL varieties and that of learner varieties.[5] The only finding that runs
counter to this general tendency concerns the more frequent use of innovative
prepositional verbs such as *discuss about*, which have a higher frequency in
ESL varieties, where their establishment as features has been analysed under
the label 'nativised semantico-structural analogy' (cf. Mukherjee & Hoffmann
2006, 161–167). Another important finding of her study is the observation that
variation in ESL and EFL varieties results from existing variation in ENL varieties. When two constructions compete, speakers of ESL and EFL varieties are
likely to select the construction that is most regular from a language-internal
systematic perspective (cf. Nesselhauf 2009, 23; cf. the subsequent discussion
of the regularity of *have to* compared to *must*). This finding emphasises the

---

4 Even more recently, Gilquin (2015) published a paper presenting case studies that illustrate
   similarities and differences between ESL varieties and learner Englishes and Percillier (2016)
   presents an in-depth analysis of common structural features in the ESL varieties SgE and
   MalE, and Indonesian learner English.
5 Note that Deshors's findings on the dative alternation in ENL, ESL, and EFL varieties do not
   indicate that ESL varieties occupy an intermediate position between ENL and EFL varieties
   but suggest that ESL and EFL varieties "are intermingled rather than grouped together according to 'type'" (Deshors 2014, 298).

importance of Mufwene's language-internal ecology for the selection of variants from the pool in ESL varieties (cf. Mufwene 2001, 192; cf. Section 3.3).

In 2011, almost 30 years after the paradigm gap between ESL varieties and learner Englishes had been identified, Mukherjee and Hundt published an edited volume with the aim of 'bridging the paradigm gap' with studies that integrate research on ESL varieties with research on learner Englishes. These types of studies are still rare today.[6] Mukherjee and Hundt surmise that ESL varieties have not been analysed within the SLA framework for ideological and political reasons, because of the

> linguistic taboos, especially on the part of the researchers interested in second-language varieties of English to establish these New Englishes as full-fledged varieties with the potential to develop endonormative and local standard and norms. These emerging local standards and norms should not be conflated, in their view, with the error-focussed description and analysis of foreign language learners' output as a deviation from the exonormative norm.
>
> MUKHERJEE & HUNDT 2011, 1–2

One of the studies of the volume that takes an integrated view on ESL varieties and learner Englishes is Biewer's (2011) analysis of modal auxiliaries in ESL varieties from an SLA perspective. She analyses the use of *should, must, need, ought to, need to, have to, have got to*, and *be supposed to* in newspaper data from BrE, AmE, NZE, FijE, SamE, CookE, SgE, PhilE, and GhanE in the period from 2004 to 2009. In terms of frequency, she finds greater variability in ESL varieties than in ENL varieties (cf. also Nesselhauf 2009), for example in terms of the frequency rankings of the different modal auxiliaries. Thus, she finds a more widespread use of *must* compared to *have to* and *have got to* in GhanE and SgE (cf. Biewer 2011, 22; cf. Section 5.2). Biewer refers to Huber and Dako, who claim that the more widespread use of *must* in GhanE results from different politeness strategies in the use of directives (cf. Huber & Dako 2008, 370), which "are uttered more openly than in western societies" (Biewer 2011, 26). In a similar vein, I argued that cultural reasons may be at the heart of the particularly high frequency of *must* in SgE in the previous section.

Biewer also analyses the function of *must* and finds that all varieties use deontic *must* more often than epistemic *must* and that the proportion of deontic

---

6 Cf. Schneider (2012) for an analysis of similarities between World Englishes and ELF in light of SLA principles, such as simplicity, generalisation, redundancy, regularisation, analogy, and isomorphism.

must is particularly high in all ESL varieties (except CookE), ranging between 88% and 91%. Biewer argues that the predominantly deontic use of *must* in most ESL varieties may point to SLA principles at work by arguing that root *must* represents the unmarked choice that learners acquire first (cf. Biewer 2011, 26).

In a third step, Biewer also analyses the context in which *must* is used and shows that different varieties of English weaken or strengthen the force of deontic *must* differently (cf. Biewer 2011, 26–27). The use of the passive to weaken the strength of obligation is a common strategy in FijiE, SamE, PhilE, and GhanE, e.g. *This must be done*. SgE instead shows strategies to strengthen the force of obligation by collocation with *never* or *can* (e.g. *You can – and must – mitigate this roguish image*, cf. Biewer 2011, 26). A strategy used to weaken the force of obligation in SgE is the use of the existential construction, e.g. *If change there must be, it is more in style* (cf. Biewer 2011, 26). However, judging from a comparison between the proportions of existential *there* in ICE-SIN and ICE-GB, this strategy is not significantly more often adopted in SgE, with proportions in both varieties at 2%. In GhanE, *must* is often used in pseudo-exhortations (e.g. *We must act now*) (cf. also Section 9.2 for a similar preference in BrE). Biewer links her findings to SLA principles. She explains the prevalence of *should* with the Shortest Path Principle, which holds that speakers will choose the modal verb that corresponds most directly to their L1 (cf. Biewer 2011, 14). The low frequency of *ought to* is explained by avoidance of redundancy, as *ought to* is synonymous with *should* and therefore 'redundant' (cf. Biewer 2011, 27). She accounts for the deontic bias of modal auxiliaries with the Transfer to Somewhere Principle (cf. Andersen 1983, 178), which holds that transfer will take place if there is a similar structure in the L1 (cf. Biewer 2011, 14) and with Markedness Theory, which states "that less marked features in world languages are less complex and more frequent" (Biewer 2011, 15) and therefore acquired first. As *must* is more frequently used in its deontic function than in its epistemic function in all varieties under analysis (cf. also Figure 26 in Chapter 5), learners acquire deontic *must* as the unmarked case first. This may also have to do with the fact that "deontic meaning is easier to grasp than epistemic meaning" (Biewer 2011, 16). While SLA principles proved to be relevant to the frequency of the modal verbs and the distribution of their functions, they could not explain the various strategies that speakers employ to strengthen or weaken the force of *must*. Biewer shifts from an SLA perspective to a cultural perspective when she explains these strategies with differences in politeness principles in ESL varieties, where local norms are likely to develop because English is used by speakers from the same cultural background (cf. Biewer 2011, 28; cf. also Meierkord 2016, 227). The development of local politeness norms is less likely in EFL varieties, where English is predominantly used for international communication. In Section 3.2.1, it was shown that HKE resembles EFL varieties in some aspects, which is why it might be the case that the high frequency of deontic *must* could be rather a result of learner mechanisms than acculturation, which might explain the high frequency of deontic *must* in SgE, which has reached the stage of Endonormative Stabilisation. For ESL varieties, Biewer argues that "[t]here will be a difference between more autocratic/conservative societies and more democratic societies in the usage of modals of obligation and necessity" (Biewer 2011, 28; cf. also the discussion about cultural motivations in Section 7.2 above).

The findings from previous studies at the interface of EFL and ESL varieties can be applied to the findings of this study. The predominance of one modal marker in terms of frequency can be seen in the use of *have to* as the most frequent expression in strong deontic modality (cf. Figure 26 in Chapter 5). The predominance of *have to* over *must* may reflect a learner's strategy to prefer the form that has fewer exceptions in use, as it has a regular verbal paradigm and can occur in all tenses. It seems to be the 'safe choice' in a situation where a decision between *must* and *have to* has to be made, because *have to* can replace *must* in almost all cases, while the reverse is not the case. This is also why some EFL teachers recommend teaching *have to* for the expression of strong deontic modality, e.g. "it is probably a good idea to teach *have to* for obligation because it is nearly always correct whereas *must* is often inappropriate".[7] This also ties in with Nesselhauf's observation about phraseological variation in ESL varieties and learner Englishes: "[w]hen semantically similar expressions compete, it is the language-internally most regular one that is favoured in both types of varieties" (Nesselhauf 2009, 23). The particularly high frequency of *have to* in ICE-HK also seems to be the result of the application of the Shortest Path Principle. As explained before, the Cantonese verb *yiu* is the translational equivalent of *have to*, which is reinforced by the adverb *yātdihng* ('certainly') to express the meaning of *must* (cf. also Section 6.2 on the structure of the domain of obligation and necessity in Cantonese). This means that *yiu* is the default form to express obligation and necessity, which may explain why *have to* is used more often than *must* in HKE.

Although *have to* is used more often than *must* as an expression of deontic modality in HKE, the frequency of *must* is also considerably higher than that found in ENL varieties. This is also true for the other two ESL varieties (cf. Figure 26 in Chapter 5). A finding that was explained by different pragmatic norms

---

7 This recommendation is given for example by Tim Bower, Course Director of the Executive School at International House in Hastings (cf. http://www.onestopenglish.com/methodology/ask-the-experts/grammar-questions/grammar-teaching-the-modals-ought-to-should-must-and-have-to/146365.article (last access: 19/02/2018)).

for the use of the core modal grounded in cultural differences (cf. Section 7.2). Another similarity to Biewer's findings is the deontic bias of *must* in ESL varieties. All ESL varieties showed a higher proportion of deontic readings of *must* than the ENL varieties, although this bias was more pronounced in ICE-HK and ICE-SIN than in ICE-IND*. The predominance of deontic *must* in all ESL varieties was linked to SLA principles by Biewer (2011), as detailed before.

In first-language acquisition, epistemic modality develops after deontic modality, a fact explained by the cognitive development of children, which is at first ego-focused (cf. Stephany 1995, 106; Hickmann & Bassano 2016, 431–432). In SLA, adult learners instead show a different cognitive development and both modalities are present from the beginning of the acquisition process (cf. Stephany 1995, 111).

> While epistemic modality is most relevant for the cognitively and socially mature adult, the cognitively immature and socially dependent child is more concerned with deontic and dynamic modalities.
> STEPHANY 1995, 116

Indeed, epistemic modality is expressed by modal auxiliaries only later on in the acquisition process, as is also the case in first-language acquisition (cf. Stephany 1995, 112; cf. also Choi 2006, 143). In the beginning of acquisition, epistemic modality is expressed lexically by verbs of thinking or adverbs, while deontic modality is already expressed by modal auxiliaries (cf. Stephany 1995, 116). Stephany explains the emergence of modal auxiliaries with epistemic meanings after the expression of epistemic modality by full verbs in SLA with the syntactic and semantic complexity of epistemic modal auxiliaries:

> the speaker's comment, by a separate proposition, such as 'I think' is less complex in a syntactico-semantic sense than its integration into one and the same clause together with the propositional content.
> STEPHANY 1995, 117

With regard to a possible transfer of these SLA processes to processes at work in ESL varieties, Biewer states that

> [a]lthough constraints on the acquisition of modals in terms of cognitive abilities and input must be different for ESL, the steps and underlying strategies of SLA may be the same – also because the learner has been successful with these strategies in the acquisition of his [sc. or her] first language.
> BIEWER 2011, 16

ESL speakers therefore probably pass the stages identified for first-language acquisition and SLA and it is conceivable that they also use lexical expressions for epistemic modality at first, especially when they need to acquire epistemic meanings of modal auxiliaries 'from scratch' if their L1s do not provide a template with both readings.

The mapping of one form with one meaning, i.e. *must* with a deontic reading, may lead to lexicalisation of epistemic modality (cf. Williams 1987, 182). This split expression of deontic and epistemic modality by different linguistic means reflects the learner's tendency to avoid plurifunctionality (cf. Biewer 2011, 16). A first indicator of the possibility of transferring SLA principles to ESL contexts is Williams's observation that modality is expressed in a separate proposition with phrases such as the discourse marker *I think* in SgE (cf. Williams 1987, 185;188). This suggests that speakers of SgE apply the principle of maximum salience, as epistemic phrases or adverbs can stand in utterance-initial position (cf. Williams 1987, 188; Biewer 2015, 94). Lexicalisation can also be observed in other areas of the tense-aspect-modality system in SgE, such as in the marking of the perfect by means of the temporal adverb *already*. This analyticity may also be strengthened by the typological profile of the Chinese substrate. This means, more generally, that SLA principles and transfer principles may work in tandem. In the case of *must*, we saw that speakers of ESL varieties with an L1 that shows bifunctional forms, expressing deontic and epistemic meanings, are more likely to use epistemic *must*, whereas speakers of ESL varieties with an L1 that shows a monofunctional form are less likely to use epistemic *must*. This means that SLA principles may be reinforced by transfer principles and cultural motivations, thus jointly pushing *must* towards a deontic reading in their varieties of English (cf. also Biewer 2011, 19, who also argues for a reinforcement of SLA principles by transfer).

Sometimes transfer principles may also counteract SLA principles, as is the case in the use of *need to* in ICE-HK and ICE-SIN. Based on the rather recent emergence of the form in ENL varieties (cf. Figure 32 in Chapter 6) and its marginal status in the group of modal and semi-modal verbs of obligation and necessity (cf. Figure 26 in Chapter 5), *need to* is a likely candidate for further marginalisation in a process of simplification of the modal system in learner varieties. And while the low frequency of *need to* in IndE indeed suggests such a scenario, the comparatively high frequencies of *need to* in HKE and SgE do not point to a simplification process at work. This simplification process has probably not taken place in HKE and SgE because the frequencies of *need to* are reinforced by similar structures in the L1s of the speakers (cf. Section 7.1 on transfer).

The low frequencies of *have got to* in ICE-HK and ICE-IND* may also point to simplification processes of the modal system with the aim of avoiding redundancy. *Have got to*, which is already a marginal member of the group of modal and semi-modal verbs of obligation in ENL varieties, is further margin-alised in ICE-IND* and ICE-HK. ICE-SIN instead shows a comparatively higher frequency of *have got to* compared to the other ESL varieties, which may be a result of the functions English performs in the Singaporean context. While English is predominantly used in formal domains in IndE and HKE, it fulfils broader functions in Singapore, probably also due to the fact that not all speak-ers have the same mother tongue here (cf. also Sections 3.2.1–3.2.3). So, while informal conversations are often not held in English but in Cantonese in Hong Kong, they may be held in English in Singapore as the lingua franca between the different ethnicities. Thus, although English is predominantly used in for-mal contexts, where formal language is most appropriate, in Hong Kong and India, it is also used in everyday communication in Singapore and has probably developed more informal styles there, which favour the use of *have got to*. This means that the functional expansion of English in the later stages of Schnei-der's (2007) model may be important for the emergence of more colloquial features. In the case of HKE, the simplification of the system may also be an indicator of its less advanced stage in Schneider's (2007) model as a variety that is sometimes considered to be in between EFL and ESL status.

One may surmise that another reason for the low frequency of *have got to* in HKE and IndE are prescriptive pressures, which may be more relevant in varieties that have not reached the stage of Endonormative Stabilisation. Furthermore, prescriptive rules are part of second-language learning in the classroom. But although it is tempting to integrate prescriptive pressure into explanations for the low frequency of this semi-modal verb, the apparent-time studies do not indicate this, as the decrease of this semi-modal is gradual rath-er than steep (cf. Section 8.3). Instead it may well be the case that speakers are less exposed to features of colloquial English based on the acquisition of English in the classroom where standard English is taught. Early instances of *have got to* show that it was typical of non-standard speech, which is why it might not have been used in the formal teaching of the language at that time in Hong Kong (cf. Section 6.1.3). This ties in with Schneider's observation that

> [i]n exploitation colonies, with primarily scholastic transmission of English through the education system, as for instance in India or Malaysia, mostly standard patterns have been preserved, so that in these countries even nonstandard uses which are otherwise extremely common and widespread, such as multiple negation, are exceptional.
>
> SCHNEIDER 2007, 101

Apart from differences in the distribution of the forms and their corresponding functions, SLA principles may also be at work in the emergence of innovative forms, such as the co-occurrence of *must* with *have to* to maximise salience, e.g. (150).

(150) <$Z> So why did you go to Disney in Europe <$A> Uh is one of the famous tourist site And I think I *must have to* go there (ICE-HK:S1A-080)

However, I only found three instances of this type of 'double modal' marking (cf. also (46) and (47) from ICE-IND* in Chapter 4), which means that this type of learner phenomenon has not achieved the status of a feature in any of these varieties, probably because this phenomenon is more readily recognised as a non-standard feature by speakers and therefore avoided than the overuse or underuse of standard forms and their respective functions.

To summarise, SLA phenomena, such as the avoidance of exceptions, the order of acquisition, simplification processes, and processes that maximise salience may help to understand some of the corpus findings, such as the high frequency of *have to*, the deontic bias of *must*, the low frequency of *have got to* in ICE-IND* and ICE-HK, and the (albeit rare) occurrence of double modal constructions.

7.4   Cognitive Principles

BrE, HKE, IndE, and SgE all showed a predominance of deontic *have to* over deontic *must* in spoken language, and a predominance of deontic *must* over epistemic *must* in spoken language and written language, irrespective of their type (i.e. ENL vs. ESL) (cf. Figure 26 and Figure 30 in Chapter 5). These similarities may point to general cognitive processes that are at work in the selection of these variants.

The predominance of deontic *have to* over deontic *must* is probably a result of its frequency, because the more frequent variant has a higher chance of selection than the less frequent variant (cf. Biewer 2015, 86). Its higher frequency in turn may be linked to its comparatively lower degree of cognitive complexity compared to *must*. *Have to* has a regular verbal paradigm and can be used in almost all contexts, whereas *must* has a defective paradigm and is more restricted in terms of its use. This may mean that the use of *have to* requires less cognitive effort on the part of the speaker, as it is more regular and therefore more flexible. As *have to* is only rarely used with an epistemic meaning, the choice for deontic *have to* over deontic *must* may be further conditioned by its monosemy, which allows the learner to map one form with one meaning (leading to increased transparency, cf. the principle of maximum transparency mentioned above, cf. Williams 1987, 178; cf. also Biewer 2015, 90).

The deontic bias of *must* can probably also be explained by general cognitive processes. Deontic *must* is used with a higher frequency than epistemic *must* in all varieties under analysis and is therefore more likely to be selected. This distribution may have to do with differences in the complexity of cognitive processing in deontic and epistemic modality. Deontic *must*, which takes narrow scope over the proposition, as it forms part of the proposition, may be marked by a lower degree of cognitive complexity than epistemic *must*. Epistemic *must* takes wide scope over the proposition; this means that epistemic *must* operates outside the proposition by expressing an evaluation of the truth of the proposition. This difference in scope can be shown in utterances where *must* is ambiguous between the two readings, such as in (151).

(151) That is sad because aside from questions of style and culture, Singapore's political system *must* have room for more opposition – good opposition (ICE-SIN:W2E-010).

In (151), we can interpret *must* in terms of narrow-scope deontic modality. Its deontic meaning can be paraphrased with 'it is necessary for Singapore's political system to have more opposition'. However, *must* can also express wide-scope epistemic modality in (151), as its meaning can be paraphrased with 'it is necessarily the case that Singapore's political system has more opposition'. If the context and/or linguistic structure (e.g. co-occurrence of epistemic readings with the progressive aspect) cannot help to disambiguate the statement, the deontic interpretation may be the default interpretation, because it is less complex in terms of structure and therefore easier to process. This would mean that deontic modals constitute the default case, while "[e]pistemic modals are considered to be more marked in comparison to their root syntactic variants, owing to the complexity of their cognitive processing" (Teržan Kopecky 2008, 123). Biewer follows a similar line of argumentation when she states that deontic *must* has a higher chance of selection because it is the unmarked form (cf. Markedness Theory, cf. Biewer 2011, 16). This 'selectional advantage' results in a higher frequency of unmarked deontic *must*, which in turn leads to a deeper entrenchment of the deontic meaning for the form *must* (cf. Schneider 2007, 110).

As a summary, it can be concluded that cognitive processes of speech processing and speech production may be the reason behind the predominance of deontic *have to* over deontic *must*, and of deontic *must* over epistemic *must* in all varieties of English. It was argued that deontic *have to* is the unmarked case in the pair of deontic *have to* and deontic *must*, and that *must* in deontic meaning is the unmarked case in the pair of deontic and epistemic *must*. In both cases, the unmarked case is cognitively less complex and therefore easier to process and to produce, which results in a higher frequency of the unmarked cases compared to their marked counterpart.

7.5 Summary

After the contributions to the pool of variants by the three contributors were discussed in the preceding chapter, four selection principles were proposed that may have guided the selection process of the variants as features of the newly emerging variety were examined in more detail in this chapter. First, transfer principles were considered in Section 7.1 and it was shown that the transfer of the epistemic function to modal *must* in the ESL variety was facilitated by the presence of an equivalent form with deontic and epistemic meaning in the L1s of the speakers. Transfer could therefore explain what the state of the historical input variety could not, i.e. the higher frequency of epistemic *must* in IndE with speakers whose L1s also encoded deontic and epistemic readings in one form. Transfer principles were also shown to be relevant to account for the greater use of the semi-modal verb *need to* in HKE and SgE, where the L1s of the speakers have similar structures.

As a second principle of selection, cultural motivations were discussed in Section 7.2 with a special focus on the high frequency of deontic *must* in SgE. It was argued that obligational practices differ across varieties depending on the construal of the self. Obligational practices are less marked in those societies where individuals construe themselves as a part of the larger group (i.e. 'interdependent' construal of self). Obligations expressed with *must* may not have the same pragmatic force in these societies compared to those marked by an independent construal of self that place a higher value on autonomy and in particular the freedom from imposition of others.

In a third step, I had a closer look at SLA strategies apart from transfer in Section 7.3. The high frequency of *have to* was analysed in terms of the learner's choice for the more regular form over a more irregular form (i.e. *must*). Furthermore, the order of acquisition of modal functions in first- and second-language acquisition offered a plausible explanation for the deontic bias of *must* in many ESL varieties. Studies on the acquisition of modal meanings suggest that deontic readings of modal auxiliaries are acquired earlier than epistemic readings, which are initially expressed by lexical means. Learners at first avoid using modal auxiliaries in more than function in order to enhance transparency. As ESL varieties are ultimately also learner varieties, it may well be that we can find traces of these acquisitional processes in the new varieties. Another SLA principle that could explain part of the findings was 'simplification', which may be the reason behind the marginalisation of minority variants of the modal system (*need to* and *have got to*), which became especially visible in IndE.

Finally, cognitive principles of speech production and processing were discussed in order to account for similar tendencies across different types of varieties (i.e. ENL and ESL) in Section 7.4. Cognitive principles, such as the choice of variants with a higher frequency over variants with a lower frequency, were considered to be relevant to the explanation of the high frequency of *have to* in all varieties of English and the predominance of a deontic reading of the core modal verb *must*. The higher frequency of these variants was linked to the lower degree of cognitive complexity in speech production and processing of these variants compared to the higher degree of cognitive complexity involved in producing and processing the less frequent variants.

The analysis of the frequency and use of the modal and semi-modal verbs of obligation in terms of a competition-and-selection process allowed for the modelling of the restructuring process taking place in the development of ESL varieties. The four different selection principles are supposed to reflect important aspects of the restructuring process in which ESL varieties are involved. As ESL speakers constantly draw on their multilingual repertoire including their L1s and English, transfer was discussed as an important selection principle at work. Cultural motivations were discussed to account for processes of the acculturation of English to local needs. The discussion of SLA processes was supposed to shed light on variation according to variety type (ENL vs. ESL), and finally universal cognitive processes were discussed to account for general tendencies identified in all varieties under analysis.

As the various cross-references in this chapter indicate, these processes cannot always be neatly distinguished, because they interact in various ways (for example, frequency and markedness are also relevant to SLA). The principles may therefore reinforce each other, for example in the case of the deontic bias of *must* in SgE. This is an example of multiple causation because transfer principles, cultural motivations, SLA principles, and cognitive processes work together here. However, the principles do not always reinforce each other, as becomes visible in the case of the comparatively high frequencie of *need to* in HKE and SgE. SLA processes (and the rather recent emergence of *need to* in BrE) would lead one to expect a low frequency of this variant in HKE and SgE in terms of a simplification process. However, syntactic and semantic similarities between the substrate languages and English facilitated transfer. In this case, the relative weighting of the principles seems to indicate that transfer principles may override more general SLA principles.

The four selection principles that were discussed in this section represent only some of the many selection principles that are conceivable (cf. Schneider

2007, 110–111 for a more comprehensive list of determining factors in the selection process, and Biewer 2015, 83–114 for selection principles relevant to
SPE). As has been mentioned, the functions of English in the countries and
also the time depth of English in these countries are important external factors
that condition variation and change in these varieties (cf. Sections 3.2.1–3.2.3).
These factors reflect the external ecology where English has developed and can
be considered as a frame within which the competition-and-selection process
takes place. Apart from regional variation in the frequency and use of the modal
and semi-modal verbs between the varieties, varieties also show internal variation according to language-internal factors and language-external factors. An
important language-external dimension of internal variation may be the age of
the speaker, because synchronic variation according to age can be an indicator
of ongoing diachronic language change. The next chapter will analyse whether
similar processes of diachronic change to those identified in ENL varieties can
also be observed in ESL varieties by adopting the apparent-time method.

CHAPTER 8

Apparent-time Developments

Linguistic change can be studied in real time and apparent time. Real-time studies sample language data from a speech community at different points in time. If these studies interview the same speakers from the same speech community at different points in time, they are referred to as panel studies. If they interview different but comparable speakers from the speech community at different points in time, they are called trend studies. Both panel studies and trend studies use diachronic language data to study language change. But there is also the possibility of studying language change in progress on the basis of synchronic language data, at least if the language of speakers of different age groups is recorded. This is possible because diachronic change presupposes synchronic variation and variation according to age can shed light on the presence and on the direction of linguistic change in progress. This method is especially promising for the investigation of ESL varieties where diachronic data are still largely missing. Here, the apparent-time method may be an effective method for obtaining empirical evidence for ongoing language change and thus for bridging the 'diachronic gap' in WE.

8.1 The Apparent-time Method in Sociolinguistics

The apparent-time method has been an established analytical tool in sociolinguistics since Labov applied it to findings from his study on Martha's Vineyard in 1963. But he was not the first linguist who used the apparent-time construct for analysing change in progress. Gauchat had already used this method in 1905 in his study on vowel changes in the Swiss village of Charmey. Gauchat's (1905) apparent-time findings were corroborated by Hermann (1929), who revisited the community several years later, thus providing early support for the validity of the method. Since then, linguists have repeatedly tested apparent-time findings against real-time data and have shown that the apparent-time method is a compelling tool for identifying linguistic change in progress (cf. Trudgill 1988; Bailey et al. 1991).

The apparent-time method is based on the assumption that speakers acquire the features of their language during childhood and do not radically change them after they pass the critical period. This means that the language spoken by younger speakers reflects a more recent state of the language and

© KONINKLIJKE BRILL NV, LEIDEN, 2018 | DOI:10.1163/9789004381520_009

the language spoken by older speakers an older state of the language. Differences in the use of a feature between younger and older speakers may therefore indicate ongoing language change (cf. also Blondeau 2013, 501). A pattern where younger speakers use a variant more often than older speakers indicates that the variant is on the rise in real time, while a pattern where older speakers use a variant more than younger speakers indicates that the variant is on the decrease in real time. As such, variation in the use of a variant according to different age groups may be an indicator of ongoing language change.

> The apparent time construct takes age as a proxy for the passage of time, concluding that differences across generations of adults from a single speech community mirror actual diachronic developments.
>
> RAVINDRANATH & WAGNER 2016, 265

But not all variation that is correlated with age is necessarily indicative of language change in progress. Some stable variables show a pattern of age-graded variation, which repeats itself in every generation and which does not lead to a diachronic change where one variant replaces the other over time (cf. Labov 1994, 84). This means that "individuals change their linguistic behaviour throughout their lifetimes, but the community as a whole does not change" (Labov 1994, 84). An example of a stable variable that shows age-graded variation is the (ing)-variable, which shows the typical pattern of age grading with stable variables in the form of a u-curve, with a high rate of the non-standard variant [ɪn] in younger speakers and older speakers and a low rate in middle-aged speakers. These changes are usually explained by the varying societal pressures for different age groups to conform to the standard language, which is greatest for middle-aged speakers (cf. Chambers & Trudgill 1998, 79). Studies that analyse variation according to age therefore need to take into account both possibilities, i.e. linguistic change at the community level and linguistic change at the individual level. Tagliamonte regards the distinction between these two as "one of the major issues in contemporary sociolinguistics" (2012, 247).

Changes in the use of variants over the lifetime of a speaker contradict the hypothesis of relative stability of the vernacular and may therefore challenge the basic assumption of the apparent-time construct. This is why age-graded variation and generational change have long been perceived as opposites. However, Labov argues that the two phenomena may indeed be simultaneously involved in some types of linguistic change (cf. Labov 1994, 97). In a comparison between the findings from 13 apparent-time studies and findings from follow-up studies on these, Sankoff finds four studies where age grading is involved in linguistic change (cf. overview in Sankoff 2006, 114). However, she does not find a single case where age grading takes place without linguistic change. This is why she concludes that

> apparent time is a truly powerful concept in locating the presence of change. In other words, a researcher who locates a gradient age distribution in a new community under study is virtually assured of having identified change, whether or not age grading is also involved.
>
> SANKOFF 2006, 113

Furthermore, recent studies that identify age-graded variation within linguistic change show that older speakers change in the direction of the generational change, which means that the presence of age grading does not imply that no change is taking place but that apparent-time studies make a rather conservative prediction about the rate with which a change is taking place (cf. Sankoff & Blondeau 2007, 582). If speakers follow a communal change of a rise of a variant as they get older, their use of this variant was actually lower when they were younger. This means that the rate of change identified in an apparent-time study may actually be lower than the actual rate of change in real time (cf. also Sankoff & Blondeau 2007, 582).

8.2   The Apparent-time Method in Corpus Linguistics

As detailed above, the apparent-time construct is widely adopted in sociolinguistics. Tagliamonte (2004) and Tagliamonte and D'Arcy (2007) employ this method for studying changes in the modal domain in York English and Toronto English. They find a decrease in the proportion of *must* and an increase in the proportion of *have to* in both varieties of English. The proportion of *have got to* instead was only found to be on the rise in York English but not in Toronto English. Both studies are based on data that were obtained in sociolinguistic interviews using Labovian techniques. This type of language data differs strongly from corpus data, which is why it is questionable whether the sociolinguistic method can actually be applied to corpus data.

As will be explained in Section 11.2, sociolinguistics and corpus linguistics have different methods of data collection because of their different research interests. Sociolinguists' primary interest lies in language variation according to social factors and in order to shed light on social variation in language they gather their data from sociolinguistic interviews with speakers whose social characteristics constitute a representative sample of the society or community as a whole. Corpus compilers are instead interested in creating a sample of the language as it is used in different situational contexts, i.e. they are interested in representing the range of text types that can be found in a language (e.g. conversations, academic writing, and creative writing). This difference in data compilation may lead to problems when transferring sociolinguistic methods to corpus data, because most corpora are not primarily designed for sociolinguistic research. This is why the social structure of corpora needs to be analysed in order to see if the transfer of sociolinguistic methods is nevertheless feasible (cf. Section 4.1.2). The comparison between the social structure of ICE-HK and ICE-IND* and census data from the two countries showed that speakers with a wide range of social characteristics that also define the population as a whole were sampled, although speakers with some characteristics are underrepresented while others are overrepresented. Despite these issues, the data were considered to be suitable for the analysis of variation along social lines. As the ICE corpora only include language data from speakers above 18, they lend themselves well to the adoption of the apparent-time method as these speakers, having passed the critical period, can be considered to have reached relative stability in their language.

An apparent-time study based on ICE-NIG by Fuchs and Gut (2015) also suggests that the transfer of this sociolinguistic method to ICE data is possible. They show that speakers below 30 use the progressive significantly more often than speakers above 50, which indicates that NigE shows a rise in the use of the progressive (cf. Fuchs & Gut 2015, 380–381). Their study shows that the apparent-time method with ICE data can be successfully adopted to obtain new insights about ongoing language change in ESL varieties. In the case of the rise of the progressive in NigE, it shows that the ESL variety is undergoing the same development as BrE (cf. Smitterberg 2005). Schweinberger (2012) also integrates information about the age of the speakers in his analysis of the discourse marker *like* in IrE. He interprets the distribution according to age in terms of age grading and shows that age grading is involved in ongoing language change that shows a rise of the discourse marker *like* in real time (cf. Schweinberger 2012, 197; cf. also the discussion about the relationship between age grading and change in progress above). Fuchs and Gut's (2015) and Schweinberger's (2012) studies show that it is worthwhile to analyse the distribution of features according to age on the basis of ICE, especially with features that are undergoing language change in ENL varieties.

One of the areas in ENL varieties undergoing language change is the modal domain (cf. Section 2.1). While there are some apparent-time studies on the modal systems of ENL varieties, there are so far no apparent-time studies on modal and semi-modal verbs in ESL varieties. In corpus-based apparent-time studies on the modal domain in ENL varieties, the apparent-time method is usually employed in order to corroborate findings from real-time studies, such as in Krug (2000), Mair (2006), and Leech (2013). Krug analyses the distribution of the semi-modal verbs *have got to* and *have to* across different age groups in the spoken demographic part of the BNC (cf. Krug 2000, 87–89). He finds that the rise in the frequency of *have got to* stops with speakers under 45 (cf. Krug 2000, 87). He also finds a saturation point for the frequency of *have to*, although it occurred earlier in time than that of *have got to*, because all age groups below 60 show approximately the same frequency (cf. Krug 2000, 88). Mair also uses the spoken demographic part of the BNC but does so in order to shed light on the development of the core modal verbs in apparent time. He shows that the frequency of *must* is decreasing between the age group 45–59 (the oldest age group, age group 60+, does not match the overall trend with a frequency that is lower than that of the second-oldest age group) and the age group 0–14 (cf. Mair 2006, 103). Leech (2013) uses the demographically sampled conversational sub-corpus of the BNC in order to find corroborating evidence for the general trend of the decrease of the core modal verbs and the rise of the semi-modal verbs. He shows that the frequency of the core modal verbs is decreasing from the age group 35–44 to the age group 0–14, which indicates a decrease of the core modal verbs after 1960 in real time (cf. Leech 2013, 113–114). By contrast, the frequency of the semi-modal verbs is increasing from the oldest to the youngest age group, i.e. it "is negatively correlated with age" (Leech 2013, 113). His apparent-time study therefore supports earlier real-time findings on the decrease of the modal verbs and the rise of the semi-modal verbs.

8.3   Obligation and Necessity in Apparent Time

The overview of studies on the modal domain in ENL varieties in Section 2.1 and the findings from the apparent-time studies mentioned before show that the modal system is an area of ongoing change in several ENL varieties. The question that these findings raise is whether the modal systems of ESL varieties show similar changes. So far, it has only been assumed that ESL varieties are undergoing the same developments in the modal domain as ENL varieties. Collins (2009b), for example, bases his whole study on modal and semi-modal verbs in WE "[o]n the relatively safe assumption that the rise of the quasi-modals [...] is also occurring in the other Englishes of the world" (Collins 2009b, 285). However, empirical evidence for this claim has been missing up to now.

In order to provide empirical evidence for changes in the modal domain in ESL varieties, information about the age of the speakers from the ICE-HK and ICE-IND* metadata were used to construct an apparent-time scenario of the developments of the modal and semi-modal verbs of obligation and necessity. For the apparent-time studies, only the spoken part of the respective corpora were used, because written language is much more standardised than spoken language. This also ties in with Schneider's observation that "written forms tend to be neutral and 'international', while spoken realizations manipulate local forms and orientations" (Schneider 2011, 343). Furthermore, written language may undergo several stages of editing in which different speakers are involved, which makes it difficult to attribute language use to just one writer. For this reason, I established the frequencies of use of *must, have to, have got to,* and *need to* across the age groups by normalising the raw numbers by the number of words spoken by the speakers of the respective age groups. Figure 46 shows the normalised frequency on the y-axis and the age groups in descending order on the x-axis. The arrangement of the age groups in descending order visually represents the implications of the apparent-time findings for real-time language change. In order to make the findings comparable to findings from ENL varieties, Figure 46 includes all modal and semi-modal verbs in both deontic and epistemic function, as in Leech et al.'s (2009) study.

The developments in apparent time show a strong decrease of the core modal verb *must* from an M-co of 101 in the age group 56–60+ to an M-co of 23

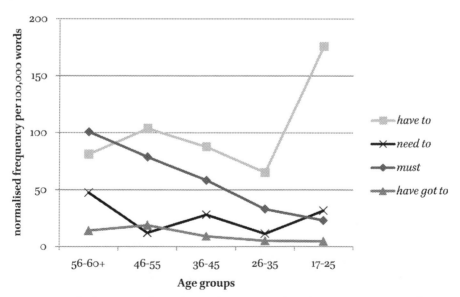

FIGURE 46   The frequency of *must, have to, have got to,* and *need to* in apparent time in the spoken section of ICE-HK (cf. Table 31 in the appendices).

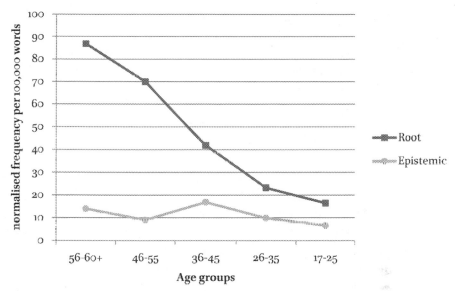

FIGURE 47 The frequency of root *must* and epistemic *must* in apparent time in the spoken
section of ICE-HK (cf. Table 32 in the appendices).

in the age group 17–25, which corresponds to a decrease of *must* in real time by
-77% in the time period between the 1950s to the 1990s. If the senses of *must*
are analysed in apparent time, we can observe a similar pattern to those found
in the ENL varieties AmE and BrE in HKE (cf. Figure 47). Root *must* is decreasing sharply from the oldest to the youngest age group, whereas epistemic *must*
shows a slight increase from the oldest age group to the age group 36–45, before joining in the decrease of root *must*.[1]

---

1 It needs to be mentioned that the language-external factor 'register' also plays an important
   part in the use of epistemic *must*, with the general tendency that more informal spoken text
   types (e.g. private dialogues) show a higher frequency of epistemic *must* than more formal
   spoken text types (e.g. scripted monologues). Despite this broad tendency, there are regional
   differences in the register distribution of epistemic *must* between the spoken sections of ICE-
   HK, ICE-IND*, and ICE-GB. The most striking difference lies in the lower share of epistemic
   must compared to deontic *must* in the private dialogue sections of the two ESL varieties
   compared to the ENL variety. If we expand our view beyond spoken language, we can identify
   written text types where epistemic *must* is almost non-existent, such as the text type 'instructional writing', while it predominates in creative writing. Detailed analyses about the register
   distribution between the two functions of *must* are beyond the scope of this study because
   this study takes function rather than form as the starting point of analysis and therefore
   does not treat epistemic *must* and deontic *must* as realisations of one and the same variable.
   However, the above-mentioned observations reveal that an analysis of regional register variation in the use of *must* might be interesting.

If we take a look at the proportions of root *must* and epistemic *must*, we can see that the proportions are approximating over time. While *must* expresses root readings in 86% of the cases in the oldest age group, the share of root readings drops to 71% in the youngest age group. This means that as a result of the general decrease of *must*, which is stronger in its root sense, the proportion of epistemic uses is rising in apparent time from 14% in the oldest age group to 29% in the youngest age group, although its frequency is on the decrease between the age groups 36–45 and 17–25.

If we now focus on the competition between the variants expressing deontic modality only (cf. Figure 48), we can see that deontic *must* has a higher frequency of use, with an M-co of 87, than *have to*, with an M-co of 81 in the oldest age group. If we compare this to the frequency distribution of *must* and *have to* in the youngest age group, we can see a strikingly different distribution. The youngest speakers use *must* with an M-co of 16, while they use *have to* with an M-co of 176. The difference in the use of *must* and *have to* between the oldest and the youngest age group is statistically significant at the p<0.0001 level (2×2 χ^2 test). But while the frequency of *must* is decreasing in a gradual manner from the oldest to the youngest age group, the frequency of *have to* does not show a monotonic increase as it is decreasing between the age groups 46–55 and the youngest age group. If we disregard the frequency of the oldest age group because it is strongly underrepresented in ICE-HK (cf.

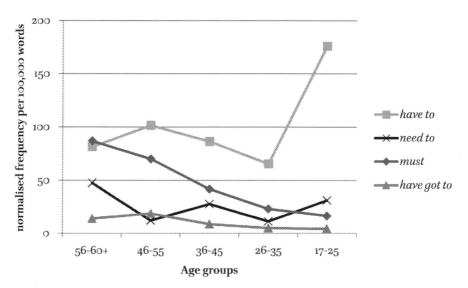

FIGURE 48   Modal and semi-modal verbs expressing deontic modality in apparent time in the spoken section of ICE-HK (cf. Table 33 in the appendices).

Section 4.1.2), we can identify a u-curve pattern that is typical of age-graded variation, with a middle-aged trough and an adolescent peak (cf. Downes 2005, 224). An analysis of the development in apparent time according to gender shows that the u-curve pattern is the result of an overlay of two u-curve patterns in the speech of male and female speakers, as can be seen in Figure 49.

Female speakers show a decrease in the frequency of *have to* in the age group 36–45, while male speakers show a decrease in the age group 26–35. Both genders show the highest frequency of *have to* in the youngest age group, although the peak is slightly higher with female speakers. If we are dealing with an age-graded pattern, this means that male speakers reduce their use of *have to* earlier in life than female speakers. If the distribution across age groups is not a pattern of age-graded variation, we may interpret it differently. If we interpret the pattern as a pattern of communal change rather than age-graded variation, we see that female speakers changed their use of *have to* earlier than male speakers. But without real-time data, it cannot ultimately be decided whether we are dealing with a change in progress or age graded variation that repeats itself in every generation or indeed a combination of the two processes, as has been found in other studies (cf. Sankoff & Blondeau 2007, 582).

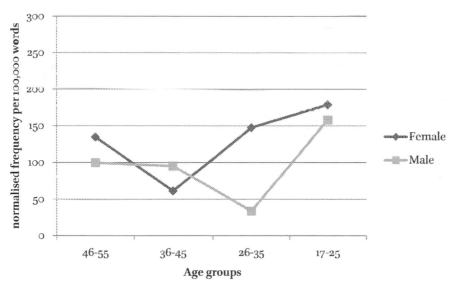

FIGURE 49   The frequency of *have to* in apparent time in the spoken section of ICE-HK according to gender (cf. Table 34 in the appendices).

If age grading is involved in the rise of *have to*, the question arises why speakers of different age groups change their use of *have to* during their life-time. One explanation could be that *have to* is associated with informality and therefore avoided in more formal contexts where English is predominantly used in Hong Kong. For middle-aged speakers, the pressure to use a more formal register is arguably stronger because of their involvement in the workforce, for example in business interactions. However, paradoxically, this does not mean that they use the more formal variant *must* more often. Instead, all variants expressing deontic modality (except for *need to*) are on the decrease between the age groups 46–55 and 26–35 (cf. Figure 48). This pattern may have to do with changing societal roles of the speakers with increasing age. An important cultural value in Singapore is respect for the old, which also becomes obvious in Chinese sayings such as *Having an old person at home is like having a treasure* or *If you don't listen to old people, you'll be taken advantage of or disadvantaged* (cf. Wong 2014, 86). These sayings show that it is believed that younger people can learn from older people, who are considered to be more experienced and therefore more knowledgeable because of their age (cf. Wong 2014, 86–87). Older people may therefore assume the role of advice-giver for the younger with increasing age, which may explain why older speakers express obligations and advice more often than middle-aged speakers (cf. Figure 48). Despite the dip in the frequency of *have to* in the middle-aged groups, it increases strongly overall and shows a particularly high frequency in the youngest age group. This particularly high frequency may be partly conditioned by the overrepresentation of the youngest age group in the private dialogue section of the corpus. Several conversations in this section of the corpus deal with external requirements the speakers have to fulfill in terms of obligations towards the family, school, university, or the job. This topic may have boosted the frequency of *have to* in the youngest age group. To take into account the simultaneous effect of the predictors on the dependent variable, I performed multivariate analyses (cf. Chapter 9).

While the frequency of the semi-modal *have to* is on the rise in apparent time, the frequency of the semi-modal *have got to* is declining from an M-co of 14 in the oldest age group to an M-co of 4 in the youngest age group. Its frequency shows that it is a minority variant for the expression of deontic modality and that it is declining gradually from the oldest to the youngest age group with the exception of a small peak in the age group 46–55. This small peak is generated by just one speaker (S2A-027A), who uses 12 out of 25 tokens of *have got to* in this age group. A closer look at the metadata reveals that the speaker received part of his tertiary education in the UK, where he may have changed his usage patterns to conform to BrE usage patterns. If the tokens of *have got to* that were produced by this speaker are excluded, we can see a gradual decline in frequency from the oldest to the youngest age group.

The semi-modal verb *need to* is also on the decline from an M-co of 48 in the oldest age group to an M-co of 31 in the youngest age group. However, the decline of this semi-modal verb does not proceed in a gradual way from one age group to the next. Its frequency distribution across the age groups is marked by strong fluctuations, visible in the zig-zagging line in Figure 48. This indicates that there is no clear tendency in terms of its development and might mean that it occupies a functional niche. *Need to* expresses obligations that are considered to be beneficial to the hearer (cf. also Nokkonen 2006, 67). Its implied meaning therefore squares well with the Chinese cultural value of attentiveness and sensitivity to the needs of others (cf. Section 7.2).

The apparent-time development of the frequencies of use of deontic *must*, *have to*, *have got to*, and *need to* showed that the frequency of *must* is decreasing, while the frequency of *have to* is increasing. This means that *must* and *have to* represent the general trend of the decrease of the core modal verbs and the increase of the semi-modal verbs identified in BrE and AmE (cf. Leech et al. 2009, 116). The semi-modal verb *have got to*, which is only rarely used in HKE, does not follow the trend of the rise of the semi-modal verbs, because it is on the decrease in apparent time. For the semi-modal verb *need to*, no clear trend in apparent time could be identified. The finding contradicts the hypothesis of

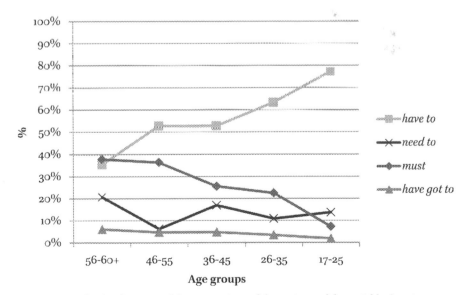

FIGURE 50   The development of the proportions of the variants of the variable deontic modality in the spoken section of ICE-HK (cf. Table 35 in the appendices).

the rise of *need to* in positive polarity contexts in HKE, which was formulated on the basis of frequency comparisons in spoken and written language (cf. van der Auwera, Noël & De Wit 2012, 71). Having established the developments in normalised frequencies, we can now take a closer look at the proportions of each variant in each age group (cf. Figure 50).

The development of the proportions shows a gradual decrease of the proportion of the core modal verb *must* that makes up 38% in the oldest age group but only 7% in the youngest age group. The semi-modal *have to* instead shows the opposite trend, as its proportion rises from 35% in the oldest age group to 77% in the youngest age group. Conversely, the proportion of the semi-modal verb *have got to* is on the decrease from 6% to 2% from the oldest to the youngest age group, as is the proportion of the semi-modal verb *need to* from 21% to 14% from the oldest to the youngest age group. The gradual decline in the proportion of *have got to* from one age group to the next shows a steady decrease of the semi-modal verb. The proportion of *need to*, however, shows more fluctuation, which makes it difficult to ascertain the directionality of change for this semi-modal verb. This means that HKE is indeed following the decrease of the modal verbs and the rise of the semi-modal verbs if the frequencies and proportions of the main competitors of the field, *must* and *have to*, are considered.

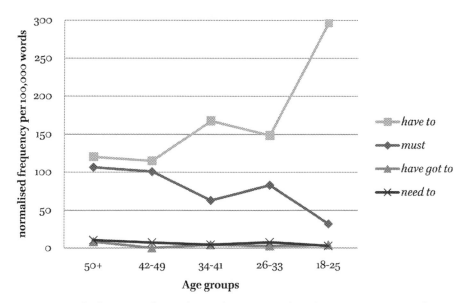

FIGURE 51   The frequency of *must, have to, have got to*, and *need to* in apparent time in the spoken section of ICE-IND* (cf. Table 36 in the appendices).

As a second analysis, the apparent-time developments of *must, have to, have got to*, and *need to* were examined in ICE-IND*. The frequency distribution of all forms irrespective of their reading can be found in Figure 51.

The frequency development of *must* in apparent time in the spoken section of ICE-IND* also shows a strong decline of the core modal verb from an M-co of 106 in the oldest age group to an M-co of 32 in the youngest age group. This corresponds to a frequency change of -69.8% in the time period between the 1960s and the 1990s and clearly contradicts Loureiro-Porto's hypothesis that IndE "resist[s] ongoing linguistic changes, such as the decline of the core modal *must*" (cf. Loureiro-Porto 2016, 148). It also contradicts Mair's assumption that the decrease of *must* "has bypassed Indian English" (Mair 2015a, 135), which was formulated on the basis of frequency comparisons between the Kolhapur Corpus and ICE-IND.[2]

Although the findings for ICE-HK and ICE-IND* are not directly comparable because of the different age groups, the decrease in ICE-HK is stronger than in ICE-IND* and also leads to a lower frequency of *must* in this variety, which also has to do with the deontic bias of *must* in ICE-HK. Epistemic *must* is more often used in ICE-IND* than in ICE-HK but shows a very similar frequency distribution across the age groups, as can be seen in Figure 52.

While root *must* is declining most sharply between the age groups 42–49 and 34–41 from an M-co of 84 to an M-co of 34, epistemic *must* is still on the rise with an M-co of 17 in the age group 42–49 and an M-co of 29 in the age group 34–41, until it follows the decline of root *must* down to an M-co of 15 in the youngest age group, after a peak in the age group 26–33 with an M-co of 37. This development clearly shows that the decrease of root *must* is stronger than the decrease of epistemic *must* and that epistemic *must* follows the route of development of root *must* at a later stage (cf. the discussion of the 'contamination' hypothesis below). While *must* is on the decline overall, the proportion of

---

2 Mair compares the frequency of *must* in the Kolhapur Corpus from 1978 to the frequency of *must* in the written part of the ICE-IND corpus from the early 1990s, although the corpora differ with regard to their structure. However, even if the frequencies of *must* are only analysed in those text types that can be found in both corpora in about the same proportions (i.e. A Press reportage (24%), K Fiction (32%), and J Learned (44%) from the Kolhapur Corpus with W2C (25%), W2F (25%), and W2A (50%) in ICE-IND*), there is no significant difference at the p<0.05 level between the two corpora (with an M-co of 71 in Kolhapur and an M-co of 56 in ICE-IND* (Log-likelihood test). If only the frequency change in Fiction is analysed, there is even an increase in the use of *must* from an M-co of 90 to an M-co of 100, although this is insignificant at the p<0.05 level (Log-likelihood test). The findings suggest that the time period of roughly 12 years that lie between Kolhapur and ICE-IND* is probably too short to find significant changes in the modal system.

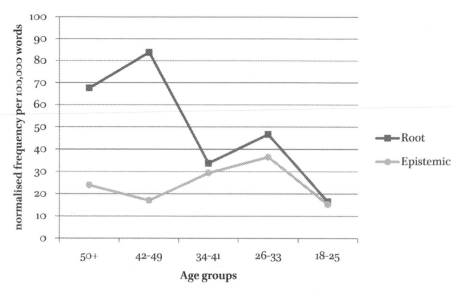

FIGURE 52   The frequency of root *must* and epistemic *must* in apparent time in the spoken
              section of ICE-IND* (cf. Table 37 in the appendices).

epistemic *must* is on the rise, from 26% in the oldest age group to 48% in the
youngest age group.

   With regard to the functions of *must*, both ESL varieties show an initial
rise in the frequency of epistemic *must*, although the increase in frequency is
stronger in IndE. Both varieties are also marked by a turning point in one of
the middle-aged groups (age group 36–45 in ICE-HK and age group 26–33 in
ICE-IND*), after which the frequency of epistemic *must* decreases and follows
the path of deontic *must*. Leech et al. also observe a decrease in the frequency
of both deontic and epistemic *must* in their analyses of BrE and AmE based on
the BROWN family of corpora and describe the decrease of epistemic *must* as a
result of "contamination by the dramatic fall of deontic *must*" (cf. Leech et al.
2009, 88). They also observe that epistemic *must* did not decrease as strongly
as deontic *must* from 1961 to 1991, which they relate to the near absence of
other forms that express logical necessity (cf. also the infrequent use of *have to*
with an epistemic reading in Figure 26 in Chapter 5). As *must* is on the decline
overall and is decreasing more strongly in its epistemic sense in all varieties,
it is likely that the proportions of root *must* and epistemic *must* will converge
over time in the ESL varieties, as is the case in BrE, where the proportion of
epistemic *must* in the youngest age group is such that the deontic meaning of
must is no longer predominant (cf. the cross-over pattern in Figure 53). If the

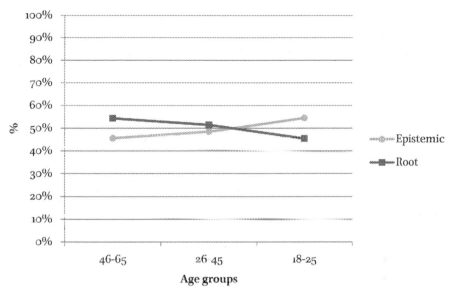

FIGURE 53   The proportion of root *must* and epistemic *must* in apparent time in the spoken
section of ICE-GB (cf. Table 38 in the appendices).

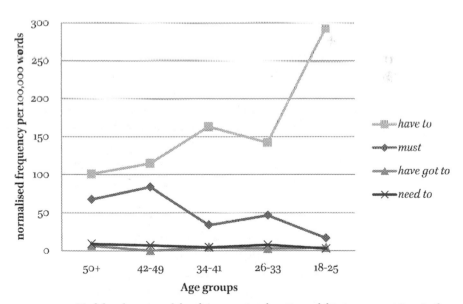

FIGURE 54   Modal and semi-modal verbs expressing deontic modality in apparent time in the
spoken section of ICE-IND* (cf. Table 39 in the appendices).

process continues in this direction, it is likely that *must* will become mono-semous at a later stage of its development and only function as an epistemic marker, with its deontic function fully transferred to the semi-modal *have to* (cf. also van der Auwera, Ammann & Kindt 2005, 258; cf. also discussion in Section 10.3).

If we now focus on those variants that express deontic modality in ICE-IND* and exclude variants with an epistemic reading, we can see the frequency distribution in Figure 54. The frequency of *must* is decreasing from an M-co of 68 in the oldest age group to an M-co of 17 in the youngest age group. The changes in the frequency of *must* and *have to* from the age group 34–41 to the age group 26–33 that run counter to the overall trends are not significant (Log-likelihood test).

If we compare the frequency development of the two apparent-time studies from ICE-HK (cf. Figure 48) and ICE-IND*, we can see that the starting point of the decrease of *must* in the synchronic snapshot of ICE-IND* is lower than that of ICE-HK (with an M-co of 68 for the age group 50+ in ICE-IND* compared to an M-co of 87 in the age group 56–60+ in ICE-HK). The end point of the decrease in the snapshot of ICE-IND* and ICE-HK can be found at roughly the same frequency in both varieties, with an M-co of 17 for the age group 18–25 in ICE-IND* and an M-co of 16 for the age group 17–25 in ICE-HK. The frequency of *have to* shows an increase from the oldest to the youngest age group from an M-co of 101 to an M-co of 292. Compared to ICE-HK, the starting point of the development in the snapshot of ICE-IND* is higher with an M-co of 101 in the age group 50+ as opposed to a starting point with an M-co of 87 in the age group 56–60+ in ICE-HK. This means that ICE-IND* is marked by a stronger rise of *have to* than ICE-HK, which may have to do with differences in the structures of deontic modality between ICE-IND* and ICE-HK. In ICE-IND*, competition in the field is practically limited to the core modal verb *must* and the semi-modal verb *have to*, as the semi-modal verbs *have got to* and *need to* are only minority variants here. In contrast, the frequency of *need to*, which speakers may choose in place of *have to* in some cases, is higher in ICE-HK, which then results in a lower frequency of *have to*. The findings also show that *need to* is on the decrease in IndE, contradicting earlier hypotheses about a rise of the semi-modal verb in this variety on the basis of differences according to mode (cf. van der Auwera, Noël & De Wit 2012, 71).

If we take a look at the rise of *have to* according to gender, we can see that young females lead the change towards innovative *have to* (cf. Figure 55), as was also the case in HKE. This gender pattern is the classic pattern of a change from below found in apparent-time studies of 'Western' varieties of English (cf. Labov 2001, 279–283; cf. also Section 4.3.1). But females have not always been at

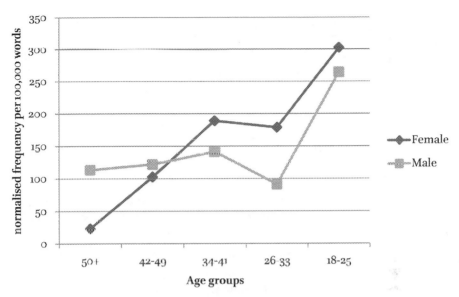

FIGURE 55   The frequency of *have to* in apparent time in the spoken section of ICE-IND*
according to gender (cf. Table 40 in the appendices).

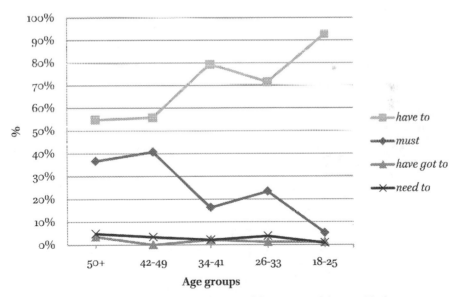

FIGURE 56   The development of the proportions of the variants of the variable deontic modality in the spoken section of ICE-IND* (cf. Table 41 in the appendices).

the forefront of change in the case of *have to* in IndE. In the age groups 42–49 and 50+, male speakers show a greater use of *have to* than female speakers. The pattern suggests a delayed onset of female lead that may reflect societal changes towards increasing female access to hitherto male-dominated domains of English (cf. Sharma 2011 for a similar reversal of the gender pattern in the accent repertoires of British Asian English speakers).

Having established the development of the frequency of the variants in apparent time, we can now turn to the changing proportions of the variants of deontic modality in apparent time (cf. Figure 56). The oldest age group uses *must* in 37% of the cases when they express deontic modality, while the youngest age group uses *must* in only 5% of the cases. This contrasts markedly with the development of the proportion of *have to* in apparent time. The oldest age group uses *have to* in 55% of the cases as an expression of deontic modality, while the youngest age group uses it almost exclusively, i.e. in 93% of the cases. If this distribution is juxtaposed to that found in ICE-HK, we can see that the oldest age group still shows a slight preference for *must* over *have to*, with 38% of *must* compared to 35% of *have to* in ICE-HK, while the youngest age group prefers *have to* over *must*, with a proportion of 77% for *have to* in comparison with 7% for *must*. In contrast to the data from ICE-HK, the preference for *have to* in the youngest age group of ICE-IND* is therefore stronger than that identified for the youngest age group of ICE-HK. In ICE-HK, the choice is not as strongly restricted to the core modal *must* and the semi-modal *have to* as in ICE-IND*, which may be the reason why the preference for *have to* is less

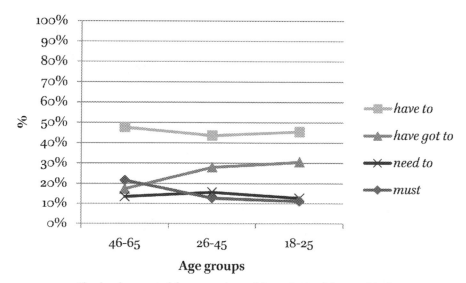

FIGURE 57   The development of the proportions of the variants of the variable deontic modality in the spoken section of ICE-GB (cf. Table 42 in the appendices).

pronounced in the youngest age group in ICE-HK than in the youngest age group in ICE-IND*. If we compare the proportions of the variants in apparent time in ICE-HK and ICE-IND* to the proportions found in ICE-GB, we can see that the proportions of *must* and *have to* do not diverge as strongly in the youngest age group of ICE-GB as in the youngest age groups of ICE-HK and ICE-IND* (cf. Figure 57).

In ICE-GB, the youngest age group uses *must* in 11% of the cases when they express deontic modality, using *have to* in 46% of the cases. That the divergence of the proportions of *must* and *have to* is less pronounced in ICE-GB may have to do with the higher proportion of *have got to* in BrE, which is used in 31% of the cases where speakers of the age group 18–25 express deontic modality. Because *have got to* is only a minority option for expressing deontic modality in the youngest age group in ICE-HK and ICE-IND*, with only 2% and only 1% respectively, these speakers show a stronger preference for *have to* than speakers of BrE.

A comparison between the development of the normalised frequency in apparent time in ICE-GB and in the ESL varieties is not possible because ICE-GB does not have a separate header file with the information of the speakers that would permit the calculation of the number of words per speaker as the basis for normalising frequencies across the age groups. But there are real-time studies on spoken data from BrE that can be used for comparison. Leech et al. analyse the use of the modal and semi-modal verbs in spoken BrE on the basis of two comparable mini-corpora, DSEU from the 1960s and DICE from the 1990s. These contain approximately 140,000 words each, from LLC and ICE-GB respectively. Their study shows that *must* is on the decline and *have to* is on the rise from DSEU to DICE, and that both trends are more pronounced in these spoken data than in the written data they analysed (cf. Leech et al. 2009, 284;287). The frequency of *must* decreased by -58%, while the frequency of *have to* increased by +32% between the 1960s and the 1990s (cf. Leech et al. 2009, 284;287).

These findings can be compared to the findings from ICE-HK by restricting the analysis of the frequency to the thirty-year period between the age group 46–55 to the age group 17–25 corresponding to the diachronic gap between DSEU (1960s) and DICE (1990s). We can identify a decrease of *must* by -71% from the age group 46–55 to the age group 17–25 in HKE. The increase of *have to* between these age groups is +69%. This means that the changes in the frequencies of *must* and *have to* are more substantial in spoken ICE-HK than in data of spoken BrE. The same is true for ICE-IND*, where we can see a change in the frequency of *must* by -68% and an increase in the frequency of *have to* by +158% between the age groups 42–49 and 18–25. This may mean that the decrease of the core modal verbs and the rise of the semi-modal verbs actually proceeded faster and not slower in ESL varieties than in BrE in this time period, a finding that contradicts general perceptions about the 'conservative' nature of these varieties.

8.4   Summary

To summarise, the apparent-time studies on the basis of the spoken sections of ICE-HK and ICE-IND* suggest that the ESL varieties follow the trend of the decline of the core modal verbs and the rise of the semi-modal verbs, with a decrease in the use of *must* and an increase in the use of *have to*. The findings also indicate that the core modal *must* is strongly decreasing in its root sense, while its epistemic sense is first seen to rise but then follows suit. Young female speakers are leading the rise of innovative *have to* in both varieties although female speakers have not always been in the lead, at least in IndE. With regard to the other two semi-modal verbs, *have got to* and *need to*, no increase could be identified.

As the findings presented in this chapter are solely based on apparent-time evidence, it is necessary to test them against real-time evidence, as soon as diachronic corpora for the ESL varieties become available (cf. *The Diachronic Corpus of Hong Kong English* (DC-HKE), Biewer et al. 2014 and *The Diachronic Corpus of Indian English* (DiCIE), Berardo & Calabrese 2012; cf. also Section 11.1.1). This chapter has shown that age and gender are important factors determining variation between *must* and *have to* in ICE-HK and ICE-IND*, but they are clearly not the only factors that are relevant. The next chapter will therefore take a closer look at the alternation between *must* and *have to*, the two main competitors in the field of deontic modality, by taking into account language-internal and language-external factors that may determine the choice for *must* over *have to*.

CHAPTER 9

Competition between *must* and *have to*

This chapter focuses on the competition between *must* and *have to* as expressions of deontic modality. The analyses in Chapter 8 have shown that age and gender are factors that influence the choice between deontic *must* and *have to* in HKE, IndE, and BrE. However, as the analyses in the previous chapter are based on mono- and bivariate analyses, the role of these two factors has to be analysed when other language-external and language-internal factors are included (cf. Schilk's 2015, 351 critique of Lange's study). In order to model the effect of several predictors on the choice between *must* and *have to*, I performed binary logistic regression analyses on the basis of the data (cf. also Section 4.3.2). This method makes it possible to identify the effect of a predictor, while at the same time controlling for the effects of other predictors. Furthermore, it also makes it possible to consider interactions between the predictors.

The first section of this chapter will introduce important aspects of binary logistic regression that are necessary to understand the models in the subsequent sections. After that, I will present findings from multivariate analyses that shed light on the local and global characteristics of the competition between *must* and *have to* in Sections 9.2 and 9.3. First, I will take a closer look at the local characteristics of the alternation in spoken HKE, IndE, and BrE, when I analyse the effects of age, gender of the speaker, text type, and type of subject (Section 9.2). Second, I will perform a multivariate analysis on the basis of the complete dataset in order to analyse the global characteristics of the alternation between *must* and *have to* (Section 9.3). This will include an analysis of the effects of the language-internal predictors 'type of subject' and 'semantics of the verb' as well as the language-external factors 'text type' and 'variety'. The aim of the global analysis is to specify remaining '*must*-friendly' contexts. I will summarise the main findings in the last section of the chapter and discuss their relevance for the broader picture (Section 9.4).

9.1 Some Basics of Binary Logistic Regression

Logistic regression models the relationship between a categorical dependent variable ('response variable') and independent variables ('predictors') (cf. Levshina 2015, 253; cf. also Section 4.3.2). In the present study, the dependent variable can take on two values, i.e. *must* or *have to*, i.e. the dependent variable

© KONINKLIJKE BRILL NV, LEIDEN, 2018 | DOI:10.1163/9789004381520_010

is a binary nominal variable, which is why the models presented in Sections 9.2 and 9.3 are called 'binary logistic regression models'.[1] I fitted binary logistic regression models by using the lrm and glm functions from the packages "rms" and "stats" in R (cf. Harrell 2017; R Core Team 2016).[2]

An important prerequisite for logistic regression is that independent variables do not correlate strongly with each other (cf. Szmrecsanyi 2006, 54). The interdependence between different independent variables can be checked by calculating the variance inflation factor (vif) (cf. Field, Miles & Field 2012, 322). In all examples, this factor was lower than 5, which represents the conservative threshold for multicollinearity. This shows that multicollinearity was not a problem for any of the models. A problem of multicollinearity could have occurred if I had included both mode (spoken vs. written) and text type in one model because they measure similar phenomena and therefore correlate strongly with each other. Another assumption of logistic regression is that the data points of the dataset should be independent of each other (cf. Levshina 2015, 271). Two data points are for example dependent on each other if they are produced by the same speaker or in the same text. However, as many different speakers are represented in ICE and many different texts are included due to the maximum size of 2,000 words, the data points can be considered to be largely independent of each other. This means that no assumption of logistic regression is violated and that it is a feasible method for the data at hand.

I fitted several models to the data. In those cases where there was no significant difference between two models, I chose the model that had fewer predictors in line with the preference for parsimonious models ('Occam's razor', cf. also Section 4.3.2). Relevant predictors of the models were identified by stepwise backwards selection, i.e. all predictors were initially included in the model and subsequently discarded to arrive at the best and most parsimonious model. The output of these fitted models then allows us to identify in what way the different levels of the significant predictors affect the choice of *must* as opposed to *have to*. One level of the predictors serves as the reference level, for example speakers in the age group 17–25 in the predictor 'age' in ICE-HK. Specifying one value as the reference level permits the comparison between the reference level and each value of the predictors but also the comparison between the values of the predictors that are not part of the reference level. I set those

---

1   The main competition between expressions of strong deontic modality takes place between *must* and *have to*, as has been shown in Chapter 5. Multinomial regressions were tested but not considered feasible because the comparatively low frequencies of *have got to* and *need to* led to small values or missing values for some levels of the predictors.

2   I also fitted mixed-effect models (cf. Bates et al. 2015) with speaker and verb as random effects to the data but including them as random effects did not improve the models.

levels of the predictors as reference levels that favour the use of *have to* most in order to receive informative coefficients for the choice of *must*. These are the youngest group in the predictor 'age', female in the predictor 'gender', private dialogue in the predictor 'text type', and category M (movement, location, travel, and transport) in the predictor 'semantics of the verb'. In the case of the type of subject, I compared the uses of non-generic first, second, and third person subjects to generic subjects in order to find out about the strength of obligation expressed. The strength is greater with non-generic subjects than with generic subjects and strongest with second person non-generic subjects and least strong with third person non-generic subjects (cf. also Section 4.3.1). It is important to mention that the choice of the reference level does not affect the statistical model and can therefore be set according to the research question.

The output of the model provides coefficients for the values of the predictors. The coefficients are log odds, i.e. the logarithmic values of odds. Odds are the ratio of the frequency with which an event occurred calculated against the frequency with which that event did not occur (cf. Levshina 2015, 261). This value shows which event is more likely to occur. In our case where there is only a binary choice between *must* and *have to*, the odds for *must* can be calculated by dividing the frequency of occurrence of *must* by the frequency of occurrence of *have to*. For example, in spoken ICE-HK, deontic *must* occurred 287 times and deontic *have to* 855 times. This means the odds for *must* in spoken ICE-HK are $287/855 \approx 0.34$. Odds can take on values between 0 and larger than 1. Odds between 0 and 1 indicate that the chance of the second event occurring is greater than the chance of the first event occurring. In our case, the odds for *must* are 0.34 and therefore between 0 and 1, which means that the chance of *have to* occurring is greater than the chance of *must* occurring in spoken ICE-HK. If odds are above 1, the chance that the first event occurs is greater than the chance that the second event occurs (cf. Levshina 2015, 261). The odds of *have to* in spoken ICE-HK can be taken as an example here, with a value of $855/287 \approx 2.98$. This value indicates that the chance of the occurrence of *have to* is three times greater than the chance of occurrence of *must*. If odds are 1, the chance of occurrence of the two events is equal, e.g. $855/855 = 1$ (cf. Levshina 2015, 261). This means that odds of 1 represent the turning point between a higher chance that the second event occurs and a higher chance that the first event occurs. Using the logarithmic function for odds, the reference point of 1 is moved to 0, so that it is possible to determine the chance of occurrence of the events by inspecting the signs in front of the figures. The log odds of the odds for *have to* in Hong Kong are $\log(2.98) \approx 1.09$. A positive value of log odds indicates that the inspected event occurs with a greater probability, while a negative value of log odds indicates that the non-inspected event occurs with a greater probability (cf. Levshina 2015, 261). The log odds are given for each value of the predictors and the intercept model. The log odds of the intercept specify the chance of occurrence of *must* when all the values of the predictors are at reference level. For the models of this study, this means that the predictor 'age' is set to the level of the youngest age group, the level of 'gender' is female, the level of 'text type' is private dialogue, and the level of 'subject' is generic. In the case of the model for spoken HKE, the intercept model has a negative log odds value of ≈-2.91, which indicates that *have to* is more frequently used than *must* in the intercept model.

Apart from the log odds, the output of logistic regression models (cf. Table 43 and Table 44 in the appendices) also reports standard errors, z-values, and p-values. Standard errors represent the distribution of the data points around the mean. High standard errors are usually indicators of data sparseness or multi-collinearity (cf. Levshina 2015, 263). The z-value is a measure that reports the deviance of the estimate from the mean. The p-value indicates the likelihood that the result is due to chance. Apart from specifying these values, the output of the lrm function also produces statistics about the model, for example the model likelihood ratio test, which tells us whether the model is significant in general tested against the null model without any predictors (cf. Levshina 2015, 258). All models that are presented are significant. Apart from this, the output also provides goodness-of-fit statistics. The C-index reports the proportion of the times when the model predicted a higher outcome of *must* when *must* was actually used in the data and a higher chance of *have to* when *have to* was actually used in the data. A C-index of ≥ 0.7 provides acceptable discrimination (cf. Levshina 2015, 259). All models except for the model glm.GBs2 included in Figure 58 have a C-index above 0.7.

9.2 Local Competition between *must* and *have to*

This section discusses findings from three multivariate analyses based on data from the spoken sections of ICE-HK, ICE-IND*, and ICE-GB. The analyses are restricted to HKE, IndE, and BrE because ICE-SIN does not provide information about social factors of the speakers and the spoken component of ICE-USA* only yielded 15 tokens of *must*, a figure that is too low to allow for statistical modelling. The low figure is still interesting because it attests to the strong decrease of *must* in spoken AmE, but also to the informality of SBC compared to the spoken parts of the other ICE corpora (cf. also Section 4.1 for the comparability between SBC and the spoken ICE corpora).

Figure 58 visualises the log odds for *must* in the three models, glm.HKs2, glm.INDs2, and glm.GBs2, representing the regression models fitted to the

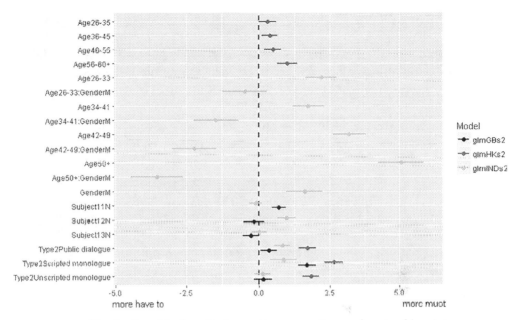

FIGURE 58   Visualisation of the log odds for *must* to compare the use of *must* and *have to* in
            spoken HKE, IndE, and BrE (cf. Table 43 in the appendices) (cf. Wickham 2009 for
            visualisation with "ggplot2").

spoken ICE-HK, ICE-IND*, and ICE-GB data respectively. The points show
the value of the coefficients and the lines indicate the standard error. It is immediately obvious that the coefficients of the predictor values that represent
smaller categories, for example the category of males above the age of 50,
show higher standard errors than larger categories. This means that we can
be less confident about the estimate of the coefficient in these groups, often
due to comparatively stronger internal heterogeneity. Three language-external
predictors and one language-internal predictor and the interactions between
them were tested for all models: age of the speaker, gender of the speaker, text
type, and type of subject. In addition to these predictors, the predictor 'language family of the L1 of the speaker' was also tested for the spoken ICE-IND*
data. Initially, I intended to integrate the L1 of the speakers in the model but
soon realised that data sparseness was an issue in this predictor. Given India's
highly multilingual situation, it does not come as a surprise that some categories were too small to perform statistical analyses (cf. also Section 3.2.2 on the
language situation in India). This is why the different mother tongues of the
speakers were subsumed under their language families. However, the findings
indicate that the language families of the speakers' L1s do not affect the choice
between *must* and *have to* in a significant way. Similar issues of data sparseness

as in the category L1 of the speaker occurred with the category 'semantics of the verb', which turned out to be too fine-grained after sub-setting the data to the spoken sections of each corpus. The models could have profited from using a semantic verb classification with fewer values, for example Vendler's (1967) categorisation according to the aktionsart of the verb or more data points (cf. Section 11.1 for the potential of GloWbE with regard to this predictor). In order to work with maximally large categories, I refrained from using more fine-grained classifications of the predictors 'text type' and 'type of subject'. As can be seen in Figure 58, not all predictors that were tested turned out to be significant for all varieties. Some predictors were discarded in the stepwise backward selection of the models. Furthermore, not all levels of the predictors emerged as significant and I will focus on those that significantly affect the choice of *must* over *have to*.

The predictors that remained in the model for spoken HKE (glm.HKs2, dark grey lines) are 'age of the speaker' and 'text type'. The positive log odds value for *must* in the oldest age group (56–60+) indicates that the chances that *must* occurs in this age group are higher than in the age group 17–25, i.e. the reference level. If we compare the log odds of this age group to the other age groups, we can see that the values become larger the older the speakers get, although the oldest age group is the only age group that displays a significant relationship. The findings therefore confirm that age plays an important role in the alternation (cf. Section 8.3), even when the effect of register is simultaneously taken into account.

Variation according to text type shows that the log odds for *must* in all text types, public dialogue, scripted monologue, and unscripted monologue, differ significantly from the reference level 'private dialogue'. The preference for *must* is strongest in the text type 'scripted monologue', which represents a special type of spoken register that is less interactive and more elaborate than the other spoken text types (cf. Xiao 2009, 436; cf. also Section 4.3.1). This means the text type 'scripted monologue' is the most formal spoken text type represented in ICE. Private dialogues and scripted monologues represent the two poles of the formality cline in the spoken section of ICE, with unscripted monologues and public dialogues in between these two poles, the former being more formal than the latter. The formality cline can be correlated with the log odds for *must* in unscripted monologues and public dialogues, although the difference between unscripted monologues and public dialogues is not particularly pronounced. Especially noteworthy in comparison to BrE is the comparatively greater chance that *must* occurs in public dialogues (cf. (152) and (153)). This might reflect cross-cultural differences in obligation practices. While the direct expression of obligations in public speeches may constitute the marked case in societies with an independent construal of self, it may be the unmarked case in societies with an interdependent construal of self (cf. Section 7.2).

(152) We *must* do more for these people when these people clamor for subsidies (ICE-SIN:S1B-051)

(153) Sir it is my fervent belief that we *must* maintain this obsession [...] (ICE-SIN:S1B-060)

This line of argumentation is corroborated by the fact that a similar pattern can be found in IndE, a variety that has also developed in a society in which individuals construe themselves as strongly dependent on the group (cf. glm.INDs2, light grey lines) (cf. (154)).

(154) So friends we *must* come <,> together we should march ahead for the self-reliance (ICE-IND*:S1B-057)

Apart from the predictors 'text type' and 'age', 'gender' and 'type of subject' turned out to be significant predictors in the model for the spoken ICE-IND* data. Gender only emerged as a significant predictor once an interaction between age and gender was included. With regard to age, we can see that all age groups differ significantly from the youngest age group (18–25). As in HKE, we can see that the chance that *must* occurs becomes greater the older the speakers are, visible in the consistent increase in the value of the log odds from one age group to the next older age group. With regard to gender, we can see that male speakers show a positive log odds value for *must*, indicating that they use *must* more often than female speakers. This finding corresponds to the gender pattern in changes from below, identified by Labov, in which female speakers are more innovative than male speakers (cf. Labov 2001, 279–283; cf. also Section 4.3.1).

However, when the interaction between age and gender is analysed, the picture becomes more complex. Against the expectation that the oldest group of male speakers would be the most conservative compared to the youngest group of female speakers, we can see that the older male speakers get, the more innovative they are with reference to the youngest female group, indicated by the negative log odds in the age groups 34–41, 42–49, and 50+ of male speakers. This indicates that the oldest male group is more innovative than the youngest female group. As has been speculated before, this may have to do with less restricted access to English-dominant domains for male speakers some decades ago (cf. 'the late female lead pattern' in IndE in Section 8.3; cf. also Section 4.1.2 for the gender distribution in the spoken text types of ICE).

With regard to the type of subject selected, we can see that *must* correlates with second person non-generic subjects compared to generic subjects in spoken IndE. When *must* occurs with this type of subject, it expresses strong obligation (cf. example (55) in Section 4.3.1). Although the combination of *must* and second person subject may represent the cognitive prototype of the use of *must* (cf. Coates 1983, 33), it is not the most typical combination in terms of frequency, as Figure 59 shows.

Must is predominantly used with non-generic third person or generic subjects, which express weak obligation. The distribution of *must* identified in Figure 59 supports claims about the decrease of the core modal *must* and the rise of the semi-modal *have to* as a result of the process of 'democratisation of discourse'. Contexts that seriously threaten the democratic interaction between speakers in 'Western' cultures are exactly those contexts where a direct obligation is imposed on a hearer by a speaker, i.e. contexts with non-generic second person subject. It is argued that *must* is replaced with *have to* in these contexts in order to establish a 'more equal' relationship between the speaker and the hearer (cf. Smith 2003, 253). By contrast, it is interesting to see that exactly these contexts favour *must* in IndE.

As I have argued in Section 7.2, I assume that obligations are perceived differently in cultures with an independent and cultures with an interdependent construal of self. While obligations threaten the negative face of speakers from cultures with an independent construal of self, for example in Britain, obligations may appeal to the positive face of speakers from cultures with an interdependent construal of self because they strengthen the interconnectedness of the self with the group. Telling others what to do or to think may be perceived as an act of caring rather than an act of imposing one's will and views on others. These cultural differences in the illocutionary force of *must* may also underlie the preference for *must* in public dialogues in IndE, which emerges as the only text type that significantly favours *must*.

If we take a look at the regression model for the spoken BrE data (glm.GBs2, black lines in Figure 58), we can immediately see that age did not emerge as a significant predictor for BrE. Type of subject and text type were the only significant predictors for the selection of *must* over *have to*. With regard to subject selection, we can identify a correlation between first person subjects (*I*, *we*) and *must* compared to generic subjects. This means that *must* is used to express self-imposed obligations on the speaker and his or her hearers, i.e. in median obligation contexts that are less strong than those contexts with second person non-generic subjects and stronger than contexts with third person non-generic or generic subjects. In the predictor 'text type', scripted monologue showed a greater chance of *must* occurring than private dialogue, a finding that was explained earlier with reference to the formality of this spoken text type.

The findings from the multivariate analyses indicate that the modal systems in spoken HKE and IndE are undergoing change, as becomes visible by the fact that age turns out to be a significant predictor of the choice between *must* and *have to*. In BrE instead, age is not a significant predictor of the choice between *must* and *have to*, indicating that the change has reached a saturation point in spoken BrE (cf. Krug 2000, 88). By contrast, text type emerges as a strong predictor in all varieties, demonstrating that register differences play a pivotal role in the selection of *must* over *have to*, with the general tendency that more formal registers favour the use of *must* (cf. also Biber et al. 1999, 494; Biber 2004, 196). However, despite its comparatively less formal character compared to unscripted and scripted monologues, public dialogues were shown to favour the use of *must* in the two ESL varieties, which was linked to differences in the illocutionary force of *must* in these societies.

9.3   Global Competition between *must* and *have to*

Having identified local characteristics of the alternation between *must* and *have to* in spoken HKE, IndE, and BrE, I now turn to more 'global' characteristics of the modal/semi-modal verb alternation by inspecting the complete dataset with all tokens of *must* and *have to* in deontic function (N = 6,092). As not all corpora provide metadata about the speakers and those that do are not comparable in terms of their classification in some categories (e.g. different age groups in ICE-HK, ICE-IND*, and ICE-GB), language-external social factors were not included in this statistical model. This means that 'text type', 'type of subject', and 'verb semantics' were tested as predictors. This time, the large database permitted the inclusion of the predictor 'semantics of the verb'. Apart from these three predictors, 'variety' was also included as a predictor in order to see whether significant regional differences exist between the reference level BrE[3] and the four other varieties, AmE, SgE, IndE, and HKE when several other predictors are analysed simultaneously.

The reference level for 'text type' is again private dialogue but the model now also includes written text types because it is based on the complete dataset from the spoken and written parts of the corpora. The reference level for the category 'semantics of the verb' is category M, which includes verbs expressing movement, location, travel, and transport. As the analysis of *must* vs. *have to* according to the semantics of the following verb has shown, this class strongly favours the use of *have to*, in particular in collocations with verbs of moving,

---

3 Cf. Section 2.4 for a critical account of taking BrE as the comparative foil against which New Englishes are defined.

coming, and going (M1). Category Y yielded too few tokens to be included as a level of the predictor 'semantics of the verb' because it comprises verbs related to scientific and technical jargon, such as *download* or *double-click*. Category Z, which includes performative verbs, such as *thank* or *admit* in (155) and (156), also had to be excluded because *must* represented the only choice in these contexts (cf. 'envelope of variation' in Section 4.3).

(155) Oh forgive me <indig> yaar </indig> I also *must thank* you for giving me about the knowledge about humour (ICE-IND*:S1A-001)

(156) But I *must admit* this is more likely to remain a dream than become a reality (ICE-IND*:W2B-002)

The exclusion of verbs from category Z does not, however, affect formulaic expressions with verbs of saying, such as the phrases *I must say* or *I have to say*, which are tagged separately with Q for the semantic category language and communication. Although from a linguistic perspective it would also be feasible to include the verbs *thank* and *admit* in the broader category of language and communication, the distinction of the tagger between these two categories reveals an interesting pattern. *Have to* has started to make inroads in formulaic expressions of *must* with verbs of saying but not yet with verbs that denote other performative acts, such as *thank* and *admit*. This may be related

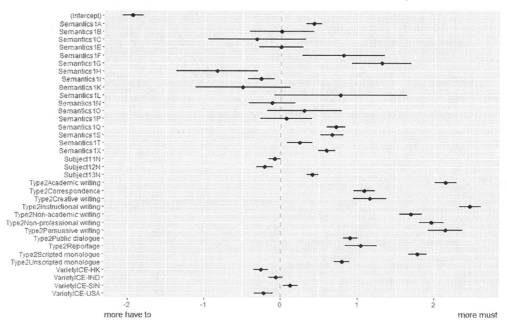

FIGURE 59   Visualisation of the log odds for *must* in all varieties (cf. Table 44 in the appendices).

to the fact that verbs of saying played a major role in the grammaticalisation of *have to*, as *say* was the most frequent collocate of *have to* together with *do* in Shakespeare (cf. Krug 2000, 60). All other levels of the predictors have been retained, as can be seen in Figure 59.

With regard to the semantics of the verb, five semantic categories significantly increase the chance that *must* occurs rather than *have to*. These are category A (general and abstract terms), category G (government and public), category Q (language and communication), category S (social actions, states, and processes), and category X (psychological actions, states, and processes). A closer look at the categories will show with which verbs *must* is likely to co-occur. The first category A is a very broad category. In this category, we can see a strong preference for *must* with the stative verb *be* (cf. (157)).

(157) Brigadier-General George Yeo said the basic approach *must be* one of openness and tolerance (ICE-SIN:S2B-019)

Another semantic category of the verb with which *must* is the preferred choice is the semantic category G. This category comprises verbs of law and order, such as *enact, register,* or *license* (cf. (158)). These verbs often occur in the passive (cf. (158)).

(158) Boats and vehicles used for transport *must be licensed* to carry passengers. (ICE-SIN:W2D:005)

The verbs of this category are similar to the verbs of permission from category S, which also includes other verbs relating to social actions, states, and processes, such as *let, help,* or *encourage*. These verbs often co-occur with *must* when it is preceded by the personal pronoun *we* in public dialogues (cf. (159)).

(159) We *must encourage* the more able to do their best for themselves and Singapore (ICE-SIN:S2B-048)

Apart from these types of verbs, *must* is also favoured with verbs of thinking and knowing from category X, e.g. (160) and (161).

(160) Now I think *I must* really *think* first of migrating you know (ICE-SIN: S1A-004)

(161) And we *must bear in mind* uh we have very much nineteen ninety seven (ICE-HK:S1B-040)

Furthermore, it is favoured with verbs of saying from category Q, such as *say* in (162) and *confess* in (163).

(162) I *must say* that the Harbour looks more like a nullah ['stream'] now (ICE-HK:S2B-029)

(163) I *must confess* though I don't belong to south but still I too am fond of (ICE-IND*:S1A-072)

These contexts represent cases that have been referred to as formulaic uses of *must*. Studies on other varieties of English confirm that these contexts are remarkably resistant to change (cf. Trousdale 2003, 276–277; Jankowski 2004, 92; Tagliamonte & D'Arcy 2007, 73–74). In dialects such as Tyneside English, where *must* almost exclusively functions as a marker of epistemic modality (cf. Section 2.1), almost all remaining cases of deontic *must* are used in these contexts (cf. Trousdale 2003, 276–277). The persistence of *must* in these contexts is "typical of obsolescing features – they often get left behind in islands in the grammar as discourse 'chunks'" (cf. Tagliamonte & Smith 2006, 355). In my data, these contexts still show the dominance of *must* but instances of *have to* can also be found (cf. (164)).

(164) This is a funny [sc. way] of enjoying your freedom I *have to say* (ICE-HK:S1B-038)

This suggests that we are dealing with a rather late stage of grammaticalisation of *have to* because we can see "that even islands eventually succumb to the waves of change" (Tagliamonte & D'Arcy 2007, 73). Judging only from the more widespread occurrence of the phrase *I have to say*, it can be assumed that *have to* has grammaticalised furthest in BrE. To summarise, we have seen that *must* co-occurs with the lexical verb *be*, with 'administrative' verbs, verbs that express social actions as well as verbs of thinking and saying.

   If we take a look at the subject selection of *must* compared to *have to*, we can see that *must* favours non-generic third person subjects compared to generic subjects (cf. also Loureiro-Porto 2016, 161). These contexts express weak obligation compared to stronger contexts with first and second person subjects. Furthermore, Loureiro-Porto argues that the preference for third person subjects in the use of *must* indicates a higher degree of grammaticalisation of the core modal verb compared to the semi-modal verbs (cf. Loureiro-Porto 2016, 161; cf. also Section 2.2). It is interesting to see that early instances of epistemic *must* occurred with subjects in the third person (cf. Section 6.1.1), indicating that third person contexts might represent a bridging context where epistemic uses developed from strongly grammaticalised deontic uses. This may mean that epistemic uses of *have to* developed in the same contexts after *have to* started to expand its use to third person subjects (cf. Section 6.1.2 for early uses of epistemic *have to* with third person subjects). It is also interesting to see that early attestations of epistemic *must* collocate with *be* (cf. Visser 1969, 1810), which is still a preferred usage context of deontic *must*, as has been mentioned earlier. This may mean that contexts in which *must* occurs with third person subjects and *be* represent later grammaticalisation stages of the modal verb that are only gradually overtaken by *have to*, once its grammaticalisation proceeds further.

Having discussed the language-internal predictors 'semantics of the verb' and 'type of subject', we can now turn to one of the two language-external predictors, namely 'text type'. Register differences play an important part in the alternation between *must* and *have to*. In its deontic function, *must* is more rarely used in conversation than *have to* but more often so in academic prose (cf. Biber et al. 1999, 494; Biber 2004, 196). This means that we can expect to see a correlation between the formality of the text type and the occurrence of *must*, with more formal text types favouring *must* over *have to*. If we take a closer look at Figure 59, the formality cline may indeed explain a substantial part of the findings. Private dialogues, the text type that favours *have to* most strongly, is taken as the reference level. As the chance that *have to* occurs in private dialogues is so high, all other text types have a positive log odds value for *must*, indicating that *must* is preferred in comparison to the reference level. The log odds values suggest a categorisation into four groups of text types (cf. Table 12). The first

TABLE 12   Classification of text types according to log odds for *must* and formality

Text type	Log odds (higher values = more *must*)	Formality (higher values = higher formality)
Unscripted monologue	< 1.0	2
Public dialogue		2
Reportage	> 1.0	5
Correspondence		3
Creative writing		2
Non-academic writing	> 1.5	4
Scripted monologue		4
Non-professional writing		4
Persuasive writing	> 2.0	4
Academic writing		5
Instructional writing		4

group with log odds below 1.0 includes unscripted monologue and public dia-logue. The next group of text types has log odds of over 1.0 and comprises the text categories reportage, correspondence, and creative writing. The group with the second highest chance of occurrence of *must* contains non-academic writing, scripted monologue, and non-professional writing, with log odds higher than 1.5. The group with the highest chance of occurrence of *must* includes persuasive writing, academic writing, and instructional writing, with log odds higher than 2. If we compare the formality of the text type by drawing on Xiao's classifi-cation of the texts across Factor 1 ('interactive casual discourse vs. informative elaborate discourse') (cf. Figure 23 Section 4.3.1), we can see that the log odds of the text types correlate with their formality (cf. Table 12). The general tendency that becomes visible is that those levels with a high degree of formality marked by higher numbers in the column formality (1 = most informal to 5 = most for-mal) have a higher chance of occurrence of *must*, i.e. higher log odds.

The group with the highest log odds includes academic writing, which is one of the two most formal text types according to Xiao's classification (2009, 436). This also aligns well with Hundt and Mair's description of this genre as 'up-tight', meaning that it is more reluctant to change than other genres (cf. Hundt & Mair 1999, 236). While the frequency of *must* in this genre is rather unsur-prising given its formal nature, it is more surprising that instructional writing and persuasive writing are also found in this group, although they are classi-fied as less formal than academic writing (cf. Xiao 2009, 436). This means that formality is not the only factor that contributes to the '*must*-friendly' nature of these text types. The content of the text types also plays a decisive role. *Must* is the preferred choice in the two text types included in the broader category of 'instructional writing', i.e. 'administrative writing' and 'skills and hobbies' that set out rules. Typical examples of these uses can be found in (165) and (166).

(165) Holiday leave *must* normally be taken during the vacation periods. (ICE-SIN:W2D:006)

(166) For those not fortunate enough to have balconies, windowsills will do, but when the plants are watered provision *must* be made to catch the surplus, so a suitable trough and a means to drain are needed. (ICE-SIN:W2D-016)

Must is also employed in persuasive writing, where speakers want to persuade their audience of their views, an aim that can arguably best be achieved by employing the subjective function of the modal verb as a tool of stance-taking to express a sense of urgency, as can be seen in (167) .

(167) Clearly, the government and businessmen *must* examine the underlying factors and offer an explanation. (ICE-IND*:W2E-007)

The group with the second highest log odds, i.e. above 1.5, behaves exactly as expected given its position on the formality cline. However, the group with log odds above 1.0 shows no clear correlation with formality except for the text type 'correspondence'. The log odds for the text type 'reportage' do not correlate with the high formality of the text type. This means that this text type is paradoxically marked by a high formality but low likelihood of occurrence of *must*. This dissonance might be explained by the 'agile' nature of newspapers, which represent a genre that is very open to language change and therefore receptive to innovative *have to* (cf. Hundt & Mair 1999, 236; cf. also Smith 2003, 251 for the strong rise of *have to* in the press section from LOB to FLOB). It more readily accepts change than fiction, as can be seen in the lower log odds of reportage compared to creative writing. The groups whose log odds are closest to private dialogues are unscripted monologues and public dialogues, which again points to a correlation between the occurrence of *must* and the formality of the text type.

A look at regional variation reveals that AmE, IndE, and HKE show a more restricted use of *must* than BrE. SgE is the only variety where the chance that *must* is used is greater compared to BrE (cf. also Section 5.2.1). However, only the use of *must* in HKE is significantly different from the use of *must* in BrE when other factors are taken into account at the same time. As has been shown in Section 5.2.1, HKE is marked by a particularly high frequency of *have to*. I have argued that the high frequency may be linked to SLA principles; more precisely the application of the Shortest Path Principle. That HKE turns out to be the only variety that is significantly different from BrE may therefore be linked to its special status as an ESL variety with EFL characteristics (cf. Section 3.2.1). This may mean that learner effects may be stronger in HKE than in any other variety of English that has been analysed.

9.4   'Glocal' Competition between *must* and *have to*

This chapter has offered an insight into the factors that jointly condition the alternation between deontic *must* and *have to*. After introducing logistic regression as a statistical model, the findings from four multivariate analyses were discussed. Section 9.2 detailed the local characteristics of the alternation between *must* and *have to* in spoken HKE, IndE, and BrE. The findings showed that 'age' only turned out to be a significant predictor of *must* in the two ESL varieties and not in BrE, which suggests that the change is still going on in spoken HKE and IndE but not in spoken BrE. Another shared characteristic of the two ESL varieties was the significant preference for *must* in public dialogues, which was linked to cross-cultural differences in the perception of strong obligations between speakers of the ESL varieties and speakers of BrE. The subject selection of *must* in IndE also called for a cultural explanation, as *must* is preferred in IndE with second person subjects, a context that represents a potentially face-threatening situation in 'Western' varieties of English. In Section 9.3, I took a closer look at the 'global' characteristics of the alternation between *must* and *have to*. The findings showed that *must* is preferred with the stative verb *be*, administrative verbs, and verbs that relate to social actions as well as verbs of thinking and saying. Furthermore, *must* is most frequently used with third person subjects and in more formal text types, especially in those formal text types that are resistant to change. The findings also indicate that HKE is the only variety that turned out to behave rather differently from BrE.

After summarising the major findings, the question that arises is how the findings from the local and global analyses form an integrated and meaningful whole that characterises the alternation between modal and semi-modal verbs. The analysis of the competition between *must* and *have to* according to age in spoken HKE, IndE, and BrE has shown that age only plays a significant role in the two ESL varieties. This indicates that these spoken varieties are currently undergoing language change. Assuming that the decrease of *must* and the rise of *have to* started in spoken language, it may well be the case that this change has passed spoken language in BrE and 'moved on' to written language. This may mean that we are indeed observing different stages of language change in spoken BrE, HKE, and IndE. While all age groups differed significantly from the youngest age group in IndE, only the oldest age group differed significantly from the youngest age group in HKE. We can therefore hypothesise that the current state of the modal system in HKE represents a later stage of the process than the state in IndE.

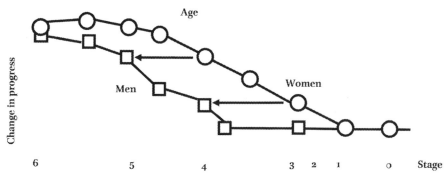

FIGURE 60   A six-stage model of gender relations in linguistic change from below (adapted from Labov 2001, 309).

This is further supported by the fact that gender only turned out to be a significant factor in IndE, as a closer look at gender patterns in different stages of linguistic changes from below reveals (cf. Labov 2001, 306–309; cf. Figure 60). Although the model has been developed on the basis of the spread of sound changes, it might also have explanatory power for the spread of grammatical changes that are below the level of consciousness.

Judging from the gender patterns shown in Figure 60, differences in the significance of the predictor 'gender' may reflect differences in the stage of linguistic change. Gender is a significant predictor at the intermediate stages of language change but not a significant predictor at the initial or final phases of linguistic change. The gender differentiation from the medial stages is resolved once the change nears completion. This may mean that in the varieties in which gender did not appear as a significant predictor, linguistic change has not started yet or is nearing completion. As neither age nor gender emerged as significant predictors in spoken BrE, it can be argued that the change has reached completion there, while this is not yet the case in HKE, where a significant correlation between the use of *must* and the oldest age group could still be identified. However, as gender was not a significant predictor, the linguistic change may be further advanced in HKE than in IndE, where we can still observe the association between the conservative variant *must* with male speakers, which points to the fact that spoken IndE is at one of the medial stages of linguistic change and thus ties in nicely with the finding that all age groups differ significantly from the youngest age group. Although the specific gender pattern in IndE does not exactly correspond to the one shown in Figure 60, the detectable effect of the social dimension 'gender' may still be used to further specify the status of language change in this variety. While the linguistic change has already reached completion in spoken BrE, it is moving towards completion in spoken HKE, whereas it is in 'full swing' in spoken IndE (despite claims to the contrary, cf. Mair 2015a, 135; Loureiro-Porto 2016, 148).

If this scenario is valid, it means that the varieties under investigation ultimately develop in the same direction with regard to the reorganisation of the modal systems, a point that has also been raised by Mair on the basis of BrE and AmE data (cf. Mair 2015a, 124). Mair argues that regional contrasts between BrE and AmE are temporary phenomena, "as the two varieties are moving in the same direction and towards the same goal" (Mair 2015a, 124). On the basis of this finding, he also hypothesises that regional contrasts will not play a major role in postcolonial varieties of English in the long run because the changes in the modal system "were set in motion before BrE and AmE diverged and the newer colonial and post-colonial Englishes emerged" (Mair 2015a, 124).

My findings furthermore indicate that this general global trend is mediated through register. The analysis according to text type showed that the change proceeds with different speeds through the text types, starting in spoken language and moving on to other informal text types until slowly reaching more formal text types. While the formality of the text type and openness to change are decisive factors in the replacement of *must* by *have to*, the function of text types is also crucial, as the reluctance to replacing *must* with *have to* in text types such as 'instructional writing' and 'persuasive writing' indicates.

As the change proceeds through the text types, *must* becomes more and more specialised. It is used more frequently with third person subjects, i.e. in contexts that denote rather weak obligation. With regard to the semantics of the verb, we can see that formulaic expressions with verbs of saying remain key contexts of *must* that are most strongly resistant to substitution by the semi-modal verb *have to*.

Finally, the analysis shows that it may not be so wrong after all to postulate a cline of advancement on which the varieties can be positioned. At least on the basis of empirical evidence concerning linguistic changes in the modal system, we can propose the following cline: BrE>HKE>IndE because the findings indeed indicate that all varieties undergo same restructuring processes, albeit at different speeds. But it is important to note that the basis for positing such a cline in this study would be quite different from the basis in other studies because it is one thing to identify a cline of advancement on the basis of empirical evidence and quite another to postulate it without testing its validity on the basis of data (cf. the discussion in Section 2.4).

CHAPTER 10

Thematic Conclusion of the Study

The present study has analysed variation and change in the modal systems of WE, with a focus on the group of modal and semi-modal verbs of obligation and necessity in BrE, AmE, HKE, IndE, and SgE. In this chapter, I will detail in what way the present study has increased our knowledge about the three key notions of the study: 'variation', 'change', and 'modal system(s)'.

As revealed in the literature review, there is only limited research on the modal systems of ESL varieties, while there is extensive research on ENL varieties. It therefore does not come as a surprise that research on ESL varieties strongly builds on insights from ENL varieties. However, in my view this has not always been beneficial for understanding the modal systems of these varieties. Whereas recent studies on ENL varieties have devoted special attention to developments in the modal system, the basis for quantitative diachronic studies of ESL varieties is still largely missing. Despite this problem, there are many studies on ESL varieties that take a diachronic perspective on synchronic data. These studies assume – rather than investigate – that the same developments as in ENL varieties have also taken place in ESL varieties. Although changes have not been empirically tested, hasty explanations for these assumed changes have already been put forward or rather simply been transferred from studies on ENL varieties. This means researchers have tried to integrate the triad of 'colloquialisation', 'Americanisation', and 'democratisation' into their studies on modal systems of ESL varieties. However, several arguments speak against taking such an approach. First, it is still unclear whether ESL varieties are really undergoing the same process of reorganisation. Second, explanations that have been proposed to account for the reorganisation of the modal system in ENL varieties are not necessarily transferable to the ESL context.

For instance, the process whereby written norms approximate to spoken language stands in sharp contrast to the assumed conceptual writtenness of spoken language in several ESL varieties. Additionally, the process of 'Americanisation' in ENL varieties might have its equivalent in a process of 'Briticisation' in some ESL varieties that orient themselves towards the norms of their historical input varieties. Finally, it has been argued that 'democratisation' seems to be a particularly 'Western' cultural explanation for changes in the modal system because it is strongly tied to an independent construal of the self, which is why Leech also refers to this process as 'individualisation' (cf. Leech 2003, 237). This brief discussion shows the problems involved when

© KONINKLIJKE BRILL NV, LEIDEN, 2018 | DOI:10.1163/9789004381520_011

transferring insights and explanations from ENL varieties directly to ESL varieties without reconsidering their validity.

I have argued that it is more effective to analyse variation in ESL varieties from an internal rather than an external perspective. Such a perspective can raise new questions and review old ones that have not been solved by the direct transfer of findings from ENL to ESL varieties. A question that awaits further research, as it has obviously not figured prominently in the ENL context, concerns the influence of the first languages of the speakers in ESL contexts. Apart from this issue, it is also important to review old questions that were considered solved by some researchers. The most important of these is whether the modal systems of ESL varieties are also undergoing language change. I have claimed that both questions can be tackled by integrating language-external factors into studies on L2 varieties. The integration of information about the speakers' first languages helps us to improve our understanding about the nature of substrate influence on the modal systems of ESL varieties, while information about the speakers' age can be the key to identifying recent language change.

The focus on the internal heterogeneity of ESL varieties seeks to counterbalance large-scale regional comparisons that analyse ESL varieties as largely homogeneous entities. The new perspective allows us to see different layers that constitute these varieties. Metaphorically speaking, this approach resembles the analysis of geological rock strata, which can give us evidence of their internal structure and can serve as an indication of their development. Each stratum was deposited at a certain point in time and shows internal homogeneity but is different to the next stratum. The characteristics of each stratum can therefore be used to shed light on the development of a rock through time. A distant external perspective instead would not permit this analysis and creates an image of a monolithic entity, thus creating homogeneity where in reality there is considerable heterogeneity.

In this chapter, I will describe in what way the adoption of such a variety-specific sociolinguistic perspective has led to an increased understanding about the modal system of English. I will review the main findings with regard to variation and change in the modal systems of ESL varieties and propose avenues for further research in Sections 10.1 and 10.2. In the remainder of the chapter (Section 10.3), I will discuss the wider implications of the findings for our general understanding of the structure of the English modal system.

10.1   Variation in the Modal Systems of WE

I analysed variation in the modal systems of ESL varieties by applying Mufwene's (2001) Feature Pool Model. As described earlier, this model postulates that

languages and varieties that come into contact in the formation of ESL varieties feed features into a pool. In the case of the ESL varieties under analysis,
these languages and varieties are the input variety BrE, the substrate languages,
and the hypercentral variety AmE (cf. Chapter 6). Their features enter a competition-and-selection process during which they are deconstructed and reconstructed in a process of bricolage. Some of these features ultimately prevail
over others on the basis of specific selection principles (cf. Chapter 7) and form
the structure of the newly emerging variety. A closer look at the structures of
the modal systems of the ESL varieties in comparison to the structures of the
modal systems of BrE and AmE (cf. Chapter 5) has shown that the end products of the selection process of each variety are highly idiosyncratic, which
suggests that it makes sense to take the influence of several factors into account (cf. Biewer 2015, 83–114).

My findings indicate that all varieties use *must* as the main expression of
epistemic modality and only rarely employ the semi-modal verbs in this function. It was argued that the absence of the semi-modal verbs in epistemic function in the historical input varieties conditions their limited use in the ESL
varieties under analysis. However, the study also revealed differences between
the ESL varieties with regard to the use of *must* as a marker of epistemic modality. IndE shows a more widespread use of epistemic *must* than HKE and
SgE. The historically later state of the BrE input variety to SgE and HKE could
not explain the difference because epistemic *must* was on the rise between the
points in time when English stabilised in India in the middle of the 18th century and in Singapore and Hong Kong in the second half of the 19th century. It
was therefore argued that other factors that pertain to the specific context of
ESL varieties must be analysed to account for these findings.

A typological overview revealed that the encoding of epistemic and deontic
modality in one form is the exception rather than the norm in the languages
of the world, so that the structure of English turns out to be 'the odd one out'
world-wide. This highlights once more the importance of questioning basic
assumptions of the ENL perspective. By incorporating information about the
speakers' mother tongues, I was able to pinpoint substrate influence, which
was particularly instructive in the case of IndE, where researchers often only
look at Hindi as the most frequently spoken language of the subcontinent. By
contrast, my approach leads to a more sophisticated treatment of substrate
transfer and could also be effectively used for other varieties of English that
developed in highly multilingual contexts (cf. Mohr 2016, 166–167, who mentions the issue for the African context).

The analyses have shown that the structures of the substrate languages play
a key role in the development of the functions of *must*. Speakers of HKE and
SgE whose substrate languages encode deontic and epistemic modalities in

different forms were shown to be less likely to use epistemic *must*. The same is true for IndE speakers with an Indo-Aryan language background. The English varieties spoken by these speakers have a hybrid structure. They use *must* in both functions as 'pre-structured' by the input but as a result of inheritance from the structure of the substrate languages strongly prefer it in its deontic function. This means BrE adds epistemic and deontic *must* to the feature pool, while the substrate languages add an epistemic adverb and a deontic modal verb. The superstrate form is then selected but altered in the competition-and-selection process by restricting its function to deontic modality through the influence of the substrate languages. After this process of bricolage, *must* enters the structure of the new variety as a hybrid construction with the form inherited from the superstrate and the function taken over from the substrate languages. By contrast, IndE speakers with a Dravidian language background show no deontic bias for *must* because their first languages also encode epistemic and deontic modalities in one form. Hence, speakers of Dravidian languages feed a form with both readings into the pool, which matches both functions of *must* in the superstrate. As a result, both readings surface in IndE.

On the basis of these findings, it would be interesting to extend the analysis to other ESL varieties, for example to PhilE. Given that ICE-PHI provides metadata about the speakers, including information about their mother tongues, a study of this kind could be realised on the basis of ICE. It would also be compelling to analyse the functions of *must* in multilingual countries from other regions of the world, for example African countries such as Tanzania, Nigeria, and Ghana. While the metadata of ICE-EA do not seem well-suited for such an endeavour because they do not include information about the speakers' first languages, the newer ICE-NIG and ICE-GH provide information about the speakers' multilingual repertoires.

Apart from investigations of ESL varieties, an analysis of modal systems in other contact varieties of English might be revealing. It would be intriguing to compare the structures of EFL varieties of learners with typologically different language backgrounds regarding the encoding of epistemic and deontic modality, for example varieties of German learners with varieties of Chinese learners. Furthermore, a look at creoles might also be inspiring. In JamC, for example, two different (though clearly related) forms express epistemic and deontic modality; *mosa* is used to express epistemic modality, whereas *mos* is used for deontic modality (cf. Durrleman-Tame 2008, 31–32).

Apart from varieties of English that have evolved in high-contact situations, low-contact situations also provide interesting areas for the investigation of the distribution of epistemic and deontic *must*. As the literature overview in Section 2.1 has shown, some dialects of native varieties of English show a restriction of *must* to epistemic uses (cf. Trousdale 2003, 277–278; Beal, Burbano-Elizondo & Llamas 2012, 67; Fehringer & Corrigan 2015, 361), which contrasts strongly with the distribution identified in ESL varieties and also standard ENL varieties. These findings suggest that it is worth analysing whether the intensity of language contact proves to be an important factor in the distribution of the functions of *must* in different varieties of English.[1]

To complement the findings about *must*, it would also be worthwhile discovering more about the distribution of the senses of *may*. As the data from WALS in Section 6.2 indicate, only a few languages feature an overlap for both necessity and possibility (cf. Section 1.1), while more languages show a partial overlap, and most languages display no overlap at all. It would therefore be interesting to see whether language contact restructures both necessity and possibility, for example if speakers of IndE with a Dravidian language background also use *may* more often in epistemic function.

The profound influence of the substrate languages on the structure of the modal system in ESL varieties suggests that it may be interesting to include other non-verbal expressions of modality, especially if one considers that the 'verbiness of modality' is a European feature (cf. van der Auwera, Ammann & Kindt 2005, 261). This seems particularly promising, given the observation that the substrate languages of HKE and SgE use adverbs to encode epistemic modality. Such an analysis would be in line with recent directions in the study of English modality (cf. Leech 2013) and would build a bridge to typology (cf. van der Auwera & Plungian 1998).

Apart from regional variation in the use of epistemic modality, the findings also revealed variation in the use of the expressions of strong deontic modality. Interestingly, all ESL varieties were marked by a higher frequency of expressions of deontic modality compared to the ENL varieties. This finding was linked to cultural differences in obligation practices, which may be less marked in cultures with an interdependent construal of self, where individuals do not strive as strongly towards independence from others (cf. Markus & Kitayama 1991). The analysis shows that an independent construal of self is not universal and not even the prevalent form in societies world-wide. Together with the finding about the rather exceptional structure of English regarding the encoding of epistemic and deontic modalities, it clearly indicates that it is problematic to restrict one's view to ENL varieties and their cultures because we might

---

1 It may also be the case that the different functions of English in dialects and ESL varieties play an important role in the distribution of epistemic *must*. In dialects, English is primarily used in informal conversations whereas in ESL varieties English is primarily used in formal conversations.

be inadvertently taking the extraordinary case as a point of reference. This also shows that it is necessary to reflect on the acculturation of English in L1 varieties as well and not only on the cultural impact on the structure of English in L2 varieties. This would ideally happen before applying cultural explanations to ESL varieties that are strongly bound to the ENL cultural context.

The study has also demonstrated that ESL varieties differ from each other in their use of certain expressions of deontic modality. IndE is characterised by a modal system that is largely restricted to the use of the modal *must* and the semi-modal *have to*. It has been argued that the state of the historical input variety may be the reason why the minor variants *have got to* and *need to* are particularly rare in this variety. *Have got to* is also rare in HKE, which might point to the influence of learner mechanisms because learners tend to simplify the system when more than one variant is used for the same function. By contrast, speakers of SgE use the semi-modal *have got to* with a higher frequency that is comparable to the frequency in BrE. It has been argued that the selection of this variant is conditioned by the external ecology of English in Singapore, where it has considerably expanded its function (cf. Section 3.2.3) and is even used for informal conversations, which favour the use of this variant. Another interesting observation has been made with regard to the frequency of *need to* in HKE and SgE. Although *need to* has only recently joined the group of semi-modal verbs in positive polarity contexts, it is quite frequently used in these varieties. A linguistic analysis of their Sinitic substrate languages suggested that the high frequency is probably another product of substratum influence because Cantonese and Mandarin have forms that resemble *need to* syntactically and semantically.

Apart from the differences in the use of the minor variants of the system, all varieties behaved alike in using *must* and *have to* as the main markers of strong deontic modality. Furthermore, all ENL and ESL varieties preferred deontic *have to* over deontic *must*. Cognitive processes have been proposed to explain this universal tendency. It has been argued that the use of *have to* is cognitively less complex because it has fewer exceptions than *must* and can be used in more contexts. This may be the reason why speakers resort to *have to* more often than to *must* in spoken interactions. The widespread use of *have to* in ESL varieties may also be linked to learner mechanisms, as learners prefer forms that are most regular from a language-internal point of view, that have fewer exceptions, and that are more frequently used. This means that the structure of the input variety, i.e. an aspect of the internal ecology, may play a decisive role in the emergence of new varieties (cf. Nesselhauf 2009, 23).

As the brief review of the main findings about regional variation reveals, *must* and *have to* are the main variants of strong deontic modality in all varieties. I therefore focused on the direct competition between the two variants to identify contexts in which *must* is preferred over *have to*. First, I took a closer look at the local competition between the two variants in spoken BrE, HKE, and IndE. The availability of metadata for the three ICE corpora representing these varieties made it possible to analyse the influence of both language-internal and language-external factors on variation. This study represents the first attempt to account for social factors in explaining variation in deontic modality in ESL varieties, as language-external factors have been largely neglected in research so far.

With regard to language-internal predictors, it was shown that IndE demonstrates a preference for *must* after non-generic subjects in the second person (i.e. *you must*). This finding stands in stark contrast to the subject selection of *must* in other varieties of English, where it is often used after third person subjects (cf. Leech et al. 2009, 114 on the subject selection of *must* in ENL). The finding suggests that IndE actually favours *must* in contexts where it would most likely be replaced by the 'more democratic' *have to* in ENL varieties. In terms of the language-external factor 'text type', we can see that HKE and IndE both prefer *must* over *have to* in public dialogues. These different discourse practices have also been ascribed to disparities between obligation practices in different societies. The finding therefore emphasises once again that we need to be cautious about 'importing' cultural explanations from the ENL to the ESL context.

The analysis of the competition between *must* and *have to* in the complete dataset revealed that the language-internal factors 'type of subject' and 'semantics of the verb' are important in the selection of *must* over *have to*. *Must* is more often used in third person contexts and certain verbs are more likely to co-occur with it than with *have to*. These are the lexical verb *be*, 'administrative verbs', verbs that refer to social actions, and verbs of thinking and saying.

It has also been shown that register is a crucial factor in the alternation between *must* and *have to*. More informal registers such as private dialogues favour the use of *have to*, while more formal registers such as academic writing prefer the use of *must*.[2] Furthermore, openness of the specific text type to innovative forms turned out to be an important factor in the alternation. It has been found that reportage, which is considered to be an 'agile' genre (cf. Hundt & Mair 1999, 236), favours the use of *have to* despite its rather formal characteristics. In light of these findings, it is important to include register as

---

2   With regard to this, it is interesting to see that the integrated grammar check in some text processing programs marks instances of *have to* and suggests replacing them with the modal *must* or *should*. This might also have an influence on the maintenance of *must* in more formal text types (cf. Curzan 2014 for the normative power of the Microsoft grammar checker).

a factor in studies on the use of modal and semi-modal verbs (cf. Biber 2004; Bowie, Wallis & Aarts 2013).

An analysis of the influence of the language-external factor 'variety' has shown that HKE is the only variety that behaved markedly differently from BrE regarding the use of deontic *must* and *have to* when several predictors were analysed simultaneously. HKE is marked by a very high frequency of *have to*, which was explained with reference to learner mechanisms. It could therefore be that the idiosyncratic profile of HKE with regard to its use of *must* and *have to* reflects its EFL-like status (cf. Section 3.2.1). As HKE was the only variety whose use of deontic *must* and *have to* contrasted markedly with BrE, it follows that the other ESL varieties do not differ strongly from BrE with regard to their choices between *must* and *have to* in deontic modality when the predictors 'text type', 'semantics of the verb', and 'subject' were simultaneously analysed. However, one of the profound differences between the ESL varieties and BrE concerning the use of *must* and *have to* relates to the impact of the social factor 'age of speaker', as will be explained in the next section.

10.2   Change in the Modal Systems of WE

The apparent-time studies show that the modal systems of the two ESL variet-ies HKE and IndE are also undergoing language change. In epistemic modality, we can observe that *must* is initially on the rise in HKE and IndE. This rise is stronger in IndE than HKE because the structure of the Dravidian substrate languages arguably acts as a catalyst. However, after a while epistemic *must* joins the general decline of the core modal *must*. This pattern resembles the pattern that has been observed in BrE, where it has been argued that epistemic *must* is 'contaminated' by the strong decrease of deontic *must* (cf. Leech et al. 2009, 88). This shows that similar processes of language change are taking place in different types of Englishes.

The same is true for changes in deontic modality, where we have observed that the ESL varieties follow the trend of their native counterparts, i.e. the decrease of the core modal verbs and the rise of the semi-modal verbs, with regard to their use of *must* and *have to*. The youngest female group of speak-ers shows the most extensive use of *have to* in both varieties, which suggests that ESL varieties display the same gender pattern that has been identified for changes from below in ENL varieties. However, a closer look at the gender-specific use of *have to* in IndE shows that females have not always been at the forefront of change and that male speakers adopted the innovative variant ear-lier than female speakers. This pattern of a late female lead was interpreted in terms of changes in the role of women in these societies, where females have not always had access to English. Although a rise in the frequency of *have to* could be observed in the ESL varieties, which indicates that they are undergoing similar restructuring processes as ENL varieties, no corresponding rise could be identified for the semi-modal verbs *have got to* and *need to*.

As these findings are only based on apparent-time evidence, they should be tested on the basis of diachronic databases as soon as they become available. Despite this limitation, it has been demonstrated that the method of using the ICE metadata for identifying recent change in ESL varieties is very effective and should become the conventional method for extrapolating change from synchronic data because it has been shown to produce findings in accordance with real-time evidence and is therefore more reliable than any of the previous methods that have been devised. Applying the apparent-time method to studies of other variables can provide new avenues for future research on ESL varieties, in particular with regard to the analyses of variables that are known to show age-specific variation and/or undergo language change in ENL varieties (e.g. quotative *be like* or the genitive alternation). The results from such studies could throw further light on the validity of Labov's gender patterns for varieties of English that have emerged in different cultural contexts (cf. Labov 2001, 279–283; cf. also Section 4.3.1). The apparent-time findings from IndE at least indicate that their validity is strongly tied to 'Western' gender roles. However, more findings about more variables are needed to confirm this hypothesis.

Age has been analysed as one factor among others in a multivariate analysis of the alternation of deontic *must* and *have to*. The analyses indicate that age turns out to be a significant factor in the spoken ESL varieties HKE and IndE but not in BrE. It has been argued that the process of language change has already come to a conclusion in spoken BrE, where the rise of *have to* has been shown to have come to a halt. By contrast, it is still in progress in spoken HKE and IndE, although it has proceeded further in the former than in the latter. While in HKE only the oldest age group differed significantly from the youngest age group, all age groups behaved significantly differently from the youngest age group in IndE. Furthermore, it has also been observed that IndE shows gender-related variation in language change, whereas HKE showed no interaction between age and gender. As gender differentiation tends to occur in the medial stages of linguistic changes, it has been argued that this supports the impression that HKE has proceeded further in this type of linguistic change because gender differences seem to have neutralised in this variety.

As variation and change are closely linked and diachronic change presupposes synchronic variation, it makes sense to jointly discuss the findings from this section and the previous section. Given that HKE and IndE are undergoing change in spoken language and language change seems to have stopped in spoken BrE, it seems likely that innovations proceed at different speeds through the varieties and are furthermore mediated through register. This means spoken HKE and IndE are still undergoing a reorganisation in the modal system while this change has 'moved on' to other text types in BrE. However, in all varieties *have to* has not yet considerably advanced to more formal registers, where *must* remains the predominant choice. Especially contexts in which *must* is used in formulaic expressions with verbs of saying and thinking have proved to be strongly resistant to change. Nevertheless, even these contexts are not withstanding change, which becomes apparent in the fact that the choice of *must* is no longer categorical in these contexts.

Apart from these particular findings concerning developments in the modal systems of these ENL and ESL varieties, my findings can also be used to refine Schneider's (2007) model because they show that sociolinguistic variation according to mother tongue, age, and gender of the speaker occurs in varieties that have not yet reached Schneider's Differentiation phase. My findings therefore blend in well with Huber's findings about established sociolinguistic variation in the phonology of GhanE, a stage 3 variety, lending support to his claim that "sociolinguistic variation […] has to be expected from early on in the development of a New English" (Huber 2014, 104). The conflict between my findings and the expectations created by Schneider's model probably stems from differences between the nature of the variants that I analysed and those that Schneider envisages in the last stage of his model. It is likely that he has variants in mind that are actively employed for identity functions, which presupposes awareness of the variant and its association with a specific social group on the part of the speaker (cf. Section 11.2.2 for examples with these kinds of variants and also Schneider 2007, 86–87 for more salient lexico-grammatical features). This is not the case with more subtle frequency differences or shifts in frequency, which could only be revealed by means of corpus-linguistic techniques. It is rather unlikely that speakers are aware of frequency differences in the use of epistemic *must* and relate a higher frequency of it to speakers with a Dravidian language background. Similarly, speakers are probably not aware of the changing frequency of *have to* and consequently do not associate its use with young females (cf. Figure 45 in Chapter 7 for an unclear association of the use of *must* with speakers of a certain age band in the questionnaire data).

10.3   Modal System(s) of WE

In ESL contexts, we can observe the emergence of a new modal system as a product of the interaction between the BrE modal system and the modal systems of the substrate languages. The findings show that some parts of the modal system are more heavily influenced by the structures of the substrate languages, while others are profoundly shaped by the structure of the superstrate variety.

In epistemic modality, we have observed that the emerging modal system is characterised by English forms which seem to derive their functions from the substrate languages. This means that the new modal system displays hidden hybridity, with overt English forms carrying covert functions from the substrate languages (cf. Spears's 1982, 850 notion of 'camouflaged forms').

In deontic modality, we can observe that the modal system of ESL varieties seems to inherit the predisposition for language change from the superstrate variety. This squares well with Mair's claim that the 'germ' for changes in the modal system already formed part of the historical input varieties of the New Englishes, which is why all varieties are undergoing the same restructuring process (cf. Mair 2015a, 124). This means the potential for change in the modal system seems to be realised irrespective of the context to which English is transplanted and it seems that even cultural factors do not prevent the germ from 'sprouting' but can only accelerate or slow down its 'growth'. If the trend identified in the apparent-time studies continues in the same direction, it might mean that *must* will decrease further in ESL varieties and that this process will only be slowed down by its high frequency in these varieties, which has been related to the socio-cultural context. However, it also means that *have to*, which is already frequently used in ESL varieties, will become even more frequent. If Mair is right and the English language is undergoing drift in the modal system and the trends identified in the apparent-time studies continue, *must* will continue to decrease most strongly in its deontic sense. This would imply that *must* will move towards monosemy over time, a trend which seems to be well advanced in some low-contact British dialects (cf. Trousdale 2003, 277–278; Beal, Burbano-Elizondo & Llamas 2012, 67; Fehringer & Corrigan 2015, 361). In some high-contact ESL varieties, this scenario is rather difficult to imagine because the influence of the substrate languages has resulted in the development of a deontic bias of *must*. But language change seems to work against the maintenance of this particular trait because it has been shown that HKE also faces a strong decline of *must* in its root use. If the trend continues, a comparatively low frequency of epistemic *must* might still remain as a characteristic trait, however.

The study has shown that regional differences can only be revealed on the quantitative level, suggesting that Nativisation processes take the form of frequency differences at the grammatical level, which can only be identified with the help of corpus-linguistic techniques. This 'quantification' of variation is probably one of the most significant contributions that corpus linguistics has made to the study of WE. Findings produced with the help of these methods have changed our perception of postcolonial varieties of English by showing that very often these varieties are not radically different from ENL varieties, at least not as different as earlier descriptions of these varieties in the form of impressionistic feature lists made us believe. My results regarding changes in deontic modality point in the same direction and inspired by similar debates in creole studies it might therefore be worth reconsidering the question of 'exceptionalism' in the context of ESL varieties. The focus on differences between ENL and ESL varieties probably also stems from the ENL-based perspective on varieties of English, in which New Englishes are negatively defined in terms of their divergence from ENL varieties (cf. Section 2.4). Saraceni aptly calls this perspective on WE 'the spot the difference approach' (2015, 80). Maybe it is time to shift the perspective and take similarities between ENL and ESL varieties more seriously in order to refine our general understanding of language change, not just in English deontic modality.

Despite the emergence of English varieties in markedly different sociohistorical settings, we can see that deontic modality is restructured in a similar way to ENL varieties. This indicates that processes of language change in deontic modality do not seem to be stopped or reversed by the influence of cultural factors. Instead, the influence of culture merely appears to lead to the acceleration or deceleration of linguistic change in strong deontic modality. If this scenario is valid, it is questionable whether cultural explanations such as 'democratisation' that have been proposed in the context of ENL varieties were ever strong enough to actually initiate linguistic changes in the modal system. Even though this cultural explanation was not considered to be applicable to the ESL context, these varieties still exhibit the same restructuring process of the modal system. There are two ways of reconciling this discrepancy. Either the cultural explanations that have been put forward for ENL varieties are indeed transferable to ESL varieties or cultural explanations do not initiate the restructuring process, not even in the ENL varieties. Based on my analyses, I would favour the second line of argumentation and propose that cultural changes are not the trigger for linguistic changes in the deontic domain although they can accelerate or slow down these linguistic processes. For the ENL context, this may mean that cultural changes towards more democratic ways of interaction that have started to run parallel to existing linguistic changes may have accelerated the process of language change, while different obligation practices in ESL varieties may have decelerated the process of linguistic change.

If language-external changes are not the cause of linguistic changes in the deontic domain, the question necessarily arises what then conditions the rise of *have to*. Could it be the case that the English language possesses a dynamic of its own in the reorganisation of the modal system which is independent from external factors? (cf. Sapir's 1921, 150 notion of 'language drift' and Mair's 2015a use of the term in the context of restructuring processes in the modal domain above). If so, what language-internal reasons might have conditioned the rise of *have to*?

The closer look at the historical development of the modal system in Section 6.1 revealed that *must* follows the path from deontic to epistemic modality and shows early epistemic uses in the 14th century. My findings from ARCHER reveal that epistemic *must* is on the rise from 1600 to 1849 and that *have to* starts to increase strongly in frequency in the middle of the 18th century. If there is a causal relationship between these types of changes, it could be that the development of epistemic *must* and its following rise in frequency created an imbalance in the system. *Must* was more and more often employed in its epistemic function, which might have triggered the grammaticalisation of *have* as a new deontic marker. Once this new marker entered the system, it fulfilled the old function of *must*. The structure that has been found in some BrE dialects, where *must* is almost exclusively employed as an epistemic marker today, might support this line of argumentation (cf. Trousdale 2003, 277–278). Furthermore, cross-linguistic evidence suggests that similar restructuring processes have taken place in other languages, where new forms have entered the system, for example in Catalan. Van der Auwera, Ammann, and Kindt's description of the modal system in Catalan suggests that speakers of this Romance language formerly used the modal verb *deure* (< Latin *debēre*) for the expression of deontic modality, which is now restricted to epistemic use, while deontic readings are now expressed by the newer form *haver de* ('have of') (cf. van der Auwera, Ammann & Kindt 2005, 259). Of course, such a hypothesis represents only one way of interpreting the wider implications of the findings and needs to be thoroughly tested by further research.

What is more, we can only arrive at more general hypotheses like these by analysing many instances of how speakers of different varieties use English because interaction between speakers is ultimately the locus of change. The combination of sociolinguistics and corpus linguistics in ESL research can therefore go a long way towards generating new hypotheses about the structure of the English language (cf. also Section 11.2). My particular findings about the modal systems of HKE, IndE, and SgE may be a first step in this direction.

Methodological Implications of the Study

After the thematic conclusion of the study, I will take a step back and discuss its wider methodological implications for the field of corpus linguistics. In particular, I will discuss the contribution of my study to two methodological issues that are of interest to the wider corpus-linguistic community. One of these issues is the debate about small and big data, which has figured prominently in corpus linguistics in recent years. The second issue concerns the interface between corpus linguistics and sociolinguistics.

In Section 11.1, I will critically discuss the commonly held assumptions that small data are necessarily more beautiful and that bigger data are automatically better data with reference to the potential and limitations of the two corpora that represent bigger and smaller data in the study of WE, i.e. GloWbE vs. ICE. In Section 11.1.1, I will add another dimension to the discussion, which is 'richness' of data. Rich data in corpus linguistics can be defined as data that consist of more than simply textual data. For the purposes of this study, the richness of ICE in the form of the metadata was exploited in order to correlate the use of linguistic variants with broad social categories such as age, gender, and mother tongue. In this way, my study combines corpus-linguistic techniques with sociolinguistic approaches.

The interface between the two approaches will be discussed in Section 11.2 by analysing similarities and differences of corpus-linguistic and sociolinguistic approaches to language. While some researchers argue that corpus linguistics and sociolinguistics have drifted apart in recent years, others claim that there is now more room for corpus-based sociolinguistics due to independent developments in the field that have led to a rapprochement (cf. Section 11.2.1). I will evaluate these two positions by reviewing recent studies conducted at the interface of corpus linguistics and sociolinguistics. After that, I will discuss possible ways of pushing the limits of research at the interface (cf. Section 11.2.2).

I will then summarise the main points of the discussion and draw a conclusion about the methodological implications of the study in Section 11.3.

11.1   Small is More Beautiful? Bigger is Better?

The advent of big data such as the *Corpus of Global Web-based English* (GloWbE, cf. Davies 2013) has divided the corpus-linguistic research community into

© KONINKLIJKE BRILL NV, LEIDEN, 2018 | DOI:10.1163/9789004381520_012

broadly two camps, those who believe that smaller corpora are 'more beauti-ful' (cf. Hundt & Leech 2012) and those who believe that bigger data equal better data. In the following section, I will discuss the two general statements with regard to well-known dimensions of corpus design to specify which di-mensions make small corpora more beautiful and bigger corpora better. Apart from size, corpora can be analysed with regard to corpus balance, representa-tiveness, tidiness, and richness, a dimension that I will add to the discussion in Section 11.1.1.

I have already introduced the structure of ICE in Section 4.1. To compare the two corpora, a short introduction of GloWbE is necessary. GloWbE was released in 2013 and has a size of 1.9 billion words and contains language data from 20 different English-speaking countries. It represents six ENL varieties from the United States, Canada, Great Britain, Ireland, Australia, and New Zealand, and 14 ESL varieties from India, Sri Lanka, Pakistan, Bangladesh, Sin-gapore, Malaysia, the Philippines, Hong Kong, South Africa, Nigeria, Ghana, Kenya, Tanzania, and Jamaica. The texts of this mega-corpus come from 1.8 million web pages; 60% of these "from informal blogs, and the rest from a wide range of other genres and text types" (Davies & Fuchs 2015, 1).[1] The aim was to "achieve a roughly 60/40 mix of informal and somewhat more formal lan-guage" (Davies & Fuchs 2015, 4). In terms of size, GloWbE is 150 times larger than all ICE sub-corpora added together (cf. Davies & Fuchs 2015, 25).

The first dimension along which the two corpora can be compared is therefore obviously size. The ICE project currently comprises 16 corpora. Those component corpora that have been completed consist of one million words each. ICE was originally intended to be a database for comparative analyses across varieties of English. Several studies put the idea of ICE as a re-source for the analysis of regional variation across Englishes into effect, for ex-ample large-scale comparative studies on grammatical variation across a wide range of national varieties (cf. Rautionaho 2014; Werner 2014). These stud-ies can therefore draw on a comparatively large database, even though this database might still be too small for lexical studies (cf. Davies 2018, 20). Ad-ditionally, more and more studies have started to use sub-corpora. By using sub-corpora (or even sub-sections of ICE component corpora), the database necessarily becomes smaller, which limits the features that can be studied.

---

1 Note that Loureiro-Porto provides different statistics for the distribution of the two sections on the basis of a word count of the two sections, while the 60/40 distribution is an estimate on the basis of the number of web pages downloaded for each section (cf. Loureiro-Porto 2017, 456). According to her word count, the proportion of blogs is considerably lower than the estimated 60%, with a mean proportion of 44% (cf. Loureiro-Porto 2017, 467).

While the size of one million words is large enough for most types of grammatical studies (cf. Davies & Fuchs 2015, 2), it is too small for phenomena with low or medium frequency, in particular for the analysis of lexical features (cf. also Loureiro-Porto 2017, 448, note, however, that Biermeier 2008 studies word formation processes in New Englishes based on ICE).

GloWbE is about 150 times larger than all ICE-sub-corpora added together and covers more varieties than ICE, with additional sub-corpora for Pakistan, Bangladesh, Malaysia, and South Africa (cf. Davies & Fuchs 2015, 25), which is why size is definitely one of the biggest advantages of GloWbE over ICE. The size of GloWbE makes the analysis of low- and mid-frequency language features possible, "including variation in lexis, morphology, (medium- and low-frequency) syntactic constructions, variation in meaning, as well as discourse and its relationship to culture" (Davies & Fuchs 2015, 1; cf. Davies 2018, 20–28). Recent studies that have made use of the size of GloWbE are Horch's (2017) study on conversion and Terassa's (2018) study on morphological simplification in Asian Englishes.

For the purposes of my study, the use of GloWbE would also have substantially increased the database. This becomes immediately evident if we just compare the frequencies of the modal verb *must* in ICE-IND* and the IN section of GloWbE. In ICE-IND*, we can find 888 tokens of modal *must* compared to 55,121 tokens in the IndE section of GloWbE, i.e. more than 60 times more tokens in GloWbE than in ICE. With such a high number of examples, automatic tagging becomes necessary (or a sample has to be taken, although this would go against the big data idea). Automatic tagging seems to be especially promising for the language-internal factors 'grammatical person', 'verb', and 'verb semantics' in my study (cf. Section 4.3.1). The search for pronouns in L1 or L2 position before the modal or semi-modal verbs may be used to code the grammatical person of the pronoun subjects. Extraction of words in R1 or R2 position as well as a combination of search strings such as *must have been* or *must be* + V-*ing* may be employed to extract the main verbs, whose forms may be lemmatised afterwards. Furthermore, the semantic tags may be retrieved automatically. By contrast, the automatic annotation of language-internal factors for which the context must be taken into account is much more difficult to realise. This is especially true for the annotation of the functions of the modal verbs (i.e. deontic vs. epistemic) and the reference of the subject.[2] Even though epistemic readings of modal verbs typically occur in certain syntactic environments, e.g. with the perfect or the progressive, these contexts are not determinative (cf. (9) and (10) in Chapter 1). What complicates matters further

---

2 Another possibility of specifying meanings of modal verbs in larger databases may be the use of semantic vector spaces (cf. Hilpert and Flach 2017).

is that there are differences in the expression of the perfect, for example in the lexical expression of the perfect with *already* in SgE and the progressive aspect, for example in case of its extended use as an imperfective marker in IndE (cf. Sharma 2009). Similar problems might arise in the annotation of 'subject reference'. Here, variable article use in some ESL varieties (cf. Sand 2004) can cause severe problems when the coding is done automatically. For example, a definite article may be used for nouns with generic reference, such as in (168) (cf. Sand 2004, 290; cf. also (187)).

(168) *The girls* tend to fair [sic!] better in these subjects. (ICE-SIN:W1A-007)

The second dimension along which ICE and GloWbE can be evaluated is 'balance', i.e. the range of text types included in the corpora. In terms of corpus balance one of the strong selling points of ICE is that the majority of texts in ICE represent spoken language (cf. Davies & Fuchs 2015, 26). The availability of spoken language data is especially valuable for variation studies as spoken language is less monitored than written language. Furthermore, the availability of both spoken and written data in ICE allows for the investigation of variety-internal variation according to mode. This makes ICE a valuable database in the recent shift from a focus of intervarietal differences to intravarietal differences in WE, a trend that has for example been identified by Mukherjee and Schilk (2012, 194). The structure of ICE not only makes it possible to analyse variation according to mode but also according to text type. As texts from 32 text types are selected to represent the English variety in its entirety, the ICE corpora can be classified as 'multi-purpose general corpora' (cf. Rissanen 2000, 8).

In terms of corpus balance GloWbE differs strongly from ICE, as it only represents online language. But exactly this register – if one can speak of a homogenous register at all (cf. Biber, Egbert & Zhang 2018) – has been missing from the ICE design so far, which is not surprising given that the design of ICE was finalised at a period of time when computer-mediated communication did not play the role it does now.[3] Today many researchers and project members of the ICE community strongly recommend the inclusion of digital texts in future ICE corpora (cf. Kirk & Nelson 2017; Loureiro-Porto 2017, 468). Loureiro-Porto for example concludes her comparative study on ICE and GloWbE by advocating that

> the future of ICE should include web registers alongside the text types included so far. This would provide a more comprehensive representation

---

3 But note that some ICE corpora include emails such as ICE-JA and ICE-UG in the category W1B (Correspondence).

of the national varieties of English than current versions of both ICE and GloWbE.

LOUREIRO-PORTO 2017, 468

When we analyse the potential of GloWbE with regard to corpus balance for the purposes of the study, we can see that GloWbE would not have permitted me to analyse differences in the distribution of modal verbs according to mode (cf. Chapter 5), as the corpus only includes written text samples. However, the composition of GloWbE with 60% blogs and 40% 'general web pages' still makes an analysis of differences in genre distribution possible. The distribution into more informal blogs and more formal general web pages is supposed to reflect the ICE composition, with 60% spoken language and 40% written language (cf. Davies & Fuchs 2015, 3–4). However, it needs to be taken into account that blogs cannot be equated with spoken language. Peters argues that while the language used in informal blogs may be similar to spoken language on several dimensions, it is not the same as spoken language as "the discourse of blogs is not contextualized like face-to-face conversations or even distanced conversation by phone or radio" (Peters 2015, 42). As neither blogs nor general web pages are part of the common ICE design (cf. Section 4.1), it would be interesting to compare the genre distributions of the modal and semi-modal verbs in the two genres of GloWbE. If the classification of the two genres in terms of their formality is valid and offline and online genres behave similarly, we would expect to find a lower frequency in the use of deontic *must* and a higher frequency in the use of the semi-modal verbs in the blog section than in the general section (but cf. Loureiro-Porto 2017, 459 for findings that indicate similarity between the two sections of GloWbE, at least with regard to the frequency of informal oral linguistic features). Furthermore, it would be interesting to analyse how the GloWbE genres position themselves on the cline of ICE genres from informal private conversations to formal academic writing in terms of their frequencies of modal and semi-modal verbs (cf. Section 4.3.1).[4]

Ultimately, it would also be interesting to analyse modality in the various sub-registers of the broad category 'General' in GloWbE. This would of course presuppose an analysis of the different types of texts included in this section. Such an analysis has been performed by Biber, Egbert and Zhang (2018), who let end-users classify web pages with regard to predefined hierarchical register categories. Their results indicate that most of the texts, i.e. roughly a third, in the general section of GloWbE can be classified as 'Narrative' (including news

---

4 For such an analysis, it would make sense to base the study on more recent ICE corpora such as ICE-NIG to avoid interpreting underlying diachronic differences as genre differences.

reports/news blogs, sports reports, personal blogs, historical articles, fiction, and travel blogs) followed by the category of 'Informational Description (or Explanation)' (including descriptions of things, encyclopaedia articles, research articles, descriptions of people, information blogs, FAQs) with 15% (cf. Biber, Egbert & Zhang 2018, 86–87). The category of 'Opinion' is the next largest category in the general section of GloWbE making up 11% and including reviews, personal opinion blogs, religious blogs/sermons, and advice as sub-registers (cf. Biber, Egbert & Zhang 2018, 86–87). Other more minor register categories are 'Interactive Discussion', 'How-To/Instructional', 'Informational Persuasion', 'Lyrical (Songs/Poems)', and 'Spoken' (cf. Biber, Egbert & Zhang 2018, 86). The largest sub-register in GloWbE is news reports and news blogs, which ties in with Nelson's assumption that newspapers can be more easily found on the internet than other text types such as students' writing, fiction, and business letters (cf. Nelson 2015, 39). Nelson also suggests that administrative writing belongs to those text types that are more readily found on the internet (cf. Nelson 2015, 39), but the findings from Biber, Egbert, and Zhang show that instructional writing only makes up about 2% of the data in the general section of GloWbE (cf. Biber, Egbert & Zhang 2018, 86).

Given the composition of the general section of GloWbE with a large number of texts in the register of reportage, we would for example expect to see a higher probability for the occurrence of *have to* compared to that of *must* in the general part of GloWbE (cf. Section 9.3). In future studies, it would be interesting to analyse regional variation in the composition of the general section in GloWbE. Heterogeneity in text types may have important ramifications for intervarietal comparisons, as some varieties might have more texts from one category than another, which would lead to comparability issues. However, this is not just an issue for the bigger GloWbE corpus, as recent research on the homogeneity of ICE registers has shown (cf. Vetter 2017). Nevertheless, as ICE adopts a more fine-grained distinction than GloWbE, it is probably the case that it less prone to regional variation than GloWbE. Furthermore, it must also be taken into account that the same register might be characterised by different communicative styles in different varieties of English (cf. Biber, Egbert & Zhang 2018, 100–108; cf. also Section 4.3.1 on the more informational and less interactional style of the registers in ICE-IND).

While ICE has an advantage over GloWbE in terms of its balanced design, GloWbE might fare better with regard to the dimension of 'representativeness' when defined in terms of how representative the samples of speakers in ICE and GloWbE are of the population as a whole. The texts in ICE come from speakers who have received their secondary education in English, with the exception of public figures, who have been included irrespective of their

educational background (cf. Greenbaum 1996b, 6). The language data therefore only represent the English variety spoken by a small proportion of the
population in these countries and often do not offer an insight into the more
basilectal end. This is also what Mair observed before the advent of GloWbE.
Even so, it has to be noted that knowledge of English is of course strongly correlated with level of education in these countries.

> [T]he focus of current corpus-based research on New Englishes is very
> much on the Standard English end of the sociolinguistic scale. ICE cor-
> pora document the English of educated users of the language, and not of
> others.
>
> MAIR 2011, 212

Some of the limitations of ICE in this regard are balanced out by GloWbE,
which contains language material that was included irrespective of the social
backgrounds of speakers. This is why GloWbE can probably cover a broader
spectrum of lects spoken in the respective countries (even though access to
the internet and censorship are clearly delimiting factors). However, it has to
be acknowledged that more basilectal data in online corpora are not always in
dicative of the inclusion of a wider range of social groups, as Mair observes in
one of his studies (cf. Mair 2011). He finds a higher frequency of creole forms
in his *Corpus of Cyber-Jamaican* (CCJ) than in the private dialogue section of
ICE-JA but notices that the conclusion that this finding is related to the inclusion of different speakers in both corpora does not seem to be valid, as both
corpora seem to reflect the language use of educated, middle-class speakers
(cf. Mair 2011, 219–221). He therefore concludes that "the same type of speaker
is apparently more ready to draw on JC [sc. Jamaican Creole] when using the
computer keyboard than when speaking in face-to-face interaction" (Mair 2011,
221). It might therefore be the case that online corpora are more representative
of more basilectal ends of varieties but not necessarily more representative of
the wide range of speakers of these varieties.

In terms of representativeness of the English variety in GloWbE, it must also
be acknowledged that the types of texts that can be found in GloWbE represent self-generated content by speakers, for example in the form of blogs. It
may therefore reflect more authentic contexts of English language use (despite
the restriction to online language) than the predetermined categories in ICE.
In Section 4.1, problems involved in finding suitable texts for specific ICE categories were outlined. These problems have to do with the bias of ICE towards
L1 text categories, which may be less representative of language use in L2 contexts. This leads to the fact that certain text types are simply not available in the

L2 country or are not text types in which English is typically used. Private conversations are a case in point given that they are often held in indigenous languages, especially in countries where the majority speaks a common language. For the ICE-HK component for example, corpus compilers tried to tackle this issue by recording conversations with a native speaker of English to elicit conversations in English rather than in Cantonese. The self-generated content in GloWbE instead reflects self-chosen contexts of English language use. Moreover, as the webmasters and bloggers were not systematically observed by linguists when they created the web content, issues relating to the observer's paradox might be less problematic in the GloWbE data (cf. Labov 1972, 209). By contrast, the content of some private conversations from ICE clearly shows that speakers are acutely aware of being recorded, which might change their behaviour (and also language), as can be seen in examples (169) and (170).

(169) Just don't laugh yaar so much yeah because that will be recorded (ICE-IND*:S1A-053)

(170) Okay history on on Friday parang it's so weird I'm talking to a tape recorder (ICE-PHI:S1A-017)

While concerns regarding the observer's paradox might be less relevant to the linguistic data in GloWbE, this does not imply that writers in GloWbE use language in the way they would in naturally occurring conversations, given that the language in blogs may be quite stylised.

Furthermore, in terms of representativeness of the corpora, it has to be noted that ICE as a general corpus might be representative of the English variety spoken in the respective countries but not of the more complex linguistic situation in these multilingual countries. As the corpora consist primarily of English texts, they do not accurately portray the pervasiveness multilingual practices such as code-switching (cf. Mair 2015b, 30). Still, an analysis of code-switches also seems to be possible on the basis of the ICE corpora, as switches into the local languages are also attested here, for example in (171) from English into Tagalog.

(171) And then he says <indig> Hindi ko nga ho alam ba't ginaganito nila ako e </indig> (ICE-PHI:S1A-036)

Despite the inclusion of words or even phrases and sentences in indigenous languages in ICE, Mair recommends a fundamental rethinking of corpus design for L2 varieties of English.

> Future corpora of Indian, Nigerian or any other kind of second-language
> English should, unlike the ICE sub-corpora, be conceived as multilingual
> corpora from the very start, and the contact languages with which Eng-
> lish interacts should stop being treated as 'extra-corpus' material.
>
> MAIR 2011, 234

In GloWbE instead, multilingual practices might be more adequately represented, also because longer stretches in the indigenous languages are not treated as extra-corpus material, so GloWbE "does not artificially sanitise the data"
(Mair 2015b, 30), as can be seen in example (172) from the Indian component
of GloWbE.

(172) I want a Punjabi *jatt sona, laraka, aprni marji karan vala* and smart
      (GloWbE-IN, G)

With increasing size, data usually become less tidy (cf. also Horch 2017, 86–87).
Smaller data are often 'tidier' because researchers can rigorously select them
for inclusion (cf. also Hiltunen, McVeigh & Säily 2017). In the case of ICE, texts
were only included if the speaker was classified as a speaker of the variety.
The ICE corpora target speakers who are above 18, have received secondary
education in English, and are 'natives' of the variety (cf. Greenbaum 1996a, 6).

> 'Native' for our purposes means either that they were born in the country
> concerned, or if not, that they moved there at an early age and received
> their school education through the medium of English in that country.
>
> NELSON 1996, 28

Despite this high level of control, some speakers in the corpora do not meet
the criterion of 'being a native of the variety', as has been shown by the inclusion of Australian speakers in the sports commentaries section of ICE-HK
in Section 4.1. While most texts in ICE were carefully selected on the basis of
the speakers' profiles, texts are assigned to a particular variety on the basis of
Google's classification in the case of GloWbE. An important parameter that
is used by Google is the country top-level domain (e.g. ".hk", ".sg"). For sites
that have other top-level domains such as ".com", Google relies on information
about the location of the server, links to the website, and visitors of the website to identify the country of the website (cf. Davies & Fuchs 2015, 4). Despite
the possibility of misidentification, Davies and Fuchs claim that they "have
yet to find a single website whose country has not been correctly identified
by Google" (Davies & Fuchs 2015, 5). The accuracy of classifying web pages by
country seems to be quite high, which means that linguistic data are reliably

assigned to speakers of the variety. However, this procedure is not perfect. Even though a web page as a whole can be correctly assigned to a country, this does mean that all its content has been produced by speakers of the variety (cf. also Davies & Fuchs 2015, 26), for example when speakers of another variety comment on texts; example (173) may be a case in point. The comment is part of the Indian section of GloWbE, even though the writer him- or herself states that he or she is from Guatemala.

(173) I know for sure Guatemalan sinkhole wasn't photoshopped. I saw it live.
      I'm from Guatemala LOL! (GloWbE-IN, G)

Furthermore, some texts do not even seem to have been directly produced by humans but rather represent computer-generated language, as the following example shows.

(174) String – message to be used when validation fails when 'is' param is used
      when validation fails when 'is' param is used (DEFAULT: " Must be is! ")
      tooLowMessage (optional) (GloWbE-IN, G)

While small does not always equal tidy (cf. Section 4.1.1), the general tendency holds, and it can be safely assumed that the careful selection of texts in ICE makes it generally less likely that they include data from speakers who are not speakers of the variety in question. Furthermore, due to the size of ICE, it is easier to acquaint oneself with the data and account for biases within it (cf. Section 4.1.2), something that is much more difficult with bigger databases such as GloWbE, where 'size' takes precedence over 'tidiness'.

Apart from the dimensions of 'size', 'balance', 'representativeness', and 'tidiness', GloWbE and ICE can also be compared with reference to a number of idiosyncratic features. These include the speed in corpus compilation, the date of compilation, the 'synchronicity' of the data, and the processing of corpus data. First, a pragmatic advantage of GloWbE is that its corpus compilation proceeded faster because the internet data had already been publicly available (cf. also Loureiro-Porto 2017, 449–450). The efficiency in corpus compilation becomes immediately obvious when one compares GloWbE's collection period of one month to the years that ICE teams have spent on collecting linguistic data and obtaining copyrights. This clearly shows the efficiency of corpus compilation on the basis of internet data: in one month it was possible to compile a corpus which is more than 150 times larger than all 'traditional' corpora collected over the last 20 years together. Corpus compilation based on publicly available data proceeds faster because copyright clearance may be less of an issue, while consent agreements are usually obtained for every speaker in smaller corpora such as ICE. However, the issue of copyright clearance in itself might raise ethical concerns in bigger corpora such as GloWbE. Even though the data are publicly available, it might not be the case that individual writers would give their consent for the inclusion of their language data in a corpus if they were asked (cf. also Mair 2011, 218 for this ethical dilemma with the data of participants in the discussion forums, and Garcia et al. 2009 for an ethnographic perspective on 'lurking' and the distinction between private and public spaces online).

A second issue concerns the date of corpus compilation and the 'synchronicity' of the data. GloWbE was compiled in 2013, i.e. roughly 20 years after the first ICE corpora, although it has to be stressed that there are also more recent ICE corpora such as ICE-NIG. Furthermore, the data from the web pages were downloaded at one period of time, i.e. in December 2012. Although this does not necessarily imply that the texts were actually written in 2012, as posting dates in forums indicate; the data might still be 'more synchronic' compared to the text data in the ICE project. As more and more ICE teams are joining the ICE project, it now has an internal time gap of 25 years (cf. also Section 4.1).

Finally, another pragmatic selling point of GloWbE is its online interface. Davies stresses the great convenience of GloWbE's interface when he states that "researchers simply enter a word or a phrase into the corpus, and they can then see the frequency in each of 20 different countries" (Davies 2018, 20). Such an interface is not yet publicly available for all component corpora in the ICE project, even though it has already been developed under the name *ICEonline* at the University of Zurich (cf. Kirk & Nelson 2017), the new 'home' of ICE.

As ICE and GloWbE differ with regard to the dimensions of 'size', 'balance', 'representativeness', and 'tidiness', comparative studies that use both GloWbE and ICE are very important for assessing the influence of these differences on research findings. So far, there are only a few comparative studies and they have produced conflicting evidence. In a comparative study on grammatical variation, Heller and Röthlisberger show that studies on ICE and GloWbE yield remarkably similar results, for example in the similar weighting of predictors in the genitive and dative alternation (cf. Heller & Röthlisberger 2015).

Loureiro-Porto's (2017) study also compares findings from ICE and GloWbE for the varieties BrE, IndE, HKE, and SgE with regard to three areas of investigation: (1) frequency and collocational patterns of modal verbs of necessity, (2) the spoken and informal character of the blogs in GloWbE in comparison to the spoken data in ICE, and (3) the vernacular and global characteristics of both corpora.

Her study shows that ICE and GloWbE yield similar findings with regard to collocational preferences of modal and semi-verbs of necessity but differ with regard to the frequencies of these verbs, which Loureiro-Porto attributes to structural differences between the two corpora rather than to the diachronic gap between the compilation dates of the two corpora (cf. Loureiro-Porto 2017, 452–453). With regard to the second area of investigation, viz. the orality and informality of blogs, Loureiro-Porto finds that the frequency of informal oral features such as the discourse marker *you know* is higher in the spoken section of ICE than in the blog section of GloWbE. The frequency of these markers in the blog section of GloWbE is similar to that found in the written section of ICE (cf. Loureiro-Porto 2017, 499–450). Furthermore, Loureiro-Porto does not find a difference in the use of her list of informal oral features between the two sections of GloWbE, i.e. blogs vs. general web pages (cf. Loureiro-Porto 2017, 459). As a third area of investigation, Loureiro-Porto presents a case study on the local and global characteristics of ICE vs. GloWbE by analysing the normalised frequency of 37 local words (e.g. *brahminhood* in IndE or *shophouse* in SgE) and the ratio of Americanisms based on a list of 113 lexical pairs (e.g. *center* vs. *centre* or *car park* vs. *parking lot*). She concludes that "there is a higher probability of finding regional lexical features in ICE than in GloWbE (although, of course, GloWbE yields more occurrences [...])" (Loureiro-Porto 2017, 463). With regard to the ratio of Americanisms vs. Briticisms, she finds that the share of Americanisms is larger in GloWbE than in ICE for all four varieties (cf. Loureiro-Porto 2017, 465). She explains the more 'global' lexical structure of GloWbE in terms of audience design in response to a wider, less locally based audience (cf. Loureiro-Porto 2017, 465).

Based on the differences of findings in most of her case studies, Loureiro-Porto concludes that "the differences between GloWbE and ICE are too pervasive to consider these two corpora equivalent alternatives for any linguistic study" (Loureiro-Porto 2017, 468). More comparative studies on ICE and GloWbE which analyse other linguistic features are needed to assess the impact of the differences in corpus size and balance on research findings.

The discussion has shown that smaller and bigger corpora have their own potentials and limitations and that smaller is not always more beautiful and bigger not always better. The benefits and limitations have to be carefully considered and this process is necessarily tied to the research question at hand. While size can be a very important dimension for the study of low-frequency linguistic features such as lexical ones, it might be less relevant in the analysis of high-frequency linguistic features such as grammatical ones where a smaller corpus such as ICE produces enough tokens for analysis. In my study, size was not the most important dimension when dealing with modal and semi-modal verbs, which are quite frequent. Instead, the possibility of analysing the distribution of these verbs across various text types tipped the scale in favour of

ICE. In other words, 'balance' and especially 'richness' outweighed 'size' with regard to my research question. However, for other types of research questions, GloWbE might be the better choice (cf. Section 11.2.2 for the potential of GloWbE for future sociolinguistic research). Furthermore, a decision between the smaller ICE and the bigger GloWbE does not always have to made, as the corpora complement each other nicely, given that GloWbE includes digital texts, which have not been included in ICE so far. This is why there is a clear incentive for more comparative studies on ICE and GloWbE, which would also help to pool the strengths of both corpora and unite the two camps in an effort to make the most of what is available to us.

11.1.1   Smaller vs. Bigger vs. Rich Data

As the preceding discussion has shown, comparisons between ICE and GloWbE have strongly focused on the dimension of size, more specifically on the size of the textual data. An important dimension that has been missing from the discussion so far is the dimension of data richness. Rich data (also 'thick data') in corpus linguistics can be defined as follows:

> [R]ich data contains more than just the texts; for instance, it may include metadata on prosody and gestures, or written language conventions [...]. This is further supplemented by analytic and descriptive metadata linked to either entire texts or individual textual elements.
>
>   HILTUNEN, MCVEIGH & SÄILY 2017

So far, only a few corpora exist that implement rich data such as gestures. A recent project, the *Corpus of Academic Spoken English* (CASE), is currently being carried out at Trier University of Applied Sciences (cf. Brunner, Diemer & Schmidt 2017). Neither ICE nor GloWbE contains information about prosody and gestures (with the exception of prosodic annotation in SPICE-Ireland). However, what both corpora offer is information about paralinguistic features such as laughter, as examples (175) from ICE-IND* and (176) from the Indian component of GloWbE show, although it has to be noted that we are dealing with different types of data here. While the transcriber added information about paralinguistic features in the case of the first example (*<O> laughter </O>*) from the spoken section of ICE-IND*, the writer of the second example from the Indian subsection of GloWbE added the metalinguistic commentary (*LOL*) him- or herself.

(175) People they go and sit there and they enjoy the whole day after ten O'clock late in the evening only they go back home *<O> laughter </O>* (ICE-IND*:S1A-001)

(176) I know for sure Guatemalan sinkhole wasn't photoshopped. I saw it live.
   I'm from Guatemala *LOL*! (GloWbE-IN, G)

While it can be argued that both ICE and GloWbE are rich in representing paralinguistic discourse features, only ICE has the additional advantage of offering
rich biodata about the speakers in the text. One major drawback of GloWbE
for the purposes of my study was that the available metadata on GloWbE are
restricted to information about the textual data (information about the country, genre, title, and source). Even though it is possible to retrieve information
about the authors of the texts via the URL in some instances, this is not always
the case. What complicates matters further is that some texts are not available anymore, either because the websites are no longer online or because the
access to the content is not freely accessible anymore. This is especially problematic for the replication of studies that take into account the larger context
in their analyses, although they could still rely on the full-text offline version
of GloWbE. Even if the source text is available, this does not guarantee that
we can find information about the writer of the text because some texts are
signed by a body rather than an individual and because bloggers write under
pseudonyms, which do not have to reflect social characteristics of the writers
themselves (even though they may still be interesting from the perspective of
stylistic practices, cf. Section 11.2.2). This means that we have to go a long way
to retrieve information about social characteristics of the speakers or are often
not able to find biographical information at all.

   This methodological difference in corpus compilation has important theoretical implications because the data in GloWbE more strongly dissociate language use from speakers and are therefore comparatively 'faceless' compared
with the data in ICE, which also raises questions of research ethics as the individual whose language use we study is pushed into the background.[5] It is
difficult to assess whether the dissociation of language use from speakers is an
intentional move towards a more 'objectified' and 'de-individualised' database
that abstracts a 'system' from the idiosyncrasies in an individual's behaviour in
line with research practices in statistics or whether it is an unintentional side-
effect of the quantitative turn. Be this as it may, a far-reaching consequence of
the separation of language use from its speakers is that it has produced quite a

---

5   It has to be noted that opponents of this view may adopt the reverse line of argumentation,
    especially with reference to the privacy of research findings on the basis of 'de-individuated',
    i.e. 'faceless' and cumulative, datasets. They could argue that the separation of language use
    from speakers might not raise ethical concerns exactly because individual speakers do not
    surface in studies. But this argument cannot always be used against 'more individuated' da-
    tabases because speakers usually either give their consent for including private information
    or are anonymised in these databases.

number of studies adopting a global rather than local perspective on varieties. The availability of big data has therefore often led to a 'distant reading' of the data, i.e. the adoption of a bird's eye perspective on variation. While the speaker might not surface in the textual data in some big datsets, this does not imply that close reading of the data is prevented because big corpora may still allow us to investigate the personas which speakers construct by exploiting linguistic variation, which also makes them relevant to third-wave type of sociolinguistic corpus-based studies (cf. Section 11.2.2). This means that studies on big data do not generally have to be restricted to analysing variation in the macro-context with quantitative methods but can also analyse variation in the micro-context with qualitative methods (cf. also Friginal & Bristow 2018, 5). Even though these types of studies are rare, it does not mean that they are not possible at a conceptual level. Nonetheless, even if such an approach is taken, an important drawback of GloWbE remains that the personas cannot be directly linked back to the speakers who constructed them. In work on the *Corpus of Cyber-Nigerian* (CCN), this shortcoming was corrected by reading the posts of the most productive participants for sociodemographic information about their locality and gender, with the caveat that self-disclosure might not correspond with reality in some cases (cf. Mair 2013, 266–267).

In contrast to this, a major benefit of the rich metadata in ICE is the possibility of constructing apparent-time scenarios by analysing the distribution of variants across different age groups. As ICE and GloWbE are both synchronic and not comparable, the availability of the ICE metadata may be crucial in bridging the 'diachronic gap' in WE. The working environment for corpus-based diachronic investigations of ESL varieties is currently improving, visible also in the contributions to Collins's (2015) *Grammatical change in English world-wide*. Some diachronic corpora representing ESL varieties are already available and several more are in the making. The compilation of Phil-BROWN (cf. Collins, Borlongan & Yao 2014), for example, has now made the diachronic study of PhilE possible. Furthermore, several diachronic newspaper corpora are available, for example for the diachronic study of HKE (cf. Noël & van der Auwera 2015), and the Englishes spoken on the Bahamas and Trinidad and Tobago (cf. Hackert & Deuber 2015), and BlSAfE (cf. van Rooy & Piotrowska 2015), although these corpora are not representative of the varieties in their entireties (cf. also Leech's 2011 discussion of Millar's findings based on the TIME corpus).[6] Diachronic corpora representing the varieties HKE (cf. Biewer et al. 2014), IndE (cf. Berardo & Calabrese 2012), and SgE (cf. Hoffmann, Sand & Tan 2012) are currently in the making. As these corpora are not yet available, this

---

6   The corpus for BlSAfE also includes fiction apart from newspapers.

study has tried to fill the gap by exploiting the ICE metadata, in particular the information given on age and gender of the speakers in order to analyse ongoing language change on the basis of synchronic data. The distribution across the different age groups helped to identify ongoing language change, and information on gender helped to illuminate its nature, because sociolinguists have shown that typically, different gender patterns occur in changes from above and in changes from below.

Furthermore, the ICE corpora offer the possibility to study the influence of the speakers' mother tongues. It was shown that the information about the speakers' mother tongues provided in the metadata of some ICE corpora can help to refine discussions on substrate influence in varieties of English that emerged in multilingual settings such as IndE by identifying correlations between the use of linguistic features and the particular L1s (cf. Sections 6.2 and 7.1). The information therefore enables the researcher to adopt a much-needed typological perspective on variation in ESL varieties. The richness of metadata is therefore a strong selling point of ICE because they make it possible to integrate broad social categories, which "have not figured prominently in the study of deontic modality" (Tagliamonte & Smith 2006, 369). They therefore allow for a sociolinguistic-cum-corpus-linguistic approach to variation.

11.2   Sociolinguistics and Corpus Linguistics

Variationist quantitative sociolinguistic and corpus-linguistic approaches to language show several similarities. Both fields[7] are interested in the empirical analysis of naturally occurring language data, and both try to find reasons for variation by finding systematic quantitative differences in language use and correlating them with independent variables (cf. also Kendall & van Herk 2011, 1). Variationist sociolinguistics and corpus linguistics therefore share a quantitative approach to researching linguistic variation. In terms of factors contributing to variation, sociolinguistic studies tend to foreground the effect of language-external factors, while corpus-linguistic studies tend to foreground the effect of language-internal factors. While sociolinguists are primarily interested in factors such as 'social class', 'age', and 'gender', corpus-linguists often analyse language-internal factors of variation such as 'animacy', 'final sibilancy',

---

7   Comparing sociolinguistics and corpus linguistics is not a case of comparing like with like, as sociolinguistics can be considered to be a theory or model of language, while corpus linguistics is rather a methodological approach to the study of language (cf. Friginal & Bristow 2018, 4).

or 'givenness' in the genitive alternation. Apart from the quantitative orientation, corpus linguistics and sociolinguistics also share an interest in the influence of context on linguistic choice ('situational variation') in terms of stylistic differences in sociolinguistics and differences according to text types in corpus linguistics (cf. also Romaine 2008, 105; Finegan & Biber 2001, 239–241).

Despite their common interests, there are also considerable differences between the two fields. These differences start with different procedures for data collection. While sociolinguists collect their data in sociolinguistic interviews and with other ethnographic methods, corpus linguists compile authentic language data from natural speech situations without adopting these techniques. Sociolinguistic interviews are aimed at generating a dataset for the analysis of a specific variable, for example the pronunciation of the variable (ing) (cf. Torgersen, Gabrielatos & Hoffmann 2018, 176); whereas corpus linguists collect their data without a specific variable in mind but with the aim of representing the entire variety. Sociolinguistic datasets are therefore often smaller and not fully transcribed. Furthermore, they come from more 'local' contexts compared to conventional corpora. Sociolinguistic datasets usually represent the non-standard speech of a speech community (e.g. Labov 1963 for changes in the onset of diphthongs in the speech community of Martha's Vineyard or Labov 1972 for rhoticity in New York City), while conventional corpora usually represent standard varieties of English (cf. Romaine 2008, 97; Mair 2009a, 40, 2009b, 7; Kendall 2011, 368). Hence, Kendall emphasises that conventional corpora aimed at representing national varieties of English "are by necessity somewhat normative and exclusive – they downplay and/or normalize over the true diversity of language at a national scale" from a sociolinguistic perspective (Kendall 2011, 363). Nevertheless, it must be stressed that there are also corpora that represent non-standard language, such as the *Freiburg Corpus of English Dialects* (FRED). Furthermore, conventional corpora usually sample variability in language "ordered along the dimension of register or genre, not the dimension(s) of social variation" (Kendall 2011, 363). This is why the representativeness of conventional corpora in terms of social characteristics of the speakers needs to be scrutinised before sociolinguistic methods are applied (cf. Section 4.1.2).

Sociolinguistic datasets and conventional corpora also differ in terms of their availability to the public. Sociolinguistic datasets are usually proprietary, while conventional corpora are (usually) available to the public (cf. also Kendall & van Herk 2011, 3). Furthermore, sociolinguists and corpus linguists are also separated by their objects of study because sociolinguists have mainly focused on phonological variation while corpus linguists have primarily dealt with lexical and grammatical variation (cf. Romaine 2008, 101; Torgersen, Gabrielatos & Hoffmann 2018, 176). The differences show that "the methodological toolkit of sociolinguists when investigating phenomena of spoken language has largely been different from the approaches employed by corpus linguists" (Torgersen, Gabrielatos & Hoffmann 2018, 176).

Given the similarities and differences between the two approaches, the question arises as to where the potential for the development of an interface between them lies.

11.2.1   *Potential and Limitations*

The question of an interface between corpus linguistics and sociolinguistics has been discussed by representatives of the two fields. While corpus linguists have asked themselves how sociolinguistic methods can be implemented in corpus-linguistic studies (cf. Mair 2009a, 2009b), sociolinguists have wondered how corpora can be used for sociolinguistic studies (cf. Baker 2010, 1; cf. also Bauer 2002; Romaine 2008; Kendall 2011; Kendall & van Herk 2011; Baker 2014; and recent contributions in Friginal 2018).

Recent discussions about the relationship between corpus linguistics and sociolinguistics come to different conclusions concerning the potential for sociolinguistic corpus research or corpus-based sociolinguistics. Mair and Torgersen, Gabrielatos, and Hoffmann maintain that there are new possibilities for studies at the interface of corpus linguistics and sociolinguistics (cf. Mair 2009b, 7–8; Friginal & Bristow 2018, 6; Torgersen, Gabrielatos & Hoffmann 2018, 176). Mair argues that studies at the interface have been facilitated by recent developments in both fields: on the one hand, the compilation of non-standard and spoken language corpora, on the other hand, a broadening of research interests in sociolinguistics, with an increasing interest in written language, public speech, and computer-mediated communication (cf. Mair 2009b, 7–8). He therefore argues that

> [t]he successive widening of the database both in corpuslinguistics and in sociolinguistics has led to a blurring of formerly fixed boundaries and the emergence of a contact zone between the two subfields.
>
> MAIR 2009b, 8

Kendall instead does not see an expansion of this 'contact zone' but rather a growing divergence between the two fields. He argues that sociolinguistics has diverged more widely from corpus linguistics in recent years because of increased interest in 'third-wave' type of studies (cf. Kendall 2011, 370). In his line of argument, he refers to Eckert's (2012) account of the development of variationist sociolinguistics, in which she categorises studies in the field into three broad progressive tendencies ('waves'). The first wave is characterised by studies that correlate linguistic variation with broad static social categories such as social class (cf. Eckert 2012, 88–91). The second wave analyses more local categories that establish the macro-categories of the first wave with the help of ethnographic methods (cf. Eckert 2012, 91–93). The third wave focuses on interactive stylistic practices and therefore places more emphasis on the agentive role of the speakers in constructing personas by drawing on linguistic variation (cf. Eckert 2012, 93–97). Kendall argues that sociolinguistics has recently drifted away from corpus linguistics with the trend towards more 'third-wave sociolinguistic studies', which are usually qualitative in orientation rather than quantitative (cf. Kendall 2011, 369).

This leads him to conclude that corpus linguistics and sociolinguistics were closer to each other before this recent trend, stating that "[f]irst wave, and to a lesser extent second wave, sociolinguistic research would appear to fit comfortably within a corpus linguistics mold" (Kendall 2011, 369). Several studies including this study can be classified as corpus-linguistic sociolinguistic studies of the first wave. Three other studies may serve as an example of this type of study here. Nevalainen (2000) analyses the role of gender in the *Corpus of Early English Correspondence* (CEEC) in the generalisation of the object pronoun form *you*, the diffusion of the third person singular suffix, and the replacement of multiple negation with single negation and non-assertive indefinites. Säily (2011) analyses gender-based variation in the productivity of the suffixes *-ness* and *-ity* in the demographic part of the BNC. Another study that can be classified as a corpus-based sociolinguistic study of the first wave is Nokkonen's (2010) study on *need to*, which investigates the role of age, gender, and social class on the use of the semi-modal verb. Apart from these studies on the ENL variety BrE, there are also a number of studies of this kind on ESL varieties, as Section 4.1.1 has shown. These studies attest to the possibility of conducting research at the interface of corpus linguistics and sociolinguistics of the first wave, i.e. by correlating the use of linguistic variants with broad social categories. But the question arises whether sociolinguistic studies of the second or third wave are also possible on the basis of corpora.

Research on stylistic variation in settings where English competes with a local pidgin or creole (English as a second dialect, ESD) has shown that corpus-based research in the spirit of third-wave sociolinguistics is generally possible. Deuber (2014) for example analyses stylistic variation along the creole continua of Jamaica and Trinidad with regard to grammar, and shows – among other things – how speakers draw on different variants from the continua to construct their identities. While her study is based on spoken text categories from ICE-JA and ICE-Trinidad & Tobago (ICE-T&T), Hinrichs (2006), Mair (2011), and Moll (2015) analyse style-shifting between JamE and JamC in computer-mediated language in the framework of third-wave sociolinguistics.

Furthermore, Mair (2013) analyses the use of Nigerian Pidgin English in the *Corpus of Cyber-Nigerian* (CCN), which is built from posts to a discussion forum. He views the discussion forum as a virtual community of practice and analyses the way in which participants use (and apparently also learn) pidgin here (cf. Mair 2013, 268–271). He also studies what kind of language ideologies prevail with regard to NigE and how speakers' language use conflicts with their language ideologies (cf. Mair 2013, 272–274).

As the brief overview here and in Section 4.1.1 on sociolinguistic corpus-based studies on WE has shown, most studies integrating sociolinguistic approaches in corpus linguistics on varieties of English can be classified as first-wave type sociolinguistic studies, as they correlate (mostly grammatical) variants with broad social categories, such as age and gender. However, a few examples of third-wave type of corpus-based studies can also be found, even though they have developed a strong focus on ESD varieties.

11.2.2 *Pushing the Limits*

Having discussed the potential and limitations of research at the interface of corpus linguistics and sociolinguistics by reviewing and classifying existing studies, I would like to consider how the limits of a corpus-based sociolinguistic approach can be pushed. Generally, two ways of extending the 'sweet spot' of this approach are conceivable: (1) broadening the objects of investigation and (2) adopting sociolinguistic methods of the second and third wave in corpus-based studies.

With regard to the first of these, two corpus projects deserve special mention that may facilitate the sociolinguistic analysis of areas beyond grammar. These are SPICE-Ireland (cf. Kallen & Kirk 2012) and ICE-NIG (cf. Wunder, Voormann & Gut 2010). SPICE-Ireland (*Systems of pragmatic annotation in ICE-Ireland*) is a richly annotated version of the spoken component of ICE-IRE. It provides pragmatic annotations of utterances by identifying the illocutionary force of every utterance on the basis of an analysis of the context of the respective utterance (cf. Kallen & Kirk 2012, 35). The annotation is based on Searle's (1976) classification of illocutionary acts. Apart from the annotation of speech acts, SPICE-Ireland also features prosodic annotation for some texts, in particular marking of intonation contours. SPICE-Ireland marks pitch accents of utterances and intonational phrase boundaries (cf. Kallen & Kirk 2012, 36). Additionally, SPICE-Ireland provides annotation of discourse markers such as phrasal discourse markers (e.g. *you know*), lexical discourse markers (e.g. *sure*), and phonological discourse markers (e.g. *oh*) (cf. Kallen & Kirk 2012, 41–51). Furthermore, SPICE-Ireland also offers annotations of quotative verbs and makes available tags that indicate the end of sentences (cf. Kallen & Kirk 2012,

54–58). These include variable tags (such as question tags as *isn't it* or sentence tags as *do you know*), invariant tags (such as *yeah*, *okay*, *right*), and vocative tags (such as personal names, terms of endearment).

If we assess the sociolinguistic potential of SPICE-Ireland, we can see that it raises several possibilities for sociolinguistic studies. The rich pragmatic annotation of SPICE-Ireland in terms of speech acts can for example be used to address the sociolinguistic topic of politeness by analysing differences in pragmatic conventions across varieties of English (cf. Ronan & Schneider 2017). Furthermore, the prosodic annotation could be used to account for social variability in prosody, a topic that has for example recently received attention in sociolinguistic research on ethnicity (cf. Newmark, Walker & Stanford 2016). The strongest potential for sociolinguistic analysis probably lies in the annotation of quotative verbs, which have proved to be a fruitful area of research in sociolinguistics (e.g. Tagliamonte & Hudson 1999; Buchstaller 2014). The annotation of all quotative verbs is clearly an asset, as it allows researchers to study the competition between different quotative verbs, including those that only rarely occur in quotative function. This makes it possible to analyse the competition between quotative verbs with regard to language-internal factors such as 'person of the subject', 'tense/time', and 'content of the quote'. Furthermore, the availability of metadata about the age and gender of speakers facilitates the analysis of language-external factors as well. The quotative system has also sparked an interest in corpus-based studies on varieties of English, visible in Höhn's (2012) study on quotative *be like*, *go*, and *say* in IrE and JamE, or in Mair's (2009a) study on quotative *be like* in ICE-JA. It would furthermore be interesting to analyse the quotative system in ESL (rather than ESD) settings. To illustrate the potential for studies of this kind, the quotative system of ICE-PHI can serve as an example. In PhilE, we can see that the quotative system has also been restructured, as *be like* competes with *say* and zero forms but also with *tell* as a quotative verb (cf. (177); cf. also D'Arcy 2013, 497). Furthermore, Tagalog quotative verbs are also employed as matrix verbs or English matrix verbs occur with quotations in Tagalog, e.g. (178) and (179).

(177) She *tells* me don't involve my boy friend [sic!] because it doesn't involve him (ICE-PHI:S1A-004)

(178) <indig> *Sabi ko* </indig> I hope I don't meet him (ICE-PHI:S1A-036)

(179) Uh hum so I *said* <indig> ano ba </indig> (ICE-PHI:S1A-006)

The examples show that the quotative system in this ESL variety is also characterised by a competition between local, localised (*tell*), and global quotatives.

An analysis of the repertoire of quotatives by individual speakers may lead to further insights into the functional distinction between these quotatives in the potential negotiation of a local vs. a global identity. Speaker $A in the text file S1A-015 might prove to be an interesting example. She uses *be like* with a very high frequency, which is probably a stylistic move with the aim of evoking an image of a 'young' and 'hip' identity fitting quite well with her profession as a DJ. Based on the remark by Loureiro-Porto on the more global outreach of blogs in GloWbE compared to private conversations in ICE, it would be interesting to see whether the quotative systems represented in GloWbE are indeed characterised by a higher frequency of quotatives such as *be like* than those in ICE (cf. Loureiro-Porto 2017, 465). Such an analysis of course needs to take into account that the findings might indicate diachronic differences rather than differences in the structure of the data if data from older ICE corpora are compared with data from GloWbE.

The second project that has enormous potential for corpus-based sociolinguistic studies of regional varieties of English is the ICE-NIG project. It is the first ICE corpus to make the audio files of the spoken files available to the research community and to provide time-aligned transcriptions of the audio data (cf. Wunder, Voormann & Gut 2010). The availability of the audio files and the transcriptions make fine-grained sociophonetic analyses of regional accent features possible, for example with tools such as Praat (cf. Schützler 2015 for an analysis of Scottish StE). The digitisation of the sound files of other ICE corpora is currently being debated and could lead to a growing rapprochement between corpus linguistics and sociolinguistics by facilitating the analysis of phonological variables on the basis of corpora (cf. also Romaine 2008, 110).

Besides making rich data available to the research community, another way of pushing the limits of corpus-based sociolinguistics is by adopting 'second-' and 'third-wave' sociolinguistic methods in the analysis of existing corpora. While it is quite straightforward to devise sociolinguistic studies of the first wave on the basis of corpus data that link the use of linguistic variables to broad social categories (cf. Sections 4.1.1 and 11.2.1), it is probably more difficult to realise second- and third-wave type of sociolinguistic studies on the basis of corpora.

Sociolinguistic studies of the second wave adopt ethnographic methods to investigate linguistic variation in locally-defined categories (cf. Eckert 2012, 91). The question is whether these types of studies can be carried out on the basis of corpus data at all. While it is conceivable that ethnographic methods such as participant observation can be used in the compilation of corpora whose linguistic data are collected in face-to-face contact, it is much more difficult to conduct this type of ethnographic study based on computer-mediated language use without personal contact with the speakers/writers. This means that traditional ethnographic methods have to be adjusted for the study of on-line communities and their (stylised) language use (cf. Garcia et al. 2009 for a discussion of ethnography on the internet; cf. also Androutsopolous 2006, 423–425). This way, it might for example become possible to identify differences in language use by contributors to online forums that are related to meaningful categories emerging in the forum. Furthermore, an analysis of language variation in computer-mediated communication from the perspective of social networks might prove to be interesting (cf. Paolillo 2001 for a network approach to language variation in a chatroom). However, it needs to be taken into account that the language used in forums and blogs is often stylised and cannot be equated with an individual's language use in naturally occurring conversations, which has been the prime interest in second-wave type of studies.

A third-wave type of approach to online language use therefore seems to be most promising to account for the stylistic practices of participants in computer-mediated communication. With regard to the representation of a certain identity by exploiting linguistic variation, online communication heavily relies on non-standard spelling. From a sociolinguistic perspective, respellings which index certain social categories may be of special interest, including representations of local pronunciations such as TH-stopping and TH-fronting, non-rhoticity, and representations of the FOOT-GOOSE merger in examples (180), (181), and (182) from the Nigerian component of GloWbE.

(180) The problem *wif* girls *dis* days is *dat dey* want *d* perfect guy *wif* perfect life etc. (GloWbE-NG, G)

(181) U guys talkn against chris did not *undastand* him dat's y; *rememba*, he didn't say it's gud (GloWbE-NG, G)

(182) But wen its sometin *gud*, dey knw how to say all sorts of rubbish (GloWbE-NG, G)

It would be interesting to see which features are recurrently employed by writers to index 'Nigerianness' (or social values other than locality) and together constitute a register of NigE by drawing on the theories of 'indexicality' and 'enregisterment' (cf. Silverstein 2003; Agha 2003; Johnstone, Andrus & Danielson 2006). In the Singaporean context, it is interesting to see that 'Singaporeanness' is often expressed by the use of Singlish. An important part of the Singlish register seem to be discourse particles, in particular *lah*, which is why they in turn can be used to express a Singaporean identity (cf. also Leimgruber 2013, 106).

But it also has to be noted that the use of Singlish features is not only employed to express locality but can also express a range of other social values, as can be seen in example (187) (cf. also Podesva 2011, 45). Investigating WE within the framework of indexicality and enregisterment could add a constructivist perspective on place-making in WE and create an emic counter-narrative against the etic distinction of varieties in terms of political boundaries of the nation state (cf. also Saraceni 2015, 184), which prevails in corpus linguistics. This is also one of the important points made by studies that investigate indexes of 'Jamaicanness' and 'Nigerianness' by speakers from the diaspora (cf. Mair 2011, 2013). In his study on the use of NigE and Nigerian Pidgin English by participants of a virtual community of practice in an online forum, Mair concludes that

> there is no longer a supposedly natural link between Nigerian English and the territory of the nation state Nigeria, or between pidgin and its West African regional and social base.
>
> MAIR 2013, 275

Moreover, by investigating discourses about the constructed local variety, speakers' language ideologies could be unveiled. To illustrate, the following examples from GloWbE can be used (cf. (183) to (187)).

(183) Hong Kong english proficiency is slight back to the stone ages which will hinder if not terminate Hong Kong students to compete in the scientific world. (GloWbE-HK, B)

(184) By default, Microsoft Word uses United States English. You can select British English or any other variety you wish (unfortunately, Hong Kong English is not available). (GloWbE-HK, G)

(185) Some Indians complain that English brings in too much Western thought, but English in India also exports a vast amount of Indian culture and thought [...]. (GloWbE-IN, G)

(186) Singlish is basically chinese people speaking english badly. it is a nonsensical form of english with chinese grammar and intonation ... it is what happens when an uneducated chinese person is forced to write english word-by-word using a chinese-english dictionary. (GloWbE-SG, B)

(187) The sentences in Singlish are usually short, sharp and straight to the point, just like Singaporeans. (GloWbE-SG, G)

Example (183) can best be read as a discourse about falling standards of English in Hong Kong, pointing to the persistence of the complaint tradition in this variety (cf. Section 3.2.1). Example (184) represents the discourse about recognising Hong Kong English as a variety of its own (cf. Section 3.2.1). Example (185) from a web page of an academic online journal dovetails with the discourse about the relationship between the use of English and 'Westernisation' in India (cf. 3.2.2 for its historical roots). The last two examples represent discourses about Singlish. Example (186) is an example of the commonly held deficit view that Singlish is 'bad English', while example (187) points to the identitary function of Singlish (cf. 3.2.3 for the rejection of Singlish by the government vs. the covert prestige it enjoys in the population). From the perspective of indexicality, this example is very interesting because the linguistic structure of Singlish is considered to index the efficiency of Singaporeans.

The brief analysis of these examples reveals that the investigation of linguistic features from the perspective of indexicality and enregisterment in blogs and internet forums in GloWbE may forge an important link between corpus linguistics and sociolinguistics. However, the challenge GloWbE poses to the researcher interested in such an endeavour lies in the fact that researchers have to remain on the level of the persona rather than the speaker, unless they extract sociodemographic information about the speakers from the many sources in GloWbE to link stylistic practices to speakers. Furthermore, language material from one specific blog or discussion forum could prove to be a more valuable database for such an endeavour because it would allow for an investigation in terms of a virtual community of practice, as has been carried out in the case of CCJ and CCN (cf. Mair 2011, 2013).

11.3   Summary and Conclusion

This chapter has discussed the methodological implications of the study with particular reference to two issues, i.e. the question of data size and the interface between sociolinguistics and corpus linguistics.

First, the potential and limitations of the smaller ICE and the bigger GloWbE for studies in WE were assessed (cf. Section 11.1). In terms of the dimension of size, it has been noted that the size of ICE is not necessarily a delimiting factor for the analysis of high-frequency features but rather more so for low-frequency ones. This means that GloWbE will probably become the choice for studies that focus on lexical variation. For high-frequency items instead, GloWbE poses additional challenges to the researcher who will have to implement automatic coding in his or her study. I illustrated difficulties in the area of the coding of aspects of linguistic features which show different patterns in ESL varieties.

The discussion also emphasised that size is only one dimension along which the two corpora can be compared. While size might be an advantage of GloWbE, balance is a benefit of ICE, as it represents a wide range of text types and does not focus only on digital texts. Nonetheless, the electronic texts in GloWbE add an important text type to the study of varieties of English, as digital texts have not been included in the common ICE design so far.

With regard to representativeness, it has been shown that GloWbE might be more representative of the wide range of speakers of the variety and might also be more representative of how English is used by these speakers in self-chosen contexts of use. This characteristic has the potential to redress the bias towards the inclusion of relatively fixed L1 text types in ICE. Moreover, ICE corpora are normative in the sense that they focus on the standard pole and the English variety only rather than considering more basilectal speech and the multilingual repertoires of speakers, while GloWbE is less normative in this regard by including more non-standard and local language material without marking it as extra-corpus material.

Concerning the dimension of 'tidiness', we could observe that bigger data are usually less tidy, for example with regard to the inclusion of speakers who are not speakers of the variety in question in GloWbE. Apart from that, GloWbE and ICE were also compared in terms of the speed in corpus compilation, the date of compilation, the 'synchronicity' of the data, and the processing of corpus data. With regard to the efficiency of corpus compilation, GloWbE was shown to have a competitive edge over ICE, as corpus compilation on the basis of publicly available internet data can proceed much faster. Furthermore, the data in GloWbE are more recent and can be considered to be temporally more homogeneous than the data in ICE. Finally, comparative studies across a wide range of varieties of English are also easier to realise with the convenient BYU interface of GloWbE. Based on the comparison of ICE and GloWbE, it was concluded that the pros and cons of each corpus should be carefully weighed with the research question in mind. Moreover, it was stressed that a decision does not always have to made and researchers should take advantage of the rich resources available to them for the study of varieties of English. Further comparative studies on ICE and GloWbE could also yield illuminating insight into the similarities and differences between the two datasets.

After a comparison of the two corpora along the dimensions of size, balance, representativeness, and tidiness, I introduced the dimension of data richness in Section 11.1.1. Data richness was defined as the availability of data about the textual data. Regarding this dimension, ICE has the special advantage of

providing rich biodata about the speakers of the texts, which allow for the inclusion of these broad social categories in research. It was argued that language
change can be investigated in the absence of diachronic corpora by integrating
information about the age and gender of speakers. Furthermore, information
about the speakers' mother tongues was considered crucial for shedding light
on the factor of substrate influence, which is often assumed but rarely systematically investigated in studies about ESL varieties. The availability of the
rich metadata therefore facilitates the integration of broad social categories in
corpus-based studies on WE.

In the second part of the chapter (cf. Section 11.2), I discussed the relationship between corpus linguistics and sociolinguistics in more detail by outlining
similarities and differences between the two approaches. While corpus linguistics and sociolinguistics have certain similarities, for example the interest in
naturally occurring language data and the quantitative approach to variation,
they also differ in significant ways, for example regarding a focus on phonology
in sociolinguistics vs. a focus on grammar in corpus linguistics or the analysis
of language-external factors of variation in sociolinguistics vs. the analysis of
language-internal factors of variation in corpus linguistics.

In Section 11.2.1, I showed that researchers have different opinions about the
current possibilities for research at the interface of corpus linguistics and sociolinguistics. Some researchers believe that there is increasing potential for
work at the interface of corpus linguistics and sociolinguistics, while others
believe that there is a growing alienation between the two fields. I have shown
that two types of studies can be identified at the interface so far. The first type
includes studies that analyse grammatical variation by correlating variants
with broad social categories ('first wave'). The second type of studies, focus on
stylistic practices, in particular in the use of English along an English-based
pidgin or creole. Most of these studies have explored variation along the lines
of third-wave sociolinguistics on the basis of computer-mediated communication, which is why they attest to the ongoing rapprochement of the two fields.

After identifying the status quo, I discussed ways in which research at the
junction of corpus linguistics and sociolinguistics can be extended further in
Section 11.2.2. First, I identified possibilities of expanding the objects of investigation in corpus linguistics, for example by making use of the possibilities
corpus projects such as SPICE-Ireland and ICE-NIG offer. I claimed that the
pragmatic annotation of SPICE-Ireland and the availability of audio files of
texts in ICE-NIG may be crucial resources for developing corpus-based sociolinguistic studies that go beyond grammar by permitting the investigation of
pragmatic and phonological variation in WE. As a second way of pushing the
limits of corpus-based sociolinguistics, I investigated possibilities of conducting

corpus-based research with second- and third-wave sociolinguistic approaches in mind. I showed that while GloWbE does not permit the integration of speaker biodata in analyses, it can still be used to analyse stylistic practices of speakers in the expression of aspects of their identities. The brief analysis of non-standard spellings and language ideologies in online communication illustrated the potential for applying recent sociolinguistic theories such as indexicality and enregisterment to corpus data of WE and forging the link between corpus linguistics and sociolinguistics.

To conclude, one might speculate that my study is one that could constitute an early study in corpus-based sociolinguistics once the field becomes established in the future because it combines earlier approaches of both fields in the shape of a grammatical study on small data with a first-wave approach to variation. Nonetheless, it may be an important step in the development of the field as the basis for future corpus-based studies that go beyond grammar, beyond small data, and beyond sociolinguistic variation according to broad social categories. I therefore believe that an exciting time lies ahead for corpus-based sociolinguistics in the study of varieties of English.

Appendices

Chapter 3

TABLE 13   Number of speakers aged 5 and over by usual language/
            dialect (Hong Kong Census of Population 1991, Census
            and Statistics Department) (cf. Figure 6)

	Number of speakers
Cantonese	4,583,322
English	114,084
Fukkien	99,045
Hakka	84,134
Chiu Chau	72,812
Putonghua	57,577
Other Chinese dialects	52,210
Others	34,398
Shanghainese	34,078
Sze Yap	22,415
Japanese	8,895
Filipino	5,939

TABLE 14   Language attitudes towards IndE (cf. Figure 7)

Statement	strongly disagree (1)		disagree (2)		neither disagree nor agree (3)		agree (4)		strongly agree (5)		Total	
1	2%	(1)	17%	(9)	4%	(2)	60%	(31)	17%	(9)	100%	(52)
2	0%	(0)	13%	(7)	13%	(7)	60%	(32)	13%	(7)	100%	(53)
3	4%	(2)	25%	(13)	10%	(5)	41%	(21)	20%	(10)	100%	(51)
4	8%	(4)	26%	(14)	15%	(8)	43%	(23)	8%	(4)	100%	(53)
5	0%	(0)	22%	(11)	22%	(11)	49%	(25)	8%	(4)	100%	(51)
6	8%	(4)	8%	(4)	19%	(10)	53%	(28)	13%	(7)	100%	(53)
7	21%	(11)	38%	(20)	17%	(9)	19%	(10)	4%	(2)	100%	(52)
8	13%	(7)	38%	(20)	25%	(13)	19%	(10)	4%	(2)	100%	(52)
9	2%	(1)	12%	(6)	40%	(21)	37%	(19)	10%	(5)	100%	(52)

TABLE 15   Ten most frequently spoken mother
                tongues in India (India Census of
                Population 1991, Government of India,
                Ministry of Home Affairs) (cf. Figure 8)

	Number of speakers
Hindi	233,432,285
Bengali	66,552,894
Telugu	65,900,723
Marathi	62,421,442
Tamil	52,886,931
Urdu	43,358,978
Gujarati	40,335,889
Kannada	32,590,177
Malayalam	30,325,637
Oriya	27,586,476
English	178,598

TABLE 16   Resident population aged 5 years and above
                by language most frequently spoken at home
                (Singapore Census of Population 1990, Singapore
                Department of Statistics) (cf. Figure 10)

	Number of speakers
Chinese dialects	949,264
Mandarin	567,041
English	451,051
Malay	341,825
Tamil	69,395
Other Indian languages	15,658
Others	2,318

Chapter 4

TABLE 17   Representativeness of spoken ICE-HK with regard to the social
dimension age as measured against data from the 1991 Census (cf. Figure 15)

Age	ICE-HK	1991 Census
17–25 | 20–24	243,461 (31%)	430,199 (11%)
26–35 | 25–34	142,366 (18%)	1,178,288 (30%)
36–45 | 35–44	220,064 (28%)	891,032 (22%)
46–55 | 45–54	133,000 (17%)	487,658 (12%)
56–60+ | 55–60+	35,705 (5%)	973,546 (25%)
Total	774,596 (100%)	3,960,723 (100%)

TABLE 18   Representativeness of spoken ICE-HK with regard to the social dimension gender
as measured against data from the 1991 Census (only people aged 20 or above)
(cf. Figure 17)

	Female	Male	Total
ICE-HK	354,904 (46%)	422,167 (54%)	777,071 (100%)
1991 Census	1,961,215 (50%)	1,999,508 (50%)	3,960,723 (100%)

TABLE 19   Representativeness of spoken ICE-IND* with regard to the social dimension age
as measured against data from the 1991 Census (cf. Figure 19)

	ICE-IND*	1991 Census
18–25	78,325 (16%)	137,692,515 (29%)
26–33	79,389 (16%)	93,160,375 (20%)
34–41	91,902 (19%)	87,619,819 (18%)
42–49	70,439 (14%)	47,592,356 (10%)
50+	143,840 (30%)	52,586,094 (11%)
60+	17,887 (4%)	35,607,475 (7%)
70+	3,167 (1%)	14,699,654 (3%)
80+	2,393 (0%)	6,374,511 (1%)
Total	487,342 (100%)	475,332,799 (100%)

TABLE 20   Representativeness of spoken ICE-IND* with regard to the social dimension
            gender as measured against data from the 1991 Census (only people aged 18 or
            above) (cf. Figure 21)

	Female		Male		Total	
ICE-IND*	207,810	(32%)	442,314	(68%)	650,124	(100%)
1991 Census	231,447,438	(48%)	248,580,519	(52%)	480,027,957	(100%)

TABLE 21   Corpus balance with regard to the social dimension mother
            tongue in the spoken section of ICE-IND* (cf. Figure 22)

Languages in ICE-IND*	Number of words	
Marathi	94,757	(24.6%)
Kannada	75,465	(19.6%)
Hindi	37,853	(9.8%)
Tamil	36,787	(9.5%)
Malayalam	29,487	(7.7%)
Telugu	26,905	(7.0%)
Punjabi	23,023	(6.0%)
Konkani	20,616	(5.3%)
Bengali (Bangla)	9,683	(2.5%)
Oriya	6,785	(1.8%)
Gujarati	5,246	(1.4%)
Urdu	4,437	(1.2%)
Kashmiri	3,347	(0.9%)
Manipuri	2,365	(0.6%)
Sindhi	2,298	(0.6%)
English	1,348	(0.3%)
Naga	1,280	(0.3%)
Angami	1,069	(0.3%)
Tulu	727	(0.2%)
Assamese	722	(0.2%)
Khasi	672	(0.2%)
Nepali	475	(0.1%)
Total	385,347	(100%)

Questionnaire
Connotations of the (semi-)modal verbs of obligation and necessity in Indian English

Beke Hansen

March 2015

Researcher: Beke Hansen, hansen@anglistik.uni-kiel.de
Institution: English Department, University of Kiel, Germany

Description:
This questionnaire is part of my PhD project, which deals with grammatical variation in the English varieties spoken in Singapore, Hong Kong, and India. The goal of this questionnaire is to find out what speakers of these English varieties associate with the use of certain modal and semi-modal verbs and investigate whether there are cultural differences in the connotations of these auxiliary verbs.

Participants are asked to fill in the questionnaire, which includes evaluation of statements tasks, discourse completion tasks, and word association tasks. It takes approximately 15 minutes to complete the questionnaire.

Privacy:
The data collected in this questionnaire will be used for academic purposes only and treated anonymously.

Statement of Consent:
I agree to participate in the above-named research project under the terms described above. I understand that my participation is entirely voluntary, and that I have the right to withdraw from participation at any time. If I have questions, comments, or concerns about this research project, I may contact the researcher at any time.

❑ I agree to the above-named terms.

In answering the questions, please give the answer that applies to your own speech, not the speech of others, or what you think your speech "should" be. There are no right or wrong answers.

Part 1: Varieties of English
Please read each statement below and then use the scale to indicate your personal degree of agreement or disagreement with each statement. Please select only one response for each statement.

1. Varieties of English					
	strongly disagree	dis-agree	neither agree nor disagree	agree	strongly agree
a) Indian English is a standard variety of English such as Australian English, Canadian English or American English.	❑	❑	❑	❑	❑
b) Indian English is different from British English.	❑	❑	❑	❑	❑
c) Indian English originates from the Indian people, so it can give me a feeling of belonging.	❑	❑	❑	❑	❑
d) As an Indian, I try to speak British English.	❑	❑	❑	❑	❑
e) American English is more colloquial than British English.	❑	❑	❑	❑	❑
f) As an Indian, I try to speak Indian English.	❑	❑	❑	❑	❑
g) I do not feel that I belong to any English-speaking community, because English is not my mother tongue.	❑	❑	❑	❑	❑
h) As an Indian, I try to speak American English.	❑	❑	❑	❑	❑
i) British English is more correct than American English.	❑	❑	❑	❑	❑

Part II: Obligations in the Social Context

Imagine you are in the situation described below. Indicate which statement describes your thoughts best. Please select only one response.

2. Situation A: Your parents tell you to go abroad for one year. What would you think?	
a) I think they want me to go abroad because they think that I benefit from it.	❑
b) I think they want me to go abroad because they think that they benefit from it.	❑
c) I think they want me to go abroad because they think that they and I benefit from it.	❑
d) I think they should not tell me what to do because I am old enough to decide on my own.	❑
e) I think I will go abroad because I have got the opportunity to do so.	❑

Part III: Discourse Completion Tasks

Imagine you are in the situations described below and interact with an English-speaking person from India. Please write down what you would say in each situation.

3.	Situation B: You are at home with your flatmate and the doorbell rings. It's 3 o'clock in the afternoon and one of your friends wanted to come around at 3 o'clock. What would you say to your flatmate as the doorbell rings?

_____

_____

4.	Situation C: Your roommate had a party yesterday and left the kitchen in a mess. You want to cook with your friends. What would you say to your roommate to make him/her tidy up the kitchen?

_____

_____

5.	Situation D: You are shopping with one of your friends and your friend tries on a shirt and is unsure whether it's a good idea to buy that shirt. You think it looks good on him/her. What would you say to your friend to make him/her buy the shirt?

_____

_____

Part IV: Word Associations

Please indicate which associations you have for each verb. You can choose more than one association for each verb.

6. Word Associations					
a) *must*	❑ American	❑ British	❑ formal	❑ informal	❑ spoken	❑ written
b) *have to*	❑ American	❑ British	❑ formal	❑ informal	❑ spoken	❑ written
c) *have got to*	❑ American	❑ British	❑ formal	❑ informal	❑ spoken	❑ written
d) *'ve got to*	❑ American	❑ British	❑ formal	❑ informal	❑ spoken	❑ written
e) *gotta*	❑ American	❑ British	❑ formal	❑ informal	❑ spoken	❑ written
f) *need to*	❑ American	❑ British	❑ formal	❑ informal	❑ spoken	❑ written

Part v: Personality Characteristics

Please rank the personality characteristics of each person based on the utterances given.
Example: If you think the speaker of the utterance "You must help me out with this!" is very
friendly, you would tick '5'. If you think the speaker is unfriendly but not very unfriendly,
you would tick '2'.

7.	Speaker 1: "You must help me out with this!"

	1	2	3	4	5	
unfriendly	❑	❑	❑	❑	❑	friendly
insincere	❑	❑	❑	❑	❑	sincere
not helpful	❑	❑	❑	❑	❑	helpful
poorly educated	❑	❑	❑	❑	❑	highly educated
not proficient in English	❑	❑	❑	❑	❑	proficient in English
not authoritative	❑	❑	❑	❑	❑	authoritative
close	❑	❑	❑	❑	❑	distant
insecure	❑	❑	❑	❑	❑	self-confident
inexperienced	❑	❑	❑	❑	❑	experienced
young	❑	❑	❑	❑	❑	old

8.	Speaker 2: "You have to help me out with this!"

	1	2	3	4	5	
unfriendly	❑	❑	❑	❑	❑	friendly
insincere	❑	❑	❑	❑	❑	sincere
not helpful	❑	❑	❑	❑	❑	helpful
poorly educated	❑	❑	❑	❑	❑	highly educated
not proficient in English	❑	❑	❑	❑	❑	proficient in English
not authoritative	❑	❑	❑	❑	❑	authoritative
close	❑	❑	❑	❑	❑	distant
insecure	❑	❑	❑	❑	❑	self-confident
inexperienced	❑	❑	❑	❑	❑	experienced
young	❑	❑	❑	❑	❑	old

9.	Speaker 3: "You've got to help me out with this!"						

	1	2	3	4	5	
unfriendly	❑	❑	❑	❑	❑	friendly
insincere	❑	❑	❑	❑	❑	sincere
not helpful	❑	❑	❑	❑	❑	helpful
poorly educated	❑	❑	❑	❑	❑	highly educated
not proficient in English	❑	❑	❑	❑	❑	proficient in English
not authoritative	❑	❑	❑	❑	❑	authoritative
close	❑	❑	❑	❑	❑	distant
insecure	❑	❑	❑	❑	❑	self-confident
inexperienced	❑	❑	❑	❑	❑	experienced
young	❑	❑	❑	❑	❑	old

Part VI: Personal Information

10.	Personal Information

Name	_____
Age	
Gender	M / F
Nationality	_____
Ethnicity	_____
Mother Tongue(s)	_____
Occupation	_____
Email Address	_____

Thank you for your participation!

If you have any questions, suggestions or concerns, do not hesitate to contact me:

Beke Hansen
(Signature)
(Contact details)

If you have any questions or comments regarding this questionnaire, please write them down in the space provided. I appreciate your feedback.

_____
_____
_____
_____
_____

FIGURE 61   Structure of questionnaire A.

Part I (as above)

Part II: Discourse Completion Tasks

Imagine you are in the situations described below and interact with an English-speaking person from India. Please write down what you would say in each situation.

1.	Situation A: You are at home with your partner and the doorbell rings. It's 3 o'clock in the afternoon and one of your friends wanted to come around at 3 o'clock. What would you say to your partner as the doorbell rings?

_____

_____

2.	Situation B: Your son had a party yesterday and left the kitchen in a mess. You want to cook dinner for your family. What would you say to your son to make him tidy up the kitchen?

_____

_____

3.   (as above)

Part IV: Differences

Is there a difference between the following three sentences? If so, how do they differ?

3.	Differences

a) "You must be back by 10 o'clock!"
b) "You have to be back by 10 o'clock!"
c) "You have got to be back by 10 o'clock!"

_____

_____

Part v: Personality Characteristics

*Please rank the personality characteristics based on the utterances given. Imagine **your
boss** is the speaker.*

*Example: If you think your boss is very friendly when he/she says "You must help me out
with this!", you would tick '5'. If you think your boss is unfriendly but not very unfriendly
when he says "You must help me out with this!", you would tick '2'.*

---

4.   Boss: "You must help me out with this!"

	1	2	3	4	5	
unfriendly	☐	☐	☐	☐	☐	friendly
insincere	☐	☐	☐	☐	☐	sincere
not helpful	☐	☐	☐	☐	☐	helpful
poorly educated	☐	☐	☐	☐	☐	highly educated
not proficient in English	☐	☐	☐	☐	☐	proficient in English
not authoritative	☐	☐	☐	☐	☐	authoritative
close	☐	☐	☐	☐	☐	distant
insecure	☐	☐	☐	☐	☐	self-confident
inexperienced	☐	☐	☐	☐	☐	experienced
young	☐	☐	☐	☐	☐	old

---

5.   Boss: "You have to help me out with this!"

	1	2	3	4	5	
unfriendly	☐	☐	☐	☐	☐	friendly
insincere	☐	☐	☐	☐	☐	sincere
not helpful	☐	☐	☐	☐	☐	helpful
poorly educated	☐	☐	☐	☐	☐	highly educated
not proficient in English	☐	☐	☐	☐	☐	proficient in English
not authoritative	☐	☐	☐	☐	☐	authoritative
close	☐	☐	☐	☐	☐	distant
insecure	☐	☐	☐	☐	☐	self-confident
inexperienced	☐	☐	☐	☐	☐	experienced
young	☐	☐	☐	☐	☐	old

6.	Boss: "You've got to help me out with this!"					

	1	2	3	4	5	
unfriendly	❑	❑	❑	❑	❑	friendly
insincere	❑	❑	❑	❑	❑	sincere
not helpful	❑	❑	❑	❑	❑	helpful
poorly educated	❑	❑	❑	❑	❑	highly educated
not proficient in English	❑	❑	❑	❑	❑	proficient in English
not authoritative	❑	❑	❑	❑	❑	authoritative
close	❑	❑	❑	❑	❑	distant
insecure	❑	❑	❑	❑	❑	self-confident
inexperienced	❑	❑	❑	❑	❑	experienced
young	❑	❑	❑	❑	❑	old

Part VI: Personality Characteristics

Please rank the personality characteristics based on the utterances given. Imagine one of your colleagues is the speaker.

Example: If you think your colleague is very friendly when he/she says "You must help me out with this!", you would tick '5'. If you think your colleague is unfriendly but not very unfriendly when he/she says "You must help me out with this!", you would tick '2'.

7.	Colleague: "You must help me out with this!"					

	1	2	3	4	5	
unfriendly	❑	❑	❑	❑	❑	friendly
insincere	❑	❑	❑	❑	❑	sincere
not helpful	❑	❑	❑	❑	❑	helpful
poorly educated	❑	❑	❑	❑	❑	highly educated
not proficient in English	❑	❑	❑	❑	❑	proficient in English
not authoritative	❑	❑	❑	❑	❑	authoritative
close	❑	❑	❑	❑	❑	distant
insecure	❑	❑	❑	❑	❑	self-confident
inexperienced	❑	❑	❑	❑	❑	experienced
young	❑	❑	❑	❑	❑	old

8.	Colleague: "You have to help me out with this!"

	1	2	3	4	5	
unfriendly	❑	❑	❑	❑	❑	friendly
insincere	❑	❑	❑	❑	❑	sincere
not helpful	❑	❑	❑	❑	❑	helpful
poorly educated	❑	❑	❑	❑	❑	highly educated
not proficient in English	❑	❑	❑	❑	❑	proficient in English
not authoritative	❑	❑	❑	❑	❑	authoritative
close	❑	❑	❑	❑	❑	distant
insecure	❑	❑	❑	❑	❑	self-confident
inexperienced	❑	❑	❑	❑	❑	experienced
young	❑	❑	❑	❑	❑	old

9.	Colleague: "You've got to help me out with this!"

	1	2	3	4	5	
unfriendly	❑	❑	❑	❑	❑	friendly
insincere	❑	❑	❑	❑	❑	sincere
not helpful	❑	❑	❑	❑	❑	helpful
poorly educated	❑	❑	❑	❑	❑	highly educated
not proficient in English	❑	❑	❑	❑	❑	proficient in English
not authoritative	❑	❑	❑	❑	❑	authoritative
close	❑	❑	❑	❑	❑	distant
insecure	❑	❑	❑	❑	❑	self-confident
inexperienced	❑	❑	❑	❑	❑	experienced
young	❑	❑	❑	❑	❑	old

Part VII: Personal Information (Part VI above)

Thank you (as above)

Beke Hansen
(Signature)
(Contact details)

Feedback (as above)

FIGURE 62   Structure of questionnaire B (only items that differ from Questionnaire A).

TABLE 22 UCREL Semantic Analysis System (USAS) tagset

A General and abstract terms

A1	General
A1.1.1	General actions, making, etc.
A1.1.2	Damaging and destroying
A1.2	Suitability
A1.3	Caution
A1.4	Chance, luck
A1.5	Use
A1.5.1	Using
A1.5.2	Usefulness
A1.6	Physical/mental
A1.7	Constraint
A1.8	Inclusion/exclusion
A1.9	Avoiding
A2	Affect
A2.1	Affect: Modify, change
A2.2	Affect: Cause/connected
A3	Being
A4	Classification
A4.1	Generally: Kinds, groups, examples
A4.2	Particular/general; detail
A5	Evaluation
A5.1	Evaluation: Good/bad

H Architecture, housing, and the home

H1	Architecture and kinds of houses, etc.
H2	Parts of buildings
H3	Areas around or near houses
H4	Residence
H5	Furniture and household fittings

I Money and commerce in industry

I1	Money generally
I1.1	Money: Affluence
I1.2	Money: Debts
I1.3	Money: Price
I2	Business
I2.1	Business generally
I2.2	Business: Selling
I3	Work and employment
I3.1	Work and employment generally
I3.2	Work and employment, etc.
I4	Industry

K Entertainment, sports and games

K1	Entertainment generally
K2	Music and related activities
K3	Recorded sound, etc.
K4	Drama, the theatre, etc.

S Social actions, states, and processes

S1	General
S1.1	Social actions, states, and processes
S1.1.1	General
S1.1.2	Reciprocity
S1.1.3	Participation
S1.1.4	Deserve, etc.
S1.2	Personality traits
S1.2.1	Approachability and friendliness
S1.2.2	Avarice
S1.2.3	Egoism
S1.2.4	Politeness
S1.2.5	Toughness; strong/weak
S1.2.6	Sensible
S2	People
S2.1	People: Female
S2.2	People: Male
S3	Relationship
S3.1	Relationship: General
S3.2	Relationship: Intimate/sexual
S4	Kin
S5	Groups and affiliation
S6	Obligation and necessity

TABLE 22　UCREL Semantic Analysis System (USAS) tagset (*cont.*)

A5.2	Evaluation: True/false	K5	Sports and games generally	S7	Power relationship
A5.3	Evaluation: Accuracy	K5.1	Sports	S7.1	Power, organizing
A5.4	Evaluation: Authenticity	K5.2	Games	S7.2	Respect
A6	Comparing	K6	Children's games and toys	S7.3	Competition
A6.1	Comparing: Similar/different	**L Life and living things**		S7.4	Permission
A6.2	Comparing: Usual/unusual	L1	Life and living things	S8	Helping/hindering
A6.3	Comparing: Variety	L2	Living creatures generally	S9	Religion and the supernatural
A7	Definite (+ modals)	L3	Plants	**T Time**	
A8	Seem	**M Movement, location, travel, and transport**		T1	Time
A9	Getting and giving; possession	M1	Moving, coming, and going	T1.1	Time: General
A10	Open/closed; hiding/hidden, etc.	M2	Putting, taking, pulling, pushing, etc.	T1.1.1	Time: General: Past
A11	Importance	M3	Vehicles and transport on land	T1.1.2	Time: General: Present; simult.
A11.1	Importance: Important	M4	Shipping, swimming, etc.	T1.1.3	Time: General: Future
A11.2	Importance: Noticeability	M5	Aircraft and flying	T1.2	Time: Momentary
A12	Easy/difficult	M6	Location and direction	T1.3	Time: Period
A13	Degree	M7	Places	T2	Time: Beginning and ending
A13.1	Degree: Non-specific	M8	Remaining/stationary	T3	Time: Old, new, and young; age
A13.2	Degree: Maximisers	**N Numbers and measurement**		T4	Time: Early/late
A13.3	Degree: Boosters	N1	Numbers	**W World and environment**	
A13.4	Degree: Approximators	N2	Mathematics	W1	The universe
A13.5	Degree: Compromisers	N3	Measurement	W2	Light

A13.6 Degree: Diminishers
A13.7 Degree: Minimizers
A14 Exclusivisers/particularisers
A15 Safety/danger
B The body and the individual
B1 Anatomy and physiology
B2 Health and disease
B3 Medicines and medical treatment
B4 Cleaning and personal care
B5 Clothes and personal belongings
C Arts and crafts
C1 Arts and crafts
E Emotional actions, states and processes
E1 General
E2 Liking
E3 Calm/violent/angry
E4 Happy/sad
E4.1 Happy/sad: Happy
E4.2 Happy/sad: Contentment
E5 Fear/bravery/shock
E6 Worry, concern, confident
F Food and farming
F1 Food
F2 Drinks

N3.1 Measurement: General
N3.2 Measurement: Size
N3.3 Measurement: Distance
N3.4 Measurement: Volume
N3.5 Measurement: Weight
N3.6 Measurement: Area
N3.7 Measurement: Length & height
N3.8 Measurement: Speed
N4 Linear order
N5 Quantities
N5.1 Entirety; maximum
N5.2 Exceeding; waste
N6 Frequency, etc.
O Substances, materials, objects, and equipment
O1 Substances and materials generally
O1.1 Solid
O1.2 Liquid
O1.3 Gas
O2 Objects generally
O3 Electricity and electrical equipment
O4 Physical attributes
O4.1 General appearance, etc.
O4.2 Judgement of appearance

W3 Geographical terms
W4 Weather
W5 Green issues
X Psychological actions, states, and processes
X1 General
X2 Mental actions and processes
X2.1 Thought, belief
X2.2 Knowledge
X2.3 Learn
X2.4 Investigate, examine, test, search
X2.5 Understand
X2.6 Expect
X3 Sensory
X3.1 Sensory: Taste
X3.2 Sensory: Sound
X3.3 Sensory: Touch
X3.4 Sensory: Sight
X3.5 Sensory: Smell
X4 Mental object
X4.1 Mental object: Conceptual object
X4.2 Mental object: Means, method
X5 Attention
X5.1 Attention

TABLE 22   UCREL Semantic Analysis System (USAS) tagset (*cont.*)

F3	Cigarettes and drugs	
F4	Farming and horticulture	
G Government and public		
G1	Government, politics, and elections	
G1.1	Government, etc.	
G1.2	Politics	
G2	Crime, law, and order	
G2.1	Crime, law, and order: Law and order	
G2.2	General ethics	
G3	Warfare, defence, and the army, etc.	
O4.3	Colour and colour patterns	
O4.4	Shape	
O4.5	Texture	
O4.6	Temperature	
P Education		
P1	Education in general	
Q Language and communication		
Q1	Communication in general	
Q1.1	Communication	
Q1.2	Paper documents and writing	
Q1.3	Telecommunications	
Q2	Speech acts	
Q2.1	Speech, etc.: Communicative	
Q2.2	Speech acts	
Q3	Language, speech, and grammar	
Q4	The media	
Q4.1	The media: Books	
Q4.2	The media: Newspapers, etc.	
Q4.3	The media: TV, radio, and cinema	
X5.2	Interest/boredom/excited/energetic	
X6	Deciding	
X7	Wanting; planning; choosing	
X8	Trying	
X9	Ability	
X9.1	Ability: Ability, intelligence	
X9.2	Ability: Success and failure	
Y Science and technology		
Y1	Science and technology in general	
Y2	Information technology and computing	
Z Names and grammar		
Z0	Unmatched proper noun	
Z1	Personal names	
Z2	Geographical names	
Z3	Other proper names	
Z4	Discourse bin	
Z5	Grammatical bin	
Z6	Negative	
Z7	If	
Z8	Pronouns, etc.	
Z9	Trash can	
Z99	Unmatched	

Chapter 5

TABLE 23   Modal and semi-modal verbs of obligation and necessity in ICE-GB, ICE-USA*,
             ICE-HK, ICE-IND*, and ICE-SIN, normalised frequency per 100,000 words,
             absolute frequency in brackets (cf. Figure 25)

	ICE-GB	ICE-USA*	ICE-HK	ICE-IND*	ICE-SIN
must	63.7 (637)	42.9 (279)	74.2 (742)	83.2 (832)	86.9 (869)
have to	52.7 (527)	51.4 (333)	114.2 (1,142)	110.7 (1,107)	85 (850)
have got to	21.6 (216)	18.0 (117)	7.5 (75)	3.3 (33)	17.6 (176)
need to	15.8 (158)	25.6 (166)	29.3 (293)	7.9 (79)	24.8 (248)

TABLE 24   Modal and semi-modal verbs of obligation and necessity and their senses in ICE-
             GB, ICE-USA*, ICE-HK, ICE-IND*, and ICE-SIN, normalised frequency per 100,000
             words, absolute frequency in brackets (cf. Figure 26)

		Root		Epistemic		Unclear	
ICE-GB	must	42.2	(422)	20.4	(204)	1.1	(11)
	have to	50.1	(501)	1.9	(19)	0.7	(7)
	have got to	21.3	(213)	0.3	(3)	0	(0)
	need to	15.8	(158)	0	(0)	0	(0)
ICE-USA*	must	31.4	(204)	10.9	(71)	0.6	(4)
	have to	49.2	(319)	2.2	(14)	0	(0)
	have got to	16.9	(110)	1.1	(7)	0	(0)
	need to	25.6	(166)	0	(0)	0	(0)
ICE-HK	must	57.4	(574)	15.2	(152)	1.6	(16)
	have to	113.3	(1,133)	0.9	(9)	0	(0)
	have got to	7.3	(73)	0.2	(2)	0	(0)
	need to	29.1	(291)	0.2	(2)	0	(0)
ICE-IND*	must	57.3	(573)	23.1	(231)	2.8	(28)
	have to	106.9	(1,069)	2.3	(23)	1.5	(15)
	have got to	3.2	(32)	0.1	(1)	0	(0)
	need to	7.9	(79)	0	(0)	0	(0)
ICE-SIN	must	70.7	(707)	14.4	(144)	1.8	(18)
	have to	83.8	(838)	1.1	(11)	0.1	(1)
	have got to	17.6	(176)	0	(0)	0	(0)
	need to	24.8	(248)	0	(0)	0	(0)

TABLE 25　Modal and semi-modal verbs of obligation and necessity and their senses in the spoken section of ICE-GB, ICE-USA*, ICE-HK, ICE-IND*, and ICE-SIN, normalised frequency per 100,000 words, absolute frequency in brackets (cf. Figure 27)

		Root		Epistemic		Unclear	
ICE-GBS	*must*	24.8	(149)	21.7	(130)	1.7	(10)
	have to	60.5	(363)	2.8	(17)	1.2	(7)
	have got to	33.3	(200)	0.5	(3)	0.0	(0)
	need to	16.8	(101)	0.0	(0)	0.0	(0)
ICE-USAS*	*must*	6.0	(15)	18.1	(45)	1.2	(3)
	have to	85.5	(213)	4.8	(12)	0.0	(0)
	have got to	42.2	(105)	2.0	(5)	0.0	(0)
	need to	34.1	(85)	0.0	(0)	0.0	(0)
ICE-HKS	*must*	48.3	(290)	14.2	(85)	1.8	(11)
	have to	147.8	(887)	1.2	(7)	0.0	(0)
	have got to	11.2	(67)	0.3	(2)	0.0	(0)
	need to	31.2	(187)	0.2	(1)	0.0	(0)
ICE-INDS*	*must*	61.0	(366)	26.2	(157)	4.2	(25)
	have to	150.8	(905)	3.2	(19)	2.5	(15)
	have got to	5.0	(30)	0.2	(1)	0.0	(0)
	need to	9.0	(54)	0.0	(0)	0.0	(0)
ICE-SINS	*must*	70.7	(424)	14.0	(84)	2.8	(17)
	have to	112.8	(677)	1.8	(11)	0.2	(1)
	have got to	26.5	(159)	0.0	(0)	0.0	(0)
	need to	28.5	(171)	0.0	(0)	0.0	(0)

TABLE 26　Modal and semi-modal verbs of obligation and necessity and their senses in the written sections of ICE-GB, ICE-USA*, ICE-HK, ICE-IND*, and ICE-SIN, normalised frequency per 100,000 words, absolute frequency in brackets (cf. Figure 30)

		Root	Epistemic	Unclear
ICE-GBW	*must*	68.3 (273)	18.5 (74)	0.3 (1)
	have to	34.5 (138)	0.5 (2)	0.0 (0)
	have got to	3.3 (13)	0.0 (0)	0.0 (0)
	need to	14.3 (57)	0.0 (0)	0.0 (0)
ICE-USAW*	*must*	47.3 (189)	6.5 (26)	0.3 (1)
	have to	26.5 (106)	0.5 (2)	0.0 (0)
	have got to	1.3 (5)	0.5 (2)	0.0 (0)
	need to	20.3 (81)	0.0 (0)	0.0 (0)
ICE-HKW	*must*	71.0 (284)	16.8 (67)	1.3 (5)
	have to	61.5 (246)	0.5 (2)	0.0 (0)
	have got to	1.5 (6)	0.0 (0)	0.0 (0)
	need to	26.0 (104)	0.3 (1)	0.0 (0)
ICE-INDW*	*must*	51.8 (207)	18.5 (74)	0.8 (3)
	have to	41.0 (164)	1.0 (4)	0.0 (0)
	have got to	0.5 (2)	0.0 (0)	0.0 (0)
	need to	6.3 (25)	0.0 (0)	0.0 (0)
ICE-SINW	*must*	70.8 (283)	15.0 (60)	0.3 (1)
	have to	40.3 (161)	0.0 (0)	0.0 (0)
	have got to	4.3 (17)	0.0 (0)	0.0 (0)
	need to	19.3 (77)	0.0 (0)	0.0 (0)

Chapter 6

TABLE 27   Development of *must* in its root and epistemic meaning between 1600 and 1999 in
           ARCHER, normalised frequency per 100,000 words, absolute frequency in brackets
           (cf. Figure 33)

Period	Root	Epistemic	Unclear	Total
1600–1649	114 (98) 90%	13 (11) 10%	0 (0) 0%	127 (109) (100%)
1650–1699	88 (231) 79%	21 (55) 19%	2 (6) 2%	111 (292) (100%)
1700–1749	79 (203) 74%	26 (68) 25%	1 (3) 1%	107 (274) (100%)
1750–1799	79 (220) 73%	28 (78) 26%	1 (2) 1%	108 (300) (100%)
1800–1849	76 (205) 66%	37 (100) 32%	2 (6) 2%	115 (311) (100%)
1850–1899	57 (155) 61%	35 (96) 38%	1 (3) 0%	93 (254) (100%)
1900–1949	97 (260) 74%	32 (85) 24%	1 (4) 1%	131 (349) (100%)
1950–1999	80 (211) 75%	26 (68) 24%	1 (2) 1%	106 (281) (100%)

TABLE 28   Development of *must* in its root and epistemic meaning between
           1750–1799 and 1850–1899 in ARCHER, normalised frequency
           per 100,000 words, absolute frequency in brackets (cf. Figure 34)

Period	Root		Epistemic		Unclear	
1750–1799	79	(220)	28	(78)	1	(2)
1850–1899	57	(155)	35	(96)	1	(3)

TABLE 29   The rise of *have to* in ARCHER, normalised
           frequency per 100,000 words, absolute
           frequency in brackets (cf. Figure 35)

Period	Root		Epistemic	
1600–1649	3	(3)	0	(0)
1650–1699	2	(4)	0	(0)
1700–1749	2	(4)	0	(0)
1750–1799	5	(13)	0	(0)
1800–1849	11	(30)	0	(0)
1850–1899	32	(88)	0	(0)
1900–1949	48	(129)	0	(0)
1950–1999	64	(169)	6	(2)

TABLE 30   Personality characteristics associated with *must* in the sentence
You must help me out with this! (cf. Figure 45)

	very un-X	un-X	neither X nor un-X	X	very X	Total
friendliness	16% (6)	13% (5)	21% (8)	16% (6)	34% (13)	100% (38)
sincerity	3% (1)	3% (1)	40% (12)	33% (10)	20% (6)	100% (30)
helpfulness	0% (0)	18% (5)	32% (9)	36% (10)	14% (4)	100% (28)
education	7% (2)	0% (0)	48% (13)	44% (12)	0% (0)	100% (27)
English proficiency	4% (1)	18% (5)	32% (9)	43% (12)	4% (1)	100% (28)
authority	3% (1)	7% (2)	17% (5)	24% (7)	48% (14)	100% (29)
closeness	17% (5)	28% (8)	14% (4)	24% (7)	17% (5)	100% (29)
self-confidence	3% (1)	17% (5)	31% (9)	24% (7)	24% (7)	100% (29)
experience	11% (3)	11% (3)	50% (14)	18% (5)	11% (3)	100% (28)
age	18% (5)	14% (4)	39% (11)	18% (5)	11% (3)	100% (28)

Chapter 7

TABLE 31   The frequency of *must, have to, have got to,* and *need to* in apparent time in the spoken section of ICE-HK, normalised frequency per 100,000 words, absolute frequency in brackets (cf. Figure 46)

	56–60+	46–55	36–45	26–35	17–25
have to	81.2 (29)	103.8 (138)	87.7 (193)	65.3 (93)	175.8 (428)
need to	47.6 (17)	12.0 (16)	28.2 (62)	11.2 (16)	31.6 (77)
must	100.8 (36)	78.9 (105)	58.6 (129)	33.0 (47)	23.0 (56)
have got to	14.0 (5)	18.8 (25)	9.1 (20)	4.9 (7)	4.5 (11)

TABLE 32   The frequency of root *must* and epistemic *must* in apparent time in the spoken section of ICE-HK, normalised frequency per 100,000 words, absolute frequency in brackets (cf. Figure 47)

	56–60+	46–55	36–45	26–35	17–25
Root	86.8 (31)	69.9 (93)	41.8 (92)	23.2 (33)	16.4 (40)
Epistemic	14.0 (5)	9.0 (12)	16.8 (37)	9.8 (14)	6.6 (16)

TABLE 33   Modal and semi-modal verbs expressing deontic modality in apparent time in the spoken section of ICE-HK (cf. Figure 48)

	56–60+	46–55	36–45	26–35	17–25
have to	81.2 (29)	101.5 (135)	86.3 (190)	65.3 (93)	175.8 (428)
need to	47.6 (17)	12.0 (16)	27.7 (61)	11.2 (16)	31.2 (76)
must	86.8 (31)	69.9 (93)	41.8 (92)	23.2 (33)	16.4 (40)
have got to	14.0 (5)	18.8 (25)	8.6 (19)	4.9 (7)	4.1 (10)

TABLE 34   The frequency of *have to* in apparent time in the spoken section of ICE-HK according to gender, normalised frequency per 100,000 words, absolute frequency in brackets (cf. Figure 49)

	46–55	36–45	26–35	17–25
Female	134.5 (45)	61.3 (45)	147.4 (61)	178.7 (361)
Male	99.6 (88)	95.3 (144)	33.7 (27)	157.9 (67)

TABLE 35   The development of the proportions of the variants of the variable deontic modality in the spoken section of ICE-HK, absolute frequency in brackets (cf. Figure 50)

	56–60+	46–55	36–45	26–35	17–25
have to	35% (29)	53% (135)	53% (190)	63% (93)	77% (428)
need to	21% (17)	6% (16)	17% (61)	11% (16)	14% (76)
must	38% (31)	36% (93)	26% (92)	22% (33)	7% (40)
have got to	6% (5)	5% (12)	5% (17)	3% (5)	2% (10)
Total	100% (82)	100% (256)	100% (360)	100% (147)	100% (554)

TABLE 36   The frequency of *must*, *have to*, *have got to*, and *need to* in apparent time in the spoken section of ICE-IND*, normalised frequency per 100,000 words, absolute frequency in brackets (cf. Figure 51)

	50+	42–49	34–41	26–33	18–25
have to	120.3 (173)	115.0 (81)	167.6 (154)	148.6 (118)	296.2 (232)
must	106.4 (153)	100.8 (71)	63.1 (58)	83.1 (66)	31.9 (25)
have got to	8.3 (12)	0.0 (0)	4.4 (4)	2.5 (2)	3.8 (3)
need to	10.4 (15)	7.1 (5)	4.4 (4)	7.6 (6)	2.6 (2)

TABLE 37   The frequency of root *must* and epistemic *must* in apparent time in the spoken
            section of ICE-IND*, normalised frequency per 100,000 words, absolute frequency
            in brackets (cf. Figure 52)

	50+	42–49	34–41	26–33	18–25
Root	67.5 (113)	83.8 (59)	33.7 (31)	46.6 (37)	16.6 (13)
Epistemic	23.9 (40)	17.0 (12)	29.4 (27)	36.5 (29)	15.3 (12)

TABLE 38   The proportion of root *must* and epistemic *must* in apparent
            time in the spoken section of ICE-GB, absolute frequency in
            brackets (cf. Figure 53)

	46–65	26–45	18–25
Epistemic	46% (47)	49% (33)	55% (18)
Root	54% (56)	51% (35)	45% (15)
Total	100% (103)	100% (68)	100% (33)

TABLE 39   Modal and semi-modal verbs expressing deontic modality in apparent time
            in the spoken section of ICE-IND*, normalised frequency per 100,000 words,
            absolute frequency in brackets (cf. Figure 54)

	50+	42–49	34–41	26–33	18–25
have to	101.0 (169)	115.0 (81)	163.2 (150)	142.3 (113)	292.4 (229)
must	67.5 (113)	83.8 (59)	33.7 (31)	46.6 (37)	16.6 (13)
have got to	6.6 (11)	0.0 (0)	4.4 (4)	2.5 (2)	3.8 (3)
need to	9.0 (15)	7.1 (5)	4.4 (4)	7.6 (6)	2.6 (2)

TABLE 40   The frequency of *have to* in apparent time in the spoken section of ICE-IND*
            according to gender, normalised frequency per 100,000 words, absolute frequency
            in brackets (cf. Figure 55)

	50+	42–49	34–41	26–33	18–25
Female	23.3 (5)	102.6 (26)	188.9 (80)	178.6 (83)	302.3 (175)
Male	113.3 (163)	122.0 (55)	141.3 (70)	91.1 (30)	264.3 (54)

TABLE 41   The development of the proportions of the variants of the variable deontic
            modality in the spoken section of ICE-IND*, absolute frequency in brackets
            (cf. Figure 56)

	50+	42–49	34–41	26–33	18–25
have to	55% (169)	56% (81)	79% (150)	72% (113)	93% (229)
must	37% (113)	41% (59)	16% (31)	23% (37)	5% (13)
have got to	4% (11)	0% (0)	2% (4)	1% (2)	1% (3)
need to	5% (15)	3% (5)	2% (4)	4% (6)	1% (2)
Total	100% (308)	100% (145)	100% (189)	100% (158)	100% (247)

TABLE 42   The development of the proportions of the variants of the variable deontic
            modality in the spoken section of ICE-GB, absolute frequency in brackets
            (cf Figure 57)

	46–65	26–45	18–25
have to	48% (124)	44% (120)	46% (61)
have got to	17% (45)	28% (77)	31% (41)
need to	13% (35)	16% (43)	13% (17)
must	22% (56)	13% (35)	11% (15)
Total	100% (260)	100% (275)	100% (134)

Chapter 8

TABLE 43   Visualisation of the log odds for *must* to compare the use of *must* and *have to* in spoken HKE, IndE, and BrE (cf. Figure 58)

glm.HKs2/lrm.HKs2

have to	863				
must	287				
LR chi2	211.10				
C	0.763				
(Intercept)		Log odds	Std. error	z-value	p-value	
		−2.9025	0.2120	−13.688	0.0000	***
Age	26–35	0.3059	0.3078	0.994	0.3204	
	36–45	0.3792	0.2760	1.374	0.1694	
	46–55	0.4942	0.2898	1.705	0.0882	
	56–60+	1.0038	0.3556	2.823	0.0048	**
Type2	Public dialogue	1.7101	0.3080	5.552	0.0000	***
	Scripted monologue	2.6493	0.3407	7.777	0.0000	***
	Unscripted monologue	1.8359	0.2914	6.300	0.0000	***

p-values: *** p<0.001, **p<0.01, *p<0.05

glm.INDs2/lrm.INDs2

have to	665				
must	199				
LR chi2	173.73				
C	0.786				
(Intercept)		Log odds	Std. error	z-value	p-value	
		−3.8956	0.4921	−7.916	0.0000	***
Age	26–33	2.2013	0.5490	4.010	0.0001	***
	34–41	1.7323	0.5545	3.124	0.0018	**
	42–49	3.2057	0.5879	5.453	0.0000	***
	50+	5.0586	0.8049	6.285	0.0000	***

glm.INDs2/lrm.INDs2 *(cont.)*

Gender	M	1.6110	0.6423	2.508	0.0121	*
Subject1	1N	−0.1068	0.2235	−0.478	0.6327	
	2N	0.9753	0.3225	3.025	0.0025	**
	3N	0.0263	0.2602	0.101	0.9194	
Type2	Public dialogue	0.8255	0.2769	2.981	0.0029	**
	Scripted monologue	0.8606	0.4822	1.785	0.0743	
	Unscripted monologue	0.1254	0.2769	0.453	0.6506	
Age	26–33:GenderM	−0.4802	0.7613	−0.631	0.5282	
	34–41:GenderM	−1.4664	0.7829	−1.873	0.0611	
	42–49:GenderM	−2.2216	0.7885	−2.817	0.0048	**
	50+:GenderM	−3.5287	0.9249	−3.815	0.0001	***

p-values: *** $p<0.001$, **$p<0.01$, *$p<0.05$

glm.GBs2/lrm.GBs2

have to	363
must	158
LR chi2	53.06
C	0.687

(Intercept)		Log odds	Std. error	z value	p value	
		−1.4737	0.2642	−5.578	0.0000	***
Subject1	1N	0.7022	0.2449	2.867	0.0041	**
	2N	−0.1740	0.3729	−0.467	0.6408	
	3N	−0.2855	0.2839	−1.006	0.3146	
Type2	Public dialogue	0.3512	0.2797	1.256	0.2093	
	Scripted monologue	1.6928	0.3158	5.360	0.0000	***
	Unscripted monologue	0.1451	0.3083	0.471	0.6380	

p-values: *** $p<0.001$, **$p<0.01$, *$p<0.05$

TABLE 44   Visualisation of the log odds for *must* in all varieties (cf. Figure 59)

glm.all/lrm.all

have to		3,821				
must		2,271				
LR chi2		1,031.5				
C		0.738				
(Intercept)		Log odds	Std. error	z-value	p-value	
		−1.9428	0.1350	−14.3900	0.0000	***
Semantics1	A	0.4279	0.0985	4.3430	0.0000	***
	B	0.0073	0.4216	0.0170	0.9862	
	C	−0.3182	0.6392	−0.4980	0.6186	
	E	0.0005	0.2922	0.0020	0.9986	
	F	0.8094	0.5373	1.5060	0.1320	
	G	1.3103	0.3862	3.3930	0.0007	***
	H	−0.8375	0.5333	−1.5700	0.1163	
	I	−0.2615	0.1766	−1.4810	0.1387	
	K	−0.4986	0.6191	−0.8050	0.4206	
	L	0.7752	0.8626	0.8990	0.3688	
	N	−0.1186	0.3039	−0.3900	0.6963	
	O	0.3068	0.4854	0.6320	0.5273	
	P	0.0697	0.3382	0.2060	0.8367	
	Q	0.7197	0.1251	5.7510	0.0000	***
	S	0.6645	0.1505	4.4140	0.0000	***
	T	0.2439	0.1675	1.4560	0.1455	
	X	0.5959	0.1127	5.2890	0.0000	***
Subject1	1N	−0.0803	0.0781	−1.0290	0.3036	
	2N	−0.2092	0.1077	−1.9430	0.0520	
	3N	0.4148	0.0763	5.4360	0.0000	***

Type2	Academic writing	2.1508	0.1444	14.8930	0.0000	***
	Correspondence	1.0897	0.1366	7.9790	0.0000	***
	Creative writing	1.1638	0.2180	5.3400	0.0000	***
	Instructional writing	2.4696	0.1417	17.4280	0.0000	***
	Non-academic writing	1.6950	0.1452	11.6740	0.0000	***
	Non-professional writing	1.9644	0.1600	12.2800	0.0000	***
	Persuasive writing	2.1460	0.2252	9.5290	0.0000	***
	Public dialogue	0.9096	0.0920	9.8900	0.0000	***
	Reportage	1.0459	0.2074	5.0420	0.0000	***
	Scripted monologue	1.7883	0.1188	15.0520	0.0000	***
	Unscripted monologue	0.7959	0.1004	7.9280	0.0000	***
Variety	ICE-HK	−0.2537	0.0925	−2.7420	0.0061	**
	ICE-IND*	−0.0568	0.0936	−0.6070	0.5441	
	ICE-SIN	0.1338	0.0970	1.3800	0.1677	
	ICE-USA*	−0.2179	0.1257	−1.7340	0.0829	

p-values: *** p<0.001, **p<0.01, *p<0.05

List of Databases, Software, and R Packages

Anthony, L. (2014). AntConc. Version 3.4.3. Tokyo, Japan: Waseda University. Available online at URL: http://www.laurenceanthony.net/software (last access: 19/02/2018).

[ARCHER-3.2] (Lancaster). *A Representative Corpus of Historical English Registers*. Version 3.2. 1990–2013. Originally compiled under the supervision of D. Biber and E. Finegan at Northern Arizona University and University of Southern California; modified and expanded by subsequent members of a Consortium of Universities. Current member universities are Bamberg, Freiburg, Heidelberg, Helsinki, Lancaster, Leicester, Manchester, Michigan, Northern Arizona, Santiago de Compostela, Southern California, Trier, Uppsala, Zurich.

Bates, D., M. Maechler, B. Bolker & S. Walker (2015). Fitting linear mixed-effects models using lme4. *Journal of Statistical Software*, 67(1), 1–48. doi:10.18637/jss.v067.i01.

Bolt, P., K. Bolton & J. Hung (2006). *The ICE-Hong Kong Corpus*. Version 1. Retrieved from URL: http://ice-corpora.net/ice/download.htm (last access: 19/02/2018).

Davies, M. (2013). *Corpus of Global Web-Based English: 1.9 billion words from speakers in 20 countries*. Available online at URL: http://corpus.byu.edu/glowbe/ (last access: 19/02/2018).

Du Bois, J.W., W.L. Chafe, C.F. Meyer, S.A. Thompson, R. Englebretson & N. Martey (2000–2005). *Santa Barbara Corpus of Spoken American English*. Parts 1–4. Philadelphia: Linguistic Data Consortium.

Harrell, F.E., Jr. (2017). rms: Regression Modeling Strategies. R package version 5.1-0. URL: https://CRAN.R-project.org/packages=rms (last access: 26/03/2018).

Meyer, C.F., H. Tao & J.W. Du Bois (2012). *The ICE-USA Written Corpus*. Version 1. Retrieved from URL: http://ice-corpora.net/ice/download.htm (last access: 19/02/2018).

Nihilani, P., N. Yibin, A. Pakir & V. Ooi (2002). *The ICE-Singapore Corpus*. Version 1. Retrieved from URL: http://ice-corpora.net/ice/download.htm (last access: 19/02/2018).

[R Core Team] (2016). *R: A language and environment for statistical computing*. R Foundation for Statistical Computing, Vienna, Austria. URL: http://www.R-project.org (last access: 26/03/2018).

Scott, M. (2004). WordSmith Tools. Version 4. Oxford: Oxford University Press.

Shastri, S.V. (1986). *Kolhapur Corpus of Written Indian English*.

Shastri, S.V. & G. Leitner (2002). *The ICE-India Corpus*. Version 1. Retrieved from URL: http://ice-corpora.net/ice/download.htm (last access: 19/02/2018).

[Survey of English Usage] (1998). *The ICE-GB Corpus*. Release 1. London: University College London.

Wickham, H. (2009). *ggplot2: Elegant graphics for data analysis*. New York: Springer.

Bibliography

Agha, A. (2003). The social life of cultural value. *Language & Communication*, 23(3–4), 231–273. doi: 10.1016/S0271-5309(03)00012-0.

Alo, M.A. & R. Mesthrie (2008). Nigerian English: Morphology and syntax. In R. Mesthrie (Ed.), *Varieties of English 4: Africa, South and Southeast Asia* (323–339). Berlin: Mouton de Gruyter.

Alsagoff, L. & H.C. Lick (1998). The grammar of Singapore English. In J.A. Foley, T. Kandiah, Z. Bao, A.F. Gupta, L. Alsagoff, H.C. Lick, L. Wee, I.S. Talib & W. Bokhorst-Heng (Eds.), *English in new cultural contexts: Reflections from Singapore* (127–151). Singapore: Oxford University Press.

Andersen, R.W. (1983). Transfer to somewhere. In S.M. Gass & L. Selinker (Eds.), *Language transfer in language learning* (177–201). Rowley, Mass.: Newbury House.

Anderwald, L. (2002). *Negation in non-standard British English: Gaps, regularizations and asymmetries*. London: Routledge.

Anderwald, L. (2016). *Language between description and prescription: Verbs and verb categories in nineteenth-century grammars of English*. Oxford: Oxford University Press.

Andronov, M.S. (1996). *A grammar of the Malayalam language in historical treatment*. Wiesbaden: Harrassowitz.

Androutsopolous, J. (2006). Introduction: Sociolinguistics and computer-mediated communication. *Journal of Sociolinguistics*, 10(4), 419–438. doi: 10.1111/j.1467-9841.2006.00286.x.

Archer, D., A. Wilson & P. Rayson (2002). Introduction to the USAS category system. Retrieved from http://ucrel.lancs.ac.uk/usas/usas%20guide.pdf (last access: 19/02/2018).

Ashcroft, B., G. Griffiths & H. Tiffin (2000). *Post-colonial studies: The key concepts*. London: Routledge.

Asher, R.E. (1985). *Tamil*. London: Croom Helm.

Bacon-Shone, J. & K. Bolton (2008). Bilingualism and multilingualism in HKSAR: Language surveys and Hong Kong's changing linguistic profile. In K. Bolton & H. Yang (Eds.), *Language and society in Hong Kong* (25–51). Hong Kong: Open University of Hong Kong.

Bailey, G. & J. Peoples (2013). *Essentials of cultural anthropology* (3 ed.). Belmont: Wadsworth Cengage Learning.

Bailey, G., T. Wikle, J. Tillery & L. Sand (1991). The apparent time construct. *Language Variation and Change*, 3(3), 241–264. doi: 10.1017/s0954394500000569.

Baker, P. (2010). *Sociolinguistics and corpus linguistics*. Edinburgh: Edinburgh University Press.

Baker, P. (2014). Corpus linguistics in sociolinguistics. In J. Holmes & K. Hazen (Eds.), *Research methods in sociolinguistics: A practical guide* (107–118). Malden, Mass.: Wiley-Blackwell.

Balasubramanian, C. (2009). *Register variation in Indian English*. Amsterdam: John Benjamins.

Bao, Z. (2010). *Must* in Singapore English. *Lingua*, 120, 1727–1737. doi: 10.1016/j.lingua.2010.01.001.

Bao, Z. (2015). *The making of vernacular Singapore English: System, transfer, and filter*. Cambridge: Cambridge University Press.

Bao, Z. (2016). Convergence-to-Substratum. Paper presented at ISLE 4, Poznań.

Barber, C. (1997). *Early Modern English*. Edinburgh: Edinburgh University Press.

Barrett, R. (2014). The emergence of th Kortmann, K. Burridge, R. Mesthrie e unmarked: Queer theory, language ideology, and formal linguistics. In L. Zimman, J.L. Davis & J. Raclaw (Eds.), *Queer excursions: Retheorizing binaries in language, gender, and sexuality* (195–223). Oxford: Oxford University Press.

Bartlett, J.R. (Ed.) (1848). *Dictionary of Americanisms: A glossary of words and phrases, usually regarded as peculiar to the United States*. New York: Bartlett & Welford.

Bauer, L. (2002). Inferring variation and change from public corpora. In J.K. Chambers, P. Trudgill & N. Schilling-Estes (Eds.), *The handbook of language variation and change* (97–114). Malden, Mass.: Blackwell.

Bautista, M.L.S. (2004). The verb in Philippine English: A preliminary analysis of modal *would*. *World Englishes*, 23(1), 113–128. doi: 10.1111/j.1467-971x.2004.00338.x.

Beal, J. (2004). English dialects in the north of England: Morphology and syntax. In B. Kortmann, K. Burridge, R. Mesthrie, E.W. Schneider & C. Upton (Eds.), *A handbook of varieties of English* (Vol. 2: Morphology and syntax, 114–141). Berlin: Mouton de Gruyter.

Beal, K. (2012). Is it truly unique that Irish English clefts are? Quantifying the syntactic variation of *it*-clefts in Irish English and other post-colonial English varieties. In B. Migge & M. Ní Chiosáin (Eds.), *New perspectives on Irish English* (153–177). Amsterdam: John Benjamins.

Beal, J., L. Burbano-Elizondo & C. Llamas (2012). *Urban North-Eastern English: Tyneside to Teesside*. Edinburgh: Edinburgh University Press.

Berardo, S.A. & R. Calabrese (2012). Nativising English: Evidence from a diachronic corpus of Indian English (DiCIE). In G. Maiello & R. Pellegrino (Eds.), *Database, corpora, insegnamenti linguistici* (35–53). Fasano: Schena Editore.

Bernaisch, T. (2015). *The lexis and lexicogrammar of Sri Lankan English*. Amsterdam: John Benjamins.

Bernaisch, T. & C. Koch (2016). Attitudes towards Englishes in India. *World Englishes*, 35(1), 118–132. doi: 10.1111/weng.12174.

Bhatt, R.M. (2008). Indian English: Syntax. In R. Mesthrie (Ed.), *Varieties of English 4: Africa, South and Southeast Asia* (546–562). Berlin: Mouton de Gruyter.

Biber, D. (1988). *Variation across speech and writing.* Cambridge: Cambridge University Press.

Biber, D. (2004). Modal use across registers and time. In A. Curzan & K. Emmons (Eds.), *Studies in the history of the English language II: Unfolding conversations* (189–216). Berlin: Mouton de Gruyter.

Biber, D., S. Conrad & R. Reppen (1998). *Corpus linguistics: Investigating language structure and use.* Cambridge: Cambridge University Press.

Biber, D., J. Egbert & M. Zhang (2018). Using corpus-based analysis to study register and dialect variation on the searchable web. In E. Friginal (Ed.), *Studies in corpus-based sociolinguistics* (83–111). London: Routledge.

Biber, D., S. Johansson, G. Leech, S. Conrad & E. Finegan (1999). *Longman grammar of spoken and written English.* London: Longman.

Biermeier, T. (2008). *Word-formation in New Englishes: A corpus-based analysis.* Berlin: LIT.

Biewer, C. (2009). Modals and semi-modals of obligation and necessity in South Pacific Englishes. *Anglistik*, 20(2), 41–55.

Biewer, C. (2011). Modal auxiliaries in second language varieties of English: A learner's perspective. In J. Mukherjee & M. Hundt (Eds.), *Exploring second-language varieties of English and learner Englishes: Bridging a paradigm gap* (7–33). Amsterdam: John Benjamins.

Biewer, C. (2015). *South Pacific Englishes: A sociolinguistic and morphosyntactic profile of Fiji English, Samoan English and Cook Island English.* Amsterdam: John Benjamins.

Biewer, C., T. Bernaisch, M. Berger & B. Heller (2014). *Compiling The Diachronic Corpus of Hong Kong English (DC-HKE): Motivation, progress and challenges.* Paper presented at the ICAME 35, Nottingham.

Blaut, J.M. (1993). *The colonizer's model of the world: Geographical diffusionism and Eurocentric history.* New York: The Guilford Press.

Blondeau, H. (2013). Studying language over time. In R.J. Podesva & D. Sharma (Eds.), *Research methods in linguistics* (494–518). Cambridge: Cambridge University Press.

Bock, H. (1931). Studien zum präpositionalen Infinitiv und Akkusativ mit dem *to*-Infinitiv. *Anglia*, 55, 114–176. doi: 10.1515/angl.1931.1931.55.177.

Bolton, K. (2000). The sociolinguistics of Hong Kong and the space for Hong Kong English. *World Englishes*, 19(3), 265–285. doi: 10.1111/1467-971x.00179.

Bolton, K. (2002). Hong Kong English: Autonomy and creativity. In K. Bolton (Ed.), *Hong Kong English: Autonomy and creativity* (1–25). Hong Kong: Hong Kong University Press.

Bolton, K. (2003). *Chinese Englishes: A sociolinguistic history.* Cambridge: Cambridge University Press.

Bolton, K. (2012). Language policy and planning in Hong Kong: The historical context and current realities. In E.-L. Low & A. Hashim (Eds.), *English in Southeast Asia: Features, policy and language in use* (221–238). Amsterdam: John Benjamins.

Bolton, K. & B.C. Ng (2014). The dynamics of multilingualism in contemporary Singapore. *World Englishes*, 33(3), 307–318. doi: 10.1111/weng.12092.

Bowerman, S. (2008). White South African English: Morphology and syntax. In R. Mesthrie (Ed.), *Varieties of English 4: Africa, South and Southeast Asia* (472–487). Berlin: Mouton de Gruyter.

Bowie, J., S. Wallis & B. Aarts (2013). Contemporary change in modal usage in spoken British English: Mapping the impact of 'genre'. In J.I. Marín-Arrese, M. Carretero, J. Arús Hita & J. van der Auwera (Eds.), *English modality: Core, periphery and evidentiality* (57–94). Berlin: Mouton de Gruyter.

Brinton, L.J. (1991). The origin and development of quasimodal *have to* in English. Paper presented at ICHL 10, Amsterdam.

Brown, P. & S.C. Levinson (1987). *Politeness: Some universals in language usage.* Cambridge: Cambridge University Press.

Brunner, M.-L., S. Diemer & S. Schmidt (2017). '...okay so good luck with that ((laughing))?' Managing rich data in a corpus of Skype conversations. In T. Hiltunen, J. McVeigh & T. Säily (Eds.), *Studies in Variation, Contacts and Change in English* (Vol. 19: Big and rich data in English corpus linguistics: Methods and explorations). Helsinki: VARIENG. Retrieved from http://www.helsinki.fi/varieng/series/volumes/19/brunner_diemer_schmidt/ (last access: 19/02/2018).

Bruthiaux, P. (2003). Squaring the circles: Issues in modeling English worldwide. *International Journal of Applied Linguistics*, 13(2), 159–178. doi: 10.1111/1473-4192.00042.

Buchstaller, I. (2014). *Quotatives: New trends and sociolinguistic implications.* Malden, Mass.: Wiley-Blackwell.

Buschfeld, S. (2013). *English in Cyprus or Cyprus English.* Amsterdam: John Benjamins.

Buschfeld, S. & A. Kautzsch (2017). Toward an integrated approach to postcolonial and non-postcolonial Englishes. *World Englishes*, 36(1), 105–126. doi: 10.1111/weng.12203.

Bybee, J.L. & W. Pagliuca (1985). Crosslinguistic comparison and the development of grammatical meaning. In J. Fisiak (Ed.), *Historical semantics, historical word formation* (59–84). Berlin: Mouton de Gruyter.

Bybee, J.L., R.D. Perkins & W. Pagliuca (1994). *The evolution of grammar: Tense, aspect, and modality in the languages of the world.* Chicago: University of Chicago Press.

Calle-Martín, J. & R.-B. Jesús (2017). Third person present tense markers in some varieties of English. *English World-Wide*, 38(1), 77–103. doi: 10.1075/eww.38.1.05cal.

Cedergren, H.J. & D. Sankoff (1974). Variable rules: Performance as a statistical reflection of competence. *Language*, 50(2), 333–355. doi: 10.2307/412441.

Chambers, J.K. & P. Trudgill (1998). *Dialectology* (2 ed.). Cambridge: Cambridge University Press.

Choi, S. (2006). Acquisition of modality. In W. Frawley (Ed.), *The expression of modality* (141–171). Berlin: Mouton de Gruyter.

Close, J. & B. Aarts (2010). Current change in the modal system of English: A case study of *must, have to* and *have got to*. In U. Lenker, J. Huber & R. Mailhammer (Eds.), *English historical linguistics 2008* (Vol. 1: The history of English verbal and nominal constructions, 165–181). Amsterdam: John Benjamins.

Coates, J. (1983). *The semantics of the modal auxiliaries*. London: Croom Helm.

Collins, P. (1991). The modals of obligation and necessity in Australian English. In K. Aijmer & B. Altenberg (Eds.), *English corpus linguistics: Studies in honour of Jan Svartvik* (145–165). London: Longman.

Collins, P. (2005). The modals and quasi-modals of obligation and necessity in Australian English and other Englishes. *English World-Wide*, 26(3), 249–273. doi: 10.1075/eww.26.3.02col.

Collins, P. (2007a). *Can/could* and *may/might* in British, American and Australian English: A corpus-based account. *World Englishes*, 26(4), 474–491. doi: 10.1111/j.1467-971X.2007.00523.x.

Collins, P. (2007b). Modality across World Englishes: The modals and semi-modals of prediction and volition. In C.S. Butler, R. Hidalgo Downing & J. Lavid (Eds.), *Functional perspectives on grammar and discourse* (447–468). Amsterdam: John Benjamins.

Collins, P. (2009a). *Modals and quasi-modals in English*. Amsterdam: Rodopi.

Collins, P. (2009b). Modals and quasi-modals in World Englishes. *World Englishes*, 28(3), 281–292. doi: 10.1111/j.1467-971X.2009.01593.x.

Collins, P. (2013). Grammatical colloquialism and the English quasi-modals: A comparative study. In J.I. Marín-Arrese, M. Carretero, J. Arús Hita & J. van der Auwera (Eds.), *English modality: Core, periphery and evidentiality* (155–169). Berlin: Mouton de Gruyter.

Collins, P. (2014). Quasi-modals and modals in Australian English fiction 1880–1999, with comparisons across British and American English. *Journal of English Linguistics*, 42(1), 7–30. doi: 10.1177/0075424213512857.

Collins, P. (Ed.) (2015). *Grammatical change in English world-wide*. Amsterdam: John Benjamins.

Collins, P. & X. Yao (2012). Modals and quasi-modals in New Englishes. In M. Hundt & U. Gut (Eds.), *Mapping unity and diversity world-wide: Corpus-based studies of New Englishes* (35–53). Amsterdam: John Benjamins.

Collins, P., A.M. Borlongan & X. Yao (2014). Modality in Philippine English: A diachronic study. *Journal of English Linguistics*, 42(1), 68–88. doi: 10.1177/0075424213511462.

Croft, W. (2000). *Explaining language change: An evolutionary approach*. Harlow: Longman.

Crowell, T.L. (1959). *HAVE GOT*, a pattern preserver. *American Speech*, 34(4), 280–286. doi: 10.2307/453706.

Crystal, D. (1997). *English as a global language.* Cambridge: Cambridge University Press.

Curzan, A. (2014). *Fixing English: Prescriptivism and language history.* Cambridge: Cambridge University Press.

D'Arcy, A. (2013). Variation and change. In R. Bayley, R. Cameron & C. Lucas (Eds.), *The Oxford handbook of sociolinguistics* (484–502). Oxford: Oxford University Press.

Davies, M. (2018). Using large online corpora to examine lexical, semantic, and cultural variation in different dialects and time periods. In E. Friginal (Ed.), *Studies in corpus-based sociolinguistics* (19–82). London: Routledge.

Davies, M. & R. Fuchs (2015). Expanding horizons in the study of World Englishes with the 1.9 billion word Global Web-based English Corpus (GloWbE). *English World-Wide*, 36(1), 1–28. doi: 10.1075/eww.36.1.01dav.

Denison, D. (1993). *English historical syntax: Verbal constructions.* London: Longman.

Denison, D. (1998). Syntax. In S. Romaine (Ed.), *The Cambridge history of the English language* (Vol. 4: 1776–1997, 92–329). Cambridge: Cambridge University Press.

Depraetere, I. & S. Reed (2006). Mood and modality in English. In B. Aarts & A. McMahon (Eds.), *The handbook of English linguistics* (269–290). Malden, Mass.: Blackwell.

Depraetere, I. & A. Verhulst (2008). Source of modality: A reassessment. *English Language and Linguistics*, 12(1), 1–25. doi: 10.1017/S1360674307002481.

Deshors, S.C. (2014). A case for a unified treatment of EFL and ESL: A multifactorial approach. *English World-Wide*, 35(3), 277–305.

Deuber, D. (2010). Modal verb usage at the interface of English and a related creole: A corpus-based study of *can/could* and *will/would* in Trinidadian English. *Journal of English Linguistics*, 38(2), 105–142. doi: 10.1177/0075424209348151.

Deuber, D. (2014). *English in the Caribbean: Variation, style and standards in Jamaica and Trinidad.* Cambridge: Cambridge University Press.

Deuber, D., C. Biewer, S. Hackert & M. Hilbert (2012). *Will* and *would* in selected New Englishes: General and variety-specific tendencies. In M. Hundt & U. Gut (Eds.), *Mapping unity and diversity world-wide: Corpus-based studies of New Englishes* (77–102). Amsterdam: John Benjamins.

Diaconu, G. (2012a). Assessing subjectivity and objectivity in modal expressions from New Englishes: A multivariate analysis. In D. Tizón-Couto, B. Tizón-Couto, I. Pastor-Gómez & P. Rodríguez-Puente (Eds.), *New trends and methodologies in applied English language research II: Studies in language variation, meaning and learning* (37–72). Bern: Lang.

Diaconu, G. (2012b). *Modality in New Englishes: A corpus-based study of obligation and necessity* (Dissertation). Freiburg i. Br.: University of Freiburg. Retrieved from http://www.freidok.uni-freiburg.de/volltexte/9596/ (last access: 19/02/2018).

Diaconu, G. (2015). The dynamics of obligation and necessity in the New Englishes: The case of *have to* in ICE. In R. Calabrese, J.K. Chambers & G. Leitner (Eds.), *Variation and change in postcolonial contexts* (127–147). Newcastle upon Tyne: Cambridge Scholars Publishing.

Dollinger, S. (2008). *New-dialect formation in Canada: Evidence from the English modal auxiliaries*. Amsterdam: John Benjamins.

Downes, W. (2005). *Language and society* (2 ed.). Cambridge: Cambridge University Press.

Dryer, M.S. & M. Haspelmath (2013). *The World Atlas of Language Structures Online*. Leipzig: Max Planck Institute for Evolutionary Anthropology. Available at http:// wals.info (last access: 19/02/2018).

Durrleman-Tame, S. (2008). *The syntax of Jamaican Creole: A cartographic perspective*. Amsterdam: John Benjamins.

Eckert, P. (1996). Vowels and nail polish: The emergence of linguistic style in the preadolescent heterosexual marketplace. In N. Warner, J. Ahlers, L. Bilmes, M. Oliver, S. Wertheim & M. Chen (Eds.), *Gender and belief systems: Proceedings of the Fourth Berkeley Women and Language Conference* (183–190). Berkeley: Berkeley Women and Language Group.

Eckert, P. (2012). Three waves of variation study: The emergence of meaning in the study of sociolinguistic variation. *Annual Review of Anthropology*, 41, 87–100. doi: 10.1146/annurev-anthro-092611-145828.

Edwards, A. & S. Laporte (2015). Outer and Expanding Circle Englishes: The competing roles of norm orientation and proficiency levels. *English World-Wide*, 36(2), 135–169. doi: 10.1075/eww.36.2.01edw.

Ehrman, M.E. (1966). *The meanings of the modals in present-day American English*. The Hague: Mouton.

Evans, S. (2000). Hong Kong's new English language policy in education. *World Englishes*, 19(2), 185–204. doi: 10.1111/1467-971x.00168.

Evans, S. (2009). The evolution of the English-language speech community in Hong Kong. *English World-Wide*, 30(3), 278–301. doi: 10.1075/eww.30.3.03eva.

Evans, S. (2013). The long march to biliteracy and trilingualism: Language policy in Hong Kong education since the handover. *Annual Review of Applied Linguistics*, 33, 302–324. doi: 10.1017/s0267190513000019.

Evans, S. (2014). The evolutionary dynamics of postcolonial English: A Hong Kong case study. *Journal of Sociolinguistics*, 18(5), 571–603. doi: 10.1111/josl.12104.

Evans, S. (2015). Modelling the development of English in Hong Kong. *World Englishes*, 34(3), 389–410. doi: 10.1111/weng.12154.

Evans, S. (2016). *The English language in Hong Kong: Diachronic and synchronic perspectives*. London: Palgrave Macmillan.

Facchinetti, R. (2003). Pragmatic and sociological constraints on the functions of *may* in contemporary British English. In R. Facchinetti, M. Krug & F.R. Palmer (Eds.), *Modality in contemporary English* (301–327). Berlin: Mouton de Gruyter.

Fairclough, N. (1993). *Discourse and social change*. Cambridge: Polity Press.

Fehringer, C. & K. Corrigan (2015). 'You've got to sort of eh hoy the Geordie out': Modals of obligation and necessity in fifty years of Tyneside English. *English Language and Linguistics*, 19(2), 355–381. doi: 10.1017/s1360674315000131.

Field, A., J. Miles & Z. Field (2012). *Discovering statistics using R*. Los Angeles: Sage.

Filppula, M.J. (2014). HAVE TO vs. HAVE GOT TO in British and Irish English(es). Paper presented at ISLE 3, Zurich.

Finegan, E. & D. Biber (2001). Register variation and social dialect variation: The register axiom. In J. Rickford & P. Eckert (Eds.), *Style and sociolinguistic variation* (235–267). Cambridge: Cambridge University Press.

Fischer, O. (1994). The development of quasi-auxiliaries in English and changes in word order. *Neophilologus*, 78(1), 137–164. doi: 10.1007/bf00999959.

Fischer, O., A. van Kemenade, W. Koopman & W. van der Wurff (2000). *The syntax of Early English*. Cambridge: Cambridge University Press.

Fleischman, S. (1982). *The future in thought and language: Diachronic evidence from Romance*. Cambridge: Cambridge University Press.

Fodor, J.D. & M.R. Smith (1978). What kind of exception is *have got? Linguistic Inquiry*, 9(1), 45–66.

Francis, W.F. & H. Kučera (1979). *Manual of information to accompany a standard corpus of present-day edited American English, for use with digital computers*. Providence, Rhode Island: Department of Linguistics, Brown University.

Friginal, E. (Ed.) (2018). *Studies in corpus-based sociolinguistics*. London: Routledge.

Friginal, E. & M. Bristow (2018). Corpus approaches to sociolinguistics: Introduction and chapter overviews. In E. Friginal (Ed.), *Studies in corpus-based sociolinguistics* (1–15). London: Routledge.

Fuchs, R. & U. Gut (2012). Do women use more intensifiers than men? Investigating gender and age-specific language use with the International Corpus of English. Paper presented at ICAME 33, Leuven.

Fuchs, R. & U. Gut (2015). An apparent time study of the progressive in Nigerian English. In P. Collins (Ed.), *Grammatical change in English world-wide* (373–387). Amsterdam: John Benjamins.

Gao, G. & S. Ting-Toomey (1998). *Communicating effectively with the Chinese*. Thousand Oaks, California: Sage.

Garcia, A.C., A.I. Standlee, J. Bechkoff & Y. Cui (2009). Ethnographic approaches to the internet and computer-mediated communication. *Journal of Contemporary Ethnography*, 38(1), 52–84. doi: 10.1177/0891241607310839.

Gauchat, L. (1905). L'unité phonétique dans le patois d'une commune. In H. Morf & L.P. Betz (Eds.), *Aus romanischen Sprachen und Literaturen: Festschrift Heinrich Morf zur Feier seiner 25jährigen Lehrtätigkeit von seinen Schülern dargebracht* (175–232). Halle: Niemeyer.

Gilquin, G. (2015). At the interface of contact linguistics and second language acquisition: New Englishes and learner Englishes compared. *English World-Wide*, 36(1), 91–124. doi: 10.1075/eww.36.1.05gil.

Gisborne, N. (2009). Aspects of the morphosyntactic typology of Hong Kong English. *English World-Wide*, 30(2), 149–169. doi: 10.1075/eww.30.2.03gis.

Görlach, M. (1987). Colonial lag? The alleged conservative character of American English and other 'colonial' varieties. *English World-Wide*, 8(1), 41–60. doi: 10.1075/eww.8.1.05gor.

Gotti, M., M. Dossena, R. Dury, R. Facchinetti & M. Lima (2002). *Variation in central modals: A repertoire of forms and types of usage in Middle English and Early Modern English*. Bern: Lang.

Gramley, S. & K. M. Pätzold (2004). *A survey of Modern English* (2 ed.). London: Routledge.

Greenbaum, S. (1988). A proposal for an international computerized corpus of English. *World Englishes*, 7(3), 315. doi: 10.1111/j.1467-971x.1988.tb00241.x.

Greenbaum, S. (1990). Standard English and the International Corpus of English. *World Englishes*, 9(1), 79–83. doi: 10.1111/j.1467-971x.1990.tb00688.x.

Greenbaum, S. (1991). ICE: The International Corpus of English. *English Today*, 7(4), 3–7. doi: 10.1017/s0266078400005836.

Greenbaum, S. (1996a). Introducing ICE. In S. Greenbaum (Ed.), *Comparing English worldwide: The International Corpus of English* (3–12). Oxford: Clarendon Press.

Greenbaum, S. (Ed.) (1996b). *Comparing English worldwide: The International Corpus of English*. Oxford: Clarendon Press.

Gries, S.T. (2013). *Statistics for linguistics with R: A practical introduction* (2 ed.). Berlin: Mouton de Gruyter.

Gronemeyer, C. (1999). On deriving complex polysemy: The grammaticalization of *get*. *English Language and Linguistics*, 3(1), 1–39. doi: 10.1017/s1360674399000118.

Groves, J.M. (2011). 'Linguistic schizophrenia' in Hong Kong. *English Today*, 27(4), 33–42. doi: 10.1017/s0266078411000514.

Gumperz, J.J. & R. Wilson (1971). Convergence and creolization: A case from the Indo-Aryan/Dravidian border in India. In D. Hymes (Ed.), *Pidginization and creolization of languages: Proceedings of a conference held at the University of the West Indies, Mona, Jamaica, April 1968* (151–167). Cambridge: Cambridge University Press.

Gupta, A.F. (1998). The situation of English in Singapore. In J.A. Foley, T. Kandiah, Z. Bao, A.F. Gupta, L. Alsagoff, H.C. Lick, L. Wee, I.S. Talib & W. Bokhorst-Heng (Eds.),

English in new cultural contexts: Reflections from Singapore (106–126). Singapore: Oxford University Press.

Hackert, S. (2014). The evolution of English(es): Notes on the history of an idea. In S. Buschfeld, T. Hoffmann, M. Huber & A. Kautzsch (Eds.), *The evolution of Englishes: The Dynamic Model and beyond* (282–300). Amsterdam: John Benjamins.

Hackert, S. & D. Deuber (2015). American influence on written Caribbean English: A diachronic analysis of newspaper reportage in the Bahamas and in Trinidad and Tobago. In P. Collins (Ed.), *Grammatical change in English world-wide* (389–410). Amsterdam: John Benjamins.

Hackert, S., D. Deuber, C. Biewer & M. Hilbert (2013). Modals of possibility, ability and permission in selected New Englishes. In M. Huber & J. Mukherjee (Eds.), *Studies in variation, contacts and change* (Vol. 13: Corpus linguistics and variation in English: Focus on non-native Englishes). Helsinki: VARIENG. Retrieved from http://www.helsinki.fi/varieng/series/volumes/13/hackert_deuber_biewer_hilbert/ (last access: 19/02/2018).

Halliday, M.A.K. & E. McDonald (2004). Metafunctional profile of the grammar of Chinese. In A. Caffarel, J.R. Martin & C.M.I.M. Matthiessen (Eds.), *Language typology: A functional perspective* (305–396). Amsterdam: John Benjamins.

Hardt, M. & A. Negri (2001). *Empire*. Cambridge, Mass.: Harvard University Press.

Haspelmath, M. (2004). On directionality in language change with particular reference to grammaticalization. In O. Fischer, M. Norde & H. Perridon (Eds.), *Up und down the cline: The nature of grammaticalization* (17–44). Amsterdam: John Benjamins.

Haspelmath, M., M.S. Dryer, D. Gil & B. Comrie (Eds.). (2005). *The World Atlas of Language Structures*. Oxford: Oxford University Press.

Hausknecht, E. (Ed.) (1885). *Floris and Blauncheflur: Mittelenglisches Gedicht aus dem 13. Jahrhundert; nebst litterarischer Untersuchung und einem Abriss über die Verbreitung der Sage in der europäischen Litteratur*. Berlin: Weidmann.

Heath, J.G. (1984). Language contact and language change. *Annual Review of Anthropology*, 13, 367–384. doi: 10.1146/annurev.anthro.13.1.367.

Heine, B. (1993). *Auxiliaries: Cognitive forces and grammaticalization*. Oxford: Oxford University Press.

Heine, B. & T. Kuteva (2005). *Language contact and grammatical change*. Cambridge: Cambridge University Press.

Heine, B. & T. Kuteva (2010). Contact and grammaticalization. In R. Hickey (Ed.), *The handbook of language contact* (86–105). Malden, Mass.: Wiley-Blackwell.

Heller, B. (2014). Automatic n-gram analysis (ANGA) on the basis of Biber et al.'s (1999) lexical bundle categories. Paper presented at ICAME 35, Nottingham.

Heller, B. & M. Röthlisberger (2015). Big data on trial: Researching syntactic alternations in GloWbE and ICE. Paper presented at the From Data to Evidence Conference: Big data, rich data, uncharted data, Helsinki.

Herat, M. (2015). *Be going to* and *have to*: A corpus study of Sri Lankan English usage in comparison to British and American English. In C. Suárez-Gómez & E. Seoane (Eds.), *Englishes today: Multiple varieties, multiple perspectives* (103–126). Newcastle upon Tyne: Cambridge Scholars Publishing.

Hermann, E. (1929). Lautveränderungen in den Individualsprachen einer Mundart. *Nachrichten der Gesellschaft der Wissenschaften zu Göttingen: Philosophisch-historische Klasse*, 11, 195–214.

Hermerén, L. (1978). *On modality in English: A study of the semantics of the modals.* Lund: Gleerup.

Hickmann, M. & D. Bassano (2016). Modality and mood in first language acquisition. In J. Nuyts & J. van der Auwera (Eds.), *The Oxford handbook of modality and mood* (430–447). Oxford: Oxford University Press.

Hilpert, M. & S. Flach (2017). From big data to small data and back again: Using token-based semantic vector spaces for corpus-linguistic analyses. Paper presented at BICLCE 7, Vigo.

Hiltunen, T., J. McVeigh & T. Säily (2017). How to turn linguistic data into evidence. In T. Hiltunen, J. McVeigh & T. Säily (Eds.), *Studies in variation, contacts and change in English* (Vol. 19: Big and rich data in English corpus linguistics: Methods and explorations). Helsinki: VARIENG. Retrieved from http://www.helsinki.fi/varieng/series/volumes/19/introduction.html (last access: 19/02/2018).

Hinrichs, L. (2006). *Codeswitching on the web: English and Jamaican Creole in e-mail communication.* Amsterdam: John Benjamins.

Ho Abdullah, I. (1993). *The semantics of the modal auxiliaries of Malay.* Kuala Lumpur: Dewan Bahasa dan Pustaka, Ministry of Education.

Hoffmann, S., A. Sand & P. Tan (2012). The Corpus of Historical Singapore English: A first pilot study on data from the 1950s and 1960s. Paper presented at ICAME 33, Leuven.

Höhn, N. (2012). And they were all like 'What's going on?': New quotatives in Jamaican and Irish English. In M. Hundt & U. Gut (Eds.), *Mapping unity and diversity world-wide: Corpus-based studies of New Englishes* (263–290). Amsterdam: John Benjamins.

Hopper, P.J. (1991). On some principles of grammaticization. In E.C. Traugott & B. Heine (Eds.), *Approaches to grammaticalization* (Vol. 1: Focus on theoretical and methodological issues, 17–35). Amsterdam: John Benjamins.

Hopper, P.J. & E.C. Traugott (1993). *Grammaticalization.* Cambridge: Cambridge University Press.

Horch, S. (2017). *Conversion in Asian Englishes: A usage-based account of the emergence of new local norms* (Dissertation). Freiburg i. Br.: University of Freiburg. Retrieved from https://freidok.uni-freiburg.de/data/12910 (last access: 19/02/2018).

Huber, M. (2014). Stylistic and sociolinguistic variation in Schneider's Nativization Phase: *T*-affrication and relativization in Ghanaian English. In S. Buschfeld, T. Hoffmann, M. Huber & A. Kautzsch (Eds.), *The evolution of Englishes: The Dynamic Model and beyond* (86–106). Amsterdam: John Benjamins.

Huber, M. & K. Dako (2008). Ghanaian English: Morphology and syntax. In R. Mesthrie (Ed.), *Varieties of English 4: Africa, South and Southeast Asia* (368–380). Berlin: Mouton de Gruyter.

Huddleston, R.D. (1980). Criteria for auxiliaries and modals. In S. Greenbaum, G. Leech & J. Svartvik (Eds.), *Studies in linguistics: For Randolph Quirk* (65–78). London: Longman.

Huddleston, R.D. & G.K. Pullum (2002). *The Cambridge grammar of the English language*. Cambridge: Cambridge University Press.

Hundt, M. (2004). Animacy, agentivity, and the spread of the progressive in Modern English. *English Language and Linguistics*, 8(1), 47–69. doi: 10.1017/S1360674304001248.

Hundt, M. (2009). Colonial lag, colonial innovation or simply language change? In G. Rohdenburg & J. Schlüter (Eds.), *One language, two grammars? Differences between British and American English* (13–37). Cambridge: Cambridge University Press.

Hundt, M. & G. Leech (2012). 'Small is beautiful': On the value of standard reference corpora for observing recent grammatical change. In T. Nevalainen & E.C. Traugott (Eds.), *The Oxford handbook of the history of English* (175–188). Oxford: Oxford University Press.

Hundt, M. & C. Mair (1999). 'Agile' and 'uptight' genres: The corpus-based approach to language change in progress. *International Journal of Corpus Linguistics*, 4(2), 221–242. doi: 10.1075/ijcl.4.2.02hun.

Imperial, R.A. (2014). Lexical variation in Philippine English: The case of deontic MUST and HAVE TO. *Philippine Journal of Linguistics*, 45, 1–18.

Jain, U.R. (1995). *Introduction to Hindi grammar*. Berkeley: University of California, Center for South Asia Studies.

Jankowski, B. (2004). A transatlantic perspective of variation and change in English deontic modality. *Toronto Working Papers in Linguistics*, 23(2), 85–113.

Jenkins, J. (2003). *World Englishes: A resource book for students*. London: Routledge.

Jespersen, O. (1940). *A modern English grammar on historical principles. Part 5: Syntax* (Vol. 4). London: Allen & Unwin.

Jespersen, O. (1954). *A modern English grammar on historical principles: Part 4: Syntax* (Vol. 3). London: Allen & Unwin.

Johansson, S. (2013). Modals and semi-modals of obligation in American English: Some aspects of developments from 1990 until the present day. In B. Aarts, J. Close, G. Leech & S. Wallis (Eds.), *The verb phrase in English: Investigating recent language change with corpora* (372–380). Cambridge: Cambridge University Press.

Johansson, S., G. Leech & H. Goodluck (1978). *Manual of information to accompany the Lancaster-Oslo/Bergen corpus on British English, for use with digital computers*. Oslo: Department of English.

Johnson, D.E. (2009). Getting off the GoldVarb standard: Introducing Rbrul for mixed-effects variable rule analysis. *Language and Linguistics Compass*, 3(1), 359–383. doi: 10.1111/j.1749-818x.2008.00108.x.

Johnstone, B., J. Andrus & A.E. Danielson (2006). Mobility, indexicality, and the en-registerment of 'Pittsburghese'. *Journal of English Linguistics*, 34(2), 77–104. doi: 10.1177/0075424206290692.

Joseph, J.E. (2004). *Language and identity: National, ethnic, religious*. Basingstoke: Palgrave Macmillan.

Kachru, B.B. (1983a). *The Indianization of English: The English language in India*. New Delhi: Oxford University Press.

Kachru, B.B. (1983b). Models for non-native Englishes. In K. Bolton & B.B. Kachru (Eds.), *World Englishes: Critical concepts in linguistics* (Vol. 4, 108–130). London: Routledge.

Kachru, B.B. (1985). Standards, codification and sociolinguistic realism. The English language in the Outer Circle. In R. Quirk & H.G. Widdowson (Eds.), *English in the world: Teaching and learning the language and literatures* (11–36). Cambridge: Cambridge University Press.

Kachru, B.B. (2005). *Asian Englishes: Beyond the canon*. Hong Kong: Hong Kong University Press.

Kachru, Y. (1980). *Aspects of Hindi grammar*. New Delhi: Manohar.

Kachru, Y. (2017). World Englishes, pragmatics, and discourse. In M.J. Filppula, J. Klemola & D. Sharma (Eds.), *The Oxford handbook of World Englishes* (272–290). New York: Oxford University Press.

Kallen, J.L. & J.M. Kirk (2012). *SPICE-Ireland: A user's guide: Documentation to accompany the SPICE-Ireland corpus: Systems of pragmatic annotation in ICE-Ireland*. Belfast: Cló Ollscoil na Banríona.

Kendall, T. (2011). Corpora from a sociolinguistic perspective. *Revista Brasiliera de Linguística Aplicada*, 11(2), 361–389. doi: 10.1590/s1984-63982011000200005.

Kendall, T. & G. van Herk (2011). Corpus linguistics and sociolinguistic inquiry: Introduction to special issue. *Corpus Linguistics and Linguistic Theory*, 7(1), 1–6. doi: 10.1515/cllt.2011.001.

Kirk, J.M. & G. Nelson (2017). The International Corpus of English (ICE) project: The next 25 years. Paper presented at ICAME 38, Prague.

Kirkpatrick, A. (2007). *World Englishes: Implications for international communication and English language teaching*. Cambridge: Cambridge University Press.

Kirkpatrick, A. (2012). Theoretical issues. In E.-L. Low & A. Hashim (Eds.), *English in Southeast Asia: Features, policy and language in use* (13–31). Amsterdam: John Benjamins.

Kirkpatrick, A. (2015). World Englishes and local cultures. In F. Sharifian (Ed.), *The Routledge handbook of language and culture* (460–470). London: Routledge.

Kortmann, B. (2006). Syntactic variation in English: A global perspective. In B. Aarts & A. McMahon (Eds.), *The handbook of English linguistics* (603–624). Malden, Mass.: Blackwell.

Kretzschmar, W.A. Jr. (2002). Dialectology and the history of the English language. In D. Minkova & R. Stockwell (Eds.), *Studies in the history of the English language: A millennial perspective* (79–108). Berlin: Mouton de Gruyter.

Krishnamurti, B. & J.P.L. Gwynn (1985). *A grammar of modern Telugu*. Delhi: Oxford University Press.

Krug, M. (1998). *Gotta* – the tenth central modal in English? Social, stylistic and regional variation in the British National Corpus as evidence of ongoing grammaticalization. In H. Lindquist, S. Klintborg, M. Levin & M. Estling (Eds.), *The major varieties of English: Papers from MAVEN 97, Växjö 20.-22. November 1997* (177–191). Växjö: Växjö University Press.

Krug, M. (2000). *Emerging English modals: A corpus-based study of grammaticalization*. Berlin: Mouton de Gruyter.

Krug, M. & K. Sell (2013). Designing and conducting interviews and questionnaires. In M. Krug & J. Schlüter (Eds.), *Research methods in language variation and change* (69–98). Cambridge: Cambridge University Press.

Labov, W. (1963). The social motivation of a sound change. *Word*, 19(3), 273–309. doi: 10.1080/00437956.1963.11659799.

Labov, W. (1972). *Sociolinguistic patterns*. Philadelphia: University of Pennsylvania Press.

Labov, W. (1994). *Principles of linguistic change* (Vol. 1: Internal factors). Oxford: Blackwell.

Labov, W. (2001). *Principles of linguistic change* (Vol. 2: Social factors). Oxford: Blackwell.

Lai, M.-L. (2008). Language attitudes of the first postcolonial generation in Hong Kong secondary schools. In K. Bolton & H. Yang (Eds.), *Language and society in Hong Kong* (453–486). Hong Kong: Open Hong Kong University Press.

Lakoff, G. & M. Johnson (1980). *Metaphors we live by*. Chicago: University of Chicago Press.

Lange, C. (2012). *The syntax of spoken Indian English*. Amsterdam: John Benjamins.

Lange, C. (2017). Indian English or Indian Englishes? Accounting for speakers' multilingual repertoires in corpora of postcolonial Englishes. In A. Nurmi, T. Rütten & P. Pahta (Eds.), *Challenging the myth of monolingual corpora* (16–38). Leiden: Brill.

Łęcki, A.M. (2010). *Grammaticalisation paths of* have *in English*. Frankfurt a. M.: Lang.

Lee-Wong, S.M. (2000). *Politeness and face in Chinese culture*. Frankfurt a. M.: Lang.

Leech, G. (1983). *Principles of pragmatics*. London: Longman.

Leech, G. (2003). Modality on the move: The English modal auxiliaries 1961–1992. In R. Facchinetti, M. Krug & F.R. Palmer (Eds.), *Modality in contemporary English* (223–240). Berlin: Mouton de Gruyter.

Leech, G. (2004a). *Meaning and the English verb* (3 ed.). Harlow: Pearson Education Limited.

Leech, G. (2004b). Recent grammatical change in English: Data, description, theory. In K. Aijmer & B. Altenberg (Eds.), *Advances in corpus linguistics: Papers from the 23rd International Conference on English Language Research on Computerized Corpora (ICAME 23), Gothenburg 22–26 May 2002* (61–81). Amsterdam: Rodopi.

Leech, G. (2011). The modal verbs ARE declining: Reply to Neil Millar's 'Modal verbs in TIME: Frequency changes 1923–2006'. *International Journal of Corpus Linguistics*, 16(4), 547–564. doi: 10.1075/ijcl.16.4.05lee.

Leech, G. (2013). Where have all the modals gone? An essay on the declining frequency of core modal auxiliaries in recent standard English. In J.I. Marín-Arrese, M. Carretero, J. Arús Hita & J. van der Auwera (Eds.), *English modality: Core, periphery and evidentiality* (95–115). Berlin: Mouton de Gruyter.

Leech, G. & N. Smith (2009). Change and constancy in linguistic change: How grammatical usage in written English evolved in the period 1931–1991. In A. Renouf & A. Kehoe (Eds.), *Corpus linguistics: Refinements and reassessments* (173–200). Amsterdam: Rodopi.

Leech, G., M. Hundt, C. Mair & N. Smith (2009). *Change in contemporary English: A grammatical study*. Cambridge: Cambridge University Press.

Leimgruber, J.R. (2009). Ethnicity as a variable in Singapore English. Paper presented at ICLCE 3, London.

Leimgruber, J.R. (2013). *Singapore English: Structure, variation, and usage*. Cambridge: Cambridge University Press.

Leimgruber, J.R. & L. Sankaran (2014). Imperfectives in Singapore's Indian community. In M. Hundt & D. Sharma (Eds.), *English in the Indian diaspora* (105–130). Amsterdam: John Benjamins.

Levin, B. (1993). *English verb classes and alternations: A preliminary investigation*. Chicago: University of Chicago Press.

Levshina, N. (2015). *How to do linguistics with R: Data exploration and statistical analysis*. Amsterdam: John Benjamins.

Levshina, N., D. Geeraerts & D. Speelman (2014). Dutch causative constructions: Quantification of meaning and meaning of quantification. In D. Glynn & J.A. Robinson (Eds.), *Corpus methods for semantics: Quantitative studies in polysemy and synonymy* (205–221). Amsterdam: John Benjamins.

Li, D.C.S. (2008). The functions and status of English in Hong Kong: A post-1997 update. In K. Bolton & H. Yang (Eds.), *Language and society in Hong Kong* (194–240). Hong Kong: Open University of Hong Kong Press.

Li, C.N. & S.A. Thompson (1989). *Mandarin Chinese: A functional reference grammar*. Berkeley: University of California Press.

Lim, L. (2000). Ethnic group differences aligned? Intonation patterns of Chinese, Indian and Malay Singaporean English. In A. Brown, D. Deterding & E.-L. Low (Eds.), *The English language in Singapore: Research on pronunciation* (10–21). Singapore: Singapore Association for Applied Linguistics.

Lim, L. (2009). Revisiting English prosody: (Some) New Englishes as tone languages? In L. Lim & N. Gisborne (Eds.), *The typology of Asian Englishes* (97–118). Amsterdam: John Benjamins.

Lim, L. (2014). Yesterday's founder population, today's Englishes: The role of the Peranakans in the (continuing) evolution of Singapore English. In S. Buschfeld, T. Hoffmann, M. Huber & A. Kautzsch (Eds.), *The evolution of Englishes: The Dynamic Model and beyond* (401–419). Amsterdam: John Benjamins.

Lim, L. & U. Ansaldo (2016). *Languages in contact*. Cambridge: Cambridge University Press.

Lin, H. (2001). *A grammar of Mandarin Chinese*. Munich: Lincom Europa.

Lorenz, D. (2013). *Contractions of English semi-modals: The emancipating effect of frequency* (Dissertation). Freiburg i. Br.: University of Freiburg. Retrieved from https:// freidok.uni-freiburg.de/data/9317 (last access: 19/02/2018).

Loureiro-Porto, L. (2009). *The semantic predecessors of* need *in the history of English (c.750–1710)*. Malden, Mass.: Wiley-Blackwell.

Loureiro-Porto, L. (2013). *[T]he figure sixty forty seven forty five...*: Modals of necessity in Hong Kong and Indian English. Paper presented at ICAME 34, Santiago de Compostela.

Loureiro-Porto, L. (2016). (Semi-)modals of necessity in Hong Kong and Indian Englishes. In E. Seoane & C. Suárez-Gómez (Eds.), *World Englishes: New theoretical and methodological considerations* (143–172). Amsterdam: John Benjamins.

Loureiro-Porto, L. (2017). ICE vs GloWbE: Big data and corpus compilation. *World Englishes*, 36(3), 448–470. doi: 10.1111/weng.12281.

Low, E.-L. (2010). English in Singapore and Malaysia: Similarities and differences. In A. Kirkpatrick (Ed.), *The Routledge handbook of World Englishes* (229–246). London: Routledge.

Luke, K.K. & J.C. Richards (1982). English in Hong Kong: Functions and status. *English World-Wide*, 3(1), 47–64. doi: 10.1075/eww.3.1.04kan.

Lyons, J. (1977). *Semantics* (Vol. 2). Cambridge: Cambridge University Press.

Mair, C. (1997). Parallel corpora: A real-time approach to the study of language change in progress. In M. Ljung (Ed.), *Corpus-based studies in English: Papers from the seventeenth International Conference on English Language Research on Computerized Corpora (ICAME 17)* (195–209). Amsterdam: Rodopi.

Mair, C. (2004). Corpus linguistics and grammaticalisation theory: Statistics, frequencies, and beyond. In H. Lindquist & C. Mair (Eds.), *Corpus approaches to grammaticalization in English* (121–150). Amsterdam: John Benjamins.

Mair, C. (2006). *Twentieth-century English: History, variation, and standardization.* Cambridge: Cambridge University Press.

Mair, C. (2007). British English/American English grammar: Convergence in writing – Divergence in speech? *Anglia*, 125(1), 84–100. doi: 10.1515/angl.2007.84.

Mair, C. (2009a). Corpus linguistics meets sociolinguistics: Studying educated spoken usage in Jamaica on the basis of the International Corpus of English. In T. Hoffmann & L. Siebers (Eds.), *World Englishes: Problems, properties and prospects* (39–60). Amsterdam: John Benjamins.

Mair, C. (2009b). Corpus linguistics meets sociolinguistics: The role of corpus evidence in the study of sociolinguistic variation and change. In A. Renouf & A. Kehoe (Eds.), *Corpus linguistics: Refinements and reassessments* (7–32). Amsterdam: Rodopi.

Mair, C. (2011). Corpora and the new Englishes: Using the 'Corpus of Cyber-Jamaican' to explore research perspectives for the future. In F. Meunier, S. De Cock, G. Gilquin & M. Paquot (Eds.), *A taste for corpora: In honour of Sylviane Granger* (210–236). Amsterdam: John Benjamins.

Mair, C. (2013). The World System of Englishes: Accounting for the transnational importance of mobile and mediated vernaculars. *English World-Wide*, 34(3), 253–278 doi: 10.1075/eww.34.3.01mai.

Mair, C. (2014). *Do we got a difference?* Divergent developments of semi-auxiliary (*have*) *got* (*to*) in British English and American English. In M. Hundt (Ed.), *Late Modern English syntax* (56–76). Cambridge: Cambridge University Press.

Mair, C. (2015a). Cross-variety diachronic drifts and ephemeral regional contrasts: An analysis of modality in the extended Brown family of corpora and what it can tell us about the New Englishes. In P. Collins (Ed.), *Grammatical change in English worldwide* (119–146). Amsterdam: John Benjamins.

Mair, C. (2015b). Responses to Davies and Fuchs. *English World-Wide*, 36(1), 29–33. doi: 10.1075/eww.36.1.02mai.

Marckwardt, A.H. (1958). *American English.* New York: Oxford University Press.

Markus, H.R. & S. Kitayama (1991). Culture and the self: Implications for cognition, emotion, and motivation. *Psychological Review*, 98(2), 224–253. doi: 10.1037//0033-295x.98.2.224.

Matras, Y. (2009). *Language contact.* Cambridge: Cambridge University Press.

Matras, Y. & J. Sakel (2007). *Grammatical borrowing in cross-linguistic perspective.* Berlin: Mouton de Gruyter.

Matsumoto, Y. (1988). Reexamination of the universality of face: Politeness phenomena in Japanese. *Journal of Pragmatics*, 12(4), 403–426.

Matthews, S. & V. Yip (1994). *Cantonese: A comprehensive grammar.* London: Routledge.

McWhorter, J.H. (2012). Case closed? Testing the feature pool hypothesis. *Journal of Pidgin and Creole Languages*, 27(1), 171–182. doi: 10.1075/jpcl.27.1.07mcw.

Meierkord, C. (2016). Speech acts in Ugandan English social letters: Investigating the influence of sociocultural context. In C. Meierkord, B. Isingoma & S. Namyalo (Eds.), *Ugandan English: Its sociolinguistics, structure and uses in a globalising post-protectorate* (227–248). Amsterdam: John Benjamins.

Mesthrie, R. (2006). Contact linguistics and World Englishes. In B.B. Kachru, Y. Kachru & C.L. Nelson (Eds.), *The handbook of World Englishes* (273–288). Malden, Mass.: Blackwell.

Mesthrie, R. (2008a). Black South African English: Morphology and syntax. In R. Mesthrie (Ed.), *Varieties of English 4: Africa, South and Southeast Asia* (488–500). Berlin: Mouton de Gruyter.

Mesthrie, R. (2008b). Synopsis: Morphological and syntactic variation in Africa and South and Southeast Asia. In R. Mesthrie (Ed.), *Varieties of English 4: Africa, South and Southeast Asia* (624–635). Berlin: Mouton de Gruyter.

Mesthrie, R. & R.M. Bhatt (2008). *World Englishes: The study of new linguistic varieties.* Cambridge: Cambridge University Press.

Meyerhoff, M. & N. Niedzielski (2003). The globalisation of vernacular variation. *Journal of Sociolinguistics*, 7(4), 534–555. doi: 10.1111/j.1467-9841.2003.00241.x.

Millar, N. (2009). Modal verbs in TIME: Frequency changes 1923–2006. *International Journal of Corpus Linguistics*, 14(2), 191–220. doi: 10.1075/ijcl.14.2.03mil.

Mitchell, B. (1985). *Old English syntax* (Vol. 1: Concord, the parts of speech, and the sentence). Oxford: Clarendon Press.

Mohr, S. (2016). From Accra to Nairobi: The use of pluralized mass nouns in East and West African postcolonial Englishes. In D. Schmidt-Brücken, S. Schuster & M. Wienberg (Eds.), *Aspects of (post)colonial linguistics: Current perspectives and new approaches* (157–188). Berlin: Mouton de Gruyter.

Molencki, R. (2002). The status of *dearr* and *þearf* in Old English. *Studia Anglia Posnaniensia*, 38, 363–380.

Moll, A. (2015). *Jamaican Creole goes web: Sociolinguistic styling and authenticity in a digital 'Yaad'.* Amsterdam: John Benjamins.

Mufwene, S.S. (1996). The founder principle in creole genesis. *Diachronica*, 13(1), 83–134. doi: 10.1075/dia.13.1.05muf.

Mufwene, S.S. (2001). *The ecology of language evolution.* Cambridge: Cambridge University Press.

Mufwene, S.S. (2006). Race, racialism, and the study of language evolution in America. Retrieved from http://mufwene.uchicago.edu/publications/RACE_RACIALISM_LANGUAGE_EVOLUTION.pdf (last access: 19/02/2018).

Mukherjee, J. (2007). Steady states in the evolution of New Englishes: Present-day Indian English as an equilibrium. *Journal of English Linguistics*, 35(2), 157–187. doi: 10.1177/0075424207301888.

Mukherjee, J. (2010). The development of the English language in India. In A. Kirkpatrick (Ed.), *The Routledge handbook of World Englishes* (167–180). London: Routledge.

Mukherjee, J. & S. Hoffmann (2006). Describing verb-complementational profiles of New Englishes: A pilot study of Indian English. *English World-Wide*, 27(2), 147–173. doi: 10.1075/eww.27.2.03muk.

Mukherjee, J. & M. Hundt (Eds.). (2011). *Exploring second-language varieties of English and learner Englishes: Bridging a paradigm gap.* Amsterdam: John Benjamins.

Mukherjee, J. & M. Schilk (2012). Exploring variation and change in New Englishes: Looking into the International Corpus of English (ICE) and beyond. In T. Nevalainen & E.C. Traugott (Eds.), *The Oxford handbook of the history of English* (189–199). Oxford: Oxford University Press.

Müller, F. (2008). From degrammaticalisation to regrammaticalisation? Current changes in the use of NEED. *Arbeiten aus Anglistik und Amerikanistik*, 33(1), 71–94.

Myhill, J. (1995). Change and continuity in the functions of the American English modals. *Linguistics*, 33(2), 157–211. doi: 10.1515/ling.1995.33.2.157.

Myhill, J. (1996). The development of the strong obligation system in American English. *American Speech*, 71(4), 339–388. doi: 10.2307/455712.

Nelson, G. (1991). *File header information.* London: Survey of English Usage, University College London.

Nelson, G. (1996). The design of the corpus. In S. Greenbaum (Ed.), *Comparing English worldwide: The International Corpus of English* (27–35). Oxford: Clarendon Press.

Nelson, G. (2003). Modals of obligation and necessity in varieties of English. In P. Peters (Ed.), *From local to global English: Proceedings of Style Council 2001/2* (25–32). Sydney: Macquarie University, Dictionary Research Centre.

Nelson, G. (2015). Responses to Davies and Fuchs. *English World-Wide*, 36(1), 38–40. doi: 10.1075/eww.36.1.02nel.

Nesselhauf, N. (2009). Co-selection phenomena across New Englishes: Parallels (and differences) to foreign learner varieties. *English World-Wide*, 30(1), 1–26. doi: 10.1075/eww.30.1.02nes.

Nevalainen, T. (2000). Gender differences in the evolution of standard English: Evidence from the *Corpus of Early English Correspondence. Journal of English Linguistics*, 28(1), 38–59. doi: 10.1177/00754240022004866.

Newmark, K., N. Walker & J. Stanford (2016). 'The rez accent knows no border': Native American ethnic identity expressed through English prosody. *Language in Society*, 45(5), 633–664. doi: 10.1017/s0047404516000592.

Nkemleke, D.A. (2005). *Must* and *should* in Cameroon English. *Nordic Journal of African Studies*, 14(1), 43–67.

Noël, D. & J. van der Auwera (2015). Recent quantitative changes in the use of modals and quasi-modals in the Hong Kong, British and American printed press: Exploring the potential of *Factiva®* for the diachronic investigation of World Englishes. In P. Collins (Ed.), *Grammatical change in English world-wide* (437–464). Amsterdam: John Benjamins.

Noël, D., B. van Rooy & J. van der Auwera (2014). Diachronic approaches to modality in World Englishes: Introduction to the special issue. *Journal of English Linguistics*, 42(1), 3–6. doi: 10.1177/0075424213512655.

Nokkonen, S. (2006). The semantic variation of NEED TO in four recent British corpora. *International Journal of Corpus Linguistics*, 11(1), 29–71. doi: 10.1075/ijcl.11.1.03nok.

Nokkonen, S. (2010). 'How many taxis there needs to be?' The sociolinguistic variation of NEED TO in spoken British English. *Corpora*, 5(1), 45–74. doi: 10.3366/cor.2010.0003.

Nokkonen, S. (2012). NEED TO and the domain of business in spoken British English. In S. Hoffmann, P. Rayson & G. Leech (Eds.), *English corpus linguistics: Looking back, moving forward: Papers from the 30th International Conference on English Language Research on Computerized Corpora (ICAME 30), Lancaster, UK, 27–31 May 2009* (131–147). Amsterdam: Rodopi.

Nokkonen, S. (2015). *Changes in the field of obligation and necessity in contemporary British English: A corpus-based sociolinguistic study of semi-modal NEED TO* (Dissertation). Vantaa: Société Néophilologique.

Nwoye, O. (1992). Linguistic politeness and socio-cultural variation of the notion of face. *Journal of Pragmatics*, 18(4), 309–328. doi: 10.1016/0378-2166(92)90092-p.

Olavarría de Ersson, E. & P. Shaw (2003). Verb complementation patterns in Indian Standard English. *English World-Wide*, 24(2), 137–161. doi: 10.1075/eww.24.2.02ers.

Oyserman, D., H.M. Coon & M. Kemmelmeier (2002). Rethinking individualism and collectivism: Evaluation of theoretical assumptions and meta-analyses. *Psychological Bulletin*, 128(1), 3–72. doi: 10.1037//0033-2909.128.1.3.

Palmer, F.R. (1979). *Modality and the English modals*. London: Longman.

Palmer, F.R. (2001). *Mood and Modality* (2 ed.). Cambridge: Cambridge University Press.

Pandharipande, R.V. (1997). *Marathi*. London: Routledge.

Pang, T.T.T. (2003). Hong Kong English: A stillborn variety. *English Today*, 19(2), 12–18. doi: 10.1017/s0266078403002037.

Paolillo, J.C. (2001). Language variation on Internet Relay Chat: A social network approach. *Journal of Sociolinguistics*, 5(2), 180–213. doi: 10.1111/1467-9481.00147.

Parviainen, H. & R. Fuchs (2015). Indian English as a super-central variety: Diffusion of clause-final focus particles in Asian Englishes. Paper presented at ICAME 36, Trier.

Percillier, M. (2016). *World Englishes and second language acquisition*. Amsterdam: John Benjamins.

Perrault, S.J., K.M. Doherty, D.B. Justice, M.L. Novak & E.W. Gilman (Eds.). (1989). *Webster's dictionary of English usage*. Springfield, Mass.: Merriam-Webster.

Peters, P. (2015). Responses to Davies and Fuchs. *English World-Wide*, 36(1), 41–44. doi: 10.1075/eww.36.1.02pet.

Plag, I. (2011). Creolization and admixture: Typology, feature pools, and second-language acquisition. *Journal of Pidgin and Creole Languages*, 26(1), 89–110. doi: 10.1075/bct.57.05pla.

Plank, F. (1984). The modals story retold. *Studies in Language*, 8(3), 305–364. doi: 10.1075/sl.8.3.02pla.

Podesva, R.J. (2011). The California vowel shift and gay identity. *American Speech*, 86(1), 32–51. doi: 10.1215/00031283-1277501.

Preston, D.R. (1999). A language attitude approach to the perception of regional variety. In D.R. Preston (Ed.), *Handbook of perceptual dialectology* (Vol. 1, 359–373). Amsterdam: John Benjamins.

Quirk, R., S. Greenbaum, G. Leech & J. Svartvik (1985). *A comprehensive grammar of the English language*. London: Longman.

Rajadurai, J. (2005). Revisiting the Concentric Circles: Conceptual and sociolinguistic considerations. *Asian EFL Journal*, 7(4), 111–130.

Rajalahti, K., H. Parviainen & J. Klemola (2012). The modal and quasi-modal verbs of obligation and necessity in the English varieties of Singapore, India and the Philippines. Paper presented at ICAME 33, Leuven.

Rautionaho, P. (2014). *Variation in the progressive: A corpus-based study into World Englishes* (Dissertation). Tampere, Finland: University of Tampere. Retrieved from http://tampub.uta.fi/handle/10024/96287 (last access: 19/02/2018).

Ravindranath, M. & S.E. Wagner (2016). Sociolinguistics: Language in social environments. In K. Allan (Ed.), *The Routledge handbook of linguistics* (264–280). London: Routledge.

Rice, W. (1932). *Get* and *got*. *American Speech*, 7(4), 280–296. doi: 10.2307/451908.

Rissanen, M. (2000). The world of English historical corpora: From Cædmon to the computer age. *Journal of English Linguistics*, 28(1), 7–20. doi: 10.1177/00754240022004848.

Romaine, S. (2008). Corpus linguistics and sociolinguistics. In A. Lüdeling & M. Kytö (Eds.), *Corpus linguistics: An international handbook* (Vol. 1, 96–111). Berlin: Mouton de Gruyter.

Ronan, P. & G. Schneider (2017). Directive speech acts in SPICE Ireland and beyond. Paper presented at ICAME 38, Prague.

Rosenfelder, I. (2009). Rhoticity in educated Jamaican English: An analysis of the spoken component of ICE-Jamaica. In S. Hoffmann & L. Siebers (Eds.), *World Englishes: Problems, properties and prospects* (61–82). Amsterdam: John Benjamins.

Ross, C. & J.-h. Sheng Ma (2006). *Modern Mandarin Chinese grammar: A practical guide*. London: Routledge.

Rossouw, R. & B. van Rooy (2012). Diachronic changes in modality in South African English. *English World-Wide*, 33(1), 1–26. doi: 10.1075/eww.33.1.01ros.

Sailaja, P. (2009). *Indian English*. Edinburgh: Edinburgh University Press.

Säily, T. (2011). Variation in morphological productivity in the BNC: Sociolinguistic and methodological considerations. *Corpus Linguistics and Linguistic Theory*, 7(1), 119–141. doi: 10.1515/cllt.2011.006.

Sand, A. (2004). Shared morpho-syntactic features in contact varieties of English: Article use. *World Englishes*, 23(2), 281–298. doi: 10.1111/j.0883-2919.2004.00352.x.

Sankoff, G. (2006). Age: Apparent time and real time. In K. Brown (Ed.), *Encyclopedia of language and linguistics* (2 ed., Vol. 1, 110–116). Amsterdam: Elsevier.

Sankoff, G. & H. Blondeau (2007). Language change across the lifespan: /r/ in Montreal French. *Language*, 83(3), 560–588. doi: 10.1353/lan.2007.0106.

Sapir, E. (1921). *Language: An introduction to the study of speech*. New York: Harcourt, Brace.

Saraceni, M. (2015). *World Englishes: A critical analysis*. London: Bloomsbury Academic.

Schiffman, H.F. (1983). *A reference grammar of spoken Kannada*. Seattle: University of Washington Press.

Schiffman, H.F. (1999). *A reference grammar of spoken Tamil*. Cambridge: Cambridge University Press.

Schilk, M. (2011). *Structural nativization in Indian English lexicogrammar*. Amsterdam: John Benjamins.

Schilk, M. (2015). Book review: Claudia Lange. 2014. *The syntax of spoken Indian English*. Amsterdam: John Benjamins. *English World-Wide*, 36(3), 348–355. doi: 10.1075/eww.36.3.03sch.

Schmied, J. (1996). Second language corpora. In S. Greenbaum (Ed.), *Comparing English worldwide: The International Corpus of English* (182–196). Oxford: Clarendon Press.

Schneider, E.W. (2003). The dynamics of New Englishes: From identity construction to dialect birth. *Language*, 79(2), 233–281. doi: 10.1353/lan.2003.0136.

Schneider, E.W. (2007). *Postcolonial English: Varieties around the world*. Cambridge: Cambridge University Press.

Schneider, E.W. (2011). Colonization, globalization, and sociolinguistics of World Englishes. In R. Mesthrie (Ed.), *The Cambridge handbook of sociolinguistics* (335–353). Cambridge: Cambridge University Press.

Schneider, E.W. (2012). Exploring the interface between World Englishes and Second Language Acquisition – and implications for English as a Lingua Franca. *Journal of English as a Lingua Franca*, 1(1), 57–91. doi: 10.1515/jelf-2012-0004.

Schröter, V. (2018). *"Where got such thing one?" A multivariate analysis of null subjects in Asian Englishes* (Dissertation). Freiburg i. Br.: University of Freiburg.

Schulz, M.E. (2012). The development of possessive HAVE GOT: The path (not) taken. *Journal of Historical Pragmatics*, 13(1), 129–146. doi: 10.1075/jhp.13.1.06sch.

Schützler, O. (2015). *A sociophonetic approach to Scottish Standard English*. Amsterdam: John Benjamins.

Schweinberger, M. (2012). The discourse marker LIKE in Irish English. In B. Migge & M. Ní Chiosáin (Eds.), *New perspectives on Irish English* (179–201). Amsterdam: John Benjamins.

Seargeant, P. (2012). *Exploring World Englishes: Language in a global context.* London: Routledge.

Searle, J.R. (1976). A classification of illocutionary acts. *Language in Society*, 5(1), 1–23. doi: 10.1017/s0047404500006837.

Sedlatschek, A. (2009). *Contemporary Indian English: Variation and change.* Amsterdam: John Benjamins.

Seggewiß, F. (2012). *Current changes in the English modals: A corpus-based analysis of present-day spoken English* (Dissertation). Freiburg i. Br.: University of Freiburg. Retrieved from https://freidok.uni-freiburg.de/data/9654 (last access: 19/02/2018).

Selinker, L. (1972). Interlanguage. *International Review of Applied Linguistics in Language Teaching*, 10(3), 209–231. doi: 10.1515/iral.1972.10.1-4.209.

Setter, J., C.S.P. Wong & B.H.S. Chan (2010). *Hong Kong English.* Edinburgh: Edinburgh University Press.

Sharma, D. (2009). Typological diversity in New Englishes. *English World-Wide*, 30(2), 170–195. doi: 10.1075/eww.30.2.04sha.

Sharma, D. (2011). Style repertoire and social change in British Asian English. *Journal of Sociolinguistics*, 15(4), 464–492. doi: 10.1111/j.1467-9841.2011.00503.x.

Siegel, J. (2008). *The emergence of pidgin and creole languages.* Oxford: Oxford University Press.

Siemund, P. (2013). *Varieties of English: A typological approach.* Cambridge: Cambridge University Press.

Silverstein, M. (2003). Indexical order and the dialectics of sociolinguistic life. *Language & Communication*, 23(3–4), 193–229. doi: 10.1016/s0271-5309(03)00013-2.

Smith, N. (2003). Changes in the modals and semi-modals of strong obligation and epistemic necessity in recent British English. In R. Facchinetti, M. Krug & F.R. Palmer (Eds.), *Modality in contemporary English* (241–266). Berlin: Mouton de Gruyter.

Smith, N. & G. Leech (2013). Verb structures in twentieth century British English. In B. Aarts, J. Close, G. Leech & S. Wallis (Eds.), *The verb phrase in English: Investigating recent language change with corpora* (68–98). Cambridge: Cambridge University Press.

Smitterberg, E. (2005). *The progressive in 19th-century English: A process of integration.* Amsterdam: Rodopi.

Spears, A.K. (1982). The Black English semi-auxiliary *come. Language*, 58(4), 850–872. doi: 10.2307/413960.

Speelman, D. (2014). Logistic regression: A confirmatory technique for comparisons in corpus linguistics. In D. Glynn & J.A. Robinson (Eds.), *Corpus methods for semantics:*

Quantitative studies in polysemy and synonymy (487–533). Amsterdam: John Benjamins.

Sridhar, S.N. (1990). *Kannada*. London: Routledge.

Sridhar, K.K. & S.N. Sridhar (1982). Bridging the paradigm gap: Second-language acquisition theory and indigenized varieties of English. In B.B. Kachru (Ed.), *The other tongue: English across cultures* (91–107). Urbana: University of Illinois Press.

Standop, E. (1957). *Syntax und Semantik der modalen Hilfsverben im Altenglischen: Magan, motan, sculan, willan*. Bochum-Langendreer: Poeppinghaus.

Stephany, U. (1995). Function and form of modality in first and second language acquistion. In A.G. Ramat & G.C. Galèas (Eds.), *From pragmatics to syntax: Modality in second language acquisition* (105–120). Tübingen: Narr.

Strang, B.M.H. (1970). *A history of English*. London: Methuen.

Subrahmanyam, P.S. (1974). *An introduction to modern Telugu*. Annamalainagar: Annamalai University.

Sun, C. (2006). *Chinese: A linguistic introduction*. Cambridge: Cambridge University Press.

Swanton, M. (Ed.) (1978). *Beowulf*. Manchester: Manchester University Press.

Sweetser, E.E. (1990). *From etymology to pragmatics: Metaphorical and cultural aspects of semantic structure*. Cambridge: Cambridge University Press.

Szmrecsanyi, B. (2006). *Morphosyntactic persistence in spoken English: A corpus study at the intersection of variationist sociolinguistics, psycholinguistics, and discourse analysis*. Berlin: Mouton de Gruyter.

Taeymans, M. (2004). An investigation into the marginal modals DARE and NEED in British present-day English: A corpus-based approach. In O. Fischer, M. Norde & H. Perridon (Eds.), *Up and down the cline: The nature of grammaticalization* (97–114). Amsterdam: John Benjamins.

Tagliamonte, S. (2004). *Have to, gotta, must*: Grammaticalisation, variation and specialization in English deontic modality. In H. Lindquist & C. Mair (Eds.), *Corpus approaches to grammaticalization in English* (33–55). Amsterdam: John Benjamins.

Tagliamonte, S. (2006). *Analysing sociolinguistic variation*. Cambridge: Cambridge University Press.

Tagliamonte, S. (2012). *Variationist sociolinguistics: Change, observation, interpretation*. Malden, Mass.: Wiley-Blackwell.

Tagliamonte, S. & A. D'Arcy (2004). *He's like, she's like*: The quotative system in Canadian youth. *Journal of Sociolinguistics*, 8(4), 493–514. doi: 10.1111/j.1467-9841.2004.00271.x.

Tagliamonte, S. & A. D'Arcy (2007). The modals of obligation/necessity in Canadian perspective. *English World-Wide*, 28(1), 47–87. doi: 10.1075/eww.28.1.04tag.

Tagliamonte, S. & D. Denis (2014). Expanding the transmission/diffusion dichotomy: Evidence from Canada. *Language*, 90(1), 90–136. doi: 10.1353/lan.2014.0016.

Tagliamonte, S. & R. Hudson (1999). *Be like* et al. beyond America: The quotative system in British and Canadian youth. *Journal of Sociolinguistics*, 3(2), 147–172. doi: 10.1111/1467-9481.00070.

Tagliamonte, S. & J. Smith (2006). Layering, competition and a twist of fate: Deontic modality in dialects of English. *Diachronica*, 23(2), 341–380. doi: 10.1075/dia.23.2.06tag.

Terassa, L.A.M. (2018). *Morphological simplification in Asian Englishes: Frequency, substratum transfer, and institutionalization* (Dissertation). Freiburg i. Br.: University of Freiburg.

Teržan Kopecky, C. (2008). Indefiniteness and imperfectivity as micro-grammatical contexts of epistemicity in German-Slovene translations. In W. Abraham & E. Leiss (Eds.), *Modality-aspect interfaces: Implications and typological solutions* (119–145). Amsterdam: John Benjamins.

Torgersen, E., C. Gabrielatos & S. Hoffmann (2018). A corpus-based analysis of the pragmatic markers *you get me*. In E. Friginal (Ed.), *Studies in corpus-based sociolinguistics* (176–196). London: Routledge.

Traugott, E.C. (1972). *A history of English syntax: A transformational approach to the history of English sentence structure*. New York: Holt, Rinehart and Winston.

Traugott, E.C. (1989). On the rise of epistemic meanings in English: An example of subjectification in semantic change. *Language*, 65(1), 31–55. doi: 10.2307/414841.

Traugott, E.C. & R.B. Dasher (2002). *Regularity in semantic change*. Cambridge: Cambridge University Press.

Traugott, E.C. & P.J. Hopper (2003). *Grammaticalization* (2 ed.). Cambridge: Cambridge University Press.

Traugott, E.C. & E. König (1991). The semantics-pragmatics of grammaticalization revisited. In E.C. Traugott & B. Heine (Eds.), *Approaches to grammaticalization* (Vol. 1: Focus on theoretical and methodological issues, 189–218). Amsterdam: John Benjamins.

Trousdale, G. (2003). Simplification and redistribution: An account of modal verb usage in Tyneside English. *English World-Wide*, 24(2), 271–284. doi: 10.1075/eww.24.2.07tro.

Trudgill, P. (1988). Norwich revisited: Recent linguistic changes in an English urban dialect. *English World-Wide*, 9(1), 33–49. doi: 10.1075/eww.9.1.03tru.

Trudgill, P. (2000). *Sociolinguistics: An introduction to language and society* (4 ed.). London: Penguin Books.

Tully, M. (1997). English: An advantage to India? *ELT Journal*, 51(2), 157–164. doi: 10.1093/elt/51.2.157.

van der Auwera, J. & A. Ammann (2005). Overlap between situational and epistemic modal marking. In M. Haspelmath, M.S. Dryer, D. Gil & B. Comrie (Eds.), *The World Atlas of Language Structures*. Oxford: Oxford University Press.

van der Auwera, J. & A. Ammann (2013). Overlap between situational and epistemic modal marking. In M.S. Dryer & M. Haspelmath (Eds.), *The World Atlas of Language*

Structures Online. Leipzig: Max Planck Institute for Evolutionary Anthropology. Retrieved from http://wals.info/chapter/76 (last access: 19/02/2018).

van der Auwera, J. & V.A. Plungian (1998). Modality's semantic map. *Linguistic Typology*, 2(1), 79–124. doi: 10.1515/lity.1998.2.1.79.

van der Auwera, J. & M. Taeymans (2006). More on the ancestors of *need*. In M. Rissanen & R. Facchinetti (Eds.), *Corpus-based studies of diachronic English* (37–52). Bern: Lang.

van der Auwera, J., A. Ammann & S. Kindt (2005). Modal polyfunctionality and Standard Average European. In A. Klinge & H.H. Müller (Eds.), *Modality: Studies in form and function* (247–272). London: Equinox.

van der Auwera, J., D. Noël & A. De Wit (2012). The diverging *need* (*to*)'s of Asian Englishes. In M. Hundt & U. Gut (Eds.), *Mapping unity and diversity world-wide: Corpus-based studies of New Englishes* (55–75). Amsterdam: John Benjamins.

van der Gaaf, W. (1931). *Beon* and *habban* connected with an inflected infinitive. *English Studies*, 13, 176–188. doi: 10.1080/00138383108596584.

van Linden, A. (2012). *Modal adjectives: English deontic and evaluative constructions in synchrony and diachrony*. Berlin: Mouton de Gruyter.

van Olmen, D. & J. van der Auwera (2016). Modality and mood in Standard Average European. In J. Nuyts & J. van der Auwera (Eds.), *The Oxford handbook of modality and mood* (362–384). Oxford: Oxford University Press.

van Rooy, B. (2010). Presidential address delivered at the City University of Hong Kong, Hong Kong, on December 4, 2008, at the 14th annual meeting of the International Association for World Englishes: Social and linguistic perspectives on variability in World Englishes. *World Englishes*, 29(1), 3–20. doi: 10.1111/j.1467-971x.2009.01621.x.

van Rooy, B. & C. Piotrowska (2015). The development of an extended time period meaning of the progressive in Black South African English. In P. Collins (Ed.), *Grammatical change in English world-wide* (465–484). Amsterdam: John Benjamins.

van Rooy, B. & R. Wasserman (2014). Do the modals of Black and White South African English converge? *Journal of English Linguistics*, 42(1), 51–67. doi: 10.1177/0075424213511463.

Vendler, Z. (1967). *Linguistics in Philosophy*. Ithaca, New York: Cornell University Press.

Vetter, F. (2017). Exploring corpus homogeneity: Press editorials in the British, Canadian and Jamaican components of the *International Corpus of English*. Paper presented at BICLCE 7, Vigo.

Visser, F.T. (1969). *An historical syntax of the English language* (Vol. 3, 1: Syntactical units with two verbs). Leiden: Brill.

Visser, F.T. (1973). *An historical syntax of the English language* (Vol. 3, 2: Syntactical units with two and with more verbs). Leiden: Brill.

Warner, A.R. (1993). *English auxiliaries: Structure and history*. Cambridge: Cambridge University Press.

Wasserman, R. & B. van Rooy (2014). The development of modals of obligation and necessity in White South African English through contact with Afrikaans. *Journal of English Linguistics*, 42(1), 31–50. doi: 10.1177/0075424213514588.

Werner, V. (2014). *The present perfect in World Englishes: Charting unity and diversity* (Dissertation). Bamberg: University of Bamberg Press.

Westney, P. (1995). *Modals and periphrastics in English: An investigation into the semantic correspondence between certain English modal verbs and their periphrastic equivalents*. Tübingen: Niemeyer.

Weston, D. (2015). The lesser of two evils: Atypical trajectories in English dialect evolution. *Journal of Sociolinguistics*, 19(5), 671–687. doi: 10.1111/josl.12162.

Wiedenhof, J. (2015). *A grammar of Mandarin*. Amsterdam: John Benjamins.

Wierzbicka, A. (1985). Different cultures, different languages, different speech acts: Polish vs. English. *Journal of Pragmatics*, 9(2–3), 145–178. doi: 10.1016/0378-2166(85)90023-2.

Wierzbicka, A. (1991). *Cross-cultural pragmatics: The semantics of human interaction*. Berlin: Mouton de Gruyter.

Wierzbicka, A. (1997). *Understanding cultures through their key words: English, Russian, Polish, German, and Japanese*. Oxford: Oxford University Press.

Wierzbicka, A. (2006). *English: Culture and meaning*. Oxford: Oxford University Press.

Williams, J. (1987). Non-native varieties of English: A special case of language acquisition. *English World-Wide*, 8(2), 161–199. doi: 10.1075/eww.8.2.02wil.

Winford, D. (2017). World Englishes and creoles. In M.J. Filppula, J. Klemola & D. Sharma (Eds.), *The Oxford handbook of World Englishes* (194–210). New York: Oxford University Press.

Wong, J.O. (2004). Cultural scripts, ways of speaking and perceptions of personal autonomy: Anglo English vs. Singapore English. *Intercultural Pragmatics*, 1(2), 231–248. doi: 10.1515/iprg.2004.1.2.231.

Wong, J.O. (2010). The 'triple articulation' of language. *Journal of Pragmatics*, 42(11), 2932–2944. doi: 10.1016/j.pragma.2010.06.013.

Wong, J.O. (2014). *The culture of Singapore English*. Cambridge: Cambridge University Press.

Wunder, E.-M., H. Voormann & U. Gut (2010). The ICE Nigeria corpus project: Creating an open, rich and accurate corpus. *ICAME Journal*, 34, 78–88.

Xiao, R. (2009). Multidimensional analysis and the study of World Englishes. *World Englishes*, 28(4), 421–450. doi: 10.1111/j.1467-971x.2009.01606.x.

Xiao, Z. & A. McEnery (2005). Two approaches to genre analysis: Three genres in modern American English. *Journal of English Linguistics*, 33(1), 62–82. doi: 10.1177/0075424204273957.

Zhang, Q. (2014). *Investigating Hong Kong English: Globalization and identity*. Bern: Lang.

Index